Oundle

Memories and Moments

A Peek into the Past

Anna Fernyhough

First published in Great Britain in 2018 by Fast- Print Publishing,
Peterborough, England.
http://www.fast-publishing.net/bookshop

ISBN **978-178456-555-8**

This book is dedicated to family and friends.
Living or not - you are forever in our memories.

...oooOOOooo...

"I am grown old and my memory is not as active as it used to be. When I was younger I could remember any thing, whether it had happened or not; but my faculties are decaying now and soon I shall be so I cannot remember any but the things that never happened. It is sad to go to pieces like this, but we all have to do it." *Mark Twain (1907)*

...oooOOOooo...

Part of the proceeds for this book will be donated to the
Oundle and District Care Committee and Volunteer Action Oundle.

CONTENTS

5

List of Photographs

I appreciate the many photographs that were shared with me, but unfortunately some were similar and on others the printing quality and clarity would not stand reproduction.

The photographs in this edition are reproduced with kind permission of the following (identified by their initials): Andrew Spurrell, Angela Hudson, Ann Greetham (*née* Colclough), Arthur Ball, Barbara Mudza, Cheryl Forscutt, Chris Denley, Chris York, David Wills, Diane and Sue Wyles, Hetty Bell, Jill Giddings, Joyce Hardick, Margaret Brewster, Marilyn Smith, Oundle Town Council, Oundle Museums Trust, Oundle School and the Worshipful Company of Grocers, Sharon Cottingham, Sue Young, Reinette Broadhurst, Thelma Quinn, Tim and Ginger Lee, Wendy Bollans.

List of Maps

Drawn by A. Fernyhough (based on sources from Oundle Museum and courtesy of Oundle School Archives). Others, with kind permission from the Oundle archive and Oundle School Worshipful Company of Grocers. Figure 7 kindly produced by S. Cottingham.

Note: The chapters in this book are organised by main streets and thoroughfares. If a smaller road dissects or leads away from the main route, I have grouped it within the section on the road and listed it under the same chapter heading.
Maps are not to scale.

Foreword

I am from Oundle and my mother's family stretches back into Oundle's past. I grew up in North Street and went to the local schools. I left to train as a teacher, gain a master's degree, then work in Spain, USA and Ethiopia, but always looked forward to coming home.

It had been in my mind for many years that I should write down the memories from the older generations of the town before they are forgotten. My mother and her friends talk about their youth, which inspired me to write about the streets, people and their lives. I have gathered their recollections and greatly enjoyed talking with our residents. I thank you for taking part and sharing your memories, stories and anecdotes with me and apologise for any repetition. It is impossible to share everything that has been said or given to me, but have done my best to recall and represent the memories shared. One of my favourites is that someone (who wishes to remain nameless) believed that a friend of the family didn't like dogs – as he was "Douglas"!

In early 2017 I met Margaret Brewster for a coffee. We got along well and discussed my ideas for a book. Margaret sourced the register and has been marvellous with her help and encouragement. Meanwhile, I have collected recollections of people and worked on organising this data. If readers should find information in this book that does not match their memory of events or people I ask them to bear with me, as these recorded memories are personal recollections from primary sources. Whenever possible, these were confirmed using the registers, census, almanacs and other secondary sources. I wish to thank the Oundle School archive, town museum and news chronicles for sharing their collections with me. The staff at Fast-Print Publishing has given help and advice in facilitating the publishing of this book.

I wish to thank Joyce Hardick, Angela Hudson, Sue Crick and Cheryl Forscutt for their significant contributions, photographs and memories. (Cheryl also kindly lent me her Oundle Directories.) Particular thanks go to my life-long friend, Sharon Cottingham for her continuous help, support and organisational skills (and to Reinette Broadhurst for sorting photographs). Especial thanks to Margaret Brewster for her additional research. I also wish to say a huge thank you to my sons, Mark for proof-reading and editorial comments and to Kit for cover design, art, support and encouragement. Diversity is our strength. All of the above will, no doubt, breathe a sigh of relief when this book is finally published. Lastly, I hope that this book will be enjoyed by all who read it. My heart is in Oundle no matter where I go or what I do.

Anna (2017)

Message from a friend and supporter:

I first met Anna when she bought my book, 'A Collection of Oundle Families'. We sat in the Talbot enjoying a coffee as we talked about her idea of collecting as many memories about life in Oundle. I encouraged Anna's enthusiasm. At our next get together we discussed how to get the project started. My input has been to visit Anna when we spent hours collecting wonderful details from Oundle residents' past and present. On occasions we roamed around the fascinating streets in Oundle, some with tiny lanes leading off where more cottages had been built. Being local, Anna has been able to collect most of the memories from people. I have been able to supply the pre-World War II (WWII) details of who was living where in Oundle. In addition, I have written an article that shows the residents of Latham hospital and Laxton hospital through the census years.

Margaret (2017)

...oooOOOooo...

OUNDLE ORIGINS - ON THE BANKS OF THE NENE

Oundle has been continuously occupied since the Iron Age. The first mention of Oundle is from the "Anglo-Saxon Chronicle" when it appears as Undala or (the Roman) Undalum.[1] The most common assumption is that the end of Oundle's name comes from 'doel', meaning 'a dale' or valley. M.W. Brown suggests that this topography is apparent to anyone entering the town from the west. Professor W.W. Skeat further suggested that the beginning of the town name was short for 'Unnan' (a form of 'Unna'), which is a man's name. Skeat says that this name "is on record". The meaning of Oundle is thus, "Unna's dales". We can assume that prior to the Roman arrival, the valley leading down to the river was the territory of a man named Unna.[2] History surrounds us as we endorse our 'Undala' and 'Undalum' Saxon town heritage that began prior to the spread of the Roman Empire.

The Roman roads around the Oundle area include Roman-built Watling Street, which crossed the county of Northamptonshire in a north-west direction near Towcester. The 'Via Devana' was a similar road running parallel to Watling Street. It crossed Watling Street somewhere between Rockingham and Oundle. Ermine Street was on a more northerly route. It crossed the north-eastern extremity of Northants by Castor, which was on the river Nene between Peterborough and Stamford. In Roman times the sizeable settlement was near the Ashton junction to Oundle (by the 'Riverside Inn').

The revered monk, Bede in his eighth century history of England[3], wrote that Saint Wilfrid died 'in his monastery' in Oundle. Accounts tell that St. Wilfrid was buried here and a chapel built to honour him on a small knoll beyond Saint Sythe's Lane (roughly the site of the current Church). Oundle was a monastery town from around the seventh century, which had a community of Benedictine monks, dependents of Medeshamstede (Peterborough) Abbey, who supplemented their income by eel-fishing in the River Nene. The monastery was sacked,

---

[1] Rev. M.W. Brown, 'Northamptonshire', Cambridge Press, discusses Oundle's name derivation.
[2] Ibid. Oundle Master, M.W. Brown, 'Northamptonshire', pp.58-59 (1911).
[3] 731 A.D.

then restored in 966 AD. Oundle held a 'good market' (dating to before 1066) and has a parish Church of a similar age. In the tenth century Oundle's name had changed from 'Undala' to 'Undela'. By the fourteenth century it was 'Oundel' (and thereafter was changed to Oundle when spelling developed uniformity).

Medeshamstede (Peterborough) was affected by the Black Death in the mid-1300s, but Oundle was largely unscathed. It is assumed that the Oundle monks were fairly solitary and isolated. Although during the reign of Henry VIII, in 1545 Sabine Johnson from Polebrook, wrote that 'Ripen hath buried one of plague and at Oundle they die still very sore. I fear this town' (of Glapthorn) and a month later she reiterated that 'At Oundle they die sore', showing that Oundle was not always free from the plague.[4]

An early Peterborough Abbey charter portrays a mediæval Oundle of around five-hundred people (including cloth-workers, a skinner, a smith and two masons). The thirteenth-century was a period of prosperity for our monastery. Mediæval Oundle had stone buildings[5] and was on the road to prosperity. In 1278, Abbot Richard gained the rights to a tithe of all venison killed within the royal forests of Northamptonshire, which meant that the monks had a share of venison or the money from its sale to locals. Abbot Richard stopped the hand-worked grindstone mills used by the people of Oundle as he felt it was a threat to the Lord's mill. The king repelled Peterborough Abbey from running a prison and from holding courts to gain rights to the possessions of felons. Felons, outlaws and fugitives who gained sanctuary in the church already submitted to banishment and lost their personal property. This is one way in which the local monastery gained funds. The king granted an exchange of land and woods to Abbot William Ramsey (1471-1496). In 1477, he gave licence to confiscate the local church and gift it to Oundle monastery, providing the vicarage was sufficiently endowed and money was distributed to the poor.[6]

---

[4] *Letters and Papers, Foreign and Domestic,* Henry VIII, Vol.4, 1524-1530, XX (2), pp.641-654.

[5] John Leyland, 1503-1542 (under Thomas Cromwell) made 5 volumes of itineraries of his UK journeys, noting religious antiquities and land, until his insanity and early death. His works are held in the Bodleian Library, Oxford.

[6] www.british-history.ac.uk/vch/northants/vol.2/pp.83-95

From around the fourth-century until the Reformation, England was largely of the Roman Catholic faith. Protestantism spread shortly after German, Martin Luther, reformed ideas of unethical practices in the Catholic faith of 1517. In the early 1530s, Henry VIII married Anne of Cleves and the dissolution of the monasteries was well underway. There had been a wealthy monastery and rectory here since the days of Henry's first wife, Katherine of Aragon. The new bishopric of Peterborough Abbey was restored in 1541, around the time when Oundle Manor was included in the dowry of Katherine Howard. Henry VIII wooed and married Katherine Howard in 1542, when she was just sixteen and he was forty-nine. (Their marriage lasted just over a year.) Catherine Parr (Henry's final wife) was then gifted the Manor until her death in 1548, when it was granted to John Russell the Earl of Bedford, by Henry's son, Edward VI. (The Russell family made their home near to the town.)

Thomas Austell's survey (of 1565) listed town properties (street-by-street) and shows that the central layout of Oundle has changed very little over the centuries.[7] Oundle land and property was owned by a few prosperous families who controlled the town's market assets. Local workmen and their families lived in tenanted, tithed and rented homes. (See consolidated maps of on town development.)

A twelfth century charter for Oundle "market and toll" confirms that dues were paid to Peterborough Abbey from Oundle assets.[8] These payments continued until the mid-sixteenth-century. Elizabethan and Stuart prosperity (mid-1500s to 1700) encouraged rebuilding. Old mediæval houses were modernised, demolished or rebuilt. Advances generated a tanning trade in the 1500s as water was free, and accessible from springs, wells and the river Nene. This led to advances in local industries, including malting and brewing. Small cottages were constructed for the mill and farm workers who were employed by the wealthy landowners. These small cottages and grand town-houses expose the wealth and influence of bygone families (Whitwell, Bramston and Creed, amongst others). Whose affluence is due (in part)

---

[7] Oundle's housing boom in the early twenty-first century was the largest since its initial development in Roman times.

[8] VCH Northamptonshire, iii, p. 89; P.H. Sawyer, Anglo-Saxon Charters: an annotated list and bibliography, Royal Historical Society no. 787; London, 1968.

to our fertile land and river location. The number and quality of workmen's cottages (dating from 1600) alongside the houses of wealthier residents show an affluence in a thriving town. Buildings were in-filled and crowded into narrow spaces in the streets and back lanes. Growth at the town edge was halted by a river boundary (except near to the access bridges). Fields were not enclosed until the 1800s, when strip-farmed fields were fenced-in and the backs of the tenant (burgage[9]) plots were settled and steadily used to expand the town.

Growth and development continued. By 1700, Oundle's range of trades had grown to include shoe-makers, fell-mongers, a tanner, a turner, a hemp-dresser and rope-maker, slaters, watchmakers, inn-keepers, fish-mongers, a miller, grocers, a 'jockey' (probably a horse-dealer), glovers and a gunsmith. John Clifton[10] recorded daily life and included local floods, fairs, bull-running, illnesses (smallpox), gardening and local Oundle characters. (By 1800 local production included bobbin lace-making.)

From the 1700's (to as late as the 1960s) travelling rag-and-bone men, grindstone knife-sharpeners ("sharper than you could do yourself"[11]), strawberry sellers, horses, barrows and carts and flocks of animals in transit from one field to another were regularly seen in Oundle streets. Calling out to trade their wares to householders. During the mid-1700s, the local rag-merchant was Laurence Landen. He also made toys out of wood and scrap-materials and sold them to Oundle people.

Roads were updated by the Turnpike Trust and the Enclosure Act of 1807 changed land management. By 1812 the town had 2,000 people clustered along 'High Street' (now North and West Streets), on both sides of Saint Sythe's (St. Osyth's)[12] Lane, in a narrow span of houses on the southern end of East Back Way (East Road), plus a few on the eastern side of Mill Road.

Unpaved cart and foot routes led to nearby villages. An essential road led from the mills on the old Barnwell Road via Elmington to

---

[9] Burgage plots were leased in lieu of work payments; as a tenure of land or property held in return for service or rent.

[10] John Clifton was a master-carpenter, sexton and diarist. He worked for the Church.

[11] Wendy Bollans, family memories of Arthur Chester.

[12] This lane was recalls Osgyth (a local 7th-century saint and princess).

Peterborough.[13] Jessie Watts-Russell (1786-1875) built a prestigious 'Market House' (town hall) around the time of the Improvement Act (1825) and gives us an ideas as to Oundle prosperity at the turn of the nineteenth-century. By 1831 the census lists 2,308 inhabitants. The railway station was opened in 1845 (and cut-back in 1964).[14]

Oundle grew steadily after the wars. The number of residents was 4,834 in 2001 and 5,735 in 2011, with a current population around 6,000.[15] According to census data, Oundle had 1,933 houses in 2001 and had grown by nearly two-hundred extra houses by 2011. The census suggests that as the resident population grew, medical (and care) establishments were cut (from forty in 2001 to thirty-four by 2011).[16] The number of roads with new housing have doubled since 1960. Oundle is a continually growing town.

One of Oundle's facets is the public school. The presence of the school could be described as 'Marmite', as people either love it or not. Nevertheless, the town definitely would be 'poorer for it' if the school had not existed. Many beautiful Oundle buildings have been preserved by the School. In 1892, Frederick William Sanderson was employed as the head of the independent School. He spent his time transforming and enhancing the school and town until his departure in 1922. The Cloisters and School House (1883) were built before, but the Great Hall, Science Block, Yarrow Gallery and the Milton Road boarding houses were all built during his Headship. Oundle School bought some of the finer, old houses, such as Cobthorne and built new edifices that were crafted to enhance the town. Education was key within the town. By 1971, innovation was clear with the construction and opening of Prince William School and a Middle School. The school was at the forefront of the state school change that lasted for almost fifty years, until three-tier schooling collapsed. The changes and reverse in Oundle's educational planning meant that Middle School children were re-spread in the town Primary and Senior School, creating two-

---

[13] Thomas Eyre's map of Northamptonshire, 1779.
[14] In 1964 regular trains ceased, except for a few 'laid on' for students attending boarding-school (until 1972). www.disused-stations.org.uk/o/oundle
[15] For accessible census data, see www.oundle.gov.uk
[16] Mark Felton on behalf of 'Transition Oundle', 6th August 2014.

tier instruction once again. 'Time will tell' if this was a wise and edifying decision by the local education authority.

In this work I intend to cover two aspects of research: to explore the older, original streets and to look at the people and families who lived in them, through their written and oral memories. There is much to discover as we uncover the strata of townsfolk, dwell in their memories, appreciate what came before and glimpse at what is to come.

CHILDHOOD

Perceptions of childhood are linked to family and home, with notions of having a good childhood inextricably linked with well-being (happiness and welfare). There are many theories related to childhood and growing-up, but in general I believe that the majority of Oundle-born people or those who grew-up in the vicinity have largely happy memories to relate. With fresh-air and fields, access to shops, historic sites and amenities just a short distance away: Oundle changes with the seasons and its townsfolk. The 1960s generation recall playing in fields, cycling, blackberry-picking, scrambling in hay-ricks, gardens and fields and sometimes, 'scrumping' apples. Whereas youth of the 1950s recall walking or cycling to Peterborough and Thrapston to use the juke-box. From the war years, people recall nostalgic fetes and dances; then practising for air and land attacks, rationing and having less to eat, but also with wistful memories of childhood fun and games.

Lives were enhanced by theatrical plays at the Victoria Hall, at the Stahl Theatre and escapist films watched in the Victoria Hall of the 1960s. The Gilbert and Sullivan players and their predecessors at the

Oundle Operatic Society of the 1930s (which met at Cobthorne) gave life to the town. In 2014 Constance Peploe celebrated her hundredth birthday. She celebrated the two wars by her birth in 1914 and her marriage to Leslie Peploe in 1939. (Les died in 1988.) In her younger days Constance spent much of her time taking part in the Oundle Operatic Society, which she loved. To show her spirit was still keen she did a tandem sky-dive when she was ninety-two!

Youth for some residents held the excitement camping and cooking-out in Miss Strong's East Road garden in the 1960s. For others, it was reading of mysterious places to go far away, whilst safely closeted in the library. Clubs offered a range of activities for the more boisterous; training and exercise in football, cricket, rugby, swimming, tennis, bowls and golf. Simply put, if you did not join any – you missed out!

...oooOOOooo...

Playing in the Street in the 1930s - Joyce Hardick (née Gaunt)

Joyce Hardick recalls that "children were always allowed to play out in the road with the neighbours children until the lamp-lighter came". The Gaunt's were no exception. Safety was not considered an issue at the time, as everyone knew each other well. Streets were very quiet by early evening, as most of the horses and carts would be home by five o'clock for their tea and "not very many people owned cars in those days". Joyce said that at twilight "the man came along to light the gas street lights and all of the children would want just a few more minutes of play before going indoors". Joyce said that "parents used the lamp-lighter's arrival as a guide to what time it was for their children to come in and go to bed. Once we were indoors it was off to bed with a favourite toy. Firstly, we needed to find our 'Nightdress case' (which was like a small bag) for keeping nighties and pyjamas inside that was left out on the bed, but out of sight. Then it was off to bed with us".

...oooOOOooo...

Memories of an Oundle Doctor and his Family - Andrew Spurrell

Oundle vet, Andrew Spurrell has lived here for all of his life and is now in his early eighties. Andrew's grandfather was Mr Cheney. He rode in the Grand National at Aintree twice and was a Fotheringhay farmer. Andrew's mother, Marjorie, and her two sisters grew up there. She was a professional ice-skater. She skated as its popularity rose in the 1920s. The "Pictorial and Descriptive Guide to London" in 1935, noted the importance of ice-skating along with listing all the indoor ice-skating rinks in the city. Marjorie and her friend, Peggy Skinner, attended the Wembley fair in 1928 and gave 'exhibitions' in a frozen tank of water.

Andrew's maternal grandparents were the Cheney family. Their three daughters were educated at the school in Townley House. They attended school with Joan Hickson (an actress who is best remembered for her T.V. role as 'Miss Marple'). Norah Cheney trained as a doctor, Helen stayed at home (to look after her parents) and Marjorie trained as a Norland Nanny, but chose skating instead. Andrew recalled that the Cheney ladies were very determined. His aunt, Norah, ground-breaking as one of the first qualified British women doctors. Norah Acheson (née Cheney) lived in Aldeburgh, Suffolk. She worked at the Elizabeth Garret Anderson cottage hospital, which was founded by the very first British woman doctor. Nora was quite a character. Andrew mentioned that she "went out in her coat and curlers when called to a night-time emergency". She went up a ladder to do a rescue in her coat over her nightdress, and called out to those below, "Avert your eyes, I'm going up". She went out in the lifeboat in the war years. When she retired the press ran a story: "Danger, Doc Norah barred from the sea".

The Spurrell line originally lived in Carmarthen, Wales. Andrew's grandfather, Walter (Dr Ivor Spurrell's father) was a printer. He published the definitive English-Welsh dictionary (called 'Spurrells'). The 'House of Spurrell' printers and publishers was established in 1840 by William Spurrell (1813-89). He worked for Bradley & Evans publishers in London (1835-1840) before returning to Wales to set up his own business. He owned and edited *Yr Haul* (The Sun) from 1857-1884. William married Sarah Walter in 1846. Their children were well-educated, particularly Edith Spurrell (1848-1908), Dr Charles Spurrell (1866-1949) and Walter Spurrell (1858-1934). Hence, Mr William Spurrell & Son ran his own printing and publishing firm that lasted from 1840 to 1969.

Walter joined his father, William in the business and later took over from him. He published records (1911-1929), journals (c. 1914) and English-Welsh dictionaries (1916). Walter married Florence Mary Turner in 1893 and their son, Hugh William Spurrell inherited the family papers when Walter died (1934). Then, the business was sold. Ivor Pritchard Spurrell had no interest in the family business. Encouraged by Walter, Charles and Ivor trained as doctors.

Andrew's father, Ivor P. Spurrell, came to Oundle in the 1920s.[17] He and his brother (Charles) had trained as doctors in London, but contracted tuberculosis.[18] They came 'to the country' to recover from TB and lived with their uncle, Dr Bernard Rowath Turner (and his wife, Emma) at 22 Benefield Road, now called "Turners" (that overlooking the fields to the south). In Oundle Ivor met Marjorie Cheney and they were married in 1934. Ivor was the Oundle School doctor. He and Bernard worked with and consulted medics, including Nurse Pailing and Mr Whitwell from the St John's Ambulance (and local pharmacist).

Andrew P. Spurrell was born in 1936. After his birth Mrs Allaby was hired as his nanny. She spent her life caring for Oundle children. Photographs show her holding baby Andrew in St. Anne's House gardens. She cared for Andrew and his sister, Judith, from when they were babies until they went to school.

The Spurrell family kept terriers. Family photographs show Andrew and his sister, Judith, in 1938, playing in the back garden at St Anne's, school days and ponies. The "growing-up" years were fun. Andrew reflects on parties and dog shows (that were held on 'Home Close').

Andrew recalls a little school named "St. Anne's in the Grove" (to the rear of Queen Anne's house). It was "The Miss Oliver's' school" (run by sisters) with its "very small classes and garden parties". Andrew enjoyed attending "Miss Oliver's, which was in the buildings at the back of our Queen Anne's garden". It had small classes and the children were all friends. Andrew can still name those in his class in this elite Milton Road School. Mrs Harris worked for the school and her husband was a housemaster at Oundle School. Members of his class included David Reece (the bursar's son), Hugo Bevan and Mary Capron from Southwick.

Andrew's first home was in St. Anne's House. It has quite a history and was owned by a lawyer, Thomas Burton in the 1700s. He was John Clifton's friend. (He lived just across the road.) Thomas' will from March 1784 is kept by the National Archives in Kew. He is listed as

[17] Andrew Spurrell, personal history.
[18] Tuberculosis is contagiously spread through micro-droplets released into the air. If untreated it spreads via coughs, sneezes, spitting, speaking, laughing and singing.

"Thomas Burton, Gentleman of Oundle".[19] His house was given a "new face" in 1824.

While the Spurrell family were living at Queen Anne's (house), Alec Benjamin Wright (1895-1970) was the local dispenser. The entrance to the surgery was on the side, in the lane. Andrew played with Charles Wyatt, the son of a lady-doctor who came as a war-time replacement when Andrew's father was sent away. Charles was just one day older than Andrew and they became friends.

During the war, Ivor Spurrell was the Officer-in-Charge of the military hospital in Leeds Castle, Kent. Around this time, during the war years, the family nanny grew to know Clark Gable. He visited the house on occasions while the family were away and the nanny happily plied him drinks with Dr Spurrell's half-bottle of brandy!

From 1942-47, Andrew was at preparatory school in Swanage, Dorset. His father went away during the war, but his grandmother stayed in Oundle, so they had to get a bigger house. They decided Cobthorne was too small as there was not enough room for the horses. Lime house had enough space at the back for gymkhanas in the war years. This was before the family moved to Lime house (then just one large house). Miss Strong bought the house in East Road from the Spurrell family. It was by the corner where the ARP station and Council Offices were. There was an observation-post in the school playing fields and the ARPs would take turns to bicycle up and observe.

The British Legion fete was held in Lime House as it had plenty of land attached. The family enjoyed living here and liked to entertain guests. Andrew has a photograph, taken in the garden at Lime House, showing 'M', Lady Ethel Wickham (of Cotterstock Hall; whose father had fought at Waterloo in 1815), Mrs Myers and Michael. (Miss Margaret Ring was Lady Ethel's housekeeper and cook. Kathleen Shiels recalls having tea with her at Cotterstock Hall on a Sunday afternoon after attending Church.)

Andrew has a film of him as a toddler being towed in a box on the ice of the frozen river Nene. With a skater mother Andrew also learned to skate. He remarked that "we saw much more snow in those days".

---

[19] The Public Records Office (PRO), PROB 11/1114/260.

Andrew recalls that when in his teens, "on the 26th December 1952 the deep water started to freeze" so he and a boy from Glapthorn went onto the ice. Three days later the lad sadly drowned. "On the 3rd January 1953, Mr Harris the housemaster at Oundle School, declared that it was fit to skate on the gravel pits from the 5th. The gravel-pits had frozen, but not the river." (It had frozen in 1903 when his grandmother (1903) ice-skated from Fotheringhay to Oundle and back.) While looking at Andrew's many wonderful family albums of photographs, he lovingly remarked that "Granny resembles the Giles' cartoon with her floppy hat and long dark coat". After perusing the photo's I agreed, she did!

Andrew reflected that the Jubilee bridges have long gone. Before the river was re-routed and drained in parts, people swam there if they didn't have access to Oundle School pool, which was an outdoor pool. This was a good place to walk the family terriers. Dr Robin Acheson and his wife (Andrew's maternal aunt), Norah, came to stay in Oundle and fell in love with one of their family's Jack Russel puppies. She kept him and named him 'Snooks', as the family ate tinned African 'snook' (a soapy-tasting fish) during WWII. She returned to Aldburgh hospital with the pup (where she worked as a doctor). Whenever she was out 'on call' in her cart, she always had him with her. Snooks the dog is honoured in death with his bronze statues at the hospital and on the sea front.

The memorial of the Oundle dog 'Snooks' was unveiled in 1961 in memory of doctors Robin and Nora Acheson who established the hospital. The statue 'vanished' (2003) so a copy was cast. As the original was returned, the town has two statues of Snooks! One is in the infirmary garden. He frequented it with his owners and "without their hard work and dedication" the hospital would not exist. An identical statue stands on the sea front. Snooks attended call-outs with Nora, but Andrew's wife, Nita, recalls that he was a 'bit snappy'![20] Apparently, "In death he is much calmer and more frequently rubbed than he ever was in life". "Generations of children have patted his nose, to the point where he is quite glossy"! The statue tribute reads" Snooks - This memorial was erected by the people of this borough to

---

[20] Andrew and Nita are the president and a vice-president of the Oundle and District Dog Training Society.

Dr "Robin" PM Acheson who cared for them from 1931 to 1959 and to Dr Nora, his wife, who died 1981 whilst still caring."

...oooOOOooo...

Memoirs - Angela Hudson (née Taney)

Angela says that she was very fortunate to be born and brought up in Oundle and has consequently seen many changes. She lived and grew-up in a terraced house on Gordon Road and "can just remember the fence across the end of the road with fields beyond".

Angela said that "during the war we had nurses from Glapthorn Road Hospital billeted with us. They were lively young girls who had boyfriends among the military personnel stationed around here. The GIs gave them extra food, as they had plenty. The nurses kindly gave it to mother so she often gave parties for them. Unfortunately, I was asleep upstairs in my cot. At one of the parties, two boys were drying the washing-up and there was one spoon left, so, to be absolutely fair, they dried one side each".

After the war, Angela recalls that Gordon Road was extended and built into a horse-shoe shape. The road was built by prisoners of war (POWs). "Some of our neighbours would give cups of tea to the POWs. Once the houses were built, many children came to live in them. The road was not as congested as it is now. I think only two people had a car so it was wonderful to play rounders', cricket, skipping, hopscotch, marbles and ball games against the walls of the terraced houses in the older part of the road. Sometimes, especially after Sunday dinner, we were told to play elsewhere as some of the residents had gone to bed for an afternoon nap".

There was a recreation ground on Herne Road[21] and Angela remembers the swings and a seesaw. "I also recall being taken there for firework displays as behind this were allotments. One day there was great excitement when we were going to have our own recreation ground on our doorstep. Swings, slides, Dutch-swings and so on, were being erected in the War Memorial Field. Queues of children formed

---

[21] Cheryl said, "... before the bungalows were built, it had a corrugated, green fence around it, by Kath Rowse's house (now Moisey)."

to have a go on everything. In the summer the hay was cut in the field, so we built houses and camps with it".

There was a cattle market in Oundle, behind Pick Arthey's garage. It was "mainly used on Thursdays, after the noon market bell tolled to start the livestock market. The rest of the week it was quite quiet. Cowboy films were all the rage at the time and the way the cattle market was laid out lent itself for being a ranch. Although it was supposed to be out of bounds, if we climbed over a barbed wire fence and then an iron fence we could get in. One day we were having a wonderful time when suddenly some police officers appeared through the gate from New Road. We all turned and ran home and hid in my small bedroom. My sister happened to be in the street playing with her friend and, much to her surprise, got told off even though she wasn't there. She was wearing a dress exactly the same as mine. Mother made all our clothes".

Angela recalls that the Victoria Hall "showed films three times a week on Mondays, Wednesdays and Saturdays. There were three prices: 10d (pence), 1/9 and 2/6.[22] We were allowed to go to the six o'clock performance on a Saturday. We would leave home at 5 p.m. and walk to town, enter the sweet shop called 'The Chocolate Box' (where 'Harpurs' jeweller and antiques shop [5a] is now). We would buy salted peanuts and honeycomb candy and then queue up. We knew if we were early we could get seats in the back two rows of the 10d, which were canvas and more comfortable than the wooden seats in front".

There was a town swimming pool in those days. Angela said, "We would go down the track, now called Bassett Ford Road, and come to a stile. Once over the stile, we would cross two wooden bridges, called the Jubilee Bridges (built to commemorate Queen Victoria's Jubilee). One went over the river and the other one over a backwater, where we could paddle and make reed boats. The course of the river has been altered since then and the bridges demolished. We then crossed the field, went over another small bridge and there was the pool. It was

---

[22] The denominations of coins: include the penny, two pence, three pence, six pence, shilling (12 pence), florin (24 pence), half-crown (30 pence), crown (5 shillings or 60 pence), half-sovereign (120 pence) and sovereign (240 pence or £1). Calculated in 2005 values are not comparable. Written, coinage is separated by a dash (£/s/d).

quite large with a path all around it and a terraced area to sunbathe on, with changing huts. There was also a shop selling pop, crisps and other items. There was 'Pop' in a bottle with a marble to seal the air in the 1950s and, by the 1960s, 'pop' with a wire cage that flipped to keep the fizz in. There was a lifeguard and generations of Oundle children learnt to swim there".

Angela recalled that "when you had learnt to swim well, you could then swim in the river, which had a diving board. Older boys put on diving displays from the top of the locks. They climbed up and dived in formation, probably thinking they were Tarzan. One man in particular we named 'Goldfish' as he would show-off on the lock, waiting for everyone to look at him before diving in. Teenagers would come from Peterborough and camp in the fields adjoining the river. The pool was fed with river water. Unfortunately, it became too polluted to use. The Council couldn't afford to put in a purifying plant, so it was closed down. It was a very sad day". (The pool is still extant, but overgrown and neglected).

In the 1960s the Youth Community Support Agency (YCSA) raised money to build a new pool on St. Peter's Road. Angela took her children to it. "It was very well kept, with a shop and gardens around it". She said, "I don't know why it closed". The Tennis Club now covers the area. She recalled that "A friend of mine's aunt had a rowing boat, which was moored under an arch of the North Bridge opposite Oundle Boat Club. We could swim so we were allowed to go with them. We took a picnic and swimming costumes, then took it in turns to row up to Ashton overflow (it is more like a weir now). We tied the boat up and got changed behind some bushes. There was a shallow part of the river, a bit like a beach, where we paddled and swam. We could also walk through the actual overflow. Sometimes we took the boat the other way to Cotterstock".

"The only time we were not allowed to wander in the countryside was in 1952, when the horrific murders happened in Ashton. An elderly couple, Mr and Mrs Peach were murdered with an axe. They lived just outside the village in a lonely cottage and were discovered by a butcher from Brudenell's (now Trendall's) delivering the meat on a Saturday morning. Scotland Yard came to investigate, but the murderer was never apprehended. There were many rumours as to who it was, but nothing was ever proved. I believe that the couple are buried in Fotheringhay Church yard".

Many celebrations were held for the coronation in June 1953. Angela said, "My sister, two friends and I won first prize in our class in the Fancy Dress Competition, dressed as the emblems of the four countries of the UK – Rose, Daffodil, Thistle and Shamrock. The dresses were made of crepe paper".

"As children we went to Sunday-school. We went quite often to St. Peter's, but sometimes to the Methodist and Congregational Chapels. The deciding factor was which one had the best Christmas party or summer outing. When we were older, we had a keen interest in Evensong at St. Peter's Church (not due to Canon Downe's sermons), but because Oundle school boys would be going to chapel at the same time and we would meet them coming from all directions. In those days the boys were not allowed to speak to local girls, so we would only look".

Angela recalled that the local shops have changed a great deal. "At one time we had three wet-fish shops, which also sold fish and chips". (The Stoke's, Ganderton's and Shutt's all had a fish stores and sold ice from 74 West Street.) They were all located in West Street, beyond the International Stores (now Oxfam). The Co-op was where the Italian Restaurant (formerly 'Artizan' gifts) is now. "We had three butchers, two green-grocers, two sweet shops, two or three bakers, two iron-mongers, two newsagents (one of which belonged to Anne and Ruth Leayton's family) and a saddlers. The Gas and Electricity Boards had shops too. Boots the Chemist was where Simmonds' was and there was also a chemists called Whitwell's (by the war memorial; now 'Boots'). There was also a drapers, a haberdashers and three banks. The Amps family had a grocer shop and Cotton's shoe shop was here. There were more public houses. One, the 'Waggon and Horses' (on the West Street and Mill Lane corner) had a paddock on which the fair was erected. The circus also visited the town. South Bridge Close is built on the paddock it used. The Women's Institute hut was also on South Road". Every shop had its own character and smell. Today they are sadly uniform!

From the age of five to eleven, Angela attended the primary school on Milton Road. She remember the "lovely May Day celebrations and the concerts that were put on". As she had passed the eleven plus, she went to the High School in Wellingborough and travelled to school by train. "You could also take the train from the station near North Bridge to Peterborough. Doctor Beeching wielded his axe on the line in the sixties. Since then the station has been converted into a house. On several occasions we watched elephants belonging to Roberts' Circus being led from the station to their winter quarters at Polebrook".

Angela reminisced, "When we were old enough my friends and I went to the Youth Club, run by the late Reg Sutton and Captain Lacey. It was held in the Drill Hall, which still belonged to the Territorial Army. When I was sixteen, I was allowed to go to dances in the Victoria Hall and the Drill Hall. We learnt all the ballroom dances until suddenly Rock 'n' Roll took over. People came from Peterborough, Corby and all around. We had a fantastic time, jiving the night away in stiletto heels and very tight or very full skirts. Soft drinks and sandwiches were served. We didn't need anything else for a wonderful night out".

Angela's first job was working in the office of Smith's Brewery on North Street. "At one time it was one of the largest employers in the town. The brewery was taken over by 'W. and R.' when I worked there and then by Courage, I believe. Eventually, it closed and the buildings on North Street and Blackpot Lane were completely demolished and houses built on the land. It was a very happy time I spent there; we were like one big family".

Angela's father, Albert Taney and his brothers and sisters were born and brought up in Oundle, as was their mother before them. Angela recalled that "it was a very proud moment for the family when Taney Court was named after my aunt, May Taney, who lived in that spot on East Road for most of her life".[23]

...oooOOOooo...

---

[23] Ellen May Taney ('May') was born in 1891; family information with thanks to Angela Hudson.

Recollections from Hetty Bell

Hetty Bell was born in 1929 at 1 Rock Road. She was the daughter of William (1888-1960) and Alice Bell (née Ely; 1890-1956). William and Alice were married in Bourne, Lincolnshire in 1915. Her siblings, Charles (1919), Cecil (1921) and Evelyn (1926) were all older than Hetty. This is the first on the terrace of houses after the 'jitty'. (Not to be confused with the 'light-house' tall, corner building that is in New Road.) At the time of her birth there were just a few other houses nearby. The Glapthorn Road had a few houses clustered by the mill, but the views from Hetty's Rock Road house were all of fields. These were "all ups and downs, stray ground and nothing else there." She said, "We spent times playing in the fields".

Hetty remarked on the speech days of years gone by. She said, "When we were younger the public school boys' parents would come for speech weekends and stayed in the local houses. Quite a lot used to stay in Rock Road. They were provided with bed-and-breakfast and an evening meal." "Dad used to grow new potatoes, carrots and peas and he would sell them at speech weekend to the parents. The money he raised used to pay for a holiday for the family. So, we went away to the seaside." "On the Saturday evening, the local families went up the road to go to watch the people going in to the Great Hall in their furs and posh clothes. The Great Hall hasn't changed, except the railings are missing from outside the other part of the school. Some parents had caravans to stay in on the Home Close".

Her father worked in the RAF in the war. When she was four years of age, Hetty's family moved to New Road where, at that time, there were "only the two identical houses". She said that they lived "on the other side from Rock Road and the top houses came down to the Caborne's house. That was once two houses that had been made into one; where Orchard Close is now, behind Mike Clack's old house. There was waste ground, but then there were just the two houses. I think this was where Mrs Cheetham lived". There are now five bungalows on the land that was the garden of Michael Clack's old house at 6 New Road. Hetty said, "There wasn't a bungalow there then. The rest of the hillside was made up of garden-allotments. Dad had three allotments and grew a range of vegetables". Hetty recalls that on the corner of Gordon Road the current Chinese take-away was formerly Mrs Wyman's small, grocery shop. Mr Wyman mended shoes up the garden. Meanwhile, Mrs Wyman "sold everything in the shop from big glass jars. Her niece, Beryl took over running the shop and had it after she died". Many years later the shop was sold to Mr and Mrs Beech.

Hetty clearly recalled that "Millfields was an orchard with a large house (but I can't remember what the house was called. It may have just been Red House). You went up the drive and there was a lovely big garden and the large house with an orchard. I always thought that if I won the pools, I'd like to buy it." On the other side of the road, "The Weston's lived in 'the corner Lighthouse'. The house opposite on Rock Road (number 2) was the home of Charlie and Mabel Fisher. They often entertained guests in their front-room. They took in School parents for speech days and at the end of term." Just on New Road, "The Schools had chickens, but they built six houses for their workers there where there were just fields and hens. Then there were just those houses there." Hetty said, "Cars were fewer, so we played in the street". "Mrs Chown had no children, so didn't want to be disturbed by our noises when we were playing. She would come out and shout, "Go and play outside your own house". We were children, so we didn't notice any noise!"

Hetty lived in a house "rented to us by Mrs Hewitt (who was the Laundimer house-master). Dad (William) worked as a houseman for the public school". "Our neighbours were John Cunnington, who lived in the house next-door to us and Mr Collier, a policeman, who lived in the house at the top of New Road hill". (A lovely photograph shows Hetty at this time. She said that it was "taken by someone who worked with dad at Miss Davidson's drapery shop on the corner of the Market Place.")

Playing was "safe and fun" in the road as the "big dyke was open and the water ran down the middle of where the road is now. I don't think there was a path there. We would come outside, drop the sticks at the first house on the hill on New Road, and run down, round the house, to see the sticks going downhill." She recalled that "Oundle School built six houses for their workers. They are the ones that go down the right-side of New Road. Before we had all these houses we had bad winters and it snowed. We had a big sledge and we'd go down the hill on it. It was smooth. Dad went down the hill one day and his brakes didn't work and he couldn't stop so he went over the fence at the bottom".

Hetty continued and mentioned that the "field at the bottom of the road is just the same" and the "memorial field hasn't really changed at all. They have added some more play items to the other side of this, but not much has moved. The cut through to get to the park wasn't there until the council houses were built. The road turned round at the bottom as it is now."

She said that the newly-developed road (Gordon Road) "had started out with just a few houses in it, but then it was built as a loop, when they built for young married people who needed houses. Before this the Gordon Road Council houses did not exist. They were all built at the same time."

Hetty Bell - My Working Life

Hetty reflected that her "Mum died and they turned part of the orchard where she lived into housing." "At the Workhouse hospital on Glapthorn Road, they had VADs helping out". (The VADs were nurses in the Voluntary Aid Detachment, a unit that provided field-nursing aid and services to hospitals, as during the world wars the units were needed for assistance, as doctors and nurses were often abroad or at war. Hetty's mum, Alice Bell, went to Oundle hospital for respite care.

Hetty worked at the kitchen in the Middle School. She met and married, George, when she was twenty-seven (in early 1957). "I was serving him dinners at the school and that was that". She recalls that she was working with Emily Afford. "George and I got married, so after we'd had Darren someone said, 'You need to be on the list', so we went along to see Mrs Lottie Mason and signed up, as the Urban Council had decided to start putting up council houses and building was underway". Hetty alleged she wouldn't have got the council house if Lottie had not "put our names forward." Hetty lived in New Road until after she married.

George and Hetty applied for and acquired 12 Gordon Road, on the centre of the horseshoe-shaped road. Hetty said that "you went down some steps and out at the front to outside or you could go out of the side and into the garden". "There were quite big gardens that met at the back with just wire fences between them." She noted, "When we lived there, I hated it. The only good thing about it was that my sister, Mary, lived behind us. As the gardens met at the back we could talk at the fence. The Carroll's lived nearby, just past the end of the terraces, in the first of the council houses." She went on to say, "We knew all of our neighbours, but I never felt that it was really my home." Hetty said that Oundle was a "lovely little town". She went on to state her worries by mourning the green spaces. "It's getting too big. Have you seen the new houses put in just before the 'George'? I often wonder what it will be like in the future. I dread to think!"

When Cheryl Forscutt (née Miles) was a girl in the 1960's, she lived near to Hetty in Gordon Road. At that time, the view from Gordon Road was of "nothing but fields". There were fields and allotments from the southern side of the road to Blackpot Lane and fields to the west (uphill) to the Home Close and Glapthorn Road. It is worthy of noting here that allotments were "shared and allotted" between the populace, hence the name allotments. The cornfield was used as a short-cut to school in Milton Road and West Street.

The numbering for the terraced houses originally ran from 1 to 21, but after the Council houses were built, the numbering changed to incorporate both sides of the road. Therefore, what was number 11 has become 21.[24] Hetty stated, "I remember when war was declared, and we came down to the allotments out of the houses and filled sand bags with soil."

When talking about her war-time childhood, Hetty said, "I first started school at the Council School down town (where the old sec. mod was. That was the school for youngsters up to seniors. The council stepped in and turned the Church School into a primary school and turned the other one into a senior school. We used to go down the Glapthorn Road to the school. They had outside toilets and they used to freeze up. You'd have to leave your classroom in the rain and go into the open air toilets. I remember when Mrs Perring was the headmistress. She was very nice. The classrooms had a sliding wooden partition, so you could have two classes or one big one. We used to have milk every day.

---

[24] With thanks to Angela Hudson.

It was provided by the government. In the winter we'd put it on the pipes to warm. It came in little chunky bottles."

Hetty talked about the land and people of New Road. She said that "At the top of the hill on New Road there was Mr Collier (a policeman) in one and a lady from Glapthorn was in the other. They had the two houses at the top. Mr and Mrs Winham and their son, David, lived nearby". Hetty remarked that "Somebody got lockjaw from playing in the dirt on the land there. There was a big to-do about it. They tried to stop children playing there, but you know what children do". The old farm house (6) was set in a large garden from before the turn of the century, but the garden has been developed into housing since 1990s. One place the children really liked was "Mrs Wyman's shop that was on the corner". Hetty remarked that New Road, "completely ended at Gordon Road. From there on there were just fields again." (The river cow-pastures remain largely unchanged.)

Hetty said that "In Gordon Road, Mr Lesley Baxter fixed radios for a living". She mentioned that he had "a large goitre on his neck that you couldn't avoid but seeing."[25] "Les lived in a little terraced-house in Gordon Road, with his mum. He worked from home and used to fix all sorts of electrical things". "Les also fixed bicycles for the local children. "His mum, Mrs Baxter, was a widow. She was very fond of cats and had quite a few! Also in Gordon Road, were Mrs Fellows (a teacher) and her sister who lived in a house together. This is the old Gordon road loop: Mr and Mrs Jackson were in the first one and the Fellows were in the second house." Sharon Hargreaves lived with her parents George and Hetty until she married. They lived moved to a Gordon Road house in 1960.

Hetty remarked, "I love Oundle. The people are helpful and friendly here. People say "good morning" and stop to chat. I'm not sure if other places are like this."

...oooOOOooo...

---

[25] A goitre is a swelling of the thyroid gland. It causes an enlarged lump to form on the neck that moves up and down when talking or swallowing. It is usually caused by an Iodine deficiency.

Growing-up in Oundle - Sue Crick (née Crawley)

fond memories of Oundle, notwithstanding moving to
she (and her husband, Mick) retired. She recalls that
e grew up with her dad, as her dad's mum (her paternal
r) was a widow. The Crawley family girls were nurses by
profession (and bought a nursing home near Birmingham at one point).
Stanley, Sue's dad, was born in 1919. He grew-up and found work (in
his teens) in pre-war Clopton as a groom at Clopton Hall. Sue's mum
worked in service in Clopton Hall at that time, which is how her parents
first met. They married at the onset of WWII and Stanley joined the
RAF as an engineer. Sue recalls locals lining the streets for local
weddings as everyone wanted to see the 'blushing bride' as she left
the house to go to the Church.

When she grew up, Sue lived in Rock Road. The houses only stretched
as far as the end of the terraces (to what was Barbara and Stuart
Wiggins house). There were fields beyond that. Here, Sue and her
friends held their own parades and events for the people in the road.
Jill Giddings, née Plowright, would join Sue and other friends in
meeting at the mound of earth at the end of the row. They would then
play for hours in the fields. Sue says that she grew up in a treasured
time. Like others of her time, she played with friends for long hours in
the nearly traffic-free street and down by the river. She remembers
the primary school Christmas parties, where "the children were all
excited and keen. Everyone took labelled plates and cups to eat from
and party food was provided. You needed your name on your cutlery,
plate and mug to prevent them from being mislaid, as they came from
home. The name was usually written onto an Elastoplast in biro!
Parents donated a cake or biscuits, a set jelly, ice-cream or juice-
squashes to help the costs. Everyone had a wonderful time".

Sue recalls the Oundle school land by the windmill and the 'Red House'
nearby. "The Straker family and their children lived here. The house
was very tall, like the 'Lighthouse' at 4 New Road, and was made of red
brick (hence the name). Mrs Straker ran Beetle Drives in her house.

---

[26] Sue Crick is a talented Botanical Artist.

You could enter the garden via a five-barred gate which stood where the entrance to Millfields cul-de-sac is now".

Sue mentioned that "Around 1976, I remember it was a very hot day and had a touring caravan that we kept in my mother and fathers garden on North Street. They were on holiday at the time and Mick and I and our youngest son Justin, who was about six at the time, were at their house. We were cleaning the caravan and Justin had climbed up a small ladder propped up against the garden wall and he had straddled the wall. He had a long stick in his hand and calmly said to his dad there is a skeleton down here. His dad thought it was one of his imaginary stories and ignored him! He was very insistent so his dad looked over the wall. Horrified at what he saw, he made Justin get down and raced up to the Police station (there were no mobile 'phones in those days!) Within a short time there were lots of police cars and blue lights. The house and garden had blue tape all around it. It was a crime scene. Next door was a brewery house where Mr and Mrs Irving lived. They were not well known for their gardening and the very large area was overgrown. The skeleton was sitting upright against the wall and all that was left other than the bones were a watch and an empty bottle. To cut a long story short the body turned out to be Jimmy Shiels who had been a 'missing person' for over a year, but the strange thing was that he only lived a little further along North Street. The police had been searching for him for months. He was an Irish man and quite a heavy drinker, so foul play was not suspected and the police came to the conclusion that he had wandered off-course on the way home from the pub. He was identified by his dental records. Justin was interviewed by a CID officer and a female officer. They were very gentle with him, but all Justin could think to ask them was could he have the skull for his bone collection. I hasten to say they said No! Justin found this all very exciting and has never had any ill effects or nightmares. He finds it a good dinner party discussion to this day".

...oooOOOooo...

My Early Life in Oundle (1948-1957) - Sue Stamper (née Knight)

Sue Stamper said that she was "born upstairs, in the living quarters above the shop, at 36 Market Place in the summer of 1948" ('Stu-Pots of Oundle' since 1992).[27] She said that she has no memories of living there, "except for one photograph of me playing in a playpen. I would add that we were living with my grandparents, as housing was scarce after the war. We then moved to 66 and 68 Benefield Road, where my first memory is of my sister being born in 1951". Sue went on to say that she recalls her family "helping to organise a Coronation party, which was held in the Women's Institute hut on South Road, where Oundle veterinary practice is. It was a very exciting time as parties were few and far between. I remember us all getting a Coronation mug, which I still have to this day. I was miffed as I was supposed to present the Coronation Queen with a bouquet, but my sister did it instead. She was obviously cuter than me!"

Sue stated at Oundle Primary School In 1953 and remembers her first day there. "We had to sit on the floor in front of a blackboard that had all the letters of the alphabet on it. In turn, we were asked to read out each letter and, depending upon how far we got, this identified which table you sat on. We sat at four tables of four children. I recall there being about forty of us with one teacher (Miss Smith) and certainly there were no teaching assistants in those days. I remember sitting on the rug and the teacher showing us flash cards. I don't remember learning how to read, but I was a quick learner and can remember reading the 'News of the World' as a very young child and my grandmother saying that I shouldn't be reading that at my age. Even back then my rebellious side came out and I carried on doing it. In the class, we all had a tidy box, which contained all our pencils and books. I loved my tidy-box and to this day I have a love of any type of box. Christmas was magical, as we had glitter and decorations cut out and made with silver foil from the tops of milk bottles. We made lanterns covered in glitter. Oh, how I would love to have had all the fairy and princess stuff that my granddaughters had".

"Whilst I was in the reception class, I broke my arm after being swung round by an older girl. She let go of me and I fell on the playground. On

[27] Previously Oxfam, 'Number 46' outfitters is now 'Stu-Pots'.

arriving home, I was whisked off to Mrs Pailing (the St. John's Ambulance[28] lady), who said that I should be taken to the doctors'. The doctor then said that I should go to Peterborough hospital. So the next day I was taken on the bus to the hospital, where my arm was set under general anaesthetic and then I came back home on the bus. No instant treatment in those days!"

"Also, during my reception year, I was a May Day Attendant. My auntie Rose made my dress for me. I was supposed to pose for a photograph, but I flatly refused; although there is photographic evidence of me on the day. I recall attending a party in the Victoria Hall. My grandmother told me to be on my best behaviour and show good manners. We had a magician who performed on the stage and somehow I found myself on the stage as his assistant. He had a magic wand and every time I held it in my hand it collapsed, but when he took it back it retained its shape. Of course, there was laughter from the audience."

"In 1954 we moved to our own house at 18 Tilley Hill Close. We played in the fields behind the house, which belonged to Mr Ray, the milkman. We would collect rose-hips from the hedges to take to school and received money for them from the factory in Lincolnshire. We would play outside all day (weather permitting) either on the big green (around which the houses in Tilley Hill Close were built) or in the spinney on Glapthorn Road. There was a deep well in the spinney and I would always worry about falling down it. If we were really lucky, we would go to the recreation ground in New Road."

"After my brother was born we moved to a bigger house at 2 Tilley Hill Close. It was just across the road. All of our furniture was moved, courtesy of Mr Waddington and his cart. I think that he was a gas-fitter or something, so he had a cart for his business."

Sue said, "The houses were cold in those days and I remember waking up to the windows covered in frost and the curtains stuck to them. We used to breathe on the windows and melt the ice to see if it had been snowing. Getting out of bed onto the cold lino was also another

---

[28] The Order of St. John dates to around 200 A.D. The Tresham family brought knowledge of the Order to Northamptonshire. The St. John's Ambulance Brigade was created in 1887 and came to Oundle in 1895. Their office was at the Brereton Rooms, Church Street.

memory". (1947 was a particularly severe winter across the UK and snow-drifts caused towns to be cut off. Water sources and streams froze. This was repeated in the winter of 1962-1963.) Sue continued, "We would walk to and from school in little groups or if we were lucky Mr Dann would take us in his van. We used to sit in it waiting for him to come out of his house".

Sue fondly remembers dance classes. She remembers "having ballet lessons with Mrs Rawlings in the Brereton Rooms and we would go round performing at fetes and other events. I recall going to Barnwell Manor and dancing before Princess Alice, the Duchess of Gloucester. Again, my Aunt Rose made me a ballet dress out of pink silk. I had to give these lessons up when we moved away from Oundle in 1957 when my dad was promoted to a position in Norwich". Sue continually returns to visit her friends in the town whenever she can.

...oooOOOooo...

EDUCATION - OUR SCHOOL DAYS (OR DAZE!)

A History of Oundle's First Community Play-group (1963-1986)

In the early days, young children spent their days learning at either Cobthorne House Nursery School on West Street or Miss Webb's' Private School in Herne Road. That is, until Cobthorne closed. Cobthorne was run by the headmaster of Oundle School and his wife for their own children and their friends' children. In the early 1960s, it closed down for a couple of reasons: their children had passed the age of nursery schooling and the Minister of Education was putting a stop to all Local Authority Nursery School spending. Following discussions with local mothers, Dr Elizabeth Grantham, the mother of three small children of her own, began a home-based nursery school for her offspring and their friends. At the time, she and her husband, Doctor Vincent Grantham, were living in a flat above the surgery (in Queen Anne's on West Street).

In the beginning, Elizabeth used her own nursery for the six children attending the sessions. Each session meant that she had to constantly put away all the furniture and set out new items and toys for the sitting-room to be used. When the surgery was moved to larger premises in West Street, the Grantham's took the opportunity to buy the whole house. A few pieces of basic furniture were purchased from the old Cobthorne School and the sessions were run in what had been the downstairs waiting-room. This meant that all activities had to be undertaken in one room, but this removed the problem of clearing away each day. In the summer of 1963, the 'Queen Anne Play-group' was born, which was the only play-group in the whole Peterborough and Northamptonshire area.

A traditional 'Nanny', Miss Kathleen Toon, was employed to run the sessions. She was ably assisted by a couple of mothers. Parental involvement was not a large part of running a play-group at the time. Twelve children attended for three mornings each week. They paid a fee of 12/6 (twelve shillings and sixpence) for each child. Each child provided a box of crayons, half-a-pound of Plasticine (a soft, pungent, modelling material, "Oh look, Mummy, I made a snake!"), biscuits and a mug along with their fee. Days were spent in play activities that included use of home-made playdough, nursery-rhyme sessions with the accompaniment of the piano and a daily fifteen-minute viewing of BBC T.V.'s "Watch with Mother". Many recall that 'Picture Book was shown on Mondays (from 1950s), "Andy Pandy" on Tuesdays, "Bill and Ben, the Flower Pot Men" mid-week, "Rag, Tag and Bobtail" on Thursdays and the "Woodentops" on Fridays.[29] A visiting violinist and pianist would also play regularly for the children. Miss Toon encouraged the children and built their self-confidence. She always insisted on them helping to clear away the equipment at the end of the session. At the back of the house was a long garden with a sandpit, a climbing frame and bicycles. The play-group had the use of a private swimming pool and had an annual spring visit to a nearby farm to see the newly born lambs.

Elizabeth Grantham realised that her own ideas reflected those of many other mothers in the UK. At this time, like-minded mothers joined together to form the Preschool Providers Association. It coordinated policies, shared ideas and started the nationwide control on Early Years regulations that we have today. Elizabeth's nearest contact was Barbara Keeley (in Bedfordshire). Correspondence and

---

[29] The 1953-1975, BBC series for toddlers was a spin-off of BBC radio "Listen with Mother" (1951); intended for infants and mothers, it was short (15 minutes) and allowed for a nap (before bigger children finished school).

exchange of ideas and views followed. The Queen Anne Play-group also defined its philosophies and values with the support of a National Play-group Advisor, Brenda Crowe. For five years the setting provided mornings sessions (with some afternoons). For the first two years Queen Anne's was run as a nursery school, which evolved into a fully integrated National PPA group with a committee, a formal constitution and an accounting system. So renowned had it grown by mid-1960 that two play-groups began in Peterborough after Oundle visits.

The Move to Glapthorn Road Hospital (1968-1978)

As the play-group expanded, the need for larger premises became apparent. In 1968, the Social Services Department offered the play-group larger accommodation when the ground-floor flat at the Glapthorn Road Hospital became available. The premises had a kitchen, toilet, large passageway (that was sometimes used as a playroom) and two smaller rooms (that were knocked into one large room in 1969). Large boxes for climbing were kept in the passage and the newly enlarged room housed the railway, garage, Wendy-house and the large table around which at least twelve children could sit (originally purchased from Cobthorne School). The play-group had the sole use of the building, which meant that items could be left out overnight and displays could remain on the walls, easing the workload of the day. At this point, the play-group formally changed its name to "The Oundle and District Play-group Association". Toys were donated or made for the group and Secondary School boys made a set of large, wooden climbing-blocks in a community project. A lawn was laid with a sandpit and climbing frame installed. The old people's home residents next-door were an appreciative audience.

Miss Kathleen Toon (who lived nearby in Rock Road) continued to supervise the sessions with a paid helper and a mother. By 1970, the play-group had developed to teach forty-five children that aged from three to five years. The children were divided into three groups with sessions being distributed throughout the week. The older fifteen children had the option of attending on Fridays (when they did more creative work and woodwork, plus 'readiness for school' preparations such as 'shoe-lace tying'). At break times, the children collected their own mugs and biscuit tins. A cellist from Oundle School was a regular visitor, along with the police sergeant (talking about road safety). Visits

46

to the fire-station next-door and local farm continued, alongside seeing maypole dancing at nearby schools. A late-60s project was 'Swap shop', a continuous clothing sale, set up in the passage by Miss Toon. The group took quarter of the asking price, which proved a good source of income. This was temporarily halted when the ceiling fell down and required fixing! In the early-1970s, the role of play-group secretary was important for advertising and encouraging parent involvement (largely mothers). By 1975 the play-group had fifty-three children. It was full and over-stretched, so new Corby and Peterborough nurseries benefitted from those who were turned away. In 1977 the play-group and PPA joined forces. Miss Toon retired, with her contributions and character recalled with fondness for years to come.

Struggles for Accommodation (1978-1982)

In the April of 1977, there were persistent rumours of play-group accommodation being turned into an old people's retirement home, although reassurances were given that the play-group would not be evicted without a new base being provided. There were reports of a change of use for the property since 1971, but now the threat was becoming a reality. In 1980, the Oundle Road Safety Committee was formed, on which a play-group member served to forward the group's views and community involvement.

The play-group was offered the use of the Scout Hut (on St. Peter's Road). As the years progressed, it became increasingly apparent that all was not well. The cold concrete floors were causing cuts, bumps and bruises; the pilot-light for the gas blew out regularly and the room needed 'airing'. Burst pipes were common and, when the boiler was accidentally turned off the pipes froze, leaving the building without water. Nearby parents offered a 'shuttle' of buckets to keep the play-group operating.

Fletton House (1982-1986)

After four years in the Scout Hut, it was clear that a better base was desirable. In 1982, the Northamptonshire Education Services acquired Fletton House, a former hospital and workhouse that sat empty for decades on Glapthorn Road. This large, airy building had originally

47

been part of the workhouse and was latterly used as a hospital for elderly gentlemen. The Youth Club had the use of a large room in the evenings and offered to share this with the play-group. Northamptonshire County Council decorated the building and the offer was gratefully accepted. On 27th July 1982, a working party of mothers gathered at the Scout Hut to clean, sort and pack the toys. The larger apparatus was moved to its new home by tractor and trailer, courtesy of a local farmer. Fathers erected a shed and the climbing-frame before setting to work laying out the new 'Oundle and District Preschool Play-group' playground. After many years the play-group was 'home' at its base again. Helpers, Lottie Hewitson (of Berrystead Barn) and Pamela Miller (of Orchard House, Benefield Road) left to start new careers when the move took place and "were given book tokens as a 'thank you' gift". Chairperson, Linda Halton (of Kings Road) moved to Cambridge and was presented with a rose-bush. Sheila Smith took over her role as new parents and children started. In many ways it was a new beginning.

Despite its age and erected in the late-1800s, Fletton House had many advantages. It was central between the schools for ease of drop-off and pick-up. It had good washing facilities, efficient heating, wooden floors and ample storage. A single, large, sunny room housed the play-group, enabling lots of stimulating activities to take place simultaneously in one space. It is next to the town library and doctor's surgery. By the summer of 1978, alterations were in progress and temporary accommodation was investigated. Yet again, the Scout Hut was the only alternative. A shed was provided, along with some tables and chairs. An outside playground was laid and fenced in by parents. Reg Sutton (the chairman of the Scout Hut Management Committee) helped in the organisation of this. A large, hollow log became a favourite piece of apparatus. The first newsletter was produced in 1978, informing parents of events and activities and offering an exchange of views.

The Friday morning sessions for the older children continued and included cooking (popcorn was a favourite). Open days, sponsored runs and family walks were successful innovations. In 1980, the first Christmas Fayre was held and was a regular feature thereafter. The year also saw the formation of the Mother and Toddler Group sessions.

The year 1983 saw twentieth anniversary celebrations for the group and recalled pioneering days, when Elizabeth Grantham spoke on the pre-school's formation. The same year marked a change of name to "Oundle Community Play-group", which was felt to be a more appropriate name for a local, parent-run play-group. Elizabeth Grantham continued to serve on the committee for a few more years following the move from West Street and remained an advisor until the end of the century. She also advised on the National Sub-Committee for Handicapped Children and was keen to see disabled children attend play-groups. She embraces the PPA philosophy of "We accept you as you are and help you to grow".

By 1986, the play-group was happily settled in Fletton House. It was split into two groups with different supervisors. One met on Mondays, Wednesdays and Friday mornings and the other on Tuesday and Thursday mornings. Introductory sessions for the two-and-a-half year olds were held on Tuesday and Thursday afternoons. A supervisor, an assistant and a rota-duty mother took the sessions. They were often helped by Prince William School pupils and girls on the Youth Opportunity Programme.

A regular and welcome visitor was an "original old girl" from the first play-group, Carrie (Elizabeth Grantham's daughter), who brought along her baby son and played her guitar to accompany the children in singing. The committee had grown to ten members. They held regular meetings and elected new members each autumn at the AGM and had regular fund-raising events to keep funds stable. In 1986, sweatshirts with the newly-adopted teddy-bear logo were bought. (In later years, I was one of the teachers leading the pre-school from 2003-2006.)[30]

Recent History (1986 and into a new millennium)

Since the turn of this century, the building was flooded and yet again, the Pre-School had to move. This time to Occupation Road Rugby Club premises. 2014 was a year of change, as the 1800s building of Fletton House was offered to Oundle Town Council in an asset transfer by Northamptonshire County. Since then the Town Council have made the move to Fletton House. In October 2015, following an extensive

---

[30] Anna Fernyhough.

refurbishment, Fletton House was open again. New facilities, including a transformation of use of the upstairs space housing the Town Clerk and Council, meeting rooms, a dance and activity studio, an arts-and-crafts room, a ceremony room and much more has appeared within the building. Central to the building is the 'Hub' cafe, where you can relax and enjoy tea, coffee and cakes. The Preschool has recommenced work in its home-base. Changes have been made to the layout and security has been enhanced within the confines of the building and preschool play area.

Three years ago, the Manager, Gina, introduced a 'forest school' day on Thursdays each week that were run at Barnwell Park. This ended after the introduction of a wild garden with ramps and equipment that is used by the children in an area sandwiched between Fletton House and the Library.

Having endorsed new technology, the pre-school is fully in the twenty-first century. They have used an electronic tablet for the past half-decade to document and register observations and reporting for the children. Alison Flint commented that "it is lovely to see the children accessing their own pictures and notes on the iPads". Alison also mentioned that "they are often just as adept as the adults in using the equipment".[31] There has always been a threat that the Preschool would need to move to a new base but hopefully this will not happen for a very long time.

Elizabeth's dream of all children in their formative years having access to pre-school learning has come true.[32] Oundle children have entrée to enlightening play-outings with staff (and parents) to woods and fields, tea-shops, the fire-station and library and discover their world from our wonderful town.

---

[31] Alison Flint, Deputy Manager.

[32] As a qualified and experienced teacher, In 2012 I funded and founded Little Ducklings Pre-School, in nearby Barnwell. Once established and running efficiently, I handed over its management to staff (2016), whilst remaining a Director of my Company.

PRIMARY SCHOOL AND BEYOND

Local Infant and Junior Schools

Several unrestricted primary schools have functioned in Oundle. The first started in the parish church in the 1600s. As the 'National School for the Education of the Poor in the Principles of the Established Church', it was moved to behind the Talbot Inn. The Milton Road primary school was opened in in 1842. In 1872 it divided the boys and girls. The boys attended the (North Street) Latham's school in a house that also housed the head of the school. The school genders were combined in 1903 (in the Milton Road buildings).

In the 1930's Oundle had two private schools. St. Christopher's was on the Ashton Road and was known as a 'Red Cap School'. Miss Webb and her sister managed it. St. Anne's in the Grove School was located on Milton Road. More recently Laxton Junior School pupils were taught in North Street. They were moved to East Road on the advent of a new, purpose-built school. Children at the Church of England Primary School (Milton Road) moved to the Middle School buildings on Cotterstock Road in 2016.

...oooOOOooo...

David Wills' School Days

David was born in Glapthorn Road (1935) in his grandmother's house, but lived in with his parents in Yaxley until the start of the war. He moved to 9 St. Osyth's Lane into the red-brick, three-storey houses (that have since been demolished to make way for the Co-op). He said, "The house had a water supply in the upstairs bathroom, but nothing on the other floors. There was a well nearby that other houses used as well as us". David's mother did the laundry in the bath and then "lugged it down to the back-yard to be pegged on the washing line to dry in the wind and sunshine". Miss Janet Ellis lived next-door at number 10. She lived downstairs in the summer and upstairs in the winter (when the cellar floor flooded). David's family didn't use the cellar very much for this reason.

David Wills attended Milton Road Primary School when Mrs Mabel Perring was the head-teacher. David recalls being upset on his first day.

He said that he liked playing in the sand tray, so that would settle him. Mrs Batson was his reception teacher. She was with the youngest children, but there was also Miss Blinns and Mrs Turland teaching there from that same time.

Some children attended the British School. It was built in 1843 and is now a private residence. (Part of the school is now 'Spurlings', with close to thirty, new, terraced and detached houses on the site dating to circa 1996). The British School had a hard play-area and the genders were separated by an iron fence. The toilets were in a block in the playground. Next-door, was a paddock and slaughter-house that belonged to Percival John North (later H. Johnson's and 'Seven Wells') butchery. Percy was born in Oundle in 1890 and ran the butcher's shop at 8 West Street for many years. David Wills and others mentioned that the children could hear the animals lowing, but thought nothing of it at that time. Johnson's had an advertisement that mentioned that they had "only home killed meat". By the 1960s they had their own abbatoir at the bottom of their garden. Wendy Bollans recalls often visiting the Johnson family home and premises to play with their daughter, Christine. Mrs Johnson gave salutary warnings against visiting the back of the house as it would give her nightmares! Canon James L. Cartwright (1899-1978) took all of the children for school assemblies in the hall.

For David and his friends an annual highlight was May Day on the Vicarage lawn. The celebrations, sunshine, colour and pageantry were memorable. Firstly, there were many, many practices to get the dancing around the maypole perfect, with the boys sitting still on the base of the pole to keep it from toppling while dancers whirled around. (David said that he was never chosen to sit on the base.) Sometimes, but not often, the lawn in front of the Great Hall was used for the May Day parade from school, with class performances of singing and the dancing displays. In the war years children made May garlands and covered them with net. When people looked they paid for the privilege and put money into a box for the Red Cross. The May Queen and her attendants were followed from the school by crocodile-lines of classes and then the display children with their decorated prams, bicycles and garlands. The competitions (with savings-stamp prizes) challenged children to make the best garland. Children spent time preparing their exhibits at home in the days before. If the afternoon ended early, parents were allowed to take their children home before the end of school day. That was a treat.

...oooOOOooo...

Oundle Primary School (circa 1960)

The Primary School Day

After arriving in school and saying goodbye to mum, children would wait for the hand-bell to signal the start of the school day. The classes went first to their classrooms for registration, then it was time for the daily assembly. These started with each of the classes and their teachers filing (single-file) into a packed hall. Children would then sit cross-legged in neat rows, trying not to fidget. "I would roll my socks up and down my leg as I often couldn't hear what was being said". Pity went out to the child singled-out for talking or not paying attention. No-one wanted to be caught or accused of chatting, passing on notes or inattention. The general assembly theme and prayers were Christian, as St. Peter's is a 'Church School'. Children sang a hymns, learned a new song (by rote-echoing a teacher) and listened to the Headmaster. In the 1960s, Mr Denley would instruct us how to use paper towels, on having shiny shoes or our general politeness. Everyone would mumble through the Lord's Prayer before shuffling out (in crocodile-lines) to music played by Mrs Batson on the piano.

The first days of starting school in the 1960s could be quite traumatic. Crying children were foisted off on their neighbours and distant relatives to prevent their tears from infecting others. Almost everyone I spoke with recalled a day of not knowing anyone or what was going on. Most children had no idea what to expect and had never been away from their mother before. There was no such thing as a play-date or preschool then. Many people found their early days in school were an ordeal.

The primary school uniform was 'regulation-wear'. Girls wore a brown tunic-dress or pleated skirt and a white shirt under a cardigan. The boys wore a shirt with short-trousers in the summer and longer trousers in the cold winters! Children had brown blazers with a school logo (sewn on by mothers). The school badge bore the St. Peter's Crossed-Keys emblem.[33] All children wore a brown and yellow striped tie. Some had a matching scarf that was made in the school knitting class. A pair of Clarks' shoes meant a visit to Cottons' before the start of each academic year, which were often scuffed "within minutes", leaving mothers to complain about the cost. When shoes were scuffed or ruined they could be buffed, polished, patched or repaired until parents could afford a new pair. Shoes were expected to last the year! If parents found holes in their child's cardigan it was often darned or patched and reused. People did not live in a world of new, but one of repair and recycle – long before the next generation thought they had invented it.

In St. Peter's Primary School just before play-time, each day children would be given a third of a pint of milk (paid for by taxes until it was cut in the 1970s).[34] It arrived in heavy crates that were 'lugged' into the classrooms by the boys of the top form. Once inside the classroom, we would occasionally gain the privilege of being the 'milk monitor'. The chubby bottles often had their foil tops pecked open by hungry birds before it ever got to the class. Children would give out the miniature bottles to the class, along with a waxed paper straw (that went soggy through sucking!). The milk was either frozen or warm. Neither was nice. "I would give mine to anyone who wanted it. After drinking the milk we were allowed outside to play".[35]

Classes were generally conducted in silence. Hands were raised to ask a question (such as "Please, may I go to the toilet?"). Talking in the class was not permitted. If a class "deserved a reward" the teacher could dismiss the class a couple of minutes earlier than the rest of the school, which meant the playground was empty. It was a bonus to be let out early! The teachers were probably just as interested to get to the staff-room for a cup of tea. Noises outside meant that other classes were out. The class would charge out into the playground, delighted to be free to make some noise and play with their friends. Children

---

[33] The Bible, Matthew 16:19, Jesus says to Peter, "I will give you the keys of the kingdom of heaven" and hence St. Peter's crossed-keys were a symbol of the keys of heaven.

[34] Margaret Thatcher, Education Secretary in 1971 was known as "Maggie Thatcher, milk snatcher" when she axed free milk for primary school children.

[35] Oral history, Anna Fernyhough.

indulged in playing 'conkers', snail racing, 'French knitting' and 'Cats' cradle' (with bits of wool or elastic), British bulldog, 'kiss-chasing', football, skipping and a climbing trees (sometimes over concrete, as there was no health and safety!) I broke my collarbone in the playground and the playground assistant told me to do 'windmills' with my arm to make it feel better.[36] On being taken to Doctor Lewis at the end of the day he confirmed that it was a fracture. No-one, not even my parents, complained of the 'treatment' in school as our current litigation society had not taken over. After playtimes, children lined-up to go back inside their classes ready to absorb the next batch of information, often with newly bleeding knees and extraneous bumps.

There are a myriad of memories from school days. Sharon Cottingham and I recall making papier-mache puppet heads in the top class (class 1) for a puppet-show of 'St. George and the Dragon'. Hundreds of tissue-paper, cut and folded circles that required stitching together to make decorative balls. Janet Brackley recalls the wicker-baskets that held the ingredients for cookery lessons at secondary school. Sometimes a plastic cover with a slit in the top to allow the handle to pass through, kept the items inside dry when walking to school on a rainy day.

May Days

The weather was not good in 1960, so the May Day was postponed. The garlands were judged in the school hall on the day. Mrs Spurrell, Mrs Lewis, Mrs Horsford and Mrs Amps did the judging. In 1961, May Day was on the 1st May. Alan Denley wrote, "May Day Celebration held this morning on the Vicarage lawn. Nice weather, sunny most of the time. Procession moved off at 10.15 a.m. (classes moved off at 10.30 after play from 10.15 to 10.25 a.m.). May Queen: Patricia Sharpe (Cl.1), Attendants: (Cl.1) Pamela Mold, Vivian Nursey, (Cl.2) Margaret Slote, Janet Hamilton, (Cl.3) Jill Burrows, Christine Murlin, (Cl.4) Cherry Gissing, Janet Laxton, (Cl. 5) Jane Trotman, Angela Dexter, (Cl.6) Marilyn Holmes, Susan Jones, (Cl.7) Patricia (Patsy) Allen, Jennifer Hooton. Page-boy, Douglas Kirkpatrick (Cl.7). Mrs E.C. Caldwell

---

[36] Ibid.

crowned the Queen and was assisted in garland-judging by Mrs L. Mason and Mrs M.R. Irving".

The summer term 1962, began on 1st May, with 'a full staff and eleven admissions'. Mr Denley noted that Peter Hardick (in Class 2) had been absent for several months with "pernicious illness" so had home tuition. The school May celebrations were held on Thursday 3rd May. Alan Denley commented that "The school's May celebrations were held this morning. Massed Assembly for instructions, playtime 10.15-10.25. 10.30, classes moved off to Vicarage lawn. Police coverage. The May Queen and her Attendants moved away in procession at 10.45 a.m. Ideal weather, warm and sunny (the only half-day of the week like this). May Queen: Theresa Greatrex, Attendants: Irean Carroll, Nicole James (Cl.1), Amanda Fletcher, Patricia Trehearne (Cl.2), Veronica Nursey, Carla Hardick (Cl.3), Linda Crick, Janet Payne (Cl.4), Jennifer Moore, Anna Mudza (Cl.5), Amanda Burdett, Julie Clarke (Cl.6), (twins) Patricia Smith, Karen Smith (Cl.7). May Queen's Page was Andrew Limmage (Cl.6-Cl.7 till this Easter)".

In 1963, on 7th May, the May Queen was Jayne Roughton and her Page was Cary Wiggins (from the Infant Reception class). Jayne's attendants were (Class 7) Julie Bygrove and Lisa Thompson, (6) Sheila Denley and Rowena Jackson, (5) Karen Fenson and Janine Hardick, (4) Catherine Londsborough and Suzanne Skingley, (3) Kathleen Shiels, Glynis Jackson, (2) Penelope Burdett and Jennifer Rootham, then (1 - top class) Sally Underwood and Lorna Jackson. Mr Denley notes that Mrs T.A. Stretton crowned the May Queen.

Each successive year, May Day seemed to advance steadily into the middle of the month! On May Day, Wednesday 15th May 1964, Mr Denley wrote, "As usual there was no dance for class 7 (reception infants). The standard of dancing was much higher this year – possibly because two postponements allowed a little more time to rehearse. A large crowd (including several men and a preponderance of mothers) supported the event. Three children from the top class collected for expenses and between them, took £5/10s/-d". Assisting Mrs J. Horsford as judges were Mrs R.K. McMichael and Miss Irene Boult. The Queen of the May was Jane Gibbs, Queen's Page, Frederick Afford (Cl.7), Attendants: Cl. 1, Nicola Morrison, Mary Sumner, Cl. 2, Barbara Emerton, Christine Johnson, Cl. 3, Wendy Mudza, Margaret Wood, Cl.

4, Rachel Sumner, Jane Tarry, Cl. 5, Amanda Brinsley, Jayne Dexter, Cl. 6, Debra Knight, Belinda Smith, Cl. 7, Carol Emerton, Jennifer Sanders. Mr Denley continues by noting that the "Garland Winners were Richard Allen, Sandra Laxton, Julie Whight, John Whight, Caroline Williams and Stephen Molsher." He notes that "The event was over by 12.15 pm, which caused consternation in the dining hall. We had hoped to finish by 12.00 noon. However, furniture was returned, meals were cleared and afternoon school started at the proper time (1.25 pm)."

The 'Northampton Advertiser' of 3rd March 1967, mentioned that the Primary School was 'grossly over-crowed' and 'squalid' with a number of "over-flow" pupils having to be taught in the British Legion Territorial Army huts and a mobile classroom. The standards at Oundle School were compared with less well-off local schools. Reg Sutton said, "If we hadn't begun to agitate I feel we may not even have had the mobile classroom for the primary school. We are not going to stop until we get a new secondary school", but this took a further five years to achieve.

In 1967, the West Street secondary school was half the required regulation size for the number of children enrolled. There was no hall or sports hall and the art and science rooms were too small. Often children had to get chairs from another classroom in order to sit. The Territorial Army huts were used for woodwork, but were by the Drill Hall. Boys had to walk there and back for their lessons. There was no running water and the loos were in the Drill Hall and were not easily accessible.

From Alan Denley's journal (5th July 1973), "Weather note: indoor temperature 76 degrees F. has been maintained for nearly two weeks now, even throughout the evenings! Normal work has been almost impossible. It has been many years since we had a sustained spell of hot weather in summer like this. Fights in the playground are on the increase because of the heat, as well as cases of bleeding".

Almost a decade later the 22nd December 1982 was the day of Alan Denley's retirement. He wrote of himself in the third-person in his journal, "The infants and juniors, ringed by parents and teachers, assembled at 2.45 pm in the school hall to say goodbye to the

Headmaster, who is about to retire. The vicar (who is also Chairman of the School Governors), Dr Lloyd R. Caddick, spoke suitably and presented the Head with a television-set and some piano music on behalf of the parents. An original painting and a writing-case (gifts from teaching and kitchen staffs, respectively) were also on display. Mr Denley replied, touching on School history and thanking everyone for their gifts and good wishes. After the ceremony the School broke-up for the Christmas holiday and should reopen on 6th January".

Alan continued, "Having served as Headmaster of Oundle C.E. School for twenty-five years and four months, I terminated my engagement today, upon retiring from the profession. Alan Denley". This was on Friday 1st December 1982. In January 1983, Mrs Anne Fox stood-in as the Acting-Head and Mrs Joan E. Fellows assisted as the Acting Deputy.

(The current primary school head is Mrs Janet McMurdo. For some years her husband managed Prince William School.)

Snack-time!

In the 1960s, Miss Kathleen Toon was a much-loved, lunchtime supervisor who sold coconut and home-made toffee in the playground at the primary school. The cost was "tuppence" (2d) for a triangular white, paper bag". Cheryl Forscutt recalls that she made the sweets in her own kitchen at 4 Rock Road. She carried them into school in her yellow, candlewick bag to sell in the playground after the children had eaten their lunches. Sharon Cottingham recalls that "the toffee had a sweet, distinctive taste and smell and came in a choice of light and sticky or hard and dark. It was yummy! She always had a few spare bags that she gave away to the children who were underprivileged and may not have had many treats".

Primary Gym

In the 1930s, (Gertrude) Sheila Brown (now Midlane) attended the local Primary and then the Council School. She was good at sport; her father, William Brown, was a member of the Oundle Town Cricket Club for many years. In the 1960s, school children took part in the twice weekly physical education (P.E.). The classes were not taken by specialists in exercise, just the same teacher they had for everything else. Games and P.E. meant "stripping down to shorts and t-shirt no matter what the weather". If anyone forgot their kit they did the exercises in their underwear (vest and pants) or had to borrow a 'spare' pair (from a friend or the lost-property cupboard). This ensured they remembered the next time! Indoor P.E. meant bare feet or 'Plimsolls.'[37] A lack of suitable footwear was not a suitable excuse to avoid gymnastics or P.E. workouts! In the 1960s, if children could not catch a ball 'Butterfingers' was a constantly used phrase.

From the 1940s to the 1960s classes had wooden desks (with a little ink-well hole for a refillable, white, pottery ink bottle that could be filled with 'Quink' ink), with a groove for a pencil and ruler. If you felt under the base of the desk it usually had something undesirable stuck to it! Some children used a pair of compasses to scratch names on the desk's wooden surface. At other times children resorted to writing on the desk with ink instead.

By the 1960s classrooms had framed-pictures around the walls, a world globe and a large blackboard at the front. No-one bothered if children were myopic and couldn't see from the back of the room. Desks were arranged in rows and children usually had their own seat. The teachers were at liberty to separate and move the disruptive children to the front, while the others just sat where they could. Children wrote with pencil until they reached the top class. A good deal of 'pencil sharpening' went on during lessons! Children could "cause trouble by whispering to each other behind the desk lid". This may be the reason why later desks had no lid, just a slot to slide books into from the front. By the 1980s these were the norm and students were allowed to choose their own seats (usually by their friends). Children would pass notes to each other, usually on nothing of consequence. This was part of the rich tapestry of growing up. A favourite part of the school for some was the library as there were so many books to choose to look at. In the top class of primary school, if there was a wet break time, children were allowed to look at comics. That was such a treat!

School dinners were obviously quite a benefit after the war, but by the 1960s they were not as pleasant or nutritious as they sounded. Some lucky children went home for lunch, but many ate school dinners.

---

[37] Plimsolls were athletic shoes (with a canvas upper and non-slip rubber sole) developed in UK as beach-wear in the 1830s.

There was always a certain smell to the food. Children would queue up for the dinner ladies to place a ladle-full of lumpy mashed potato, boiled cabbage (or other 'greens') and non-descript meat onto your plate. The food was probably cooking and boiling since the morning break. Some children liked the food and had a favourite dish. Some recall the "semolina with a blob of jam in the centre that could be stirred to make the whole thing pink". Others liked the jam roly-poly and custard and described it as delicious. (I only stayed for lunch a couple of times and then under duress. I didn't enjoy being told that I had to eat food I didn't like.[38])

Memories when retold are good and bad. Miss Batson was not averse to whacking the entire class with a ruler. Children would line-up and hold out their hands to be struck by a twelve inch wooden ruler across their palms. Often they were punished as a whole class and not as individuals. (Especially if no-one would admit to whatever misdemeanour they were accused of.) In the war years and to as late as the 1960s, children did not so much respect their teachers as fear them. School days are something personal and individual. No two students came away with the same feelings or thoughts regarding how they hated or enjoyed school. Some teachers were favoured and friendly, whereas others were quite terrifying. Without mentioning names, students had a fair share of both personality-types during senior schooling!

One teacher who taught at the primary school for many years was Bevil Allen. His father owned the bicycle shop on the corner of North Street. Bevil had three sisters named Mary (who was always called 'Alice'), Doreen and Lorna. Bevil worked in his father's betting shop in St. Osyth's Lane, but really wanted to teach. After his father died, he sold the business to the Hardick family (1966), then he and his wife trained and taught in the local primary. Thelma Quinn is related to the Allen and (Skiba) Dyson families that are interconnected. Percy Allen was Thelma's grandfather, so Jack was Bevil's father and Gordon (Thelma's dad) was his cousin. Mavis Allen was Thelma's late-aunt (her dad's sister). Many, many families in the town have an interwoven history. This is Oundle in a nutshell!

---

[38] Anna Fernyhough, personal information.

School and Work – Dialogue with Carol Moorehead (née Wright)

Carol Moorehead attended the local schools in the 1960s and 1970s. She recalls with fondness her family trips in the 1960s to Wicksteed Park (which opened in 1921). The parkland with lakes and amusements "went on for-ever". She recalls that "school days were fun". Carol said that Miss Toon was the playground assistant she remembered most clearly "as she made snacks of toffee and fudge for the children and sold them at playtime for a penny or tuppence a twist ... and we all had rotten teeth"!

Carol particularly remembers Mary Sumner, who was in the art classes with her. She also recalls Mary being a "short-haired angel in the nativity play". She also remarked that Mary had worked with her "at the Talbot in the early 1970s" (as did I). Mary had once gone into the kitchen to collect a starter dish for a table. The chef called out the table number and what the dish was, before shoving it to Mary across the counter. She came out into the restaurant and went all around the table asking for who had ordered the "heron". It was only when she went back into the kitchen with it that she realised that it was 'Rollmop herring'![39]

Carol recollects working with Lesley at the Coffee Tavern. She also has fond memories of working with her aunt "Minnie" (in the 1960s and 1970s), who "always had a fag hanging out of her mouth, but made excellent trifles"! During her time at the Talbot she worked with Ray Gray, the wine waiter. He had a penchant for young girls working there and teased them. Overall, it was a time of growing up and having fun. Carol (née Wright) and Lawrence Moorehead have lived in Springfield Road and Rockingham Hills. They married in Oundle in 1982.

...oooOOOooo...

Memories from Cheryl Forscutt (née Miles)

Cheryl recalls her first infant teacher was Miss Barrett. She always came into school and gave "Quality Streets" sweets to the children in her class. Mrs Batson had some favourite children who gained much of the praise. Others were given an immediate "naughty boy" reputation,

---

[39] Anna Fernyhough, personal history.

at the tender age of five.[40] In the second year in school two "Mrs Fellows" were teachers. This could have been confusing, but one was nice and one was not! Mrs Anne Fox taught the first year children of the junior school. Mrs Turland's class followed. They were situated in the long verandah rooms to the right of the building (from the front view) that were roofed, but open-air. (This was later altered to a glassed-in corridor).

On the way home, children of the 1960's could go into the town or cut through the fields to get home quickly to the council houses in the newer estates of Springfield and Gordon Roads. By the age of thirteen Cheryl was working, serving lunches at Laxton and Crosby (Fischer) for pocket-money. She recalls being taken on before she was old enough as she was "very responsible". Meanwhile, in school Cheryl was an "All England" Cross-Country runner in school. She took on a job at the Talbot, where she recalls working with Minnie Walker. As she talks she summons-up a taste-memory of Minnie's chocolate gateau, sherry trifle, crème caramel and the smell of curling the warm butter. She also recalls a small kitchen fire that occurred in the late-1970s, when a thermostat on the fryer overheated and burst into flames. It required the local firemen to put it out! Cheryl left school in 1976 and married in 1982. Her memories of school and work pleasures are clear and vibrant.

School Conversations with Diane Hammond (née Wyles) & Sue Wyles (*et.al.*)[41]

While having a convivial group chat in the Coffee Tavern, Margaret Slote recalled that she was "not very fast" in school and was once hurt in the school playground. She was taken home, but had to leave her bicycle behind. This possibly bothered her more than the injury! Many others recall being injured or knowing people who were injured by accidents with hockey or cricket balls during games in the Secondary Modern School.

Sharon Jackson (now Cottingham) was in Mrs Turland's class (aged 8). According to Sharon's mother, Teresa, her conductive deafness was

---

[40] Cheryl says that her twin brother, Michael, was one of these.
[41] Including Sharon Cottingham, Margaret Slote and Anna.

caused by a "build-up of chalk in her ears" (as she was a board-monitor and cleaned the dusty chalk-board)! On consultation, their doctor said that this was not the cause – "and the recurring tonsillitis was not caused by school either". Teresa was not amused.

Mrs Fellows and Mrs Turland were teachers and sisters. Teachers took turns with 'playground duty' at play-times. Each day the children lined-up by the wide gap in the stone wall before being allowed (class by class) into the class rooms. Mrs Fellows had said to walk to, but not go inside, the classroom. The statement on that day could not have been very clear, as some children went in and Sharon followed. Sharon was smacked for going inside. On arriving home her mother asked her about the day, so she went to the school to complain. A short time later the incident was mentioned in front of the class by Mrs Turland. This humiliated Sharon, but left no lasting effect as she was later chosen as 'Head Girl'.

Diane ('Di') Wyles said that she that those not enamoured of school "counted down the days until you left". She said, "You could leave school as soon as you got a job. So, I got a job with the dentist and left school at Easter, so didn't do any exams." Her sister, Susan (Sue) said, "I'm not good at mental arithmetic as I can't see figures. In Mrs Titman's class, you had to shout out the answers and I couldn't do it as I'm a visual person and not quick with auditory". "I'd never heard the term A-levels before leaving and when I left school I felt a complete and utter dunce, but have found out that I'm not". Sue continued, "If you were good at maths in school, you were working in Barclays before you knew it. For children who could not keep up with the work, humiliation was fair game. There was favouritism in all schools. I was not a favourite! Certain people were always chosen for everything and I wasn't one of them".

May Day was a time of delegation: dance, sing, sit on the pole-base, may attendants, page boy and May Queen. Margaret Brewster was voted to be an attendant and was very surprised. (She appears in the May Day photograph in this volume.) Margaret said that she had "white strap-over shoes that were fantastic, like fairy feet, as I always had sensible shoes." As stated earlier, this was a time when children had a single pair of shoes. "If you ruined them you were in trouble with your family as they were meant to last the year." May Day meant constant practises. While "Mrs Batson played the piano and we all learned to dance round the maypole". All non-dancers sang as children skipped round: "1 and 2 and 3 and 4; Take your ribbon and turn round. 1 and 2 and 3 and 4; Bow to your partner or curtsey to the floor."

Miss Parker (from the Barnwell Station House) was a teacher in Oundle Secondary Modern. It was said that she would 'jab' children if they worked badly. Several ex-pupils mentioned that some teachers of the 1960s had an issue with enunciating and spitting as they did so, thus it was not advisable to sit in the front row! Others noted that the 1960s school governor, Miss C. Capron, made open remarks regarding the local children and suggested that they needed only a rudimentary education as they would "only work in the fields and shops". This view now seems very limited, but at the time was a parochial "way of the world".[42]

In the senior school, boys did woodwork and girls took sewing classes. "It took two years to make something in the dress-making classes". Sharon said that her mother, Mrs Jackson, was a seamstress so could not bear the "waste of time that it took to make a peg bag or dress"! "We all made awful psychedelic 1960s dresses"! The treddle sewing-machines were hard to work and threading them was always a problem, plus "using your feet to push the low-treddle, while feeding material through under the needle was a coordination skill too far"! This was a time of "no waste" that had persisted since the 'make do and mend' war era. Parents were not 'spend-thrifts'. Sue said, "Parents bought us skirts that were very long in the first year, but we were still wearing them in the fourth year". This was likewise for blazers, which were expensive. (Sharon has a photograph of the secondary school students wearing multi-dot skirts and their uniform blazers.)

Sue recalls Mr Jakes, who was a judge in the literature festival. "We had to stand in the corridor and read aloud." Mr Jakes said, 'That would have been absolutely perfect if you had been a little slower', so I did it like he said and I think I got a first."

---

[42] Living at Southwick Hall and teaching at Oundle Secondary Modern (1960s) was Mrs 'Kath' Whiley. She was a warm, encouraging, helpful teacher. She also gave her time working in Oxfam.

Sharon remembers her new, black-patent shoes (circa 1970). At a point when Sharon and I were on a temporary ban from meeting, we met and walked to Polebrook. When we were running across a ploughed field (somewhere we shouldn't have been), Sharon said, "That just felt like I lost the heel of my shoe". We found it, hobbled home and Sharon's mother returned the shoes and got her money back on them! (We never said where we had been.)

Margaret said, "I've been very lucky with my growing up. I had a very happy childhood." … "Apart from when I was in Miss Smith's class and I wanted to go home for lunch, but she wouldn't let me".

…oooOOOooo…

Memoirs of the 1960s and 1970s

Many people remember their days at school, no matter which school they attended: Oundle Church of England Primary, the Secondary Modern (Council), the (now defunct) Oundle and Kings Cliffe Middle School, Prince William School, Laxton Junior or Oundle School. They are remembered with opposing outlooks; either "happy days" and "those were the days!" or "I couldn't wait to leave" and "glad those days are gone"! Opinions differ also in which subjects are liked and disliked the most and there are individual reasons for each of these.

Ann Greetham (*née* Colclough) lived in Oundle until 1966. She attended the Milton Road Primary School and the Secondary Modern School in West Street. Ann says that she has very good memories of her days spent in the town. She still meets friends in Oundle and has not moved very far, as she resides only two miles away!

Sharon Cottingham (Jackson) attended both primary and secondary schools in Oundle, before growing up, marrying and teaching in them. When she was in the primary school she said it took some years before the realisation "that on my first day in school, Mrs Fox had not given me an elf jigsaw with hundreds of pieces" (more probably nine to twelve pieces) and "when I cried she slapped me across both knees and my older sister, Glynis, had to be called for". Sharon remembered the 1960s Primary boys being sent out to lug the crate of milk inside. "In the winter the milk was so icy that bottles had to be put onto the radiator pipes to thaw! In the spring, the bluebirds would peck open

65

the silver foil tops for a drink". No-one wanted the pecked bottles, so it was "first come, first served"! "Students who didn't have a taste for milk had no choice. We were required to drink it". (Di Wyles recalled that she was one of those children.)

Any first day at school in the 1950s and early 1960s was sure to be fairly traumatic. There were no pre-schools or nurseries to cushion the way. Suddenly, girls were dressed in "special clothes" that consisted of an itchy tunic or gym-slip[43], a white shirt, a knitted cardigan, a tie and some white ankle socks. It was not much easier for the boys! Various comments from friends included, "Everything felt scratchy and new". Clothing was not at all like the comfortable outfits worn at home. "We had to walk to school, whatever the weather." "We learned to cross the main roads with the other children".

Many recollect learning to read with the old 'Beacon Readers' and 'Janet and John' books of the 1960s or vocal lessons along with "Singing Together" on the radio (where children learnt many "songs from the past"). If children were very fortunate the teacher on duty would let them collect or ring the big, brass hand-bell to summon the children to line-up ready to go into class. Children's playground games played included marbles, cats-cradle, French-knitting, skipping alone and in small groups (with singing rhymes). More boisterous games that were recalled included 'Kiss Chasing' in the playground. This was basic 'tag chasing' with a kiss to "pass on"! The concrete and grass playground had a row of big, shade trees along the western side for hiding behind or sitting under. "If you fell over, someone would take you to a teacher, who found some cotton wool and disinfectant to clean you up and put a plaster on your knee". This practice has so changed!

Mrs Perring, Mr Venner and Mr Denley were the head-teachers from the 1940s to the 1960s. All are well remembered with affection by those who attended the primary school in Milton Road. The reception teacher at the time of Mr Venner was Miss Smith. Mrs Bateson and Mrs Turland taught during the era "under Mr Venner and Ben (slap your thigh) Rowbottom" and with Alan Denley. Mr and Mrs Denley

---

[43] A gymslip was a sleeveless tunic (pinafore dress) that was part of a girl's school uniform.

came to Oundle around 1957. Many people remember Mr Denley as a "very tall, slim and well-dressed man". "A kind and thoughtful headmaster", "slightly obsessed with hand washing and how many paper towels were used, but lovely all the same". Mrs Denley was a "gentle, likeable lady". Catherine Denley believes that "dad would've been really chuffed" to know that so many people remembered him with such fondness.

Jane (Marks) Brooks lived at number 21 North Street, just opposite the Denley's house. She lived with "Granny Bunning" until she moved to Tilley Hill Close (when she was eleven). Jane recalls the day that the Denley family moved in. Her mother looked after the "young baby for them". This was the youngest child in the family, Sheila! Jackie Hilliam attended Oundle primary and the secondary schools. She mentioned that she was "uninterested" and 'bored' with school, so "always hated school", yet (despite this) "Mr Denley was always my favourite". Carole Rowsell understood that "Everyone had to have shiny shoes!" and "I remember being a Prefect and having to go to Mr Denley to ask which hymns we were having in assembly". Carole also affectionately recalls the teaching couple, Mr and Mrs Allen.

On the reverse side of these nostalgic memories, one contact said that "after a year at the senior school under Mr Evans, I still hadn't learnt how to read and write." Another remarked, "One of those things that reminds me of school is that awful smell of sawdust on vomit." Children are at times sick in school and before the development and use of chemical cleaning materials the school caretakers used sawdust (which was plentiful) on any offending mess. Yuck! The primary and secondary schools each had a sick bay, but rarely a nurse. Often children would be sent there to 'have a lie down' while their parents were contacted. (This was much harder for schools in the days before telephone or mobile usage and often a sick or injured child just had to wait until the end of the day before being collected from school and taken to see a doctor.) There was usually at least one person in the school at any one time with a broken arm or a sprained ankle!

Many students who attended the Oundle Secondary School (from the 1930s to 1972) recall "Miss Gale". Margaret Gale was a form teacher for the intake year 'A' stream and was considered to be quite strict. She had grown-up in an era when children did not answer back and did as they were asked. She expressed concern that if girls rested their heads on their hand (with an elbow on the desk) it looked lazy and would "ruin their posture". Her sentiment was that "necks were designed to support heads so there is no need to prop it up". During the year of 1966 (or early 1967) she spotted Jennifer Moore with her head propped on her hand. She promptly walked up to Jenny and slapped her around the head with the class register. Now, at this time I was keen on writing, but not very astute![44] I proved this as, later the same day, in Miss Gale's English class I wrote an essay about her hitting Jenny. I believe that I was quite outspoken about the "smack on the head with a big blue book" and suggested what medical issues could arise as a result. On her reading the essay that I had handed in to her, Miss Gale was not best pleased. I was frog-marched to Mr Whyte's office and left to await my parents (who were called in). Neither appeared to side with me (as in these days there was an intrinsic respect for teachers). I was informed that Miss Gale no longer wanted me in her class. I was demoted into the B-stream (until the fourth form, when everyone had forgotten and I was moved back to the A-stream again!). I was quite contented and made other friends. Miss Gale forgot my "misdemeanour" and I got along very well with her from then on. It was only in later life that I realised I was in the right all along. No great harm was done as I enjoyed being awarded school prizes each year and when I grew-up I trained and toiled as a teacher!

...oooOOOooo...

Gordon Edwards - Early Life in Oundle

Gordon Edwards stated, "I was born in Glapthorn in 1947. My father, Harold Edwards, came from an old Glapthorn family. My mother, Christina, was the daughter of the farm manager at the Capron estate in Southwick. Dad and mum met before World War Two at a whist drive (a card game tournament) in Southwick. They married in 1946, when dad returned from the war. These are memories from the first twenty years of my life growing-up in and around Oundle. I left the town to go to University in 1967".

---

[44] Anna Fernyhough.

Gordon's parents "lived for a short time in Glapthorn after I was born. They then moved to Barnwell Camp, which was a collection of WWII army huts along the road between Barnwell and Oundle. There is a garden centre now on the site. These huts were made available for families during the housing shortage after the war – but they were very primitive. My brother, Brian, arrived in 1950 when we were at Barnwell camp. The conditions at home meant that mum had to have Brian in Thorpe Hall, near Peterborough. We moved to Oundle in 1953 when I was six".

The Edwards' first house in Oundle was at 20 Rock Road. It was a "small terraced house with no running water, coal fires, gas lighting and a cellar which housed a colony of rats. The toilet was at the bottom of the garden was a twenty-yard walk away". Gordon said, "I had the job of tending a paraffin heater in the toilet to stop it from freezing in winter. We were lucky to get the house as good friends of my parents, Syd and Amy Rowell (who lived next-door at number 18) put in a word with the landlord when it became vacant".

Some of Gordon's earliest memories in Rock Road were "of dad plumbing in a water-system with taps and putting in electric-lighting, with the aid of an electrician friend, Bill Vine. Dad was tall and was continually ruining gas-mantles by bashing them with his head, so he was pleased when we went electric. We had a large coal-fired copper in the cellar where mum did the washing every Monday morning. My brother and I had a bath in a tin tub down there once a week. Our near neighbours in Rock Road were the Rowell's, Chris and Rose Newton, the Bygraves family and Mr and Mrs Black. I was great chums with Bruce Black (who was my age) and Tony Rowell (a couple of years older)".

Upon his arrival in Oundle, Gordon entered the Church of England Primary School in Milton Road. He went into Mrs Batson's class. He said, "This was a big school by comparison with the one in Barnwell village where I'd been for a little while before we moved. We had assemblies in the morning, where Mrs Batson always played the piano. Nurse Pulley regularly attended to inspect us all for nits and bugs, examine our teeth and look into our ears! The Headmaster when I first started there was Mr Venner, who was a graduate of Durham University. When he retired he was replaced by Mr Denley, an accomplished musician, who came from Corby. Alan Denley was keen that our shoes were always well-polished and held regular inspections. His were always bright and shiny!"

"At the primary school I progressed through the classes of Mrs Turland, Miss Wagstaff and Mr Johnson. These were enjoyable years, but I was not particularly interested in school work. When in Mr Johnson's top class I managed to fail my 11-Plus exam. I was given a second chance as my birthday fell early in the school year (September) and everyone thought I should pass. But I failed again. The classes then were large (about fifty in the top class with Mr Johnson) and I just wasn't interested or stimulated enough to try hard at school work."

Gordon's best friend at the time was David Chapman (who lived in Benefield Road, opposite the Black Horse pub). Gordon said, "We spent most of our time together after school playing cricket, fishing and collecting golf balls from the grass verge outside the Golf Club (along the Benefield Road). We collected lots of balls – there were some bad golfers in Oundle at the time who regularly hit their balls into the road! We sold them to Arthur Howitt (the saddler) who sold them on to other golfers and Oundle public school boys.

Mr Howitt's shop was initially located in New Street before moving to the market place. We got sixpence or a shilling for each ball, depending upon its condition. I still recall the beautiful smell of leather, wax, 'neatsfoot' oil and other evocative items in his shop. He also sold cricket bats, so this is where my grandmother bought me my first bat. I mention cricket as at about this time it became a real passion in my life and has stayed with me ever since. David Chapman, Tony Rowell and John Belcher (who lived in North Street) were also keen and we played a lot together. In those days there were few cars on the roads and our pitch was in the road in Rock Road, just between our house (number 20) and the Newton's house (number 22). The wicket was scratched on the wall with a stone and we bowled across the road. We had to pitch it up or bowl it very short, otherwise the ball would hit the kerb! If you walk along Rock Road nowadays and look on the wall between numbers 20 and 22, you may be able to detect the faint, still present scratches of our wicket! A teacher at the Secondary Modern School was Jimmy Lowe, who lodged with the Bamford's at the end of

Rock Road (2). He would sometimes watch us playing. More about Jimmy later!"

"In 1959 I entered Oundle Secondary Modern School and went into Miss Gale's class (1A). This was a massive change as the school was so big compared with the primary school; with many children from the surrounding villages as well as Oundle. Several names from the class float across the memory: David Chapman, Victor Burns, Brian Bailey, Robert Dawson, Susan Fensom, Susan Freshwater, Wendy Slote and many more. I often wonder where they are now."

The move to the secondary school was a big change for yet another reason: "For the first time in my life it was made clear to me by my teachers that they expected me to do my best academically, try hard, concentrate, and get to grips with every aspect of school work. It's not too much of an exaggeration to say that this was a life changing experience for me – and played a big part in 'turning me around' and forming the basis of any success I've been lucky enough to achieve in subsequent years. Going to the secondary modern school in Oundle was one of the best things that ever happened to me!"

"In the late-1950s, every Friday (or Monday) we all had to put our subject books on our desks and our Welsh headmaster, Mr Kenneth D. (Chinny) Evans[45] walked around with Miss Gale to inspect each pupil's work and the score or marks and comments in the books. This was a major event every week and the praise and criticisms from the headmaster were a great motivator. He had something positive and encouraging to say to every pupil. Everyone held him in awe. He was passionate about learning and determined that his pupils should achieve their full potential in all aspects of school life. He was conscious of being in a town with a large public school as well as a boys' grammar (Laxton School) and I'm sure this motivated him to ensure his pupils didn't suffer in comparison. Coupled with this were the fortnightly 'lists' where marks were totted up for each pupil in the class and the one at the top had to take the list up to Mr Evans every two weeks in morning assembly - in front of the whole school. What an experience – which, fortunately was mine on several occasions in that first year."

---

[45] By the 1960s, Dennis Whight was the headmaster.

Gordon said, "Then there was the 'House' system, where everyone was a member of a house (I was in Richardson House) where each month house points (awarded to pupils for good academic work or other useful deeds) were totalled - and the winning house from the whole school was determined each month. We religiously recorded our house-point tally in our jotters, which were kept in the blazer pocket at all times – a firm rule! This House organisation was a wonderful system for building teamwork and allowing us to get to know pupils from other years in the school".

He recalls, "In moving up the school one naturally came into contact with the other teachers who ran my classes. There was Mr Don (2A) who was the geography master. His favourite range of mountains was McGillycuddy's Reeks in Ireland. Leo Dunham (3A) was head of Religious Studies and English. He was a real stickler for proper pronunciation of the English language! Mrs McAdam (4A) was the Deputy Head and also head of Maths. She taught algebra and geometry and I was fascinated by these subjects. Mrs Evans (the Headmaster's wife) also did a bit of supply teaching and continued to develop my love of mathematics. Other teachers who influenced me greatly were Jimmy Lowe (teaching History and coaching boy's Games) and Les Titman (who taught Woodwork)". Gordon asked, "Does anyone else remember Jimmy's 'two good facts' test in history?"

Gordon resumed discussing one of his favourite subjects - cricket (again!). He said, "Jimmy Lowe and Leo Dunham were extremely enthusiastic about the game and as a fellow enthusiast I found these two to be real soul mates of mine among the teachers. Religiously, rain or shine, Jimmy and Leo would organise cricket practice in the playground every summer's evening after school and also during lunch hours. I begged my parents to let me have school meals so that I could join in during lunchtimes, as well as after school, but we couldn't afford it and I had to walk home every day to eat!"

He remembered that "Jimmy had been a considerable player (batsman and bowler) when at Liverpool University, representing the combined English universities. During the war Jimmy was involved in an explosion that had left him partially deaf. He used this deafness as a weapon in school. Everyone knew he heard far more than he would admit and we had to tread carefully! He was the secretary of the Town Cricket Club and ensured all aspiring players at the Secondary Modern joined the Town Club. Leo was a fine left-arm spinner who got his colours at Laxton School and could spin the ball for miles. I was astonished on first meeting him – with his demonstration of bowling at a netball post twenty-two yards away and hitting it five or six times out of ten. I recall him telling me once after practice, 'After all this batting against me, Edwards, you should never get out to a left-arm spinner in the rest of your career!' Every time I faced a left-arm spinner in later years I remembered his words and had some success in making his wish come true!"

Gordon recalled that "when I was about thirteen the first call came for me to play for the Town Cricket Club in a real match. It was away against Wansford in the Sunday 2nd XI. We drove there in Oliver Walton's car and I was asked to open the batting. I stayed in a long time and got twelve. My first real cricket match! Colin Roberts, one of our bowlers, said to me when I came back to the pavilion, 'a nice little dozen, Gordon. You'll get lots more runs if you keep playing like that'. It was a matting wicket and I remember vividly the chalk dust coming up from the matting when the bowlers bowled. I've often visited that ground at Wansford in subsequent years. It's still there, more-or-less unchanged with its (now) astro-turf wicket (just behind the Haycock hotel). At about this time, as part of the Oundle 2nd XI, I recall visiting a pub for the first time in my life after a match and tasting a pint of Shandy. This was in the 'Waggon and Horses', opposite the police station and close to the Milton Road cricket ground. I also played darts and dominoes there after matches. I had become grown-up! The 'Waggon and Horses', along with several other pubs in the town, have now disappeared."

There were some fine cricketers in the Secondary Modern school at that time who also went on to play for the Town club. Gordon said, "A couple of years ahead of me was Ivan Wallis from Stoke Doyle. Ivan scored hundreds of runs over the years. Another was Peter (Whippet) Burnham from Barnwell. A beautiful player who sadly died not long ago, after building the new pavilion on the Milton Road ground - brick by brick with his own hands. Tony Rowell was a useful all-rounder and Rodney Gilbert a fine seam-bowler who also bowled off spin. Rodney and I were selected to go for County Cricket trials one year; first in

Corby and then at the County Ground in Northampton. What an experience! Jimmy drove us there in his car".

"The Town cricket club was very strong at that time, benefitting from the presence of several Oundle School masters and players from Laxton School. Dr Eric Donovan ('Don') Tagg[46] was head of Maths at the Public School: a Wiley leg spinner and solid bat. David Woodhead was a master at Laxton and a fine batsman and leg spinner (who went on to get a 'Blue' at Cambridge). Chris Oakley and Bob Cummins were very good players when they were pupils at Laxton School. Mick Henderson, who came from Bedford, was a good opening bowler and 'Duggie' Bell another solid bat. So getting into the first team at Oundle meant you could play a bit. I became a regular first team player from the age of sixteen".

When Gordon was thirteen or fourteen he "moved from Rock Road down to Gordon Road. As my grandmother (dad's mother) from Glapthorn was very ill she had to live with us. The house in Rock Road was too small, but we were helped by town councillor, Lottie Mason, to get a bigger council house in Gordon Road. It was great, as we were literally twenty-yards away from the war Memorial Recreation Ground at the bottom of New Road, where we played cricket against the wire-netting of the tennis court".

Gordon remarked that "These were hard times for us financially. Dad was working then as a mechanic at the garage at the bottom of New Road. He didn't earn much and ran two allotments, as well as cultivating our back garden to keep the family fed. Mum worked at the Berrystead boarding house, earning a little to top-up the finances. Every evening after work during the summer months, dad was on one or other of his allotments and I was dragged along to help. He carried home sacks of potatoes across the handlebars and crossbar of his bike, which he had obtained from a good friend Fred Carter, who drove the town dust-cart. The bike had been thrown out by Mr Whitwell the chemist and dad mended it. I still have the bike. It's a 'Royal Enfield'

---

[46] 1913-1988; Born in Lancashire, Eric Tagg attended Cambridge University, then taught at Oundle School (1949-1963). He married his wife 'Mike' (née Elliot) in 1939. Eric volunteered with the Oundle St. John's Ambulance service after the war.

and dates from about 1920. It is very big, as Mr Whitwell was at least 6 feet 6 inches tall!"

"At about this time (I think I was in class 3A or maybe 4A) mum and dad received a letter from Mr Evans, the Headmaster of the Secondary Modern, to ask if they could come in and see him. "What mischief have you been up to?" was their first question to me. A few days later we went along and all sat nervously in Mr Evans' office after school. I remember his words exactly: 'I simply want to ask you one thing Mr and Mrs Edwards. I know you are finding it difficult to make ends meet, but can you assure me that you won't force Gordon out to work when he leaves here. I want him to have every opportunity to continue his education as he has considerable potential and could go very far'. I was shocked. My head was spinning. So were mum and dads'. They simply said yes! Mr Evans asked me what my favourite subjects were (apart from cricket, which he knew about, but had little interest in!). I said maths and science. He then organised for me to have extra 1:1 science classes after school with Mr Blackman, the science teacher, for the best part of a year after this. So with this academic 'shot across the bows' I continued through years 3 and 4 and into the (new) 5th year. I became a Prefect and then Head Boy of the school – I'm not sure why. By this time Mr Dennis Whight had taken over as the headmaster from Mr Evans, who had retired. Mr Whight continued all of the support and encouragement."

"Mr Murcutt was the form master in the 5th year. He was an Australian (or Tasmanian?) who was happy to share banter on cricket! He smoked a lot, which wouldn't have been allowed in Mr Evans' time. Mrs Diggle taught English Literature. I can still recite some of the poems in the book 'Poems of Spirit and Action', which was a set book for the RSA Exam. Other class mates I remember in the 5th year were Bruce Black, Ruth Brudenell and Joy Smith. After I left the Secondary Modern School, mum and dad kept the promise they had made to Mr Evans. With their help and encouragement, I attended Wellingborough Technical College from 1963-65 to do GCE 'O' levels. I then went to Kettering Technical College (1965-67) to do GCE 'A' Levels."

Gordon said that during his time studying in Wellingborough and Kettering "I was living at home in Oundle. In 1963, I recollect travelling regularly by train from Oundle station to Wellingborough (on steam trains) before Dr Beeching made his cuts. Getting to Kettering later, without trains was more difficult, but I managed to cadge a lift with Carl Norwood who had a taxi contract to take kids to Kettering each day. I had also got a motorbike, which helped sometimes".

"These were busy times, for (as well as travelling to Wellingborough, Kettering, then back to Oundle daily for college study) cricket still figured prominently and I was progressing well. As well as playing for Oundle during these years, I was invited to play regularly on Saturdays for Northamptonshire Colts and several times for Northamptonshire Second X1. As part of this I was expected to attend the County Nets in Northampton on Saturdays through the winters of 1964, '65 and '66. This posed a real problem in terms of transport as dad didn't have a car. I managed the trip from Oundle to Northampton each Saturday morning through the winters mainly by hitch-hiking. I started at the Barnwell Road Bridge at the end of South Road and would, more often than not, get a lift all the way there. If not, then at least to Wellingborough or Kettering, which were both about half way to Northampton!"

Gordon has great respect and love for his parents as "During all this time mum and dad didn't ask for a penny from me, didn't force me to earn money, fed me, and showed great interest and support in everything I was doing. Dad still worked at the garage at the bottom of New Road and ran his two allotments, but he was fanatical about me taking my education as far as possible. This was partly due to what Mr Evans had said and the promise he made, but also because he (as a lad in the 1930s) was forced to leave Laxton Grammar School with no qualifications to work and support his widowed mother. He was an able scholar and this abrupt termination to his education still figured prominently in his mind and tainted his life. It was clear as to why he said 'yes' to Mr Evans!"

This is where Gordon's very detailed memories of living in Oundle come to an end. He said, "My A-levels gained me a place at Nottingham University in 1967 to read Mechanical Engineering and at that point I left the town to embark on the rest of my life!" "As the years passed, I gained B.Sc. and Ph.D. degrees in Engineering at Nottingham, achieved a lifetime ambition of playing professional first class cricket (for Nottinghamshire), married, had two boys, joined the Shell oil company and worked for them abroad for twenty years – playing cricket in virtually every country I visited!"

Gordon said, "I called in once on Mr Evans in Clevedon, near Bristol (his retirement home) in about 1975. He was pleased to hear of what I'd been doing. We visited mum and dad in Oundle regularly and they enjoyed seeing their grandchildren growing-up. I returned to the UK in 1996 to live in Gloucestershire and take up a position at Bristol University." Gordon retired in 2015.

He mused on the passing of his parents. He said, "Dad died in 2005 and mum in 2016. (Their ashes are in Glapthorn Church yard.) I visit their grave whenever I can to say thanks. I have a look around as I pass through Oundle on my way. There were many changes in the town since I lived there. Many have been for the better. The Secondary Modern School is no more, but Oundle Town Cricket Club is happily still flourishing!"

...oooOOOooo...

A Potted History of the Denley Family from Chris Denley

Chris' father, Alan Denley, was born in 1926 in the nearby village of Aldwincle. Alan's own father Albert (Bert) was also born there in 1898. Bert's parents (Albert and Esther) came to Aldwincle in the late-1800s from Northleach, Gloucestershire.

Albert was a stonemason. He secured a job as Lord Lilford's personal stonemason (hence Albert's move to Northants). Esther (née Eyraud) from St Etienne in France, had been a chambermaid in Brockhampton Hall, Gloucestershire, before their marriage. Their son, Bert served as a soldier in WWI. He was a painter and decorator, who married Sophie West, a seamstress from Burton Latimer. When Alan was small they moved to the West family home in Duke Street, Burton Latimer. Alan went to Kettering Grammar School and attended (early, due to the war) Borough Road Teachers' Training College, London. He began teaching (aged nineteen) at Samuel Lloyd School in Corby, where he met Marjorie Judd (from Hertfordshire), who was a young teacher (aged twenty-one). They married in 1947 in Burton Latimer church, during his army national service.

77

Alan became deputy-head at a Secondary School in Corby (situated close to the steelworks). Aged 31, he became the Head-teacher of Oundle, St. Peter's Church of England Primary School in 1957. He and Marjorie had three children. Chris was born in Brigstock in 1951, Catherine was born in Kettering St Mary's Hospital in 1954, and Sheila was born in our council house in Rockingham Road, Corby, in 1957. The family moved to Oundle from Corby when Chris was six. Sheila was a baby when they moved to Latham House in North Street (26). All three children went to the primary school in Milton Road (known locally as the 'Top School') where our Alan was the Head.

Chris said, "I went on to Laxton Grammar School, then on to Queen Mary College, London University, to study Mechanical Engineering. Catherine went to Corby Grammar School, then to Trinity College of Music, London, to study singing and piano". Sheila attended Kettering High School, then Hull University to study mathematics. Catherine married Miles Golding and lives in Hertfordshire and they have three sons: Olly, Oscar & George. Sheila is married to George E. Stables and lives in Oxfordshire. Chris is married to Katrine Thomsen and lives in East Yorkshire. "We are all musicians, an inherited skill going back at least five generations that we know".

Chris continued, "My grandfather, Bert Denley, had a brother (Alec) and a sister (Evelyn) from Aldwincle. Both married, but neither had children. Alec lived to be 102 years and was almost certainly the oldest ballroom dancer in the country, continuing until his 100th birthday in Irchester. Bert and Sophie are buried in Burton Latimer cemetery. Evelyn is buried in Aldwincle (All Saints) Church yard, next to her parents Albert and Esther. Alec is buried at Wadenhoe. My mother died of a brain tumour in 1976 aged 51. My father retired early in the early 1980s. He spent his remaining years in Oundle and died of a heart attack in 1997, aged 71. Both are buried in Oundle cemetery".[47]

...oooOOOooo...

---

[47] Christopher Denley grew-up in North Street. Alan, his father, was Head of Oundle Primary.

MOVING ON

Laxton and Oundle School

Oundle Grammar School was first established (in 1499) by Dame Joan Wyatt. William Laxton was educated there. He went on to endow the school in his will. Sir William died in 1556. He left property to the Grocer's Company of London, on the condition that they support a new school that replaced the one he formerly attended.

By 1876 the school had grown very large, so was split into two schools: Laxton and Oundle. The former was for clever day-boys (generally local) and the latter was for boarders (who were expected to go on to University and greater things).[48] The town hall (the upper floor of the guild-house) and Long Room were used for Laxton boys and new buildings were added for Oundle School boys. The lower floor held the almsmen from Laxton Hospital. A new portion of the school was built on New Street in 1883. The school is governed by a Royal Charter that dates to 1930. It was amended by a supplemental charter in 1999.

Oundle School is recalled (by some boarding students) as being "hard and inflexible", particularly during the war years. The boys were expected to develop into 'tough gentlemen'. They had cold-water baths each morning. The hours of study were long and the food was described as 'unappealing and unappetising'. Students were meant to 'enter as boys and leave as men, ready for anything'.

Bevil Allen[49] and David Wills[50] were day-boys in Laxton School during the war years (after passing the entrance exam). Mr Sidney J. Leech (1892-1979) was the headmaster and Thomas Stretton his deputy. Lessons were mainly taught in the Long Room.[51] In the 1930s there were around thirty boys in each class. In the winters, the rooms were heated by open fires. As the buildings were tall, the heat dissipated and the boys felt cold. The Cloisters (below the Long Room) were open to

---

[48] "A History of the Oundle Schools", William G. Walker, for 'The Grocers' Company' by Hazell Watson & Viney Limited, 1956.
[49] Bevil Allen, personal history.
[50] David's father, Chris, b. 1906, determined he "would be happy and do well".
[51] The Queen Mother visited Oundle in 1956. The long-room now bears a plaque commemorating 400 years of schooling.

the air which created a wind-tunnel. It has since been glazed for warmth. David recalled that one year the boys couldn't write as ink froze in their inkwells.

Local boys deemed sufficiently educated to pass their 'Eleven Plus' examinations could attend the 'Laxton' part of Oundle school. The school accommodated fee-paying students and those who succeed in passing the entrance examination. There was once a gulf between the town and school, but this is slowly being eroded. Current students take part in and organise community events (particularly for the elderly). This would have been frowned on in the past when boys were not even allowed to talk with the townsfolk. For the first time, in the 1990s girls were admitted to the school as day and boarding students.

...oooOOOooo...

A view of Oundle in the late 1800s from Oundle School

John Gatherer Lowdell (1859-1934) was born 'at sea' off the coast of Greece. Known as 'old Horny' (a small, bespectacled man), he was a much-liked master at Oundle School. John first lived at 100 North Street (1881). He married Florence (1865-1929) in 1886, when she was twenty-one. They had three sons, Alan, Arthur and Donald. The family lived at 44 (Woodland House) Glapthorn Road. John changed his last name from Hornstein to Lowdell (his wife's maiden name) after WWI.

John Lowdell worked under various heads. The first was the Reverend St. John Reade, whom he greatly liked. Lowdell was in charge of the boys' studies (across the road from New House) in the Albion Rooms. He penned his thoughts about his Oundle memories. He wrote that when he first arrived in Oundle, "broad, deep trenches bordered the narrow pavements and involved, when crossing the street, perilous climbs over earth embankments or treacherous foothold across slippery planks". This was due to drain replacement and new school building. He suggested that the town was reluctant to have the new drainage, as it was happy with its "primitive cess-pits".

In North Street, Wise's, "also known as Wightman House" was part of the premises of "a plumber and house decorator's business, carried on

80

by Widow Wise, a respected, motherly soul." The building was later used for School junior assistants. "Avondale House, now numbered 35, was the boarding house of the Grammar School boys and further along, I was shown Laxton House, now called Cottesmore, which was then one of the three boarding houses of the new school." Lowdell went on to say that "At an island site nearby was a heterogeneous mass of buildings, soon to be demolished to make room for the present Jesus Church." (He alleged it was a rambling mass of buildings, with poles and ladders propped up against the outer walls. The principal occupant was a shoe-smith.) "On the west side, facing this island, was a modern two-storied building, then called Albion Rooms. It had failed as a workmen's coffee tavern and recreational club, and was used partly for the Grammar School classes and as an art studio."

His friends included Nelson Frederick Cobbald (who married to Clara in 1889 and had a son, Ernest Barham Cobbald, born in Oundle in 1891). Cobbald taught maths and science. He "lodged in Folkestone Villas in the street, now vanished, opposite the vicarage, the lower rooms of which was fitted up with a few shelves and cupboards" and other scientific equipment. Mr Hansell was the housemaster of Laxton House (which, at the time, was named Cottesmore). Francis King, "a musician, devoted to Haydn or Aden, as he called him" built a row of villas (Haydn Terrace). During Lowdell's time here, mortar boards were abolished in favour of a "black school cap and the school badge" and in 1884, owing to the head's views on alcohol, beer was no longer supplied to prefects at supper time.

Lowdell wrote of the market of "farmers and villagers from a far flung neighbourhood. In the early morning, booths and stalls were set up in open spaces around the market, and the roads were alive with droves of sheep and cattle and with carriers' carts lurching leisurely along, packed up with a varied assortment of goods as well as bevies of merry, chattering women. Threading their way through this traffic of man and beast the farmers, often accompanied by their wives, all in their Sunday best, came bowling along in their smart traps and gigs, hastening to arrive before the church bell was set booming at noon to announce the opening of the market."

Later, Lowdell wrote that Oundle business was "dead and few who know it today can realise its importance as an agricultural centre fifty years of more ago. Barely a dozen ale houses languish on a diminished and legally restricted trade, and the Talbot, a once celebrated posting-house, beloved of farmers and commercial travellers, has been reconditioned within as an expensive up-to-date hotel." He went on to say that "On the left, above the Talbot, was the 'Turk's Head' Inn, with its mullion windowed gable bay, moss grown, stone-slated roof and fine chimneys. Through its wide portals a cobbled courtyard, hemmed round by stables and coach houses, made a picture that was enhanced on occasions by the mellow scarlet of a farm cart tilted up in the background, a round wicker bird-cage dangling askew against a wall and a parcel of hens busily pecking up stray grains of corn. Still further to the left came two substantial houses, screening a brewery from the road and, stretching beyond them, was a low structure with mullioned windowed bays, low-pitched, irregular roof and shapely stone chimneys. A narrow passage way led to what was once the vicarage kitchen garden with its vine-clad gardener's cottage at one end. Garden and cottage were hidden from view by the 'Red Lion', a double-fronted hostelry fronting a wide stable yard and premises."

Lowdell stated that the vicarage, "nearly opposite the Red Lion, was a prosaic looking edifice". "Below it was the 'White Hart' Inn of grey stone with bays, mullion windows and roofs of the thin flaked stone, known as Collyweston slate, characteristic of older Oundle." The White Hart "block concealed a noisesome pig market [that] was reported to have been the decisive factor in establishing a new School in the town itself, rather than on the roomier site, offering unlimited scope for future developments, which was acquired by the Governors at the north west confines of the town and now occupied by the Field Houses and playing grounds". The lawns, Great Hall and its rooms were formerly "occupied by a congeries of insignificant houses and cottages, fronting some barns and stackyards." The farm was presumed to have been part of the lands associated with the Berrystead. Blackpot Lane was, in the 1870s, "an almost impracticable track, the steeper half of which was largely used as a dump for discarded household utensils". Milton Road was described as "the North Backway", "a rough, rutty, cart road, lined, as it still is on its south side, by the long field." On the north side of the "North Backway" there were large "town allotments, now occupied by the science block, Yarrow Museum, the School chapel and sundry private houses". Beyond the allotments the two boarding houses and playing-field land is where there "were cornfields and pastures called Shaman's and Blott's lands".

He says that a "ramshackle building ... that was interesting for its associations with coaching days, has ... been transformed as a grocery store. The flat fronted stone structure, once a bank, and now part of a Council school, built in its old world garden at the back, has lost the massive hood with a winged cherub's head that stood over its doorway, which was protected by a stout low wooden grille."

Parsons lived comfortably, with "roomy parsonages", "a large staff of in-door and out-door servants" and took time out to hunt, "two or three days a week and were good shots." The Michaelmas fair was a fun occasion, but the Statute fair was much more serious. Would-be servants (labourers and housemaids) attended the Statute fair, "lining the streets looking for domestic work". They could be hired for wages from eight to sixteen pounds a year. Lowdell wondered if domestic service was akin to slavery, as mistresses were not always thoughtful of their staff. John Lowdell was a forward thinker and a credit to the school and town.[52]

...oooOOOooo...

---

[52] Reproduced with thanks to the Oundle School Archive.

School House in the 1920s - by A. Plowright[53]

The Oundle School Archivist, Elspeth Langsdale kindly shared Mrs A. Plowright's memories. In these 'Ada' described a time when Frederick Sanderson was the Head of Oundle School (1891-1922). She wrote: "My sister-in-law worked at School House for about seventeen years as private maid to Mr & Mrs Sanderson and later to Dr & Mrs Fisher. They had a wonderful cook; she also cooked everything on a large range. As well as cooking for the boys, the family and the staff, she did a dinner party almost every week as Mrs Fisher liked entertaining. The Lord Mayor of London and lots of titled people were included. The cook also made lots of jam as the different fruit came into season; she also pickled eggs for cooking. There were no freezers, but everything seemed to be nice and fresh with the lovely homemade taste". "Mrs Sanderson was very, very strict in every way, but Mrs Fisher wasn't quite so fussy. This was, of course, before the Headmaster lived at Cobthorne. The cook could rest from 4 pm to 6 pm each day and then be ready for the boys' evening meal at 7 pm. Apart from that, she only had the same time off as the other staff. They were a very happy crowd."

Mrs Plowright wrote: "I used to pop in to see my sister-in-law and it always seemed a lovely atmosphere. Several of the maids slept at the top of School House and others were along Church Street in the old men's Latham Hospital. There were about seven maids in all. They only had one half-day's break a week and every other Sunday afternoon. Apart from that, they didn't come out of the house at all unless there was any special function and then they must be in by 10 o'clock."

She continued, "Speech Day was a big day for Oundle. Lots of parents came by train on Friday night and stayed at the Talbot Hotel and other large houses. Quite a lot stayed in cottages with no modern conveniences at all, but they seemed to manage quite well. We used to go and sit on the Great Hall wall on the Saturday evening to see the fashions as the parents arrived for the Concert. A catering firm from Cambridge used to do the tea in a very large marquee on School House lawn. However, it brought a lot of excitement into the town and extra

---

[53] Ibid. With thanks to the Oundle School Archive.

trade for the shops. Everything is so different now, but we cherish these memories."

...oooOOOooo...

Senior School Days and Teenage Years

Oundle's sprawling private school is comprised of many 'houses' (established in Tudor times). The town ran a Council School that could not compete with small classes, specialist teachers and new equipment. Its recent transformations have helped with some more successful than others! The state secondary school was established at St. Peter's Church in the 1600s. It moved to behind the Talbot and was known as the 'National School for the Education of the Poor in the Principles of the Established Church' (also known as the 'Church School', 'Council School' or 'County Modern'). Milton Road School site opened in 1842. In the 1870s, co-education was halted when class sizes grew. The girls remained in Milton Road and the boys were relocated to Latham's School at 26 North Street. The children were allowed to reunify in Milton Road in 1903. They were generally well-behaved as the well-known saying ran: spare the rod and spoil the child.

Local school teachers were bothered by the limited health service usage, so made an appeal to parents in 1940. Parents attended the prize giving at the end of the school year at Oundle Church of England School and, with her captive audience, Mrs Perring (the head) asked them to use the town medical and dental services for the sake of their children. Just two years previously there had been a case of tetanus that been left untreated, so thirteen year-old James Winham died. James was the son of Albert and Constance Winham (née Knowles) who lived at 13 New Road, Oundle. The coroner declared that tetanus was the cause, yet could easily have been prevented.

In 1886 a boy from Dryden House (North Street) climbed the outside of the Parish Church spire. There he fixed his school cap to the weather vane, where it remained until it was blown off and picked up in North Street. In 1890 the cap was fixed there again. A steeplejack named Upchurch climbed the spire to retrieve it. (Years later, he fell from a

85

Church steeple and died.) The cap is kept for posterity and is held in the Oundle School archive.[54]

During the war the local children had some classes in Old Dryden House and others in West Street. The children continued their schooling in West Street until Prince William School (PWS) opened in 1971. The PWS and Middle School were formed to create a new, local, three-tier, state-school system. The primary school in Milton Road is a Church of England controlled school. Following a re-organisation of local state education in 2015, the primary school expanded and functioned on two sites; with pupils aged four to seven remaining at the primary and children aged eight to eleven taught at the former Middle School on Cotterstock Road. St. Peter's Primary School closed in July 2016, along with Oundle and Kings Cliffe Middle School, when the three-tier system drew to an end.

In the 1960s the Secondary Modern School produced an annual magazine, "The Undela". Students produced articles for this early version of a year book. Its production was overseen by the Head, Mr Dennis 'Chalky' Whyte. Some of his comments are very revealing: "Mr Marshall was a victim of the flu epidemic. During his absence some of the boys helped with the stoking" (presumably to keep the heating going), "The door handles of our classroom has met with an accident and is waiting to be replaced. Many is the time when one of us has had to climb through the window and open the door from the inside, because the door handle has been mislaid"! "Strip lighting has been installed in classrooms, the library and small hall" and "... during the holiday, workmen pulled down the old toilets and installed a completely new drainage system".[55] A comment regarding hockey in the School Team reads: "Diane Wyles ... plays well as a rule, but sometimes seems overawed by the occasion"! Reading the comments seems like a social comment on the times: Granville Wiggins (in 3A) wrote a poem about "Scrumping", Barry Marshall wrote a piece on "An evening with Arthur Negus" (antiques expert on "Going for a Song"), Sheila Peterson wrote about "The Old People" (student community help) and Beverley Roberts wrote about the "Robert Brothers Circus" (her father and uncle) and how much school she had missed while

---

[54] Elspeth Langsdale, Oundle School archives.
[55] 'The Undela', volume 2, no.6, July 1969, p.4, and volume 3, 1970.

travelling each year. Others wrote about noisy neighbours, nature, moving house, sporting and House achievements, a trip to Peterborough *son-et-lumiere* with Mr and Mrs Titman, bed-times, going to the hospital, Brian Edwards (a leaver) joining the Metropolitan Police force as a cadet, Roger Burrows joining the Navy, Gerald Langley reading Physics at London University and working with the Admiralty Underwater Weapons Establishment. Finally, there were advertisements reading, "When you are ready to leave school and are looking for a job try: Denton's (Footwear) Closing Department. Training is given for various operations in the Closing of Shoe Uppers". There were also "Toetectors" shoes in the yard! Forms were listed in the magazine as 'A', 'L' or 'Remove' (singling out children who were streamed as able or not!) These are moments captured and gone, perhaps for the better.

The uniform was a maroon blazer, maroon tie (for girls and boys), grey or black trousers for the boys and blue and white spotted skirt for girls. There seemed to be no real pattern description for the girls' skirts. They appear to have worn any shade of blue (usually Royal Blue) and the spots could be anything from giant spots to miniature dots. Everyone wore white shirts. They usually had a pocket on the breast for pens and other useful bits and pieces, although blazer pockets were better for these.

Each student had a pencil case with their own equipment inside: pencils, fountain pens, cartridges of ink, sharpener, eraser, a protractor and a pair of compasses. Often our text books had the times tables (multiplication) on the back cover. We were expected to cover our books with clear paper or wrappers to keep them clean and help them to last. I know that many of us still keep our school hymn book and Bible (that were given to us on the first day in school). Others keep memories of the flag-pole 'decorations' at the end of the summer terms.

These were the days of 'Izal', a non-absorbent toilet paper (that was more useful as tracing paper than as a wipe!). It was also the time of toilet cistern-tanks placed high above the toilet bowl (in a cold, outdoor loo as they would were insanitary when inside the house). At home at night the choice was often no better: to walk down the garden path to the outhouse or use the 'guzunder'[56] (a pee-pot that goes under the bed!). A toilet flush was achieved by 'pulling the chain', which the older generation can't forget. My mother still mentions that she has 'pulled the chain' when the loo clearly has no wooden-handle on a chain, as modern conveniences have a handle or push button flush. This persisted until the late-1950s and early 1960s.

New indoor toilets were a function of wealth. Toilets were steadily moved to inside houses and schools. Health and Safety was important and the water-supply plumbing and sewers were no longer linked. Gender roles made a change in the war years with women's suffrage and voting rights. Women were no longer chattels in a marriage, but part of a team. The community changed its perception of itself and transformed accordingly. Appliances have come a long way, but still have far to go.

After the wars, sports and exercise were raised in our consciousness as being essential to good health. The range of physical activities offered in schools, gym's and recreational centres now far extend from those of the past. In 2000 the Head of Prince William School (PWS) deemed that the school should offer rowing to its students. With the Amateur Rowing Associations Project 'Oarsome', PWS and Oundle Town Rowing Club was established.

Laxton Junior School opened in 1973 as a (fee-paying) preparatory day-school for local children. It accepts both girls and boys (aged four years and upwards) and prepares them for Laxton Senior education. Firstly it was based at Old Dryden in North Street, then it moved to its current East Road purpose-built location in 2002. In the same year, almost as a mark of the millennium, the governing body merged Laxton Grammar (deemed a day-pupil house) into 'Laxton House'; in the House-system in Oundle School. In 1998, the School's Oscar Radio station began broadcasting for pupils and the town. It is one of the longest-running school FM radio-stations broadcasting in this country.

...oooOOOooo...

---

[56] Thanks to Tina Wallman.

Evacuees and Teachers - Joyce Hardick (née Gaunt)

When Joyce was at the senior school in the late-1930s, some older children came to Oundle as evacuees from a school in Barnsbury, Islington in London. She remembers that they wore green uniforms. A teacher who accompanied them was an art teacher named Mr Green. Joyce found him "very frightening, as he would shout at the boys and cane them regularly". He liked Joyce's surname 'Gaunt' and said Joyce came from royalty. This statement embarrassed Joyce. He insisted that she had people named Edward, John and George in her family, descendants of 'John of Gaunt'.

A nicer teacher was Miss Caldwell. She was the shorthand and typing teacher, who came to school with the evacuees and is remembered as "a very nice lady" as she encouraged Joyce towards her career. Joyce's first job was to work in the Glapthorn Road Hospital offices. She didn't like the job, so soon left. Throughout the war years Joyce worked at the Land Settlement Association in Cotterstock Road.

...oooOOOooo...

Further Education

Some children recall travelling to school in Oundle on the steam train! Others recall walking (in the cold, slippery winter streets) in short socks and skirts. For four years Diana Leigh (1938) travelled on steam-trains from Oundle to Northampton as a student at the School of Art. She says that she has "such happy memories" of this. Of the trains in the late-1950s and she said, "It took an hour and five minutes to travel from Oundle to Northampton. I loved the steam train".

In 1970 the only way for local teenagers who attended the Secondary Modern and wanted to gain 'O' and 'A' levels, was to catch Carl Norwood's mini-bus into Kettering or Corby technical college. (One of the reasons why I decided to not be a 'local' foundation art student in Northampton was that by the 1970s, it involved a long bus ride via Kettering bus station, with a change of bus to Northampton. Then all the way back again after a long day.) After Beeching's cuts there were no Oundle trains, so a bus or mini-bus was the only feasible means of transport.

School Punishment in the 1950s and 1960s

Virginia Francis recalled that teachers at the County Modern "made you stand outside the door if you had done something they didn't approve of". (Sometimes they forgot they had sent you there!)

Sharon Jackson (now Cottingham) recalls that in Oundle Primary School in the early 1960s, one teacher 'spanked' her with a flat, open hand that was so hard that it left an imprint on her leg. The mark was still evident when she arrived home. Her mother was so incensed by the sight of this that she went to the school and heartily complained that "no-one could do that" to her child.

On another day the whole class was punished when the teacher couldn't locate the culprit of a classroom misdemeanour. Memories of the actual issue has been long forgotten, but the unfair punishment has lasted a lifetime!

By 1986, beatings in state schools (or strapping with a belt) were legally discontinued. A year later using the cane was banned. Yet, the ban did not include fee-paying schools until 1998. Many non-westernised schools round the world have yet to follow suit as individual countries approve legislation.

My School Days by Chris Denley

Chris Denley said that he distinctly remembers his first visit to Oundle. "I was five or six when my mother took me for a day visit, shortly before we moved there in 1957. We were living in Corby and waited at the Bus Station. All the Corby buses were the green United Counties type, but to my great excitement a red bus rolled up, the first I'd seen there. The Eastern Counties service 313 to Peterborough dropped us at the Oundle Motors bus stop, from where we walked to see my mother's friend Mrs Beech, mother of Helen and John. Whilst cooking us roast lamb, Mrs Beech taught me to make fresh mint sauce, my first culinary experience, which I have remembered ever since. It was also my first meeting with Helen, who was to become a school friend. My father became the headmaster of the primary school so, some weeks later, we moved to Latham House, North Street. Coming from a modern council house in Corby, this seventeenth century house lacked any kind of charm at the time, as it was cold, damp and full of mice and spiders.

We kept cats that soon kept the mouse population down, but the huge spiders were a constant companion. I never learned to like them".

Chris found that school days were an ordeal. "I have very few happy memories. I am dyslexic and dyspraxic. At that age I'd never heard of such words, but discovered at the age of about three that I was very easy to beat up, and (at seven or eight) that I struggled with reading. I was in Mrs Batson's class and was very jealous of Pauline Dexter, who happily read her way through a book, when I was desperately trying to get to the end of a page to have the satisfaction of turning it over. As to physical coordination, I cannot throw, catch, kick or bat a ball. This was a great source of ridicule, attracting descriptions like butter-fingers, spastic, weedy, useless, pathetic. This often led to social rejection and physical bullying. Thus school taught me a lifelong hatred of football and cricket. It is still to my great regret and resentment that throughout school my teachers never bothered to recognise or coach me through any of this".

Despite Chris' father being the headmaster, he found that this carried no favours. He recalled that "at the primary school there were some very nice teachers and some awful ones. My favourite was Miss Green (Joyce). She was smiling and delightful, clearly enjoying the company of us six-year olds. She taught me the long method of subtraction, 'borrow-payback takeaways'. I remember one day in summer, a butterfly landed on a terrified boy's shirt. I think it was Michael Friday. Miss Green managed to calm him down until it flew away. Nice chap though, Michael. I met him again twenty years ago. Joyce Green used to occasionally baby-sit for us. We went to her wedding when she became Mrs Lane. Then there was the terrifying and perverted Miss Smith from the class below. She was the ugliest woman ever, with goofy teeth. She taught us one day when Miss Green was away. One young lad was deemed to be naughty. She hauled him out to the front, stood him on a chair and removed his clothing from the waist down before spanking his bare backside. It's still hard to believe this actually happened. Imagine a male teacher had done that to a girl. He would have been locked up before the day was out. Miss Smith left soon afterwards. She was replaced by the much nicer Ann Thurlow, who became Mrs Fox. Young Miss Rees, a lovely red-haired Welsh girl, was on the staff for a short while before disappearing very suddenly without explanation. A rumour went around that she was pregnant. Rather than celebrating new life as would happen nowadays, I presume she had been deemed shameful and unceremoniously 'asked to leave'. In Mrs Turland's class, I sat next to my friend Nicola James. I often wonder what happened to her. Mrs Turland could be unpredictably vicious. It was early spring and the daffodils were out, so we did poetry and she read the Wordsworth poem. We were then asked to write our own poem about daffodils. But we were to be original, to write something different. I wracked my brains, having no skills in imaginative writing. At home we had wondrous displays of daffodils in the garden. Most were the usual yellow type, but there were other varieties too. Outside the back door there was a spread of blooms with white petals and yellow trumpets. I'd write about those as I thought that would be original. So I started, "Daffodils are white with yellow trumpets ...", and was promptly stumped. I could not think of a suitable rhyme for trumpets and could not compose a sensible second line. Mrs Turland came to inspect our progress. My one line was clearly insufficient, and my description of these daffodils was in her eyes completely incorrect. So she picked me up by the lapels and shook me very hard. Thus I learned to hate poetry."

He went on to say that there were two girls, "fraternal twins, who were slow learners and must have had severe psychological problems. I think they were illegitimate, but we children were sheltered from such taboo information. Both girls wet themselves daily, so Mrs Turland sat them isolated at the front of the class as they stank. It was an awful way to treat them. They left after that year, we weren't told where they went to. I hope it wasn't to some ghastly institution. Other teachers were Miss (Yvonne) Wagstaff, who was very nice, and Mr Johnson, who wasn't. I suspect much will be said elsewhere about the latter: there have already been many comments on Facebook. Suffice it to say that he was unpredictably frightening, as you never knew where you stood or what you might be randomly punished for. He had his favourites, usually bright girls. But he also had a liking for spanking boys in front of the class. One regular recipient of this treatment was rammed so hard against the desk over which he was bent, that it caused him severe abdominal pain, so that he was bent double on returning to his desk".

Chris stressed that despite the bullying from some of his peers, there were also "some very nice kids I grew up with. I sometimes bump into some of them in Oundle. There were also some good memories from primary school. Music was always good fun and hands-on. We did "Singing Together" with the radio (the 'wireless'), where some of our traditional folk songs were passed on. We also took part in percussion, recorders and the school choir. May Day was a wonderful tradition with its many commemorative photos. We learnt maypole dances and elected the May Queen. There were also the skipping games and songs played predominantly by the 5 to 7-year-old girls. I remember one lovely tune – "Wallflowers growing up so high", they would sing. Each year-group taught the words to the one below, then stopped as they got older. Thus the tradition only existed in that age range, but had probably been in the playground for decades. Like May Day, I suspect it's all gone now".

He recalled that the children used "ink wells and wooden-handled pens you dipped. One girl chewed her pen shaft so much it shrank to half its length. She must have consumed the rest. I think it was Jean Prior, sorry Jean for reminding you of this! But we were only nine. We also had the third-pint milk bottles every day. Winters were freezing in those days and milk bottles were put on the radiator-pipes to thaw. The milk tasted ghastly. It snowed every winter and there was frequently a hard frost, when you could make great playground slides by polishing the ice with your feet".

His final year was in the very early sixties, towards the end of the rock and roll era. Chris said that he "We loved to sing the Cliff Richard songs and I remember doing the twist with Theresa Greatorex in the playground while we sang 'The Young Ones'."

Parents were oblivious to what it was like for their children as "next came the infamous Laxton Grammar School. A seven-year prison sentence would have been preferable! It was a brutal and tyrannical regime, run by an aloof, uncaring headmaster called Stretton, whom we feared. His only apparent concern was that he was seen to run a tight ship. Corporal punishment was routinely used as a first resort. I was twice a recipient without any warning and in neither case was it remotely justified. Rather than encouraging those who struggled, the philosophy of the school was to embolden and coach those who had obvious talent and ignore and punish the rest. At Laxton, the bullying was considerably worse, physically and mentally. It could come from my peers, the older boys, the prefects or the staff. Worst of all, it came from so-called friends. I had my equipment vandalised, money "borrowed" and not paid back, food taken, homework borrowed for copying then "lost" and I was forced to "own up" for things I hadn't done. On one occasion, I was forced onto the floor face-down, had the perpetrator's knée forced into my back, whilst he shoved his bubble gum down my neck so that it stuck in my hair and inside my collar. Ironically, the natural survival mechanism is to attempt to befriend bullies, make them laugh. In this way they are less likely to abuse."

Academically, Chris "excelled at some subjects and made little progress in others. This I now know is a recognisable trait of dyslexic children. It should have rung alarm bells with the staff, but it did not. I cannot read thick blocks of text and there is no logical reason why. History was the worst subject. We had a strict and utterly boring teacher called Mr. Brown. I lived in dread of the weekly homework, which was to read the next chapter in the bloody awful book and learn it for a test. If we got less than 3 out of 20 in the test, we were punished. Most times I got either extra work or detention. Brown never taught me any history, he taught me to hate it. For Tuesday afternoon recreational activities, I never dared volunteer for any of the more exciting activities for fear of predictable jeering and peer group rejection. I was therefore put into the reading group. Hell. A senior boy was put in charge, a thug named Johnson. He sat at the front with his newspaper and feet on the desk. When he came round to check on us, he noted my unsurprising lack of progress through my book. "Are you still on Page 40?" he said, rolling up his newspaper with which he thwacked me several times round the head".

Chris says that he is an instinctive musician who was "better than most at singing in tune", but for some unknown reason, he was not selected for the school choir, so "was devastated, as I was sent off to read instead! We had music classes as part of our normal lessons, in which we learnt the history of Beethoven's life and so on. Thoroughly uninteresting. There was no hands-on instrument-playing or singing like there had been at primary school. There was not even any music theory. The chap who came top of the class wasn't at all musical; he just came first at everything, so any practical music education was denied me at Laxton. Instead, I subconsciously learnt of music by myself and absorbing all about harmonies from hymn tunes, my father's excellent piano playing, the BBC Light Programme and, of course, the Beatles".

He recalled that his class "had quite a good French teacher, Mr Gresty, whose lessons were fun, but his discipline wasn't great and he dished out lines quite a lot. One kid called James was given lines more than anyone. James wrote out extra lines in his spare time to build up a ready supply, so that when Gresty said, "Right James, 100 lines, I must not talk in class", he simply went to his file, retrieved the pre-written lines and handed them in. The school had its own scout troop, also run by Gresty. I enjoyed scouts as we learned about navigation and camping. We were proud of our tidy scout hut, until Gresty left and was replaced by a new guy, who was a complete 'wally'. He bought an old car in bits and dumped it all over the scout hut floor, intending one day to teach us motor mechanics, which he never got round to doing. Our once-proud scout troop deteriorated rapidly and I ended up hating it."

Chris said that his art lessons "were a farce". "The teacher was (supposedly) a noted artist called MacKenzie. He had no interest in teaching and rarely turned up to lessons. If he did, he spent most of the time outside in the Church yard with a fag. We just threw paint around or skived off. One good trick was to stick paper to the electric potter's wheel and splodge paint onto it to make circular patterns at high speed. All that lovely equipment and no-one ever taught us to make a pot. Games were hell. No-one wanted me there and even I didn't want to be there. As I got older, I learned to skive off. Most of the time I wasn't reported. We had a very good gymnastics teacher, Mr. Hogg. I was rubbish, but he never looked down on you if you struggled. In the summer he took us swimming. I liked that as I could swim".

Chris' escapes from the "stresses of school life were essentially solitary". He said, "I went out on my bike round the lovely Northamptonshire villages or on a sunny afternoon, sat on the crossing-gates on the footpath to Ashton, watching sand-martins flying around and waiting to see the steam-trains go by on our lovely little railway-line from Northampton to Peterborough, before it was closed by the infamous, short-sighted and vandalistic Beeching Plan".

Chris' friend, David Allen bought a guitar and lent it to him. He recalled that "within a week I could play it better than he could. We formed a band called 'The Etc.', playing the hits of the sixties. We were quite good and had an excellent singer, Duncan Laxton. We had a lot of fun playing at the Youth Club in the Market Place building on a Saturday night. Thus began a lifelong passion for playing the guitar. As I improved, there was only one guitarist around who was better, an older Oundle School boy called Chris Sansom with whom I was briefly to become acquainted before he left school. He could play like Eric Clapton and I vowed to do the same. As I quite quickly became a proficient blues guitarist and, with the realisation by many that I could do something that they couldn't, the bullying disappeared. Suddenly I was looked up to. One lad called Squires, who had previously, continually sneered at me suddenly blushed bright red and walked to the other side of the street. This kind of situation was something I was unhappy with and believe it is better be liked for who you are than for what you can do (and not be disliked for what you can't do)".

Chris recalls school punishments delivered via "a feared prefect system". He remembers that there were "two ranks of prefect, school prefects and house prefects. All could dish out punishment, but the school prefects could use the cane. There were some particular thugs amongst their number. The aloof Stretton should have known better than to appoint them, but then he was no better himself. One nasty piece of work called Woods, caned me for no reason whatsoever: I despise him to this day. As I reached the sixth form, Stretton made me a house prefect and I was surprised and flattered, but vowed not to emulate some of my predecessors. I did not entirely succeed as the system dragged us into its traditional ways, with expectations on us to maintain discipline. To my regret there were times when I was unfairly nasty. As school years progressed, social life began to pick up. There were parties where there were some of my early encounters with girls and with alcohol. My first visit to a pub took place at the age of fifteen. John Jellis and I went to the Angel for a half of bitter. Three old blokes were playing dominoes. We knew them all and we were concerned our presence would be reported. Then the police sergeant came in wearing his uniform. He knew our dads, so we were now seriously worried. He went round to the barrel-room with the landlord, Tony Moore. I think he too had an illicit pint! Nothing was said".

Chris considers that "So much of my time at Laxton had been wasted and could have been better spent had the school been better organised and actually cared for children and education. Instead they crammed our heads full of stuff, brainwashed us with Church of England beliefs and right-wing politics. There was no social education whatsoever and absolutely no careers-advice. There were no girls, so we were an academic elite, male community; a very narrow cross-section of society. All of the down-to-earth people we knew from primary school who went to the state schools seemed to have a more well-rounded education and we saw less of them. We were taught by individuals who segregated themselves from the Oundle community. This "Town and Gown" mentality had been inherited from Cambridge University. Yet, I believe the school has improved since then. Had there been league tables then Laxton would have come out on top, as these only assess only things that put schools (like Laxton) at the top. League tables are a self-justifying, meaningless, circular argument. The School was not an education, it was mentally damaging at an important and formative time of life. Yet, one thing that it sparked in me was an interest and fascination with mathematics. This formed the basis of my careers as a teacher and an engineer. I learnt far more in spite of Laxton than from it. I am a guitarist in many styles: rock, blues, folk and jazz; a mandolinist, bassist, composer, fluent German speaker, mountaineer, fell-runner and marathon-runner, little of which can I attribute to Laxton School".

...oooOOOooo...

Secondary School

Heather Rice attended the Secondary Modern from 1964 to 1968. Her first form teacher was Mr Murcutt, who suggested that children should be "all be lined-up and shot". Her next form-teacher was Mrs Titman. She asked, "Who could forget Mr Blackman? We didn't dare give him any cheek". Sharon Jackson and I fondly recall him as a quiet man, with a wry, dry sense of humour. He was softly-spoken and "knew his stuff" on the subjects of biology and environmental science. His laboratory

97

held cages and vivariums with locusts, rats and other creatures, although it seems that only Mr Blackman experimented or dissected these within his own interests as I do not recall the students doing so.

All of the girls made a peg bag (to the same design) and a tray-mat using embroidery threads on 'Binka' sewing fabric. This was to practice a variety of stitches, sewing patterns and techniques (as a sampler) that could be used in finer work. To some degree, this practice (for girls) had been continued since Tudor times.

Girls were expected to make their own spotted, school-skirts and cookery pinafores. They were started was in the first sewing and needlework class, at the start of their first term in the Secondary school. By the mid-1960s the skirts and pinafores could be made at home by mothers (or bought). The clothing made in these years were tunic-style mini-dresses with a large bauble or ring attached to the front zip.

Janet Brackley (née Chapman) remembers the girls in her class making their own school skirts and dresses from scratch. "We had three patterns and materials to choose from; then were left to get on with it!" She remembers her "Nan hemming mine by hand...", whereas, Jackie Ganderton and Marion Rowell (née Rawlings) recall "happy times: boys gardening and girls' cookery". School was not always a preparation for life. "We grew up fast after leaving school." (Jackie and her secondary school teacher, Miss Margaret Asplin, both married in 1965.) Margaret became Mrs Ward and taught 'domestic science' (cookery) in the 1960s. She said that all of her students were girls, with one exception. There was one boy who wanted to learn to cook. His parents supported him in this and he was permitted to join in. Margaret Saunston (née Asplin, later Mrs Ward) still lives in Oundle. She grew up in Rock Road and then Gordon Road. (Later, she married Mr Keith Saunston). An ex-pupil of hers said, "It is always quite difficult for students to start calling a teacher by a new name and converting Miss to Mrs, but we got used to it!" For many years she worked at the local library. Margaret continues to enjoy cooking and keeping active. She takes an active role in the many town social groups, the Historical and (MID-NAG) Archaeological Society.

Nigel Wiggins said that in the senior school during the early 1960s, there was "a Welsh headmaster, Kingsley Davies ("Chinny") Evans, who closed his eyes when he caned you." Jean Donegani said, "I was no angel, so one day I told Mr Johnson just that. That ended up with me bent over his knee in front of the class as he smacked me with his gym shoe. I didn't tell my mum as I thought she might smack him back" and she didn't need the subsequent wrath from her mother! Sue Crick agrees with Nigel, in that she was caned by him "on three occasions". Alan Box stated, "Who would have thought a man who read "Tarka the Otter" to a class could be so awful?" All the things experienced "would get you put in jail now". Jean (Donegani), said the Geography teacher was "nice enough, but had a real good aim with chalk and the eraser. He could reach all areas of the classroom. We learned how to duck really fast."

In the early 1960s, Mrs Murkett (a "meek, polite and nice lady") taught Religious Instruction. Her husband, Mr 'Mickey' Murkett, taught geography. He was ex-army and scared the classes as he was a bully. If a child didn't know the answers he would launch at them, threaten to tear up a sheet of paper and scatter it to the winds, then make the child pick up every last bit (no matter if it flew on to the roof!). His threats were not carried out, but he would throw chalk at individuals and sometimes larger items. He once "hit a boy from West Street (Mick Stokes) on the head with a big Bible". Luckily, most of the teachers were not so intimidating and their teaching methods were to coax and reward rather than punish.

One teacher was Mrs Pauline Turner. She was the wife of the vicar of Woodnewton. She would invite students in the sixth form to the vicarage for tea. Sharon Cottingham and I would cycle over and have tea. She taught English and dispensed careers advice. I felt that she was outspoken, thought-provoking and usually fair. She was a great help and encouragement in sending Sharon and I on to University in the 1970s. Without her help it would have been harder to achieve. She taught in the secondary modern school then transferred to Prince William School.

Leo Dunham had names for each of his students (which was probably a mnemonic for their names to help him remember them). He particularly enjoyed going out with his classes into the countryside.

"He would take all of us (with no health and safety issues) on our bikes, visiting local churches and looking at the 'panoramic view' of Oundle from the near Biggin Grange"! Besides teaching music and cricket, Leo was outgoing and sang in the Gilbert & Sullivan Society. Despite his avant-garde methods, Sue Crick disliked Leo Dunham. She said, "He laid me across the desk and continually thrashed me with a hockey stick, but I am still here to tell the tale. We were very tough and it prepared us for a tough world. Maybe that is why we don't drop at the first hurdle". The alternative view is that of Anton Lang, who said that "Leo Dunham was the Mr Chips of his day and a tutor of a past era that was blessed with respect and peaceful intentions. I loved the man and, despite the occasional chastising, had a huge respect for him throughout my days at OMS and beyond as a young adult alongside another, slightly older one. He would always stop on his bicycle to greet me if he saw me walking, ask how I was doing in 'the big world outside school' and would always have a parting smile. What an absolute gem of a tutor and one of the last bastions of chivalry that clung on to an older (and milder) world. 'New Boy' will ALWAYS be my name (the very same 'Chips' afforded to one of the characters in the James Hilton story) and it was an honour to have been bestowed with such. He once asked if I was familiar with 'Oberammergau' and 'The Passion Plays'? At the tender age of twelve or thirteen, I had no idea why he would ask such. It was only when I embarked upon my career in the world of theatre that I fully understood why he would ask this."

By the 1970s, the Secondary School headmaster was Mr 'Chalky' Dennis Whyte. Most teachers had their own forms for registration and general teaching styles. Those most recalled were: Mr Leo Dunham (music and boys sports), "Chinny" Evans (who still administered the cane), Miss Margaret Gale (art), Mrs Titman (maths and girls sports), Mr (Jimmy) Lowe (history), Mr George Blackman (science), Mrs McAdam, Mr Titman (woodwork and technical drawing), Mr Hyatt and Mrs Dunham, who was "a nice lady". Christine Cunnington said, "I remember Mike Stokes who was a big Rolling Stones fan". Many recall that their father, mother, they and their offspring were all taught by Miss Gale, Leo Dunham and Jimmy Lowe, from the 1940s until they retired in the 1970s. Just prior to the move to Prince William School, young Miss Beale (Mrs Lewis) and Mr Richard Underwood and other newly-qualified staff began their teaching careers in the old Secondary Modern School.

School Memories from the 1980s

Prince William School senior school is located in the south-eastern outskirts of Oundle. The school, built in 1971, was opened by Prince William of Gloucester. At that time it was named Oundle Secondary School. The prince was frequently seen (as was his younger brother, Richard) shopping in the town. His family home, Barnwell Manor, is only a couple of miles to the south (along the A605). Prince William was killed in an air crash less than a year after the school opened. His brother, Prince Richard, attended to re-commemorate the school in his brother's name in early 1972. In 2015 the school reopened as an academy under Mr McMurdo.

Prince William School (PWS) now caters for students aged eleven to eighteen (as a recent Northamptonshire educational move changed local schooling from three-tier to two). In the early days of PWS, there were temporary mobile-classrooms at the School and limited teaching staff. Reforms in 2015 meant that PWS reverted from an upper-school (aged 13-18) to a secondary (11-18). After almost two-hundred years, Oundle Primary transformed from a lower-school to a full primary and moved to the former Oundle and Kings Cliffe Middle School site on Cotterstock Road.

Headmaster Chris Lowe, MBE, ran PWS from its inception. He recalled that on a day when he was showing new, prospective parents around the school and praising its quiet countryside location, a student came running into his office in a panic. "Help", she said, "One of the girls has been shot". (The local game in the woods nearby were ripe for bagging.) Chris, without turning a hair, said, "Don't tell me, go and tell the deputy-head!" I wonder if those parents actually enrolled their child! Chris is to this day, a fondly-remembered headmaster. (Post scriptum: the 'shot' student survived.) In the summer of 2017 he visited Oundle to celebrate his eightieth birthday with staff and friends.

Perceptions of the past give recollections of summers with long, warm and sunny days. A time when the school holidays meant roaming free all day with friends. When our parents rarely knew where we were as long as we were happy and busily involved. We would often take a packed lunch and off we would go. Sharon Jackson and I would take our bicycles to ride to all of the local villages, very much like our parents had done before us.[57] With busier roads and faster cars this practice seems to have dwindled to some degree in recent years.

MEMORIES OF WAR AND PEACE

Three Memorials to the Fallen of Oundle and Ashton

The first Oundle war memorial stands in the centre of town. It is a traditional monument that commemorates the dead from the conflicts of the First (1914-1918) and Second (1939-1945) World Wars. There are sixty-eight names listed on the memorial for the first war and twenty-seven for WWII. Half-way up on all sides of the pillar are bronze laurel wreaths, and below them are inscriptions of the names and ranks of the fallen men of WWI. They are ordered under the service in which they served. The names the fallen of WWII are listed on the sides of the top step. In the 1960s, this memorial had metal chain around it, which has since been removed.

The second Oundle war memorial commemorated is known now as the recreation ground or pocket park. It comprises of sporting space and play activities. The third is the Oundle School Chapel, a grade-II listed chapel, which was built as a memorial to the fallen. Construction started in 1922. This building is in the last cohort of Gothic Revival churches in England.

With WWI fought in the years 1914-1918 (which ceased in 1918 with a formal declaration in 1919) and WWII from 1939-1945, the town centre war memorial commemorates both wars and reads: "In Grateful Memory of the Men of Oundle and Ashton who gave their lives in the Great War 1914-1919. Greater love hath no man than this that a man lay down his life for his friends".[58] The names of local men who died during the world wars are listed on the memorial.

---

[57] Anna Fernyhough, personal history.
[58] Germany surrendered on 11th November 1918. The fighting stopped while peace terms were negotiated. In June 1919, Germany and the Allied Nations formally signed the Treaty of Versailles to end the war.

The 80 Men Listed on Oundle and Ashton Town War Memorial

Much has been already written in books on Oundle concerning the sad loss of life in the two world wars. As a continuing tribute, listed here are the names in memory of the men we lost.

Men listed are: C.E. Afford, R. Barrett, I. Bell, A.F. Bennett, C.J. Bennett, J.E.F. Boulter, T.G. Chaplin, A.E.G. Coombs, S.J.T. Cooper, T.L. Cooper, E. Cottingham, J.E. Crawley, W. Craythorne, F.H. Cullop, P.E. Cullop, H.N. Curtis, T.P. Elllis, F.E. Garrett, M.W. Gurton, H.B. Hancock, J. Hill, J. Hunter, W. Johnson, G. Lacey, P. Beresford-Lees, T.J. Leverett, R. Lilleker, B.F. Loakes, H. Malsbury, C. Mancktelow, H.G.M. Markham, D.W. McMichael, J. Mears, M.J. Miskin (Military Cross), P. Munds, F.C. Norbury, A. Page, F. Peacock, F, A. Phillipson, F. Phillipson, F.H. Preston, J.T. Pridmore, F.W. Rollerson, J. Roughton, R.B. Sanderson, R.B. Seaton, J.W. Sexton, C. Sharpe, W. Sharpe, W.E. Sharpe, B.L. Siddons, A.E. Smith, A.J.S. Smith, E.P. Smith, F. Smith, G.E. Smith, J.H.M. Smith, T.E Smith, W. Stafford, C. Stretton, P.J. Stretton, S. Swann, S.H. Taylor, H. Titman, G.A. Tryon (Military Cross), C.L. Vear, F. Whistlecroft, G.H. Williamson (Military Cross), E.A. Bennett, J.G. Brown (Distinguished Conduct Medal), F.G. Edwards, E. Hendry, W. Horsford, W. Marshall, A.E. Moisey, D. Monk, C. Vipan, G. Waite, A.W. Wilson and S. Wright.

Oundle War Memorial was cleaned in April 2017. Here, but unnamed, I also wish to pay tribute to the many men who returned, but for them and their families, life was never the same again.

The 960 Men Listed as Dead from Oundle School, WWI Memorial

Nine-hundred and sixty men died during WWI, who were educated at or served on the staff of the School. They were stationed all over the world and two-hundred and twenty-two were killed in action or died of their wounds. Two-hundred and two were decorated for their valour and eighty-seven have no known grave. The oldest man to die was aged forty-five and they youngest was seventeen. They were a tribute to Oundle, their school and their country.

I believe what José Narosky wrote in 2010 is true, "In war, there are no unwounded soldiers".

...oooOOOooo...

Cut-backs and Supplementing Supplies

In 1939, when WWII began, the first product to be controlled was petrol as stocks were low and supplies were not being delivered to the country. In early 1940, bacon, butter and sugar were also rationed, followed smartly by ration regulation of meat, tea, jam, biscuits, cereals, cheese, eggs, lard, milk, plus canned and dried fruits. Ration books were issued with coupons that could be used weekly. These were introduced for items that could not be transported easily or that were in short supply as men left to fight in the armed services. With a short supply of farm workers, food pricing rose. Shipments from other areas of the country was problematic with a lack of men to transport it. Plus, there were no further imported foodstuffs from abroad. Rationing was a means of sharing food evenly and fairly, although there was some swapping of coupons for items that may be considered more desirable.

During WWII, one governmental concern was that the Germans would send paratroopers into Barnwell to kidnap Prince Henry (the Duke of Gloucester) and Princess Alice and their family (as, their son, Prince William, was born at the end of 1941.) In her memoir, Princess Alice mentions that in the event of this happening there were no instructions on what to do, but she was issued with a Welsh detective as a guard, who ubiquitously accompanied her throughout the war years. Almost every household in Oundle had an evacuee or an evacuee family (including the elderly grandparents who had left the cities)[59]. The Gloucester's and their household did likewise. They took in three evacuee children then, later, a couple more. The younger men who worked at Barnwell Manor were sent to war. The retired men who were left were asked to dig up the gardens and plant potatoes. Princess Alice agreed as to why this had to happen, but was sad to see a tended garden dug up. During the Battle of Britain, Lady Ethel Wickham visited from nearby Cotterstock and lent a hand at helping on a partridge-shoot (to supplement the food stocks). According to Princess Alice's memoirs, this was not very successful - as Lady Ethel was around ninety years old at the time.[60] (See Andrew Spurrel's photograph of Lady Ethel

---

[59] David Wills, personal information.
[60] Princess Alice, daughter of the 7th Duke of Buccleuch (1901-2004). 'Memoirs of Princess Alice, Duchess of Gloucester', Collins, London, 1983. pp. 122-126.

in the garden having tea.) The whole area 'mucked in to help out' in some way or another.

It is notable that Lady Ethel's daughter, Molly, was in charge of the St. John's Ambulance nurses. Ethelreda Gordon ('Ethel', 1864-1961) was the last child of the Marquis of Huntley. He never saw her as he died a just couple of months before her birth. In 1884, at the age of nineteen, she married Colonel Henry Wickham (who died in Oundle, in 1933, aged 77). Ethel helped to form the Northamptonshire District Nursing Association in 1903. During the influenza epidemic she nursed the people of Oundle and Barnwell. With Lady Lilford she established the Oundle Music Festival. She enjoyed local hunts and was said to have been a very competent and fearless horsewoman. She was also spotted in the town riding a motor-cycle! It was said that Percy Amps would stop serving his customers to serve her whenever she entered his shop. On her death in Cotterstock Hall in 1961 the hall was sold to the Capron family.

An enduring recollection is that women of the 1940s would use tea-stain to colour their legs and paint a brown line (as straight as possible) down the backs of them using eye-liner to create the 'seam' of (fake) stockings. This was one of the lengths women went to when deliveries of 'nylons' were in short supply.

...oooOOOooo...

My Family: Lucjan Mudza and Arthur Chester

My grandfather, Arthur Chester lived in Cherry Orchard, Benefield Road, after marrying the love of his life, Dorothy Nicholson, in St. Peter's Church in 1924. They had known each other for just a few months before they decided to wed. Arthur married Dorothy (née Nicholson) on his return from WWI. They had one child, Barbara, who was born in Cherry Orchard in 1930 and lived there for the first few months of her life. In 1952 Barbara married a Polish naval cadet, Lucjan Mudza, who had been stationed at nearby Lilford. They met for dances in Peterborough with other young people from the area.

My father, Lucjan Mudza was brought to the UK as a Naval Cadet at the end of the war. He was proud to learn a new language and use it for the rest of his life. His first revisit to Poland was in the late 1960s.

At this point, he found that his nearest surviving relatives were his cousins, whom he believed were all dead. He remained close to his cousin, Jasia (pronounced 'Yasha') for the remainder of their lives. The war had taken his parents and his little brother. This left Lucjan with awful, muscle-locking, stress symptoms. In contradiction to the generally held belief that only gypsies, vagrants and Jews died in the war camps, when the Russian army invaded Poland it transported many families living on the eastern border into the death camps of Russia. His family were reasonably wealthy, farming, middle-class Roman Catholics. The family farm is now in USSR, owing to the border changes after the war. Towards the end of the war Stalin's secret police (the NKVD) took custody of Polish prisoners from the Red Army. They had a web of reception-centres and transit-camps allowing transport of Polish citizens to prisoner-of-war camps in western USSR. The soviets carried out a series of mass executions of Polish nationals by the NKVD (the "People's Commissariat for Internal Affairs"). The Katyn War Cemetery and its Polish military personnel graves are near Smolensk, Russia and was where the (1940) massacre of 4,412 Polish officers took place. This is where Lucjan's father, Stanisław, met his end. Lucjan's father, an army Major, was shot along with other army officers Katyn. His brother, Henryk, died in Siberia of malnutrition aged around eleven years. This was followed by the death of his mother, Maria, whom family say "died of a broken heart", believing that her family were all dead. Lucjan (aged around fourteen or fifteen) was alive and was taken overland through Turkmenistan to Egypt by In December 1939, General Sikorski visited Moscow for the Polish government to propose and agree the Sikorski-Maisky pact with the Soviet Union (August 1941)[61]. Stalin invalidated the partition of Poland, declared the Russo-German Pact of 1939 void and released thousands of Polish prisoners from Soviet camps, who were subsequently sent (overland) to areas short of armed forces. General Władysław Anders oversaw this. Lucjan rarely talked of his time in the camps, but once commented that if the older men had not taken pity on the young and shared their meagre potato rations, he and other boys would have died. Lucjan became a naval cadet in the cluster sent to the Middle

---

[61] Roman Wapiński, *Władysław Sikorski*, Polski Słownik Biograficzny, zeszyt 154 (T. XXXVII/3), 1997, p. 474.

East and was brought to England for further training. After the war he made many German friends, but no Russian ones.

Lucjan met Barbara Chester at a dance. They married in 1952. Barbara and Lucjan had two daughters, firstly me[62], then Wendy. Barbara had no siblings, but says that she was "not bothered" about this as she had nineteen "close" maternal-cousins living nearby (sixteen children of matriarchal step-aunt, Doris Hooton), three cousins ('Charlie' Nicholson's children), plus a cousin, Martin Bateman, the son of her paternal aunt (Dora Chester).

Barbara's grandma, Frances Palmer, was born in Oundle in 1874. She married in Oundle, but shortly thereafter moved to Worksop with her husband, Charles Nicholson. Sadly, he died aged just twenty-six, leaving Frances with their two infants. Charles was almost three and Dorothy only a few months old (in 1899) when her father died. The family returned from whence they had come, where they had family to help and support them. Dorothy appears on the census in Oundle, aged one. Frances married Thomas Craythorne. He was the only father that Charles, Dorothy and Doris knew (yet biological father to only Doris).[63]

My grandfather, Arthur Chester grew up with six siblings: Stanley, Minnie, George, Mabel, Harold (Arthur's twin) and Dora. Their formative years were in Shropshire, yet many lived in Oundle for at some time in their lives. Arthur's daughter, Barbara recalls her 'Grandma Chester', who took her to a park in Manchester to hear the band play in the bandstand. (She enjoys band music to this day.) Arthur and his brothers all fought in WWI. His eldest brother, Robert Stanley Chester, was shot through the neck while fighting in France. He survived, but he could never yawn or cough. He was awarded a certificate for bravery on the battlefield. His youngest sister, Dora said, "Mother had it framed and insisted on it being hung on the sitting-room wall." Stanley recovered from his war wound and married his

---

[62] Anna Fernyhough, personal history.

[63] My family, Thomas and Frances Craythorn, their daughters Dorothy (Chester) & Doris (Hooton), Arthur Chester & Lucjan Mudza are buried in Stoke Road cemetery, along with many other members of the Hooton family.

nurse, Marjorie. Arthur's sister, Minnie, lived in Oundle before finally settling in Peterborough. She married 'Uncle Mac' (Arthur McNuff; 1891-1969). He also fought in the war. When the British were evacuated in Gallipoli he fell into a trench and broke his ankle. He recalled being afraid that he was going to be left behind, but returned to England safely. My grandad called his sister "Minnie Minervah" and "Minnie Mariah" (probably as a tease). She lived above the North Street sweet shop (30) for a time (before she ran Barnwell post office when it was at the bottom of the hill). In the early 1930s, Dorothy would walk her toddler, Barbara, across the road to see her aunt. Both Percy Arnett and Barbara Chester recall the shop beneath the flat as having "nice windows that were full of treats and sweets".

Arthur's brother, George (1895-1962), served as a Lieutenant in the Ontario Regiment of the Canadian Army. He served in France, where he was wounded and lost the use of his left arm. Arthur said, "It was no good to him ... and he had a hole above his heart". George was awarded the Victory Medal and the British War Medal. Post-war, he moved to British Columbia where his mother's sister, Auntie Polly, lived. He remained in Canada for the rest of his life and working in the salmon fisheries.

Mabel Chester (1898-1974) married Charles Fisher. After their marriage, they lived on the corner of Rock Road (first at 'the lighthouse' on New Road [1930] and then at number 2 [1932]). I have a photograph of my mother, Barbara, aged around two or three standing in the garden. In 1985, my mother recognised the house and interior from her childhood in the 1930s as belonging to Auntie Mabel and Uncle Charlie. Elderly town residents recalled the Fisher's throwing parties and hosting dinners. Their large wedding present box of monogrammed cutlery is mine and has returned to its original home in the house!) The women in the family knitted for the war effort: socks, gloves, scarves and balaclava hats! The family all sent their men and saw them return. The only non-returnée was Harold, their young brother.

Arthur's 1914-1918 War

Harold and Arthur were identical twins and were the youngest boys in the family. They were born in 1899 and signed up to go to war when they were seventeen. The twins believed that they were about to take part in a brave and worthwhile war against a common enemy, so 'took the King's shilling'[64] (his words). Arthur returned partly blinded, minus his twin and with a very different opinion of war. Arthur said that they were both shipped to France before their seventeenth birthday. He recalled that in the trenches, he had very little sleep. He remembered building bridges that were promptly blown to pieces after completion. He said that half of the time the shells landing around them were from their own side. During the war nothing was glamorised as it is in the movies. Grandad said, "We were in a big forest place. We had pick-axes, we had shovels; we had everything. We'd got to cut our way through to make a passage-way. We were at one end and the 'Jerries' were at the other end. As we were going, our artillery were supposed to put a barrage over the top of us to stop him (the German army) from coming. You could see towards their line. Instead of that, all of our own shells dropped right where we were. We lost one half of us from our own shells!"

The army would "advanced a hundred yards to be sent back again the same distance". Lice and mites bothered the soldiers in the trenches and they ached with inflamed limbs from a lack of movement and the damp conditions. Grandad said they were "never dry". The winter sounded severe. Harold became ill after three weeks back at the Front and died aged 18. Arthur said that he never saw him again after Harold became ill. He recalled, "We went out on the same cattle truck, together". Harold contracted "Double Pneumonia" (a lung infection that affected both lungs and caused respiratory problems).

Arthur said, "We joined the battalion, coming out of the line, coming back for a rest. Then we had to march so many kilometres further on. That's what soldiers did." The soldiers marched in order, with a full pack that was "A good weight." Conditions were bad and Grandad believed that numbers were inestimable as "No-end died with

---

[64] A colloquial saying regarding the payment of a shilling (5p) offered to low-paid workers to leave their trade.

pneumonia". He said, "We were both together in the same platoon. We re-joined the mob on the front-line. That night he was taken bad and couldn't get his breath". Arthur said that Harold was "...really bad all night, I was bathing his head ... but I couldn't report him 'til morning. As soon as I could, I took him to the orderly's place where you report sick. They took him in and that was the last I'd see of him". He regretted, "I wasn't with him when he died." Arthur never saw his brother again.

After his twin's death, Arthur continued to fight at the front with his entrenched regiment. He was subsequently poisoned by 'mustard' gas before being returned across the Channel (via several hospitals) for specialist medical treatment, assessment and recuperation. (I think that this was near to the end of the war.) He said, "I was gassed and couldn't see. Even now, they didn't cure me eyes ... no. They helped, so that I could see a bit. Then I was taken from the hospital area at the Front, to the coast and on the boat home; then to Scotland, then to Manchester (to mother) and attended the eye hospital. And they did not cure it. They used to put alum in them, every day, and it gradually cleared. By the time I was married my eyes were ... oh, the whites were nothing, but like fire. Red. They still irritate. I wasn't fit or right to fight again with me eyes, but (later) they sent me back out to France, guarding prisoners. I used to take them out and work a night on, going round the camp and walking around the outside; you know, seeing no-one had escaped. Then you'd be on one night and you'd have the day off. The next day you'd be taking them out and pulling all the big dugouts down. Oh, they were big dugouts that the German soldiers had. Much better than ours. They had pianos and everything in there!"

At the end of the war, Arthur found Armistice Day "a quiet affair". He was stationed at a British coastal camp in Redcar. He said, "A group of us were gazing out to sea, watching submarines come in, when word went around that the war was finished. We had a great sing-song that night." When asked if the war was worth the loss of life, he always said a loud, "No".

Arthur was effectively blind for over six months (with burning pain and the whites of his eyes invisible for "red"). He suffered from 'nerves' and 'the shakes' for most of his life, particularly if cold or after swimming. His 'suffocated' lungs were damaged too and doctors advised him to take light, active employment outdoors to help his chest; hence grandad's decision to become a gardener.

(None of the Chester family truly recovered from the death of Harold.) Harold died in April 1918, aged eighteen. He is buried in the Somme war graves in Gézaincourt, near Doullens, France. It was sad to go to visit his grave with my family in the 1980s. Grandad, sadly never visited. The cemetery was begun in April 1918, after the German attack in Picardy, so Harold was one of the first soldiers to be buried there. Both twins were in the 19th Battalion of the Welch (Welsh) Regiment. Arthur outlived his twin by almost seventy-three years. For many years Arthur laid the British Legion wreath at the war memorial as Oundle's oldest Somme survivor.

Arthur Chester served in the Home Guard in WWII. He donated his spare pots and pans for collection to be taken and made into "guns and munitions". Although he believed the war was a great waste of life, Arthur thought it an honour to place a wreath at the Oundle memorial each Armistice Day. He missed his twin, Harold, until the day he died. He died in 1991 at home in North Street.[65]

Post-War

After the war, recuperation, and subsequent marriage, Arthur worked as a gardener near to his new home in Oundle, Northamptonshire. He often helped the local vet, Mr Smith, when "cutting the pigs" (castration). On one occasion, he saved the vet's life by fending off an attacking boar) he became the head-gardener at a local manor house in Stoke Doyle, near Oundle. He was a keen outdoorsman (bringing home little surprises, plus exploring the bluebell woods and pointing out other wildlife). One day he arrived home and remarked, "I've got something for you in my jacket pocket". On dipping my hand inside I pulled out a handkerchief. I was really not please to discover that his false teeth were inside. When he saw my face, Grandad said, "Not that pocket!" He had brought me a live mole that had been trapped and

---

[65] Arthur's youngest sister, Dora, was ten years younger than him; she died aged 99 years 11 months, after upholding that she didn't want to live to be a hundred!

caught in his work in Stoke Doyle.[66] It was amazing. I am sure that today not many children have such an interesting way of learning about their environment. My mother, also a keen gardener, probably got her skills in planting from her father.

Grandad was accident prone. His dentist must have been so tired of him. Once, when riding home on his bicycle, he sneezed out his false teeth and rode over them, which meant a trip to the dentist. Later, we went out to Oxford in dad's car. On the way home, Grandad wanted to stop for what he called a "Jimmy Riddle" (rhyming slang from the war). He came back and on almost arriving home announced we needed to go back and find the field! He had lost his teeth there! This meant another a trip to the dentist.

Things grandad liked that may help readers to recall their own memories include: "A nice dripping sandwich" (pure fat on bread, with a little salt; not considered healthy now). Liquid 'Camp' coffee, was a brown, sweetened liquid used in the war years, which I think was made from chicory. Grandad always made his 'coffee' with a spoonful of 'Camp' and a mug of hot water. (I always preferred the exotic looking label to the taste). He also liked Jacobs' cream crackers with a triangular (Kraft) "spreading cheese" on the top. I can still smell the toast, which he made on the end of a long toasting-fork in the front of the parlour fire. It was spread with lashings of butter, alongside a glass of Robinson's barley water. We would watch "Doctor Who", "Dad's Army", "Top of the Pops" and "Adam Adamant" on the television in the 1960s.

Arthur loved and was proud of his family. He had an infectious, merry laugh and I recall him chatting and playing with his grandchildren when eighty and ninety. His pleasures were simple: laughing and enjoying a 'nice piece of cake'. My children, Mark and Kit, and my sisters' eldest daughter, Helen, called him "big grandad" as he was their "great grandad", but he was small, probably no more than five-foot-four in height. (By our teens, Wendy and I were his height or even slightly taller!) I am sorry to say that Amy, his final grandchild, missed meeting

---

[66] Arthur was a pacifist at heart and he loved nature. He went with me to release the mole in the fields beyond the football field on Station Road. To this day, I still smile when I see mole-hills.

him in person by just two months. Before he died, Grandad asked Wendy, "What do you think you'll have?" and Wendy replied, "Another girl". Arthur was a memorable, gentle, charming 'gentleman' character. He would always devalue himself and say that "the smart twin died early". He was gentle and kind, which is how "we will always remember him".

…oooOOOooo…

Arthur Ball's Memories of His Grandfather, Robert Edward Butt

My grandfather, Robert Butt, known as Bob, was one of the old Oundle characters. He lived in Inkerman Place before moving to a council house, 113 Benefield Road, for the rest of his life. This was a time when Oundle School had their own power-station in Blackpot Lane. He worked here until he retired. Every time there was a thunder storm, he jumped on his bike and raced down to the power-station to ensure there was no interruption to the school power-supply. In his free time, Bob played football for Oundle Town Football Club.

Bob served in the army in WWI, during which, he was at the battle of Mons and was taken prisoner. He then spent some time in a wartime camp in Grevelejren, Denmark. (He was a member of the Yorkshire Regiment, but I don't know why that was his chosen regiment). Denmark had been occupied by German forces since 1940. He was sent to defend the Fortifications of Copenhagen and lived in the camps that were barracks. Arthur believes that his grandfather was in this concentration camp: "The main parts of the Grevelejren, camp were divided into the Greve Camp and the Barfredshøj Camp".[67] When Bob came back after the war and his time spent as a POW, he returned to work at the Oundle School Power Station in Blackpot Lane (where he worked until he retired). He was the first ever Scout Master in Oundle and was presented with his certificate of office, signed by Lord Baden Powell. He had four daughters and a son. The only one who remained in Oundle was my mother, Grace. The others all married and moved away".

Arthur recalls that Bob "was an expert shot with a twelve bore and always had several dogs and ferrets, which he used to catch rabbits".

---

[67] http://www.vestvolden.info/Eng/Eng_Tune_lejre.htm

Arthur's favourite story about him includes Peter Scott. "As a boy, Sir Peter Scott attended Oundle School and befriended my grandfather. Occasionally, when the boys were allowed to go walking in the countryside around Oundle. Sir Peter and a friend would collect my Grandfather's ferrets and spend the afternoon hunting rabbits. Of course, this was against all the school rules. To keep the ferrets concealed, he cut a hole in the lining of his blazer and placed them inside. In his autobiography, he mentions having the ferrets inside the lining of his blazer when he and a friend bumped into the Headmaster on the Oundle North Bridge. While they chatted to each other, the ferrets were wriggling around at the back of his blazer! I don't think the boys were ever found out!"

He said, "When my grandfather was in hospital just before he died, Sir Peter sent him a signed autobiography, which was later passed onto me as the only ornithologist in the family". "When my grandmother, who was a bit of a dragon, gave him a hard time he would turn off his hearing-aid and take refuge in the nearby 'Black Horse' pub[68] in Benefield Road, where he was a member of the darts team."

...oooOOOooo...

War-Time Recollections from Bevil and Margaret Allen

While growing up in the war years, Bevil and his family lived at 27 Benefield Road. It was a double-fronted house with railings that were removed in the war. The government had an obligatory need for iron gates and railings, so these were cut down with axle-grinders, dumped temporarily in the Market Hall and then the pile of scrap-metal was taken away to foundries (where some of it was used for munitions to help the war effort in the early 1940s). Bevil said that "what was left outside the house were blobs where the welding chip cut off the upright rails". He noted that after the war, they didn't replace them and no-one brought any back!

Bevil said that his father and Mr Williams (his friend) were air-raid wardens during WWII. One day his father came home shaken. He told his family that when they were walking down the Benefield Road towards the centre of town, "a plane came over and machine gunned

---

[68] Arthur Ball went on to say, "Sadly, the pub no longer exists" (family history).

straight down West Street and hit one of the balustrade balls on the top of Danford's Yard". Apparently, they were so shocked they threw themselves flat at the edge of the road.

"The first week of rations came in a cardboard box that was placed on the kitchen table." Bevil commented that they said, "We can't live on that; there is only a tiny bit of butter". Bevil said that he would "cycle to the station to get the train to Wellingborough. It felt like a long journey. Trains were not fast and there was always a walk or bicycle ride at the end".

His father and uncle owned a shop in North Street, called "Allen Brothers". Bevil attended Laxton School in the town as a day boy. On leaving school he worked for his father. He met his future wife, Margaret, at a dance in Thrapston and 'courted her'. They married in Warmington and the couple are still inseparable. After their marriage, they both worked in Bevil's father's betting shop as his parents "died early".

Bevil's father ran the St. Osyth's Lane betting shop (a designer-shop named 'Grot" [2015]), that is accessed via an alley to the left of the shop-front window. Bevil worked in his parents' betting shop. When they died, Margaret and Bevil took over the business. They were not contented in doing so, but felt they should continue the Allen business. From 1966 to 1969, Bevil and Margaret went to college to train to teach. They both taught in Oundle Primary School after qualifying in 1969.

Margaret Allen (née Burdett) came from an educated and musical family. She played the piano and loved music. She was born in Oundle (delivered by Dr Spurrell) then lived elsewhere until 1950, when she married Bevil. Her widowed father taught in Victoria School in Wellingborough. He retired at the start of the war. Her mother had died when she was eight years old, so she mostly recalls her 'Gran Sharpe' who lived in Oundle "in the last house in Gordon Road" (10). She later moved to a bungalow on New Road. Margaret remembered the Beech family's shop on the corner, as a "treasure box, selling all sorts of groceries and sweets".

Bevil, a skilled violinist, briefly appeared (playing his violin) in the 1972 film "The Ruling Class" (a British black-comedy starring Peter O'Toole, Alastair Sim and Arthur Lowe). When Bevil and Margaret moved from the Benefield Road house, they moved to Glapthorn Road (by Tilley Hill Close). Their children (David, Ruth and Richard) camped in the field behind the house with their friends and often played with them there. One of their friends, a boy, was bitten by a sheep. This land and its livestock belonged to Des (Desmond) and George Ray. There is now a new lane at the north-western edge of Oundle that has been named Old Farm Lane. Six large, barn-style houses were built (in 2016) on this land that once belonged to the Ray family.

Living near to fields had its drawbacks and bonuses: Cattle roamed in the field at the back of the houses. One day the gate was left open and the plants in the Allen's garden were all trampled. A bonus was that manure from the farm was used to fertilise nearby gardens. Margaret Brewster's father, George Slote, knew the Allen family well. Bevil recalled that they would 'hide' George in their house when he wanted a break from work. He would say, "Don't tell them I'm here". There was a spinney with a spring and a pond. The pond had been dug out as the land was 'brick drying land'. Sadly, the barn for bricks was later demolished. The houses in the road now extend well beyond where the cows were in pasture.

Bevil asked if we knew some of the Prisoners of War (POWs) who came to Oundle and the surrounding villages. He informed us that, as there was a lack of agricultural workers, the senior school students and POWs were set to work in the fields as labour. Bevil recalls them working on his uncle's farm in Stoke Doyle. "They were collected in the morning and taken back in the evenings on the back of a lorry. They seemed happy to be doing some beneficial work and they were treated well". There were Italian and German prisoners (they were boarded in Warmington, Barnwell and other local villages). Fletton House also boarded WWII German P.O.W.'s who were sent to help out at local farms.

Bevil talked about Margaret's family. Margaret's grandma was the daughter of Joshua Phillimore (who was born in 1814 in Eversholt, Woburn) who wrote several diaries. These have been copied for their posterity and antiquity by Woburn Abbey. Margaret said that "Joshua was a very fine artist who was related to the Duchess of Bedford" (wife of John Russell, the sixth Duke). "She was associated with a scandal of the time" (possibly as a child born outside of her wedlock to the Duke). Joshua was well-treated, educated well and was taught to paint at the hand of the famous. (The Duchess of Bedford was a great patroness of the arts, and had a longstanding relationship with the painter, Sir Edwin Landseer). Joshua's works of art are in the style of Landseer (and some were direct copies), so were always left unsigned. Joshua gave these paintings to family members. Some were passed down to the many branches of Margaret's family. Margaret has an enchanting and clever replica of 'A Distinguished Member of the Humane Society' by Sir Edwin Landseer painted by her ancestor.[69] Joshua's original works are held in high regard by the Allen family.

Bevil showed his interest in garages and cars. He mentioned that in the 1960s, Willmot's garage stood across the road from Milton Road and in the Benefield Road. The Ashworth's first owned the garage, then it became Francis and Marshall's garage. (Now it is the site of townhouses). Bevil recalled that there was a food shop near St. Wilfrid's Church (on West Street) and a garage next-door at the end of West Street. The shop was handy as the Benefield Road families did not need to walk all the way into town for groceries.

Bevil was very proud of his grandad, who was a postman. He worked in East Road, not far from the exit to the current Co-op and near to Jean Donnegani's garage. Bevil mentioned his attachments to the May fetes run by the Home Farm Trust that took place on the Home Close. Bevil was a member of the Trust. He organised and ran the fetes (and raised over £40,000 for a special needs home that his daughter, Ruth, attended). There were spaces on the field for other charity stands. The summer festivals were very well attended and people had money to spend in the 1960s and 1970s. He recalls that Pam Miller (whose husband was the head of music in Oundle School) served on the committee. He remarked, "They were good times and fun".[70]

…oooOOOooo…

---

[69] The original is in the Tate; first exhibited 1838.
[70] Bevil and Margaret gave kind permission to use their information (some has been shared with other authors).

Home and School in the War Years - Elsie Bladon (née Arnett)

Elsie Arnett and her siblings grew up at 15 Benefield Road, which was part of "Cherry Orchard". There were five children in the family: Joyce, Percy (Perce), Kay, Elsie, Jean and Brian. Elsie was born in 1935. Her parents were Herbert and Gladys (née Coles). Herbert worked at the Stewart and Lloyds Steel Works in Corby. Elsie recalls that as children, they played outside most of the time. She still has her whip and top and explained how the children would colour the top with coloured chalks, which made a pretty pattern as it spun. They made use of the things around them and could make a sledge from old bits of wood when it snowed.

The children often went over the road and down to the allotments on the south side of Benefield Road to play. They would then walk up to the top of the field to slide down on their sledges, under a wire and into the brook. Her Mum was not happy when Elsie went home wet through! They were collectors of bits and pieces they found and were interested in wildlife around the town edges as they 'would always play out'. Home was warm, but Elsie recalls that the family toilet was at the bottom of the yard. There was no indoor plumbing other than a tap.

At the Council (Secondary) School, Elsie recalls that she was caned twice by Mr Evans, due to talking in class. Thankfully, the corporal punishment practice is no longer tolerated. In state and nationally-funded private schools, corporal punishment was outlawed by the Parliament in 1986. Teachers were considered 'in-loco-parentis', which meant that they could deliberately hurt children in response to undesired behaviour while in school. This meant that (legally) they could smack across the child's buttocks or on their hands with a cane, wooden stick, paddle, slipper or strap. More often than not, it was with the slim, wooden yard-stick, used for drawing straight lines on the blackboard that was "near to hand". Elsie Bladon recalls her punishment, but said there were other children who were caned much more frequently. Later, the Arnett family moved to the house to the other side of the road.

...oooOOOooo...

Barbara Mudza (née Chester)

School Life with my Cousins

Dorothy Chester (née Nicholson) and Doris Hooton (née Craythorne) were half-sisters. As Dorothy's father had died before she was a year old, her mother remarried Mr Craythorne. When grown and married, Dorothy had one child and Doris had sixteen children. The cousins all played as a group and went to both the primary and secondary schools together. Dorothy's daughter, Barbara Chester and her many Hooton cousins were close. Barbara said that she was never lonely as she always had her cousins, who behaved like sisters to her. She was closest in age to Maureen, Audrey and Sheila, but they all looked out for each other. They shared holidays and the occasional "overnight stay", together. They played together in the holidays, evenings and weekends and went to school as "one big happy family".

Molly Slater would walk Barbara to school (as she was in the year above and lived in the same road). Barbara recalls "walking knee-deep in snow up Blackpot Lane to get to school". When Barbara was at the Council School in the early 1940s, the class were lining up to go into Miss Gale's classroom. Barbara Carter talked and Miss Gale said, "Who was that talking?" Someone said, "It was Barbara", so Miss Gale picked on the first "Barbara" she saw and instructed her to go to the Headmaster (Mr Evans). "What are you here for?" he asked. Barbara replied, "Someone was talking, but it wasn't me, it was Barbara Carter". Mr Evans told her to go back to her class. (Luckily, she didn't get the cane.)

Farm Work and 'Mum on the Horse's Bum'

During WWII, girls from the Council School were sent to aid the delivery-workers' rounds, to help with livestock and vegetable (potato) picking on the local farms around Oundle. At one point, Barbara's friend sat on the back of a horse that was pulling a cart. The friend had a secure seat, but the horse had Barbara on its rump. She slipped and fell off. The cart wheel went over her hip and thigh. She had a mark on her hip for a long time and suffered some "side effects that were forgotten over time".[71] (These were before the days of health and safety!)

Heacham Holidays

Just after WWII, cousins, Audrey Hooton (aged 17) and Barbara Chester (14 at that time) went on an annual holiday with Barbara's parents. Audrey would borrow her aunt, Dorothy's five-pound flat iron to straighten her dresses when they unpacked. They caught a train from Oundle and, after a couple of changes, they would arrive for their stay in the chalet bungalows of Heacham. On their arrival, the girls would heat the flat iron on the gas cooker and spit on it to see if it was hot enough to iron with. "If it bubbled then it was". At the end of the holiday, Audrey announced, "Well, I've had a lovely time and I've still got five pounds in my suitcase". Her aunt, Dorothy, said, "What? I thought you said earlier that you were broke." Audrey burst with laughter, as what she had in her case was the five pound flat iron.

...oooOOOooo...

Valerie Hillyard (née Leigh) - Home and Family

The house at 34 North Street was a pub called the 'Carpenters Arms'. (It is grade-II listed.) The front of the building is sixteenth-century and the back of the house is seventeenth-century. Valerie Hillyard said, "There were stables down the yard that had a mounting block. Two cottages also stood down the yard. The stable lads and grooms stayed in the first cottage and the horses were stabled at the bottom on East Road". Any visitors stayed in the inn. After its years of functioning as an inn, Doctor Turner owned the house (Valerie believes that he possibly moved from here to Duck Lane). When the Hillyard family moved in to the house their son, John, was eleven. (He arrived at the house with his parents over seventy years ago). His mother was a widow when John and Valerie married, so the couple moved in with her. Nearby, Valerie's aunt (née Leigh) and uncle kept the 'Half Moon Inn'. She recalls that it was "where Joe Brudenell worked, next-door to where he kept the engines going".

---

[71] Information from Barbara Chester.

Valerie's sister, Diana is a talented artist and runs an art class every Tuesday afternoon at the Football club. Diana has previously run an evening art class at PWS, but when the class ceased "(as dad was alive in those days) he said to use the football club, so Diana did". Val remarked that "the community enjoy the lessons and Len Rutherford (the vet) has been attending the classes for many years."

Valerie's (and Diana's) paternal grandfather, James Leigh, lived in Polebrook and was a stone-mason. Val's parents were coaxed by 'Button' Horn[72] to buy two houses that were being built (9 and 11 East Road). He said they "needed to buy them as they were a damn good buy". They were made from stone and brick from Ashton Manor. Ralph was born in 1909 in Oundle. He bought the East Road houses with the little money he had, but as he was getting married he needed somewhere the live. Phyllis and Ralph Horn married in 1936. The family lived at 11, which was altered over time. The family rented number 9 to a couple who pitched water over the fence at the children. Val said that they didn't understand children as they had none of their own. Val and Diana attended Oundle primary school. Their father, Ralph Leigh, was a veteran of North Africa. He met Mussolini and saw the bombing of Dresden. He came to hate war. Ralph worked for Emap, the regional newspaper publishers. Val's brother did an apprenticeship with Emap then worked there until his retirement.

Ralph was a prisoner of war in Dresden, Germany. Val reflected that "He had a very hard time and lost his golden hair through the stresses of that awful time. We went to bed every night and looked out of the back window at the church and prayed for dad. We had no idea if he was dead or alive. He saw Dresden burn in 1945, but we didn't know that he was there until afterwards. Mum received a letter to say that he was missing in action, presumed dead. I will always remember sitting there in the bedroom and praying for him every night." She recalled, "In mum and dad's East Road house, we used to sit in the bedroom (11) that was at the back. We could see the church steeple. We would say our prayers overlooking the land that is now the ugly Co-op. That is where there were pretty cottages that were full of history and shouldn't have been pulled down". She said that "One of the

---

[72] Valerie said that (in her mother's side of the family), the Horn name had no 'e', but has been spelled differently by others.

stories about them is that the executioner (Mr Bull or his assistant) stayed in one of the cottages for a couple of nights before the execution of Mary Queen of Scots (1587). There were three cottages in the back and three on the front. The back-yard had chickens in the war years as everyone had chickens." Mr Palmer lived at the front by the Hooton's.

"My dad, Ralph Leigh, was on his way home after being a prisoner of war in Germany during the war. My uncle took us to get dad from the station. He first collected Diana and me from the primary school in Polebrook, then drove to collect dad in his bread van. Dad once had bright yellow hair and my sister and I didn't want to look at him as his hair had all fallen out. When we got back to Polebrook School they had (literally) put the flags out for him. He made a speech there, then we came into Oundle. Val remarked that the Spurrell's lived where Lady Tara Becher lived in Lime House. The house is divided into smaller dwellings now, but at the time the Spurrell family owned the lot. They had gone out and put flags and bunting all over the road to celebrate dad's safe return to East Road. As his hair was falling out, we girls went upstairs and hid in the bedroom. We didn't want to look closely at him."

On his return after the war, Ralph Leigh "was a busy man who immersed himself into doing everything he could". Ralph kept horses in the Webb's field (by the Redcap school), which the Leigh girls called "The Webbery". The children either walked to the school here or were taken there by horse and cart.

Ralph ended up the Chair of the Football association in Oundle, Peterborough and Northants. The original football field was on the right at the top of Benefield Road, in the same field as Mushie the lion ("only he was here after the footballers gained the new field on Station Road"). Val recalls that as a child she would say goodnight to 'Mushie' every night from their back-bedroom in East Road, when the lion lived adjacent to them in Easton's Yard (where the Co-op car park is now).

"My grandparents lived in one of the council houses in East Road (54) and mum was brought up there." Val and Diana's maternal grandparents were Lyla and William "Button" Horn. "In WWI, Button was on horseback with the mounted cavalry. He continued his love of

122

horses when he returned from France". "Grandad kept about eight ponies and charged half-a-crown per-hour for tuition and lessons in his riding school. Susan Head (from the fruit shop) and all of the local famer's children attended the pony club. They all rode there. Grandad taught the two Princes of Gloucester, Prince William and Prince Richard, how to ride. When there was a gymkhana they were allowed to ride our small grey pony and we weren't allowed to ride whenever the Gloucesters' wanted him." (No wonder they won all the trophies!) Vet, Leila (née Hillyard), his great-granddaughter continues this interest today and recently attended the horses of the Household Cavalry in Hyde Park, London. She has three children with her husband, David, (two boys and a new baby girl, Eliza) and maintains horses for herself and ponies that her children can ride. David is a doctor. The whole family had a 'horsey heritage'. Grandfather, Button Horn married Lyla and they were contentedly "long-lived" together with their family. Val's parents, Phyllis (née Horn) and Ralph lived into old age. Val mentioned that Ralph died about fifteen years ago (aged 84) and Phyllis died later.

Valerie remarked, "Life has changed in Oundle. We never celebrated Halloween like they do today. Recently, robbers blew up the Co-op cash machine with gas canisters. At 3 a.m., we heard the explosion from our house. Diana said that all of East Road residents got up, wondering what had happened." "We had no local policemen to deal with it as they've all been moved to Corby. Oundle has changed and it is dreadful." Despite this unwanted change to the town's character, Valerie and John have wonderful memories of their lineage and their growing family not too far away.

…oooOOOooo…

Sue Stamper (née Knight) – Home and Family

Mr Cook George Afford and Ellen Afford, his wife (who married in 1882) lived at 34 East Road. Their daughter, Clara Afford (1882-1976) was run over by a vehicle at the top of New Road, when she was going to throw sticks into the stream. Their son, who was known by his second name (Ernest), fought and died in WWI. Private George Ernest Afford of the 1st Northamptonshire Regiment appears first on Oundle

123

and Ashton War Memorial. He was "killed in action" on 9th September 1916, aged 28. His body was never found.

Ernest was born in Oundle and grew up on West Street. His registered occupation that was listed when he was conscripted was "gardener". He was conscripted in May 1916 and died in the battle of the Somme after a month of fighting. He is commemorated on Thiepval Memorial, to the Missing of the Somme, France. His sister, Grace, and younger brother, Albert Percy Afford (1892-1966) lived with the family. They had several Oundle homes during their lives. In 1891 they lived in West Street, then Benefield Road in 1901, then at 5 Burnham Terrace, East Road by the time of the 1911 census.[73]

Sue Stamper was born at 36 Market Place in the flat above a carter's (who delivered goods in a horse-drawn cart, from the shop that is currently "Stu-pots"). At that time there were two flats on the upper floor. In 1939, Mr Albert and Emily Afford and Mr Cook George Afford (1856-1951) and his wife, Ellen Sophia Clarke (1859-1930) lived here. Miss Rose E. Afford was born in 1932. She married Percy Clark in 1954 (and thus, is Gillian Black (née Clark)'s and Sue's aunt). She mentioned that Nigel (Afford) worked at Brudenells and at the Co-op. Rose lived at 51 Rock Road for many years. Sue recalled that around this time her mother was an auxiliary nurse at Fletton House. She said, "I recall the old soldiers sitting on a seat outside Fletton House. They lived at the "Spike". There were flowers growing out of the wall and they are still there now, forty years later." The family had evacuees during the war and "Gran would cook at the primary school for them".

Sue lived in the Market Place for two years before moving to 66-68 Glapthorn Road. She later lived at 18 Tilley Hill Close (no longer living with her grandparents who, by then, lived nearby at 2 Tilley Hill Close). When they moved house they took their belongings across the Glapthorn road on a trolley. Sue recalls, "We lived near to Susan Fenson and Karen Fenson, whose dad was a policeman. They lived in Tilley Hill Close and attended the same school." In the primary school, Sue recalls being together in Mrs Turland's class. She also reflected

---

[73] See https://fisharebest.webtrees.net/individual.php?pid=i5333&ged=genesis

that, "Mrs Batson always played the piano. Mr Venner was a lay-preacher at the Jesus Church when it was Church of England."

When speaking of days when she was not in school, Sue recalled "going primrosing in Biggin Woods, gathering bunches of leaves around the outside of the flower bunches. Then they could be put into our baskets and sold." "On May Day, we made garlands. The maypole was always fun to dance around and we had lots of practices in the school hall. The maypole stood wrapped up in paper in the corner for the rest of the year." Sue said that her class "We had 'Activity' and 'Tidy Boxes' in our reception classroom with Miss Smith. Miss Smith had these on the carpet and used flash cards she held up to get us to identify. She always wore a cardigan done up at the back with a set of pearls around her neck. We had to line up in front of the teachers to go in and out of the classroom." She remembers that "Those who went to Sunday-school won all of the prizes". When Sue was nine years old her family moved to Norwich. Sue said, "Dad worked with the Inland Revenue, so we moved to where they needed us." Four years later, they were living in Bolton.

...oooOOOooo...

Sharon Cottingham (née Jackson)

Sharon's father, Frank Robert Jackson was born in 1919. He became a member of the 5th Northants Territorial Army. He "joined up" at the age of fifteen, but hid his age. A number of events were planned for King George V and Queen Mary on their Silver Jubilee (25th) celebration tour in 1935. Frank was one of six local men chosen to parade for Royalty when they visited Peterborough on the tour. (The King had visited Peterborough in 1934 by Royal Train and did so again in 1941.)

Recollections of Dad, Frank Jackson

Sharon looked to the years between 1956 and 1966. She said, "When I was little, my Dad worked six days a week". The legacy of the tuberculosis Frank had contracted just before WWII was a weakened chest. "On his left-side only half of his lung worked. This was discovered when Dr Lieber listened to his chest and was shocked. He sent Dad for an x-ray and it showed a dark mass where the base of his lung had calcified. Dad worked so hard, despite his medical history, that it is understandable our garden was not a mini-allotment, even though we were a large family".

She continued, "At one time he drove for Taylor's of Castor, Ailsworth and Stibbington and later, Dad worked for Northamptonshire County Council rising to Foreman-Fitter Mechanic. In the winter of 1963, when the snow was banked high on Glapthorn Road, we hardly saw Dad. His hands were rough and bled from the amount of grit that he shovelled. Later, he would be out before dawn, sending out the grit lorries that kept the roads clear. By this time they had heated cabs and machines that spread the grit. Over the years he was so dedicated that his boss, Mr Thompson, put him forward for an OBE. It did not matter to Dad that this was not successful, he was proud that 'Thommo' had proposed him for the honour. We still have the letter".

"At the East Road depot, Dad worked with his brother, Bernard, who drove a road-roller. He also worked with Mick Crick, who was a great friend. They were respectively called 'Big Unc' and 'Little Unc'. Dad worked with Arthur Shawley and (amongst others) Eric Mould, whom his work-mates knew as 'Tarzan'."

Box Brownie

The Jackson family lived at 43 Gordon Road. Mr and Mrs[74] Harold Edwards lived at 49. Sharon remarked that "Mum and Mrs Edwards were both Scottish and enjoyed sharing the magazine 'Peoples Friend' and 'The Sunday Post'. One day Mrs Edwards came round with some photographs. They had found an old box-brownie camera and although the film was over fifty years old, they had the film developed and the photographs were fine. Who were the young lads on the picture? The cottage in the background was Melton Cottage in Glapthorn. Mr Edwards told his wife that the young man was Frank Jackson! Mrs Edwards brought the photographs to our house to share them with Mum and Dad and Harold was correct. The young lad, aged 11, was my Dad. Dad said that he "was dressed ready for Scouts", hence the shorts and plimsolls. The other young lad was Willie Buick".

---

[74] Harold and Christina were married in Oundle in 1946.

White Gate-Posts

In the 1940s and 1950s 'drink driving' was not an offence. Sharon said, "My dad and Mr Crawley, known as 'Crump', had been for a few drinks at the 'Wheatsheaf' pub in Thurning, run by dad's brother, Herbert and his wife, Gwen. As they arrived back at Crump's garage on Glapthorn Road, by the windmill, my Dad commented that he didn't remember the white gates. They had taken a left instead of a right and had driven onto the Public School pitch and had driven between the rugby posts".

Growing Up

Sharon remarked that "when walking to and from school, we, Jackson girls (Lorna, Glynis, Sharon, Rowena and Maria) were 'looked after' by all of the Mums, Aunts, and Grannies. Few, if any, dads walked children to school in those days as they worked. If you were carrying your coat and it was cold you would be told to put your coat on. Looking back, I see it as a sort of collective parenting, all of the mums were looking after you and you treated them with respect and bided what they said".

Sharon recalled an experience that taught her a salutary lesson. She said, "As I walked home from school one day, I stroked Miss Ward's dog, except that I got it wrong, it was not Miss Ward's friendly dog. It was Gertie Brown's dog and who'd had an operation on his head. Unfortunately he bit me and my hand filled with blood. I dashed home and was taken to the doctor, but it was not serious. The following day Gertie Brown came around with a small box of chocolates for me. Mum let me have them all. Not at once, but I did not have to share with my sisters and little brother, Robert. The following day in assembly, Mr Denley talked about the danger of stroking stray dogs".

'Light Bulb' Moments

As we grow we realise our misconceptions of things in the past. Sharon reflected on "two major 'lightbulb' moments concerned my first school day and the death of my Nan Jackson. I recall that I believed I was given a jigsaw of hundreds of red and green gnomes to sort and put together on my first morning at school and I could not do it. I became upset and would not stop crying, so was slapped across the knees. My sister, Glynis, was sent to comfort me".

"When I was about twelve years old, I realised that the jigsaw probably only had a few gnomes on it and that I was upset as it was my first day at school. The memory of the slap is exact though."

The other recollection is of "an afternoon when Lorna, Glynis and I had tea at the Latham's Alms House with Nan Jackson, peaches and evaporated milk. We had been given new pinnies by Nan when we had tea. I think that is why the visit stayed in my mind. Sadly, Nan died shortly after this and I believed that the doctor had told her not to eat tinned peaches! At the same time as discovering my 'puzzle' error, I realised that Nan had not died from eating peaches. She had simply died shortly after our visit and I had wrongly put two and two together".

Sharon said, "It was a long time before I knew that my Dad, Frank Jackson had nearly died from tuberculosis in his twenties. He was saved by the new 'wonder drug' Penicillin.[75] He told us that the patients who were the most seriously ill were in the beds next to the nurses station, which had glass panels so that the patients could be observed at all times".

Sharon went on to say that "on several occasions he woke up to find the bed opposite empty as the patient had died during the night. He was greatly relieved when his bed was moved away from the big glass windows. He returned home to Elmington Cottages with his Mum and brother(s) while recuperating. His 'bedroom' was a shed, where one wall had been replaced with sacking for a sanatorium effect! One night he rang the bell relentlessly, so Nan sent Uncle Horace (I think it was Horace) to see why. Outside, the snow was blowing-in off the field and onto Dad's bed. The icy blast did no great harm and he recovered. Later, Auntie Jessie (Jessie Richmond, née Roughton, dad's cousin) told me that Dad's girlfriend, May, had died of tuberculosis. In Jessie's words, 'She had holes in her lungs the size of half-crowns'."

Recorder Group, 1966

Sharon recalled that "in September 1966, I started at Oundle Secondary Modern School". "The school only had enough recorders for a group every four years. As the eldest pupils left the school, the new

---

[75] Penicillin was developed in 1928.

intake had an audition for the recorder group. Luckily I started the year that the new intake had a chance to learn to play the recorder". She continued, "Quite a few people find recorder playing a little amusing, I was just grateful that I learnt how to read music and play an instrument. When I left the school in 1971 I was able to play the descant, treble and tenor recorder. I had gained first place in the Treble recorder solo at Oundle Music Festival (Yes there was more than one entrant!) and played solo at the School 'Prize Giving' in the Victoria Hall". She went on to say, "My parents showed great restraint while I learnt how to play, as did the neighbours. However as I walked down to Mrs Beech's one day Mr Quincy (who lived at 23 Gordon Road) came out and gave me 'Teddy Tail's Book of Children's Songs', so he too had heard me learning to play and I still have the book". Sharon learned to play the recorder and sang in the choir. For a time she was a campanologist at Oundle Church. She enjoys music to this day.

...oooOOOooo...

OCCUPATIONS AND TRADE

Earning a livelihood

Guilds existed in the past to pay for the livelihoods of priests, who prayed for the souls of their patrons and parishioners. The Tabret (Tabard or Talbot) Inn in Bury (New) Street was a likely asset and income provider in Tudor times.[76]

Much more recently, in 2017, Oundle was named by the press[77] as one of the best places to live in the Midlands. Oundle is a desirable market town, with low crime rates, reasonable house prices and range of schools to choose from. Employment available, if not in Oundle itself, it is in nearby towns and cities. Oundle has range of local shops, offices, trades and businesses. As in the past, this lends itself to interest from those outside the town.

...oooOOOooo...

---

[76] "The Talbot Hotel Eatery and Coffee House, A Brief History, by Will Swales, p. 4. Courtesy of the Talbot Hotel Management.

[77] Sunday Times, March 2017; Country Life, August 2017; this information was also repeated in the Northants Telegraph.

Susan Young – Memories of Grandmother, Mrs Norman

For most of her formative life, Susan (Sue) and her brother, Philip Norman, lived with their parents above the green-grocer's shop (as they were "purveyors of fruit and vegetables and, later, flowers and garlands") in the Market Place. The shop was formerly the cobbler and the saddler's shop. Mr Howitt lived next-door. Old Mrs Norman (senior) lived further down West Street from her son and his wife. She ran a furniture shop.

Shops in the 1960s and 1970s had window-dressing competitions. One year, the elderly Mrs Doreen Norman (senior) dressed in a crinoline dress and full-regalia sat in a displayed chair in the furniture shop window. When the judges came around, she sat very still and they admired how life-like the display was. She made them all jump when she suddenly waved at them! Doreen May Norman (née Jackson) was born in 1917 and died in 1973. What an amazing character she was.[78]

...oooOOOooo...

Sam York's Work Years (1940s-1980s) by Grandson, Chris York

Chris explained, "My grandfather, Sam York, was commonly known as 'Ernie'. He lived in Lutton in 1929 and worked on the land driving a Fowler steam-engine, ploughing many fields in the area. He went on to help with constructing the runways at Polebrook airfield when World War II broke out. He also had a fish-and-chip van and ran his own business. The van caught on fire in Ashton just a few years after the war." Chris has a photograph showing the fish and chip van. Ernie is standing next to a fireman who was "intent on putting out the fire inside". Sam said that it shows that "Ernie is wearing the Trilby hat he always wore when leaving the house, right up to the day when he passed away."

Chris mentioned "The steam-engine that Ernie drove was later captured with him in a photograph (taken in 1970s at Lilford Park), when he was happily reunited with his engine after 40 years." Chris

---

[78] From a 'chat' in the road, 20th July 2017.

said that "Ernie drove the buses for Eastern Counties until he retired. Ernie went on to drive the Alec Head school buses in Oundle, until he finally gave up bus-driving at the age of 75. He died, aged 89, in Oundle in 1995."

...oooOOOooo...

Denton's Shoe Factory

Mr and Mrs Butler ran a shoe shop, by the Norman family's fruit shop and Crown Court. They lived at the back in a cottage. Many women of the 1940s worked in the shoe factory in the mews, just off West Street (opposite Queen Anne's House). Barbara Chester worked there from the age of fifteen. She recalls, "there was a drive to go down to reach the factory", which adjoined the back of the main house. Mick Crick was born in the kitchen of the house at the front of Denton's (currently a music shop that repairs brass instruments). The shoe shop was at the front and the shoe factory was attached to it. The shop had a cobbler, who repaired the shoes that people brought in. They later moved to the shoe factory when a new building was constructed at the back.

When it was built, the new factory was owned by Denton's, but when new parts of shoes were needed (if Denton's of Rushden had no more), the parts were obtained from John White's. Inside the building were many different types of machine. As each woman worked a machine that made a different part of the boots and shoes, some made the back strips, others the toe or sides. There were trimmers to cut the rough cotton and leather off the shoes. All of the workers were women, except for Mr Butler, who ran the factory for the shoe companies. Mr and Mrs Butler lived in the house with their two, small daughters. Tea and lunch breaks were welcomed. The shipment lorry driver was a man, who delivered the leather goods and then took the completed uppers away to Rushden to have their soles fitted. The factory survived until around the mid-1960s.[79]

The row of buildings at the front of the factory were both, homes and shops. Mr Charles Thurlby was the caretaker. Number 109 was Thurlby's residence in the 1960s. Jerry Thurlby is part of this family. His parents were Charles T. Thurlby ('Charlie') and his wife, Ida (née

---

[79] Oral history, Barbara Mudza.

Barrett). Their first two offspring died, but these were followed by several healthy babies: Sylvia, David, Ronald, Christine, Michael and Jeremy. Jerry (born in 1941) was the youngest of their children. He left Oundle over a half-century ago, but recalls it with nostalgia. (Many people who went to Oundle primary school in the 1960s will probably remember his nephew, Frank, who grew-up in New Road.)

The main shoe sales were at the front (right) in Anthony Moore's cobber's shop. The footwear shop was here until the 1970s. It then became David (known as 'Dave') Kirkpatrick's barber's shop during the 1970s and 1980s. His daughter, Jacqueline Kirkpatrick (later Mrs Brian Head) took over running her father's shop in the 1980s. She ran the hairdressers for men and women. After some years Jackie moved away. In the late 1960s and early 1970s, her younger brother, Douglas ('Dougie') gained a reputation for annually climbing the town Christmas tree in the Market Place. Sometimes causing as much grief to himself as to the tree!

...oooOOOooo...

Marilyn Smith (née Haynes) - My Working Life

Marilyn worked at the 'Coffee Tavern' from around the age of 13 to 15. She worked there on Saturdays as she was still at school. She worked alongside Janet Pope and with Peter and Sheila Hooton. She recalls that Peter had a naughty sense of humour, just like the rest of his family. She returned to work there when her children were at the primary school. These were the days of the juke box in the back with the latest records, Coca-Cola served in bottles with a straw.

Marilyn recalls that there were fights every Saturday afternoon after the pubs shut (around 2.30pm). She was a teenager, so was a little worried by the occurrences. Doris Hooton, Peter's mother, didn't stand any nonsense. She would appear and whack the drunken fighters around their legs and ankles with a broom! They soon left the premises!

Janet Pope worked for Peter and Sheila at 'Coffee Tavern' café for many years. Clare, Joanne and Sarah Hooton lived upstairs with their parents. Hairdresser, Ruth lived next door. She married Carl Norwood and had a daughter, Jayne, who continued to run the hairdressers in Jericho from the late-1900s.

Meanwhile, Marilyn worked at Madeline Sewter's nursery school during the 1970s, until her sons started at the primary school. Marilyn then worked as the manager of "Number Forty-Six" in the Market Place for eight or nine years. This menswear shop was administered by Marilyn after Mary Cotton left to go to Canada. Charles Lane (Rothschild) owned the business and hired managers. He had around five other stores around the country. The trendy men's clothing shop eventually closed in the early 1980s.

FAITH, HOPE AND CHARITY

Oundle Churches

Originally St. Peter's Parish Church was of the Roman Catholic denomination, but in the reign of Henry VIII shifted to the newly founded Anglican Church of England. The building has an amazing 210-foot spire, which is a local landmark and dates to the thirteenth Century. It is a useful visual guide for anyone unfamiliar with the Oundle road layout as it is the tallest spire in Northamptonshire.

The site of the 'Jesus Church' was known as 'Chapel End' as it gained its name from the St. Thomas of Canterbury Chapel, which stood here in mediæval times. It has often been said that Oundle "had more pubs than churches", but the town has truly thrived on both. They likewise both have raised local revenue. Churches are often related to giving and are at the heart of fundraising for the poor and needy, just as politics and faith are also connected.

In 1800s there were three non-conformist Churches, plus the current Jesus Church (built by the Watts-Russell's as an Anglican Chapel). Oundle was the centre of Poor Law Union. A parliamentary report from 1777 recorded that the parish workhouse could accommodate up to forty-five inmates. The poor-rate expenditure for 1833-1835 was 13 shillings and 2 pence per-head annually. Oundle workhouse was demolished in 1970s and its chapel converted into a private residence.

The 21st December (the winter solstice) has lost its original alms-giving tradition. In the 1700s the longest night and shortest day was known as 'Mumping Day'. It was the feast day for 'doubting Thomas'. The poor and destitute of Oundle joined in with the Church and local benefactors aware of the date and its significance for the poor. It was a day when the lowly people of the parish were expected to go mumping (begging for alms). On St. Thomas' day 1782 (Mumping day) John Clifton wrote in his diary that "wretches" usually left "to go sliving about, but nobody went". This may be that fewer people were in the need of alms or and the poor houses did not permit their inmates from doing so. In the 1930s the workhouse master and matron were Mr Albert and Mrs Rose Belton. (They had married in Oakham in 1924.) Tramps were steadily seen less often in the district, which was good news for the workhouse.

Charity Shops and Charitable Foundations

There are a number of charity shops and charity ventures in Oundle. There are currently three spread between the market square and West Street. Several alms houses have been endowed here, along with school trusts. Two workhouses were here for the poor and destitute of the town and surrounds. Local schools take part in fundraising ventures and often send senior students to less wealthy countries to take part in building schools and hospitals. Oundle Volunteer Action is a local charity that supports the elderly, those who are unwell, disabled or disadvantaged in Oundle, Thrapston and the local villages.

The Austell survey has a reference to the pre-Reformation 'Our Lady of Oundle' guild hall that was bought by "Mr Laxton somtyme maior of London". Before the Reformation there was a small guild school held in Oundle Parish church, but Sir William Laxton's will (1556) instructed purchase of the guild house to be used as a grammar school (with accommodation for 'seven poor honest men'). It was on the Church yard site of the current school cloisters and library. In 1611, equally kind favours were shown to Oundle women in the 'gift' of Latham's Hospital (North Street) to the town when the Reverend Nicholas Latham founded alms house for women and school (in the hospital premises). Today, Latham's Hospital still fulfils its purpose of providing a home for elderly ladies. Parson Latham's Bluecoat school merged with the Oundle Church of England School at the end of the 1800s.

In 1544, Thomas Franklyn bequeathed his lands to start a charity from the sale of his lands as poor relief. Around the same time as Nicholas Latham made his bequest, the Feoffees and Overseers of Oundle raised and donated funds to the poor in the 1600s. Some funds were raised through rental of their estates and lands. Around this time, Thomas Franklyn's endowment was first administered by the Feoffees. They were a Christian charity who donated Bibles and money to the church, gave alms to the poor and distributed loaves to the needy on St. Thomas' (Mumping) day. In 1791 the society paid to help repair the town bridges and fix the drains. They continue to be active in the town and annually give to charities, including a small sum of money to the elderly over the Christmas period.[80] Like other societies, they met in the Tabard during the early days, but by the mid-1800s they were meeting in the Church.

John Clifton's will (from January 1723) presented three-hundred pounds to the "Feoffees of the Town Estates to distribute the interest for the benefit of two poor blind people and among deserving old men". It was recorded that a sum of five pounds, five shillings and four pence was dispensed in lieu of this in 1924.

Under direction of the Northamptonshire County Court "holden at Oundle 17 April, 1860" the Vicar and Churchwardens were appointed as Trustees of the Charity of Miss Charlotte Simcoe, "the endowment of which consists of £500 Consols with the Official Trustees of Charitable Funds producing £12 10s. 0d. yearly in dividends, which is distributed in flannel to about 100 recipients".[81] During her life Charlotte Simcoe resided in the Rectory on North Street.

A workhouse report from the building destined to be the 'Victoria Inn' of West Street states that "It is now five years since this Town, burthen'd with the Poors taxes, resolved in a Vestry to purchase a House for the Maintenance and Employment of the Poor, who were as full of Idleness, as they were of Complaints, and they chose seven Governors and Trustees, beside the two Overseers, who are chosen Annually; there is a Master and Mistress appointed to take Care of Provisions for the House, and to keep those employed, who are able

---

[80] Oral history, Barbara Chester.
[81] http://www.british-history.ac.uk/vch/northants/vol3/

to work; there are now in the House, six old Men, five old Women, and nine Children; the Women and Children are employ'd in Spinning and Knitting: And the Men and Boys, who are able, are sent to Plow for the Farmers, and feed and look after their Cattle at home; the profits from their labour, which is generally about six Shillings per Week, the Master of the House accounts for once a week to the Trustees; and the Expences of the House, which he also lays before them is usually about 40 shillings. The Overseer's Bill before used to rise to half a Crown in the Pound per Annum often, and seldom or never less than 2 shillings, they now come to no more than 10d. or 11d., so that, upon a fair Calculation the Town is eased of two Thirds of their Charge, and yet I assure you the Poor are provided for in a very plentiful manner, and have everything necessary or convenient in Life."[82] The West Street poor-house provided lodging for up to forty-five inmates. This seems crowded by today's standards!

Paine's and Latham's trusts funded Oundle alms houses that gave the local (women) somewhere safe when they were spinsters or widowed and alone. This was support for our town and made it worth living in. Oundle's Cottage Hospital, Fletton House, plus the larger workhouse in Glapthorn Road housed old men. Some had been institutionalised since childhood. The building was constructed around 1900. Later, nearby Abbot House was built for ladies. It later admitted both sexes.

Charity Fundraising

Prince William School students participate in the Duke of Edinburgh Award programme. They support a number of charities, including 'Jeans for Genes', annual fundraising campaign for genetic disorders and 'Red Nose Day' that tackles poverty and a range of other national and worldwide issues. Fundraising offers students the chance to enjoy working with their peers and benefit others and their good cause.

The 'Oundle School sleep out' in 2017 helped to raise awareness and funds for St. Basils'. It is a charity that helps prevent youth destitution by offering lodgings, skills and support to runaways and young homeless people. The 'Oundle School Mencap Holiday Community'

---

[82] 'An Account of Several Workhouses for Employing and Maintaining the Poor' published, anonymously, by SPCK (the Society for Promoting Christian Knowledge). This account is of Oundle from 7th December, 1724.

(OSMH) hold residential breaks for children with learning disabilities and have provided parent respite (for over thirty years). The OSMH organise volunteers and rely on donations to fund their projects.[83]

Oundle Charity fundraising occurs in many ways. Oundle Tennis Club, a non-profit organization raises funds for the Cure Parkinson's Trust by conducting events. In 2018 the events will culminate in a sixty-mile coastal walk. Oundle Young Farmers Club hosts events for people aged between 10 and 26 with an interest in the countryside and rural issues. It promotes social life and encourages members to put something back into the community. After raising funds from 1966, the Round Table ceased its work here in 2010. Oundle and District Care requests annual Christmas gifts of money to aid those in Care and in need of medical equipment. They also provide flowers and fruit to locals who are unwell or bereaved. The Christmas Appeal always has a generous response with kind donations from locals.

...oooOOOooo...

Charity Fundraising, Life and "Aunt Marjorie" by Robin Moore

When the 'Angel Inn' publican, Tony Moore died, his son, Robin, dedicated his life to walking to raise funds for charities, Cancer Research UK and Sue Ryder (supporting those who with terminal illness).[84] He has walked around UK and New Zealand, Spain, France and many other places to publicise cancer research and to raise charity funds. Although Christine (Moore, née Thurlby), Robin's mum, moved to Cornwall some years ago, Robin has recently moved to take care of her (2007). He no longer lives in the town, but pays regular visits.

In October 2014, Robin walked 1,000 kilometres from Oundle to Ypres. He later followed the 1914 allied frontline from Switzerland to Ypres for his charities. A "Pilgrimage of War and Words" was his third trek, associated with Ypres in Flanders and referencing the Great War. This journey was a poignant reminder of "sacrifices made by soldiers on the Western Front and conveyed a message of peace and hope". Robin supports the Peterborough Cancer Treatment Appeal that is dedicated to raising funds for equipment used in diagnosis and treatments of

---

[83] oundlemencap.co.uk
[84] For walkers there is a local Walking group and Kettering Ramblers' Association.

cancer in NHS hospices (Stamford and Peterborough). Robin completed his task by hosting a charity 'gig' in Oundle.

Robin and the Moore family are fondly remembered by the people of Oundle. Particularly remembered is Robin's aunt, Marjorie (Jones; née Thurlby), who grew up in Oundle and was a 'Cadbury Angel' in the 1930s. When she died, Robin wrote about her as "The end of an era for an iconic Cadbury's Lady".[85] She is recognised for her work at Cadbury's chocolate factory and was well-loved by friends and family. "Auntie Marjorie" supported of Robin's charity walks and Macmillan Nurses (after her husband, Eric Jones died in 2000). After her own death in 2015 (aged 91), Marjorie left a £10,000 legacy to MacMillan's. Robin remarked that, 'She often spoke to me about her delightful days as a youngster at Cadbury's where she was for all of her working life – barring the war years.' In her own words, she described the wonderful experiences she had in a bygone age of simplicity and fun.

Marjorie left Oundle and started work at Bournville in 1937, aged 14. "I met Phyllis Palser and we became lifetime friends. My first job was sorting nuts and raisins and by the end of my work years I had moved to quality control. As a teenager we cycled to Ullenhall to stay in a cottage owned by the Cadbury's family. We looked after ourselves and I remember cycling to Henley where we enjoyed one of its famous Dairy Ice-Creams! During the war, part of the factory was closed due to the difficulty in obtaining the ingredients. Phyllis and I went to do war work at 'Birmetals' in Woodgate. I wanted to go into the ATS because I was a sportswoman, but there were no vacancies then. At 'Birmetals' we made pipe-work for our war effort and for us it was only a bike ride from home. My job was operating the overhead crane, although I needed to be athletic to climb down by rope when there was an air-raid, which was a frequent occurrence!"

"We missed the sport at Cadbury's, but formed a cricket team so as to keep our interest alive. Towards the end of the war I met my husband Eric. In 1944, we were able to return to Cadbury's where our pensions had been kept on for us and we were able to resume our sporting

---

[85] Robin said, "My aunt is on my father's side and features in the book 'Cadburys Angels', but I think extracts of her diary may be found on my website under Cancer Charities".

activities. The facilities were great and we loved the sport; we played netball, cricket and hockey; often against other firms and after we enjoyed a lovely tea. I also learnt to swim at Cadbury's; taught by Miss David and swam once a week for several years. The family were lovely people and were interested in everything we did. I remember Miss Dorothy riding her bike down Bournville Lane; she was just one of use really. When I got married I was given a carnation and Bible by Mr Laurence and, after 25 years of service, I received a gold watch by Mr Adrian. It still works too! I always loved buying the waste bags of chocolates from the factory shops. By the time I retired, after 43 years, I had worked all round the factory: starting in cocoa and finishing in the laboratory doing quality control! The last time I spoke to Phyllis on the phone, we both agreed those were the best years; especially playing cricket at Bournville!" When Marjorie died, Robin wrote a poem to commemorate the passing of his beloved aunt.[86]

Robin walked around the UK in 1997 raising funds for Macmillan Nurses. Robin raised thousands of pounds over the past twenty years by trekking over 25,000 miles. He supports fundraising evenings with local volunteers.

Robin said, "My aunt was always there for me; she would help fund some of my walks and was grateful for the care she received from the Macmillan Nurses when Eric was suffering from cancer. She supported them every year after and I hope that her legacy will make a difference to humanity. God bless her and Macmillan Nurses too!" Robin completed over twelve fundraising walks, covering in excess of a thousand miles. Eight of his walks were completed in honour of Cancer Charities.[87]

HELP IN A CRISIS – THE EMERGENCY SERVICES

Andrew Spurrell has a photograph of The Duchess of Gloucester inspecting the personnel at Oundle's First-Aid Station at the 'Public Institution' in Glapthorn Road on a Sunday afternoon in October 1939. She was met at the entrance gates of the institution, then accompanied by Oundle's Divisional Superintendent and First Aid

---

[86] Robin's tribute to Marjorie's life "where she saw friends as extended family".
[87] Support Robin through www.justgiving.com/Robin-Moore2.

Commandant, Mr Frederick William Whitwell (1905-1973). He was congratulated by Her Royal Highness on the town's "excellent turn-out". Mr Whitwell introduced the chairman of Oundle Urban Council, Mr S. Bennett J.P., and the Clerk to the Council, Mr C.A. Pulley. The occasion demonstrated the medical station and skills of the teams who served in local emergencies. The day was recorded in the local press and in photographs taken by Dr Ivor Spurrell.

Ambulance Services

In 1939 the Oundle Ambulance workers were reviewed in the local paper. The "Happy Division" praised its leaders at the annual general meeting of the Oundle Division of the St, John Ambulance Brigade. This was held on at the "Board Room" and was "presided over by Dr Arthur Forbes Elliott, who was supported by Sergeant E.M. Hill."

Prior to 1940, doctors were paid for their consultations and for any medicines supplied. This was paid for by each customer. People were often in need of serious treatment, but could not afford a large bill if it was presented to them by hospitals and clinics. To help with this, Friendly Societies were created. Before national insurance was established these were set up to help with patient payments.[88] These were mutual associations (in the 1800s) that provided sickness benefits, pensions and life assurances. They were registered under the Friendly Societies Act of 1974 and more recently the Act of 1992. As there were no free medical services the doctors had to be paid by their customers. To help with payments the societies would collect a few pennies weekly to pay the costs if they were ill. They also gained grants for dental and eye treatments.

Oundle Oddfellows charity lodges helped in these circumstances. The National Friendly Society had a branch in Oundle for customer deposits. Pubs and inns would run clubs that collected payments for the same. Clubs from these would last a calendar year and usually paid out for illness. At the end of each year, had the money not been used, the surplus was paid back to customers, which "was as a good

---

[88] The National Insurance Act of 1911 first offered 'worker' health insurance. In 1946 the modern welfare state was founded.

Christmas bonus"![89] Oundle hostelries and inns acted as meeting-places for charity societies. The local Oddfellow group was based at the "Red Lion", the Provident Society at the 'Nag's Head' and the Tradesmen's Friendly Society at the 'Ship'.

Community First Responders

Oundle 'Community First Responders' (CFR) are local volunteers, trained by the East of England Ambulance Service to get to emergencies in the vital minutes before an ambulance from Peterborough or Kettering arrives. Their role is to help to stabilise the patient and provide appropriate care until the more highly skilled ambulance crew arrives on scene to take over treatment. Oundle First Responder Scheme has run (24 hours per day) since 2003. In late 2003, Dr Stovin called a meeting to ensure their beepers would not be turned off overnight and this has contributed to saving lives. The scheme is funded by donations and the Council.

Fire and Rescue Services

The Fire Station was in the town centre during the 1880s, but was moved to its new site on Glapthorn Road in the 1970s. "The Northamptonshire Fire Brigade and the separate Northampton Borough Fire Brigade were created in 1948 by the Fire Services Act of 1947. In 1974, the Northampton Fire Brigade was merged with Northamptonshire Fire Brigade to create the present service. Oundle has a retained fire service. It is financially supported by the National Fire Fighters Charity.

In 1935, Oundle Volunteer Fire Brigade had Harry Taney and Bill Taney as crew. Both went on to become Fire Chief Officers.[90] Angela Hudson is proud to be related to Harry and Bill. They served in the fire service for many years and attended the cottages in East Road where their grandmother had lived. The cottages that caught fire were demolished to build 'Taney Court'. (See the Taney brother photographs.)

---

[89] Leslie Black mentions this too in pamphlet, "My Oundle". Arthur Chester paid into these on his return from WWI. He suffered from mustard-gas related issues with his eyes that required attention for some time after.
[90] Angela Hudson (Taney), family history.

Many families have worked for the emergency services. The Cunnington family are most notable. They lived in Oundle since the 1840s and celebrate five generations of firemen. Joyce Marriot was one of Oundle's first female fire-fighters who still resides locally. In the 1960s the fire-station was located centrally (where the 'Stafford and Brown' shop was previously). The Denley children loved to hear the old war fire siren, as they could hear it from their house in North Street. Sheila says, "We would race out to see firemen, Mr Shiels (Patrick, Kathleen and Desmond's dad) haring up North Street on his bike. If we were allowed, we would run after Mr Shiels and try to get to the fire-station before the engine left. This was when the station was in the Market Place. Of course, we never wished for a bad fire, but we just loved it when the fire-engine came out with its sirens and lights and just travelled about fifty yards across the road to the chip shop to yet another chip fat fire. There were groans and cheers from the onlookers."[91]

Pat Coles proudly tells of her brother, David Midlane, who was a member of the voluntary fire service. The fire-station is currently staffed by seven members of the community who give up their time to maintain the fire-station. It often struggles to find enough people to cover the daytime shifts. Periodically they advertise for new recruits as they have done for many years previously. In 2015 the police and fire service nucleus for Oundle had its official opening at the Fletton House 'hub', after a major refurbishment it served as a base for community groups, including the police and fire officers. (See the photograph of Oundle Fire Service 1969-70.)

At Christmas 1969, the Oundle fire station crew and their wives held their "Annual Dinner and Dance" at the Talbot Hotel. A photograph of the occasion shows (left to right): David Cunnington, Molly Cunnington, Effie Cunnington, John Cunnington (standing), Noel Marshall, George Slote, Ellie Marshall, Nancy Slote, Margaret Marshall and Harry Marshall. On a photograph of the Northamptonshire Fire Brigade in 1970: (back l-r) George Slote, Ron Cunnington, Terry Wells, David Midlane, Ivor Scillitoe, John Cunnington, Stuart Wiggins, Michael

---

[91] Sheila Denley, personal history.

Shiels and Bert Burdett. At the front (l-r) are Bob Burdett, Percy Cosham, Jim Bunning, Noel and Harry Marshall.

It is said that in the winter times, the fire station at 4B Glapthorn Road has heated floors to keep the engines ready to go in the event of an emergency.

My time in the Fire Service by Joyce Marriott

Joyce Marriot noted a few of her memories of her time with the Fire Brigade as "twelve-and-a-half years were some of the best times of my life". She said that "back in my childhood we lived in a cottage over the road from the farm where I grew up. One winter we had a bad chimney fire and the Oundle Fire Brigade came. As in many old cottages there was one big beam across the chimney-breast and it caught alight and had to be removed. The crew were there for hours, demolishing the stonework and exposing the chimney-breast. I was in my pram, aged about two and apparently screaming the house down. According to my mother, I was petrified and wouldn't look at the big, black, sooty hole where our fireplace had been. Even now I get a shiver down my spine with things that are sooty or jet black.

A few years on, I suppose I would have been about six years old and we had moved to live in the farmhouse. My brother, two of our friends and I had some packets of caps that we put in our toy cap guns. We thought that if we set fire to the whole roll at once it would go with a big bang, so we went across to the stack yard to get a small handful of straw. We moved away from the barn before lighting the straw and putting the roll of cap in it. Obviously a few yards was not far enough as all that happened was a sort of big *'fizz'*, then our small fire went across to the loose straw on the ground and within seconds the whole stack and barn was ablaze. I ran as fast as my little legs would go, and called for Mum. I asked her to bring a bucket of water as the barn was on fire. She ran and looked from the back door, "You'll need more than a bucket to put that out", she shouted, as she got straight on the phone and dialled 999. Three fire engines came. Once it was all under control two were sent back, leaving the Oundle crew there all night damping down. I was sent to a friend of my Mum's for the night and came back the next morning. I was frightened to go to see what damage we had done, but remember having a sly look and seeing a lot of small wads of hay and straw still smoking where they hadn't finished damping down. The only thing I remember was sitting on the fire-engine to have my picture taken with the big wheels of its wheeled escape ladder at the rear. This must be where I got the taste to join the Fire Service".

She said that almost twenty years on, in the spring of 1985, the fire station were desperately trying to recruit some new members. "I was already married to one of them, who had two brothers serving alongside him, so I knew quite a lot about the job, besides knowing socially other members and their partners. It was something I had been mulling over in the back of my mind for some time. They had some firemen who worked out of Oundle so could not provide cover during the day. This was known as 'limited cover'. What they needed was someone who could give 'twenty-four-hour cover'. I lived about five-hundred yards from the fire station and worked less than half a mile away, so I was fine for cover (with my employer consenting). I had thought perhaps they wouldn't want a woman to join. Even with all the publicity about equality around at that time, even if legally they couldn't refuse me, there might be a few of them with doubt in their minds. So I decided the best thing to do was to go to the station and put it to them. I explained that I thought I could do the job, but if anyone had any doubts or objections about me joining, then I wouldn't pursue it and would have no hard feelings. I left it for them to mull over for the evening and went home to await the verdict. To my relief they all seemed happy for me to join. As long as I could do the job (and drink the odd pint of beer or two). So I filled in the application forms. The next step was to run it past my employer, as it would mean my dashing off at a seconds notice or if I got a call in the night I might be late in to work or, as it happened on a couple of occasions, not arrive for work at all. They were happy for me to do it so there was only one thing left for me to do, 'Now, where did I put those forms?'"

Before joining the brigade, Joyce performed basic tests that she had to pass alongside a medical. "At that time there was a minimum height limit of five feet six inches, which may be where I could come unstuck. I was five feet four and a half inches. If I really stretched my neck I could almost manage five foot five. As I passed the other tests, I think they gave me the benefit of the doubt to see if being an inch short gave any problems. I'm glad to say a couple of years later they scrapped the height restriction for retained firefighters. Whether or not I had anything to do with this decision I'll never know. My employer signed a form to agree and on 5th May I was a member of Northamptonshire Fire Brigade or Fire and Rescue. Then the training started. We drilled every Wednesday evening from 7pm to 9pm so, for the next six weeks, I learnt where and what every piece of equipment was on the appliance (or wagon as we called it). I also had to tie a few basic knots, learn how to run-out hose properly and use the standpipe, key and bar. This is what is used to connect the hose to the water-main and turn the water on. I also had to be able to recognise the officer's rank markings, after all I would need to know if I bumped into the chief wouldn't I? This happened sooner than expected".

"Every year we put aside one week for street collecting for the National Benevolent Fund Widows and Orphans Appeal. We went out collecting each evening around the villages and finished the week in the town centre on Saturday morning. The collection week happened to coincide with my six week training. As I didn't have a uniform yet, I was left to look after the wagon and listen for the radio while they went off collecting around the housing estate. If there was a call for them on the radio I was to give a quick blast on the two tones and one of them would come running. While sitting in the cab learning for my test, along came an ice-cream van that stopped a few yards down the road. I thought to myself, "Should I or shouldn't I?" for all of five seconds before giving in to temptation to buy a cornet with a chocolate flake in it. It was perfect for a warm evening, so I parked my butt in the rear cab with my legs swinging out the door like a big kid and got stuck into my cornet. I noticed a car pull up behind the wagon and a man in a shirt, tie and black blazer got out. At first I thought 'Perhaps he's come to get an ice cream too', then he walked up to me, gave me a strange look and asked where everyone was. I told him and he wandered off to find them. A few minutes later Graham and 'the man' came around the corner chatting. The man went to his car and drove off. Graham came over and asked what I was up to when the 'Chief' arrived! My mouth dropped open, 'CHIEF', I gasped, oh no! I had been, swinging my legs out of the side-door while licking an ice cream cornet! A fat lot of good it is learning rank-markings when he turns up in a plain blazer, I thought."

Joyce said that she "also had another little incident in my first six weeks, which is known to all and sundry as 'My passing out parade'. Every year we would do the odd exercise involving the neighbouring stations. On this occasion it involved Thrapston too. It was held at the Oundle boat factory. I was told that, as I didn't have all of my fire kit yet, I could go and observe. I was getting quite excited at the thought of my first exercise involving another station. However, my full time job at the garage required me to go to fetch a trailer from the other side of York. I set off as early as I could, only stopping for a cuppa on the way back, as driving doesn't make you very hungry, just tired. The traffic was quite heavy on the way back, but I arrived home in time to grab a quick shower and sandwich. It wasn't a warm evening, so I wrapped up warmly as I was going to be standing about. However, John (our sub-officer at the time) had very different ideas and got me involved in running out a hose, making up and so on. At the end of the exercise, everyone stood 'easy' while we were debriefed and the officers pointed out our mistakes – if any. Well, a combination of no proper food or drink all day, wrapping up and getting too hot, meant that I had the most embarrassing moment of my career. While listening to what the officers were saying, I started to feel a bit iffy. I tried to move from one foot to the other, hoping I'd be okay. Then a darkness started closing in. I tried to blink it away, but to no avail. I felt very wobbly. The darkness continued to close in, then - SPLASH. The next thing I saw were Stuart, Graham and John's faces peering down at me, while loosening my clothes to let some air circulate. I remember thinking to myself, 'Oh no, what have I done?' I apparently rocked to-and-fro a couple of times, then passed out, falling straight back into a puddle. After walking about for a while I was back to normal. I was almost sent for another medical, but after explaining the day's events; they gave me the benefit of the doubt. This was known for many years as my 'passing out parade'."

"At last my six weeks were over and the day of my test had arrived. The Station Officer arrived and briefly ran me through how the test would be run, then we got started, doing all the things I had been practising for. I was running out hose, tying knots, and was asked to fetch certain items of equipment from the appliance. I had to know exactly where they were and be able to go straight to them as if I had my eyes shut. In between doing these tasks, he was firing questions at me. I felt that everything was going quite well and, when he asked what different types of hoses were on the appliance, I reeled them all off, one after the other. Then I got cocky and came out with 'radiator hose and brake hose', to which the officer smiled and said, "Ok, I think that will do. I'm pleased to say that you've passed." At last I was going to *ride*. We managed to rustle up a fire-fighting tunic and leggings to go with my helmet and boots I already had. All I needed was my bleeper. I was given the usual warning speech that was given to every new recruit about safe driving and "don't go mad", but there's such a rush of adrenalin when you get that first call, that all goes out of your head. So that's it. I'm now a fire-fighter 'on call' and all I have to do now is wait for my first 'shout'."

Training and Learning

Joyce recalls the days that went by when she kept checking that her bleeper was working. "At last, I was at work when "bleep-bleep-bleep". Everyone gave a cheer as I ran to my car and raced to the fire station. Most of the others were already there, but they shouted at me to grab my kit and get on. My heart was racing as I finished getting dressed in the back of the wagon. Stuart sat next to me and said, "There's no need to panic, you've got until Kings Cliffe to get yourself sorted" (ten minutes away). Once settled, helmet on, tunic done up to the neck, gloves on, I was ready for action. My head was racing. We arrived only to find out it was a false alarm. I was so disappointed, but thought it was better this way than to have a huge factory fire and running round like a headless chicken. My next couple of call-outs were AFA's (automatic fire alarms). Was I ever going to see any flames, or make a rescue? Finally it came, a chimney-fire ... an ordinary, run of the mill, chimney-fire, but it was very exciting for me. Over the next three months, I had more calls and tried to learn as much as possible from my colleagues so as not to look too green when on basic training. This came round very quickly. 9th to 13th September 1985. I looked forward to it, but was worried that I hadn't enough knowledge. Up bright and early on the Monday morning, shirt pressed, shoes shining. I set off to the station to book on duty with control and pick up all my gear. The course was held at Rothwell station, which was hardly the nicest station. I made friends and after the first day I realised there was nothing to worry about, as we were all in the same boat. The course went back to basics and taught us from scratch. Running out hose again and again, for about half a day. Another half-day doing 'carry down'. We were lucky to be able to do 'live' carry down, as we had a visit from the H.P. (hydraulic platform) and the poor 'volunteer' was strapped into the safety harness attached to the H.P. We managed without any major accidents, but by the time we all got to the bottom, our legs were like jelly. I was to find out, when back on station, that a live carry-down is so much better and easier than using a dummy. The dummy doesn't bend in the right places and is awkward. Many a time I've seen it dropped, usually in temper when it wouldn't bend as it should. Another day we learnt a few knots and used them with equipment. The best day was when we had to do ladder drills. Oundle carried a 13.5 metre ladder for all the high buildings. Most other retained pumps only use a 10.5 metre ladder that can be carried by two people, but the 13.5 is a four person ladder. I was the only person on the course to have worked with one. I don't think some had even seen one. The rest looked in amazement, "God, how do you use this thing?" one of the lads asked. "It's quite easy once you get used to it and don't forget I've got to learn your 10.5 too", I replied. There was a lot crammed into a week and I'm pleased to say I passed, which was not the case for all. Back in Oundle I was eager to put my new-found knowledge into practice. Every time a new recruit is on a training course they come back to home ground with a new way of doing things and end up teaching the old dogs new tricks."

Joyce said that as the weeks and months went by, "the time came for my next course: Breathing apparatus-B.A. The first part of the training was held at Rushden Station, as it is the location of the specially built 'smoke house'. It has a normal house layout with a stair to the first floor and then a ladder into the loft space. The difference being it's all built of concrete, specially designed to withstand very high temperatures from the fires that are lit inside. It has a control-room where temperatures can be monitored and, in the case of an emergency, big extraction fans to disperse the smoke in seconds. Although some days it was tough going, I thoroughly enjoyed it. You are never alone in B.A. and I teamed up with a guy from Raunds most of the time. We had a few trips off station. One day we went to St. Crispin's in Northampton to use one of their old buildings. Chris and I were first to find the casualty, high on a window ledge. It was one of

148

our instructors, but we had to treat him as a real casualty. We needed more help so we clapped our hands to summon some assistance from another team as we had been taught. Another team of three heard us and came to assist. After explaining what the situation was, we all entered into discussion as to how we should get him down from the ledge and who should have his arms and who should have his legs. Then somebody disagreed with someone else and it all started again. In the end the lights came on and we were all called outside for de-briefing (or a rollicking). "It took a minute to find the casualty, but unfortunately he died while waiting for his rescuers to stop arguing about who was carrying his arms and legs!" Point taken, and never to be forgotten."

"Another fun day was in the high expansion foam. The ground floor of the smoke house was filled to the ceiling with foam. We were sent, in twos, to find B.A. tallies. These are flat pieces of plastic about 15c.m. by 4c.m. and are normally attached to your set until you enter a job. Being in foam is as claustrophobic as thick smoke, if not more so. Again Chris and I teamed up. I got down on my knees and grovelled around a bit. We soon found our first tally and took it outside to the E.C.O. (entry control officer) who promptly sent us straight back in. We were soon back out with another. After we had found them all it was time to wash off the foam. We had the shower from the chemical unit set-up in the drill yard that was connected directly to the hydrant. It was so cold! After completing the course I had to get in many hours of wearing, cleaning, testing and operating the entry control-board as possible. All this was recorded in a log book. I was allowed to wear 'a set' at an incident after it was made safe for damping down and such like. The last part of the course was at a weekend. There was a written test and on the 26th November 1986 I was fully-qualified to wear breathing apparatus."

Another hurdle for Joyce came in 1992. She said that was "when I went on an HGV (Heavy Goods Vehicle) course to allow me to drive the appliance. I was there with a full-time fire-fighter from Corby. The driver training and run-up to the test was fine. We both had a few minor faults, but in general all went well. Then came the day of the test, a final run-through in the morning, lunch, and then the test. Geoff, our instructor, left us to decide who went first, but did not want the second person to know how the first got on until we had both finished. He thought it might interfere with concentration. I wasn't at all worried about who was going first, but my mate was. He was in such a panic, he asked if he could go first, as he didn't think he could wait any longer. So off he went. I had another cuppa and a chat with a few of the guys and then went out into the yard to wait my turn. I saw the lorry drive in and saw them going through the final questions. When the door opened, a beaming smile across the yard, "I crashed", he shouted and laughed. I took it that he had failed. It turned out that he was driving through a village with a single-track road and there was a parked builder's lorry. He had to go right up the opposite verge to pass it, which made the lorry lean over even more and just touched it. FAIL! Anyway, off I went. Everything seemed fine, until turning back into the test centre. It was a very tight turn and a miracle if anyone did it perfectly. It could only be done if there were no parked cars. However, there were parked cars and I had no option than to run my nearside rear-wheel over the edge of the curb. I made all the necessary checks and observations before doing so and made sure that the examiner saw me doing it. The examiner realised the necessary checks were done to the best of my ability. He had no other choice but to let me hear those magic words, "I'm pleased to say that you have passed". I was still not allowed to drive on 'blues and twos' as a 'red driver' has to do an Emergency Fire Appliance Driving (EFAD) course. This is to instruct in emergency driving. I did this a couple of months later. It needs renewing every three years. I did quite a lot of driving as not many others had an HGV licence."

Memorable Incidents

Joyce and the fire-crew attended a house-fire at Kings Cliffe in the early hours of one morning. "It was the week I was on my B.A. course and during the day we had lectures on the different cylinder capacities and how a neighbouring County may have different capacity cylinders, so calculations are different. In this case, the entry control officer (E.C.O.) would have the B.A. boards from both counties. We pulled up outside the premises and immediately sent in a B.A. team comprising of two wearers. I was E.C.O. when a crew from Stamford arrived and another team of two were ready to enter. I saw they had different sets to ours and I took charge of both boards. I was quite pleased with myself as I was all clued-up on what to do, as it was only a few hours earlier that I had received instruction as to what to do if this situation arose. Luckily, although it could have been a nasty fire, we arrived in time. Although it damaged some floorboards and joists, it didn't have time to really catch hold."

"The next was one I'd rather forget, when we were alerted to Warmington Mill, I drove, which meant that on arrival I would be pump operator. Approaching on the A605, we saw the issue as smoke was billowing across from the mill. It was so thick that I couldn't see the road in front of me and had to slow down until we were through it. When we got to the mill it was well alight. Norm was the Officer in Charge (OIC) and made it 'pumps six' before he went off to 'suss out' the job. The rest ran out the hose and got stuck in. I called Mo back as the tank supply wouldn't last long and we would have to set up the equipment to pump from the open water-supply that I just happened to be parked next to. We connected up the lengths of hard suction to the pump, dropped the strainer into the water (by which time we had quite an audience from the village). I then gently pulled the throttle back to increase the rev's to priming speed and waited for the change in engine-noise that was an indication of the pump priming, usually only a few seconds. I soon realised this hadn't happened and checked the gauges to confirm my misgivings. I called Mo back, as it would need two of us to get the light portable pump off, but first we checked all the connections other basics before we tried again. The outcome was the same. The water in the tank was diminishing fast and we still had no other supply of water, so I knocked down the revolutions as much as I dared (to conserve water as much as possible) and we set about connecting up the LPP. This can be connected to the main pump and used to prime it, then it can be disconnected, as once primed the pump will function. While we were setting up the LPP, the crowd of villagers had realised that all was not as it should be. Some of the older men, who seemed to think they knew it all, shouted, "The water's not deep enough" (I noted that it was) or "Give it more rev's". I bit my tongue to stop from exploding at them and concentrated on the job in hand. I had pumped from open water on numerous occasions and knew that there was a fault with the main pump. We had the LPP all connected and Mo increased the rev's, but still no joy. Time was running out, so we decided to forget using the main pump, just use the LPP (although this only had half the output of the main pump). The main was 500 gallons per-minute and the lightweight only 250. This was better than nothing, not forgetting we had six more appliances on the way to assist. We swapped over the suction-hose and tried to prime, but still we had a problem. We were now getting very frustrated. The know-it-all's from the village were still putting in their 'two-penneth'. Norm kept shouting for more water, my fuse was getting shorter and shorter. Mo and I checked through everything again, but to no avail. Just as the tank gauge reached empty, I heard the Thrapston pump siren coming down the lane and breathed a sigh of relief. It turned out that the priming-wheel was slipping on the main pump and there was a gasket and joint leak and letting air in on the LPP. Wonder what the chances are of both pumps going defective at the same time again. I pity the poor person it happens to next time as it certainly had us pulling our hair out. This was one day to forget."

Joyce said, "We had the occasional stack fire, which kept us out all night, but the longest job I was on was twenty-nine hours. It wasn't a stack, it was floods. It was about 8 pm and the rain was coming down heavily. We were called to Polebrook. The water ran down the road resembling a river. The brook that runs through the village had burst its banks. The people in the cottage next to it were starting to panic, the garage was already flooded and now it was up to their back-door step and there was no sign of stopping. We left some of our crew there and the rest of us went through the village helping people in need. I volunteered to check the pub, even if it was on high ground, (it was getting near closing time). I managed a swift drink in there before carrying on with my duties. After a few hours, we were re-directed and re-directed again - pumping out floods. We went to Glapthorn Road in Oundle, Cotterstock, and Elmington for most of the following day. Finally, around 10 pm, as we were reversing into the fire station the radio burst to life again. "Proceed to a flooded cellar in Yarwell". We were all knackered, had 'made do' with a few sandwiches all day and now we were off again. Before we left the station, I grabbed the bottle of Scotch from the cupboard and thought we could all do with a drink. I asked 'Grubby' on-route what the address was and recognised it immediately. The whisky went straight to our heads as we hadn't had any proper food. When we pulled up I was feeling quite 'squiffy'. The 'flooded cellar' wife heard how long we had been out and what we had been doing. She said, "Let me make you a nice cup of coffee". She decided we needed warming up a bit so she topped them all up with whisky. Before we left her husband said, "Of course, you'll all join me for drink before you leave". Luckily that was the last job; after 29 hours."

Annual Inspection!

"Each year the brigade had an inspection by the Home Office Inspectors (HMI). They were usually in the county for a week. We had heard that it was HMI week and there were rumours of an exercise being planned, but you know what rumours are like. I was at home watching the T.V. one evening when my 'alerter' (pager) went off. We were to go to Corby station on stand-by. All the way there we were sure it was something to do with this exercise everyone had been talking about, just as we got to Weldon we heard our call sign on the radio. We were to go to an address in Corby to a chimney-fire. Luckily, one of our crew knew the address and we weren't far away. When we arrived it was out, so there was nothing to do, just check it was out and make sure all was okay. Then it was all aboard to continue our journey to Corby station. Nearly there when control called us on the radio again to proceed to a make pumps TEN at 'Golden Wonder', which of course we were all convinced was an exercise. As there were already so many appliances there, the radio was going mad. Norm decided they were seeing how far they could go with putting control under pressure. We were all very relaxed about the whole thing until we pulled up at the factory and Norm said, "Ooohh, look, it's not an exercise. There's flames through the roof!" So we took absolutely no notice of rumours after that."

"Another funny incident was when we were called to some rubbish in a farmers dyke, at the edge of a field. I hadn't been in very long as John was the Sub-Officer. We dressed in our fire kit and got on the wagon. John was the last to arrive, as he lived he furthest away, so he grabbed his kit and jumped on. He was getting all his kit on and was rummaging round in a mad panic. "I've lost me welly! Who's got me welly?" We were all laughing in the back, as this wasn't the first time he had left some kit behind. He went to a job once and left his helmet back at the station. Anyway, the farmer turned up and John commandeered one of his 'green wellies'. We were then all invited back to the farmhouse for a drink and food, where John returned the borrowed Wellington boot."

She said that "whenever there was a call to a Public House there was always a fight to attend, as you knew that there would be a free drink or two in it. This obviously applied to officers too, as when the Ashton 'Chequered Skipper' caught fire, lots of officers turned up. We originally got the call as a chimney fire. Even though it was a thatched roof, we had dealt with chimney fires there in the past. However on this occasion, when we pulled up we saw flames licking over and along the apex of the roof. "Bloody hell, make pumps!" "How many?" I shouted back. I made the decision of six in the end. Before we had hardly stopped moving, I was on the radio to book 'in attendance and make pumps'. A few years previously I had been there, but the thatch was only alight at one end by the chimney stack, so we were able to cut a break in the thatch and save three-quarters of it, but this time, in seconds it was ablaze from end to end and the place was gutted."

A very 'Sticky End' (literally!)

"We were called to Thrapston to assist with a fire at the sweet factory. It was a bitterly cold winter evening and water quickly turned to ice. We had the worst of the fire extinguished and were damping down. As a factory, they bought everything in bulk, so there were pallets stacked with large sacks of sugar, coconut and such like. Some of the sacks were fire-damaged and the contents spilled, so the ingredients, mixed with the water we used, meant we were all in a mess: ankle deep in sticky gunge. It was a laugh at first, but with the cold air it soon got beyond a joke. The only nice thing about it was we all smelt nice and 'sweet'."

Standbys

Joyce mentioned that when the crew were sent on standby to another station if they were attending a large or time-consuming job. "It was sometimes dull, but we would try and make the most of it. One night we were sent to Corby. You always had a good nosey-round as soon as you arrived and four of our crew found the dormitory and went to bed! Mo and I had a game of cards and messed about. Then we found the switch for the tannoy. Just as the rest were falling asleep a rather loud announcement came over the speakers. "The train for Kettering is now departing from platform five". You could hear moaning and swearing, even though they were on a different floor from us. We made a cuppa and poked around a bit more. We found an old chemical protection suit previously used for training. Mo got kitted-up in it and crept into the dorm where they had all dozed off again. He wandered round moaning with his arms out like a ghost. I didn't think he'd get out alive this time, but he did, so we decided not to risk another prank and let them all sleep. We carried on playing cards and just as they had got off to sleep again, control rang to say we could return to Oundle. That's life in the Fire Brigade!"

...oooOOOooo...

The Police Service

The Northamptonshire and County Constabulary was started in 1840, with a force of only twenty-eight policemen.[92] In 1974, the force was renamed as the Northamptonshire Police. The county has over a thousand police officers today, with around five-hundred civilian staff. Initially, very few towns in the county had patrol cars. In Victorian times, police transport was by horse and buggy-cart. In the 1950s, all visits to local areas were made on foot or by bicycle. This was replaced by a motorcycle fleet in the early 1960s. The first radio-patrol cars appeared over a decade later. Most towns had a small gaol for 'rowdy' townsfolk or 'dangerous' criminals. Serious arrests were not frequent. Police officers reported back in emergencies by using the blue police telephone boxes (as seen most recently on "Dr Who"). These have gone from usage since the development of walkie-talkies and mobile 'phones. Women police constables appeared in the years after WWII.

Oundle police station was positioned at 4B Glapthorn Road, but its staff and placement were steadily eroded, inversely, as the town has grown! The Police Station closed its drop-in counter for locals and is now located in Fletton House (opposite the existing Oundle police station building), the "operational base for officers in the town." The police team cover Oundle and the surrounding villages. To report a crime

---

[92] "A pictorial history of 150 years of the Northamptonshire Police (1840-1990)" booklet, Northamptonshire Police, 1990.

telephone '101' (or in an emergency - 999) to talk to the police, who then relay the message to the local police.

In 1952 and 1953 the Oundle police were busy with the "Ashton murders". The lodge deaths were never solved (and remain a cold-case). The murder victims were found in their own home on 25th October 1952. They were game-keeper, George "Harry" Peach (64) and his wife, Lilian (67), who were discovered in their Ashton cottage at the eastern edge of the village.[93] Harry had been bludgeoned with a claw-hammer whilst in bed. Lilian, in an adjacent room, saw the intruder and is thought to have fought with him.[94] Still alive, she was rushed to Peterborough Hospital, where she lost consciousness and died several hours later. The police did not have the opportunity to question her. Butchers' rounds-man, Lawrence Wright, called at the cottage to deliver a Sunday joint and raised a query. He left the meat at the "The Three Horseshoes" pub ("Chequered Skipper") and returned to the butcher's shop in Oundle as he didn't get an answer to his knock on the door. Publican, Frank Slater, was worried as he had not seen Harry go to work, so went with others to the cottage and subsequently raised the alarm.

There was little evidence, with no major signs of disorder, but for a pantry broken window and palm-print on the window-sill, which police assumed was the culprit's access point. The local community and the police were shocked. All local householders were finger-printed and questioned as in the police inquiry. A week later, a claw-hammer was found in a cabbage-patch nearby. Robbery was ruled out as the intruder had not searched inside. The Scotland Yard inquiry detectives had an incident-room at Oundle police station, where over 500 people were interviewed, including the (overseas) residents of Polebrook Worker's Hospital and Molesworth aerodrome and American base. There were no tyre-tracks, but police took over 2,000 fingerprints, including those from estate workers, "suspicious persons" and itinerant travellers. Harry was wounded when serving in the Northants

---

[93] Joyce Gaunt left her job in the brewery in 1946. In 1947 she visited London with Jack Peach's girlfriend. She said they were well-remembered as a normal family with a sad end.
[94] An Oundle woman recalled that "Lily was wearing metal curlers that had been battered in, so was unable to talk before she died".

Regiment in WWI. He walked with a limp and the couple slept in separate rooms owing to his leg injury. People talked about the "Darby and Joan murders" and, with Oundle being what it is, everyone had an opinion. (Some quite spurious and others clearly eliminated from the police inquiries.) The case was never solved.[95]

In July 2016 the local police, paramedics and ambulance crews were called when a school bus overturned while taking children from Oundle to the villages. Police hurried to the crash to find nearly fifty local children had injuries from not wearing belts.

In early 2017, the National Grid used Fletton House as a customer base on the first floor to advise and update Oundle residents of the town-wide gas problem.[96] The local police assisted with organising the influx of gas crews from all around England when Oundle had "gas issues" (from a Thursday to Saturday) in January 2017, when we were cut off from the national gas supply. Over forty engineers from the National Grid were called in to visit each of our homes to turn off the gas supplies (and return to those they could not gain access to), then to visit again to turn everyone on again. They went to over ninety-percent of properties. This was a successful repair job and the people of Oundle grouped together to ensure everyone was looked after. Neighbours and friends lent each other heaters and blankets to keep warm. The Warmington garage was handy for getting coal for heating, for those lucky people who still had a coal fire.[97] During the year, Oundle retired Police Constable Gerald Fensom, died (aged 82).

Oundle police have attended fundraising Conker Championships in Ashton since 1965. When the Ashton World Conker Club contest outgrew its village, the events were moved to Southwick. The World Conker Championships take place annually on the second Sunday of October. This and other events are supported by all of the emergency services. Long may they remain to serve Oundle.

...oooOOOooo...

---

[95] See: 17 October 2002. Article by Tony Smith in the "Northampton Chronicle".
[96] See section on Emergency Services in this book.
[97] Anna has a coal fire: a bonus when the central heating was off.

LOOSE DAYS OF LEISURE

The First Oundle Brownie Pack and Girl Guide Company
- Wendy Bollans

Oundle's "Brown Owl" was established by Miss Boult in the first half of the twentieth century. She was aided by Miss Wood (the District Captain), Miss Spurling (Lieutenant and Tawny Owl) and the Misses Barton and Leverton (cadet helpers). Most 1960s Scouts, Cubs, Brownies and Guides remember doing a "Bob-a-Job" with her. This was when the members went around to family, friends and the local community to raise annual funds by giving service, helping people, by doing small community jobs. Each person was paid a 'bob' for each job they did (a 'bob' was a shilling; five new pence). Miss Boult encouraged others to take up Guiding and was supportive of their efforts.[98]

When 'Miss Strong' moved to Oundle, she established her position working with the Girl Guides and Brownies. She hosted them in her garden, where they pitched tents and did outdoor cooking and crafts. She also hosted fetes in the garden in the 1960s and 1970s.

The first time that Wendy ever camped in the Lime House garden was around 1969, when there was a District Camp held there. Joselyn Locke was the patrol leader. Under the trees at the back of the garden was a small spinney, where cooking took place. When the Guides were cooking, a group of boys (which included Johnny Lewis) noticed the smoke and looked over the wall. They joked with the Guides (whom they knew well) that they would come at night to let their tents down. Wendy awoke to see stars and when she noticed that the tent was missing, woke Joselyn. Joselyn thought she was being attacked by a giant snake, but it was only the tent pole! They woke the others, but could not wake Rosemary Moynehan, as she was a sound sleeper. Five of the six in the patrol put the tent up again around Rosemary, who continued sleeping.[99] The Guides made sure that Miss Strong remained unaware of the incident.

Years later, Wendy took her own patrol leader's camp permit and continued to camp here. In these days, Wendy did a paper-round from

---

[98] Wendy Bollans, personal history.
[99] Ibid.

James' the newsagent, doing alternate weeks with Rosemary. (The early morning newspaper delivery circuit was from West Street, the School houses, around the Jesus Church and up Inkerman Way. Once done she would go home and back to bed.) Wendy arranged the camping weekends for when it wasn't her turn "to do the papers". Rather than going through the garage, it was easier to not let Miss Strong know what they were doing. Rosemary, unfortunately, was not good at climbing walls. She was okay getting down, as the inside garden-level was higher than the South Road path, so getting back in was a challenge. She was a great supporter of Wendy and the Guides who visited. Joan always enjoyed seeing the girls and hosting them in her spacious garden.

The Brownies divided in 1967 as the pack had expanded. The 1st Oundle Pack's twenty Brownies met on Wednesdays at the primary school, then after the summer of 1967, met in the newly built hut on St. Peter's Road. (This is no longer extant and was just behind the water pumping station, where there are now flats.) The very first Brown Owl, Miss Irene Boult, retired just before 'Thinking Day'[100] after running the pack since May 1929. Mrs Gibbs and fourteen Brownies became the new Brown Owl and the 2nd Oundle Pack, who then met on Fridays at the new hut in St. Peter's Road. Miss Boult's retirement was celebrated by all of the group and the leaders. A photograph was taken of them at the occasion in early 1967.

Wendy Bollans (née Mudza) would often take groups of Guides and Brownies camping. She was particularly pleased when (in 1983) two of her charges, Helen Asplin and Clare de Heveningham, received their Queen's Guides award. At that time, Clare lived in Stoke Doyle Road and Helen at 29 Gordon Road. Her mother, Margaret Asplin (née Ward) worked as a local teacher and Brownie leader. The Brownies, their parents and friends helped celebrate as Miss Strong presented them with their royal, embossed certificates. Margaret had cooked and iced a cake for the occasion. It resembled the Guides' Trefoil. During the celebration, when asked which badge was the hardest to gain, Clare said that it was her camper's badge, as it rained all the time!

---

[100] Annually recognized world-wide on 22nd February. A practise since 1932, Thinking Day is celebrated by collecting global coinage to raise funds for Guides and Scouts.

Oundle Life Boys – Chris Beesley

Chris Beesley developed an interest in music while a member of the Oundle Life Boys. This was the 'Junior Reserve' of the Boys' Brigade, which was around in Oundle until 1960s. The group functioned like the Boy Scouts. (The Boys Brigade "Camp Commandant" in 1961 was Sir Alfred Owen, who was educated in Oundle School.) It was run by Mr (Watty) Rawlings[101] and his son, Steve, was a participant in the group. The group were often seen parading and marching through the town.

The Oundle School of Ballet

Josephine Black (née Smith) speaks highly of ballet lessons and the training given in Oundle. She learned in the Victoria Hall, but current classes are held in Fletton House. The current Oundle School of Ballet teach children the Cecchetti Method. This is a classical ballet technique and training method that was devised by Italian ballet principal and teacher, Enrico Cecchetti (1850–1928). The ballet students start early and are able to take dance examinations from five years of age. Today, classes are run by Lisa Hunter (who qualified in 1990). Like many others, Lisa began dancing under Mrs Mary-Jane Duckworth. Mrs Duckworth is the founding principal of Oundle School of Ballet and everyone speaks very highly of her. Mary-Jane was trained at the Royal Ballet School in London. She danced on a national scale. She is the chair of the Cecchetti Classical Ballet Faculty of the Imperial Society of Teachers of Dancing (ISTD). Josephine enjoys dancing and still practises today.

...oooOOOooo...

Pubs, Clubs and Dances

At one time, there were four breweries in Oundle. These were in North Street, South Road, West Street and New Street. Up to forty-five buildings have been run as pubs (throughout the aeons). A dynasty of brewers were established by Stoke Doyle farmer, John Smith and his son, John, who held a considerable amount of property in Oundle that was used for brewing.[102] The North Street brewery started operating

---

[101] Apologies if this surname is incorrect. Chris Beesley, personal history.
[102] Thanks to the National Archives at Kew and the Brewery Archives.

in 1775 and supplied the military camps at Norman Cross during the Napoleonic Wars, which increased business. Around the same era two young Oundle millers, Mr Kirby and Mr Gregory (from the Oundle mills) apparently liked to play the point-scoring card game, cribbage (sometimes called crib). They were also partial to playing bowls. Mr Kirby created a bowling green near to his 'haycock fence' and let off fireworks to celebrate his feat. (There was a previous bowling green at Bramston House, but Mr Bramston wanted redesign his garden to include a fish pond, so John Clifton removed the green).

The 'Red Lion' of New Street was owned by William Reachlous, who later moved to the Talbot coaching-inn. The Inn and Mr Barnes' Brewery stood next door to School House (where the Great Hall is now). During 1771 Mr and Mrs Crooks, the Talbot proprietors were superseded by Mr Ellis (the new landlord). Mrs Crooks had kept a firm hand on maids. One time when she was ill they became so drunk that they wrecked her mahogany card-table!

By 1812, Thomas and William Walcot (descendants of the Creed's) owned the brewery, the 'White Lion', Cobthorne and the old Rectory ('Mansion House' is now the Gascoigne building). When property owner, John William Smith died in 1897 (aged 83), his brewery was passed to his son, John 'Jack' Hume Smith (1859-1916). Jack was wealthy and lived in Cobthorne House. He was the captain of Oundle Cricket team in 1890 and continued playing throughout his life.

Richard Tibbitts (Jack's nephew) joined the company in 1837. The brewery equipment needed to run included boilers, malt-bins, mash-tuns, coppers, barrels, steam-heaters and storage tanks. Sixteen years later, the men purchased the West Street Union Brewery, closed it and used the premises. By the WWI, Tibbitts' successors, John and Mary Smith, ran the industry. John and their only son died in the war, so their manager, Basil Ludlow, took the brewery on with his other businesses (including the Talbot). His sons, Guy and Rex, continued this after his death. The Maltings closed in 1947. The townsfolk remember the huge, metal man-hole covers that enabled men to walk through from one side of the road to the other, beneath the road-surface, were removed two decades later. It is not a surprise that there was some subsidence in East Road junction with North Street twenty years ago. It could be presumed that the tunnels were not fully filled in![103]

Nene River Authority purchased the Brewery (old Rectory) stores and offices. Brewing work had endured for two centuries before closing in 1962, when the beer-producing edifices were demolished. In the 1980s housing was built on the Blackpot Lane site. Brewing in Oundle continues. In the twenty-first century we have come full-circle, as Oundle has recently revived the beer business with some success. The local brewery produces a "Jim Irving, India Pale Ale" (that was commemorates the late brewery manager). It is thought that this would have made Jim proud.

Wartime and Post-War Night's Out - Barbara Smith (née Gibson)

Barbara Smith (née Gibson) was born in 1938 into a family of nine children. She remarked that she was the seventh. She has two younger brothers and while growing-up her older sisters were aged enough to look after the younger members of the family. Her dad was Reginald Gibson and the family lived in a lodge where water had to be "pumped-up and boiled to use". Barbara married Bernard Smith in Fotheringhay and said that at that time, Fanny Adams kept the village shop. The community needed more than a local shop, so Oundle was an important hub for going to dances, films, the market and strangely enough, the post office.

Barbara said that before she was married, groups of girls from the villages would have "half-a-crown each" (about 15 pence in decimal coinage, but worth so much more) to catch the bus into Oundle. The money would "stretch to the wooden seats at the picture house" (in the Victoria Hall), an ice cream during the performance, plus fish and chips from the shop afterwards. The money covered the bus fare home afterwards too!

Her eldest sister was in the ATS[104] (and she acted as mum to the younger children). At the close of the war, she was a G.I. (a term for "Government Issue" in the military) bride and "left for America". She

---

[103] Oral history, Cheryl Forscutt.
[104] The Auxiliary Territorial Service for women.

returned once on a visit, travelling on the Queen Mary to Southampton with her daughter (aged ten at the time).

Barbara often came in to Oundle to take part in Square Dances that were taught by Margaret Titman. Mr Titman was the "caller" for the group, while his wife instructed the class. The women wore "big skirts for these dances". The Titman's sometimes travelled to the villages and taught in halls, but in the summer they danced on the lawn of the chapel in Nassington. She talked about meeting "Onslow" (actor, Jeff Hughes) who lived locally. He would often buy "a big box of chocolates and eat the ones he liked, then would give the box with the ones he didn't like to the girls in the shop". In the 1980s, when between acting jobs, he worked at Lilford Hall, then at Wigsthorpe.

Barbara Smith also remembers the "farmer on a lorry" who would collect the boys from Apethorpe borstal to do potato-picking in the fields. "They would keep the small potatoes in their pockets and would pelt local girls with them". They were scolded, "... but it didn't make much difference to them as they were wayward". (The building was restored and renamed Apethorpe Palace, recalling the 1600s when James I was a patron and visitor.)

Barbara held that life was "easy and fun". She said, "People seemed fitter in those days as they always walked for miles or used bicycles, carried heavy bags and boxes, bent and lifted all day long. No-one ever needed a gym!"

Like Barbara Smith, Gwen Mackey recalls that she came to Oundle on the bus and went to RAF Wittering (where she met her husband, Brian, at a dance in the 1950s). She said that this was a "social event that many local girls would attend". "The men would stand around the sides of the room and peruse the ladies before choosing one to dance with". Sometimes the waiting ladies wanted to be asked to dance, but if they knew that their 'partner' was not a good dancer, this was not always the case!

...oooOOOooo...

Ray Skinner - Personal Recollections of Oundle Pubs

Ray is a retired (army) parachute regiment member, who has moved to Islip. He clearly recalls enjoying a pint of beer in the 'Angel Inn' of the 1950s and 1960s with fondness. He talks about the publican's son, Robin, calling him "Tony Moore Junior". [105] He said, "I used to drink in Tony Moore's pub, 'the Angel' in the 1950s. You could walk through the door, through the shop and help yourself to a slab of cheese". He recalls, "The Old Vic' was my favourite public house. It was on the other side of the road from the Ganderton's fish and chip shop. It was very handy for a quick meal." [106] If you couldn't go there, "The Rose and Crown was spit and sawdust on one side and a nice bar on the other."

Ray recalls "the North Street Brewery had the Half Moon Bar". "The Railway Inn changed its name to the Riverside when the railway closed in the early 1960s. It was near to the Siddon's Coal Yard". "There was the old Black Horse and the White Lion, but both closed in the 1960s. Oh yes, they were the good old days".

"The Ship was a café and not a pub in those days. Weddings and Christening receptions took place there." It was very popular for daily lunches in the dining room. It also served morning coffees and afternoon teas, besides providing accommodation for overnight guests. "If you went on a pub crawl there were plenty of drinking holes to go to." Ray said, "On a visit to Oundle from one of the villages it was either walk, bus or bicycle. Sometimes you didn't drink because you could go to the cinema". The Victoria Hall was the cinema where they showed wonderful "Panoramic" films. Mr Ingram was the projectionist. (He lived in Inkerman Way.) Miss Richards, who lived next to the White Lion, was the usherette and sold the tickets. Then Chris Willis checked and took the tickets. The usherette had a reputation for "telling everyone off". "There were sometimes dances too." (In the 1960s there were dances and shows "put on at the Victoria Hall".)

---

[105] Publican, Tony Moore's son.

[106] It was not Ganderton's in those days, it was Brenda and Harry Hobbs' in 1950s and 1960s. They lived above the shop with their sons, Nigel and Christopher (who now run a fish and chip shop in Hunstanton). Susie Moore says that Harry was helping out in his son's shop even when he was in his 80s.

Ray continued by saying that "in the war time and just after it ended, people often walked in to Oundle from Woodnewton and the villages. Allen's rented bicycles and June (Gaunt) worked there. The police kept complimentary bicycles in the windy, tunnel-like, open-space under the Market Place Town Hall that people would borrow. The airmen would borrow them to get back to Polebrook airbase and just about anyone who wanted to get home after a night out. Everyone brought them back to be used again. If it was late, you could cycle home at midnight and return the bike the next day. They weren't locked up and no-one ever stole them." Ray is nostalgic when reflecting on the past. He mentioned that, "There were Oundle fights between pub goers. It could be quite rough as the night went on, but overall it was peaceful. People left their doors unlocked and open. No-one was worried. It was a much safer time in the good old days".

...oooOOOooo...

Inns and Tobacco

Today, smoking in public places is banned. From its origins in the 1600s it was adopted by some, but hated by others. King James I was outspoken about the use of tobacco and of drinking too much alcohol, when he wrote that it was "A custom loathsome to the eye, hateful to the nose, harmful to the brain, dangerous to the lungs, and in the black, stinking fume thereof, nearest resembling the horrible Stygian smoke of the pit that is bottomless".[107] In his missive he states how tobacco pipes are used between friends, also how the breath of the smoker is altered – and not for the better! To curtail tobacco use he raised import duty and tax on entry of tobacco into the country. This carried hefty punishments for those who did not pay. A legal smoking ban (the Health Act 2006) was eventually enforced in England, making it illegal to smoke in all enclosed work places from 1st July 2007. Some places introduced a ban before this, as awareness of the problems inhaled smoke caused grew. Smoking continued in pubs, clubs, bars and restaurants (except pubs those serving food) until the end of 2008. Tobacco advertising was barred gradually, starting with a ban on the

---

[107] James I of England (1604)'s paper, "A Counterblaste to Tobacco". In the same text there is also a mention of, "A branch of the sin of drunkenness, which is the root of all sins". From the collected edition of the King's "Workes", published in 1616.

use of televised cigarette advertising in 1965, to a complete ban on all tobacco advertisements in 2005. Many of the Oundle pubs were smoke-filled places and were reinvented as clean, family eating places, unlike the 'Half Moon Inn', 'Angel Inn' and other pubs around the town that were snug, small-roomed and very smoky!

The air in many was thick with hazy smoke (particularly in the evening), ceilings were marred with soot from open fires (as there was no form of central heating) and yellowed by pipe and cigarette smoke. Until the latter half of the twentieth century no-one considered it was unhealthy to smoke. The corporations generating tobacco products openly encouraged smoking. Film and television heroes made smoking appear 'cool'.

Since WWII, there were six main cigarette companies: Philip Morris, R.J. Reynolds, American Brands, Lorillard, Brown & Williamson, and Liggett & Myers (now the Brooke Group). Woodbine, Players, Camel and other cigarette brands were bought over the counter along with ales and spirits. Tobacco was the norm as they were openly advertised in pubs and shops. Children were sent to the tobacconist in the market place to buy a packet of 'fags' or 'cigs'. The law preventing the use of cigarettes, pipes and cigars in inns and bars has quietly changed the health of the clientele for the better. Pubs are now welcoming and not murky! Whole families are permitted in to eat together. Inns have changed persona to encompass the entire family, not merely a domain for men.

...oooOOOooo...

Dances and Concerts

The Victoria Hall

Through the years, Joyce Gaunt and her friends have loved to dance at the Victoria Hall and other local venues. Joyce said that she "really enjoys dancing", is active and "can still jive" (along with some of her octogenarian and nonagenarian friends). Barbara Mudza attests to this as she saw Joyce doing so at the latter's ninetieth birthday celebrations at the Golf Club in 2017.

166

The Victoria Hall has been used for concerts and dances (along with the Drill Hall) throughout the twentieth century. Even in this century (to 2017) the hall has hosted dances, which include Ceilidhs, dancing from the Fringe Festival, Zumba and other local dance classes, parties and panto's.

The shop between the Victoria Hall and the Congregational Church (now the Bazaar) was formerly Mr Arthur David Marlow and Sons.[108] It sold fruit, flowers and sweets was a handy venue for anyone attending the 'cinema'. Here audiences would stop to buy "toffees, sweets or an apple to take to the pictures".[109] Mr Marlow had a market garden in South Road, where he grew much of his produce.

Oundle School, Great Hall Concerts

During the 1960s, 70s and 80s, when the older generation complained that "the young men all look like girls", the Oundle School Great Hall was the venue of many 'pop concerts'. Whitesnake, Wild Turkeys, Genesis (Peter Gabriel – when he had hair!) in 1972 and Peter Hammill (ex-Van der Graaf Generator) in 1974, tickets were issued for Queen (but they hit the headlines that year and cancelled for coming to Oundle; despite playing at Peterborough Town Hall in 1973), Riff Raff with Oscar played in 1978 (and in Clopton in 1979), as did Harvey and the Wallbangers.

I remember sitting in the balcony seats and loving every minute. As tickets were available to locals the Great Hall was often packed. Sometimes Oundle people would travel a little further away, such as to hear Ralph McTell at the Peterborough Folk Club in Stanground (1969)[110] and to Boston Town Hall to hear Elton John (1972). These were the days when everyone sat on the floor. There were always local pubs hosting 'gigs' from up-and-coming or down-and-going bands. Bad Manners played at the Great Hall in 2006 for a charity gig arranged by

---

[108] Arthur Marlow died in 1954 (aged 78) and his wife, Alice (née Slater) in 1968 (aged 89). The shop closed and has been converted into a private house.
[109] Barbara Chester (later Mudza).
[110] Ralph McTell returned to play in Peterborough Key Theatre in late 2016. He was just as enjoyable. This time everyone sat in chairs – including him. Anna, personal history.

the landlords of the George pub, who had a former harmonica player of the band amongst his regulars.

The Sundowner Dances

During the 1960s and 1970s, Churchfield Farm (behind the Benefield Road golf course on the Lyvden road) was a favoured venue for dances and popular ('pop') bands. This annual, summer event was called the "Sundowner", as it started in the warmth of the early evening and became quite raucous as the evening progressed and as more beer was consumed. The event had a hog roast and food provided. The audience all sat on hay-bales as this event took place in a large barn.[111] These events were always very well attended by the youth of the day. It was linked to the Young Farmer's. Groups of the day included "Edison Lighthouse", who are brought to mind as singing "Love grows where my Rosemary goes"!

...oooOOOooo...

Oundle Teenagers and Bands

Most Oundle youth as some stage wished to be a pop-star, film idol or just become famous. Many of the young boys from each generation sang or, in the 1970s, played a musical instrument. One such group was organised by Chris Beesley. In the band, Chris played lead guitar, while Tim Sanders played the drums, Ian Crick on the Bass guitar, Christian and Kieran on guitar. Chris' brother, Richard Beesley, was a lead-singer and a guitarist too. According to Wendy Bollans (née Mudza) their best instrumental piece was a rendition of "Albatross".[112] The group had a following in local clubs.

The 1970s fashions were often ridiculous: hot-pants, hairy Afghan coats, very long boots and coats, cheesecloth shirts and bell-bottomed trousers! Around this time, Peter Simmonds produced two or more CDs of songs and music that he has written. 'Pete' composed and sang melodic folk songs. An Oundle group who keenly performed at functions are named the "Old Gits". They were already well beyond

---

[111] Anna, personal history.
[112] For further information, see section on Gerry Lee regarding a 'borrowed' song that he had written for Chris' group.

their teens when they got together (1998). They have specialised in playing 1950s and 1960s popular music (Buddy Holly, Rolling Stones, Beatles and so on.). Despite their now pensionable ages, they have made appearances well-into this century.

More recently there has been Fenech-Soler. This group formed in Kings Cliffe in 2006. They are currently a two-man an electropop duo: Ross and Ben Duffy, after their founding members (Daniel Fenech-Soler and Andrew Lindsay) left the band in 2016. In 2017 the 'Weekenders' played as part of the Oundle Fringe festival and at other local events. The Victoria Hall continues to host charity rock concerts. These have recently included 'A Dangerous Liaison', 'Desperate Measures' and 'Gone to the Dogs'. The Oundle Wharf has also held rock concerts for the several years. In the summer of 2016 they hosted 'Absolute Bowie' (a tribute band) along with other supporting bands.

Over the years Oundle has steadily developed its range of activities for young people who once made their own entertainment. For budding musicians the Nene Valley Music and Performing Arts Centre has its base at the primary school. Here they teach music, instruments, musical-theatre and rock. For those less musically-inclined there are always other physical and mentally-stimulating activities to occupy them. With activity clubs, art, bowling, cricket, fencing, fitness, golf, rowing, rugby, social (for young and old), squash and many, many more to choose from in the town.

…oooOOOooo…

Oundle Football and Golf Memories - Eric Heath

Eric was born in Woodston in 1926. He recalls many Oundle sporting events and the people involved in them. Eric says that "as a boy before the war, I remember Oundle as a small town that you travelled through on your bicycle on the way to Wicksteed Park. My involvement in football and golf in later years brought me into contact with many Oundle sportsmen".

Eric fondly recalls football matches. "In 1942, whilst playing for Fletton Boys Club (Peterborough) against Laxton Grammar School, we played on a sloping pitch in Milton Road. It was on the left-hand side before the cricket ground. In the Oundle team were Ken Laxton (who later played for Peterborough United, Rushden Town and Oundle Town) and Michael Amps. From 1951-60, Oundle Town played football in Benefield Road and teams changed their clothing at the 'Black Horse', the pitch being further along the road on the opposite side.

The Oundle team included Reg Norwood, Jack Hogg (who was also Secretary), Jimmy Lowe and Tommy Pope. Ralph Leigh was a local referee, also Percy Haynes. Leo Dunham, a teacher, would be riding his bike through town and would sometimes join in. In my later years in football I recall the following names: John (Crump) Afford, D. Brackley, M. Dolby, Arthur Loakes, Derek Race, Carl Norwood, Tim Eden and Nigel Wade."

An avid golfer, Eric mentioned that "Oundle Golf Course was then nine holes, later extended to thirteen and then to eighteen. I had the privilege of playing with Phil Cotton, whose name lives on in footwear in the town. Playing in the late-1970s I followed Kenneth Kaunda (president of Zambia for twenty-seven years). He was accompanied by an armed bodyguard and later joined us in the Clubhouse." Eric recalls, "On the social side, I remember the Smith's brewery at the bottom of Blackpot Lane and the nearby Half Moon pub. The landlord was Harry Brighty."

He went on to say that during the Second World War, he was stationed with his friend Derek (Perry) Dexter. They had been posted in the Gold Coast, Ghana. Then they were stationed in Edinburgh together and "at the time of our first leave, Derek invited me to his home in Warmington. We went to the 'Red Lion' public house where Sam Todd was the landlord. I became friends with the landlord's daughter, Vivian. After a period of time we fell in love, married and made our home in Warmington."

...oooOOOooo...

Oundle Town Football Club

Oundle Town Football Club was founded in 1883. From 2017 the Oundle Junior Football Club and Oundle Town F.C. merged into one club. They are now known as Oundle Town Football Club. The club house and football field is on the corner of East Road and Station Road. The club runs teams of all ages; regular adult teams, 'walking football' (senior) teams, junior teams (for boys and girls) and toddler teams (named Mini's) for children aged two to six. Matches are serious, but the club prefers to make learning fun for children. Tim Lee has a photograph of an elephant doing the 'kick off' for a match between Oundle and Peterborough. The club currently has two teams playing in the Chroma Sports and the Peterborough and District League.

...oooOOOooo...

The Cricket Club

In 1826, "The Huntingdon Journal" reported that 'The gentlemen and tradesmen of this town and neighbourhood have lately established a Cricket Club, and if we may judge from the public spirit of the projectors, little doubt can be entertained of it soon attaining great celebrity. The members exercise regularly, and a stimulus is given to their exertions by playing for suitable refreshment. The anxiety of each gentleman to become an adept in this noble game and to escape "scot free" is kept alive by this plan, and the social hour enlivened by the well-earned bowl. Yesterday a well-contested match was played for "a rump and a dozen" in which the rising merits of every player was observed with much pleasure by the spectators. After the sports of the day, the party partook of an elegant entertainment at the Dolphin Inn; the "rosy wine" was briskly circulated, "auld acquaintances were brought to mind", new friendships formed, and each aspirant departed in the evening well pleased with the harmony and goodwill which characterised their convivial meeting.'

Later, the Reverend Michael Hodgson was a fine cricketer, who formed a side who called themselves "The whack-it up-'em" team. The Reverend paid for all of the equipment and then bought everyone in the team a beer before the game began. This no-doubt either greatly aided or hindered their matches.

Val Prior recalls the 1960s, when "the best times meant going from Oundle to Barnwell and to Ashton and watching the cricket games". "Prince William came over from Barnwell to play. Ashton was busy with making cricket teas and with Pam Ray from Tansor. The pitch was beyond what's called 'Murder Cottage' and the Wold. It was always

171

sunny when the cricket group went to Sandringham estate to play cricket. These were the happiest of times."

...oooOOOooo...

The Bowls Club

The Bowls Club meet regularly at the Occupation Road bowling green and play tournaments with other clubs. Oundle Bowls Club commemorated its centenary with a Bowls England Celebration match in July 2016. Twelve counties were represented in the centenary meeting. The bowls club sprang from the Oundle Quoits Club, which was founded in 1866. It changed to lawn bowls in 1916 and made a change of name in 1954, when it became Oundle Bowls Club. In 2009, the highest winning rink was skipped by Stewart Laxton, who received the very first Bowls England Certificate of Merit Award. This is an annual bowls award. By 2016, Margaret Marlow was the local president of the club.

...oooOOOooo...

River Sports - Jay Thurlby [113]

Jeremy Thurlby (known to his friends as 'Jay') said, "I was born in June 1941 and most of my happiest memories concern my great love for the river. I vividly remember all the happy times we spent at Ashton 'overshot' or weir, in the 'shallows'. This was a large sandbank thrown up by the very strong torrents over the weir in the wintertime floods. In the summer the weir was a mere trickle and the sand bank provided a natural paddling pool, a place to catch minnows and Gudgeon in a 2lb jam-jar, baited with a few breadcrumbs and a string handle to pull the jar up fast when the bait was accepted! This was usually very successful and we could proudly display our glittering prize to the watchful grown-ups. In my case, the grown-ups were usually brothers or sisters, since I had five siblings above me! Many of us learned to swim there, although I think the old swimming pool was already in existence. I am told that I could 'swim like a fish ' when I was four and I never had any fear of the water. I had respect for the water, certainly. Years later, I was a keen angler and spent many happy hours on the

---

[113] Jeremy 'Jay' Thurlby, personal history,.

banks of the Nene or on the back waters. Just me, two dogs, my fishing rods, an old 'Oxo' tin of sandwiches and a bottle of cold tea. Bliss! My brothers and my uncle Ned taught me to fish and how to read the waters. I have always been grateful for this. I learned to love the river and all that it meant in terms of wildlife, beauty and peace. This love of the natural world has remained with me all down these long years."

Jay recalled, "I have many memories of Laxton School in the 1950s and of Tom Stretton, the then Master-in-Charge. I also worked on local farms from about twelve years of age onwards, during the school holidays. I have tales of some of the old farmers. Some were kind and always found me a job, whereas others (one in particular) were mean spirited and miserly. I have so many memories of Oundle and mentally edit them whilst gardening or walking."

...oooOOOooo...

At this point I feel it appropriate to mention the intrepid Mrs Graham of Northampton. In 1828 she attempted a trip in a balloon. It had been blown-up and arranged for two people to travel, but it had been damaged so she set off on her own! Dakard's Stamford News suggests that on her first trip she collided with a chimney and jumped out of the basket and in through the "Widow Ager's attic window". The second trip saw her land in the River Nene, near Oundle. When rescuers found the basket they started to look for a co-pilot, to be told that Mrs Graham had set off alone!

...oooOOOooo...

HOUSES AND LIFESTYLES

Housing styles and comforts have transformed throughout the ages as tastes have changed. Victorian and Georgian fireplaces were knocked out or covered-over in the 1960s and 70s, but are now being revived. In the late Victorian era, some of the more affluent houses had a form of central heating, with ducts built into their floors to carry warm air through the building. Most houses were built with small rooms to keep them warm in the colder months. In the 1960s and 1970s, people started to save and have a better income. Television arrived in most houses and solid-fuel central-heating started to become affordable and was often fired by a gas boiler. There would still have been an open fire in the living room, which may have heated the water as well (often called a back-boiler as it was by the side of or behind the fire place). The open grate was usually at the front.

Many houses had an electric fire (with two or three bars) in the main room, so the nearer you were to the fire the better on cold winter's nights. People needed to wear extra clothing to keep warm. I recall Liberty bodices were so tight and uncomfortable with loads of buttons all the way down at the front and stiff as a board. Perhaps they were warm, but they definitely were constricting. (The winter of 1963 had thick snow and was particularly cold.) The warmest room in the house was usually the kitchen as it was naturally heated when cooking. People with less wealth lived in their kitchens and kept the colder 'parlour' for entertaining guests. Then a fire would be lit in the hearth to warm the room.

By the early 1980s, most houses had central heating. Plumbing in the 1970s was also changing, with the development of indoor taps, indoor toilets and bathrooms being installed, traditions and lives altered. The installation of bathroom-toilets into houses meant that the outdoor privies and public 'jakes' (toilets in Duck Lane, Jericho, the bus depot car park in East Road and in the Crown Court yard) were no longer a necessity and slowly disappeared. Access to adjacent handwashing facilities has also improved hygiene. One benefit that is in-part due to indoor plumbing innovations is that illness and mortality has decreased.

Daily Life

Between the terraced houses and the start of the newer council houses in East Road there was a gap that "was wide enough to drive a small cart down". The post-war council houses were built with a 'wash-house'. Facilities included a lead (or copper) drum built over a brick oven construction. My grandad always talked about his 'copper', but this was the washing-machine of the day. The top was a big, copper 'wash tub' drum that was filled with a bucket, then it heated the water and boiled the clothing clean. Using the wooden clothes-tongs (to lift the hot laundry from the boiling water), a wash-board and bar of soap (or flakes) to scrub the clothes against, clothing was "scoured clean". In the council houses, "tongs were useful as the water was very hot".

174

Josephine Smith (now Black) recalls helping her mother and "feeding the washing through the mangle". I know from first-hand experience that mangles were lethal! In the early 1970s, when washing-machines were electric, some had electric mangles, rather than hand-crank ones (that were the precursors to spin-driers). I could not afford a newer machine as I was a student, but as I bent down to pick wet laundry from the water, I caught my hair in the mangle.[114] As the rollers turned, they scooped in more hair. Soon, it began tearing hair from my scalp as more and more got caught. I screamed and my husband, Tim ran in from the other room and pulled out the plug. My hair had to be cut as it couldn't be untangled from the two (mangle) rollers. Hence, I was a 'punk' before it was fashionable!

Hetty Bell recalls that "Most children (until the mid-1960s) were bathed in front of the fire in an old "copper" boiler (bath) that was filled with kettles of hot, steaming water that had been heated on the fire or on the hob of the cooker". Then, "with the metal bath having been dragged in from outside, it was Saturday night bath-night in the wash-tub". "The bigger the family the colder and dirtier the water got."[115] The detergent was a bar of hard, yellowish soap. By the middle of the twentieth century, more affluent homes had bathtubs in bathrooms and piped, running, hot water became increasingly common. In the countryside, it took a little longer before piped-water supplies and plumbing was commonplace. Saturdays were sometimes only a half day of work, especially at the turn of the twentieth century, so the afternoon off allowed time for the significant labour of drawing water, carrying and heating water, filling the bath and then emptying it after the family had had their baths. In many families it was usually the prerogative of the youngest to "go first" and when the children had been "cleaned, dried and put to bed, it was the turn of mum and dad to climb in and have a scrub".

Water wells were used and the water filtered for use, before running water was brought to housing. Sharon Cottingham recalls that her aunt had a water filter. This was the norm in the 1930's. Water was boiled and filtered through a tank. It took quite some time to filter through,

---

[114] Anna Fernyhough.
[115] Oral history, Hetty Bell.

so the children were only allowed a small cup of water if they were thirsty. There could be no waste.

Daily life altered with a move from traditional remedies, beliefs and practices to the NHS, when everyone could go to see the doctor. Medical practices became "modern", yet some parents still insisted that they could do better with the use of cloves, honey and oil. General Education did not stretch to the finesse of how the human body worked. I recall having a particularly bad earache and having warm oil poured in my ear. It did not good, but made mum feel she had done something to make it better! Mum always said that a "ginger-wine would settle the stomach". I think warm oil can't, in itself, heal a perforated eardrum, but some 'old wives' believed that a "hot toddy wouldn't do too much harm"! Likewise, shopping practices have changed. Family-owned shops in the town centre have closed and large stores opened on the periphery of the town (enabled by the ownership of cars). I was told that "in those days, mum bought a roast on Saturday and it would linger until Wednesday". Sunday lunch was a roast dinner and the leftovers would be used to make a pie, stew and sandwiches for the remainder of the week. Joyce recalled that "the Corona delivery-man came with fizzy drinks. The children would all pick their choice. My favourite was dandelion and burdock, but orange was Virginia's favourite". The bottles had flip-tops with a cage mechanism that enabled bottles to be easily opened and closed.

The folk of Oundle's world view has changed since these days. This is largely related to educational change and technical innovation (the radio, television and the internet). Oundle can still be insular and parochial, but most of the populace follow a constantly developing perspective with the rest of the western hemisphere.

Seasonal Difficulties

Mr James Gaunt was a bus driver. He was Joyce's father. Joyce said that when she was in her teens (in the 1940s), "the conductor walked in front of the bus with a torch to guide the bus in the fog and keep it on the road." With more people using his bus, Jim Gaunt was content. Joyce remarked that this was a time when "new-fangled electrical gadgets were appearing in homes." Joyce said that "everyone had a twin-tub, yet before this they had to use a copper with a mangle". In the early 1950s, the Gaunt's rented a black-and-white television from 'Owen and Hartley' and had a pink rent card for keeping a record of their weekly payments. Joyce remembers that the family had a horse and carriage ornament, which they kept on the top of their big television. Today this would not be possible, with the slim, wall-mounted sets. Joyce remarked that when she and her sister were children, "there was not a lot of spare money". Her father was always keen on a bargain and often "picked things up somewhere". She recalls a "Chatty Cathy" doll that her father brought home one day. It did chat, "... but it only spoke in Spanish"! For Christmas one year, her dad built a bookcase as the family's main present. Everyone loved it as their expectations were lower after the war. "The Christmas pillow-case held the presents and there was a sock on the end of each bed with an orange in the toe." Virginia said that there was a warning that Father Christmas would not come if children did not believe in him. She recalls that their belief was so strong that she saw him in the sky. Joyce also saw his red coat leaving the bedroom door. She said, "The world of children was special then. I always believe in Father Christmas. I saw him"!

I recall that in the early 1990s my son created a 'Santa Trap'. He tied ropes around his bed-legs, the furniture and the door. When Tim (my husband) crept inside, he fell. His comment to our youngest child was, "Don't do that, you'll kill Santa!" Santa left presents under the tree from then on![116]

"Settling Down"

Joyce Hardick reminisced that she paid a pound for a week's lodgings in the early 1940s. She said that earnings were less, so prices seem very cheap, but didn't feel cheap at the time. Food items (tea, sugar, etc.) and other groceries were delivered in large sacks. They were transported once a month by van or with a horse and a flat-backed cart. Salt was delivered in sacks and was weighed out by the 'stone'.

In North Street, the 1950s house and cottage purchase prices were as little as £100. The Mudza family took a loan from a North Street 'relative' (known as "Uncle Fred") to make their purchase and never

---

[116] Anna Fernyhough.

looked back. It took them some time to repay the debt, but the couple were very happy to have a cosy home to live in with their new baby. Barbara recalls buying a book on Oundle with an account that described her house as derelict. As it cannot be seen from the road, it was an obvious mistake, but it annoyed her. (I apologise for any similar issues that may arise in this volume.)

Hans Hardick was a German prisoner of war in WWII. He was captured in 'Operation Goodwood' in France. He held that they were 'blanket bombed' and the noise made people deaf. He came to Oundle, 'fell in love with an English lass' and married Joyce Gaunt. He did not return to Germany, but stayed and made Oundle his home for the remainder of his life; content and at home with his English wife and their four children.

Oundle is a good place to raise a family and grow old. Shops are now centrally placed, rather than having a grocer's shop in every street, but walking and driving is not difficult. Educator (and pensioner), Elizabeth Grantham, of Mill Road, said that she would like to see the "main shopping area extended to cater for all of the new people in Oundle". Oundle has always embraced change, so when Oundle population increases our services should also adapt to cope with demand.

...oooOOOooo...

The toll house and toll-gate on Benefield Road

The Market Place and old Butter Cross from the east
Shillibeer's etching from the 1820s – of Oundle (from Jericho)

The Shambles and Swann Inn from the west

The windmill, Glapthorn Road   St. Peter's Church interior

Station Road c. 1900

Oundle station c. 1960

St. Osyth's Lane cottages c. 1950

The Talbot
Courtyard,
c. 1970

The
Ship Inn,
West Street

North Street

Brewery Cottages 2017 & (below) c. 1959

Smith's brewery -
North Street, c. 1958

Smith's Brewery mineral factory works
(opposite the football field), Station Road, c. 1960

Surviving thatched cottages: North Street & Benefield Road

Percy Allen's cycle & barber shop, 1915

Splash-back, St. Osyth's Lane

Prentice's Way, Jericho

Bill Pheasant, St. Peter's Church Groundsman, c. 1950
Charles J. Douglas, clock-maker

The International Stores, West Street

Princess Alice, Duchess of Gloucester with Oundle medics

Ganderton's in West Street – fish and fowl

Laying up of Oundle British Legion Colours, 1967

Robert 'Bob' Butt (front left) at Grevelejren POW camp, Denmark

Victoria Hall dance night, 1940s

The Rose and Crown smoking-room dominoes team, early 1950s

Oundle Urban District Council, 1964

The Wiggins family of Gordon Road

Spurrell children learning to ride with Button Horn, Ashton Road

View to the south from the Gordon Road houses, c. 1960

Recreation ground, big slide, New Road, c. 1960
Phyllis and Angela Taney at the recreation ground, 1953

Drill Hall Christmas Party, early 1960s (Jackson girl's dressed alike)

Gordon Road street party, 1953

May Taney (front 2nd left) at the National School, c. 1898

School photograph, 1932   (below) Primary School, 1948

St. Peter's Primary School, Mrs Fox's class, 1961

Secondary Modern recorder group, c. 1967

(left) Sisters Doris Hooton (née Craythorne) & Dorothy Chester (née Nicholson),
c. 1907   (Right) Sisters Annie (Jackson) and Emma Rycroft (Moisey) c. 1950

Miss May Taney in 1916 and in later years

June & Joyce Gaunt in the brook (betwixt Benefield & Stoke Doyle Roads), c. 1931
(right) Barbara Chester in Rock Road, c. 1933

Reginald Melton at work for Oundle School near St Anthony's House, 1961

New Road, Coronation street party, 1953

New Road carnival float, 1975.   Mrs Allaby with Andrew Spurrell (aged 4 weeks)

Oundle School outdoor pool, 1944   Spurrell family at the pool

Mill Road (from the North), 2017

Mill Road workers cottages (from the south)

Latham's Hospital, North Street (2017)

The Union Workhouse buildings on Glapthorn Road, c. 1908

Laxton Hospital, Church Street, 1914

Mabel Fisher, Oundle Operatic Society, c. 1930

June Gaunt at work, J.H. Clarke's bicycle shop, St. Osyth's Lane

Jack and Percy Allen in their hardware store (2 North Street), 1908

Barnwell Station (became stuck on the bend) travelling north in North Street (1977)

Market Place

Market Place shops from the 1930s onwards

A coach and four visit New Street (2017)

The Bookshop and site of old fire station

The
Great
Hall

Old School Friends: Sharon Cottingham, Anna Fernyhough, Sheila Denley & Wendy Bollans at the Primary closing day.

"The Band", Ian, Tim, Chris & Kieran (c. 1970)

May Day, maypole dancers, c. late 1950s

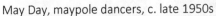

May Queen and her Maids of Honour, early 1960's

May Day garland competition

'M', Lady Ethel Wickham, Mrs Myers & Michael at Lime House

Hetty Bell (nee Carter) 1930s   Joyce Gaunt at Ashton Bridge 1948

The Primary
School on
Milton Road,
was relocated
in 2016

Arthur Chester, c. 1917   Ella Formby at the Rose and Crown, c. 1940

Frank Jackson, Territorial Army, in a parade for Royalty
Lucjan Mudza in Polish Naval Cadet uniform, c. 1950

Jill Giddings' picture of "Rosemary and Jamie at school"

Snowflake Dancers

Oundle Brownie Anniversary, Glapthorn Road, 1954

Oundle Brownie and Guiding Movement Leaders, 1967

Jubilee bridges, c. 1950

2000, Market Place millennium celebration

 A page from Joyce Hardick's scrap book - c. 1942 - "Kay Setton and her dance instructor and partner (BF)". Joce's friend, Kay was a G.I. bride and emigrated to America. "Clark Gable in his plane at Polebrook airbase" and "Visiting Clark Gable, Bob Hope, Francis Langford at the Peterborough Red Cross".

Postal workers in 1911

Frank Gaunt's bus

Frank Gaunt, wearing his bus driver's hat

Frank Gaunt (driver) & John Richardson (his conductor)

Oundle firemen with the Taney brothers (either side of Bugler)

Fire in West Street (beside Davis' paper shop)

Fire brigade (1925) Harry (front 1st r.)
and Bill Taney (2nd row 1st r.)

Fire Chief,
Alfred Taney at his house

Fire brigade 1970

Fire Station crew dinner dance, Talbot, 1969

East Road and Ashton Road street party ladies, 1953

East Rd and Ashton Road residents, Coronation party, 1953

Benefield Road, Dixon's shop and cottages
before their fiery destruction

The Red Lion in New Street (now Oundle School)

View of New Street from Oundle School

Ellen Harvey and Mushie the lion

Ellen Harvey, Mushie and Speck (the dog)

Entertaining the crowds - Captain and Ellen Harvey with Mushie

Irene Channing (née Harvey), high-wire artist with Mushie

Sam York, known as 'Ernie' - with his chip van on fire!

Betty Iliffe and Cyril Wyles, Benefield Road, 1930

Barbara Chester and Margaret Martin
(at the back of 13 North Street) in the mid-1940s

Barbara Chester, c. 1948

The Denley family (in 26 North Street), 1960

Alan Denley

The Spurrell Family, c.1914. (L-R) Andrew's grandfather, father & family: Ivor, Walter, Walter R., Hugh & Florence

(below) Lime House

Paine's Alms Houses, West Street

Mrs Rawlings dance troupe: Sheila Fox, Judith Leayton, Carolyn Colclough, Judith Welch, Pat Midlane & Rosemary Burnham (or Valerie Hastings).

The Talbot Hotel and War Memorial

Oundle Primary School (Milton Road), 1930

STREETS OF OUNDLE

Oundle's Saxon Market Charter was renewed by King Edgar in 972 A.D. and was granted to the Abbot of Peterborough. Just over a hundred years later, the Domesday Book (1085-6) records Oundle as one of five market towns in Northamptonshire. In the early 1530s, John Leland described Oundle as "al buildid of stone', while continuing to keep a 'very good market'". The whole main street (now named West and North Streets) was first named High Street, just as New Street and Church Street were Bury Street. St. Sithe's (or Osyth's) Lane, leading southward, downhill to the meadows and river, was previously named Lark Lane.

MARKET PLACE

In 1539, John Leyland reported to Henry VIII that 'Oundle has a good market' and by the mid-1600s was prosperous; selling cattle, sheep and grain. The butter-cross, the shambles and butcher's row have since faded into the past. The small town had several markets (none of them where the market is held now). There was a market formed around a 'butcher's row', Butter (or Cheese) Cross and a Bait House.[117] The butchers' row was a double row of building located roughly to the west of the central shops in the Market Place. These were permanent buildings in the centre of the roadway (opposite where the bookshop is now), which were demolished to make way new building. The first recorded bake-house was located at the eastern end of the market. Just beyond this was the Butter Market. The best illustration of this area is Shillibeer's etching from the 1820s of Oundle (from Jericho). In 1591, it had a cross covered by a "pent house" with a tall central shaft. It was topped by an octagonal, timber-framed, slate roof. Stone steps led up to a traditional mediæval market cross. People utilised this as a meeting place when they came to market from the town and nearby villages to buy their butter, milk, cheese and eggs (usually on Saturdays, but later altered to Thursdays). A livestock market augmented this in 1800. Fresh yield was placed on the steps of the cross and displayed. The butter-cross had an arched-cover forming a

---

[117] Ibid. 1150-1200; Middle English 'bait', Old Norse is 'beita' to hunt with dogs, hawks or fish bait. Caught animals are edible to 'bate' and 'bite' (see definition).

simple roof that lent shelter from the elements to traders (built later than the cross.)

The market space was repaved in accordance with the Improvement Act of 1810, when the cross and cover were dismantled. Oundle was considered "improved" after the removal of the butter-cross[118] and Shambles[119] that once dominated the market. These changes were further enhanced with the instigation of gas street-lighting. A Market House was built after the Improvement Act of 1825 on the site of a former building. Strangely enough, today's market still has a regular cheese stall in attendance since the 1970s, which is the longest consistently-running stall on the market, which parks less than a couple of hundred metres from the original butter-cross position.

The current central point hosts family shops, a local farmers' market (once each month on Saturday mornings) and a regular all-day Thursday market. Oundle boasts many traders, shops and cafés. Our continually expanding town has a population of over five-thousand people, which contrasts with the much smaller mediæval population of a mere five-hundred, which includes all of the traders (including cloth-workers, a skinner, a smith and two masons). In the thirteenth-century, each of the townspeople and traders would know each other, their history and relate to them as their own community. Today this still occurs, but to a lesser degree!

Oundle roads and their many properties have changed little since the 1600s. A few street names altered, such as Stoke Hill, which was known as "Chappel End" (*sic*.),[120] which was named for the mediæval chapel of Saint Thomas Becket.[121] Mill Road and Jericho retain their names, although the origins of the latter name has been lost.[122] It may be that its proximity to the Church was significant. (The story of the Good Samaritan was set between Jerusalem and Jericho.)[123] The Tudor and

---

[118] In some documents this is referred to as a "Cheese Cross".

[119] Butchers stalls and shops.

[120] Abbreviation: *'sic erat scriptum'* is Latin for 'thus it had been written', transcribed as in its original source, complete with errors, archaic spellings and colloquialisms.

[121] Thomas Becket was Archbishop of Canterbury from 1162 until his murder in 1170; remembered a saint and martyr in the Catholic Church and the Anglican Communion.

[122] Information with thanks to David Wills.

[123] The Bible: Matthew 20:30; Mark 10:46; Luke 18:35.

early Stuart times saw restoration and rebuilding, when old mediæval houses were demolished, modernised or rebuilt. In the 1800s, the wealthy Whitwell, Bramston and Creed families demonstrated their position in society by building to impress (for example, Cobthorne). They did not ignore their workers and built houses for them, proving they were important in the larger scheme too. Mill Road was so-named for the water-Mill nearby. Mill Road cottages have been previously dubbed 'Millionaires Row', as they were expensive to build and now even more so to buy. It is held that local historian and writer, Alice Osborn, lived in two of these converted cottages in the 1970s, no doubt inspired by her significant surroundings.[124] John Clifton was considered well-read and had a large library within his house. In one of his accounts, Clifton mentions the annual bull-running custom that was held in Oundle streets (largely, North and West streets) from the 1600s and into the 1800s. When the railway opened in 1845 it created a hub, between Peterborough and Kettering. As street names evolved, so did the people who lived in them.

Three Nonconformist Churches and the Jesus Church (originally Anglican, but now Roman Catholic) were built by the Watts-Russells'. Oundle was a centre for the Poor Law Union. Despite the workhouse being demolished, the chapel has been converted to a private house. The town has been the home to several banks over the years, which have held the accounts of Oundle residents and businesses. Some have moved to Peterborough. The National Westminster Bank and Barclays Bank remain, but the Trustee Savings Bank (which merged with Lloyds) and the Halifax Building Society and the Norwich and Peterborough Building Society (that is a trading name of Yorkshire Building Society) have all moved from the town. "Half-day closing" for the shops was on Wednesday afternoon. This gave the tradespeople a half-day without working to recompense for the extra hours worked on Saturdays to catch the trade of shoppers. After some worry that the town was in danger of losing its clientele to the supermarkets nearby, it appears that the shops have diversified and there are thriving market days (dependent slightly on the weather!) and themed, seasonal and festive markets at other times during the year.

---

[124] Oral history, Jean Atkins.

Oundle grew steadily since WWII. According to census data, in the last decade of the twentieth century the populace increased rapidly to 5,735. As the town grew, changes to housing, roads and traffic arrangements have become issues. Despite these, occasionally the town sometimes develops a calm quiet (when schools are on holiday).

The Market Place - shops and dwellings

Around the time of the Norman Conquest (1066), Oundle's market place was most likely an open space that extended to the boundaries of the church yard. From the era of King John to the reign of Edward I,[125] there were permanent tenements and shops built around the central market. As late as 1565, the wool market was open land, with a narrow row of shops running to the west of the current market place (by the centre of the market place where the ex-Town Hall' building stands). These were linked to the eastern end of the Moot Hall and visible from the horse market, just beyond. The Town Hall (used for public meetings) made several moves. Originally it was in the Guild Hall, by the Laxton Cloisters. It then moved to the Market Hall (in the centre of the town), prior to the Victoria Hall, Drill Hall, Court House and most lately, Fletton House.

The Market Place Town Hall was built in 1826. In the 1940s the large upstairs room was used by the Roman Catholic Church. Mollie Pratt (née Weston) was the last person to be christened here in 1948.[126] The Church subsequently moved to St. Wilfrid's (formerly the Zion Baptist Chapel, which was built in 1852), not far from the end of West Street, then relocated again to the current position in the "Jesus' Church". The building was originally open to the air on the lower level. It was used for housing the market stalls for the weekly market and as a useful rain-shelter for the market (and for parking shoppers' bicycles). When it was built it could be walked through from end to end, but is now enclosed and contains businesses. A clock has been added to the east-facing wall in this century.

In a prime business location, beneath the old town hall chamber is "Hair Designers". The 'Norwich and Peterborough' bank was here, but

---

[125] In 1304, Edward I granted monks free "warren" lands in Oundle and Biggin.
[126] Oral history, Mollie Pratt (née Weston).

recently closed. In the 1960s, the town hall was used on Tuesday evenings by the Youth Club. For a minimum fee, there was a pool table, dart board, chess games and a range of activities to participate in. Pop music was played; often loudly! Sometimes there were outdoor activities, such as archery, that took place near the School swimming pool. Most times were spent socialising in the sparse, upper rooms of the town hall. The 'chippy' was open when the evening ended, so it was handy to grab a snack meal on the way home. (The much older Youth Club was held at the end of West Street, between Dyson's and Inkerman Way in the Brownie and Youth Club hut. Betty Marlow and Barbara Chester attended "a couple of times as a very young-teenagers, to see what it was like".) By the 1960's, George Carter was heavily involved in the Youth Club, with Cyril and John Carroll. Mr Bell taught archery to groups on the Oundle School field beyond their swimming pool. I recall enjoying this activity, but waiting for ages for a turn (as there were a limited number of bows, arrows and targets).

Until 1830, 1 Market Place was an Inn that ran throughout the entire building. "The Swann Inn" had rooms above that were let to visitors. Now it has a small, one-bedroom flat over the shop, with views over the town centre. The main coaching entrance was on Market Place (judging from the building work this probably was where the current Optometrist is). From 1905, New Street and Market Place corner shop was owned by Frederick G. Davidson. It was a "value for money" ladies' and children's outfitters, "draper, milliner and silk mercer". (Fred died in 1942, aged 75.) The shop then changed hands several times: E.W. Davis', an Army Surplus store, a kitchen and bathroom supplier, a bridal shop, a general store and a kitchen and bathroom sales shop. The Leayton family owned and rented this eighteenth-century building when it was part of the larger, corner establishment. Since the 1980s, the building has been divided into two shops and now trades as two separate entities. The first part is currently a ladies fashion-clothing shop, 'White Vanilla'. Since 2009, another part has been 'Shaman Quinney' estate agents.

From 1900, Herbert Hunt Markham's printing business was at number 3. Herbert was born in Oundle in 1868. He married Miss Charlotte Miles in the Parish Church in 1897 and died in the town in 1948. The shop then passed to Victor Edwin Leayton (1896-1962) and his wife,

217

Ivy (née Edmonds from Brixworth, whom Victor married in the summer of 1923). They renamed the shop, "Leayton's". It is believed Victor Edwin Leayton's father (or grandfather), Orlando Leayton, was the Oundle town crier. He wore the bright, traditional livery for crier's, including a hat and a bell that alerted the townsfolk to his broadcasts. In 1859, he proclaimed news of: parades, festivals, sporting matches and current news from the town and district.

Most residents recall Leayton's newsagent and stationers' as a long-run family business. Anne L. Cooper (née Leayton) and Ruth E. Leayton (who is three years younger than her sister) are still very active in the town. Their homes are still in the Market Place. Ruth once ran the bakers' shop next-door to the newspaper shop. The bread and cakes were baked in the premises behind the shop. The sisters retired in the 1980s. In 1987, it was renamed "Oundle News". It sold magazines, papers, cards, toys, snacks, sweets and some fresh food. In 2000 it changed ownership, but retained its name.

Number 5, a late eighteenth-century building, matches the others in the row. Attached to the current newsagent's, this building was a family bakery, making and selling cakes and bread since 1910. It was first William Green's confectioners shop. In 1940, it was run by Mrs Veer (whose husband died in WWII and is listed on the war memorial). By 1950, the bakery belonged to Mr Fletton (possibly related to William Green). It had the bread ovens at the back, via a corridor flanked by the paper-shop and bakery. In the 1960s, "Fletton and Company" made iced-buns, cakes and bread for Primary School events. Nan Donegani worked in the bakery at that time. Many people who attended the Primary School recall the sweet, tasty, pink or blue iced-buns. These and other treats were made here for the school Christmas parties and were given out at the end of the event. In the 1960s, after the bakery closed, Mr John White opened an opticians in this shop. From 1995, Stephen Whitehead followed suit. This is currently "Judith Day, Opticians". This is the second-half of what was one building with the newsagents shop (with a central passage-way that leads to the rear).

Located at 7 was Cotton's "practical boot-maker" shop. Three generations ran the business (1871-July 2017), which was first sited in North Street. By 1900 it was considered a time-honoured local business, which sold footwear and repaired shoes as "R.C. Cotton and Sons Limited". Anne, a fourth-generation 'Cotton', said that she and Stuart (her dad) sensed it was a time for change. They found parallels between both old and established shoe shops. 'North Shoes' was founded by boot-makers, William and Sarah North. In 1876, they found a property for sale at Bourne from which they sold the boots and shoes they made. By 1914, demand out-stretched their cobbler employees, so goods were sourced elsewhere. North Shoes is managed by William and Sarah's great, great grandson, James.[127]

The National Provincial Bank added the current gothic-style façade in the late-1800s. Since the early 1980s, the National Westminster (NatWest) bank has traded in the Georgian building at number 9. The bank history dates to 1900. It expanded into the building to the right in the latter part of the twentieth century. In 1893, Chew and King ran a grocer's that was the right-hand part of the current bank building, which was then sold to the Northamptonshire Bank. Sadly, banks are in decline in favour of on-line and telephone banking. This Oundle branch of the bank has given its customers a final closure date of June 2018. Barclays are due to follow suit later in the year. This sadly leaves Oundle without a bank!

There is a small courtyard between the bank and the pub. In the early 1800s this was the access way to approximately eighteen small dwellings, ten on the northern side and the rest behind the pub. The building next door was extended leaving a small courtyard area where barrels were stored. It currently has metal gates.

The "Rose and Crown" Inn (11 Market Place) dates to the late-1600s. The poet, John Clare (1793-1864), stayed here when training with the Northants Militia in 1811. At that time, the landlady of the 'Rose and Crown' Inn was the widow, Mrs Kitty Britchfield.

This hostel has an interesting history as a seventeenth-century inn. It is said to be haunted by a 'White Cavalier'. The pre-WWI trade was Norwood's, followed by the Thurlow family (during and after WWII),

---

[127]   www.northantstelegraph.co.uk/news/deal-is-the-perfect-fit-for-oundle-shoe-shop

then the Gaunt's (Margaret and Frank)[128] until the early 1950s.[129] During this time, there was a "Dominoes team" and they and their friends would meet in the Rose and Crown smoking room in the early 1950s. The team won a trophy and celebration meal. Joyce Hardick has a photograph taken in the pub showing the winners.[130] By the 1990s the publican was Geoffrey Wicks (son of Malcolm and Sheila Wicks, née Hooton). Geoff said that 1992, "was incredible, seeing what was found in the ground when I put the extension onto the Rose and Crown." Recent restaurant extensions have not changed the pub's character, although subsequent landlords since may have tried. In 2013, the 'Rose and Crown' was subject to a licensing review on its rowdy and unpredictable patrons and gained a, albeit temporary, 'rough' reputation. This would probably have fit with its character in the distant past.

Number 13 is a seventeenth-century building with a very distinctive, colonnaded front. The external pillars support an enlarged upper storey that was extended forwards over the street. A rear doorway was useful when the current gap (to the school and Church) was occupied by a building. If one looks carefully at the end wall, the stonework clearly shows where the next building was attached. From the outside, it is clear where the original building was expanded and enlarged. In the early 1800s the building was owned by grocer, Samuel Anthony, who died in 1823. In the 1820s, John Jenkins ran the shop. In 1841, he passed it to his nephew, William L. Fisher, who ran a coal and timber business here. By 1858, Edward Peach lived here. He died in 1891, aged 74. Later, George Ramshay ran the shop on the ground floor as a hardware and ironmongers' and upstairs was housing for his wife, Elizabeth, and their family. He also owned the adjacent 'blacksmith forge' next door (now an alley) to the yard at the back. It was owned by George and Lizzie Ramshay until their deaths in 1906 and 1909, respectively. In 1923 Oundle School acquired the building and opened a book shop for School students. This is most certainly the best local

---

[128] Frank Gaunt died in 1973.

[129] The Gaunt family moved to 19 Rock Road in 1957.

[130] The team were (back, L-R) John Watkins (who lived in a caravan behind the 'Angel'), John Afford & his wife, Nancy (who died in 2017, aged 80), Frank Gaunt (the landlord), Mr Jackson's friend, Margaret Gaunt, Bernard Jackson. (Front, L-R) two friends, Ernie Brinsley, Arthur Loakes (of East Road), David Tortoise & Mr Mould.

shop to go to order books. In 2010, it was leased to Coleman's. "Oundle School Bookshop" has lost the word "School", but still sell books, art materials, maps and stationery.[131]

A gap between buildings now leads to the Church and Oundle School and is retained by the latter. At the rear of this in 1820 there was a house and stables. The current gap is wide enough for School vehicles to drive in with a gated front that is closed-off once each year to maintain a property ownership right-of-way. To the right, there were shops owned by Stafford and Brown; later, the town Fire Brigade with a sign over the entrance (established in 1844, the brigade had only three officers and thirteen men). The building face has reverted to a shop-front with Oundle School library to the rear (as the fire-station relocated to Glapthorn Road in the 1970s, with easier access). It is clear to see where the fire-engines were housed, as the stone rebuild is distinctively different from those around. The fire-station took the whole building that is now: 'Bespoke Outfitter', 'The Barber's Comb' (previously Mrs Whatby's wool shop) and 'Leo's Pet Supplies' (a former bakery and greengrocer). The engines were in the part that is 'Leo's Pet Supplies'. When the fire-station moved, in the early 1970s, 15 became the "Goldsmith and Bass" estate agent and auctioneer offices. Goldsmiths' has been trading since 1964.

In 1900, 15a was a motor-cycle repair shop, run by Mr Donegani, until Hooton Brothers acquired the premises. In 1939, it was (15) a hardware, grocers and provisions merchants, run by the Hooton's, who made daily deliveries to local customers.[132] The building also hosted the County Court Office in the upper floor during the war years. Later, it was Goldsmith's Auctioneers and Estate Agents, then "Romejo's" (which moved over the market place to 'Normans'). At 15a is the 'Tailor Shop' (clothing repairs and alterations) and next-door is the 'Barber's Comb' at 15b. This was where "Tatform" grocer's stood, but was demolished along with its neighbour (15c) in 1922. In the 1930s to 1960s, 15b was occupied by the Oundle Fire-station before it was rebuilt as a shop. 15c was rebuilt and incarnated as a mobile-phone shop. It was then "Finishes and Touches" hairdresser and is currently "Leo's Pet Supplies" (since 2000). This is Oundle's only pet shop.

---

131   The building is leased by Oundle School.
132   Peter Hooton believes that it eventually closed as it went bankrupt.

Number 17 was run by Mr A. Townsend. In the early twentieth century it sold lino and household items. "Townsend's" shop had windows that were in an L-shape around the corner. Ruth Keans recalls she loved this shop. It became "Oundle School sports shop", then part of Laxton House sixth-form rooms and an ICT-room. The building is at the corner of North Street, opposite Jericho and St, Osyth's Lane.

Number 19 is a listed corner-building that is part of Laxton House. It was the home to the Trustee Savings Bank (TSB) until the branch was relocated to Peterborough. Locals petitioned outside the bank, but the bank did not consider Oundle to be valid (despite redecorating the entire building before it relocated!). Many of Oundle's TSB customers moved banks rather than have to travel to Peterborough! The building was used by Oundle School "Community Action Department", until a move to the nearby Opera House (3 North Street) and is now the School Duke of Edinburgh Award Scheme office. Even numbering starts at the other end of the Market Place.

Opposite the war memorial, the even numbers begin at number 2. Number 2 Market Place was owned by William Robert Maddison, an outfitter and source of tailored clothing. He specialised in "supplying the local gentry" and selling "breeches and liveries", hosiery, "cloths for costumes" and "hand-made hunting gloves". In the 1890s it advertised as an agent of Pullar's Dye Works, Perth. (William died in 1969, aged 83). 'Quality Wear' clothing and haberdashery shop, on the corner of New Street and Market Place, was run by Miss Newborn throughout the 1950s to 1960s. In the 1960s, Dugdale's bakery was run by Frank Dugdale's daughter, Mary, who lived at the farm by Barnwell Mill. It traded as 'Cookies' (a bakery from 1995-2005) and is now 'Oundle Bakery' (selling bread and cakes). It is a quaint, old building, where the slant of the roof and style of stonework portrays an age. The outbuildings to the rear have been demolished. Tony Hilton says that he is fairly certain that this bakery had an entrance inside that led back to a coach-house.

At the front of number 4 there is a large thermometer on the wall to the left of the door. According to Wendy Bollans, "it has always worked, but many people are oblivious to it as they pass by". Number

4 was a chemist and opticians, but prior to 1824, John Henson[133] (sometimes appears as Hewson) owned the house (currently 'Boots'). It was sold by auction at the Talbot and converted into a commercial property. It was, in part, owned was a surgeon. By 1833, it was running as a pharmacy business. Henry E. Roper and his wife, Caroline (then their son, Will Roper), ran the dispensary and chemist business until 1923, when it sold to Douglas Whitwell. Mr F.W. Whitwell in the 1950s, would see customers "earlier than advertised" with appointments "made for his personal attention". In 1967, he sold the business to chemist, Michael Flower. June and Michael Flower had two children, Timothy and Teresa. The gardens at the back of the building went almost to South Road. This is where the Flower children played with their friends. Alan and Jill Stewart (managers of the Talbot hotel in the 1970s) recall their children playing there. In 1975, Anthony Hilton joined Mr Flower and, in 1984, he bought the business when Michael retired.[134] His wife, Rita assisted him with the bookwork and served in the shop. Still functioning as a pharmacy, it is part of the national "Boots" franchise. Tony Hilton considers the current Tesco and Boots buildings were built as one large house. The central doorway led to the alley between the parts (now giving access to Amps Wines), which is interesting as the building was constructed with beer and wine vaults, a dairy, a wash-house and a brew-house. Tony and Rita, his wife, lived in the flat above the shop. Since moving on, the cellars have been cleaned up and there is now a serviceable store-room and toilet downstairs. Tony noted that in the upstairs lounge, very neatly etched in copper-plate writing on the glass of the window-pane, are the words: "Peggy Hanchor - 1st May 1773". This dates the building to the reign of King George III or earlier. (It is unknown who Peggy was or why her name is engraved onto the window.)

Since 1901, Mr P.W. Amps ran a business at number 6. It started out as a house, a general store, a tea dealer's and tallow chandler's, then much later became a supermarket and wine merchants. It grew and extended over time, as the family evolved along with the products sold. At one point, John Amps' grocery store roasted coffee-beans that could be recognised all around the market area from their distinctive

---

[133] Thank you for this information, Tony and Rita Hilton, checked using Freebmd.
[134] Oral history, Tony and Rita Hilton.

smell. Behind the 'Tesco Extra' is 'Amps Fine Wines'. This is a fourth-generation, independent Oundle business. Prior to the restoration and becoming a shop, it was a pair of cottages that were owned by the chemist next-door.

At number 8, there was a 'Temperance Hotel' (like the one in North Street). At number 9 were 'Dolby and Son' (accountants) in the 1930s, now Southams' estate agents and auctioneers offices.

The 'Blue Marlin' is currently at number 10, but this was preceded by 'Fri-Fare 88' fish-and-chip shop. In the 1930s to the 1950s, this was Mr Clarke and Mr Charles J. Douglas' clock shop (a partnership that was eventually owned by 'Charlie' Douglas, a skilled jeweller, clock-maker and repairer). His advertising stated that this was a "watchmakers, jewellers, engravers and opticians". The business was long-running and had been in the Clarke family (continuously) since 1840. The shop counter ran along the wall to the left-side, rather than at the back (as it is now). "There was a large 'station style' clock on the wall which dominated the place". Besides working in his shop, he was also a Church Warden. The shop sold sweets and flowers for a short time, but a fire put paid to the business in 1973. The shop was redecorated as an accountants.

Michael Amps then bought number 10, to run as a fish'n'chip shop during the 1950s. Thereafter, Neville Ganderton bought it from him in the early 1960s and "brought a manager in". Gill said that "Inside, the picture rails and wallpaper patterns were very old-fashioned. The back of the building was added later and the right-hand side was private. To go into the house (which was at the back) you had to walk through the shop. It was then remodelled, so that you went in through a separate door at the front (as it is now). There were stairs to the upper floor. These are at the side". Gill stated, "It was converted by Richard's brother to allow for a fish and meat delicatessen, but this did not work out". She suggested that the deli did not work owing to the townsfolk who were used to getting their fresh fish from the fish van. "The building was changed back to how it was before."[135] This family fish-and-chip shop had tempted the Ganderton's to relocate from West Street. Gill is married to Neville's son, Richard. She recalled the shop

---

[135] Gill Ganderton, personal history.

had a huge grandfather clock on the wall and chatted about the family's 'Fri Fare' fish-and-chip shop. Children who attended the youth club enjoyed visiting the shop to collect a bag of 'scraps' to eat on their way home!

12 Market Place was John Eaton's ironmonger, decorator's and household supply shop, selling calor-gas and other goods in the 1940s. This narrow building stretches south to the rear. It has been much-changed inside during the last century. It was Vergette's Estate Agency, prior to a transfer to Christopher Woodford of "Woodford and Company", estate agent, property consultant and auctioneer.

Mr Walter Black ran a shoe and boot-maker business that was trading at 14 Market Place in the early 1920s. He was described as being "in the passage by Eaton's". Walter ran his small car into the passage to park! The shop he ran was sold and traded (from 1948 to June 2014) as Norman's greengrocers. It had shop number 14 on the frontage and 16 was a cottage at the rear that Mrs Shrives rented. This was accessed via a side passage. Inside, the ceilings were low. This is an indication of the age of the property, which dates to the 1600s. In one of the house alcoves there was a small dark-room where Jim Norman did his own developing. He took lots of family photographs that the family still treasure today.[136] Jim's father was an engineer with ambitions to open a shop, which he shared with his son. Prior to being a grocer, Jim had worked as a builder on the wartime Army Hospital site at Lilford Hall. After the war he moved to Oundle and established the business using local knowledge and their produce-growing contacts. Initially, the shop was rented from the Honourable Mrs Lane of Ashton by James Norman and his wife, Vera. They ran it as a shop and lived in the cottage behind the shop with their children: Sue, Dave, Phil and Hazel. The children grew up almost literally knowing the business "inside and out". They helped in the shop whilst still at school. Fresh produce was delivered from as far afield as the markets of Paris, although much of the shop stock came from nearby farms.

Number 12 was the shop-front next to Norman's greengrocers (14). It was owned by Mr Fryer of Fotheringhay. This was used as part of Norman's business as a small sweet-shop and florists until tragedy

---

[136] Sue Norman, personal history.

struck. In October 1973, a fire created a turning point for the business. It started above the three-storey building at number 12. Jim and Vera Norman and their family, who lived at the rear (in 18) were evacuated from their home, in case the fire spread and trapped them. Their living quarters were behind the shop, so the family were awakened by loud banging sounds. It was the Fire Brigade, who were trying to wake them. An American gentleman who lived above the shop at number 12 (worked at a local USAF base) overloaded the sockets with transformers, which caused the fire. It was a cold autumn night when the firemen did their rescue in the early hours of a Thursday morning. The shop lost all of its Christmas stock due to smoke and water damage, which was "quite a blow at the start of the busy period". Firemen took Sue into the building on the day after the fire. She found it "depressing to see everything blackened and ruined". The devastation the fire had caused resulted in Jim Norman closing number 12. The floristry business was transferred to number 14. Mrs Norman (senior) went to the insurance company on behalf of her son and his family "to berate them for not paying up". She threatened to chain herself to the railings of the insurers in Peterborough, then ensure that everyone knew they didn't honour their insured clients. The insurance company suddenly 'put their skates on' and promptly paid up.[137] The shop became Bulley Davey accountants, Vergettes' estate agents and, later, Woodfords'. The flats behind the shop belonged to John and Dorothy Eaton. They also owned the large property that abutted it to the rear (on South Road).

After the fire, the greengrocers had a massive makeover and the shop became self-service. When Jim retired his son, Phil, took over running the vegetable and fruit side of the business and his daughter, Sue, continued with the floristry. Jim was still evident in the shop until he died, aged 74. By the time the shop closed, the family were one of the longest-running 'Interflora' agents in the country. The family marked sixty years of selling fruit and vegetables by collecting the memories of its customers. Two children of the late Mr Norman who took over the business (who had worked there since the school days), Susan and Philip, closed the business when focus on the town-centre shifted. The family did their utmost to keep their business open, but were unable

---

[137] Sue Norman, personal history.

to compete with the strong supermarket competition nearby with their product ranges and lower prices. The Norman family celebrated sixty years of trading (1941-2008). Owing to competition from local supermarkets, which easily undercut their prices, Norman's closed in July 2014. The cottage at the rear of number 18 was the Norman family home. Jim Norman's grandson, Chris Young, continued living here until December 2014. The shop, "Romejo's gift shop", recently rebranded as "Rather Gifted".

Number 20 had a ladies' public toilet (at the back in Crown Court) and Ned Thurlby's tailor's workshop upstairs. The shop sold ladies clothing as "Parry Irving" in 1970s and "Jack's for Women" in 2005 (also selling clothing, jewellery, shoes, hats and scarves). After a time when it was vacant, in 2013 became a bakery. "The Small Bread Company" eventually closed and the shop became Paul Watts' hairdressers.

Crown Court is now a coaching-gap with rooms over an archway and either side. This was formerly the 'Crown' inn courtyard. There are now shops within it: Oundle in Stitches (previously Wall Brothers' Ice-Cream company), Dexter's restaurant (previously a pet and seed shop with a jeweller's next door) and Designer's hair-salon (previously Mr Howe's saddlers then Parry Irving's ladies' clothing shop). Crown Court (18) is separately numbered inside. 2 and 3 Crown Court trade as Dexters' restaurant and cafe (right of the arch) and number 6 is 'Oundle in Stitches' (to the left). The Crown Court area is where 'The Crown Assembly and Club Rooms' existed (at the bottom of the yard) in the 1950s. People would take their 'slate money' along to pay in to help sick people. (See Hetty Bell's description of payments into 'friendly societies' in this volume.)

Long before this it was 'The Crown Inn'. The 'Crown' hosted courtyard cock-fighting. Property was traded with an endorsing glass of wine or beer. Throngs of animals were often kept outside the two inns (to advertise the offer of prize fights).

Heather Black's family owned 'The Crown' coaching inn during the late-1800s and early 1900s. Her grandfather, Tom Allestree Cunnington (nicknamed "Tatcho") was born here in 1895. Tom wrote a short memoir on "Oundle in the Past". In it he described (when he was twenty one) how "Jerry finally got me" in 1917. He was carried to the first-aid post, where the medical officer was, surprisingly, Dr Arthur Elliott (from Oundle!). As Dr Elliott was overwhelmed with patients to attend to, he sent Tom on to another aid station. On route, Tom collapsed for loss of blood, but said that he was able to forgive and forget when he next met his doctor. Tom ran a fruit and vegetable shop in the town. Tom's birthplace was in front of the assembly rooms (where the Chamber of Trade meeting took place). The assembly rooms were used for dances, street parties and meetings. In the rear courtyard was a Health Centre (a baby clinic, where babies were weighed and mums could buy formula milk and other baby products), a jewellers and a pet shop, before reopening as a Mediterranean restaurant and courtyard cafe.

Tom Cunnington (who married Dorothy Sawford in Oundle in 1925) described nineteenth-century Oundle and stated that he was born in the 'Crown' public house. He describes his early life sitting in the crowded, beer-fumed, smokey room to eat meals. The inn has since been many shops (including a saddler's). In the 1950s, this was an ice-cream shop "Stapleton's Ice Cream", but is now 'Oundle in Stitches' (established over twenty years ago, it sells a range of patterns, wools and sewing paraphernalia).

Originally, two Inns once stood here, (numbers 20 and 22) next to each other, "The British Queen" (now Trendall's butchers shop) and the "Three Lasts", which changed its name to "The Crown". The old 'Crown' inn hosted travelling theatre companies[138] with thirty-one performances in just two-months in 1771. In the rear yard of the Inn, travelling companies produced plays, farces, songs and dances. John Smith owned this property in 1824.

Number 22 was owned by John Isham and his neighbour, John Pole, in the early 1800s. 22 Market Place was a butcher's shop that was run by Thomas Ball and Son until 1912. It was then E. Brudenell and Son family butcher's, selling pies, pasties and a range of raw meats (cut to the directions of the customers and taken home to cook). The company delivered daily to Oundle and twice weekly to surrounding villages (until 1989). In the 1930s, Mary, Margaret and Sheila Martin lived above the butchers shop with their parents. At the age of 16, David

---

[138] 'A History of Hostelries in Northamptonshire", P. Hill, p. 18.

Wills left school at fifteen and started work in Ted Freeman's builder's yard (now Coles') in West Street. After a short time overseas on National Service during the mid-1950s, he returned and wed (mid-1958) the youngest Martin daughter, Sheila. She is a talented fabric artist. Her sister, Margaret moved to live in Peterborough after her marriage to Cyril Deri. Philip and Dorothy Brudenell worked here when the shop was owned by Philip's father. Dorothy took the money at the cubicle kiosk, where customers paid for their items, while the butchers cut and packed the meat. The butchers did not touch the coinage and Dorothy did not touch or taint the meat. During this time, Josephine Black's uncle worked here. He managed very well with one arm (as the other had a 'pirate style' hook to use when working). The butcher's was run by Philip Brudenell for many years and is now Martin Trendall's business, with butchered meats, pies and a delicatessen (a runner-up in the Northamptonshire Food and Drink awards in 2012). Trendall's butchery was formed by families providing local meats straight from their farms.

Numbers 24-30 Market Place are on the corner to St. Osyth's Lane, where the current Oundle School, Bramston House-master lives. This residence was built by lawyer, Stephen Bramston, in 1701. Bramston House is a large Georgian building. It has a high balustrade that hides the roof, but has changed very little since first built, with its large, smooth, stone frontage. The land was owned by John Smith in the early 1824. It was later owned by a retired ironmonger, Charles Peach (born 1862). It was passed from Mr Peach to the Newman family, who sold the building to Oundle School. Attached to Bramston House was a bay-fronted building that was a clothing shop that was run as a Gentlemen's Outfitters.

Bramston House was purchased by the School in 1916, then internally extended by the procurement of Pettit's and Moore's shops. After the wars, 'Thomas Moore and Company' a tailor, hosier, hatter and outfitter traded here. Here, Oundle School parents bought their necessary uniforms and equipment and it is where townspeople bought their smart suits and outfits. Mr Arthur Laxton and his family lived in the premises. Arthur's children were Don, Margaret, Jean, Ken and Stewart. The shop had a door-bell concealed within the door-mat.

"In the 1930s, when walking home from school, it was a joke to push one-another onto the mat to ring the bell – then to scarper quickly!"[139]

From the 1950s to the 1960s, the proprietor was Donald A. Laxton (the elder brother of Stewart and Ken). He lived above the shop with his wife, Viva, and their children: Yvonne, Nigel and Marcia. Grandma, Gertrude Laxton, lived at the back of the premises in number 26. Sue Norman went over the road on her wedding day (from their Talbot reception) to show her dress to Gertrude. A recent comment on businesses in the area elicited the response, "The women of the Market Place were strong women: Mrs Laxton, Mrs Norman, Mrs Cotton and the Leayton girls. They really ran the place".

32 St. Osyth's Lane (which is a long-running pharmacy site for many years) was run by Mr R.M. Turner, before becoming Hall's family chemist-shop, before it became "Boots". Frank Hall and Son were chemists and the National Health Insurance and Hospital Savings Association optician in the Market Place. When 'Boots' moved to its current location, Richard and Christine Simmonds bought the pharmacy with its adjacent "Stable Cottage", "Grooms Cottage" and "Guinness Cottage". Here they offering self-catered, overnight lodgings within the cottages in their private courtyard. The shop has more recently (2006) rebranded as "Oundle Pharmacy".

Builder and wheelwright, Thomas Towndrow Gann (1864-1936) ran his business at number 34. Hayden P. Rands[140] followed with his "grate, sink, pump and stove" fitter and seller, plumber, glazier, painter, "paper-hanger" and decorators shop. Number 36 was a grocer's shop in 1937. "Maunder and Crown" held the ironmongers shop in the war years. In 1946, "Hayward and Towel" ran a decorating business. The "Avondale Restaurant" was at 34 and was run by Mrs Burdett from 1940 to the late-1950s. This property was owned by the local Rothschild and Capron families.

Number 36 was Albert and Fred Hasnip's grocery shop during the 1930s, before it became "H. and V.", an ironmonger's business. The premises are on the corner of Jericho and the Market Place. It was later

---

[139] Barbara Chester, personal history.
[140] 1937-72.

run by Mr Fitzjohn as "Forty-Six men's wear" in the early 1970s. Jean Atkins recalls when the old Oxfam shop was in what is now 'Stu-pots' (established in 1992 and run by Stuart Blow). It was rented to them as it was an empty shop that belonged to the Rothschild's. 36 Market Place was the first 'Oxfam' building. It was started as a market stall, then went into empty premises (such as our current 'Stu-Pots' shop). It was started by the Hon. Mrs (Edith) Christian Capron[141] and Miss Frances Pierce (who was in the Land Army and was staying in Southwick).[142] At times this shop has sold products from the Ashton Estates, surplus antiques, then teen-clothing and jeans. This was Mr G. Wilkinson's electrical and mechanical-engineering sales, installation, maintenance and repair shop in the 1950s.

NORTH STREET

North Street was once the main street of Oundle. It was busy with shops and people. As the town grew it inked into West Street via the market area, which bore the same name, High Street. In early times the market was nearer to the top of North Street than it is now. Most of North Street dates to the 1500s, yet some houses have incorporated walls from much earlier. The street has changed little for many centuries, yet shops came and went.

Prior to and during the 1940s, North Street was quiet as traffic mainly consisted of horse-drawn carts carrying the coal-men, the milk-men and the rag-and-bone men. There was a street water-pump located against the Church yard wall (opposite Dryden). Annual circus' came to town and travelled via North Street to West Street lodgings from the Railway sidings. When the elephants went past, householders would rush out with their dustpans and fire-shovels to collect excrement to use as nourishment for their gardens. Barbara Chester tells a story about her mum rushing out to collect dung as the circus passed through, to find that it was not as good as she had thought. In the coming weeks its 'power' completely killed her roses!

By the early 1970's traffic had increased in the town, particularly as by then we lacked any rail transport. Thelma Quinn (*née* Allen) has quite

---

[141] Edith Christian Capron (née Hepburne-Scott), 1901-1989, was married to George T.H. Capron. Their children were Rachel, Elizabeth, Bridget and George.
[142] Oral history, Jean Atkins.

a history. Her father, Gordon Allen, was Bevil Allen's cousin. Mrs Skiba (née Dyson) was another of Gordon's cousins. Fred Allen lived at Stoke Doyle Manor. Thelma has photographs from the late Nora Blunt (from Barnwell). Thelma believes that Nora attended a school in Oundle, before working in the Oundle bookshop. (Her brother was Percy Marriott.) Thelma has two of photographs showing the station building (from Barnwell) being transferred to Wansford after the railway closure. During the 1970s the bypass road had not been developed and North Street was found to be a narrow road to pass a 'station' through. Thelma Quinn commented, "Wowsers, look at the size of that lorry!" All traffic passed through the town, but there was less of it than there is today. Oundle did not have the bypass as it yet had to be built on the old rail route.

North Street (the east side from the town centre)

At the turn of the century the corner shop (2) was Tafford Whittam's corn-flour dealers. Thereafter it was John and Percy Allen's barber and bicycle shop. By the 1940s it was Mr John B.W. Allen's shop. He was a commissioning agent (testing electrical items in newly constructed buildings) and bicycle sale and repair shop at the corner of Jericho and North Street. John married Margaret Burdett in 1950 (when he was twenty-two). Bevil Allen said that his father and uncle jointly-owned "Allen Brothers", where bicycles could be bought, hired and overhauled. Bevil's uncle did most of the repairs. In the downstairs-shop, people could rent a bicycle for a shilling per day. This shop has been 'Owen and Hartley' television and electronic specialists for many years since.

After 1900 the shop at number 4 was Miss Hoyle's ladies outfitters. In the 1930s, 4 North Street was Miss Alice Lloyd's milliners. It sold balls of wool, ladies and children's wear. By the 1940s and early 1950s it had become Miss Mitchell's linen shop. Shoppers could build up a tab and put money aside for a purchase. Each week purchases were paid off in instalments. When the shop finally closed, someone remarked, "Well, you can't buy knickers in Oundle anymore!" This business was then bought by (and passed down in) the Hayward family from Tony Hayward's father. It sold wallpaper and decorating-materials, but mostly "items you could furnish your bottom drawer with". The shop served the town as Hayward's until the 1970s. This was around the time when Gwen and Tony's son, Peter, joined the Navy to "cruise around the world".

Bulley Davey chartered accountant offices are at number 6. This building was formerly used as the Urban District Council Offices. In the late-1950's it also housed Oundle library in the back rooms, before the library moved to Glapthorn Road (around 1962) to operate from a "mobile" in the doctor's car park until the new library opened in May 1981.[143] In 1964, the Urban District Council was comprised of Dennis Whight (the Secondary Modern School headmaster), R.W. Cheney, A.V. Gibbs (Clerk), B.G. Seaman (Ratings Officer), J.W. Wild (who does not appear on the photograph), Reg. E. Sutton, A.E. Lane, F.B. Bennett, A.B.A. Wright, Geoffrey M. Willimont (gargage owner and Chairman of the UDC in 1963, Rotary Club and member of the Chamber of Trade and Northants RNIB)[144], R.K. McMichael, Tom Allestree Cunnington, R.E. Catchpole (Vice-Chairman), Neville G. Ganderton, Mrs Lottie Mason and R. Carpenter. A familiar face, Allison Davies, has worked at 'Bulley Davey' as an accountant, a secretary and part of the tax department since 1992.

Old Dryden (Oundle School) is hidden behind the coach-entrance leading to its East Road gardens. It was formerly 'The Dolphin Inn' and was advertised as a "Family and Commercial Hotel, with Bath Room". It closed in 1867, when it was purchased by the independent school. In the 1940s, the secondary modern girls were taken for art classes in the building, but as it was for the boys' Public School there were no toilets available for the girls.[145] John Hadman mentioned that the toilets were outside at the bottom of the premises. They were smelly and icy in the winter, owing to their enclosed, yet outdoor position. Miss Margaret Gale, the art teacher at Oundle Council School, directed the girls in their studies in Old Dryden. According to John Hadman, if there was an air-raid the children would be rushed into the basement until it was all clear. The all-clear signal was the vicar on his bicycle using a whistle to signal the all-clear. These whistles were issued to give a distinctive piercing, double-note screech (that could be heard from a long distance away). This form of whistle has been distributed

---

[143] Thanks to Margaret Saunston (née Ward), personal history.
[144] Geoffrey Willimont died in 1992.
[145] Oral history, Barbara Chester.

to the police, firemen and ARP wardens since the 1880s. They were used during the war to direct people in the dark as they could be heard over the sounds of explosions, shouts and a general hubbub of voices.[146] The Old Dryden building later functioned as the first site of Laxton Junior School from the 1980s to the 1990s, when a new East Road site was developed.

Number 10 was originally an Inn that provided accommodation and also operated as a public house named the 'White Lion'. This building occupies a prime position facing the Church. This late-mediæval building had four new bays and an attic floor that were added in 1641. The limestone construction dates from 1661, bearing the date of its completion in 1662 (in Roman numerals on the central apex). The property has been split into two residences. Like many buildings in the town, it is retained by Oundle School.

In the 1930s and 1940s it was owned by the Burdett family. It regularly hosted the "Pig-Keepers Association" alongside other groups. The Burdett children were: Buster, Bertie and Bobby (the latter were twins). Susan ('Susie') Moore lived in North Street and recalls that her father, John Moore worked at the 'White Lion'.[147] This was the venue for Frank Jackson and Teresa Dolan's engagement celebrations. Teresa was not used to drinking spirits and so put them in Frank's pint whenever she felt that wasn't looking. He didn't notice! Frank and one of his friends spent much of the late evening "walking each other home". (At that time, Frank was a resident in Danford's Yard.)[148] When the Burdett family moved to the 'Coffee Tavern' in the Market Place they ran it as a coffee-bar and restaurant. The houses behind the 'Coffee Tavern' were also owned by the café business, but they were sold over time.[149] The 'White Lion Hotel' was used as student accommodation. (The dormer at the end slopes due to its age and other parts have had some reconstruction. The building to the left also has had some haphazard work done to the dormer framework and

---

[146] They were also used by soldiers in the trenches during the First World War.

[147] Susan Moore, personal history.

[148] Oral history, Sharon Cottingham (née Jackson).

[149] Oral history, Peter and Sheila Hooton.

bears a rough date in the concrete repair.) The sun needs to be in a late-afternoon position to be able to read these dates clearly!

Contiguous with the 'White Lion', Number 12 has the same date, 1641, on its gable end. In the 1930s, the Parish vicar was the Reverend, Canon Cartwright. When he retired, he moved out from the seventeenth-century rectory and lived in this house (to the left of the 'White Lion Inn', in the corner house on Duck Lane). In 1939 (at number 12) Percy Robert Knight (1880-1940) ran a repair and overhaul garage for cars and motor-cycles, as well as bicycles. He stocked and serviced tyres, tubes, batteries, typewriters and sewing-machines. According to the Town Directory, the business also "ground scissors and razors" and sharpened knives.

During the war years, when most homes threw open their doors for evacuee children, the Reverend Cartwright invited Joyce (Gaunt) and other children to a birthday party for their evacuees. Joyce said that despite her initial reservations that it would not be fun, it was a very pleasant, memorable and enjoyable event. By the 1950s (after Cannon Cartwright) Dr Arthur Elliott lived on the corner of Duck Lane and the Berrystead. He was a partner at the doctor's surgery. His surgery was at the back, down a corridor. Hetty (Bell) recalls his house and surgery well. When a child, she was in poor health and needed to visit the surgery and see Doctor Elliott frequently.

Arthur Elliott worked as a medic in the First World War. He wrote daily diaries during that time which can be seen on the Oundle School Archive site. He did not spend every day tending to the hurt and dying. On 11th August, 1916, he wrote: "Sanitary conditions bad – spent day cleaning up – digging latrines and burying Bosch." On 12th August he noted: "Entrance to my dug-out blown in in the night – but dug out in morning. A big H.E. [high-explosive] shell burst on parapet opposite entrance and pushed it in." The entire diary is quite harrowing to read, but gives a picture of the futility and harm of war.[150] During the 1940s and 50s, Dr Elliott lived here. For a time, Gwen and Tony Hayward lived here before they moved along the street to live in Tony's father's

---

[150] archives@oundleschool.org.uk - Oundle School Archive retains School records, including the School registers from 1626. This information and account, with thanks to archivist, Elspeth Langsdale and the O.S. Worshipful Company of Grocers.

hardware shop. In the 1960s this house was the venue for Congregational Church Sunday-school Christmas parties. Sharon Jackson (now Cottingham) and her sisters recall attending one of the parties in 1963. It sounds as if it was a fun and joyous occasions for all.

Duck Lane is mentioned in the Austell survey of 1556. The name suggests that it may have been to near to a pond with water fowl, but this was in antiquity. During the 1700s, the public 'Jakes' (toilet) was in this lane! By the 1930s, there was a small garage at the bottom of Duck Lane that did small repairs. It was tucked behind the houses as the lane curves away (parallel to North Street). The apparatus for petrol pumping and other use still remains attached to the walls. Once upon a time, there would have been tanks by the wall with a pump below. The metalwork that would have attached to the hoses is still on the wall of what is now the School Psychology Department. In the 1940s, Ken Laxton worked here as a mechanic, under the supervision of Mr Francis. As a trainee mechanic, Ken initially started work "pumping-up tyres" and looking into solving vehicle problems. He later ran this business when David Francis' father went to war. After the war, the garage business moved to Benefield Road (both the corner sales office and the workshops). Ken moved with the business and Duck Lane was closed as a business. According to Virginia Francis, "Time stood still" for the business after this.

The Berrystead is set back from the main road. Its' name denotes a nearby location to the growing cemetery site and was 'Burysted'. It was built in the late seventeenth-century as a gentleman's town-house by William Whitwell.[151] He was a London lawyer (whose ancestors built the newer parts of the Talbot). He left behind him a legacy of buildings. The Berrystead House was later owned by Thomas Hunt. In this grade-I listed building is a co-educational House, accommodating the younger boarders. I note here that Queen Victoria (Alexandrina, 1819–1901) travelled via Oundle on her way from Northampton to Stamford in November 1844. Outside the Berrystead and set into the footpath, there are cobbles with the word 'Jubilee' marked in differently coloured stones. The pattern dates to Victoria's golden jubilee in 1887. The cobbles have become worn and some have been

---

[151] Whitwell died in 1711, his son, also named William, went to Oundle School.

replaced over the years, so this is not quite as clear as it would have been at its time of design. It is said that this face of the building was once thought of as the back, as the imposing East Road lawns were considered to be the front.

Mr M.W. Brown moved from Christ's College, Cambridge to join the Oundle School staff in 1895. He was ordained three years on, at the close of 1898 and was married a couple of years later. In Sanderson's book on his work in Oundle School (The Years of Achievement, 1901-1822) the esteemed headmaster wrote that he wanted to set-up a preparatory house. In 1901, the Reverend Martin William Brown having married, moved from Laxton and "opened, with three young boys, his preparatory house in the Berrystead, an old family house, belonging to the Ward Hunt trustees, with one of the best gardens in Oundle. The name of Mr. Brown's house was first given in the blue book of January 1907". In 1923, Brown's wife donated an adorned Altar Cloth to the Oundle School Chapel. Sanderson noted that since Brown had bought the Berrystead in 1911, "the plan for building a special house was never revived". By this time, the school number of pupils had "risen to one hundred and eighty: with the consent of the Committee there were forty-six at School House, thirty-two at Dryden, eighty-two in the hostels (but two were to be absent for the term) and three with Mr. Brown; there were also seventeen day boys". Housing was gradually becoming an issue as pupil numbers increased. Sanderson wrote that "Lodgings had been taken for three masters in the old Sidney, which was not the Company's property and in part had reverted to the name of Knaptoft, given by Mr. Willson to the building of 1640. But, after paying for the temporary chapel and the hostel kitchens, the Court of 18 December 1901 unanimously decided to defer all new outlay on buildings at Oundle to a more convenient season."[152]

Flanked by Berrystead and Laundimer Houses is a smaller and less-noticeable school building. Known as Mowbray's, it was once run as a "Temperance Hotel" alcohol-free inn. Mr Charles Henry Curtis (a plumber and decorator) ran his business from here in the 1930s. David Wills' maternal grandmother ("Mrs Curtis") lived in Mowbrays and ran

---

[152] Sanderson p.508-9.

the Temperance Hotel and cafe. Unlike other Oundle inns this one did not serve alcohol, hence the name. Mowbray's cafe originally had a bow-window looking out into the street, but this has been altered. Temperance Societies and Hotels were created in direct response to drunkenness and other excesses. The British Association for the Promotion of Temperance was established in 1835 and promoted abstinence from alcohol and clean living. Meanwhile, non-conformist groups' lobbied parliament to bring about laws to limit alcohol sales. The Temperance Hotel may have attracted some customers and put off others![153]

It later became as the business premises for Mr Manning and Mr Brice, who were (1960s) plumbers and decorators. When Oundle School purchased the building it was renamed 'Mowbrays'. This occurred in the 1970s, in memory of an 'Oundle old boy', Kenneth Mowbray. Kenneth attended Dryden House from 1910 to 1914 and was a keen cricket player. He was killed in action (on 9th April 1917) while leading his men in an attack in the Battle of Arras. He was aged just 20.[154]

Sue Crick (née Crawley) said, "You may think this strange, but I love refectory eating". She mused that "it may be due to the fact that I grew up in a public school town and have enjoyed refectory meals on many occasions". Sue continued, "One of my early recollections of a refectory was in the late-1950s, when I was a young teenager and worked in the dining room of Bramston House at Oundle School". Sue continued, "At the time, the dining-room was on the upper floor and the kitchen was in the basement, therefore everything had to be sent up to the dining-room on a manually-operated dumb-waiter. On a Saturday evening my workmates and I would take along a change of clothes so that we could rush off after work to the local 'hop'.[155] The fashion of the day was bright, fluorescent pink petticoats, which looked like a mass of candy-floss and made your skirt stick out. My friends dared me to get in to the dumb-waiter. As I was never the one that stood at the back of the crowd, in I got. I was soon comfortably in position. My naughty friends pulled on the ropes and before I had time

---

[153] Oral history, David Wills.
[154] With thanks to Oundle School: Recollections from WWI and K.J.W. Mowbray, C. Pendrill, Yarrow Fellow.
[155] Dance.

to shout at them, I arrived in the dining room looking like a mass of pink froth. The boys thought it was hilarious, banged the cutlery on the tables and made a lot of noise. The stern housemaster, the Reverend P.O.C. Edwards did not think it funny and gave me the sack on the spot."[156]

In 1976, Josephine Black (née Smith) worked in the refectory (situated to the back of this building). She was sixteen years old. Mowbray House was where the permanent kitchen staff resided. Lodgings freely came as part of the modest salary, so did not constitute as rent. Health and Safety was 'out of the window'! For a fire escape from the top floor, the means of escape was a wide canvas strap-belt. This was attached to the eaves of the roof and was housed in a black, leather box with a sturdy 'tool-box' style clasp. It was by the windows so that, in the instance of fire, it could be placed around the body like a waist-band. Josephine explained that the general idea was that "you stepped out onto the roof and abseiled down to the ground". (No-one had tried it.) Josephine also recalls that on the third floor, above the street level, there was a small door that opened between the eaves of the two rooves, adjacent to Mowbray House. The tiny door led to a 'sun-trap' world unseen and out onto a gulley (that made for an excellent place to lie down out of sight) where the girls could sunbathe "and get frazzled".[157]

The 'serving' job in the refectory entailed, wiping down the long tables, counting and polishing the cutlery, then setting out the cutlery on the tables, followed by stacking the plates near to the serving-hatches. Then despatching food from the hot-plate surface onto plates (after the chefs had cooked it) once the boys had entered the separate, House dining-rooms. Josephine said, "To fill the jugs of milk for the tables you had to get it from a churn in the walk in fridge". She felt that "it was a bit scary to go into the fridges, but lovely and cool when the kitchens were so hot. If only they had extractor fans in those days!" Whilst still at school in the 1970s, Maria Jackson worked in the refectory during the weekends to earn extra pocket-money. One day, she put the dessert plates into the hotplate in error (as it was jelly for dessert). A boy laughed at her, so she slapped him. Mr Shingles, the

---

156 Sue Crick, personal history.
157 Josephine Black (née Smith) personal history.

housemaster, did not chastise Maria as he said the boy had been rude![158] Maria was quite a character. (Many years later she was driving to work when a policeman waved at her. She politely waved back. On arriving at work she found that the policeman had actually been trying to flag her down!)

When Josephine first started work at the refectory, her wage was £12 per week [cash in hand for forty-two hour working week]. This was an improvement from the shilling per week people earned in 1900. The cost of living has changed dramatically. In the 1950s, a Dinky toy cost 3/6d (three shillings and six pence). It cost a "guinea for a jacket" (twenty-one shillings) in 1963.[159] In the early 1970s, the wage for working in the refectory for Sunday morning to the first part of the afternoon was 50 pence per hour for part-time, local staff (and this was usually seen as pocket-money for local school girls).[160]

One of the incarnations of the "Coffee Tavern" was situated in 'Mowbrays' in 1886. The Women's Temperance Society held their meetings here. In the early 1900s, Edward P. Monckton and his family owned Laundimer and Mowbrays. The Grocer's Company purchased these buildings as part of the School. Both had pedestrian access to East Road and North Street. This was changed long ago. In mid-2017, Mowbrays needed updating, which included removing the Meeting Room toilet partitions to create space for a shower room. New toilets and a new sick-bay with a shower and 'wash-room' are planned for the new surgery. The plan is to make an opening between the buildings by removing some of the stonework, which will be later reused to complete the door surrounds. The contiguous refectories for the Laundimer, Berrystead and Old Dryden staff-families and boys are located and accessed between 'Mowbrays' and Laundimer House buildings.

Laundimer House was built in 1810 as part of the School boarding-houses for boys. It has extensive outside grounds that stretch to East Road. (These can be reached via a gate in Duck Lane.) To the rear is an enclosed garden, a football pitch and tennis court. Mr Michael Shiels

---

[158] Family history, Sharon Cottingham (née Jackson).
[159] Oral history, Dr Richard B. Allen.
[160] Anna Fernyhough.

(from 50 North Street) was the Laundimer Houseman in the 1960s and 1970s. Laundimer House was the residence of Fitzpatrick Henry Vernon (Lord Lyvden, 1804-1900; died in Kensington, aged 96). He lived in the house from the 1860s to the 1880s, with his wife, Albreda. (The couple married in 1853. Albreda died in 1891, aged 62). Albreda Vernon was named Albreda Elizabeth Wentworth-Fitzwilliam. She was born in 1829. Her parents were Charles and Mary Fitzwilliam. 'Robert' (later Baron) Vernon-Smith was the Member of Parliament for Northamptonshire in the mid-nineteenth-century). Laundimer House (Master's residence) was acquired by the School in 1916.

Latham's Alms Houses

The House for Laundimer is attached to number 24 (Parson Latham's Alms Houses). These are gated, with a courtyard at the front and gardens stretching to East Road in the rear. Latham's Hospital was founded in 1611 in North Street and is grade-II listed. The alms-houses were partially rebuilt in 1830. The northern part was a 'Blue Coat school' to the mid-nineteenth-century. The building consists of an E-shaped two storey building with gables facing the street to either side of elaborate gateways. The material used was pre-used limestone. The mullioned windows give an indication of the age of this large house. Latham's Hospital continues to provide a home for elderly ladies, but the Bluecoat school merged with Church of England Primary School in the late nineteenth-century and closed in 1905. The two courtyards are entered via stone gateways, decorated with a cross and an eagle standing over a baby in swaddling clothes (a crest of the Latham and Stanley families). Parson Latham (buried in Barnwell) founded the Oundle Hospital with a constitution giving authority to local 'hospitals' with specific eligibility for locals. At that time a 'hospital' was a place of refuge for the poor, disabled or elderly, rather than a medical establishment. Parson Latham had already (through his Will) had a similar mission in his home village, Barnwell, of alms-houses (around a courtyard) and school (in 1604; currently leased by the Duke of Buccleugh Trust to Little Ducklings Pre-School). All of the Parson Latham charities that were established are each managed by individual groups of Trustees.

Sharon Cottingham's 'Nan' (Annie Jackson) lived for a while in these Alms Houses. Sharon recalled her visit to Annie and new 'pinnies' she and her sisters were given (see earlier in this volume).[161] On my part, I recall crossing North Street (from my grandparent's house) to go to the Hospital alms house to talk with Miss Ginny and also to Miss Mary-Jane Cates (who died in 1968, aged 84) through her road-side window. 'Auntie Ginny', who was related to the Craythorne family, was a very frail and gentle lady. A sensory memory is that she smelled "a bit like Parma-violets". She would wave at people she knew and would to lean on her stone window-ledge passing her time talking with people who went by. Elderly ladies continue to live here until they are too ill or infirm (when they are transferred to a care-home or hospital).

In the 1930s Mr and Mrs Perring lived at number 26, in what was then a tithe-house for primary school heads. (It bears the same swan coat-of-arms above its gate as the alms houses.) As Mrs Perring was the headmistress she and her family lived at 26 as part of a financial arrangement for each primary school head to reside here.

The 'Blue Coat School' was also housed here. It had the space for 'thirty poor men's sons, chosen out of the town of Oundle'. Parson Latham's Hospital Trust now manage his educational foundation and award grants towards the costs of further education for applicable children of the town. There is also an allowance for school equipment that can be applied for from the Trustees. Head-teacher, Mabel Perring invited local children to her house at weekends and for entertainment and exercises. The Denley family lived in the same house for many years. There is an enclosed staircase to the left of the courtyard that led up from the courtyard to the bedrooms. This had previously been the route upstairs to the classrooms and the coat hooks for the children's coats are still there on the walls of the staircase. Sheila Denley believes that the house was downstairs and it is believed that there was an art school held in the house at some point. (After Alan Denley retired, Parson Latham's alms houses have occupied the old school house and its garden.)

During the 1930s & 1940s, number 28 belonged to the butcher, Frank Seaton. (His son, Robert Seaton and his siblings grew up here.) Their shop was easily located with a ceramic pigs' head (with an apple in its mouth) clearly displayed in the large window. The meat was delivered

---

[161] Pinafores or aprons.

around the back in East Road and then was carried into the shop via the house corridor. Number 32 has a large window and, in the 1950s, it was Mr and Mrs Horner's shop. Percy Arnett recalled that "In North Street, there was Seaton's butchers' passageway, then a sweet shop with paned-windows." The Carpenter family lived at number 30 from the 1950s to 1970s. It once had a shop-front with large windows that were replaced with new stone work.[162] The external, lower walls and windows have been modernised and altered. Peter Hooton recalls that his family ran the original 'Coffee Tavern' here and it kept the name when it moved to the market place. The upper floors still demonstrate some original masonry. Miss Valerie Carpenter and her elderly father, John, lived here from the 1950s to the 1970s. Their house was divided into flats, so they rented a flat to the local USAF families. Until her death in the 1990s, Valerie was a stalwart of the Oundle and District Care Committee.

Sellers' fruit shop and Young's sweet shop were based somewhere along this stretch of the road. In the 1930s, 32, sold a large range of hardware items: lamps, buckets, and other tools, nails, screws and fasteners. Number 34 was originally an Inn named "The Carpenter's Arms". It had stables behind, adjoining East Road that was the Hillyard family home for over fifty years. The workshops are still intact. The main room in the house is carefully crafted with pine panelling and the finish of the internal decoration is old. Number 36 is currently being restored. Philip Slater[163] (who married in 1905 and died in 1973) and his wife, Alice, lived here in the 1950s. (Ted Hooton was a lodger for a short time.) Mr Slater worked at Oundle School. Barbara Chester would cross the road to play the piano with their daughter, Molly. The passage-way to the back of 34 and 36 led to the washroom and then to some one-up one-down cottages. These caught fire and needed restoration work.[164] In the 1950s and 1960s, number 38 was rented to American families from local air bases. The Hillyard family (née Leigh) moved here post-marriage. Attached to the rear of the North Street house is 'Hillyard's of Oundle', a wholesale plant nursery, accessed from East Road. The house had a small, self-contained building at the

---

[162] Oral history, Peter Hooton.
[163] His sister is Ruth Keans.
[164] Oral history, Matthew G. Seward.

back, which has been periodically rented.[165] Numbers 40 to 44 were also once shops.

From 1930 to the 1950s, number 46 sold plumbing, buckets, sinks and baths, yet this house deserves much more of an accolade, with a history that dates to the sixteenth-century and probably earlier. The original plot was owned with Havelock cottages, plus 29 and 31 East Road, which have, since, been separately sold. The house was held by Solomon Pierce, who bought "East Court House" (with Havelock cottages, to the rear, formerly named "East Court Cottages"; which may have been 'converted' from 'barn buildings' at one time). The building was initially L-shaped with a garden to the front left side, where a similar half to the house now stands. To the inside-right stands the main hall, above which (upstairs) was the parlour. 46 North Street has a well-documented history dating from the sixteenth-century. There was a 'drastic' rebuild in 1700, but the earlier beams and south-end front-room survived.

In 1736, the house and cottages were bequeathed to offspring and were divided into three: Thomas Cooke, Lyonell Cooke and Elizabeth Asquith-Dodson (née Cooke) owned the parts. The timber-framed, small-hall house was where people could congregate. It comprised of a hall, house and solar above. Originally black-and-white, the current frontage was added around 1850. It remains one of the oldest houses in North Street. Its original beamed ceilings and walls, wide fireplace (with a single, long beam supporting the projecting breast), plaster work and stud-wall date from the early 1600s.[166]

The house hides an early-seventeenth-century priest-hole that is entered from above. The act of installing a hidden priest-hole in a house from this period strongly suggests that some of the inhabitants of Oundle hid dissenting Catholics in the late Tudor and early Stuart era. The house was split in the rebuild, with a rear kitchen. In the twentieth century, the house was "knocked through" into the two nearest cottages that now form part of the house. The whole house front is newer than its rear and the roof has curious, triangular gable-

---

[165] Molly Slater lived here. When Molly married she retained her maiden-name rather than use Ludwinowicz.
[166] With thanks to Bernard Kay.

pieces at the ends of each apex. The house has a small back-garden with a flowering fig tree.

Solomon Pierce purchased the main house along with Havelock cottages. He lived in the main house until his demise at the age of seventy. Solomon was buried by the parish Church in 1839. The property was bequeathed to his wife, Susannah. The house was then transferred to John Allen and Esther Woolley. Later, William Clark and George Ireland lived in the house, followed by George Phillips, William Stafford and 'Widow' Owen.

In 1925, it was the home of Miss Bertha Metcalfe, a spinster, before it was sold to builder, Mr William Walter Assiter. The front, right window dates to 1850, which was when the front wall was extended, but the window to the left was changed by Mr Assiter. He bought the house with 1-14 Havelock Cottages (East Road). These were used as the malting's office for a time. He sold the cottages, made alterations to the house front in 1939 and lived here until 1963. Renowned artist, Bernard Kay bought the house after moving from London. Prior to this move to the country, he spent three years in Liverpool School of Art, two years in the Royal Academy Art School and a year in Paris. Bernard's work is mainly in oils and fine etching. In his youth, he "rubbed shoulders" with many famous painters and artists, including Pablo Picasso; yet had a very special career of his own in the art field. He has exhibited all over the world and says of his sanctuary here, "I had a very good career in art for thirty-five plus years in London and didn't really like Oundle when I first visited". Yet, his home has been in Oundle for nearly forty years. He happily said that he steadily "grew to like it".

When Bernard first bought the property it came as a plot with the nearest two rear cottages. A 'private' entrance to East Road and Havelock was a public right-of-way until the 1990s. There was once an open 'paddock' alongside this, a double-gated yard, which was used for storing glass from the brewery that was to be melted down and recycled. Two 1980s in-fill houses (46b and c) stand between the original dwellings on this paddock, which were designed to merge with the existing houses.

Next-door was land where 46 a, b and c were built in the 1970s. Also once brewer's houses, 48 and 50 are two long, rubble-stone houses with bay-windows that stretched out of sight to the rear. In the 1930s, Mr Wallinger lived in both houses with its long, central courtyard (this hidden behind large doors). In the 1960s, Christine White lived in 48 with her parents. Susan Moore's sister, Carol Palmer lived in 48 later in that decade. In the 1990s, Humphrey and Joy Cruttwell lived here with their lovely court-yard garden. In the 1960s, Michael and Bridget Shiels lived at number 50, with their three children. Michael and his wife were originally from Ireland (one from the North and one from the South). The family were a mainstay of St. Wilfrid's Church. Michael worked as a caretaker for Laundimer House. There was a large workshop inside the compound on the right (dating to its time as an ironmonger or ferrier) and the yard stretched all the way to East Road.

The four terraced cottages (by the current traffic lights) are stone workmen's houses dating to the 1600s. The oldest of the group is south of the others. The one nearest to the corner of Fotheringhay Mews is slightly younger. The beams in the oldest denotes their construction at around 1520. By the twentieth century they were owned by the local brewery.

At one time, Smith's brewery was the foremost employer of townspeople. The 'brewery people' (workers and their families) lived in these cottages in the 1920s to 1960s. In the 1960s they had mains-piped water outside, but not indoors. Around the same era, electricity had been installed in them. During the latter days of the John Smith's brewery the four families were Ida Faulkner and her family, Joe Condor and his family, John Lilley and his family and Mrs Denny and her family. Mrs Lilley was a great friend of Mrs Betty Pope (from 39). They frequently met for tea and a chat at each other's houses. North Street is a very convivial street, but perhaps that is the nature of old Oundle.

In the 1970s, these ancient houses were rented out to USA air force personnel who were stationed in Molesworth and Alconbury, along with their families. I recall babysitting for two of the families who lived there, Glenda and Mike Way and their three children, Terri, Tobi and Michael Junior. The stairs would always creek when tiptoeing upstairs to check on the children and I was worried it would wake them! When the United States Air Force Alconbury branch cut its staffing, the small houses were less in demand from American short-term visitors. The Way family returned to the States in 1974. The cottages were rented to workers of the brewery by the Ludlow family. The bath-houses for workers were located in what is now 'Fotheringhay Mews' Maltings. The hook-and-hoist with its boxed-in lift-space is still visible and retained at roof height. Bags of grain were hoisted up into the building by this apparatus. This is where the barley was taken to be crushed to make the beer. The inner workings of the buildings were remodelled around a courtyard to make pleasant town-houses. During the 1940s, behind the cottages and current brewery Maltings of Smith's was a carriage and vehicle repair shop (once the horse-yard for drays to transport and distribute the beer kegs) and a dray yard.[167]

North Street (west side)

Laxton School (which is now the day student part of Oundle School) is the first building on this side of the road. It has a door near to the bus stop at the corner of North Street. This was the first site of the school endowed by William Laxton. There is a phoenix holding a standard on the roof. The building on the corner is the Guildhall that was founded in 1485. This 'Guildhall School' closed during the reign of Edward VI (son of Henry VIII), when it became a grammar school for boys. The current building dates to 1855. There is a slightly faded plaque on the eastern wall (above the door) in Latin, Greek and Hebrew reminding us of the original benefactors.

Laxton School cloisters are inside the bounds of the Church yard. It dates back to the mid-1500s when Sir William Laxton, Lord Mayor of London and Master of the Worshipful Company of Grocers, endowed a 'Free Grammar School' in Oundle. In the town where he had been educated (at the original 'Gild School' founded in 1506). Prior to the Reformation a guild school was held in Oundle Parish Church. William Laxton formed a grammar school with a small number of housing places for the poor. The guild house stood on the south-east corner of the Church yard (Laxton School cloisters). The school building was

---

[167] The dray was a wagon or horse-drawn trolley. Dray horses were 'draft' horses.

rebuilt in 1855 and replaced the old school building, alms house and Guildhall on this site.[168]

The northern part of the Church yard was the site of a Royal Manor, although determining exactly where it stood is difficult. The manor, rectory, church and associated buildings and land were enclosed within a walled-boundary from the Market, North Street and Blackpot Lane to behind the current Talbot Hotel. It is also believed to be the site of the monastery that St. Wilfrid founded. In the seventh century, this was possibly the centre of the 'Province of Oundle' and was likely part of an eastern or outer-Mercian kingdom.

A Christian community built around the Church has existed in Oundle since before 709 AD, the year that Saxon saint Wilfrid died in the Church that stood on the spot where St Peter's Church building now stands. The Church is Early English. It is decorated and perpendicular in style. The masonry of the building is mainly from the 1300s, with a fifteenth-century tower. St. Peter's spire dates to 1634, when it was rebuilt. There is a small room for priests to stay in over the porch. In the 1990s, fitted carpets covered parts of the floor and chairs were bought to replace the benches. New toilets were constructed at the back of the church in early 2017.

The original graveyard extended to New Street, which was at that time called "Bury Street". Many pastors have officiated at St. Peter's, including the Reverend Hopkins (1876) Canon William Smalley-Law (early 1900s)[169], Canon Downe and Canon Cartwright (50s-60s), Canon Cockin (60s-70s), Reverend Lloyd Caddick (70s-80s) and Richard Ormston (from the 1990s and early 2000s), who was much missed on his departure to Northampton. Stephen Webster and Jema Ball currently officiate and welcome newcomers.

The Parish Church has a long-run tiny-tots group and an annual multi-denomination carol-service in the market area by the Christmas tree. St. Peter's has activities for all that include curry nights, Ploughman's suppers, walks, barn dances, an exploration and outings group hosts visits to local places of interest with afternoon tea. Joyce Tompkins

---

[168] A guildhall is a town-hall used by guilds for meetings and ceremonies.
[169] The 'Northampton Mercury' (1940) notes the death of Mrs Clara Catherine Smalley-Law, widow of Canon Smalley Law, vicar of Oundle for 26 years.

runs the Mothers' Union, an evening women's group and their speakers, a Tuesday afternoon 'social' with games, tea and cakes. Sheila Wills organises a Thursday Coffee group (that is open to all) and Latham's Teas (held for retired women) in North Street. The Green group is trying to reduce the Church's carbon footprint. Oundle Town Council and the vicars are making the Church yard wildlife friendly. St Peter's has solar panels on the roof that generate nearly half their annual electricity consumption.

A cobbled, drive leads to the old Rectory, where John William Smith (father of the brewer) lived in the late 1800s. The rectory building was used by Anglian Water, Nene River Board Offices and subsequently was destined to become the Oundle School Gascoigne building. From the 1930s to the 1960s fetes and parties were held in the gardens. As a child of the 1930s, Barbara Chester attended these fetes. She said "they sold lovely flowers in the Rectory" and recalls rolling on its grass mounds with friends. In these gardens were caged pheasants and other birds. A pond with large koi-carp was opposite the building entrance (In the 1960s). When it was the Anglian Water Authority's regional office, Ann Greetham (née Colclough) worked in the "front office". This was in the 1960s. Ann recalls that "the wall inside had a mural, painted in the war that depicted a girl in a bikini". It is probably not there now!

The houses on North Street that backed on to these grounds were frequently treated to the croaked refrains from frogs that had managed to make their way through the wall and into their gardens.[170] The "Opera" house is a small building to the rear of the North Street thatched cottage (9). It is opposite the main building and gained its name as the water company workers were in the operatic society, so company props were stored here. The Oundle Gilbert and Sullivan has been running for over sixty years. Its forbearer was the Oundle Operatic Society.

War time evacuees and their families stayed in the Rectory. A little later, it was rented to the army. They had guards on duty at the main gates. There there is an old engraving on the stone wall. This is a mileage distance marker for North Street indicating "Peterborough 13

---

[170] Oral history, Barbara Mudza (née Chester).

miles/Thrapston Cross 7¾ miles." Slightly further along the same rectory wall there is a sign for O/R (designating the gateway to the old rectory building for "other ranks")[171]. The main drive was only used by important visitors and officers. The other ranks were lower, so these men had to pass along the alleyway to the side of number 5. The rights to this way have been re-designated and this appears to be part of the access to the garden of 5.

Number 5, now called the 'Manor house', was the home of the Moore family in the 1960s. Although no longer residing in Oundle, their eldest daughter, Susan, is a mainstay of the Oundle Secondary School reunion group. She has organised several meetings for the ex-pupils of the Secondary Modern and Primary School, which have been a chance to re-meet and catch-up. She recalls her early years in the house as being quite hard. The house was large, dark and quite rambling. The family took in a lodger, Mr Ernie Brindsley, who had lost his lodgings in St. Osyth's Lane. He was, by all accounts, a difficult lodger. Susie is convinced that during the time her family lived in the house it was haunted by a "shadowy, headless man who stood in the doorway at the top of the stairs". She went on to say that "he wears a habit, like a monk, and stands, unmoving with his arms folded".[172] The house has since been remodelled to allow more light inside.

Houses 7 and 9 share a garden and are reached via an external alley door. The first house (7) faces the street, but the rear house is not seen. The first was the home of Mrs Griggs, who was distressed and gassed herself after the death of her husband. To the rear of 7 is number 9, a thatched cottage built in 1483, while 7 dates to 1600. The thatched stone cottage is two-storey with brink stacks. The front is rendered (white) with casement windows. Miss Irene Harriett Boult (1895-1974), who formed and ran Oundle Brownies, lived in this thatched cottage from the 1950s until the 1970s. She encouraged girls to take part in community work. Her thatched house is one of two that survive in Oundle, despite a proliferation of thatches in nearby Ashton, this is not endorsed in Oundle's history. Conservation work carried out

---

[171] The wall has a squad number and "O/R" (Other Ranks), denoting that ordinarily-ranked men could pass this way, whereas officers could enter via the main gate.
[172] Oral history, Susan Moore. Susie noted that Helen Lee and Jennifer Piggin (née Moore) also witnessed an apparition.

in mid-2017 included the removal of its concrete floor and internal cement-and-gypsum plaster, an extension of the chimney stack and reopening of a window in the gable wall. In her younger days, Miss Boult had worked as a children's Nanny for Dr. Fisher (Oundle School Headmaster).

Susie Moore recalls "watching Princess Margaret's wedding in Westminster Abbey" on 6th May 1960 at Miss Boult's house, "as she had a television" (that was very new to Oundle in this era) and kindly invited local families in to watch the spectacle. She loved to have visits from the local children and passed on her love of knots and Morse code to her young visitors! Wendy Bollans said that the discrete cottage reminds her of mum's house. Everything had its place as it was quite small inside. She recalled a table by the window, where she would clean the brass items and silver cutlery.[173] Using the window light meant that she could save on electricity. As a Brownie Leader she was definitely thrifty.

Number 11 in the 1940s was the home of Mrs Harris, who continuously "banged on items in her house" and on the wall of her neighbours in number 13. The residents nearby were annoyed and she was "called on by the police". (This apparently did not stop her!). It's believed that she was lonely, but would not tolerate minor disturbances. Bearing in mind that this was a time before television, it is understood that Britain is quieter in more recent years. Studies of sounds in towns and cities (kept at the British Library) indicate that technical advancements from 1940, combined with the "lost art of whistling", have reduced urban sounds to create a more peaceful environment.[174] The chirping of sparrows, jovial whistling and hiss of steam-engines were replaced by the bleep of supermarket tills and the sound of public address systems, yet noise levels in our pedestrianised town centres have reduced. This is not to our detriment. In the 1970s and 1980s number 13 was owned by the Hony family. They did not live in it, but rented it out. Viv Hony

---

[173] Oral history, Wendy Bollans (née Mudza).
[174] The British Library sound archive "Save our Sounds" project compares today's street noises with recordings from the 1940s. "Listen: 140 Years of Recorded Sound" (October 2017 to March 2018).

was a mathematics teacher at Oundle School and published books on the subject. Mrs Hony continues to live in Oundle.

Number 13 (from 1930 until the 1990s) was the home of the Chester family. Arthur Chester was, at one time, the oldest Oundle survivor of the Somme offensive. He survived mustard gassing, but lost his twin brother at the age of seventeen in the First World War (WWI). House number 13 is a storey higher than 11 and 15. I recall browning bread on a toasting-fork before an open-fire in the 'front-room' with my grandma, Dorothy. The blackened fire-back was embossed with a picture of a phoenix. When flames licked upward, the phoenix was mesmerising and magical to watch.[175] Their house had two ground-floor rooms: a 'front room' parlour and a kitchen, which served as the main living room of the house.

The wireless was kept in the kitchen. Food was kept in the outdoor 'cold-safe', just outside the back-door. It had a slab for cold-meats, cheese and butter. Milk was kept fresh in a glass bottle placed into a metal bucket filled with cold water. This was life before refrigerators and freezers! In times before electric-lights people used candles and oil lamps. "I bought an oil lamp to enhance my Victorian house, but the first time I lit it, smoke filled the room and we had to stand the lamp in the garden!"

In 1940, Mr Chester (from number 13) and other brave Oundle men, served in the WWI, then was a member of the Home Guard throughout WWII. The Home Guard were Local Defence Volunteers, responsible for protecting their home town. The men who served could not join the regular army as their jobs were necessary to keep the country running. These were often the essential farm workers, bakers, bank staff, railway workers and men too young, too old or unwell enough to prevent them joining the regular army. Mr Chester had been gassed in WWI and (aged over forty) was too old to serve in WWII. The Home Guard were given rudimentary military training. Farmers donated their shotguns and arms. At night they patrolled the town and fields, looking for enemy planes or parachutes, reporting incidents and hoping to slow any invasion forces. When his great-grandad died, my son, Mark, helped to sort and empty his house. I explained that grandad Arthur's

---

[175] Anna Fernyhough, personal history.

things would be "given to a charity, for people who may want them". Mark looked at the pile and said, "So can anyone have them?" I affirmed this and he said, "Well, I want them. Can I have his walking stick and his hat?" From that day on, Mark has had these memory items from his great-grandad.

In WWII, the families in the houses from 13 to 19 all volunteered and hosted young evacuees sent from London during the bombing. The evacuees were with them for long enough to start school and settle in so much as to call their hosts 'auntie'. Over the course of the war, Arthur and Dorothy Chester had three sets of evacuees staying with them. The first were two boys, which seemed a little inappropriate, as they had a small daughter and Dorothy was not used to bathing boys.

During the war years the early cruise-missile doodlebugs over London lessened and then renewed.[176] During these periods the children returned home to their parents. After a while, new children came. This time Dorothy was responsible for the care of two out of a family of three girls: Pearl Rochford was the eldest, Vera was a middle child and the smallest was Ruth. ('Ruthie' was aged around three or four at that time.) Pearl came to the Chester household with her little sister, while Vera (the middle child) was billeted with Fred Carter and his family who lived nearby. The family spent most of its time in the kitchen, as the front room was reserved for special days and visitors. Ruthie came in to the kitchen, where they were chatting and cooking. She immediately spotted Barbara sitting on a buffet-stool by the fire. Ruth asked if she could sit with her on the matching buffet on the other side of the fire. This then became her 'spot'. She settled quickly and asked Dorothy what she should call her as she had noticed that Barbara called her 'Mummy'. From this moment Dorothy became "Mummy Chester" to the evacuee girls. Later in the war, the girls returned to Oundle for a second stay with their host families. Dorothy was saddened that there had been a swap around that she could do little about. Ruth had been housed with their neighbours instead of with them. This did not stop

---

[176] Grace Gordine (later Fernyhough) worked in the Admiralty buildings on Whitehall, London, throughout WWII. She often talked about the Admiral she had been assigned to, who would not go down to the shelters when the air-raid sirens sounded. Instead, he would carry on working or go to the roof to watch. The V-1 flying bomb was referred to as the 'buzz bomb'. When its engine stopped buzzing it dropped.

Ruth from visiting or playing with her friend next-door. The wartime evacuation was a marked moment in all of their lives. They never forgot their Oundle hosts. It is worth noting that all four girls stayed in touch throughout their lives, even after the war had finished. To this day, Ruth and Barbara still talk on the telephone and send each other cards on birthdays and at Christmas times. Barbara Mudza (née Chester) has fond memories of the evacuees who stayed with her parents over eighty years ago. The children settled into school very well as they were often in the same classes as the children from the families they were staying with.

Another memory that Barbara remembers is being aged around ten or eleven. She went down to the river with her friends to do some "'tiddler' fishing, with nets". She recalls that on one day there were Italian prisoners of war cutting the reeds and improving the river flow. Two of them helped the girls to catch minnows and sticklebacks. The girls went home happily with their jam-jar of tiny fish. Mum, Dorothy, was not sure "what to make of this" and was worried about letting the girls return. Later, when they did, the P.O.W.s had gone further upstream with their task.

There is a salutary story of when Grandad caught his 'fake', cotton-wool, beard alight on Christmas candles in the war years. He went to a friend's party at the Denny's house at 37 North Street (subsequently demolished). As Mr Denny was in the army (so was not at home) Arthur offered to dress as Father Christmas for the family. He used fake eyebrows and glued-on a cotton-wool beard. Unfortunately, one of the lit candles fell from the Christmas tree and Arthur moved to help to extinguish the flames. Whoosh, he was alight! His wife, Dorothy, tried to tear-off the beard. Her slipper caught alight as she used it to beat out the flames, so it was quickly thrown into the snow outside. The children had quite an exciting and surprising visit from Father Christmas - and Arthur came away with some burns to remind him to be more careful next time.

At my grandparents' house in (13) North Street, there was an outdoor a stone-built 'cupboard' that was almost opposite the back-door of the house. It was used as a cold store. It was always cool, no matter what the weather was like outside. It was used for cheese, meat, milk and butter. Grandad called it the "safe" and kept a bucket of water there

254

for glass bottles to stand in. The milkman would deliver daily and the milk was placed in the cool. There was a large stone slab inside and a small-hole, wire, rigid-screen, aerated door. Grandad grew wisteria over the top (which must have also helped to keep it cool). War-time families were largely self-sustaining; supplementing purchased foods by growing their own vegetables in back gardens and on allotments. Many, including Grandad, rented a fertile patch on Blackpot Lane allotments, behind the buildings.

In 1970s, Billy Bragg (now famous for his left-wing political stance) rented number 15 and played in his band, Riff Raff.[177] He found Oundle was "not quite the headquarters of rock". In 1977, Stephen (Billy) Bragg formed a punk (and pub) rock-band: Riff Raff with Wiggy, and decamped to rural Oundle where they played at gigs in local villages: including Clopton and Brigstock. Josephine Black recalls dating the drummer, Bobby, while her flatmate dated the lead guitarist, Gary. She said they were 'groupies' and loved the music. She remembers going to London with Bobby to meet his family and had 'weird, spicy food'. The band split when Gary died. Billy returned to London and became a celebrity, but his home in North Street remains an integral part of history.

In the 1930s until the 1960s many people did not move around, but stayed in one house. At number 15, there was Arthur Frederick Marshall (known as 'Fred') and Annie Elizabeth known as "Lizzie" (née Craythorne) Marshall. I recall Lizzie making junket (a sort of milk-curd, set pudding) and asking if I would like to try it. They thought of Barbara and her family as 'relatives'. Evacuees, Joyce and Ethel, stayed with the family throughout the war and retained strong links afterwards. Lizzie and Fred, had a daughter of their own, Phyllis Craythorne (later Conder). The house had an outside 'cold store' and outside toilets at the bottom of the garden. At this point there was no indoor plumbing.

Number 17 was the home of Mr & Mrs Coles. The *Northampton Mercury* of April 1906 reported that "at Blott's farm, Oundle, Bertram Hutchinson, favoured with instructions from Mr. J.C. Siddons, will sell

---

[177] His landlord of the time said that he wouldn't ever rent his house again. He did change his mind, but the new tenant was a young lady, from local families and not in the pop business.

by auction (without reserve) on Thursday April 19th 1906, fifty Lincoln Red steers and heifers". I have tried with little success to locate Blott's land, but know that it was in Oundle. I assume that it was probably sold and built on during the twentieth century. By 1939, an old farmer, Thomas Blott had been widowed. He owned lands towards Peterborough. For a time, he lodged at 17 North Street, with Alfred and Rose Coles. Their son, Ken, married and moved from Oundle when (in 1953), he wed Margaret, the sister of their evacuee, Bill.) The house stretches to the back and has gardens behind it. The gardens link with those of numbers 11, 13 and 15 via a gate that is set into a tall wall.

In the 1930s, Mrs Jackson and her daughters, Hilary and Barbara lived at 19. Number 19 and 21 date to 1894. They both have garret (bedroom) windows in their roof spaces. Number 21 was where the Bunning family lived In the 1930s and 1940s. Evelyn and Kathleen Bunning (sisters) lived here. Evelyn later was Mrs Rootham. They were Norman Bunning's cousin (of Gordon Road). Numbers 19, 21 and 23 are terraced and identical in design. During the 1940s and 1950s Mr Mott and his son lived at number 23.

Number 25 is a large house with a drive into an L-shaped courtyard, a garden at the back and a garage in a barn-conversion. For modern families the drawback of many of these houses is a lack of car-parking. Quite often houses share a courtyard garden at the back (often via a shared passageway). If they are lucky they have a courtyard to park their cars in. The house occupants that ran businesses or were wealthier often had a carriage yard.

Captain and Mrs Barnes and their twin girls, Gwen and Judy, lived at number 25 from around the 1920s. Both girls married (one to a policeman). One sister lived in the market place over Moore's shop, while the other lived with her mother in North Street. Captain Barnes was attached to the School armoury that was located by the school swimming pool. In the mid-1940s, when the twins had children of their own, Barbara Chester became the nanny to their "two toddler boys". In the 1960s, John and Diana Rivett (née Harris) were married in Wellingborough in 1943. After the death of their middle child, David, in 1950, when he was aged just four. They settled in North Street with their children, Susan (1943) and Timothy (1953). Tim, their son (born in 1953) lives in America. For many years, Diana worked as the primary school secretary. In the 1990s, after John died, Diana sold her house to the Pearson family. She moved to the newly constructed 'Half Moon Mews' houses in Blackpot Lane and lived there for the remainder of her life.

Rex Ludlow and his brother Guy each owned four houses in the North Street. The houses were in a block. Rex had numbers 27, 29, 31 and 33. His brother, Guy, owned the brewery and houses 35, 37, 39 and 41. Plus the Talbot, which was purchased from their family in 1955. As the land was shared the initial plans and areas were not easily designated. Now that the idea of shared land has gone and ownership has taken over, measurements count.

A low, beamed roof and gated passage leads to 27 and 29. Just inside the passage-way is a small square alcove measuring not more than a foot (30 centimetres) square. It is believed that this was used storing delivered items. From the 1930s, these were combined as a house and 'barn'. This reverted back to being two dwellings in the 1990s. Grace and Larry Dexter lived here from the 1950s to 1970s. It may be that the conversion was affected by the Poll tax by re-adapting to two cottages. This reinstated their original designated numbers and saved money. Until the 1970s this house only had electric lighting downstairs. Grace and Larry took a candle to bed with them each night. When Larry died, Grace moved to live in Latham's Alms Houses.

Number 31 is a house that dates to the 1600s or earlier. It is hidden from sight of the road and looks out onto its own carefully tended garden. It was rented by Rex Ludlow until the early 1950s as a 'brewery house'. Two old ladies who were known as "the Gray sisters" lived here together in the 1920s until the mid-1940s. It is believed that Sarah Gray was blind for over forty years. She worked from home making hearth-rugs and sewing cloth pieces onto canvas as rug-backing. Barbara Mudza recalls that the younger sister worked at Coombs' solicitors.[178] It appears while they lived here they also were created millinery work. They were quite old when they moved out and the house was in need of repair. It could be that one died and the other moved, (Sarah was most probably ninety-six in 1936 and her sister around seven years her

---

[178] Oral history, Barbara Mudza (née Chester).

junior).[179] Nevertheless, Mr Lilley and his family lived here in the late-1940s and early 1950s. Mr Lilley worked for the brewery. He was 'very tall' and probably experienced problems with the heights of the ceilings (that measure only six feet up from the sloping floor). Decorating the house is problematic as none of the floors, ceilings or walls are straight! Until the late-1940s, the house had a porch over the front door and wooden shutters on the outsides of the windows. When the Ludlow brothers were old, the houses they owned were sold.

In 1955, Barbara and her husband, Lucjan Mudza, bought the house and began to make small repairs and changes. Barbara moved from number 13 after living there for twenty-five years. She is the resident who has the accolade of having lived in the street for the longest time (eighty-seven years to date). After moving here with her parents (from Cherry Orchard in the Benefield Road) in her first year. The wash-store side of the house was "knocked through" and converted into the current kitchen. The coal-shed in the garden of 31 was incorporated into use for the Pope family before the land was separated. The rooms have thick walls (with the wall between the kitchen and dining room being about three-feet wide). The stone, rear wall has a 'bulge', from perpetuity, while the doors each were (and have to be) individually constructed as they do not fit standard sizes. The front wall is constructed from multi-sized bricks. Tudor bricks are shallow with rounded right-angled edges and brickwork is characterised by thick joints of lime-rich mortar. The outside wall that adjoins 33 in the small courtyard had a well "that had been buried for years". It is now 'topped with a concrete slab'. Barbara said that "originally, it had a pump that was taken by the builders when 33 was renovated". She believes that the ground water is higher now as the well was filled-in with builders' rubble. In the 1960s a bathroom was added to 31, adjoined to the house by a small passage. Enlarged via the purchase of a strip of land, it stands where the old outdoor privy had been.

The family moved in to this small house when I, their first daughter, was a few months old. Their next child, Wendy, was born in the upstairs

---

[179] Barbara does not believe that either sister married. Another source implied Sarah was married to a grocer who ran his business from this house, also that the other woman (Anne?) was her daughter. I have no evidence for this and consider that Barbara is correct as she and her family knew the women.

bedroom. To make the house more habitable the family made some changes. Barbara said, "When Anna was a baby, my dad helped us to dig through a yard-thick, solid wall of our new home". (His intention was to make a doorway to between the current kitchen and dining-room.) "Dad suddenly said, "Look, I've found some shoes!" Apparently, as the house is at an angle and built upon a slope, "he had tunnelled up and come out upstairs, through my built-in cupboard by the fire-breast!"

On another occasion, Arthur bricked himself up in a wall. He was reconstructing his daughter's current living room and needed to brick up a wall. He did so, but forgot to climb out before he finished the job. His daughter heard, "Barbara, Barbara ...", but could not locate her dad. He was in the wall! Needless to say, he got out!

Another 'do-it-yourself' alteration idea that went wrong was when "Dad took down the very low ceiling. It was less than six feet from the floor to ceiling. We wanted to check if the height of the room could be raised to stop people from bumping their heads". No one had tried to change this since the house was built. Barbara remarked that "While removing the reeds from the ceiling-space, dad cut his arm on an old scythe-style knife that had been left in the reeds in the ceiling". The ceiling was eventually raised to its rough-cut beams by about an inch! It wasn't really worth all of the effort or stitches in the cut arm!

Annually (about a fortnight before each Christmas), Betty Pope would go "down the yard" to Gladys Humphrey's house to sweep her chimney. Gladys and her husband, Bill, (who had a wooden leg) lived at 33 North Street. It is a double-roofed house, which allowed roofers to walk between the gutters, where the rooftops meet. On one occasion when Betty went to sweep the chimney with her brushes, the rods came untwisted from their joints and left the brush stuck up the chimney. After a moment of discussion, they knocked at Barbara's door to ask if she had a ladder. She asked her father (Arthur Chester) for his ladder and queried if he could help. He brought his equipment and climbed up to get the brush-head out from the top of the chimney. Arthur (in his eighties at the time) got the brush out and then froze. He couldn't move or get down. Barbara rang her cousin, Peter Hooton, to ask him for help. His wife, Sheila, answered the phone. She had to call to Peter that his uncle was stuck up the chimney, to which he responded, "What does he think he's doing? He's not Father Christmas!" Peter helped him to climb down in tandem. As the house and gutter is not seen from the road, this event did not cause a spectacle!

From another perspective, Sharon Jackson (Cottingham) and I recall being asked if we could collect a ladder from number 13 to take to 31.[180] This was done, but was like a Laurel and Hardy sketch, as both houses were accessed by passageways. The ladder had to go out into the middle of the road to turn the corner out of one house, and into the middle of the road to go up the next passageway. Then this was repeated on the return journey. Sue Wyles later suggested, "What you really needed was a bendy ladder". The idea of a bendy ladder caused much mirth! Whenever my own children do something silly or talk of the things their great-grandad did (or things that their grandma does now) they refer to it as "the Chester gene". (I think we all suffer from this condition.)

Susie Moore recalls, "My sister, Jennifer, Anna and Wendy and me, playing on their small lawn, where we would put on a 'show' for our neighbours. We would hang a curtain or sheet on the washing-line and charge 3d ('thruppence') for people to watch. We set up the dining room chairs in a row and performed for their pocket-money". Neighbours, Betty and Tommy Pope, Gladys and Bill Humphrey, Arthur Chester and Barbara Mudza were then subjected to whatever 'play' the children would perform. I am not sure if this was a delight or a disaster, but performances would usually end in time for tea!

My grandmother, Dorothy Chester, recalled that number 33 sold hats and gloves, as it was a milliners shop in late-1800 to the 1920s.[181] Anne Cooper (née Leayton)[182] confirmed this. Her aunt "Catermole", learnt to sew there and was a milliner at 33 North Street in WWI years. The business declined in the inter-war years and the building was used as a house. It was later the home of William (Bill) and Gladys Humphrey (until the 1970s). Gladys sang loudly each morning as she did her chores in her kitchen. At that time the houses were strangely divided.

---

[180] Sharon Cottingham and Anna Fernyhough, personal memories.
[181] Oral history, Anna Fernyhough.
[182] Anne Cooper (née Leayton), family history.

Number 31 had its bedroom above number 33. Why this was so is a mystery to me. (By the 1980s the room below was purchased, making the house whole again as a two-up, two-down cottage.) Gladys loved to sing Sunday hymns on almost any day of the week and she loved listening to the "wireless". She did this while preparing her dinner,[183] or when doing her laundry at the kitchen sink. Her voice (joining in very clearly with the radio) carried all around the shared yard! Number 33 has two front doors on the front of the building and one at the rear. One front door was access for the shop customers, with the other leading to a passage within the house for the family to use. The lower walls beneath the windows were slightly reconstructed owing to erosion of the bricks in the 1960s. Gladys was a good friend and neighbour of Grace Dexter. They would walk up to the 'Rose and Crown' for a mutual 'Stout'. Gladys died in Stamford hospital in 1981. Subsequently, this bow-fronted building has belonged to Mr Aldridge (1980s) and has changed hands several times since.

Cottages 35, 37 and 39 are accessed via a roofed, white-washed passage-way. Here were several houses with a shared right-of-way to them. Number 33's shed once held a boiler (just inside) that was used by all of the adjacent householders to do their laundry. It is recalled that an elderly lady lived at 35 during the 1930s, before Mary Marshall's parents, Percy and Marjorie, lived here. Mary attended school with Barbara Chester. During the 1960s the house was rented by the Colver family. In the 1980s, number 35 was the home of Lewis (born in 1929) and Margaret Burrows and their children. In the 1930s & 1940s, the cottage where Len Denny lived (37) originally backed onto the stone rear-wall of number 31. Harvey, the son of Stanley and Leah Crawley (who lived at 47), purchased 35 and 37. The three-storey house (37) was hidden from the road, but could be seen clearly from the adjacent gardens. In the 1970s, Harvey Crawley moved in. He lived in number 35 for a very short time, while he demolished 37. The house was knocked down without talking to any of his neighbours (or, it is believed, the Council regarding its demolition). At the "top of the yard", Number 39 was rented to evacuee families in the early 1940s. Thomas Pope (known as Tommy) married Betty Brudenell (aged

---

[183] Anna Fernyhough recalls the smell of "boiled greens wafting through my bedroom window"!

twenty) in Oundle in 1943. Tommy, Betty and their three children (Janet, Doreen and Stephen) lived in this a detached, brewery-owned property. As Tommy worked for the brewery, his house "came with the job". Number 41 (opposite 35) has a room above the shared-access passageway. Barbara Mudza recalls 'Granny Marshall' who lived at number 41 in the 1930s and 1940s. This lady was related to Fred (at number 15).

George Howe and Mary Ann Harris had a son, William Carter Howe, who in turn married Elizabeth 'Eliza' Rippiner. They had ten children. William was one of the ten siblings. He was baptised in 1816 in St. Peter's Church and died in Oundle in the winter of 1893, at the age of 77. He was a stonemason by profession and his son continued this tradition. Mr Howe owned 43 and 45 North Street. He, like his father before him, worked and traded from the three-storey house (1930s to 1950s), which has quite a history and many original features inside.[184] Grave-stones were propped against the external walls of his house as examples of his trade. He had head-stones displayed inside his front windows too. There is a traditional coach-house gateway to the property.

The Georgian house, number 47, was known as the 'big doctor's house' ('big' described the house and not the doctor!). It belonged to a doctor who had been a prisoner of war in Japan during the 1940s. Doctor Lewis subsequently lived here from the 1950s to 1970s. 47 and 49 are late-seventeenth-century, stone houses with casement windows. A cobbled drive runs amid these houses, yet 47 has three-storeys and 49 (large, ex-brewery house) two. Guy Ludlow lived here before building his Blackpot Lane house (now "Gardenways"). The North Street house was later Dr Lewis' home (before his move to East Road) prior to mechanic, Stanley Crawley and his wife, Leah (née Smith), moving in with their family in the 1970s.

Befitting its status, the last house in North Street, number 51, was known as the "Head-Brewer's house". It is a two-storey, eighteenth-century house. Samuel Wigginton owned the house in the early 1800s, followed by the head-brewer, John Smith in 1817. It later belonged to the Guy Ludlow and his family. It has an arched entrance doorway and

---

[184] Oral history, Julia Langridge.

bay windows. When Basil Ludlow (father of Guy and Rex) owned the brewery, this house had railings outside (on the right by the driveway). It was much clearer to see as there was no wall or gate in the front, just a white, metal barrier. During day-time, ravens were attached to the railing. They were returned to their cages in the Rectory gardens in the evening and overnight. Brewery offices faced the drive (around the north side of the current building). Basil's office was the first on the right side of the house. The house had a builders' store behind it, plus one of the Maltings. The Head Brewer was accountable for all aspects of the beer process and production. This responsible job supported a suitably large family house to denote this management status. This house is three-storeys high with a cobbled yard (used for parking).

The tall, three-storey town-houses are set back on the hill behind a low wall. These were built in the late 1970s, on the site of the old brewery houses, general office, boiler house and 'Half Moon Inn'. in antiquity, the inn was named "The Black Pots Inn" and was subsequently renamed as the "Horse and Jockey". Its first name originated with reference to the leather-covered drinking vessels that were originally used for the ales. Leather mugs were used from the mediæval period onwards.[185] They started out as an orange-brown colour, but changed over time and usage to a blackened colour. The nearby lane to the "Black Pot" tavern, was hence re-named the Blackpot Lane. (With "Black Pot" being amalgamated into one word.) Glass bottles were used (albeit infrequently) from 1600. Glass superseded skins in the mid-1800s, when the glass-tax was repealed and the making of mass-produced, machine-blown glassware was established.[186] Bottles were cleaner, recycled and easily reused. It is just coincidental that many centuries later a tall, blackened 'pot' chimney was built on this site for the brewery.[187] In the 1960s, Mr and Mrs Earp ran the pub and 'off-licence' sales. (It is recalled by one local that "Mrs Earp was a big lady" who "ran the shop"!)

---

[185] Leather bottles were used and inns used the image on their signs to identify themselves as being Inns. There was a 'Leather Bottle' Inn in Glapthorn. In Tudor times, 'black' sealed, random-sized, leather 'blackpots' held ale. Drinkers had a literal 'skin-full' if they had literally drank too many. See P. Hill, "Hostelries", pp. 35-36.
[186] Ibid.
[187] Information by (and with thanks to) David Wills.

Wendy Bollans (née Mudza) and Sheila Denley recall that as children they would go to the pub to buy bags of peanuts at 2d ('tuppence') each. There were also three-biscuit packs for around the same price. Mrs Earp would carry items around on a tray advertising "Nestlé Milk-Maid"[188] Toffees (which may have depicted a milk-maid with her yoke around her neck and buckets hanging from it). The memories evoked are always eclectic!

Number 53, the nearest part of the new buildings to the demolished pub, has a half-moon door-plate indicating history that is passed. In the 1960s, the Inn had a small hatch in its doorway for children to reach without entering, but allowing them to purchase bags of crisps (unsalted, with little blue-twist papers containing salt) and a bottle of lemonade. This is a favourite memory of mine.[189] The pub was scheduled for preservation in the 1960s (with the 'White Lion', 'Anchor', 'Nags Head' and 'Wagon and Horses' public houses), yet it was 'long gone' before the twenty-first century.

There is a division of four ancient ways, Station Road (leading north), North Street (south), East Road (east), and Blackpot Lane (west) meet here. (This is not to be confused with the greater layout of the town where the names of the early streets and roads [or back way] denote a direction as in North, South, East and West.)

Blackpot Lane (Brewery and Brewery Cottages)

Blackpot Lane had a very tall, nineteenth-century brewery chimney that stood at the bottom of the hill. As stated earlier, it was named regarding the local inn's archaic mugs. It is presumed that many a black pot was downed-from in the North Street pub. Prior to its "Black Pot" designation, this narrow lane was known as "Dweel-Wonc Lane" ("wonc" and "dweel" being obsolete words for 'residences', as "wonc" means "a dwelling").[190] Thus, it could easily have become "Live Here Lane"!

---

188 The brand dates to 1886, Illinois, USA.
189 Anna Fernyhough, personal information.
190 'The Oxford Book of Late Medieval Verse and Prose', ed. Douglas Gray, p. 573, Clarendon Press, Oxford, 1985.

At that time there were fewer street buildings between the land owned by the Parish Church (that was a central nucleus to the town) and its Manor-house. The manor property stretched northward to Dweel-Wonc Lane from the Church yard. The lane formed part of the early Saxon settler's town boundary as, at that time Oundle was a small, wooden, walled hamlet.

At the top of the hill, opposite 'Gardenways' house is the 'Sci-Tec' and Patrick Engineering Centre were rebuilt on the old Oundle School foundry site. This was rebuilt and its technology brought up to date during 2016 and 2017. Lower on the hillside are new houses that were built on the allotments and where the old Gas Works stood in the 1880s[191]. In the 1960s Aubrey Clarke held an allotment here. The Denley family recall that Aubrey 'Clanger' Clarke was then the Tower Captain of St. Peter's Church bell-ringers, which gave him (and his wife) this nickname. He was tortured while a prisoner-of-war in Japan and after the war kept livestock and was said to have had "a lovely allotment over the road from the new houses in Blackpot Lane".[192] Most of the North Street residents rented an allotment in the 1950s and 1960s and, apparently, there was a waiting list for gardening plots. Planning permission was sought for a building development of thirty-three flats and garages. In 2006 the original building was demolished and a replacement dwelling was erected. The northern side of Blackpot Lane has terraced, two-storey houses, set beyond a grass bank. They replaced walled-allotment gardens and brewery buildings (now Kings Road).

During the 1960s passers-by would sometimes see a ladder that was placed across the road (as there was little traffic in the lane in those days). The ladders were used by the brewers for rolling the barrels over the road from the barrel sheds. The ladder kept the barrels rolling in a straight line! There were metal runner tracks embedded in the road for this too.

Only two properties were listed on the southern side of the road in 1939, which were 'Brewers' houses. These cottages were at the

---

[191] There were two gas works in Oundle in the 1880s: one in East Road and one behind the Station Road-Blackpot Lane section of the Brewery.
[192] Oral history, Gerry White.

bottom of the hill, opposite the mineral factory. Both housed tenants who worked for the brewery so they and their families lived in the rented, brewery-owned cottages. Number 1 was a thatched-bungalow, "about 200 yards up on the left" on Blackpot Lane. This first cottage was the home of John (known as 'Jim') and Gwendoline Lincoln and their children, Betty and Sylvia. John worked as a brewery, motor-transport engineer. Sylvia Burdett (née Lincoln) recalls the mid-1930s, when she "had a lovely summer house" that her father, Jim, made from an old bus. The bus had made regular trips from the Talbot to the railway station, but was no longer used, so "dad removed the wheels and axles and made it into a play house". He left the steering wheel in situ and converted it in the Brewery workshop, where he repaired vehicles. The family cottage-bungalow "had a large garden with steps up to the houses and a wall with a gate at either end". When they moved, the Emerton family lived here when Barbara and Carole were children. Wendy Bollans recalls their pet hamster playing in the doll's house.

Mrs Lee also lived on this south side of the road before she moved to East Road. In the second cottage was Albert Brookes and his wife, Marjorie, who lived with their children, Doreen and Terence. Edna Bask (later Ball), an evacuee, lived with them. Albert worked for the brewery as an electrical and general engineer. In the 1960s one of the houses was the home of a part-time gent's hairdresser, who cut hair at the weekends. Michael Shiels came here for haircuts when he wasn't working. The cottages stood beyond the Engine Room, with the constant noises of barrels and pop bottles being washed. Suds and foam often slopped across the road, either from the beer or from the cleaning sheds. Slightly behind where the tall row of town-houses now stands, were the bottled beer store, the filling sheds, the cask beer store, the wine and spirit store and an open yard with a cool-cellar beneath.

The cottages were demolished when the brewery closed and new buildings eventually replaced them. When John Smith's was purchased in 1961, there was a directive that the Oundle brewery had to close. Jim Irving worked for Smith's and was instructed to close the brewing business. Once here, he did as instructed, but refused to leave Oundle with his family. He settled fully in Oundle and was the founder of the

Gilbert & Sullivan Players in 1959 (built on the old operatic society of the 1930s).[193] Artificially-carbonated beer was first bottled in 1923. Their paired horse drays were phased out by 1929.

By 1963 the Oundle brewery was gone, but Parry and John continued to live in North Street thereafter. New town-houses stand at the front on North Street, with new terraced 'cottages' are in a new courtyard slightly behind that is named Half Moon Mews. The stone wall leading uphill remains largely unchanged. Further up the hillside is the exit from the old rectory (Gascoigne Building). 'Gardenways' is on the other side of the road from the new Oundle School science and technology building. It runs alongside the Gascoigne rear car-park. When Rex Ludlow died, his widow had a house built on this site. In 1998, changes were made to the boundary-wall and the garage-access route. The current sprawing mock-Georgian house was designed by Paul Bancroft and constructed in 2009. The external view of its garden gives glimpses of mature trees. Here, Mr Rose and his sons run their businesses.

Percy Arnett recalls that when he was a lad, the boys would "form sides and would fight using 'sticks and dustbin lids' all the way down Blackpot Lane and back up again". Lower down the hill were the iron runners and tracks that ran across the road, which were used to roll the beer barrels across from one side to the other. On the lower slope of Blackpot Lane stood the Coopers' shop (making the beer barrels), the cask washing-sheds and small brewery garden. The aroma from the brewery washing-sheds were the very distinctive smells of aromatic hops and malt. A small garden and engine-room were on the corner of Station Road, plus the brewery house where Joe Brudenell and his family lived.

Station Road

On the north side of the road, part of the brewery faced into Station Road. The first building on the corner was known as "Mr Brudenell's Engine Room". Joe Brudenell lived in the first house up the hill (from the corner) with his large family. 'His' pumping station, mineral factory and small carpenter's shop were along Station Road. New houses were

---

[193] W.J. Irving was a key member of Oundle Museum and its foundation. His wife, Parry, ran a dress shop in Crown Court.

built here in 1972. The barrel washing shed was behind the mineral factory. The brewery Maltings stopped working in 1947. (Guy Ludlow died in 1954.)

Station road began at the John Smiths' brewery and meandered to the Railway Station on the far side of the River Nene. Along the western and (after the bend in the road before it goes over the river) northern side of Station Road, there has been a dramatic change and a 'tidying' of buildings in the past few years. The road originally led past allotments on the western side of the road (and the football fields to the east). There are now houses covering the area where the allotments stood: Victoria Road, Vine Close (cul-de-sacs) and Kings Road (which leads in a curve from Station Road to Blackpot Lane). A little further along the road is also a small cul-de-sac named Bridge View, comprising of two-storey, stone and brick town-houses, most of which have a good view of the bridge!

Along the Station Road (to the bus depot by the garage) on the western edge, there was no path, just a hedge bordering the allotments, a ditch and a narrow grass-strip by the roadside. To walk here in the 1960s, one had to cross the road and walk on the football-field side. I recall that from the road the allotments could be spotted through the tall, hawthorn hedge. My grandfather had his allotment here and grew flowers, peas, carrots and potatoes. I remember when he would take me along with him as a child and I was allowed to pull up a few potatoes and help to pick carrots and peas. (I'm sure that I was easily tired of watching him cut and dig, so would wander around looking at the other interesting and attractive plots on the site.) Grandad and I would then walk back along North Street to my grandma's house (number 13) and we would 'shell the peas' ready to cook for lunch.[194] Everything that he grew there tasted fantastic.

New houses were built in the late-1970s on the old (WWI) allotments and brewery land. Victoria Road, King's Road and Vine Close houses were built on what was Smith's land since the eighteenth-century, from when it was claimed as part of the parliamentary Enclosure Acts. (Dating to when enclosed open fields and common land became the legal property of landowners, giving them rights common land.)

---

[194] Anna Fernyhough, personal history.

Previously it was common grazing land. The new road names recall three Inns that were owned by the John Smith's brewery (established in 1773). The estate was originally referred to as 'Laxton Park', recalling the Oundle-born Lord Mayor of London, whose 1556 bequest fully established Oundle School.

The first buildings in Station Road (after the allotments of the 1950s and '60s) was the Bus Depot. It closed in January 2012 and was dismantled in the early twenty-first century. The large Depot building was mostly concrete, corrugated metal with huge doors at the front to allow the buses access. I recall that several buses could drive in through the huge sliding-doors to park overnight. (My memory may be faulty at this, but it felt huge as I was just a child at the time!) Oundle services were transferred from Kettering to the Corby depot, with the closure of the Oundle outstation. I hosted services from the former Eastern Counties, 'Cambus', Oundle Bus, 'Stagecoach' and 'Viscount'. The Peterborough to Northampton 'out-station' on Station Road was demolished in September 2012, when it and the adjacent land was sold. The nearby garage (petrol, repairs and car sales) was owned by Francis and Marshall, but changed hands several times. For some time this garage was known as "Oundle Motors". They were open every day and sold Austin Ford cars. The garage hired-out cars and mini-buses. It also did "electric-spot-welding" and "pop-riveting"![195] Pick Arthey (Oundle) Limited opened in April 1986. It is currently named 'Pick Arthey, Oundle Limited' and is run by John Pick and Eddie Arthey, who are colleagues from a nearby Ford dealership who have continued this in Oundle. Behind the garage were Panther Caravans (made here in the 1960s) and later the Lo-Cost store.

The 1950s bus depot that was next to Pick Arthey garage was demolished in the early twenty-first century. New homes were built on land that had been reincarnated many times, including the old cattle yard. This was no longer used by 1960s, but the pens were still there beside a cornfield that stretched westward to the Home Close. The cattle yard became the site of a log-yard (timber yard and wood factory[196]). In the 1970s it accommodated 'Sunseekers' caravan factory

---

[195] Oundle Official Guide, 1960.
[196] Where the Miles family (of Gordon Road) bought sawdust for cleaning the hutches of their pet rabbit.

and a short-lived 'Lo-Cost' supermarket. Pick Arthey purchased some of the land for their cars (and from where the bus depot stood). (The bus depot was not located here in the 1930s, as it was in East Road, behind the current Co-operative store). The bus travelled to Kettering and local villages. Louis Hodson (born in 1854) married Elizabeth Edwards in 1882. He and their sons, Harry (born 1885) and Louis (junior, born in 1886) ran the vehicle repair garage in Station Road and were agricultural and motor engineers during the pre-war years, 1900-1914. They also operated a local bus service (1912) when vehicles were fairly new on the roads here. In 1939, Station Road only a minimum of families in residence. The garage then belonged to Mr Thomas Salisbury (Oundle Motor's Limited), but was run by the Hodson brothers. Louis Hodson (junior) married Edith Cotton in 1920 and ran a local bus from the garage around 1912. The Willimont family owned the garage after this. Fred Swann worked here with Gerry White's father. Siddons and Sons were established in 1840 as corn-feed and manure, coke and coal merchants with Depots in Oundle, Barnwell and Kings Cliffe stations. In the post-war years, 2 was Oundle Market Company Limited. Mr Raymond Clark lived at 3. Colonel Ronald King McMichael (born in 1900; married Janet MacGregor in 1929) and his family lived at 4. Many children have enjoyed playing in the field beyond their house, in the brick-built barn in the big coal yard and in the orchards beyond the house. These have all since been developed. The Nene Catchment Board (River Authority) owned 5. The courtyard has new building. Oundle Yacht Club also has a new building next to it. It is part of the malting's housing complex.

The river Nene passes under the Station Road North Bridge. It was widened in the early 1900s and needed rebuilding after the winter floods in early 1912. This bridge was repaired at least twice in my lifetime. The bridge has two inscribed stones. The older foundation stone tells that in 1570 the arches of the bridge collapsed and were swallowed by the River. They were rebuilt in 1571 (this time with limestone).[197]

---

[197] It reads, "In the yere of ouer Lord 1570 thes arches weer borne doune by the waters extremytie - in the yere of over Lord 1571 they weer bulded agayn with lyme and stonne - thanks be to God". (Note that the inscription letters are all capitalised).

The road continues past the river-side Maltings (some parts listed buildings and others newly built around 1990) and past the Oundle School boat house. (It is worth noting here that the boat house is a rather well-thatched building.) The field between the Nene River and the Oundle Station is known locally as 'the quicks'. Thomas Stone (1787) mentions the "state and management of common field lands". The "small inclosures, in flat situations, surrounded with a great number of trees and quicks, grown to a considerable height ..." [198] In 1811 (in his "General View of Agriculture of the County of Huntingdon") Richard Parkinson noted that parts of the enclosed land were divided into "fields and quicks". In "A treatise on engineering field-work: containing practical land", Peter Schuyler Bruff (1838) notes that a ditch is not always an edge to fields. In some areas "the roots of the quicks" sometimes form boundaries.

On the north-eastern side of the river is the old Railway station. Steam-trains passed and children waved to the driver and passengers (rather like a scene from the "Railway Children"). Oundle station and line were closed in the rail-network cuts in the 1960s. Baron Beeching composed a report that led to far-reaching changes in the rail-network. This was known as the "Beeching Axe". Railways countrywide were taken out of service. This was a great loss in many respects. "Going on the train or watching one go along the track was every child's idea of a treat." [199] Jean Atkins recalls arriving at Oundle Station from Wellingborough during the war. She said that "you had to count the stations as all identifying signs had been taken down to cause confusion if England was invaded".

One of Oundle's older residents said that "Everyone knew the times of the trains, as there weren't that many" and "people would walk down the cut through to the railway from the end of Herne and Ashton Roads, to avoid the long walk via East Road". Joyce Hardick recalls "using the short-cut from Ashton Road to see Queen Mary on the train". Joyce was aged about ten at the time and remembers the day

---

[198] "Suggestions for Rendering the Inclosure of Common Fields and Waste Lands: A Source of Population and Riches", Thomas Stone, Land & Tythe surveyor, Bedford. (Published in London by J. Nichols, 1787.) Especially, p. 5. (The Board of Agriculture, 1913, also mentions that these tough, river-side grasses are periodically burned.)
[199] Jean Atkins.

with pleasure as "events like this don't happen and excite local children any longer". Hetty Bell recalled that the train went "over the bridge to Northampton". She went on to say that "the soot was always terrible. You had to spit on a hanky and wipe it off".

Susie Moore reflected that the schoolboys "were a sight with their suitcases, all waiting on the platform for the train to arrive". Charlie Weatherington (who lived with his family in Gordon Road) was the signal-man at the railway station. In the late-1960s, after our line-closure, the rails were removed from the tracks. The station waiting-rooms and ticket office were subsequently converted into a very comfortable home. Much of the rail-line was turned into the new road-route for the (Oundle to Barnwell) A605 bypass.

The station building stands on the northern side of the main Peterborough route into town. Like others along the same line, the building had a waiting-room and ticket office that had been created in a Jacobean-style. The main-line and station opened in 1845 and carried passenger-trains, coal and freight from Peterborough to Northampton along the Nene Valley. From end to end the journey took one-and-an-half hours (over the "43¾ mile" track). The first line was a single track that went alongside the two-storey station house. The line was expanded in 1846 with a second platform and a simple waiting-room. The line closed in 1964 and remained neglected for many years.

Goods-yards were on each side of the line, accessed by wagon turntables connected with a crossed-line. A large goods-shed stood next to the main building and the yard had a five-ton crane. Later, another line was built and more sidings added. (They curved into the new goods yard.) Trains would shunt from one line to another at this point or spin on the turntable. There were only three steam-trains each day in 1845, but by 1883 this had risen to six.

Since the station was on the edge of Oundle, a town omnibus or post-horse could be hired from the Talbot Hotel for transport. By 1926, the goods yard had new sidings and a goods shed. As the yard-link was close to the line, the two wagon turntables were not needed and were removed. When the station closed in 1964, the station was occasionally used to ferry children in 'school student specials' at the start and end of term. This terminated when the station closed on 6th

November 1972. The station building was saved and restored as a house, while retaining much of its external 'station' character.

As a child many recall standing at the long, white gates that were closed by a signalman. These prevented anyone from crossing the tracks if a train was imminent. We would wave at the trains and get covered in black, steam smuts. There was always a distinctive 'fire' smell of the trains that passed. Joyce Hardick recalled when she worked for Bulley's (the accountants) and there were times when she would have to travel on the train to Northampton. She said that it made a "nice change from the office"! Josephine Black's recollection was that she and her brother walked down to the Elton crossing to watch the train pass on its final journey. This is a time long gone, but cherished and not forgotten.

Combined recollections of the station are of an old-fashioned waiting-room, just off the platform. Luggage, old suitcases, vanity-cases, hatboxes, milk churns and sack barrows that were awaiting a train. The inside had a toilet with an old penny slot-machine on its door. There was a large clock on the wall and a small window for ticket sales. The platform at the front of the building, faced the river and town. The (wheeled) gates were closed when the trains were coming across the eastern end of North Bridge. They were white and had a reflector on them to alert the traffic, preventing accidents when they closed at twilight or in the winter.

After moving from the house at the top of Nene View, Christopher Awdry was, for a time, the 'master' of this refurbished station. He had continued writing the 'Thomas the Tank Engine' books in 1972 when his father, the Reverend W. Awdry, retired.[200] These much-loved train stories are based on tales the Reverend told to his son, Christopher (around 1943) while recuperating from the measles. Christopher held local book-launches to publicise his 'latest' works. Very innocently and wanting to know when he had taken over the writing process, I asked, "When did your father die?" At this, he looked down his nose at me

---

[200] 'Thomas the Tank Engine' is a steam-train in 'The Railway Series' by Rev. W. Awdry. He retired from writing in 1972 when Christopher took on writing the stories.

and said, "My dear, my father believes that he is still very much alive!"[201] (Ooops!)

Nearby 'Laxton Drive' was not built until 1995. It commemorates Sir William Laxton. Formerly on this site was the coal-depot (used by passing steam-trains). The curved cul-de-sac road of thirty detached houses is considered to be part of Ashton (not Oundle) as it is geographically beyond the confines of the Nene. It is (technically) also within the town limit!

New houses (and parts of the A605 road) were built on the Roman dig site and Siddons' family coal-yard behind the station. This land was used for housing animals that came to town with the circus or were livestock transported by rail. Mona Monk worked the low-loader lorry to carry the railway items that came in by train. Ann Sauntson (née Keans) went with her mum, Ruth, on the last train to Peterborough.[202] At this point the 'Riverside' inn fell into a doldrum of disuse. In the 1930s, Mr J.H. Adam ran the 'The Railway Hotel'. He let accommodation and sold wines, ales and spirits. Until the 1970s, the proprietor of the inn was Mr E. Halstead. The pub served as the local Angling Association headquarters, providing fishing tickets and Nene licences, 'bed-and-breakfast', lunch and dinner.

A Roman town existed by the River Nene. In 1982-83, a large-scale salvage excavation was conducted by senior pupils and the Nene Valley Archaeological group. Archaeologists found the foundations of buildings, burials, pottery and jewellery. Amongst the finds was a bronze-age Beaker burial. The site remains extended under the old Oundle railway station and adjacent buildings.

An archaeological dig was essential before the current Oundle bypass could begin construction. Permission was given by the land-owner, Miriam Louisa Rothschild (the Honourable Mrs Lane), who was a zoologist, naturalist, academic and eccentric. She conducted research into parasites and their hosts and this was reflected in the Ashton estate pub the "Chequered Skipper".[203] In the 1970s the pub had a large replica of a flea above its fireplace and butterfly curtains in her

---

[201] The Reverend Wilbert Awdry, the vicar at Emneth, near Wisbech, died in 1997.
[202] Ruth Keans, personal history.
[203] Miriam Lane (née Rothschild) died in January 2005, aged 96.

honour! Ashton was a Rothschild village, created as a community facility for the tied Ashton Estate workers. A bypass road for Oundle was completed shortly thereafter on what was originally part of the train line to Kettering. Bypasses to a number of Northamptonshire's towns and villages were constructed in the 1980s and 1990s.

Since the turn of the twenty-first century, the land between the Oundle Town Football Club, the unused 'Riverside Inn' and the flood-fields has regenerated with retail businesses. On the eastern side of the Nene is the near-derelict 'Riverside' Inn. This has slowly been allowed to fall into disrepair over the past 30 years. Despite newspaper reports and local council bulletins stating that the building is due to be used, nothing has happened here for quite some time. In the autumn of 2017 the stone walls by these building and the nearby bridge wall were repaired.

The development of old Oundle Wharf has given new life to the land by the river and makes the North Bridge view of Oundle much more pleasing. The Nene Valley Brewery opened in 2012 with a revival of its brewing tradition. Nene Valley Ales 'micro-brewery' is new businesses situated by the Wharf. Nene Valley Brewery at Oundle Wharf produces a wide range of local ales and entered the century with historic and amusingly-named beers that are now Gluten Free.[204] The Wharf area and brewery holds events that include dancing and bands for the Oundle Fringe festival and other music events. Nene Valley Brewery and its co-owner, Dick Simpson, have an intriguing story. On retirement, Dick began brewing in his back garden. He then decided to open a brewery, re-establishing an important Oundle tradition from over fifty years ago.

The newer Wharf development hosts Errismore (wholesale flowers), Gorilla Cycling, an Aga shop, Amps Wine Merchants and Hambleton Bakery. The 'Tap and Kitchen' bar and restaurant has pleasant views of the river and wildlife from its outside terrace. The outdoor courtyard hosts the sale of farm produce and creative items at its Christmas markets and food festivals. A story that I was recently told made me smile, so I have included it here: An employee at a nearby Oundle business who was in need of inter-personal skill development, so had

---

[204] NVA run tours twice monthly. www.nenevalleybrewery.com/NVB/Tours.html

been sent on a two-day training course. Staff at the business were very surprised to see the person back at the desk for lunch on the first day of the course. They asked, "Why are you back so early?" to be told "in no uncertain terms" that the course was a waste of time as "there was nothing to be learnt from it"!

Jericho and Prentices Yard

Jericho has changed little for over a hundred years. It is now a grade II listed building. The dead-end alleyway may once have been a lane that led out of town. Jericho House has recently been a pottery, card shop, bakery and hairdresser. In the 1930s there were up to four neighbouring residents. Mr H. Shirley ran a gent's hairdresser's shop (which joined Mrs Shirley's ladies hairdressers yet was run separately). It became Ruth's and later Jayne's hairdressers (all generations of the same family). Mr Ruff ran the barber shop, offering prophylactics and fishing tackle from his small shop. The shop was merged into Ruth's business in the 1960s.

In 1767, Lorne House was the residence of the prominent surgeon, John Campion. He often sought help from locals (such as John Clifton) to aid him in his work. (Just as Mr Smith, the vet, did many years later!) It is a large, three-storey, grade-II listed, stone building. This Georgian house hides an Elizabethan heritage, but denotes its age with a (former) coaching yard and eighteenth-century water-pump. The rambling house has cellars and wine store. The large formal lawn and garden has a remarkable conifer tree (dating to 1870) that is believed to be one of the tallest in the county. Lorne House was a comfortable home to doctors and vets. Until his death, in 1835, the house was that of Dr John Campion. It was then willed to his nephew, John William Coventry, who changed his name in respect of his uncle to John Coventry-Campion. He was granted the rights to bear the Campion arms by King William IV in a decree from Whitehall in 1835. This was largely due to John Campion having proved himself to have been a respected Oundle surgeon. The house has a walled garden stretching alongside that of Jericho's gardens. It has been suggested that Lorne House and Jericho were once one property, as a parallel asphalt coach-track appears to straddle both sides of the adjoining wall. The wall was built between the two lines on the ground. Lorne House was split into smaller dwellings at the end of the 1800s.

By the turn of the century John M. Siddons, a surveyor, lived in Jericho (then Dr Arthur Forbes Elliott by 1911). Two sisters, Elizabeth and Ellen Prentice, lived in the back portion of the house. In 1900, Fanny Thorne lived in Lorne House, then Mrs Bell lived at (38) Lorne House in the 1930s.[205] On 11th April 1945, the *Northampton Mercury* reported that Lorne House was for sale with Berry Brothers and Bagshaw's administering the auction. The executors of the late Mrs L.F. Bell were marketing the premises and the valuable household furnishings.

'Lorne House' is interconnected to 'Lorne Cottage' (a modern, two-storey cottage). The gardens of the houses were split in the 1970s, when the vet, Andrew Spurrell, moved to the South Road surgery. On the East Road end of the garden there are new houses that were built after others were demolished in the late-1960s. Valerie Hillyard was a receptionist for the vet, Mr Smith. The garden backed onto what was once a walkway thoroughfare to East Road, via where Lorne House had its pigeon lofts. The residences (and their outside loos) were at the back of Lorne House gardens.

In 1808, when West Street was known as the High Street, (William) Thomas Prentice, an attorney, died at his home in Oundle, leaving a widow and large family. Elizabeth Brudenell (née Prentice), who was born here in 1846, appears on the 1861 census as staying with her maternal uncle, Thomas Prentice. Thomas' son, Samuel Prentice lived here all of his life and died in 1881, aged 56. He and his wife, Ann, had nine daughters. The Yard named 'Prentices Yard' is likely to have been part of this families' heritage. It is to the right of Jericho, and leads behind the Coffee Tavern and the St. Osyth's Lane shops.

In the 1930s Miss Prentice lived at number 42 and the Reverend E. Lee lived at 44. The entrance to the backs of the St. Osyth's Lane houses and premises in East Road (that led along the perimeter of Lorne House and 'Jericho East' buildings). The old 'Jericho' house is divided and named in compass point parts. It has some of its older, stone, northern side windows filled in (possibly with regards to the window tax). By the side of Allen's bicycle (electrical) shop and Jericho were the town's

---

[205] See the 1911 census and freebmd.

public toilets. These have long since been dismantled. The Berrystead and Old Dryden share a side wall with the walkway to East Jericho.

The residents in the 1970s and 1980s included Barry Haddon (circa 1988) and Mrs Watkins (who is recalled as having many dogs!) in the lane house, behind him. Access from Prentices Yard exited here (to the left of the houses). It also leads to the back entrances of shops, such as the Coffee Tavern. The entrance to the cottages led to a more enclosed passageway short-cut to East Road. Phyllis Beeby agreed that she used the short-cut route many times as a child. She said that it was the easiest way to get to the town centre. In the 1930s the cottages in the cobbled passageway housed Eleanor Harley, who lived in the cottage by Lorne House and Mrs Watkins next to her. The Beeby family lived in the house by the passage exit into East Road.

St. Osyth's Lane

St. Osyth's Lane turns downhill (north to south) from the Market Place. It covers just a short distance, but commands "oodles of history". It was originally known as St. Sithe's Lane as it was named after Osgyth, a 7th-century saint and princess. It has also been named Lark Lane. The buildings in St. Osyth's on the eastern-side begin near the Market Place. Mews Cottage is in a courtyard with small rental cottages (Oundle Cottage Breaks).

Currently, 'Number One' St. Osyth's Lane caters for meetings and support. This is the Community Project by the Oundle Baptist Church. It serves as a place to drop in for a 'chat' about financial, governmental and social problems. "Stitchat", the youth services, women, men and parenting groups meet here. The Baptist Church is temporarily served by the Reverend John and Enid Singleton since Easter 2017.

In the past, St. Osyth's Lane had very few houses on view (but more than there are now) as there were many more cottages and houses hidden behind the street terraced row. In the 1930s, number 1 was the home of Miss L. Siddons. Mr John H. Clarke (1854-1934), cycle agent and tobacconist was at 2. Mr Albert Edward Brinsley lived at 3 (born in Oundle in 1880; married here in 1906 and died here aged 74). Number 4 was the home of Mrs 'Eliza' Lane and her family. She ran a shop and business here.

At the rear of the pub there was a 'doss house', which cost very little to stay in for a night or two. The landlord of the Angel was responsible for administering the fee. He also cooked home-made faggots, which he sold around the town from his horse and cart. At 5 was W. Mann, but no-one was listed as living at 6 in 1939. Mrs Beatrice M. Clarke (1876-1959) lived at 7 and James H. Garrett (1868-1939) at 8. Number 9 was the home of Harry Taney (born in 1885). Mrs Ellis lived at 10, while 11 was the home of Cecil John Clarke. Mr Edwin J. ('Ted') Hooton (1896-1960) and his family lived at 12. He married Doris Craythorn in early 1924 and lived here with their growing family: Edwin R. (known as 'Eddie', who was born in the summer of 1924), Ralph J. (1925), Eileen E.F. (1927), Audrey (1928), Maureen D. (1931), Sheila (1932), Mavis E. (1933), Brenda M. (1935), Gwenda R. (1936), Peter R. (1938), Geoffrey I. and Jean B. (the twins, who were born in 1939), Stella P. (1932), John K. (1943) and his twin, Janice T. Hooton (1943). (Doris also gave birth to an early, still-born baby who was buried in Oundle cemetery.) Later, Doris and her family moved to Danfords in West Street. It is believed that Ted was fond of drinking in the local pubs. After many years of putting up with his behaviour, Doris moved him out. Thereafter, Ted lived on the opposite side of the street for the rest of his life. At 13 and 14 (two houses) were Mr J.C. Palmer and family. Mr F.G. Fox lived at 15. (16 was empty in 1939.) Mr C.J. Wright lived at number 17.

In the pre-WWII years the Roman Catholic Church owned number 18 and 19 (the latter was empty). Thomas Robert Craythorne and his wife, Frances (Nicholson; née Palmer) lived at number 20. Frances Nicholson (née Palmer) married in Oundle in 1896, but was widowed in 1900 when her then husband, Charles Nicholson, died suddenly (at the age of 26). She married Thomas in early 1902 and lived at number 20 with her new husband, her two children (Charles and Dorothy Nicholson) and their own child, Doris (later Hooton).

Matt Wild is in charge of Oundle Church's Youth Association. He recently ran 'Christian Options' for schools and an outreach mission to Peterborough. Thomas Reginald Norwood's taxi firm ran from here and thereafter his son, Carl, ran the business. It is next to an older building: Mr Clarke's toy shop, where June Gaunt worked In the 1940s. It became Hooton's general store. Ralph and his wife, Marie, and their four "J's" (their children were Jane, Jennifer, Julie and James) lived upstairs and at the rear of the shop. Afterwards, the Underwood family bought the business (in the late-1960s-1970s), when the Hooton's moved to open a successful hotel business in St. Hellier, Jersey. The shop took on several forms, including trading as a children's clothing store and "Jitter Tug Toys". Next-door was part of the grocery shop store-rooms, which turned into a betting shop, a pottery shop and the "Grot" shop (designer clothing). It had small, rear cottages that were accessed via a passageway that led between these shops from the street.

Next-door was the "Angel" Inn. It was managed by Mr and Mrs Tom Lane. In the 1940s and 1950s, Mrs Lane continued as the landlady at the Angel Inn (and in her grocery shop). There was a lodging house next, for 'old chaps' (which included the local rag-and-bone man). He could rent bed and breakfast for nine old pence. In her teens, Barbara Chester worked for a time in the shop at the front of the Angel. Customers entered the bar by first walking through the shop and down a short corridor. As Barbara was under-aged to serve the beer, she only served sweets, cheese and canned products. Customers came in all ages: men, women and children. Owing to her age she was also not allowed in the bar, but at times when the landlady need to "put her takings in the Market Place bank", the law "turned a blind eye" and was overlooked for short times. Barbara learned to get beer from the keg. She mentioned that the "rag-and-bone man would warm the fireside poker in the open fire and then plunge it into his beer to mull it" and change its flavour. People often thought ale was healthier when consumed warm, so there was a fondness for sweetened, warm ale and a "distinctive smell" would permeate the rooms. Barbara said that the bar and shop rooms were quite dark inside as lighting was mainly from the small windows and fire. Also, electric lights were not as efficient as they are now.

In the late-1950s and 1960s, the Angel Inn was run by the Tony and Christine Moore. By autumn 2017, the pub was in Robin Moore's thoughts as the pub freehold is for sale. Robin believes that his family pub should always remain a pub and carry its history with it.

Just past the pub was a row of terraced cottages that were demolished in the late 1960s. One had a stone lion above the door. Gwen Mackley recalls coming to Oundle when she was ten or eleven years old around (1949). She walked down St. Osyth's Lane and felt that she was as tall as the house bedrooms in the row of cottages. She could almost see inside the upstairs rooms.

Miss Gilbey (who worked at Selby's ironmongers) lived in one of the cottages. One day Ralph Hooton's sister, Jean was minding her brother's shop[206] (while he attended a local football match). Some fire-men rushed into the shop and led in Miss Gilbey. They sat her in a chair in the grocery shop and explained to Jean that Miss Gilbey's house was on fire. Jean took her into the back of the shop into the living quarters, made her comfortable and talked with her to calm her down. She realised that "the lovely lady" was clutching a cloth bag. She explained that it contained "all her money" and was the first thing she collected when her home caught alight. Jean felt great sympathy for her predicament.

On Guy Fawkes' night, huge bonfires were lit in the Hooton's big back yard, behind their St. Osyth's Lane house. Hot potatoes were baked in their embers.[207] (Excited children could use the toilet easily as the Hooton family outdoor 'loo' was approximately where the co-op toilet block is now!)

Angela Hudson tells of her great-aunt (her granny's sister), Lydia Richards, who lived on St. Osyth's Lane at the turn of the twentieth century. It was a very cold winter in 1906, but Lydia needed to go out to collect water from the well. It was icy and slippery underfoot. The well was at the back of the little shop (in the lane) and Lydia slipped on the ice, fell into the well and drowned. This tragedy occurred on 29th December 1906. She was 54 years old. Angela said it was heart-breaking as no-one knew she had fallen into the well-shaft and it was some time before they found her body. (This is approximately where the current Co-op stands.)

The newly named 'Duck's Nest' house is a private home that stands on the corner of East Road and St Osyth's Lane. Its history dates to the Stuart period. It was constructed in 1637 and bears the date and (IM)

---

206 Information with thanks to Jean Taylor (née Hooton).
207 Barbara Mudza, personal history.

on its south-facing exterior wall. Now known as the 'Duck's Nest', but in the 1800s it was the 'Anchor Inn'.

Mr Sydney P. Garrett owned the 'Anchor Inn' on the corner. He married Mabel Freestone just after the First World War, in 1919. Sid built coffins at the back during the 1930s. This had been part of a pub named "The Lamb", attached to "The Anchor" and had been extended into it. (To the rear of these houses was land where Mushie (a lion) was often parked in his lorry-cage for periods during the 1950s and '60s.) The Channing family lived near here and the adjacent yard had a short-cut passage to the red-brick flats by the 'Angel' (now a car park).

Joyce Gaunt[208] slept in the 'Anchor' end-bedroom as a child. She recalls that she was told that Oliver Cromwell had slept in this building while passing through Oundle. Like Joyce, Doreen Weston recalls sleeping in this small room in 1958. The building is a low and two-storeys high. It was originally at the end of a row of small cottages that were apparently built at in the same era. This is more than likely a truth as Cromwell came from Huntingdon and moved his troops all over the area. It is believed that Oliver Cromwell stabled his horses in Peterborough Cathedral. However, he seems to have kept his troops in check when in Oundle. His generals did not permit their militia to do this here. Nevertheless, his Puritan-minded, fighting followers did cause some havoc as they passed through the town. They seized the heavy, brass, eagle lectern from the Parish Church and threw it into the Nene. It was much too ostentatious for their tastes. It was not retrieved until the nineteenth century when the river was dredged.

The gated parking area for this building is on East Road. The gate bears a sign: "21 St. Osyth's Lane" to avoid confusion! This is the terminus of the Lane. South Road begins here. This may not have been the case in the past. There is a record of the sale of pasture land in Oundle from 1715, reports that the "Oundle, Manor of Memorandum, of the surrender by John Quincey, Customary Tenant of the Manor, of five acres of arable land in St. Syth's field in Oundle near a place called

---

[208] Joyce Hardick, personal information.

Basford[209] and two acres of greensward adjoining, into the hands of Edward Paine and Henry Jenkins".[210]

The 1881 census names the road from here on as South Back Way, which begins where 'Lime House' and 'Lime Cottage' are situated.

St. Osyth's Lane (west side, travelling south)

Once upon a time, the old Oundle streets were mud. Later they were cobbled. It's hard to believe that horses, carriages and carts travelled along these lanes and roads long before we did. As the town grew, the roads steadily improved also.

On the corner of Market Place and St. Osyth's Lane stands the imposing Bramston House. It occupies the entire western length of the lane. Bramston House is a town-house built by Stephen Bramston, who was a lawyer in the early 1700s, late into the reign of Queen Anne. The building was purchased by the School in 1916 and was extended when the School bought Pettit's and Moore's tailor and hatters' shops. To the rear are impressive gardens that had once contained a bowls green and fish ponds.

This lane has the peculiar feature of a "splash-back" (opposite 1 St. Osyth's). The wall is not straight. It is built where the garden wall meets the main building. As the Anchor, the Angel, the Rose and Crown and the White Lion public houses were a short walk, this wall convergence made a shady-corner to use when "taken-short" and "needing a Jimmy Riddle" (rhyming slang from the First World War). To deter its use as a public convenience, the wall was fitted with a buttress of sloping brickwork (a wedge set in as a fillet), to do what its name suggests – "splash-back"! Bramston House student accommodation is on the top corner of Market Place and St. Osyth's. Further down the lane (opposite the Co-op) is a sizeable compound of housing for teaching staff and their families. The bungalow on the south-eastern corner (by Lime House) housed the World War Two air-raid patrols and was a Council building. It has access onto East and South roads and St. Osyth's. The lane ceases at this junction.

---

[209] Basford or Basset Ford.
[210] From a folio signed by Quincey, Paine and Jenkins, dated 1716.

EAST ROAD (south-east side from St. Osyth's Lane)

East Road was named "East Back Way" in the 1600s. The first house, number 2, on the southern corner by the post-box (opposite the side of the 'Anchor Inn') was at one time the postal service sorting office. At another time it served as the Urban Council Offices. Mr Garner served as the ratings officer in the 1940s.

In the early 1800s, number 4 was the home of Elmer Pywell, a lawyer who owned the house and its attached cottage. Thereafter, William W. Holloway lived here with his mother, Elizabeth (in the late-1800s). In the early-1900s, this was the home of Herbert and Charlotte Markham and their daughter, Margaret. Herbert was a journalist, who worked alongside the Cheney family in producing almanacs (Markham's Almanac) in 1939. It is uncertain if this house was named 'Lime House' at this time. In the mid-1960s, Mr and Mrs Shooter made this their home. They found parking and noise while living here was an issue, so they complained about everything. After they left (until the 1970s) it was the home of Arthur Weston. Then Margaret and Alex Spotswood made this their home. Alex was a sewage-worker and Margaret was a teacher. After this, the Carter family lived here until the 1990s. The house had gardens, paddocks, a coach house (the entrance is still extant) and stabling at the rear.[211]

In 1881, Anna Theobald lived at 'Lime House' with her daughters, Elizabeth and Jean. Later, William Lenton (a seed merchant) and his wife, Ruth, lived here. By the 1920s Mr and Mrs Markham were living in this large house with their daughter, Margaret. They created a tennis court here for her and her friends to play on. A little later this was the home of the Spurrell family.

One well-loved, kindly lady who lived at Lime House was Katherine Joan Strong. Her family called her "Joan". She grew-up in Thorpe Hall (which was her family home). It was a hospital during the war years and subsequently (in the 1950s) a maternity hospital and a Sue Ryder hospice (from the late-1900s into this century). Joan Strong bought the house from the Dr Spurrell.

---

[211] Thanks to Andrew Spurrell, personal information.

Miss Strong's Story

In the mid-1800s, the Honourable Reverend William Strong renovated the family home of Thorpe Hall (on the outskirts of Peterborough). He married Miss Isabella Isham (born in Polebrook in 1816) and they had six children. On his death, the Hall passed to his eldest son, Charles Isham Strong (1838-1914), a magistrate and Lieutenant-Colonel in the militia. On the lighter side, on his travels in 1847 Germany, Sir Charles Isham Strong purchased twenty-one terracotta garden gnomes to decorate his ninety-foot rockery. He instigated a craze for decorating (or littering) gardens with these bearded, merry and mischievous garden gnomes. Sir Charles's daughters did not approve of the garden dwarfs and cleared their garden of all but one (that was lost in the undergrowth for decades). When found, "Lampy" was declared to be the world's oldest-surviving garden gnome!

Charles married Katherine Powlett (aged 26) two years before his father's death (1866) and they had two sons. Upon Charles' death in 1914 (aged 76), his eldest son, Brigadier-General William Strong inherited Thorpe Hall (1914 to 1927). He fought with its many running-costs, but eventually had to sell the house and many of its furnishings. Joan Strong and her family moved to Oundle. From 1943-1970, Thorpe Hall functioned as a maternity hospital, with many Oundle women having their babies here. In 1986 it was acquired by the Sue Ryder Foundation. In 1991 it opened as a hospice.

Miss Joan Strong retained a married couple who took on the many roles as her housekeeper, chauffer, handyman and gardener. Joan was the County Commissioner for Guiding (1941-1951). Girl-Guides of the 1960s recall that the house wooden, parquet flooring needed much polishing! Joan kept a formal garden (with flowers to cut for the house on the left of the garden path). She also grew raspberry and gooseberry bushes and rows of vegetables on the opposite side (the right). Lower down the garden was the large paddock where she held fetes, meetings and camping weeks.[212] Dr Ivor Spurrell and his family had also hosted local fetes, gymkhanas and parties in this extensive garden and Joan continued this after she had moved in. Joan lived in Lime House (4 East Road) for the rest of her life (to 1984). She never

---

[212] Oral history, Wendy Bollans.

married. During her life-time the house was quite extensive, with a huge and very useful garden at the back. The house has had small-scale and large-scale changes over the years, with the installation of indoor toilets and a change of use to the eastern part of the house, which created a new single-dwelling. A new garage was also built with vehicular access. The Joan Strong Centre (in East Road) was named as a posthumous tribute to her non-ceasing work for the youth of Oundle. Katharine Joan Strong died at Lime House in September 1984.

East Road (continued)

Combined, 'Lime House', the Georgian 'Lime Cottage' and 'St. Osyth's House' (now number 4a) were once one Joan's large house. They are listed buildings, which were given a new frontage in the 1700s. 4a, St. Osyth's House, has some windows that have been bricked in. This dates to the window-tax of 1695, when houses with more than six windows were charged a tax. If they were filled-in there was no charge. Thankfully there is no window tax today.

The large house on the bend of the road is 'Lime Cottage'. It is number 6 and was the residence of Captain Francis Rivers-Freeling (born in 1806). He was related to the Selby family by marriage. Later, Mrs Sarah Donegani (born in 1848) lived here after she was widowed. Her son, Percy, worked at the newly-founded family engineering business on the premises. The turn of the century was a time when cars were making their way into our lives. Percy was born in 1889. He worked as a motor-engineer for most of his life. His family owned the nearby garage. Percy, married Lillian (Clarrice Lillian Johnson) in 1922 and she moved in with her mother-in-law. He served as an ARP warden during WWII, as he was over fifty years of age by 1940. Percy and his family lived in the vast house. Their children were John (born in 1922), Elizabeth Joan (born in 1926; who was known by her second name) and Harold Austin (born in 1930; also known by his second name). In the 1950s John took on, ran and owned the garage. John, his wife and their five children later moved to Canada. Percy Donegani died in 1994.

There was a gated way next to this house, which led around the back of the Lewis' house, leading to a paddock where Diana Leigh (née

Horne[213]) housed her horses. William Duke (known locally as 'Bill') lived in a shed in this field. He was formerly a soldier in WWI and fought at the Battle of Passchendaele, in the third Battle of Ypres, in a campaign fought by the Allies against the German Empire. The battle took place on the Western Front from July to November 1917). During the 1960s he helped at the Angel Inn and then moved to the shed in 'Button' Horne's field. Later, Bill lodged with Dolly (Dorothy) Ingham (next to the Angel) and finished his life in a home in the 1970s. (Robin Moore describes the dwelling as "a small shed with a window and a door".) Bill drank in the Angel when he was not busy. He made his living by doing odd jobs for people who lived nearby. Times were hard for those who had returned from WWI and had no family left to care for them.

From the 1950s, Dr Michael and Mrs Kathleen Lewis lived in the big house set back from the bend (Lime Cottage at number 6), with their son, John (known as Jonny). The original house has been demolished and a new house is in its place (2016), slightly set back from the road. Number 8 were the repair-garage buildings that were owned by Percy Donegani and his family. These have since been demolished to create housing.

The Gordon Road Jackson girls' "Auntie Winnie Jackson"[214] lived in the old buildings where Taney Court now stands. Mr and Mrs Thurlby and their daughters, Christine and Marjorie, lived just along the road from her. Christine subsequently married Anthony Moore (later the publican of the Angel Inn). More houses have been built where cottages once stood. The original cottages were demolished in the 1990s when they were declared derelict, hence there are new houses forming a similar row. In the 1930s, Robert Wignall lived at number 10. He was a skilled baker.

Also in the row, at number 12 East Road was the cottage where Miss Ellen May Taney (known as May, 1891-1979) lived for most of her life. She was born over the road and moved to number 12 when she was two. She had a long, busy and active life, despite operations on her feet. She was a British Legion member and their standard bearer for sixteen years. She was the founder and secretary of the Evergreen

---

[213] Note the spelling of 'Horne' and 'Horn' is interchangeable in various documents.
[214] Oral history, Sharon Cottingham.

Club, a member of the Congregational Church "Friendly Club" and in the Mothers' Union (despite being single and never a mother!). In 1891, her parents (Alfred and Mary) lived in St. Osyth's Lane with her siblings, but by 1890, they had moved to East Road. She was the final person to live in these cottages, before moving into Latham's on North Street. Her Oundle family, especially Angela (Taney) Hudson, were honoured and delighted that the new houses were named after their grandmother's sister, who was Angela's great-aunt. (With thanks to Angela for sharing her many Taney family photographs.)

What excitement there was on 18th May 1934! There was a whist drive (a cards tournament organised by a ladies' working-party in connection with the church fete) in the Brereton Rooms, Church Street. The lucky winners were announced as being Miss May Taney, Mrs J. Hunter. Mrs E. Stafford, Miss C. King (playing as a man) and Mr J. Bull. Miss Taney was a sociable and busy figure around town. In November 1940, seventy members attended the annual meeting of Oundle Women's Institute. The official report and accounts said that the elected committee for 1941 were Mrs W. Bamford, Mrs Batson, Mrs W. Bell. Mrs J. Crawley and Miss May Taney. Further to this, the 'Peterborough Advertiser' (5th August 1955) reported that the local charity 'Collectors' were: Mrs Rawlings, Miss M. Bennett, Miss Wills, Miss J. Pox, Mrs Baxter, Miss May Taney, Miss Prldmore, Mrs Crawley, Miss Washington, Mrs Taney (of Rock Road), Miss Oliver, Mrs Read and Miss Bennett. The organiser was Mrs Markham. These ladies were a credit to their families and to the town for their good works. Miss Taney "never let the grass grow under her feet" and was always active.

Burnham Terrace dates to 1909, with newly built bungalows and houses set back from the road in the gardens of what was Bertram and Dorothy Batson's house. In the 1960s, Mr and Mrs Batson (teachers at the secondary and primary schools, respectively) lived in a house that was off East Road in a large garden. Several houses have been built upon what was their garden. These are located on a narrow lane. Nearby, there was a row of terraced houses with railings in the front, which were taken down in the war. In the 1930s, Percy Haynes lived at number 14 with his wife and their daughters, Violet and Florence (Doris). Both were born at the start of the First World War. Percy was a gardener by trade. Connie Jackson (an aunt of Robin Moore) lived here until the 1970s and Winnie Barrett lived in a house just behind this row. It was then rented to USA forces staff until the 1960s.

Number 16 was the home of Mark and his daughter, Gertrude Gale. At the start of the twentieth century, Mark worked as a railway engineer, doing maintenance and repairs as a labourer. The family took in an evacuee, Ida Violet Hodgkinson, who was twelve when WWII began. (This family is not to be confused with a family bearing the same name living at number 36, but Mark is Bessie's brother-in-law; John Gale and Mark were brothers.)

At number 18 in the 1930s, lived a widow named Charlotte Gilby and her daughter, Sarah (who was born in 1908). During her working life, Sarah was a ledger clerk. Charlotte was born in Oundle in 1867 and died in 1940 (aged 73). Robin Moore recalls that by the 1960s Sarah, who was always called 'Miss Gilby', lived alone in the corner house. By then she worked in Lane's shop (to the front of the pub). Robin reminisced that "She would often stand on the corner in her big black skirt, looking down the road. She was probably lonely after her mother died". Sarah stood waiting for people to pass the time of day with her.

In the early twentieth century number 20 was a cottage, home to Frederick and Elizabeth Sansby. Frederick worked as an agricultural labourer. His neighbours were John Fox and his wife, Mary Ann (née Horn) who lived at 22. They married in 1900. John was a general labourer on local building sites. He was an Air-Raid Precautions (ARP) Warden during the war. John looked after pigs, which he kept on his land and belonged to Colonel McMichael and his family. Edith and James Bunnings lived 24. James worked as a school caretaker and as a retained fireman for the Oundle Urban Council. Number 24 is part of the East Road new building development as the house was pulled down. In the 1930s this was a very "handy" row of houses to live in, as the row of terraced-houses had a skilled fireman (at number 24) and a "health visitor" (at 26) who would attended each mother and child after a local birth.

Numbers 26 to 36 were known as 'Burnham Terrace' and 38 to 42 were 'Rudland Villas'. After the little road to the Batson's house, there are more terraces. There is a row of six, with a gap (alley) to go through to the gardens after the first three. There is a gap before 38-40-42 that

289

are in this end block of houses. This is followed by a gateway within the structure of the buildings, with an alley to the back gardens between numbers 40 and 42. Numbers 38 and 40 had their roof-spaces converted into useable rooms at the end of the twentieth century.

Before WWI, Mrs Esther Munds lived at number 26 (the second house in the terrace). Esther was born in 1872. When living at number 26 she rented a room in her house to a female lodger. She also shared the house with her married daughter, Winifred Almond (née Munds; who was born in 1916). Their 1940s evacuee was Maureen Henaghan (born in 1933). Winifred was considered a very busy lady. She was a member of the St. John's Ambulance Brigade (Oundle Division) and was a nursing reserve. Winifred also worked as a shop assistant in the local stationers.

John Mott and his wife, Alice, lived at number 28. John was a labourer at the foundry. The history of number 30 is lost, but living at 32 was William (Bill) Cottingham and his wife Alice. Bill was a gardener at the public school. The couple took in evacuees. These included Margaret Dennison, who was aged around fourteen during WWII. His neighbours David and Ethel Allaby lived at 34. David worked as a night-watchman at the Royal Air Force depot on the Barnwell Road in Oundle. They had a teenage wartime lodger, Gwendoline Wright.

At number 36, the end house in the first terrace of six, was the home of John William Gale (born in 1871 in Oundle), his wife Bessie (née Palmer, who was born in 1887) and their daughter, Margaret. Bessie Gale was a widow with a young family, as John William Gale died in 1930 aged 48. His obituary states that he was a well-known Oundle Odd-Fellow.[215] For many years John was a member of the District Committee of Management. He was the Masonic Past Provincial Grand Master, Lodge and State Auditor and Provincial Grand of the Loyal Providence Lodge females. His daughter was known as "Miss Gale" by her pupils. She was a teacher at Oundle Secondary Modern School from the 1940s to 1960s. As she taught for many years in the same school, she often taught several generations within a family. Margaret Gale was a talented artist and long-term art and form teacher at the

---

[215] Founded during the 1700s, the Independent Order of Odd Fellows is a non-political and non-sectarian group performing charity works.

school. Margaret's line-drawing (a view sketched from East Road) was used for the logo of the Oundle Guide. It is now the logo for Oundle Town Council. Born in 1913, Margaret never married.

This terrace of houses originally had a low front wall, which has been removed. This row of terraced houses (ending at the Gale's house) was next to a row of three terraced houses with bay windows. These are adjacent to a narrow lane. It passes between the council houses and the terrace of houses. The lane now leads to Mason Close rather than to the backs and gardens of the former council houses. It previously terminated in the open fields. In the 1930s, number 38 was the home of Mary Harris (who was born in 1899). She was a widow who lived alone.

After the terraced houses in the road were three bigger houses. In the 1930s, in the first house (number 40) there lived Mrs Elizabeth Clarke (who was born in 1858). Elizabeth was a widow. She hired a "lady's maid" after her husband (John) had died. Her employed maid was Miss Freda Hasnip. She acted as both a companion and household help. It is believed that Freda was required to wear a cap and apron as part of her formal contract. In the late-1800s and early 1900s, a 'companion' was essentially (and legally) a domestic maid who was paid a salary for accomplishing duties. Usually, a companion was a maid to someone who was an invalid, "desolate" or elderly. In the pre-war years, many women were much more dependent upon their 'bread-winner' husbands. Widows often required 'company' to prevent loneliness and a 'companion-help' was often sought when travelling away from home. This lasted until the onset of war, when women were involuntarily 'trained' to be more self-reliant.

John Brown, was a police inspector in the Reserve Northamptonshire Constabulary. He lived in the third of the larger, terraced houses (at number 42) with his wife, Florence. Their daughter, Margaret, was born in 1923. In the 1960s, one family who lived in East Road were the Collis'. Ivor Collis and his wife, Dorothy, had four children, Richard, Terry, Ellen and Jeremy. They all attended the local primary school. Ivor worked for Anglian Water. When St. Peter's Road was in the process of being developed the family had a house built and they moved there once it had been completed.

East Road Council Houses started to appear in the 1930s. Built between the 1930s and 1940s, number 44 was the first of the Council Houses. It was the home to Harry Lee (born 1879) and his wife and family. He worked as an engineer at the old pumping-station in Barnwell Road, Oundle (as, originally, liquids would be 'pumped' to transfer either the foul or surface water to a local drain, manhole or sewer system. Since this time, the old pumping-station has been converted from its original use and is now a house and flat). Harry lived here with his wife, Florence (née Boulter; who was twelve years his junior) and their sons, Raymond and Brian. (Fanny Parker also lived with the family. She was four years younger than Florence, so may have been a relative.) Raymond later married and moved into the newly-built Springfield Road houses with his wife. His children (born in the 1950s) were Elaine, Marie and David.

During the 1930s, number 46 was the home of Mr Wilfred Welch. He who worked at the gas works as a gas fitter (now Waitrose). His elderly, widowed mother, Ada Welch (who was born in 1875) lived with him. Wilfred also served as a member of the Oundle Division of the St. John's Ambulance Brigade. In the 1950s and 1960s, the spot between the football-field and new Waitrose building was where the British Gas cylinder purveyor, stove shop and gas showroom 'Oundle Gas Light and Coke Company Limited' stood. My mum bought her first cooker there after marrying my dad (1952) and my grandparents shopped there long before that (in the 1930s). At the new Waitrose site, some residents opposed demolition of two ancient, late-mediæval barns that were of an age and character suitable for conservation and listing (2012). They were demolished.

During the 1960s, the fish and chip van would "stop just around this corner" into East Road for residents to buy a delicious cooked meal. This was the advent of 'fast food'. The smell of chips would permeate the area and everyone knew what day and time the van would arrive and start cooking. Queues would appear as soon as the van did. Sadly, this practice stopped when the van caught fire! Once the fish and chip shop had moved from the west end of West Street to the Market Place, its placement·was more central for people to buy their pre-cooked meals.

At number 48 was Mrs Daisy Marlow (née Green). She was a lady who worked at the Brewery Bottle Factory. Prior to 1938, when Ernest Marlow died, he and his wife lived with their six children: John, Nora, Muriel (who moved to America), Dennis, Margaret[216] and Betty. Their son, John Marlow, was in the RAF and lost his life in WWII. His is one of the names used for the House system in the Secondary Modern (Council) School as a tribute to his life and early demise in military action for his country. Ernest and Daisy housed an evacuee, Joyce Herby, in WWII.

Frank Gaunt wed in 1924 and the family lived at number 50. Frank and Margaret Gaunt and their children, June, Joyce, Jean and Alan (Malcolm), were here in the 1930s and 1940s. Joyce said that "Mum took in laundry for the Americans". "I can still smell the wash-room and laundry in the yard with its big 'copper' of boiling water and the mangle to squeeze water out of wet clothes." Frank was a bus-driver ("public-service vehicle driver"), an Oundle Urban District Councillor and a part-time auxiliary fireman. Herbert Dodsworth worked as a public-service vehicle driver (PSVD) and conductor with Frank, so rented a room from him.

At number 52 was Henry and Gertrude Toyne and their children, Brian, Barbara and Terry. Henry was a school sanatorium houseman. Their lodger, Betty Wrigley, was in the Land Army. She married a G.I. during the war and emigrated to America with her husband as an 'Army bride'. The Women's Land Army (WLA) was a British civilian organisation, which was formed during the First and Second World Wars so that women could work in agriculture and replace the men who had been "called up" to the military. Women who worked for the WLA were commonly known as Land Girls. Also living here, was Kathleen Brightman, who was a civil servant at the General Post Office.

At number 54, there was Mr William "Button" Horne and his wife, Elizabeth. He was grandfather to Valerie and Diana Leigh. Button was an auxiliary postman who was too old to join WWII, so stood in as a full-time postman for the men who left. He rented rooms in his house to James Walton. James was a general labourer. Rooms were also rented to Leonard Longmore, a riveter. Until the 1970s, everything

---

[216] Now Mrs Nelson.

from buildings and bridges, to planes, tanks and automobiles were held together with rivets. These were fastened into place by air-gun-wielding factory workers. By the twenty-first century, this has more or less given way to technological innovations. Welding and installing high-tensile bolts has taken over, as riveters seem to have disappeared.

Leonard and Gertie Crick (in the 1880s) and their children, Margaret, Mary and Ray, lived in number 56. Leonard worked on the railway engineering maintenance and repair staff. At number 58, Mr Elias Craythorne and his wife, Sarah (née Quincey) and their two "pretty and flirty" daughters, Freda (born in 1911) and Rita (born 1918), lived on the corner of Ashton Road. "Times were hard and the girls used to go potato-picking in the local fields to make a bit of extra money". (Mum recalls them doing potato-picking with her and a group of the other local girls from their school in the war, when senior school girls were allowed out in the afternoons to help the 'War Effort' in the fields along the Stoke Doyle Road. There was no maternity leave as such. Sharon Cottingham reflected that when her "aunt was heavily pregnant and she was still in the fields picking potatoes".) On 9th November 1934, Miss Freda Craythorne (the daughter of Mr and Mrs Elias Craythorne of 58 East Road), married Mr Frank C. Abbott. In 1936, Freda and Frank had a "bouncing baby girl" (named Jean) and at this time, the family were still living in the same household (at number 58). Rita married Ronald White in 1937. Elias and Sarah were long-lived and celebrated their diamond anniversary.[217]

During WWII, the Ashton Road had a road block, which was constructed in mid-July 1940 by the Central Midland Command. The carriageway was not permanently blocked, but steel stanchions and sand bags were used along with lump stone, which enabled the duty men to close the road quickly in the event of an emergency. The houses along the Ashton Road were mostly constructed in the 1930s and sold to Oundle Urban District Council. East Road and Ashton Road residents held a coronation street party in 1953 (see photograph, with thanks to Ann Greetham [Colclough]). The local families enjoyed the celebrations.

---

[217] Report from (N. M.) paper.

The footpath to Ashton village starts here (via the newly named "Old Quarry Road"). The shortest walking distance from the town centre to Ashton is along this route. The Rothschild family allowed their Manor House, over the fields in Ashton Wold, to be used as a Red Cross Hospital during WWII. The hospital acted as a convalescent home and billet. The Red Cross moved out again in 1945. The top floor of the house, where all the hospital beds were installed, was cleaned and the evidence of wartime use was removed by Mrs Lane's son. The stables were used to billet the men of the Ordnance Corps and their officers stayed in the house of one of the estate agents.[218] Miriam (Mrs Lane, née Rothschild) was a naturalist with a particular interest in fleas and butterflies. She adopted forty-nine refugee children to save them from being taken in the holocaust. It is remembered that she did not stand on dignity and always "dressed down".

Herne Park (a cul-de-sac) leads off from the mini-roundabout. It is at a junction with Ashton Road and the rest of East Road. Number 1 Herne Park is on the corner of East Road and Ashton Road. The Joan Strong Centre is the charity home of 'Oundle Rural Mind', helping people with mental health problems and offers support to sufferers of anxiety and depression, formerly "Nene Valley Mind". The Joan Strong Centre was named to commemorate Kathleen (Joan) Strong's lifetime of work supporting the Scouting movement in Oundle. (This was the way to the Recycle Centre). On the corner (just past the cul-de-sac that once led to fields and takes you to the 1990s recycle waste centre) was the site of the NCC Depot. (Frank Jackson was a worker at the Oundle Town Council depot in the 1950s and 1960s.) The vehicles were stored here along with piles of grit. When the weather was bad, the men were called in to grit the roads. This was not mechanised. Men shovelled spades full of grit onto the roads, prior to a freezing night or early in the morning before the traffic started to move.

During the war, 'Nipper' Cunnington was in charge of collections. Household rubbish and 'night soil' (excrement collected at night from buckets cess-pools and outdoor toilet ['privies'] that was used as manure) was collected in a horse-drawn ash-cart. If it was icy and slippery on the roads, the horse would be fitted with spiked shoes to

---

[218] Oral history, Bevil Allen.

prevent skidding. During the war these carts also collected paper and cardboard that was left in the Town Hall.

For many years, potatoes were grown in the fields behind the depot. 1960s teenagers were co-opted to help their mothers in the holidays for seasonal picking of potatoes and other vegetables in local fields. Potatoes were picked, weighed and added to previously picked potato bags collected by the same family. Pay was depended on how many bags (by weight) were collected. Parents would give their children some 'pocket money' from the daily wage.

The Oundle Brownie, Guide and Scout Headquarters was originally used as a Decontamination building. It is used as the local polling station for government elections. Oundle Beaver Scouts tend the Joan Strong Centre garden (planting sunflowers, beetroot, tomatoes, beans, lettuce, carrots, herbs and flowers). In November 2016, the Beavers and Cub group helped to plant crocus bulbs in St Peter's Church yard as one of their Community projects. These germinated and looked wonderful in the spring.

In 2015, Oundle Girl and Cub Scout Leader, Sheila Pick, received the British Empire Medal in the Queen's Birthday Honours List for services in Scouting. Sheila is based in the Joan Strong Centre, where she continues her excellent work with the 2nd Oundle Scout Group. She is the wife of John Pick, who part-owns the local Pick-Arthey garage on Station Road. Oundle long stay car-park is located here. It is free to park here all day.

As noted earlier, Oundle Recycle Centre was at the terminus of this road (but is now permanently closed). The nearest recycle centre is now in Weldon. This closure meant a great loss to Oundle, as it was used continuously and made life easier for the residents, who could visit with their grass and tree clippings, newspapers, glass, foil, etc. (The latter items are now collected from houses, but garden waste collection carries an annual charge.)

From the Joan Strong Centre and workshops there were fields and paddocks (over the road from the back of the Berrystead) that lie behind the contemporary buildings. A wall divides the world from the back of Berrystead. An eighteenth-century gazebo-tower is in the corner of the grounds and forms part of the wall. It was moved from Queen Anne's House and relocated here. Imposing ironwork gates with columns topped with statues stood behind Berrystead (formerly Rectory Manor). On stone pillars either side of the gates were a statue of Robin Hood (with a bow and arrows) and Little John (with his dog). In the early 1900s they were removed and sold.

A smaller, much less impressive gate in East Road was a route to the paddock field that Aubrey Clarke (locally named "Clanger Clarke" as Captain of the bell-tower at St. Peter's Church) owned. During WWII, he was taken captive and worked on the Burma-Siam railway. He took short-cuts behind his house, from Bassett Place to the East Road field, to feed his animals.

Two semi-detached cottages are still evident near Mowbray's paddock. The Oundle School Buildings Department have offices here. Laxton Junior School (the new site after a move from Old Dryden) has its own zebra-crossing. Once upon a time, under this site, were grass tennis courts (to the rear) and a paddock for goats and a pony (at the front), which lies under the current Laxton Junior School car-park. This was previously Congregational Chapel land.

There is a row of three houses further along the road. In the 1930s, Herbert (born in 1884) and Fanny Craythorne lived at number 60 with their children. Herbert was a brick layer. Their son, Herbert W., was a school caretaker. At number 62, lived John H. Wade and Frances, his wife. John was a plumber. Their daughter, Frances (born in 1912) was a poultry farmer. She later married Mr Hodges. In 1939, at 64 East Road were the Misses Roe, two spinster sisters: Ann Elizabeth Roe (a retired elementary school head-teacher) and Emma Roe (a retired infant teacher). By 1939 the couple were aged in their 70s.

Nearby there was a corrugated metal gate to a small field with trees. This is where Mr Clarke kept his chickens in the 1960s. They roosted in the trees at night time. The hens lived near a piggery that had wall-flowers growing on the walls. Sheila Denley recalls that their cats (Percy, a ginger) and William (ginger and white) were both female! William was the roof-top walker. Percy was run over on East Road and buried by Aubrey Clarke in his piggery, as he thought it was one of his cats until it sat next to him just as he'd finished. Aubrey said that he said "ere, I just buried you!' He then had to seek out Mr Denley to tell him the news. (Other Denley cats that liked to lurk in the road and nearby fields were: Tinker, Squeak, Noggins, Butch, Limpet and Agnes Flower, to name but a few.)

Number 66 was the local gas works with its small, front office and behind it was the gasometer tank (used for storing gas). The gas holder was an upturned-bell within a framework that held it as it rose and fell (depending on the amount of gas it had inside). Mr Walter H. Frost lived at (66) the gas works. He lived with his wife, Annie, and their family. Walter was the gas works distribution manager and an ARP in the war.

Just prior to the terminus of East Road (and the Waitrose store), there is a small road that leads off. This is Eastwood Road (cul-de-sac). It has a mini-roundabout allows traffic ease of access to the appropriately named, Eastwood Road, comprising of a discrete group of 'industrial units' and pre-schools. Eastwood Road is was mostly created in the early twenty-first century. It contains a collection of workplaces and small industries, including 'Classic Reclaims' (which moved from behind the old train-station), 'Oundle Carpet Sales,' Goldsmith's Auction Rooms', 'Rainbow Nursery', 'Small Wonders Nursery' (built on the site of 'Oundle Spares and Repairs'), 'Oundle Curtains' (Units 4-6) and 'Surma' Indian-food (takeaway and delivery business).

It is interesting to reflect and curious to recall that, previously, Oundle only had deliveries of (uncooked) foods until the 'Fish'n'Chip van appeared (in the 1960s), yet we have evolved from visiting the old 'chip van' to a myriad of hot food deliveries. In 2009, the corner spot was Norwood's[219] taxi-hire service, which was first established in 1945. New in-fill buildings are slowly filling spaces between the houses along East Road and Eastwood Road.

EAST ROAD (north-west side from St. Osyth's Lane)

The Duck's Nest (formerly the Anchor Inn) is on the corner (see St. Osyth's Lane) with its vehicle access and parking in East Road. A separate garage appears to adjoin number 1 East Road, which was originally the home to Raymond Mottram. Ray was in the ARP service

---

[219] Carl Norwood lived in St. Osyth's Lane for much of his life.

and worked as the Oundle postmaster. He lived here with his wife, Florence. In WWII, the ARP (air-raid precaution) wardens supervised the blackout, making sure that people did not 'show a light' at night time, for fear of bombers seeing the lights and dropping their payloads. This house was the ARP base. ARP duties included looking for enemy planes to sounding the air-raid sirens (or whistles), looking for houses that didn't 'black out' properly and 'dangerously' showed lights after dark, checking for fires and general defence regimes: practising evasion for an invasion. A motto was "be like dad, keep mum". One night, a fully loaded bomber crashed as it was about to take-off. The locals were woken by the 'terrific noise' that was heard in Oundle when all was quiet and they were in their beds.

The current house was built in 1936, according to the stonework date above the door. The house has a cottage look to it and bears the name "Fig Tree Cottage". In the early 1970s, the secretary of the Flower Arrangement Society, Mrs M.H. Holmes, lived at 1 East Road.

Next-door (number 3) appears to be missing, although there are signs of demolition on the walls. Number 5 is also missing, but the corner house is a very unusual shape from the outside, as it does not have ninety-degree corners to its walls, and may have been incorporated into the next houses. Number 7 is "Orchard Manor House". It is now a private house.

Ralph and Phyllis (née Horn) Leigh and their family (Valerie and Diana) lived at number 9 in the 1930s. Ralph was a school caretaker. Thomas Sammons (who was twenty to thirty years older than Ralph) and Leslie Andrews (six years younger) were lodgers in their house. Thomas was a riveter; a skilled job, requiring him to a work with metal inserts, hammering rivets. Leslie worked as a riveter's labourer (possibly alongside Thomas). Mr and Mrs 'Button' Horne and their children (Phyllis, Sydney and Rita) lived on the west side of the road. Since the 1960s this was home to Diana (a talented, local artist and art teacher) and her family. Mr Samuel Roughton lived at number 11. He was an elderly widower and retired gardener, who lived here with his son, Percy. The main householders were Percy Roughton (a draper's-shop assistant) and his wife, Mary. The family also supported lodgers. At number 13 was William Cottingham. He was a retired building labourer. 'The Mousehole' is part of the terrace of houses leading round the corner. Its name appears to be newer than the building. This two-bedroomed, cosy cottage has beamed ceilings. It has a new two-storey extension and small courtyard garden. Annie Neal lived with Edith Wright at number 15. They were about the same age. Annie was a single lady, who worked as an assistant in the School Tuck Shop. Later, Ann Colclough (later Greetham) lived at number 15, when it was two cottages.

In St. Osyth's Lane, roughly where the Co-op is now, stood a thatched house where Edward ('Ted') and Doris Hooton lived with their large family.[220] They delivered the Sunday newspapers around the town. During the war, no-one liked food and clothing rationing, but they understood why it was necessary. Many people kept chickens and their own livestock to supplement the ration coupon purchases. There were never enough clothing coupons, as clothing manufacturers turned their hand to producing uniforms and bedding for the troops. Those with a large family, which Doris Hooton did, would often exchange their clothing coupons with 'better off' families who had fewer children and wanted something a little nicer than the rudimentary outfits. Materials were purchased to make outfits. Barbara (née Chester) recalls that parachute materials were in high demand. Most families learned how to sew and make-do-and-mend. Their family became well-known business people around Oundle (Ralph owned his own general store in St. Osyth's Lane, Ralph then Peter had the 'Coffee Tavern' and Audrey had a small shop in Rock Road). Doris did her laundry in a shed that was joined by one wall to the house. She had chickens and fowl in a pen. When the eggs were ready to hatch, Doris put the eggs into the warm fire-grate and her niece, Barbara, recalls the fluffy chicks that often inhabited the house.

Number 17 is a stone building that is now an end-terrace, renamed "Plum Tree Cottage". It is the last house in this block as it is next to the rear entrance of the Co-operative car-park (and houses that previously stood here have been demolished). Mr and Mrs Thomas ('Tommy') Sharpe and their children, Nancy and John, lived here in the 1930s (17). Tommy was the Brewery Maltster. His wife, Annie, was a charwoman

---

[220] Anna Fernyhough. "My grandmother's step-sister, Auntie Doris Hooton, had sixteen children. My mum was an 'only child', but never felt as if she was one, as she had so many close cousins".

(cleaner). Their son, Jack, lived with them and worked as a butcher's assistant (and was an ARP messenger during the war). Their daughter, Nancy (later Mrs Brady), was born just prior to the war. (She was six years younger than her brother.) Andy Upchurch, a builder, lived here in the late-1970s and early 1980s. He conducted quite a lot of renovation to the property including excellent stonework repairs.

The two houses that follow number 17 (19 and 21) were demolished in the 1960s. John Olley (a school master of music), Joseph Mann (an Oundle School porter) and Joseph's daughter, Margaret (born in 1896) lived at number 19 during the 1930s. The last house, number 21, was the residence of Albert Arberry and his wife, Ethel (who, in time, was Ann Cheetham's grandma). Albert worked as a school caretaker in the School Chapel. Ethel Arberry was a close friend and neighbour of Miss May Taney. This was a cottage where Sharon Cottingham's "aunty Ella" lived as a lodger. Ella worked at the nearby School Refectory. Sharon said that Ella "probably had the cleanest teeth in Oundle, as when the hot wash was on in the machines, she would pop her false teeth in for a wash too"!

The original entrance for William T. Beadsworth's agricultural engineers and ironmongery was at the back of the Anchor Inn at the turn of the century. Then its right-of-way became the entrance for double-decker buses to a depot that was here from the 1930-1950s. William Beadsworth died in 1930, aged 82. It is where the Co-operative store car-park and toilet-block stand. Behind the houses (now Co-op) stood the 1960s shoe factory and the site of 'Complete Supplies Engineers' in the 1970s.

A pathway between houses gave access to St. Osyth's Lane. A bungalow in the corner of the car-park (number 21) was demolished when the Co-op was built. Oundle Registrar, Mark Fox, reflecting on his youth, said that at harvest-time the traction engines would race through the town to Bill Beadsworth's Yard in East Road (where the car-park is). The engine drivers would try to get to the repair shop first to get a faster service. David Wills said that in the noises they made were impressive and exciting, as streets were usually dark and added to the smoke, steam and golden "glow from the fire box".[221] The

---

[221] David Wills, personal history.

Hooton girls and Barbara Chester would go from St. Osyth's to the East Road Depot shed with the bus conductor, Bill, who allowed them to collect lost loose change from under the seats.

The house numbers on this side of the road resume at number 23 with a house along a short drive. Widow, Elizabeth Nickerson, lived here in the 1930s. Also here was John Sawford, who worked as a farm labourer.

Number 25 is a relatively new house, but with an older, brick portion. In the 1930s Harry Beeby and his wife, Lizzy, lived here with their two sons and two daughters. Harry was a road-work labourer and their son, Dennis, was a laboratory assistant. This was Phyllis Beeby's home. (She is now 93 and is a lively resident at Abbott House.) She grew up in East Road and was the youngest of four (born in 1924). She is proud of her brother, Dennis Beeby, who worked in the science block at Oundle School. Phyllis said that she worked as a Post Office switchboard operator.

Phyllis also mentioned that she has always loved to dance. When she was younger she attended dances "in many places", including Peterborough Town Hall. She lived in the house "in the front of the Snake's house". This later became the Watkin family's house. Living in East Road meant that she "always used the cut-through past the other houses to the cycle shop that became the electrician's" (Owen and Hartley). This right-of-way has long gone between East Road and Jericho.[222]

The 'Snake family's house' was in the back-yard of the current house on East Road (behind Lorne House). The back gate entrance to Jericho looks out on East Road. This was originally wide enough for a carriage to pass through. The interior of the garden had an asphalt drive leading to Lorne House. The interior of the gardens has been remodelled. The right side is an organised English garden. It was designed and planted by Betty Heesom in the late-1950s. She studied Vita Sackville-West's 'garden rooms' and designed her garden with this in mind. Behind the wall to the left is the garden of Lorne House. This has cottages, including number 27, behind the current buildings facing onto East

---

[222] Phyllis Beeby, personal information.

Road. At number 27 was John E. Watkins (born in 1882) and his wife, Martha (née Manning). They wed in March 1930 in Thrapston. John worked as a night-watchman and worked in the mobilisation department. They lived with John's brother, James Watkins (who was born in 1884). James who worked in the brewery as a maltster. The house was quite busy with three adults and John's three children: Millicent, John and Herbert.[223]

The rear gates and gardens of the Oundle School Berrystead House were used by Laxton Junior School when it first opened and before its move to the new premises in East Road. There is also access to the gardens via Duck Street and from Old Dryden. The small, square, eighteenth-century gazebo towers mark the property boundaries of the garden. It is believed that they were moved from elsewhere to enhance the grounds of the Berrystead House. They stand next door to the kitchens for Mowbrays, Laundimer, Berrystead and Old Dryden refectories, which are accessed via North Street. Miriam Woods noted that she was approximately seventeen years old when she worked in Oundle School refectory. She did so alongside Ann Upex. Miriam said, "On Friday evenings I was a clearer-upper". (Her mother, Dora Wood, worked at the school as a cook under Mr Thurlow.) Towards the East Road are the gardens and tennis-courts of Laundimer House.

These gardens are followed by a gravel car-park and large lawns to Parson Latham's Hospital. The rear of Latham's Blue Coat School has been linked internally with the Parson Latham gardens, making the already sizeable gardens much larger. (The Blue Coat School was later the home of the headmaster for Oundle Primary School and was a tied, job-related residence). Mr and Mrs Denley and their family lived for many years in this house. Alan Denley was the last head-teacher to live in this residence, with his wife Marjorie and their three children. This stood empty for a while, but has been incorporated into Latham's home for retired Oundle ladies next-door (as this was all part of the same property in its historic ownership).

---

[223] In 1891, their parents, Edward and Jane Watkins, lived at 11 Havelock Cottages. In 1911, the entrance to the Cottages was via North Street (on the east side). Their house was described as "South View" 11 Havelock Cottages, North Street.

Regarding the local 'Council' (Nationally-funded) school, Joyce Hardick mentioned that there were changes to the junior and the senior divisions of the school in 1939. Mabel Perring ran the school as head-teacher in 1932 to 1940. Her back gate entered onto East Road at this point. While Mrs Perring was the headmistress the Oundle 'Church School' came to be known as the Saint Peter's Church of England Primary School. Joyce Gaunt went here and had her first "Milky Way" chocolate bar on the way home! She had never tasted a bar so delicious and she was most impressed! She said, "As food was rationed, the headmistress, Mrs Perring, sold chocolate wafers to the children from a tin. Evelyn Rootham was a 'big girl' at the school and helped out."[224] The County Modern School was developed out of the Council School. The name change was major, but the location stayed the same. Croft House is a new-build house. It looks as if it was built in the 1960s, but may be older.

At number 29 were George Williamson and his wife, Phoebe (née Cooper). He was a general labourer. George married Phoebe in 1931. Their son Dennis is shown as living with or visiting his widowed, maternal grandmother, Harriett (at the time of the 1939 census register record). Harriet's late husband was Samuel John Thomas Cooper from Oundle. Next-door, at number 31, lived John G. Craythorne (born in 1877). He was an unmarried, general labourer (doing heavy work). He lived with another single man, born in the same year, John Martin. He was also a labourer in heavy work. Living with them was Henry Cates (born in 1874) and his wife, Mary (born in 1883). Henry was a house painter.

'Pettifer Drainage' is currently in the position it has held for over fifty years. Originally it is listed as being run by W. F. Pettifer and his son in 1960. The company was for complete irrigation systems, boreholes, submersible pumps, permanent mains, watering equipment, soil mechanics investigation and artesian well engineers. The company may have closed in 2006. Yet, the same family performs their work in the irrigation trade. Their delivery office is listed as being 29 Nene Valley Business Park. Progressing along the road, behind John Hillyard's house was a florists business until around 2013, when part of the trade

---

[224] Joyce Gaunt.

moved to the Wharf business area. Their business is listed at 9 Eastwood Road. 'Hillyard's of Oundle' is still a florists, dealing in wedding bouquet sales and trading in wholesale florist and horticultural supplies. The business is now run by John and Valerie's son, 'Bill'. There was a recent fire in their outer building on East Road (2016), but this was successfully extinguished by Oundle Fire Brigade.

Havelock Cottages

Havelock cottages form two lines of houses (fourteen in all), side-on to East Road that are located in a cul-de-sac. They were built during the 1700s and 1800s and renamed to commemorate Sir Henry Havelock's assistance in the liberation of Lucknow in 1857, during the Indian Mutiny. During the 1800s there were nine cottages. The former Maltings office was adjoined to them. Widow Callon, George Manon, John Bland, Rebecca Richardson, John Crooks, Mary Ann Roe, Louisa Richards, James Wade and Widow Askham lived in them when they were first built. Thereafter there was John Isham Sabin, James Todd, Mrs Roe, Mr J. Greaves, Rebecca Richardson, Mrs Brudenell, John Riddle and Henry Hill, with an unoccupied house at the end.

By the turn of the century, Charles Loakes, William Elderkin, Mr C.H. Palmer, Arthur Sharpe, Samuel Pridmore, William Pulford, Edward Watkins, George William Butt and the Widow Freer lived in the cottages. There were four other cottages erected on this site, with two under the tenure of Samuel Grooby. These were occupied by William Bossingham, William Marlow, Daniel Beeby and Henry Holdich. Then Henry Holdich, Richard Burrows, Stephen Phillipson and William Clipstone. By the end of the 1800s, the residents were Henry Holdich (born in 1841), Widow Roe, William Mason and Robert Baxter Burrows (who died in 1899).

Three further cottages were added on the site of a barn at the east end of the property. These were occupied by Daniel Dakin (died 1890, aged 69), Joseph Clipstone (who died aged 71 in 1894) and Mrs Jane Brudenell (died 1888); then later, Widow Freer, Joseph Clipstone and Mr Titman. All of this estate belonged to Samuel Pierce and was known as East Court, but this group are now better known as Havelock cottages.

The north side wall where the cottages join were partly the property of Benjamin Todd, then Mary Smith. On the south side (wall) the cottages were "bounded by the property of John William Wise, then John Hayes". By 1919, William Allen was "admitted to the premises". Numbers 1-14 Havelock and 29 and 31 East Road were still portioned together. The Havelock 'garden' was bordered by the property of neighbours, William Bertie Binder on the north side and Mary Smith (1939) on the south side.

A semi-detached house is located at 1 Havelock Cottages. Thomas Sismey and his wife, Bertha, lived here in the 1930s with their two children. Kathleen, their daughter, was born in 1925. Thomas was a general labourer in "heavy work". The dwellings are grade-II listed stone-built, worker's cottages dating to the nineteenth-century. The small, two-bedroomed cottages (lower at the east end than west) have brick-floored living-rooms (with nineteenth-century chimney-pieces), original cast-iron ranges and a pantry, lit by a shuttered-window. They have been recently renovated. At number 2 lived Blanche Hasnip (born in 1906). She was the daughter of Mary and James Samuel Green (who were originally from Great Stukeley). In 1927, Blanche married Frank L. Dent in Huntingdonshire, before the birth of their son, Reginald, who was born in 1928. By 1933, Blanche was styling herself as a "widow", yet records show Frank's death was much later! Also living at this address was Mary Green (born in 1863), who was also a widow. Blanche Dent quickly married Albert Hasnip in 1933 in St Ives, Huntingdonshire, and they rapidly had a baby girl, Constance, born in 1934. Blanche was the widow of Albert Hasnip within the same year as the baby arrived; as Albert died during 1934. In 1939 Blanche met Raymond Clarke, a widower living at 3 Station Road with his family, Kenneth and Jessie. (See Station Road.) Blanche subsequently married Raymond in 1940.

The Havelock cottages (pronounced 'hav-a-lok') have their own numbering system. At number 3 lived Alfred (Fred) Roughton (the son of Alfred and Ellen Roughton, he was born in 1890). He lived here with his wife during the 1930s. His wife was Emma K. Roughton (née Mounder). She was born in 1896. They married at the close of the First World War (1918). He worked as a night-watchman. At number 4 lived Charles (Charlie) Pridmore (born 1886). He was an unmarried, farm labourer. At number 5 there was Dorothy Rogers, who worked in the town as a 'charwoman'. (She was employed as a cleaner in people's houses and in the school offices). Arthur and Phyllis Coles lived at number 6. Arthur worked as a local general labourer. Leonard Gates was billeted with the couple during the war. (He was born in Islington, London, in 1927.)

Virginia Francis (née Gaunt) and Jackie Ganderton both recall the year 1948, when they lived with their mum and dad in 7 Havelock Cottages. At that time Olive lived in the first cottage, before moving to South Road. Molly Slater lived in another. Mrs Dorothy Black (later Miles) lived in the cottage at the top of the row and June Gaunt lived two doors down (probably number 9 or 10). Jackie recalls that the rooms were 'very tiny'. David and Olive (née Miller) Ginns lived at number 7. They had married in December 1917. David worked as a farm labourer. He died in 1944. Later in her life Olive married Mr Joseph Hollowell (in 1957). Arthur Sharpe lived at number 8. He was born in 1876 and had not married. He worked as a brewers' labourer. (Numbers 9, 11 and 12 Havelock cottages were possibly used as outbuildings at this time as there is no record of them as being lived in). Just prior to WWII, Mrs Dorothy Black lived at number 10 Havelock Cottages when she first married (after the death of Mr Black, she remarried and came to be Mrs Miles). Her daughter, Cheryl recalls that "not very far from here there was a registry office on East Road".[225] In the 1930s, Percy Brackley worked as a night-watchman (most probably for the brewery). He lived at number 13, along with other (transient) visitors. Norman Dexter lived with him and worked as an errand boy in the town. Harriet Cooper lived in last in the row of houses, at number 14. She was the householder. She was fifty-eight years old when she took in a four-year-old evacuee, Dennis Williamson, in the early 1930s. This was quite a change to her normal lifestyle!

It is perhaps worth noting that like other towns throughout the UK, there were times when Oundle residents took in and supported evacuees from London and other large cities that were in danger of

---

[225] With thanks for this information to Cheryl Forscutt.

being bombed. The evacuees stayed with the families during the war years.

Two large, modern, stone houses with garages in their drive, have been built that stand back from the road here. I believe that they are numbers 37 and 39. Next-door, there is a drive and gates to one further house. The old brewery Maltings or 'Fotheringhay Mews' have vehicle access from North Street. Four 'town-houses' stand on the site of John Smiths' land, with an interior courtyard. It is lovely that the old brewery buildings have been kept for posterity, but changed enough to allow for habitation purposes.

ASHTON ROAD

Old School Avenue, Mason and Webb Closes, Sutton Road, Old Quarry, Rowell Way and St. Christopher's Drive are all new roads that lead off from the Ashton Road. On the east side of the lane there was a local rubbish and land-fill tip over the road from the farm, in the copse, abutted to the railway line. The 'dump' was here from the 1920s to sometime in the 1960s and 1970s, when the land was cleared for development. During the 1990s, just off the Ashton Road (on the north-eastern side of East Road) there was the Oundle Area Parcel Force Sorting Office and 'Fairline Boats' (a top-of-the-range boat building business).[226] One town dump was where PGR is and another on Ashton Road. There is currently a gym and businesses with offices using the site. It has been much developed since the 1990s.

There are now many new roads and houses in this area, linking the old Ashton Road to Herne Road via footpaths. Most date to the late-1990s and early twenty-first century. There is no road link for cars, but pedestrian parents and children can walk easily to Prince William School and home again. New road names include Mason Close (named as commemoration for Lottie Mason of Oundle Council, who spent her life helping to develop Oundle), Webb Close (named for Miss Webb, who established and ran the Red Cap School), Sutton Road (named to commemorate Reg Sutton, a former Chair of Oundle Urban District Council, who had a life-time enlightening the town), The Old Quarry

---

[226] 'Fairline Boats' made British luxury motor-yachts. The business was started in 1963 by Jack Newington. The company went into administration in 2015.

(named for the old quarry that was on this site), Rowell Way (named for the farming family who lived here in the 1930s) and St. Christopher's Drive (built in 1988 and gains its name from Miss Webb's school that was here from 1933 to 1973). Old School Avenue is the on the site of the drive and grounds where Miss Webb's Victorian house (named Herne Lodge) and former Red Cap School stood.

The walk across the fields to Ashton can be a pleasure on a sunny day. The old railway tracks had been removed and the walk via Herne Road, Ashton and back via Ashton Road and East Road meant open landscape all of the way. I have always enjoyed walking in the countryside around Oundle with my family.[227] On one such occasion, while crossing the fields between Ashton and the town, my sister and I climbed over the five-barred gate while our mother, Barbara (who had a painful knee), slid under the gate. While she was doing so, a man came along with his black Labrador dog. The dog lifted its leg and had a pee by the gatepost and sprinkled on Barbara, who said, "You dirty dog! You watered me!" The man nodded and unperturbed, said, "What do you expect? You're in his usual spot!" Showing no surprise or concern ('without batting an eyelid') he then continued on his journey.

Ashton Road (west side)

In 1937, there were twelve houses in the Ashton Road. Ashton Road is linked to Herne Road and East Road by a new development that dates from 2015. New building and roads include Old School Avenue, leading to Sutton Road, Webb Close and St. Christopher's Drive (built around 1998) and Rowell Way (built circa 1995). The house numbering in Ashton Road was never odds and evens, so continues in an ordinal fashion. This road had no houses on the opposite side. They overlooked fields and spinneys (and the town dump).

The first house (1), on the corner was that of John H.E. Garner, who was born in 1890. He was a letter-press printer and journeyman. (A "journeyman" is a skilled worker who successfully completed an official apprenticeship qualification in a building trade or craft. When his apprenticeship had been served, a man is considered competent and is authorised to work as a fully-qualified employee in his field.) John

---

[227] Anna Fernyhough.

Garner's wife, Alice was born in 1897. During WWII, this family housed evacuee children who were billeted with them. One of these was Barbara Weston (who was around eight years of age when the war began). The remainder of the road was built by a private company just after the war. It was then sold to the Oundle Urban District Council. There is a cut-through via the fields to Ashton from this road, thus a reason for its name.

Arthur and Kathleen (Pat) Howitt and their son, Ronald, lived at number 2 in the 1930s. Arthur had grown up in Rock Road. He was a leather-worker and harness maker who undertook leather repairs and construction. He initially mended school satchels and leather goods at his shop in the Market Place. He later moved to a new shop on New Street (next to today's 'Coleman's'). He was a saddler and made horse bridles and harnesses. Arthur wrote "Oundle Reminiscences" in 1954, discussing life within his memory from 1879, where every shop he recalled had changed owners, with the exception of two.[228] Arthur Howitt died in 1960, aged 83.

In the 1930s at number 3, were Joseph Horne (sometimes without an 'e'; related to the Leigh family) and his wife, Evelyn. They lived with their children, Joseph and Pamela. Joseph was an auxiliary fireman and a part-time corn-cake, seed and manure merchant. Next, at number 4, lived Christopher and Doris Newton and their daughter, Christine. Christopher was also an auxiliary fire-service man. He worked as a stoker and engineer at the Oundle School Laundry. Again, in the 1930s, number 5 was the home of Mrs J. Esther Crawley. She was a widow who lived with her son, Stanley. He worked as a groom in the local hunting stables. Their lodger, Miss Marion Lilleker was around Esther's age. Marion was a tailor (tailoress) and skilled dress-maker. Mr Hubert Shirley lived next door, at number 6. He worked as a ladies and gentleman's hairdresser. His wife, Winifred, followed the same trade and assisted him, but catered only for the female clients. In 1937 number 6 was the home of Mr Charles Thurlby and his family. By 1939,

---

[228] A 16 page document: "Oundle Reminiscences" by Arthur Howitt, (pdf) 1954.

Mrs Ida Thurlby lived at 7 with her son, David and four young evacuees.[229]

Number 8 was the home of Mrs Mary A. Sharpe. She was a widow who accepted evacuees during the war years. Miss Joan Mold (as a young child) stayed with her In the 1930s. During the 1930s Charles and Minnie Beesley lived with their daughter, Wendy, at number 9. They were from the USA (and are believed to have returned after the war). Charles worked as a motor-transport driver. Derek Gray lived here as an evacuee. Next-door to the Beesleys was the abode of Percy L. Smith and his wife, Ethel. In the 1940s they lived in the first house along the lane, then moved to 10. Percy Smith worked at the International Stores on West Street as a grocery shop assistant. He luckily had a van to use for some of his deliveries. 11 was the home of Mr Patrick Woodford. He is remembered as being a clever sculptor as he made small ivory figures. He worked at the betting office (for a time) and lived with his widowed mother, Mrs R.B. Woodford. Next-door (12) was Mrs Rosina Phillipson with her son, Geoffrey, and daughter, Dorothy. Geoff was a maintenance wire-man. Mr Bertram Batson was a grocery delivery 'rounds-man' who lodged with the family. Dorothy married him in mid-1940 and as Mrs Batson, taught at St Peter's primary school. Their son, John, was born in 1946.

New roads have been built here with extensions to Oundle housing. The first of these roads is Mason Close (named after Lottie Mason). They are built on what were the council house gardens. The residents had no choice as they did not own their houses, but rented them. The Council divided the land, then sold their gardens for building plots; much to the chagrin of the house-residents.

Mrs R. Phillipson lived at number 12. Miss Webb lived at Herne Lodge. Mr J. Horn is listed (in the 1939 directory) as living in the property. Mrs Emily Webb, a widow, lived at number 13. She was born in 1862, but was widowed after her daughters, Winifred (1891) and Constance (1895) were born. She taught at and was the principal of a small private school, known as Miss Webbs' independent 'red cap' school for girls (as financed boys attended Laxton). Its correct name is the St.

---

[229] Joyce Gaunt (Hardick) and Barbara Chester (Mudza) recall that there were lots of children locally.

Christopher's School, hence the name of the nearby new road. (Doreen Allen was one of the pupils who attended this school.) The school permanently closed in the 1970s. Miss Webb's nephew, Nigel Webb, lived with her and helped to run the school. After he married, he continued to live in the large school-house along the drive with her. The Crawley family lived next-door (Stanley Crawley's parents).[230]

David Rowell's dairy farm and house were at the end of the road. Each day the Hooton girls were dispatched to collect the milk. Often, Barbara Chester would go with them. Barbara recalls that Mr Rowell had a daughter, Marion. She also remembers that "when Eileen had to go to get the milk for the family, she would collect it in a churn. She would swing it round her head and none would spill, but if her mum had ever found out there would have been trouble!"[231] One advertisement declared: "A good resolution for 1939! Drink more Rowell's milk". Mr Rowell's farm employees lived in the bungalow and a cottage on a subsidised 'peppercorn' rent[232]. In 1952, Hans and Joyce Hardick lived in the tenanted house as they worked on the farm. They were here until old Mr Rowell died "by his own hand". This is when the houses and land were sold to a local farmer. Joyce and Hans then moved to work on the Stoke Hill farm as it was owned by the same family. They then moved to the house that became part of the 'Angel Inn' (before it was converted into part of the pub). They moved on to Rock Road, Nene View and latterly, Springfield Road.[233] Proving that once you know that you love Oundle you may move house, but never leave town!

In the 1940s, people living on the farm as tenants were Mabel Briggs and her son, Thomas (who was the head cow-man), Mr Maurice Malkin, plus teenagers: Henry Kenny and Denis Stephens. This road was a short cut walk to Ashton without going along the main road. There was a railway line to cross, but in the 1980s this was converted into the main A605 link-road between Peterborough and Thrapston.

---

[230] See section, in this book, by Sue Crick on her memories.

[231] Barbara Chester, personal history.

[232] A peppercorn rent comes from (an early term) when landlords charged rent in peppercorns rather than coinage, which allowed an avoidance of tax as rent was low.

[233] They moved with their family grew. Their children are Peter, Jeanine, Bunty and Rachael.

The old road was excellent for shady nature walks and calm, sunny afternoon saunters until its alteration in the 1970s.

NEW STREET

New Street (east side from the War Memorial)

At the eastern corner of Market place and Bury Street (New Street) was a 'stocks house' and 'cage' for the punishment of offenders. Mr William Hacket was a "religious enthusiast in Oundle". (He was hanged for his faith in 1591 after "inciting fervour".)

Other issues that would have required trial and punishment were times of 'spotting of evil women'. The seventeenth and eighteenth century were rife with superstition in the rural areas. One recorded case was that of Helen Jenkenson of Thrapston (who was said to have bewitched a farmer's cattle). She was released. Mistress Mulso accused the same woman of causing her child's death and this time trial resulted in the finding of 'witch marks'.

Two local women, Elinor Shaw of Cotterstock and Mary Phillips of Oundle, were accused of selling their 'souls to the Devil, in exchange for evil powers'. They were then thought to have used their powers to hurt local people and cattle. In March 1705, they were taken to the County Assizes for "Bewitching and tormenting in a diabolical manner". The wife of Robert Wise of Benefield and a four year-old were considered 'harmed', Charles Ireland of Southwick (aged 12) was "Betwitched to death" and several animals were considered also harmed by their 'evil magic'. Elinor and Mary at first pleaded 'not guilty'. After a time, they both confessed to the crimes and were found guilty. On this there was mayhem in the courthouse. The court took no time to condemn the two. The unfortunate women were tortured, hanged until almost dead. They were then "surrounded with faggots, pitch and other combustible matter, which being set on fire, their bodies [burned and] ... consumed to ashes" (8th March 1705). This is reported to be the last ever execution of witches in England. The Witchcraft Act was repealed in 1736.[234]

---

[234] 'Ladies of Distinction in Northamptonshire', Mia Butler and Colin Eaton, 2005.

The 'Moot Hall' (court house) was a building on the corner of New Street.[235] It occupied the space of the three current premises. Later, it was the site of the 'Swann Inn' (until 1863). During the 1800s, the 'Talbot' and the 'Turk' entrances were also by the town water-pump. As water was essential for the brewing business, there were pumps by most of Oundle's breweries. Until the early twentieth century there was a local town water-pump where the current war memorial stands. Armistice Day commemorations have taken place around this memorial since the war. Townspeople congregate on this corner and in the nearby market area for meetings, coronations and memorial days and have done so for time centuries.

The New Street corner building was an outfitters. This was a much larger premises and had two doors; one into each street. By the 1970s, it was "Rachel's" fashion-clothing shop. It was named for Joyce and Hans Hardick's youngest child, Rachael. (Joyce notes that the spelling was incorrectly written [no 'e'] by the sign-makers and it was "too late to change it".) The large shop had changing rooms at the rear. When the shop closed the property was split to create two shops. The current corner-shop 'White Vanilla', sells clothes (is entered via and is numbered as being in the Market Place).

The first New Street shop since the 1990s is been a travel agency, 'Kitts Travel', 'Oundle Travel', then 'Go Cruise Travel Agency' (2012). Thomas Bell's printing shop stood next door to the Swann Inn in the 1800s. The printers and the adjacent Stamford, Spalding and Boston Banking Company was later managed by Richard Todd. He died in 1867, aged 63 (St. Peter's Church has a memorial window with information on him, his wife, Eliza; also their daughters). The original buildings were demolished in the 1860s and rebuilt.

Number 2, Barclays Bank, opened in 1911, in the Georgian building. The future may hold something completely different as banks in Oundle are all due to disappear in 2018. Number 4 is currently the home of three businesses: Hunt and Coombs Solicitor, Croesus Financial Services and Oundle Ticket Sales (for the International

---

[235] Courtesy of Rockingham Forest Trust, Historic Landscape Education Project, 2008.

Festival, Stahl theatre and local event information and tickets). Hunt and Coombs was formerly 'Hunt, Capron and Coombs'.

Numbers 6 and 8 were converted into one large room downstairs as 'China Town' restaurant and bar. The restaurant is located comfortably inside a lovely seventeenth-century building. It has two storeys and attics. At the turn of the last century, a serious fire broke out in Miss Negus' property. She ran a needlework shop, but lost her goods as the fire brigade were not able to prevent water and fire damage. They said that it was lucky that the fire was contained, as Mr Todd's gun-powder store was nearby.

Coleman's has a nineteenth-century shop-front. It has a modern shop window to the left. From the outside, it is very clear to see where the original two houses were. Number 10 was a saddlers' leather-works (in what is now the southern part of Coleman's art-craft material and office-supply shop). The saddler, Mr Howitt, shared his premises with Mr Price. In the early 1900s the shop by the corner hairdresser's was Coulson's tailor's shop. This is where Ben Thulby, a tailor (who suffered from dwarfism), later worked. Arthur Howitt moved his leather-work shop to the Market Place during the 1960s.

In the 1930s, Joyce Hardick recalls that, on Christmas Eve, the local children were invited inside the Leayton family shop (on the corner of Church Street and New Street) to peruse tables set out upstairs. They would bring their pocket money along and would look at and select gifts for their parents. These were on reduction, so that 'cheap' Christmas presents could be purchased by the local children as this was a way of giving their Christmases special meaning. This was a kindly gesture to the children of Oundle by the owners of the shop. It was well appreciated and clearly remembered.

When the Leayton family moved from here to their Market Place shop, 'Kings' of Oundle' continued trading in paper products. Printers, "Kings of Oundle" (who bought the business from Mr Leayton) extended into the neighbouring saddlers (formerly Howitt's). The proprietors, Dennis and Sheila Harris sold greeting cards, stationery, and toys. They also used "new-fangled" photocopying and faxing facilities. Oundle was entering the twentieth century! Like other shops of the day, until the

1960s it used shady, sun-canopies to prevent window goods from fading. This shop regenerated as 'Coleman's of Oundle'.

The 'White Hart Inn' was in New Street (where the Cloister buildings are). The New Street Oundle School buildings date to around 1880 and were designed by John Sebastian Gwilt. With an eye-catching gatehouse and turrets, it bear the motto "God Grant Grace" along with the Grocer's Company coat-of-arms. The camel logo (always facing left, coming from the East) is carrying two bags of pepper with "valuable cloves". The motif denotes the grocer's historic links with the spice trade. (On close inspection, one of the stone-carved camels seems to have lost part of its head!)

The gatehouse also has animal gargoyle waterspouts and a statue of Sir William Laxton in a stone-carved canopy niche. The gate-posts have old-style (electric) lamps, which match the recent 'old-style' lighting-fixtures around Oundle. The interior courtyard buildings were built at different times. Despite a Tudor style, the main building dates to the early twentieth century, whereas the adjoining two-storey house dates to 1790. The south side has a 1960 porch (in a Georgian style), while the remainder of this side of the building is from 1800.

Church Street lies between Coleman's and the Oundle School quadrangle entrance. The Oundle School entrance to the quad and the cloisters originally had a metal railing on the low walls, but it was melted down for munitions in the war. The Vicarage (used as a vicarage from the late seventeenth-century until 2015)[236] was sold as a private residence and modernised. This lies between entrance pathways that lead to St Peter's church. The old vicarage property has entrances on New Street and into the Church yard.

Oundle School properties also have access to both sides of their buildings with entrances on New Street and into the Church yard and via the Quad courtyard. The garden is recalled with love and lives in 'wonderful' memories by many people. "There was a fete every year in the vicarage garden. In June, I think? I helped on the stall for the Guides' cakes. May Day was a special time too, when we would walk

---

[236] Rev. Richard Ormston served Oundle for 13 years (2001-2014). He is Archdeacon of Northampton. The vicarage house was sold in 2015 and is now private.

from the primary school in Milton Road through to the Church Rectory garden where the May Queen was crowned. It was always a time of celebration! I just loved those days of community!"[237] Anne Grey (née Clark) said, "My favourite memory is from 1950. My brother, Peter, and I think Gill Langley received a sports trophy shield from Mr Venner, the Headmaster of the Primary School, in the old vicarage garden in New Street, where a lot of events were held for the school. The shield was presented by a lady on the board of governors, Miss Valerie Carpenter. I have very happy memories of that garden."[238]

Church Street

Church Street is a short, narrow lane, which leads to the Church and Church yard. The door by the corner is the old tuck shop entrance for Coleman's building that originally sold sweets to school children during break times. The courtyard double-doors lead behind North's shoe shop on Market Place. Number 1 is part-way along the row as back entrances have no number designations. It was constructed in 1877.

Mrs Abbott lived in (1) the Brereton Rooms in the pre-war years. (Then these rooms were also known as "the Vicar's Rooms). Around 1940 this is where the Girls' Friendly Society meetings were held. During the 1950s the rooms were necessitated by the primary school infant classes. Miss Meta Newborn led the Sunday-school meetings. It was here that she told countless allegories and Bible stories to the children. In the 1980s the Sunday-school group meetings were held here. (Possibly for fear of children's voices carrying in the service.) Number 2 is the School Deputy-head's office and Bursars' office. This was purchased and converted from its purpose as Laxton (elderly men's) Hospital. The building has an imposing stepped entrance on Church Street (Church Lane).

The School Art block is on the opposite side of the lane. Between the sixth and tenth century the northern part of Church Lane had multi-occupancy tenements that were part of the Manor grounds (leading via the Church to the Manor in the area where the currently named

---

237 Oral history, Amanda J. Delaney-Smith, 1/06/2017.
238 Ann Greetham and Angela Hudson kindly shared their dance photographs, c.1947. Angela's photograph has fairies: (row 2, L-R) Carole Crawley, Alma Black, Ann Hurley, Angela Taney, Anna Walker, Anne Clark and Irene Tyers (with bow).

'Gascoigne Building' stands). The land, mediæval church properties and vicarage were all in the control of the domain of Peterborough. The early (monastic) friars and priests conducted services for an income. The Bishop would send his fee-collectors to take away his allotted Oundle revenue, which was a 'cut' taken from the payments.

At the back of New Street tenement was a horse-market (on a long plot of land). Here, horse fairs took place, followed up in the Talbot, with a sale of the horses to the highest bidders. It was commented that the horses were paraded up and down New Street and Church Street for all to see. A new vicarage (which, in 2016 became a private house) was built on the site of the ancient Manor garden and old graveyard adjacent to the horse-market.

Laxton Hospital Alms-House, Church Lane (Church Street)

The original Laxton Hospital (Alms-House) stood in Church Lane (where the School Bursar's office is now).[239] An article in the 'Stamford Mercury' of 1828[240] suggested that not many inhabitants knew that Oundle "was once a corporate town". This suggests that most of the houses and businesses were in the control of one family. I am assuming here that this is a nod towards William Laxton, his school and hospital or the properties of the Wyatt family. The old article went on to say that this information is "incontestably proved by a curious old survey made in the reign of Queen Elizabeth" (the first) that had been perused by "our correspondent, and is now in the possession of a gentleman of Oundle". The article further stated that it was not known for how long the corporate charter or franchise has been lost. The will of Lady Jane 'Wiott' (Wyatt) is referred to in the document (dated 1506), as "she therein gives the issues of certain lands in Oundle to the Alderman of the Guild ... for charitable purposes".

This document describes the assets of William Laxton and his Guildhall: "The late Guild-hall of our Lady of Oundle, being a very fair hall, builded with freestone, and now purchased by one Mr Laxton, sometime Mayor of London, and is now made a free-school house, and lands by him are given for the maintenance of a school-master there, and the

---

[239] Just a short distance from Church Street Hospital there was the North Street 'Eye and Ear Infirmary'.
[240] 'Stamford Mercury', dated 27th June 1828.

same lyeth between the church yard on the North, and between the Lord's customary tenement called the Crown, in the tenure of Henry Chathorne, on the South." The narrative suggests that part of the ancient building attached to the church yard was "beyond memory, a free grammar-school, and the remainder of the building a hospital, called Laxton's hospital, there cannot be a doubt that this edifice was formerly the Guild-hall of Oundle".[241]

In 1901, on the event of the coronation of Edward VII, Oundle held a band-led, 'flag waving' parade that led to the Church. After the service there were sporting events laid on. The men were decked out in their familiar costumes, including gaiters and a top hat. One race at the event included the elderly gentlemen of Laxton Hospital. The inmates were Billie West, Tom Hunt, Father Allaby, Stephen Laxton, John Laxton, Joe Rowell and Stephen Coles. (Joe Rowell won the race!) When King Edward died (in 1910), George V came to the throne and the town repeated the same celebrations.

Until their 'reconstruction' in the 1800s the Wyatt chapel and Laxton school-rooms stood at the corner of the church yard on North Street. The Laxton donations (for the poor) came from a "great benefactor to Oundle, Sir William Laxton who founded an Oundle school and a hospital in the sixteenth century" for "seven aged men". He had no children, so donated for the benefit of others in his will. Until the arrival of old age pensions there was always a waiting list for placement in the alms houses. Men were allotted seven shillings weekly and a Sunday dinner. Their distinctive clothing style was of interest to visitors. The old men always attended the Parish Church on Sundays and had their own designated pews (under the pulpit).

Prior to the state old age pension bill that became law in 1908 and its first payment in January 1909, there were many more people without income in their old age. (Even then, a state pension was paid on reaching the age of seventy.) With the coming of pensions the numbers very gradually declined in alms houses. Mr Joseph Rowell was the last (see below). "Now 'seven aged men' in the town receive the weekly pension and the hospital is closed as such".

---

[241] Ibid.

In 1841, Susannah Ragsdale (aged 55) served as the Laxton Hospital Matron on Church Lane. She continued in her job until the end of her life in 1856. The retired "inmates" in her care were were almost all aged in their seventies. They were comprised of John White (aged 78), Samuel Ireson (78) who was an agricultural labourer, William Franklin (78), James Louther (70) was a glazier and John Simpson (72) was an agricultural labourer. William Fox was a 64 year-old gardener and John Wright, a 79 year-old blacksmith. The hospital matron had an assistant, Miss Mary Gann, aged twenty. Later, in the 1840s there were two new male patients listed as Rafe Dale (50) and Robert Sculthorpe (aged 30). Robert was presumably incapacitated and unable to work. The 1943 'Stamford Mercury' reported on an inquest that was held "by Mr Marshall, on the body of Sam Ireson (aged seventy-nine), an inmate of Laxton's hospital, Oundle, who, whilst apparently as well as usual and getting his supper on Thursday night the 23rd, suddenly fell back in his chair and expired. Verdict, visitation of God".[242]

In 1851, Elizabeth (Susannah) Ragsdale (aged sixty-five), a baker's widow, continued functioning as the Matron. (See above.) The all-male inmates were retired from their previous employment. John Afford (aged 85) was an Oundle stone-mason, Luke York (76) a farmer from Churchfield, Thomas Whyman (seventy-four) was an Oundle wheelwright, James Pierce (66) was a currier from March. William Allen (73) was a 'post-boy' from Oundle and William Howett (57) was a tailor from Catworth. (It is worth noting that Elizabeth Ragsdale died five years later.)

By 1861, the matron was Miss Sarah Alexander (aged 46) who originally came from Yarmouth. The seven "good" men who were listed as 'Almsmen' were Thomas Whyman (83) who was an Oundle wheelwright, William Askham (83), an agricultural labourer from Weldon, William Nichols (80), an agricultural labourer from Brigstock, Henry Ruff (80), an Oundle basket-maker, William Giddings (67), an agricultural labourer from Oundle, plus William Howitt (64) and John Staines (61) who were both tailors.

In 1871, the Matron was Mrs Eliza Tibbs. She was a widow from Fotheringhay. The inmates (all retired widowers), were comprised of

[242] *Stamford Mercury,* 31st March 1843.

men Oundle and nearby villages. Steven Coles (85; later written as Stephen Coales!) was a gardener, John Platt (80) who was a stonemason, William Tansley (a labourer and the youngest at 66). William Coulson, John Bellemey (in 1881, his name was spelled as Bellamy), Samuel Booker and John Ives were three local labourers (all aged in their 70s).

A decade later, the 1881 census recorded the first property on 'Church yard' as the School House. It faces the Church and is within the 'yard'. Church Lane is where the Laxton's Almshouse stood. The next property is listed as the 'Workman's Institute'.

In 1881, Eliza Tibbs (aged 69) was Matron. The inmates still included Stephen Coles (later written as Coales; now 95), John Bellamy (84), John Ives (85), a labourer from Glapthorn, John Steers (72), a labourer from Oundle, John Bettle (71), a labourer from Bozeat, William Martin (71), who was a groom from Leadenham and Thomas Clare (72) was a carpenter from Thornhaugh. The 'Stamford Mercury' of 1st February 1886, noted that "Stephen Coales, an inmate of Laxton's Hospital (Grocer's Company) attained his 100th birthday."[243] Perhaps gardening does keep you fit! On the day of the Michaelmas Fair in October 1889, Oundle went into mourning for Stephen Coales, aged 103 (at which point he had been living in the Laxton Hospital for almost 20 years).

The Oundle Board of Guardian's meeting perused a letter from the Rev. Mungo Travers Park (a cheerful Headmaster, later disabled) stated that William Hewitt, an inmate of the house, had been elected to fill a vacancy at Laxton Hospital (generally known as the "Old Men's Hospital"). This was recorded in the newspaper in November 1889.[244]

In 1891, an Oundle resident, Elizabeth Epps (43) was matron. She worked for the Hospital for almost twenty years before taking her own life. The inmates were all retired widowers. They were Thomas Marlow, Miles Smith, William King and George Howe (all from Oundle), William Clare, William Hewitt and William Jakeman (who came from further afield). Two years later the Northampton Mercury (January 1893) recounted the "Seasonal Benevolence" of F.W. Sanderson as

---

[243] 'Stamford Mercury', 5th February 1886.
[244] 'Northampton Mercury', 30th November 1889.

"the new master at Oundle School has given a tea, etc., to the old men inmates of Latham's Hospital. Mr Newman of Bramston House, has given a similar treat to them, and also one to the old lady inmates of Latham's Hospital. To the old men he has given a pair of gloves each and each of the old ladies has received a shawl from him".[245]

The local press reported the death of "An inmate of Laxton's hospital for Men, named Marlow, on Saturday evening died suddenly. He had been, as was his wont, assisting in some of the lighter household work and had made preparations to smoke his pipe previous to retiring to bed. Suddenly his comrades were surprised to see the pipe fall to the ground and Mr Marlow fall back in his chair. Assistance was immediately called, but Mr Somerset (medical practitioner) found that death had resulted from heart disease. The coroner, owing to this and the deceased's great age (he, being considerably over 70), deemed an inquest unnecessary". Mr Marlow's funeral took place on 5th September 1894.[246] In December 1897 "there passed away an old, respected inhabitant of the town, Mr Thomas Gann. [The] Deceased had been for some time in Laxton's Hospital. For many years he was a member of the Town Fire Brigade and on Monday at the funeral a detachment of the brigade attended as a mark of respect".[247]

In 1901, Elizabeth Epps (now aged 54) continued to serve as the hospital matron. The retired inmates in her care were Mr Miles Smith (78) an Oundle shoe-maker, Alfred Martin (83) a coach builder from Rutland, Thomas Ruff (84) an Oundle butcher, James Laxton (78) an Oundle 'jobbing gardener', George Afford (85) and John Platt (83) both were mason's from Oundle, plus Joseph Kilham (76), who was also a gardener.

Some of the newspaper reports are quite abject, announcing: "Suicide – At the Police Station on Tuesday, Mr J.T. Parker, jun, held an inquest touching the death of Mrs Elizabeth Epps (60), whose body was recovered from the river at Bassett ford on Sunday morning. Dr Turner stated that there were no marks of violence on the body, which appeared to have been in the water about twelve hours. He knew Mrs

---

[245] 'Northampton Mercury', 6th January 1893.
[246] 'Northampton Mercury', 7th September 1894.
[247] 'Stamford Mercury' 3rd December 1897.

Epps when she was matron at Laxton's Hospital. She suffered from gout, but, though she sometimes seemed depressed, he had never heard her threaten suicide. Evidence of identification was given by Frederick Barwell, verger of Jesus Church, who stated that his aunt was a widow. He understood she had a pension of 10 shillings per week. She had complained of feeling lonely. A little girl, named Lily Clipsham, who lives with Mrs Jones in West-street, said Mrs Epps came to her grandmother's nearly every day. She had tea there on Saturday afternoon. She appeared to be very low spirited, and said she did not like the thought of Christmas and the bells ringing. Others would be happy, but she was a poor old lame woman. Witness had heard her say she would do away with herself." The jury returned a sad verdict of "Suicide while temporarily insane."[248] After this sad event, advertisements were placed in the 'papers' to recruit a replacement matron: "Wanted, a capable Woman as Matron for the Laxton Hospital Oundle. Apply with testimonials to Headmaster, School House, Oundle, Norths."[249] Subsequently an announcement of employment mentioned that Elizabeth's "Laxton's Hospital" replacement was Mrs Hawkins (Hankins).[250]

In 1911, Mildred Elizabeth Hankins (aged 53) was the Matron in charge at the hospital. The widower inmates were each listed in the register as a 'Pensioner in charity Institution'. Maurice Smith (seventy-seven), Thomas Hunt (68) and William West (70) all came from Polebrook. George Allaby (was born in Spalding in 1843; was in this Hospital aged 68. He died in 1918), James Laxton (1839-1921; an Oundle man, aged 72 on his entry into the hospital in 1911), Thomas Fletton (from Benefield [1836-1915], was aged 74 on entry to the Hospital) and George Stevens (69) from Oundle. It is presumed that their place of origin was where they were born.

A photograph was taken in 1914 of the men at Laxton Hospital. It shows Mr W. Hunt, Mrs Hankins (the Matron) and Mr C. Gilby; and, in the front, Mr J. Fletton, Mr G. Allaby, Mr J. Laxton, Mr W. Stevens and

---

[248] 'Northampton Mercury', 14th December 1906.
[249] 'Stamford Mercury, 1st June 1906.
[250] 'Northampton Mercury', 6th July 1906 (Should read Mrs Hankins).

Mr W. West. It is worth noting that matron, Mrs Hankins had a son was the police superintendent in Wellingborough.

Hospital rooms were never unoccupied for very long. In 1917, it was reported that Mr Joseph Rowell (who was over seventy years old) was "selected for" a vacant room in the Laxton Hospital. It was considered important and was noted that he was "a native of the town" and for most of his life has been as a gardener at the Rectory. In 1917, "At the monthly meeting of the local Oddfellows he was presented with a walking-stick, suitably inscribed, in recognition of his work for the Providence Lodge for the past 40 years".[251] The Northampton Mercury (1934) reported that "The sole surviving pensioner of Laxton Men's Hospital left the hospital this week and is accommodated in rooms in Oundle" and that the "recent death of the matron made the change necessary".[252]

...oooOOOooo...

Data on Latham Hospital and the Almshouse Residents
(Collected by Margaret Brewster)

Marriage - On Monday, at Oundle, Mr Thomas Drage, to the widow Faulkner, of Latham's Hospital. *Stamford Mercury 24 April 1829.*

Three of the commissioners appointed to enquire into public charities have been at Oundle for upwards of a week, busily engaged in investigating the accounts and documents belonging to the various charities in that town and neighbourhood. The bailiffs of Latham's Hospital, in Oundle, have been highly complimented by the commissioners on the good management of that charity, and the correct state of the accounts. *Northampton Mercury 10 October 1829.*

In Latham's Hospital, Ann Milburn, under-warden, aged 78. Huntingdon. *Bedford & Peterborough Gazette 8 October 1836.*

To the Editor of the Mercury – Passing through Oundle the other day, my attention was attracted by a very great profusion of ornamental architecture in the gateways leading to Latham's Hospital and School in the North-street of that town, which are surmounted by a very

---

[251] 'Northampton Mercury' 9th November 1917.
[252] 'Northampton Mercury', 12th January 1934.

singular device, representing a babe in a cradle, beneath a bird with extended wings, and its beak inclined towards the child's face, - whether for the purpose of destruction or protection is not apparent. The origin of this design I was unable to ascertain; but as doubtless it has some reference to the charity, I shall feel obliged to any of your correspondents who will through your columns explain the meaning, and of the other devices, of which there are several displayed in the building; and will also state whether the expenditure is sanctioned by the Trustees. A Traveller Thrapston Feb. 13, 1838. *Stamford Mercury 16 February 1838*.

To the Editor of the Mercury – Sir – In answer to your Thrapston correspondent in last week's paper, relating to the ornamental architecture of the new gates of Latham's School and hospital, &c. at Oundle. I beg leave to say he may make himself perfectly easy as to the misapplication of the funds of that charity, the gateways alluded to being erected at the sole expense of John Smith, Esq., one of the trustees of the school and hospital – the same gentleman to whom Oundle is so much indebted for its other improvements, and I may add its present flourishing condition. Your's An Old Correspondent. Barnwell near Oundle Feb. 19th 1838. The sculpture on the stone alluded to is the crest of Latham, the founder of the charity. – Latham's Arms are, Or, on a chief indented azure three roundlets gules; crest, an eagle standing on a cradle Or, therein a child proper. *Stamford Mercury 23 February 1838*.

1841 – Elizabeth Porter aged eighty, was matron. Inmates all born in the local county were, Elizabeth Bracknell seventy-five, Catherine Island sixty-five, Elizabeth [*name illegible*] eighty, Elizabeth Harlott sixty, Ellenor Sauter sixty-five, Elizabeth Pearson sixty-five, Susannah Hill sixty-five, Sarah Chamberlain seventy-five, Ann Hopkins sixty, Susannah White seventy-five, Elizabeth King sixty, Sarah Snart eighty, Sarah Clark sixty, Sarah Colson seventy-five, Mary Bailey eighty and Elizabeth Clark seventy.

At Oundle, on the 14th inst., Catherine Island, for some years' warden in Latham's Hospital, aged 78. *Cambridge Independent Press 23 October 1847*.

1851 – Dorothy Sismey sixty-five, was Matron. The inmates also born in Oundle were Elizabeth Pearson seventy-two, Elizabeth Harlock (blind) seventy-three, Susannah Hill seventy-eight, Mary Britchfield fifty, and Elizabeth Coles sixty. Eleanor Panther seventy-six from Glapthorn, Ann Hopkins seventy-three, Sarah Clark sixty-nine, Yarwell, Ann Blackwell seventy-one, Deene, Hannah Burdett seventy-two, Hunts, Elizabeth Clipston sixty-four, Thorpe, Hannah Pepperday sixty-eight, Earls Barton, Mary Platt fifty-nine, March, Ann Wade seventy-four, Whiffen, Elizabeth Edis sixty, Deene and Elizabeth Ruffe fifty-nine Burton Lattimore. Mary South forty-four from Norfolk was the cook. Mary Ann Burbridge aged nineteen from Marholm was the housemaid.

An inquest was held at the Dolphin inn Oundle, on Tuesday, on the body of Hannah Dobson, an inmate of Latham's hospital, who died very suddenly on the 26th ult. Verdict, died of diseased heart. *Stamford Mercury 3 October 1856.*

1861 – Elizabeth Bellamy, seventy-one, from Glapthorn was Head of Latham hospital, Elizabeth Edis seventy from Deene was sub-warden. Inmates born in Oundle were Susannah Hill eighty-eight, a carpenter's widow, Elizabeth Pearson eighty-two, a coachman (domestic servant) widow, Mary Gowdey fifty-nine, a tailor's widow, Sarah Clark fifty-nine, a hospital nurse, Lucy Brudenell sixty-five, formerly a dressmaker, Celia Underwood sixty-five, formerly a seamstress and Mary Britchfield sixty, a hospital house servant. Hannah Pepperday eighty, a plaster and slaters widow from Earls Barton, Mary Platt seventy, a stone-masons widow from March, Mary Coulson sixty-six, a hospital nurse from Fotheringhay, Sarah Smith fifty-eight, a hospital house servant from Water Newton, Elizabeth Ruffe sixty-nine, a farm labourers widow from Burton Latimer, Mary Henson eighty, a shepherd's widow from Aldwinkle and Elizabeth Wood seventy-seven, a mat makers widow place of birth unknown.

During the thunderstorm last week, a chimney at Latham's hospital, Oundle, was struck by the electric fluid in a very peculiar manner: the only simile to be compared is that of cutting a loaf in a proper way. The stonework of the chimney was thrown a considerable distance, and the roof of both the school premises and the dormitories of the inmates was considerably injured. *Grantham Journal 25 June 1870.*

At Latham's Hospital, Oundle, on the 19th instant, Sarah Clarke, aged 68. *Northampton Mercury 14 January 1871.*

1871 – Elizabeth Bellamy aged eighty-one continued to be the matron with Mary Coulson aged seventy-four as vice matron. Inmates born in Oundle were Lucy Brudenell seventy-five, Mary Britchfield seventy, Elizabeth Drage seventy-seven, Mary Clarke seventy-one, Elizabeth Afford eighty-one and Charlotte Layton seventy-two. From the surrounding villages were, Sarah Smith sixty-eight, Mary Platt eighty-one, Susanna Baker seventy-two, Martha Askham sixty-seven, Sarah Ruffe sixty-nine, Mary Ann Clipson sixty-five. Harriet Sismey aged sixty was a nurse, as was Sarah Smith aged sixty-three from Oundle. Sarah Rippiner aged forty-seven from Oundle and Harriett Smith aged sixty-five from Peterborough were firewomen.

Suicide at Oundle – Mary Ann Rippiner, aged 58, an inmate of Latham's Hospital, cut her throat with a razor. *Stamford Mercury 3 January 1873.*

At Latham's Hospital, Oundle, on the 5th inst., Elizabeth Bellamy, aged 84. Deceased was for 20 years warden of the above hospital. *Stamford Mercury 14 November 1873.*

Benevolence – J. W. Smith Esq., J.P. has, at a very considerable outlay, caused hot-water pipes to be fixed in the lower rooms of Latham's Hospital, bearing the whole expense himself. *Northampton Mercury 14 March 1874.*

Latham's Hospital has been opened, and the inmates seem to have been provided with every accommodation. A special service was held in the church to celebrate the event: after which about 250 persons sat down to a tea. The new schools are progressing rapidly, and in conjunction with Latham's almshouses will form as pretty a block of buildings as are to be found in the county. *Stamford Mercury 10 October 1874.*

1881 – Mary Coulson eighty-four from Fotheringhay, Alms warden with Mary Ann Clipson eighty-one from Tinwell, as her sub-warden. Alms Women (Inmates) born in Oundle were Charlotte Laxton eighty-two, Sarah Sharpe seventy-three, Sarah Rippiner fifty-six, Susannah Freer sixty-four and Ann Ellis sixty-three. The ladies from surrounding villages were Sarah Smith eighty Waternewton, Susan Baker eighty-two Barnwell, Harriet Smith seventy-four Peterborough, Ann Hunt seventy Polebrook, Ann Sawford fifty-eight Titchmarsh, Fanny Hicks sixty-nine Glapthorn, Sarah Moulton seventy-five Weldon, Harriet Sismey seventy-one Suffolk, Lydia Smith seventy Leicester, Maria Labin seventy-one Warwick and Ann Pratt sixty-nine Benefield.

Mary Coulson died in 1885 aged eighty eight.

1891 – Susannah Freer seventy-four Oundle, was warden with Ann Sawford sixty-eight Titchmarsh, as her sub warden. Inmates born in Oundle were Sarah Rippiner sixty-six and Mary Ann Smith sixty-three. The ladies from surrounding villages were Susannah Baker ninety-two Barnwell, Sarah Smith eighty-eight Waternewton, Ann Hunt seventy-nine Polebrook, Elizabeth Clipson seventy-two Covington, Jane Spencer sixty Titchmarsh and Dorcas Wallis seventy Ashton.

An old lady named Baker died in Latham's Hospital on Monday at the ripe age of 93 years. Deceased, who had been an inmate for 29 years, was the oldest person in the town. *Stamford Mercury 12 February 1892.*

Accident – An inmate of the Latham's Hospital for women, named Mrs Sawford, on Tuesday evening fell down on some slides in the street, and broke her thigh. *Northampton Mercury 20 January 1893.*

1901 – Susannah Freer, eighty-four was warden of the hospital, she had no sub warden. Inmates born in Oundle were Fanny King eighty-three, Martha Fox eighty-four, Martha Beal seventy-six, Harriett Lilley seventy-four, Mary Ann Garrett sixty-six and Emma Britchfield sixty-two. The ladies from surrounding villages were Elizabeth Clipston eighty-two Covington, Ann Henson eighty Leicester, Mary Ann Stretton sixty-nine Barnwell and Elizabeth Drage seventy-two Peterborough.

Sudden Death – Mary Ann Garrett, an inmate of Latham's Hospital, died suddenly on Sunday morning aged 70 years. The Coroner was communicated with, but an inquest was deemed not necessary. *Northampton Mercury 8 December 1905*

1911 – Susannah Freer aged ninety-five was warden, she had Elizabeth Drage aged eighty-one as her sub warden. The only inmate born in Oundle was Emma Britchfield seventy-two. The ladies from surrounding villages were Mary Ann Stretton eighty Barnwell, Ann Green seventy-one Cotterstock, Emma Crisp sixty-three Molesworth, Caroline Kerry sixty-five Woodnewton, and Ann Henson ninety from Leicester. Alice Hill thirty-four, from Leicester was a nurse.

Susannah Freer died in 1912 aged ninety-seven.

Mr Pettit, builder, Thrapston and Oundle, has secured the contract for rebuilding Latham's Hospital for Women. *Northampton Mercury 4 April 1913.*

Mrs Rudd, late of the Oundle School Sanatorium, has been appointed Matron of Latham's hospital. There were eight applications. *Northampton Mercury 9 January 1914.*

There were five applicants for the vacancy at Latham's Hospital Almhouse and the choice fell upon Mrs Howe, widow of the late Mr John Howe. *Northampton Mercury 13 March 1914.*

Having reached the great age of 97 years in August last, Mrs Ann Henson, of Oundle died on Thursday morning at Latham's Hospital, where she had been an inmate for over 20 years. She was the oldest inhabitant of the town, and retained her faculties to the last few days. Her husband pre-deceased her about 25 years since. There are now living two sons and three daughters, and a great number of grandchildren. One of the sons, Mr Philip Henson, Peterborough, is well-known as an old guard with 50 years' service on the L. and N.W. Railway, from which he retired some year or more ago. *Northampton Mercury 14 December 1917.*

The interment took place on Friday last in Oundle Cemetery of Mrs Alice Howe, who had reached the age of 82. She was the widow of Mr John Howe, whom she had outlived by 42 years. For several years past she occupied a room which had been granted to her in Latham's Hospital, and where she passed away after a short illness. *Northampton Mercury 2 April 1920.*

PARSON LATHAM HOSPITAL – The Trustees require the services of a STRONG, ACTIVE WOMAN as Working House Matron at their Almhouse in Oundle. Help provided. Age between 30 and 50. Salary £50 per annum, with a room, firing and lighting. Candidates must be single women or widows without dependants. Particulars may be obtained from the undersigned, by whom applications in writing with copies of not more than three recent testimonials must be received not later than 5th March 1923. By order C. A. PULLET, Clerk to the Trustees. Oundle 13th February 1923. *Northampton Mercury 16 February 1923.*

Oundle Woman's death after fall – A hospital inmate's fall when on a visit to Peterborough was described at an inquest at Latham's Hospital, Oundle, on Sarah Jane Burgess, aged 75. *Northampton Mercury 10 January 1936.*

The death took place at Latham's Hospital, Oundle, of Mrs Mary Laxton, at the age of 91. She had been an inmate of the hospital for many years. *Northampton Mercury 25 February 1938.*[253]

...oooOOOooo...

The Church yard and burial ground

Throughout the years the Church yard has evolved as buildings around the perimeter developed, parts of the church were revamped and graves extended (until the grave-yard was at capacity). In 1773, Dr Walcott banned school-boys from playing the group sport of "Fives" (hand pelota) in the Church yard, as it required hitting a ball against a wall using their hands (fives were fingers) and keeping it aloft. This game was a little like an early game of squash, without the expense or purchase of a racquet.

On the left, within the church yard is the rear entrance to the Old School House. It was built in 1763 for a new headmaster and replaced a fifteenth-century building. The Reverend John James (1810-1829) lived in this property. It belonged to the Grocer's Company who had appointed him as the Master. John had resigned his fellowship at Oxford when he married (in 1810) and made the move to Oundle. As the Head of the 'Grammar School' John James and his wife lived in the old School House. During his time in Oundle the schoolboys had limited play-space so they ran and played in the church yard.

---

[253] Please note, this section is taken from the records by Margaret; she suggested that its prose should not be altered.

The Old School House building currently has a smart, bright-red door, making it a good background to use in wedding photographs. The nearby cloisters, accessed through an arch, were built in 1880 in a Tudor-style. The library and archives are next to the original cloisters and Long Room. Also in the church yard are access gates to the front and rear of the Gascoigne (old Rectory) building, as well as the rear of the newer vicarage on New Street (now a private house). The gates lead into gardens. At the turn of the century, there were also wooden gates to the steps into North Street (with an arch bearing a light to show the way).

In the 1930s, when Barbara Chester was a child, streets were generally quiet with doors left unlocked or wide open and deemed safe. She often played in the Church yard with her dog, Betty, who would sit in her doll's pram. Betty would let Barbara do anything with her, but disliked strangers. A friend visited her mother and said, "You ought to see what your daughter is doing in the cemetery. She's picking all the flowers and putting them in the doll's pram, but I can't go near her or the dog will try to protect her." So her mother collected her - and cautioned her not to pick any more flowers.

There is access to the market place via steps that takes us to a courtyard by the rear door of the Book Shop. A wide gateway leads us into the market place (formerly blocked by a contiguous building), but now a gated area that is locked once per-year ensuring the right-of-way remains with Oundle School and not the town.

New Street (west side from the War Memorial)

From the 1500s, New Street was originally named Bury Street. This has obvious connotations. One the corner is number 1. This is currently 'Beans' café. This shop was previously a newspaper and stationery shop. Prior to this, in the 1960s the Cheney family ran it as a hairdressers and tobacconists. It is currently thought to be a charming place to sit inside or out to watch the world go by whilst having a coffee tea or hot-chocolate drink! This venue is greatly enjoyed by cyclists on Sunday mornings. It is part of the route of the 'Women's Cycle Tour' as Oundle hosts the opening stage of route. It occurs annually in May and has been going since 2014. The Tour sets off from Oundle Market Place, then the riders pedal fast to Northampton, the destination of the first stage of the tour. This five-day race draws the world's top female cyclists to race against Britain's Olympic heroines. The race begins with the opening stage from Oundle to Northampton, while Leicestershire, Bedfordshire, Essex and Hertfordshire host subsequent stages in the event, with the final finish in Bury St. Edmunds in Suffolk.

Mrs Bertha Binder (wife of the late Arthur H. Binder) ran a jewellers at number 3 in the 1930s. Mr George R. Pearson ran a dental surgery upstairs. In the 1940s, it was owned by Mrs Burdett. She ran a tea-room here. Later the shop was "London Central Meat Company" and "Dewhurst's" butchers. For a time in the 1960s it was Baxter's butcher. Roger Hibbins (an insurance agent) worked in 'Number 46" (selling men's wear) in the Market Place, then ran own his insurance sales business firstly from the upstairs rooms of 'Parry Irving' by Crown Court. He then moved in to 3 New Street. He was very generous with his time for charity. He opened his shop as a Christmas grotto in the Christmas of 1987 and welcomed the Brownies and townsfolk in to visit Santa. Roger was Father Christmas. He handed out gifts and made the group laugh. Around the millennium, Roger died. His wife Judy took over the shop. Since 2013, it has been run by Judith (Judy) Hibbins' as 'Crackers' gift-shop. She is ably assisted by Elaine Bilson. The shop always has interesting and colourful window-displays of cards and knick-knacks. It is packed with purchasable gifts and has shelves full of interesting items.

The post office building dates to 1904, but Oundle has retained post-men since the end of the eighteenth century. In 1843, Mr William Danford and Mr John Eaynor were the local postmasters. (John died in 1844.) In the 1930s it was run by Raymond William Mottram (1892-1979). The building where the post office now stands was once a two-storey building with bay-windows. (It was similar in construction to the corner building, 'Beans'). I remember when I was a child, looking at the clock in the high window to see what time it was. It was always set correctly. The clock disappeared from the window sometime in the 1970s and was, sadly, not replaced. The Post Office first opened on New Street when the sorting office depot on the corner of East Road closed. This building once served as just a post office, but became a shop and post office when the current owners took over. In the 1950s, Siddon's coal merchants functioned from the post office yard. The early twentieth century, New Street post office is a Sub-Post Office and store, yet there are plans to close national post-offices. We will need to wait to see what the future will bring for Oundle post office and its building. The building forms a hub for Oundle, especially at Christmas time when people send parcels and cards. It has offered us a range of services, including car tax renewal, travel insurance, foreign currency, money-grams, stationary and greeting cards, alongside operating as a general store for other items - such as toilet roll!

Origins of the Talbot Hotel [254]

The Talbot an inn building that was erected over a thousand years ago. It was first chronicled in 638 AD, after its start as a Christian 'hospitium', dispensing ale, food and lodgings to pilgrims and travellers. (It and the nearby school buildings are not designated with numbers, so postmen lookout!) The Talbot Hotel has a rich tapestry of history. This hospitable coaching-inn has grown in affluence over the centuries. Long ago it was named the 'Tabret' Inn (after a small drum). It was later named the 'Tabbard' (a tunic from livery). It is one of the oldest surviving Inn building in Oundle and the earliest surviving hostelry in Northamptonshire.

Oundle monastery was built to the memory of St. Andrew and it is said that when it caught alight and was destroyed, the flames "passed over" the guest-house where the Bishop Wilfrid's remains stayed (our Talbot). By 700 A.D. the Tabret was a well-renowned 'rest-house' under the benefaction of the Medeshamstede (Peterborough) monks who rebuilt it. The Inn housed brethren who visited the hospital for aged mendicants (beggars) and town school for orphaned children. The hospital has closed, but the school remains under the control of the Worshipful Company of Grocers, who visited the inn whenever they were in town. The stables (for horses in transit) stood behind the building. Further along the street, the Great Hall site was where the original refectory was in Wilfrid's monastery.

It is said that William Whitwell purchased stone from Fotheringhay castle to rebuild and enlarge the Inn (1626), which at that time was named the Tabret. It seems likely that William purchased the panelling

---

[254] With thanks to the Talbot Hotel for their help and information.

333

and oak staircase from the castle. The staircase and small latch-gate is believed to have been a barrier between Mary (the abdicated Queen of Scotland) and her warders, prior to her execution in 1587. Mary is said to have been confined beyond the wicket gate with a window view of the Nene. The old, stone 'horn' (and at some point oil-cloth) windows and the coaching-yard entrance-arch are time honoured memorials to this bygone time.

Glass window-panes were limited until the seventeenth-century. Before this, windows for the common people were often covered in oil-cloth or made with horns (that had been soaked in water, flattened and made into small panes). They kept out the draught and let in an opaque light. James I of England (VI of Scotland) had the castle in Fotheringhay demolished and sold. As one teacher put it, "it was raised to the ground". He was the son of Queen Mary of Scotland who was executed here. The castle building and its history was sold (stone by stone) and then rebuilt from purchased remains forming a new source of history for Oundle, the reconstructed Talbot.

Whitwell granted the tavern-keeper a right to use his family name, coat-of-arms and logo: a Talbot passant (a dog represented as walking with the right front foot raised), hence, the name was changed. The 'Talbots' were powerful, white, hounds (with large ears and jaws) that became 'coaching dogs', brought to England by William the Conqueror.[255] Coaching dogs were bred and trained to run beside private carriages on their travels, while guarding their occupants from robbery and attack. Owned by wealthy people, traders and merchants, the dogs were trained to attack the highwaymen and their horses. A 'new' Talbot frontage was added in 1626, whereas the original building had been a wooden constructed. The building is grade-I listed as it has many features from the earlier building, including a mediæval timber-framed back range. Parts of its open passageway gallery is still visible.

The hotel has long been the Pytchley hunt meeting-spot (along with Biggin Hall). The hunt kennels their hounds in nearby Brigstock. In the spring of 2012, after a year-long closure for repairs and alterations, the

---

[255] In 1449, King Henry VI referred to John Talbot the Earl of Shrewsbury as "Talbott, oure good dogge", as a pun on his name, alluded to his family crest. A British Library document shows John with Queen Margaret and a white dog (his heraldic image).

Talbot re-opened. The rear courtyard had been restructured and its cobbled yard discretely covered by flagstones. The courtyard's eastern wall was removed and converted into an airy glass-wall. What was once a dark dining-room is a newly-constructed, millennium coffee-bar room has drawn new clients to use the hotel for meetings and convivial lunches. A mounting block stands by the entrance gateway, although few people tether their horses here or climb its steps today. It was last used when two coaches, each with four horses, visited Oundle in the autumn of 2017 on their one-week tour of local coaching inns (along the old Great North Road), in their efforts to raise awareness and money for "Help for Heroes".

On the Tabret Room's courtyard wall, a logo of three tuns (casks or barrels), John Smith's initials and 1775 are carved in stone. This stone came from the "Three Tuns Inn" (North Street), one of the first inns Smith bought here. It was taken from the wall of the demolished brewery. In the 1930s, the Talbot was managed by Miss L. Clarke. In the 1970s Alan and Jill Stewart ran the hotel (before moving to the 'Falcon' in Fotheringhay). Today, the Talbot is a pleasant venue to imbibe with coffee of something stronger. I reflect here that perhaps the 'something stronger' may be a factor in patrons and staff (particularly Minnie, in the early 1970s) seeing an apparition that they claimed was the executed queen, Mary of Scotland, on the main stairs and in the rear kitchen!

A row of buildings formerly adjacent to the Talbot included the Barnes' Brewery, the "Mermaid" and "Turk's Head" (next to North's butchers). Now, the 'study-rooms' for Oundle School are next to the Talbot. They were built relatively recently on the site the "Turks Head" Inn and a row of cottages. The Oundle School one-storey row of study-rooms (behind wrought-iron railings) is built in a 'chocolate-box style', in-keeping with Oundle's history. Listed School buildings dominate almost the entire road, from the Hotel to the corner of Milton Road. 'Folkstone Place' was once a row of Victorian terraced houses (from 1877). The end of the row was Richard Gann's furniture works. The houses were bought by Oundle School for redevelopment. In 1907 they were demolished to create the space in which to build the Great Hall. The 'Turk's Head' Inn was joined to School House, but was demolished to make space to build the Headmaster's study in 1887. It faces the cloisters, but was built after the demolition of the cottages. It has been used for a variety of functions and houses the offices of the headmaster and the school admissions department. The Great Hall was constructed in 1908. Originally it was only the central portion with lawns either side. The north and south wings were added later. Opposite the Cloisters in New Street and next to the Great Hall is School House. There has been a School House since 1556. This particular building was the abode of the Oundle School Headmaster and was as a boarding House in 1887. Mr Adam Edward Langsdale is the current housemaster in School House. He lives here with his wife, Elspeth (the School Archivist) and their children. Mr Langsdale was the Head of Biology, plus coached hockey, diving and sailing. Mr King is the head of Politics and gives support as the Deputy Housemaster. (The current house Matron is Mrs Françoise Barron.)

The Oundle School sixth-form lectures have included political speakers: President Kaunda of Zambia, the First Minister of Northern Ireland, Lord Tebbit of Chingford, Baron Patten, Baron Heseltine; James Watson (DNA discoveries) and other Nobel Prize winners; an ex-Head of the KGB and Dame Eliza Manningham-Buller (Head of MI5); scientific Professors, Stephen Hawking, Robert Winston and Richard Leakey; classical musicians, Natalie Clein, Craig Ogden and Jeremy Menuhin; novelists, Kazuo Ishiguro, Simon Winchester and Ian Hislop; Journalists, John Simpson, Michael Buerk and Martin Bell. It also included sportspeople such as Lord Sebastian Coe, Gary Lineker, Henry Winter, Hugh McIlvanney and Michael Atherton. A Sixth Form concert and a 'Concept of Remembrance' lecture are held yearly, along with memorial lectures in honour of Sir Peter Scott and Joseph Needham, prominent 'Old Oundelians'. A wonderful, memorable lecture in the Great Hall was that of Sir Wilfred Thesiger (1910-2003), when, thanks to the History Department staff, my husband, Tim and I were invited to attend his post-talk chat with the sixth form. (I believe that I was the only female present!)[256]

The Great Hall hosts the Oundle Music Festival, which is affiliated to the British & International Federation of Festivals. It was formed in 1909 with the help of Lady Millicent Lilford (of Lilford Hall) and Lady

---

[256] Anna Fernyhough, personal history.

Ethel Wickham (who was living at Barnwell Manor). The festival continues and attracts all ages and is organised by Gwen Radcliffe, Nicola Jakeways, Gill Potts and Diana Awdry (2017). This Oundle festival has provided over thirty years of concerts, theatre and community events.

The gardens to the right of the Great Hall have a discrete pathway that leads through to Milton Road. The Elliott M. Viney statue sits on the lawn, hidden from street view. Viney was an 'old boy' from School House. During the WWII he was at Dunkirk and was a prisoner of war for five years. For his efforts in these years he was awarded a DSO and MBE. Viney was the first Old Oundelian to be a Master of the Grocers Company (1970). These gardens once were the home to a caged captive monkey. No one today seems to remember why it was there, but assume it was the pet of one of the Masters' that outgrew his home. It was a favourite of the boys, who would go to visit it and watch it through the side-windows of the Great Hall.

WEST STREET

West Street (south side, travelling west)

North Street and West Street were contiguously and together were named 'the High Street'.[257] Large-scale changes occurred at the far west end of the street (where the 'Jesus Church' stands today). The Austell Survey tells of how the Chapel of St. Thomas Becket had stood there. In 1565 the area also held houses and a workshop. The Buck engraving of 1729[258] denotes that the main street stretched from north to south. The houses and workshop were replaced by the current church in 1879.

Number 2 West Street is a two-bedroom terrace house (to the rear of number 4). It is in an off-street position. A Georgian building (4) was Charles P. Berkley's property. It was then sold to Mr Charles T. Wilson (an Oundle solicitor) and his wife, Anne, whom he married in 1841. They lived with their family and their servants. Later still, Robert W. Todd ran the drapers' shop business with the help of his sister, Elizabeth. The tailor and outfitters was destined to be "Wilkins and

---

[257] The Austell survey.
[258] Samuel and Nathaniel Buck were eighteenth century topographical artists.

337

Company" (as it appears in the 1930 directory), then Mr Parker's gentlemen's outfitters. The shop supplied Oundle School uniforms and jeans to the local teenagers. Mr Parker was always very obliging and helpful. He and his wife allowed girls to try on their purchases in his front room. This was at the back of the corridor that led from the shop. The premises did have a changing cubicle in the shop, but this was for boys! On trying on clothing there in the 1960s, Wendy Bollans commented that Mrs Parker was always happy to help anyone trying on their items. She would then offer a cup of tea and a chat to accompany their purchase. This shop (in the early 2000s) was 'Dante' ladies fashions and is now the 'Air Ambulance' Charity Shop. Mr Herbert Parker and his wife lived in the upper floors of 4 and Mr Cecil W. Green (1860-1944) also resided in part second of this building (4).

Number 6 was Elijah Storey's 'General Furnishing Ironmonger' in the late 1800s and George S. Selby's ironmongers' in the pre-war years. George is remembered by many. He lived to be 90 and died in late 1952. The shop was Bridge's Ironmongers in the 1960s. At 6, the ground floor was used by 'H. Newman Limited' who ran a radio and television installation and repairs business. It is currently occupied by the Vincent Sykes solicitor's practice. At one time the building was larger as it originally incorporated the buildings used by 'Milestones' and 'Brewbabu'.

In 1966, Heather Melton worked here when it was Northamptonshire Farmer's, haulage contractors, selling grain and animal feed. 'Milestones florists' (at 6a) sells flowers that are displayed outside. The shop sells floral arrangements for a range of events. It was once part of a larger Georgian premises; a property combined with next-door. The ground floor held a shop and upstairs was the family accommodation. This grade-II listed building was Jim Selby's shop in the 1940s. His assistant was Miss Gilbey, who "wore dirty men's overalls and smelled of paraffin". She lived in St. Osyth's Lane (near to Ralph and Marie Hooton's shop). Selby's then became Newman's Ironmongers in the 1950s and 1960s. The walls were lined with shelves that were always full of items – everything from screws to ladders. The proprietor often had to climb up a ladder to reach the top shelves to get down items for purchase. After selling hardware until the 1960s, it was a successful clothing store 'Jumpers'. Then this many-roomed shop sold gifts and cards as 'Birthdays'. Number 6 is now 'Brewbabu' tea-room café. The shop stretches to the back and into the smaller side rooms. The rear was not originally used as part of the shop premises. It now has additional seating in this flourishing tea-shop business.

Mr J.W. North and Son ran a butcher's shop at number 8 during the late-1930s. It later became Mr H. Johnsons' butcher shop. His daughter, Christine Johnson attended the local schools in the 1960s. She was so polite that when walking backwards, she walked into a lamp-post, slid into a puddle at its base and apologised to the post! The shop is now 'Seven Wells' butchers. The name 'Seven Wells' comes from Stoke Doyle farm, where the cattle are raised, but the name dates to much earlier.

The Seven Wells

Between Barnwell and Oundle are seven wells and "during the ages of superstition" it was commonplace to "dip weakly infants, called berns" into their waters. It is not known where this pagan custom originated, yet it was also believed that an angel or spirit would give protective benefits to the water. So "mystical and puerile rites were performed at these springs, denominated *fontes puerorum*" and a "dark devotion" was then paid to the wells, which "grew into a continual resort of persons, productive of great disorder". A consequence of these heathen pilgrimages was that they were banned by the clergy and the Bishop of Lincoln, Oliver Sutton, around 1290.[259] The only dipping of babies we perform today is in Church at a baptism.

The current butcher's shop is managed by Robert and Sally Knight, who purchased K. Johnson & Son butchers' shop (who have traded locally since 1905). The amazing, original 'cow and piggy' tiled front of the building remains largely the same. To the right is an entrance-gateway, through which deliveries were taken. It is a listed, eighteenth-century construction. It has lovely ceramic panels on the lower front walls to illustrate its purpose as a shop. These date to the early twentieth century.

---

[259] Britton, 'A History of the County of Northampton', Vol. 3, ed. W. Page, published by Victoria County History, London, 1930.

Formerly, number 10 was a fashion-wear shop named 'Pandora Boutique'. Subsequently, it became the 'Oundle Sweet Shop'. Like the others around it this is a listed building. At 10a is the Oundle 'Candy Company' shop. It is a new, traditional sweet and chocolate store. Despite its American sounding name, a large percentage of the sweets are handmade locally. To tempt us, 'retro' items include bonbons, toffees, mint humbugs, stem-ginger, chocolate-peanuts, Nut Crunch, Turkish Delight, milk teeth, Black Jacks, Rhubarb-&-Custards, jelly-beans, fudge, Fluff, Nerds, M&M's, popping candy, liquorice, wine-gums, floral-gums, aniseed twists, candy sticks, mega-lollies and a range of chocolate treats, to name but a few. These are today's sweets from our childhood memories. Since the turn of this century the building has housed Winifred Dunkley's clothing shop, "Smiths'" delicatessen, a clothing store and a small-furnishings shop. Chris Rowell ran the Wool Shop at the rear (before moving to 'Oundle in Stitches'). It then was a chiropodist's and is now 'SA Bai Gai' Thai massage business (10c). The 'Rounded House' furnishings shop opened at 10b in 2017. Previously, this was part of a united building.

Through a fancy, Georgian passage-doorway we reach shop doors within. This is number 10. It was the home of Mr Thomas Skeffington (1864-1946) and he ran his seed and corn shop here. It was later the business premises of Siddons and Sons, coal and corn merchants in the 1930s. The coal yard was on Station Road, but its main offices were next to a jewellers. (It was "Chocolate Box" sweet shop in the 1960s). Heather Cunnington informed us that "this is the building where I worked in the 1960s and early 70s, when it was 'Northamptonshire Farmers'. It later changed to 'East Midland Farmers' with a Northampton head-office. Bradshaw's (Perio Limited) were here in the early 1960s. (Curtis', also in West Street ran a similar trade.) Part of this building was where the Bygrave's lived and, after they left, the Bayliss' lived here. Both families had lived in Oundle for quite a while."[260]

Number 12 was the Peterborough Cooperative Society. Mr Stanley Jeakins (1896-1973) was its manager in the pre-war years. The large glass-fronted building has successively served as the first 'Co-op' and the International, Bateman's Antiques, '62 Love me Do' (a 1960's style

---

[260] Kind permission of Heather Cunnington (née Melton).

retro-restaurant) and now is Salerno's family-run Italian restaurant and delicatessen, which serves traditional Italian food each day. Number 14, Haydn House, was a music shop at the turn of the century. In the 1920s, this was William H. Hinman's Temperance Hotel. This was a response to the number of inns providing a bed for the night, but which served alcohol. The hotel was for 'genteel' personages. In 1939, number 14 was the Rushden Electric Supply Company. It was managed by Mr Hector Jack MacDonald. (Hector was born in 1906 in Daventry.)

West Street houses - Anne Cooper (née Leayton)

Anne Cooper (née Leayton) lives with her sister, Ruth, above the shops in West Street. Her house was built in the 1740's, although the land was owned long before. The Skeffington family lived there before the Leayton's. When Anne and Ruth bought it (1972) the property was very delapidated. The old Co-op beneath their apartments was for sale. Its former owners couldn't get planning permission to do what they wanted to, it was put up for sale. Anne said, "It was Northants' farmers when we were children. I remember Mr Bamford working in the Co-op". (His brother lived on Rock Road.) Ann stated that "North's butchers was next door. Where 'Brewbabu' is now was Selby's hardware. They sold parafin at the side, where 'Milestones' florist is now. It has a roadside window where people can now sit for coffee. This was originally a passage with a wooden front-door".

Ann said, "The bakery was Maddison's the tailor when I was a child. It was a gentlemen's outfitters. The building that is the Air Ambulance was another tailor's. There was also the Crown Assembly meeting rooms nearby, which is where the Irvings were. The Oundle and Thrapston Council offices were at the back and the front was where Parry Irving's ladies clothing shop was. The Conservatives met at the meeting rooms and the Labour party had theirs in Ship lane – on the right hand side in the car park. The back entrance is now much further down. The Labour club building is now part of the pub accommodation, by the gate, opposite the back entrance of Cobthorne."

Returning to the street, at number 14 (on street-level) is "The Beauty Room" (for facial and body treatments). It was the home of Mr King (who owned the New Street printer's). The building was then run as the 'Commercial Hotel'. It was run by the Hinman's, who dished out excellent food and had comfortable rooms. It is also believed that a 'Commerical Bank' was also run from the building. It has since been a music shop, then a travel agency, followed by Southam's estate agents. In the 1960s it was the Coal Office (for household fuel sales and orders). By the 1980s the 'Oundle Tourist Information Centre' sold memorabilia and shared local information with visitors. Now the building hosts the 'beauty' premises.

Number 16 is Cobthorne. In the 1930s this house was the home of Mrs John H. Smith. Cobthorne House (sometimes without an 'e') is retained by Oundle School and is the residence of the Head and his family. With large gardens to the rear and a gated-stable entrance (that leads through to the back lawn from West Street) it brings back memories of its garden fetes of the 1960s. The house formerly belonged, though marriage, to the Capron family of Southwick Hall. George Capron, a London solicitor, bought the Manor of Stoke Doyle ten years before acquiring Southwick Hall for his family. He had connections with the Lynn family through his cousin, the Reverend John Shuckburgh (after whom the public houses in Southwick and Stoke Doyle are named). His second son, the Reverend George H. Capron (Rector of Stoke Doyle) succeeded him in 1872. His wife was Mary Smith, whose family lived at Cobthorne. The Southwick Capron's were involved in public affairs, acting as magistrates and sheriffs. They were associated with reformers and anti-slavery issues in the 1800s. Christopher Capron, the present owner, was the head of BBC current affairs programming before establishing his own television company. (He coaxed Alexander Solzhenitsyn to visit Southwick Hall for a rare interview.) Miss Constance Elaine Capron (1902-1981) was a governor at Oundle Secondary Modern School.

West of Cobthorn, Ship Lane dates to the formation of Oundle and leads to South Back Way (now South Road). It is adjacent to the 'Ship Inn', which is a fourteenth-century coaching-stop.[261] Although mainly seventeenth-century, it has fourteenth-century roots. This public house is probably one of the oldest in Oundle still enduring and open. It was a café and guest-house for much of it existence. The rear of 'The Ship' had a large carriage way. Here there once stood a saw-pit that

[261]   David Wills and others.

was used by Oundle wheelwrights and blacksmiths. In the 1930s and 1940s, Oundle had a blacksmith. Horses were still on the roads pulling carts and service vehicles.

The 'Ship Inn' has a long history. It dates to the fourteenth-century and carries its own ghost story and a subsequent mystery! Allegations hold that a 'former' landlord committed suicide by launching himself from the bedroom window. It is said that the "distraught owner, broke his neck on the road below" and that his "spirit has appeared many times to scare and shock past-licensees and guests". (Possibly after some consumption of the local beverage?) More recently, there were tales of a missing landlady. Several people in the town mentioned Mrs Newitt, who seems to have 'disappeared without a trace' in the late-1960s. Locals love gossip and suspect murder, as they report that she took nothing with her. No sign of her was found, she contacted none of her Oundle friends and no-one has heard from her since! (Although, it may transpire that Oundle resident, Mary Ann Newitt, who died in 1977, was this the former landlady?) John Clifton notes that there were battles in the pub between clients in 1791 with Mrs Brookshaw and Mrs Chapman, who laid into each other.

Mrs Brookes ran 'The Café' at number 18 in the pre-war years, when it hosted christening and wedding receptions. In 1938, Mrs Brookes made home-made cakes, jams, chutneys and pickles, besides running her café and guest house at the "Old Ship Inn". By 1973 it was run by co-owners, Ronald Franklin and Ian Fleming. The rustic bar is compact, but is cosy and warm with its open-fires in wintertime. Events are held in the 'long' bar behind the building (that was called the 'Longboat bar' in the early 1970s). In the 1970s, the coffee cups and saucers depicted a ship in full sail, although we really can't get much further from the sea! Number 20 is a simple stone building, similar to 18. It is attached to the inn by a high roofed entrance and carriageway, denoting its coach-house origins. This is the Ship Guest House.

Mrs Frances (Pawson (née Marlow, wife of Joseph B. Pawson) was a bootmaker who lived and worked at number 20. Number 22 was the business place of 'E.H. Lee Limited' until 1991. After a period as a haulage contractor business, retaining vehicles capable of emptying sewage buckets it became W.H. Curtis and Company (continuing from that date to the present) as an agricultural seed merchant. Curtis' have

343

been here "for as long as I remember and before" as Curtis' Seed and Agricultural Supplies Merchants have run from these premises for over fifty years.

Next-door was the 'Council School' or Secondary Modern School, with its open gateway to the former garden, classrooms and playground, which are now private housing. This school was also used by the "middle school" for a time. The Veterinary Practice operates (somewhat literally) in what was the school canteen on South Road. Access is now via Ship Lane. (The former school courtyard still has a beautiful Japanese Ginko tree growing in the garden area. (Several generations of students will recall this from their days in the school.) New residential houses have been built upon what was the playground. These can be seen clearly from the gateway on West Street or from the Vet's off South Road. The land and buildings were sold for re-development and to Oundle School.

As noted elsewhere in this book, the 'Queen Anne House' (at number 24) is a large town house. The front wall dates to 1824, as there is a date to be found on the down-pipe. The rest of the house dates to the seventeenth-century. Sadly, a new, wealthy owner thought it worthwhile to replace a seventeenth-century front during the course of a major renovation. Both end-walls have blocked-stone mullion windows. The back range (on the west side) contains a huge hearth stack. This was the home of Dr Vincent Alpe Grantham (known as 'Ben'), a general practitioner (born on 9th June 1922, he qualified at St Thomas's Hospital, London). He came to Oundle as a general practitioner in 1954 and was very well-regarded by his patients. He became the Oundle School doctor in the mid-1960s. He lived and practiced medicine in West Street for much of his life. His wife, Elizabeth, founded the Oundle Community Play-group (later a Pre-School). It is currently listed as the office address for Nene Valley Brewery in Station Road. Later the house belonged to the Spurrell family, who were also physicians.

Charles Herbert Howitt was a hairdresser. He worked and lived at number 26. 'Onkar' Indian Restaurant[262] was originally two buildings. Prior to the restaurant, in 1968 the buildings held Pearson's

---

[262] Onkar opened in 1995.

hairdressers (to the right) and Mrs Ratson's wool and good-quality 'Ladybird' children's clothing shop (on the right). They each had their own doors, but one of these has been blocked in. Gill Ganderton said, "Pearson's was where the current 'Onkar' back kitchens are. They were a salon at the back when it was a hairdressers. Mr and Mrs McAdam owned it for a time while they lived 'in a big house' in Glapthorn Road. Mrs McAdam was a (music) teacher at the secondary school. Their son, Canon Michael McAdam, lived at 5 West Street. Mrs McAdam moved to Deene Hall and ran the Guides. There were rooms that were let out upstairs from Pearsons'. They seemed to have quite a range of visitors from the town during the day. This may have been annoying as the upstairs could only be accessed via the shop!" Gill, a hairdresser, worked for Pearson's around the time of her marriage to Richard Ganderton. She is busy around the town and for many years joined the chorus of the Oundle annual pantomime. This shop was 'Oxfam' for a very short time.

The two residences (28a and 28b) form a detached, stone-house, tucked away from the road. In 1938, the shop (28) belonged to forty-three year old Mr Tom Allestree Cunnington. He was a fruiterer and florist, making bouquets and wreaths. His fresh vegetables were 'from our own garden daily'. Fruits were brought in for sale. The family also sold shrubs, trees and seeds. After Tom had retired, Mrs Richardson ran an expensive ladies-wear shop here (before it reverted to residence). Next-door, William G. White worked as a piano, wireless and gramophone dealer at number 30. This six-bedroom town house is now a contemporary and traditional art work gallery. The house has an original carriageway (via double doors). The art gallery and art sales since the year 2000. The Dolby's sell and create art, plus host art exhibitions in the small gallery at the front of the house.

In the 1960s and 1970s the building (30) was a doctor's surgery. Doctor Michael P. Lewis and then Doctor Oliver Stovin worked in this building before the surgery relocation plans were hatched. Oliver Stovin said that during his time in Oundle he has seen the development of a new Glapthorn Road surgery, an expansion in patient numbers and much change in the National Health Service. After twenty-six years as an Oundle doctor, he recently retired.

Dr Lewis wrote in the British Medical Journal (16 January 1971) on his concerns for "Hearing Aids for the Elderly". "Dr M.P. Lewis (Oundle, Peterborough) writes: I would like to draw attention to the unsatisfactory nature of the present National Health Service hearing aid, particularly when it is to be used by elderly patients. It so often happens that patients will not persevere with the aid because, on the one hand, the ear pieces are clumsy and not easy to fit into the ear and, on the other hand, the controls are small and so badly marked that it is very difficult for anyone whose senses are impaired to set the sound at the right point. ... The device for measuring the volume should I think be considerably larger and marked with some sort of elevation which could be felt with the fingers and would not require the use of an elderly person's failing sight".

The surgery, from the perspective of a child of the 1960s, was that it was full of long corridors and narrow, winding stairs. The surgery waiting room was accessed through the coach doors into the courtyard and then through a side door. It led to a small, divided waiting room. There was a barrier wall between the two parts. On the wall were a set of electric panels (basically a divided box with lightbulbs that individually lit when the doctor was free to see a patient. The system meant that a ticket was given and it was a first-come-first-served basis to gain the attention of the doctor. (The wait seemed less than waiting times today.) Then, it was through a door, past the office, down a corridor and in to see the doctor on duty. Generally patients saw their own doctor, who knew their temperament and history, as he had seen each patient since they were in utero!

Four cottages lie within the boundaries of numbers 30 and 32. They were created from a variety of outbuildings which were formerly a coach house, stables and 'groom's bothy' or hut. These were derelict when the present owners acquired the property in 1981. Thomas Weldon lived at 32 in 1939. He lived in Oundle throughout his life and died in 1949, aged 67.

Past records show that there was an ale house ("The Nags Head") on part of the site in 1795. The property appears to have been bought by a butcher, Mr Thomas Arnsby (and his wife, Elizabeth) in 1828. It is believed that Thomas was the person responsible for the demolition and rebuilding of the three-storey front of the property to create a more impressive building as befitted his status. Although the gardens ended up derelict and have since been redesigned there are still traces of the apothecary's original plant ingredients found in various parts of the garden. Thomas died in 1847 and his wife followed him ten years later.

Joyce Hardick (*née* Gaunt) and her sister, June, celebrated the Victory in Europe (VE) day in the 'Nags Head' public house at the terminus of West Street. The day was declared a public holiday and was celebrated on 8th May 1945. It marked the formal surrender by Germany and the conclusion of the war. After six years of restrictions, rationing and risks during wartime, with the end of blackouts and bombing raids, it was reasonable to see how excited people were to finally be able to let feel free at last to 'let down their hair' and enjoy living again. Joyce recalls that everyone was overjoyed and there was a "wonderful, relieved feeling".

Number 32 West Street is a two-bedroom terraced-house that was formerly part of the 'Old Hind' Inn (which is now a private house). It is grade-II listed, dating to before the seventeenth-century, as that was when it was partly rebuilt. It has a much lower roof than the adjacent buildings and seems to have a slight bend to its walls. In the latter-half of the 1700s, John and Mary Cross lived here. John was a local farmer who died in 1809. On Mary's demise the house was passed to Thomas Spencer (her nephew). The Fowler family ran a school for young ladies here, before it became a veterinary clinic under William Branford. The census shows that in the late 1800s a husband and wife team, Edward and Ann Carr continued and taught in the small school that based here. By 1911 it was the home of John Gatherer Hornstein and his wife. (They had moved here after their marriage in Brighton during 1886.) This was the home of Mr Michael McAdam, who lived here in the 1960s, followed by 'Bill' (Martin) Hillyard, who was resident here in the 1970s.

There was another part of the Inn ('Old Hind') at number 34. It was previously a part of 'The Unicorn' Inn then had changed its name to 'The Mason's Arms'.[263] The private house with its 'Old Hind' art gallery in the garden was converted from the sixteenth-century stables, from what was once the "Drover's Inn". On the 12th January 1912 the funeral

---

[263] 'Brewery Trail', Oundle Museum Trust, 1997.

and interment of Mr John Maddison of the "Old Hind" Inn was held "amid a general scene of regret". John was a popular and respected figure. Towns-people lined his final route from the church to the cemetery. Shops were closed as a mark of respect. The building was revamped as 'refreshment' tea-rooms in 1925, after it closed as a pub. This was the "Avondale" cafe. Miss Maddison lived here (34) in 1939. Later Michael Aubrey came to create his art-work. Gallery Lane is at the rear of this house (with three buildings in a complex).

Number 36 is 'Townley House'. It is a large, Georgian house set on the corner of the long drive leading down to Coles' Builder's Merchants. All adjacent land was associated with the brewing industry (from West Street to South Road). It appears to have some windows blocked (possibly due to the window tax). The property was formerly part of the Oundle Union Brewing Company that ran from 1836 to 1853 and was purchased by Smith's (and worked by association with the 'Old Hind' Inn). Townley House functioned as the brewery offices. The current staff report seeing several 'apparitions' of a man with a flat-cap and overall in the basement. This building was part of the Anchor and Smith's breweries group and subsequently ran as a private girls' school. The main door to Townley House is on the western face. In 1938, Hooper and Forsyth were dentists at 36. This building, in the 1950s and 1960s, was run by the National Health Service (NHS) and continues as a private practice. Mr Catchpole was the Oundle NHS dentist from the 1950s to 1970s. When the practice became private, it forced the opening of a new NHS dentist. Many recall Mr Catchpole's methods seem somewhat outdated. Virginia Gaunt (now Francis) was a dental assistant (1968) and remembers him being a "nice man" and, contrary to some views, said that "people loved him". [264] Many children who grew up in the 1960s have a very different opinion!

Mr William M. Freeman and Son were builders, established at number 38. William was born in 1862. He died in 1947 (aged 85). Siddons and Freeman took over as a team until 1907, when Siddons' moved businesses. They were in charge of the construction of the Victoria Hall at the turn of the century (using public funds). The Freeman family continued working as building contractors, plumbers, decorators,

---

[264] Virginia left when she married David Francis (son of the 'Francis and Marshall' garage franchise partnership).

stonemasons and blacksmiths until 1937. In the 1950's Ted Freeman Builders at number 38 (next to Townley House). This is currently Patrick Coles' building-merchant business. His builders' yard is at 38 West Street along a lengthy, southerly driveway. His wife, Pat Coles (née Midlane) said that she and her mother were born in Oundle. Mrs Gertrude Sheila Midlane (née Brown) is Pat's mother (aged 92). She has always been known as 'Sheila'. She attended the local schools and Pat followed suit. They both attended the same Church of England Primary School and Council School (Secondary Modern). Pat noted that the name had changed slightly, but the school still had some of the teachers from her mother's days who taught them both. Her brother, David, was in the voluntary fire service and set up OATS. (David Midlane now lives in Bedford.) Pat said, "Mum's father was William Brown, who played cricket for the Oundle town". Pat and Paddy have four children, still live in the town and run the builder's yard on West Street.

Mr Edward Newton lived at number 40 prior to WWII (1939). 'Melton House' (42) is a listed, two-storey residence that was built in 1800. Its side-wall suggests that there have been some building changes. The building currently houses an osteopath and other businesses. 44 is a Georgian building with brass plates and bell. 44 is an elaborate, mid-nineteenth-century, three-storey building. The Misses Haines lived here in 1938. It has two windows in Dutch gables in the roof. Above the main door there is a school coat-of-arms. There are two ball finials and two stone chimneys at the gable ends. The double-fronted building has a side-gate with wrought iron railings to the front. Mr Capron, a solicitor, owned this spacious and comfortable house and lived here. His brother was the rector of Stoke Doyle in the late-1800s. In the early 1970s, the house was rented to American Air Force families. The non-resident families were a useful source of pocket-money income to local girls who performed baby-sitting services. 46 was the home and workplace of Ambrose W. Stokes fishmongers. (Ambrose died in 1943, aged 63.)

Number 50 is a fine-stone dwelling that dates to the sixteenth century. The old terraced cottages 52, 54 and 56 are built of rubble-stone. George Martin lived at number 52, Thomas West was at 54 and Aubrey and Winifred Bamford at 56. F. Marlow and family lived at number 58.

Numbers 58 to 60 stand either side of the Danford's classy entrance driveway.

Turner's and Danford's Yards

Turner's, Setchell's and Danford's Yards are also related to individuals who lived or owned property here in the past. Setchell's Yard was named for John Setchell, son of John Setchell, a butcher. The family purchased this land in 1864. Setchell's Yard is located betwixt 76 and 78 West Street. In the late-1930s, number 1 was vacant, but Mr W. Paddington lived at 2. Mr Reginald C. Poole lived at 3. He married in Miss Ethel Palmer in 1929. They lived here together with their family. Meanwhile, Mr William Smith lived at 4 and Mr Harold (Herbert) George Upex and family at 5. The first post office was originally next door to the Turner's. The mail cart came from Peterborough with any mail for the school and town. Turner's Yard was the home of Charles John Turner, a cabinet maker, whose premises stood here at the turn of the twentieth century. Charles Turner (1858-1930) and M.M. Coles were cabinet makers, upholsterers and undertakers and house furnishers. They made and repaired baskets and cane seats. Mr Turner died in 1930, aged 72. Miss Turner lived here for a time. She was the daughter of Charles and also worked as an undertaker.

In the 1800s the Danford family lived in property that gained their name. They owned the area that came to be known as 'Danfords yard' and its adjacent land to the south (leading off from West Street). Danford House is a Georgian building with a wide-arch coach-way between two wings. It has a balustrade at roof level. Further buildings within the yard are joined by a footpath to Danford's Close. Danfords Close was constructed in the 1960s and is accessed via South Road. The Council demolished the small cottages in Danford's Yard in the early 1960s and built the new "Danford's". Mrs Lottie Mason, a well-loved, local personality and voluntary service member, lived at number 5. In 1939, Mr Albert Hall (1904-1974), who worked as a chimney-sweep, lived at 2 in Danford's yard.

The main entrance to Danford's resembles the lodge to a great house, but led to a yard with cottages. In World War II, many Oundle residents have remarked on "a Spitfire that flew down West Street chasing a German Heinkel plane". Arthur Chester was a member of the Home

Guard and was very annoyed by people rushing out into the street to watch, while he and other men of the Home Guard tried to get them back inside the buildings to safety. The plane shot off a ball from the top of Danford's gateway before continuing on its journey. Percy Arnett said that "a 1940s RAF plane chased a faster enemy plane around Oundle. It flew just above the road". He said that the German airman "used up all his bullets in West Street. It was said at the time that he was trying to get to the gas works to hit that. Later in the day, people went out into the street to look for bits of shrapnel to keep as souvenirs." Bevil Allen remarked that when he was a day boy at Oundle School "during the war years, the older 'boys' were given rifles and live rounds of ammunition". "They were sent up to the playing fields to await any Nazi paratroopers. There was not much training for it". Bevil said that the school boys "wouldn't have been much help in a crisis, but at least they felt they were doing something". He said that to settle their nerves "the Housemaster gave each boy a cigarette". He retold the story that others had mentioned by remarking that "Much later, when the plane flew over it shot the stone ball from the top of the balustrade on Danford's Yard in West Street. It was really lucky that no-one was hurt". During the 1960s, Mrs Doris Hooton and her family lived at number 60.[265] By this time, Doris' family had grown and "flown the coop". She saw several of her children pre-decease her. Towards the end of her life, Doris lived here with Eileen, her unmarried, eldest daughter. Eileen was the eldest of Doris' children. She remained with her mother for her entire life. On Doris' death, Eileen found life quite complex and lonely. She was wealthy in her own right, but never dressed or behaved as if she was. She often sat on the bench in the town centre watching people go by. Her Danfords' home was passed on to her eldest brother's children. Eileen never married and had no offspring of her own.

Number 62 is a sixteenth-century building and 64, shows restoration and new windows. Mr A. Howe lived here in 1938. The top-floor stonework is original, but the lower floor has had repairs using larger, cut stone. During the pre-war years, the business at number 64 belonged to Mr H.C. Wainer. He was a baker, confectioner and pastry cook, who made his wares on the premises. The speciality of the house

---

[265] Anna Fernyhough, family history.

was "cream meringues and buns". By all accounts his pork pies were "worth a nibble" too. Mr T. Hook lived at number 66. Reginald Lionel Crick (1893-1976) lived at number 68. Mr Charles Fears (1859-1937) lived at number 70 in the 1930s.

Alongside this is the new development of West Street Mews private houses; six detached, terraced and semi-detached residences that have been restored or built since the year 2000. Number 1 is "Wow Fitness Limited". Number 2 is a rented four-bedroom town-house and 5 is the base of a management company. Number 6, in the Mews, is a dwelling. It was a barn-conversion in 2014. It is flanked by a three-storey building (number 70) that is the current music shop. This shop sells instruments and sheet music.

In 1938, the 'Manor House' at 72 West Street was the home of sixty-five year old, Daniel James Craythorne. (He was born in 1873.) His home is an attractive, listed, Georgian town-house. It is joined to other buildings in the row. At 74, Mrs Joyce Shutt sold 'wet-fish'. She worked with badly arthritic hands and eventually moved to live in the nearby village of Wadenhoe. Patrick Winters lived here for a time before he married. His father bought the fish shop and the green-grocers' from the Stokes family.[266]

Numbers 74 and 76 are eighteenth-century listed buildings. (Please note that some of the numbers do not correspond to those in the past.) From the 1930s to the 1950's, number 76 was Mr Jack Wade's home and butcher's shop. Jack was well-liked locally. (Cheryl Forscutt noted that she was given Jack Wade's jubilee decorations.) Numbers 74 and 76 are one building. This is the current 'Green Man Antiques and Restoration' shop. (This shop was formerly run on the opposite side of the road.) The building was previously a public house named "The Green Man". As John Clifton lived at number 76, it bears the name "Clifton House". Half of the building was formerly Kirkpatrick's barber and hairdressers. It also held a tearoom. Jean Atkins[267] informed me that "Peggy Page lived here alone for some years". She also said that this house was previously a butcher's and that "Cattle were frequently kept in the back yard". Jean said that the house had a trap-door in the

---

[266] His son, Barry, grew up at numbers 46 and 48 West Street.

[267] Jean was Pearson's hairdresser's manager "for a time".

floor of the sitting-room, which went down to the abattoir below, at the back of the house. In the late-1930s, number 78 was the home of Mr Arthur George Vessey (who died in 1946, aged 75) and his wife. Mrs Elizabeth Upex lived at number 80 in the 1930s. Nurse Coates lived here thereafter.

Setchell's Yard

Setchell's Yard has old and new cottages along its length. It emerges onto West Street opposite the old Poor-House and Victoria Yard. William John Beesley lived here (although born in nearby Wadenhoe) and he followed the family trade as a blacksmith. In 1909, he married Annie Langston (a cook) and lived with her and their five children in Setchell's Yard. Their blacksmith's forge ceased to be used after WWI. The bungalow at number 2 Setchell's Yard is a listed building. In the 1930s there was no one living at number 1, but G. Collins lived at 2 and Reginald C. Poole and his wife, Ethel (née Palmer) lived at number 3. They married in 1929. At 4 were William G. Underwood and his wife, Gwendoline (née Underwood). Number 5 was the home of Harold George Upex (1895-1960). Behind Setchell's yard are the houses of South Bridge Close.

West Street: Setchell's Yard to Mill Road

West Street continues with number 80, a grade-II listed building that bears the date 1877 in a lozenge on the third storey. It is attached to a very similarly designed, listed, number 82. A lozenge on the wall shows the emblems of the United Kingdom and this same date. The 'New Yangtze River' is at number 84 West Street. The Chinese takeaway first opened in the 1980s. Before the takeaway was here, it was Mr Howitt's (the saddler) and then Joyce Hardick's house (1960s). It has a shop door and a double-door entrance to a courtyard. The second floor bears an illegible plaque (a hook has been attached to its centre). During the 1930s, 84 was W.H. Underwood's "Hunting and Company" coal merchants. Then, slightly later it was William Brown's company trading under the same name.

Next-door, at 86, the two-storey building was originally Oundle Commercial Bank. Mr G.J. Nixon's outfitters came here in 1938, before it was a pram shop. E. Walton was an electrician at Geoff Stubbs', but

Geoff has sold model aircraft, boats, radio-controlled equipment and sports equipment for nearly fifty years.

Ruth Keans recalls the Ganderton's meat shop at numbers 86 and 88. In 1939, Neville Ganderton lived at 82 (with his shop at 88). From the 1960s to 1970s, the building that is now "Just Lets" (a house rental business and estate agency) belonged to Martin Trendall's aunt, Sheila Lord, who ran a fabric and curtain shop. Later, Neville Ganderton and his family ran their 'fresh fish and game' shop here. The back-room, at that time, was part of the house. Before 1942, number 88 and 90 were owned by Mr John Barber.

By 1939, at number 90, Mr. Barber ran the florist and fruiterers and (across the road). Then numbers 88 and 90 were merged into Ganderton's game, fish and poultry store. The family then extended into 88b, formerly 'Sheila Lord Carpets' (selling household goods, carpet and curtains). Richard Ganderton, was born here, as his parents ran the shop. The family sold fresh fish and fowl to the townspeople. Neville George Ganderton and Sons of West Street had their "plucking rooms" behind the building. Later, this shop transformed into a "designer store" named "Fashions-88" (named for its number in the road) is still a shop-front and is newly extended at the rear. Joyce Hardick ran it as a boutique selling trainers, jump-suits, Asian prints, cap-sleeves and designer tops. She said that there was some opposition from other clothing trades within the town centre as they thought she would undercut their business, but she catered for "young and trendy styles" and this was not about to affect the sales of "older persons' wear" for those who shopped in the town. There had been nothing new for younger people prior to this. After a year, the business was then moved nearer to the town centre (to where Harper's Jewellers is now). The building had been divided up, so its front left, downstairs corner room was part of number 88. This has reverted to being one building since.

Very near to Ganderton's fish shop was another. This was Ambrose W. Stokes' fishmonger's shop and ice store, where he also sold game and fruit to Oundle in 1938. Many people recall Mrs Stokes serving in the shop at number 46. At the time, the sale of fish and game was highly competitive.

Mary and John Hindman's sweet shop was opposite St. Wilfrid's Roman Catholic Church (previously the Zion Baptist Chapel) and next door to the 'Wagon and Horses' pub. It was a sweet shop for many years. In the 1960s it had a myriad of large glass bottles and jars of sweets to peruse. Mary would measure out a quarter of a pound of this and a quarter of that in her scales. Sherbert in a bag and five-penny Victory V's, Cream Soda on draught and milkshakes. Kevin Holmes sold eels to Mary after he had been out night fishing in the Nene. Rachel Harris lived next door.

Barbara and Lucjan Mudza married in St. Wilfrid's in 1952. They were required to have a registrar present as my mother was Anglican and my father Roman Catholic. She felt that she had no choice, but to promise to bring up any children they would have in the Catholic faith or the wedding could not go ahead. In the 1960s, after attending each Saturday catechism class at St. Wilfrid's Church, I was allowed to spend my Saturday sixpence in the shop. It was a great treat after sitting on the hard pews in the cold church for over an hour.[268]

Small lanes and alleys reach to the back of the "virgate"[269] dwellings in Mill Lane and opposite Drumming Well Lane (on the other side of the high street). The narrow part of this lane was sometimes named Dobb's Lane, which led into Drumming Well Lane after the rear of the Talbot. Mr North (the butcher) kept his holding pens here (later part of the primary school playground). Oundle is divided into sections on the town plans from early times. One section leads from the market area, to the tenements, to Chapel End. Mrs Alice Sivers lived at number 92. She and her husband, Harry Sivers, were married in 1884. He died in 1929, aged 73. She outlived him by twenty years and died when she was aged 92. Mr Albert Alexander Moisey lived at number 94. He was born in Oundle in 1902, lived in the town for his entire life and died here in 1974.

Mr Frederick W. Litchfield ran the (former) 'Waggon and Horses Inn'. 98 and 96 were a public house known by successive names: the "Bull" (1565), the "Hind" (not to be confused with the newer inn of the same

---

[268] Oundle Museum has a display of Hinman's shop items (June 2017).
[269] A varying measure of land, around 30 acres. More a measure of tax assessment than area. A virgate was usually a quarter of a hide. (Oxford dictionary.)

name, which is an artist's residence) and "The Waggon and Horses". The corner building dates to the early 1800s, when Bartholomew Bellamy was the landlord, followed by George Afford (in 1843). The property is now a private residence.

A paddock-drive led to its rear field. During 1873 the fair men could set up their stalls in the town and on this ground. Farm workers and servants would parade and hope that they could pick up some extra work with anyone hiring. Charlie Bloom was a local 'clothier' who knew that he could sell many of his products to the labourers (often on credit) during the fair and in the lead-up to harvest time (when they would be paid and their debts settled).

Circuses and fairs were held in the field at the rear of the pub. This is where 'Mushie' the lion was a sometime resident. Behind a low wall stands a cottage with a very high chimney. It appears part of the contiguous building. The "Wagon and Horses" (number 98) was a public-house. It rented out its rear yard that was used by the circus and for fairs until as late as the 1950s. In the 1970s, Brian "Pud" Rice, ran his 'Pudding Bowl' antique shop and lived here. In 1939, 100 West Street was Dixon and Son's bakery and grocery shop. This was when the property was owned by Mr Hubert Johnson.

West Street (north side, travelling west)

On the junction of West Street and the southern end of New Street stands Oundle and Ashton's grade-II listed War Memorial. It names our local men who lost their lives (and the names of the unit they served with). There was once a town 'pump' in the centre of this junction. The War Memorial was commemorated after WWII. The pumps would force water up from the underground springs and aquifers. At one time there were water-wells in back gardens all over Oundle,[270] plus several water-pumps around the town for public use. The largest stood where the war memorial is. There was one opposite the 'White Lion' in North Street and another in New Street by the vicarage. The space where it was is still visible. Stoke Hill had a water-pump by the Jesus Church.

---

[270] Barbara Mudza knows that several of the North Street wells were filled with rubble once they were no longer in use. She believes that some house ground-water floods are a direct response of 'in-filling'.

Many people had their own well or pump. Inkerman Yard, Victoria Yard, Danford's (six houses) and Setchell's (five houses) were set around yards with shared pumps until Oundle was connected to the mains water supply (around 1896).

'Beans' corner café is an excellent position to lure recreational cyclists on fine Sunday mornings, observing as the 'world goes by'. Prior to his death in 1711, Mr William Whitwell owned this corner plot on West Street (formerly High Street) and New Street. The house bears a wall-panel in the gable that is inscribed '1626 W.W.'. (These are the initials of William Whitwell, who built all of the properties that extended to beyond the Talbot.) Part of his mid-seventeenth-century property was demolished to build the current Post Office in 1903. The street face of the Talbot ('Tabret') Inn remains unaltered since the 1600s. It is a gabled, three-storey building, with mullioned bay windows and a wide central archway. A saddler named Richard Ekins ran his leather working business from the corner shop in the 1800s. In the 1930s, Mr Raymond W. Cheney ran a hairdressers in this building. It was originally two buildings with doors leading out to both roads. These were transformed into one during the early 1960s. From then on, the shop was run as a stationary and trinket shop by the Cheney family, but the back still functioned as a hairdressers. The building has changed internally since this time. Cheney's shop exited into New Street. In the late 1960s Francis and Marshall's electrical and TV shop was in the northern end-part (of 'Beans' cafe) that opened onto West Street. The doorway still exists, but it not used. In the mid-1960s the shop conducted electrical repairs upstairs. Prior to this, it was 'W. McMichael and Sons' coal merchants (selling timber and coal), located opposite Siddons' Coal Merchants! Marjorie McMichael ran the shop, but lived in the Riverside Maltings, before moving to a nearby village with her daughter, Bridget. (When it the shop Marshall's TV repair shop.) Now, 1 West Street has a new, open-plan, one-bedroom cottage that is hidden from view and named the 'Old Brew House'. This cottage would be warm in the winters when it was built, owing to the small room size. During the late-1930s, 1 was 'London Central Meat Company' and at 3 were 'North and Perkins corn merchants'. In 1950s, Hockney's grocer's was next door.

The 'Grapevine' (number 3), was a public house that ceased trading in the 1860s. An even earlier pub on this site was the 'Beehive'. 'The Vine' has remained as the house name for this old landmark. The building was later a carpet and curtain shop, then was managed for a time as a book-shop and print sellers. Geraldine Waddington sold her lovely line-drawn prints from this shop. It currently functions as a beauty salon. It was named "Beauty with Ruth", but now trades as 'Oundle House of Beauty'.

Number 5a was run by Miss Mary Hinman as a confectioners. 'Harpurs' jewellers (5a) came from Bedford and was established in the 1950s. It was run by Peter and Pearl Hill who moved to Oundle in 2002. Their son, Nigel took on the business on their retirement. 'Martin Charles Bridal Gallery' is at number 13. From the 1960s to 1990s, this was the old 'Oundle Music' shop. It sold sheet music and musical instruments. As noted earlier, 5 was shared by W. McMichael and Son (coal merchants) and W.H. Curtis (corn merchants). At 5 West Street, Fred T. Cheshire (in 1939) was an electrical and radio engineer who made installations, fixed radio-receivers and conducted torch refills, charged accumulators and fitted cables and (lighting) lamps. Number 5 was previously Barber's greengrocers, before Mr and Mrs Norman owned it, but retained the 'Barber' name. There was a large cellar that went under the road, so floral tributes were kept here as it was so cold. It was a useful storage space. Subsequently it became a second-hand furniture shop (after William Norman, died in the mid-1960s). The shop was then run by his widow, Mrs Annie "Emily" Norman (the green-grocer, James Norman's mother).

One year when there was a town window-dressing competition Mrs Norman (dressed in Victorian costume) sat in the window. She parked herself in one of the chairs that was for sale and scared the life out of the judges when she suddenly moved! Later this shop became the 'Oundle Cobbler' shoe-shop in the 1990s and early 2000s. Number 5 is currently the Oundle Dental Practice (NHS).

The Queen Victoria Hall is at number 7. It was built in 1902 on land that had formerly been a bowling green. It has recently been refurbished. The Queen Victoria Hall was built by the people of Oundle to commemorate the reign of their late Queen. The foundation stone was laid on the Coronation Day of Edward VII, on 9th August 1902. Around

1928, the Temperance Society 'Band of Hope' meetings took place in the hall. Oundle cinema was in the Victoria hall in the 1950s and 1960s. Frank Jackson told his daughters that he remembered 'throwing popcorn' in the back row![271] I reflect on (but can't remember) being taken here to see the Disney 'Bambi' film as a very small child, but my mother, Barbara, says "We had to leave as Anna cried loudly after Bambi's parents died, so we missed the end of the film as she had to be taken home!"[272] (In recent years the Stahl Theatre has taken over as Oundle Cinema, showing films for the local population.)

St. Claires' hairdresser was formerly at 7a, left of the Victoria Hall, up a flight of six steps with a wrought-iron hand-rail. This is now closed and the small building is now private. Number 9 is a south-facing, three-storey, stone house with a slate-roof and bay-windows. It has gardens to the rear. Mr Arthur David Marlow (and son) were greengrocers. They lived at number 9 during the 1930s. He is remembered fondly for selling sweets and fruit to the Victoria Hall theatre goers. Arthur lived all his life in Oundle. He married Alice Slater in the Parish Church in 1902 and died in 1954, aged 78. Alice died in 1968, aged 89.

Number 11 is a private house, which stands next to the old United Reform Church (used from 1859-1977), formerly a Baptist Chapel that was built in 1852. It was last used as a church in the late-1960s. It has steps leading inside. From 1984 to 1989 this was 'Rachels' fashions. More recently it has rebranded as "the Bazaar" and is a small shopping arcade with a restaurant and coffee-bar (upstairs), plus Asha's Attire, Chapel Interiors and The Male Room (men's clothing) on the ground floor.

Drumming Well Lane

Drumming Well Lane accesses West Street and Milton Road. It is a pedestrian passageway and leads north to what is a 'new' Methodist church. It opened in 1985 in what was the former Telephone Exchange.

---

[271] Oral history, Sharon Cottingham.
[272] The Victoria Hall was intended for community use and its construction was funded by a group of local businessmen. In 1946, the Hall was given to trustees at the Oundle Town Council, who oversaw the refurbishment and updating of the building.
[272] Bob Baxter, personal recollection and interview 14th July 2017 and 30th September 2017.

The story has it that there was a well in Drumming Well Lane, which emanated certain noises. The beating of the drum was said to portend some great event. It was said to have been heard before the deaths of Charles II and James II. Richard Baxter (1615-1691) wrote about the lane, saying "When I was a schoolboy at Oundle, in Northamptonshire, about the [poor, migrant] Scots' coming into England, I heard a well, in one Dob[b]'s yard, drum like any drum beating a march. I heard it at a distance: then I went and put my head into the mouth of the well, and heard it distinctly, and nobody in the well. It lasted several days and nights, so as all the country people came to hear it. And so it drummed on several changes of times. When King Charles II died, I went to the Oundle carrier at the Ram Inn, in Smithfield, who told me their well had drummed and many people came to hear it. And I heard it drummed once since".[273] The well was covered in, but is memorialised by the name of its covered walk-way, Drumming Well Lane (behind the Talbot Hotel). The Talbot previously purchased a house for staff in the West Street end of this lane.

Robert (Bob) Baxter's family initially lived in Cotterstock, but moved to Oundle in the mid-1940s.[274] He may well have been a descendent of Richard Baxter (see above paragraph). Bob's father was a gardener at Cobthorne House. He took a pride in his work and the beautiful lawns, terraces and topiaries at the back of the house are a tribute to him and the other gardeners who worked here. At that time, Cobthorne had recently become the residence for Oundle School's Headmasters, who held regular summer garden-parties on its lawns. The lawns and borders needed to be perfect.

From the 1940s, the Baxter family lived in a thatched cottage at the back of the Talbot. This was situated where the rear car-park that leads to Turner's Yard lies. The low wall to the car-park marks where the house stood. It is behind Drumming Well Lane. The house was a 'stones-throw' from the corner of the lane and Skelton's bakery (where it meets West Street and is now a hairdressers), so there was a "lovely smell of bread every morning". Bob says that Skelton's was an excellent bakery selling home-cooked bread, made freshly each day on the premises. The family lived in the house at the top of the two-storey

---

[273] Richard Baxter in *"World of Spirits…"*, p. 157.

building and the bakery was in the building behind. There was an orchard at the back of the bake-house, which was next to his thatched-cottage home.

Bob also recalled that his cottage home was quite close to the British Legion hall or hut. The British Legion base has moved locations several times since. In the 1940s, they had a hut on the Primary School Playground. Turner's Yard was a right of way and local children used it as a cut-through to walk to school. Although the main gate was often closed and cars did not use it, there was a small picket gate to go through. Mr C.J. Turner was a cabinet-maker who lived in these premises, off West Street, in the 1900s.

As Bob's dad worked at Cobthorne the family rented this nearby cottage. The thatched cottage had a 'solid floor' throughout the lower rooms. In the scullery, at the back, there were old, rough, stone tiles on the floor and the room had the washtub in it. This room was the main source of heating and water for the house. The other room on the lower floor had a solid floor with lino covering it (and some carpets). It had two bedrooms that were "half in the eaves of the roof". "You went through one to get to the other. You went up the stairs to the main bedroom. Then you went through one room to get to the other, as the room of the second bedroom was off to the other side."

In his description of the house he said that "downstairs there was the front door, hall and a best room or the front-room (used at Christmas and for guest visitors), on the other side was the main living room and the scullery and kitchen at the back. Then we had a long garden which backed onto Turner's Yard. Outdoor loos and that type of thing". The scullery was used for laundry, washing-up and personal washing.

Bob said, "Drumming Well Lane has not changed that much. The new buildings behind the Talbot are where the old stable yard was. Presumably stables and a big, long L-shaped block with a hay-loft for the Talbot. There was a burial pit for offal for the bits left from the slaughtering at North's the butchers. That was at the back of the playground for the school, but it didn't belong to the school at that time. The playground didn't come all the way down to the bottom then. It was extended in the 1960s. I distinctly remember the offal pit. It was actually tight to the telephone exchange. There were two British legion huts, in two places. One was on one side of the GPO telephone place and the other was in the back of the orchard and the bakery. The final one was in the playground of the primary school."

Bob recalled that "The land around the back of the Talbot was used as part of Smith's brewery. The cottage and land was all 'Talbot' brewery land that was owned and rented out by the brewery. Our cottage, the stables, barn and yard were all owned by the brewery at one stage. The chef at the Talbot made ice-cream and you could get one if you went to the back window. The management didn't like you going down there a lot, so you had to be quite careful. I used to cycle down the Talbot yard to get to the buses to go to Peterborough in the mornings. It was cobbled then and now there's a gate. It's been opened up and there are new buildings that have been built at the back. There was once a row of cottages there, if you go right back. Reg Sutton had some of this information and had photographs of the cottage, but I don't have any. It's a great loss. There is now a new arch at the corner at the top. It was not the preferred route to the town at one time. The main carpark was enclosed within the Talbot wall. That's all disappeared now and has been forgotten."[275]

During WWII, Fred Carter, his wife and their son, Brian, lived in the cottage behind the Talbot (where the car park is now). They had an evacuee named Vera Rochford living with them. The family moved to the 'Half Moon' pub in North Street after the war.[276] In 1939 William D. Stretton lived at number 8 Drumming Well Lane. (He died in 1942, aged 81.) Bob remarked that "just over the main street, the open plot had 'Freeman and Son', builders, decorators and painters establishment (before it was Coles' builder's yard). Some of the bus drivers lived in this yard. There were lodgings there. Bus drivers and conductors were a funny bunch, but all very likeable; Bob could name some and knew the funny quirks and attributes of Bill Perkins, Sanders and Sumner. One in particular man was not a fast driver and "dawdled a bit". Bob recalled that "You knew that if it was him driving you would be picked up late and would be late for work".

---

[275] Thanks to Bob Baxter, who made efforts to call several times with information.
[276] Oral history, Barbara Chester.

Joyce Hardick's father, Frank Gaunt, "worked on the buses" and drove for Eastern Counties. He operated his vehicle alongside Bert Dodsworth and Bill Perkins, as they were his conductors. For a while during WWII, he had a female conductor from Benefield Road (Mrs Rogers). This was due to men being in short supply while the war was on. Chris and Sue York's grandad, Ernest, was known as 'Ernie'. He had a fish and chip van just after the end of WWII, which caught fire in Ashton a few years later (which Chris has photographs of). He ended his working life as a bus driver for Eastern Counties on the Peterborough to Oundle, via Warmington, route. He also drove the Alec Head school buses from Lutton until he was seventy-five.[277] Mr Leonard Vernard 'Skelton and Sons' bakery stood in the lane. Leonard was born in Oundle during 1899.

In 1939, 11 and 13 were general stores and tea rooms, respectively. They belonged to David W. Redhead and his son. They sold a range of foodstuffs including wines, spirits, cakes and confections, pies and cooked meats, chocolates and sweets. They also served teas and cold luncheons. David lived from 1878 to 1928. His son continued the business for a time after his death. His name still appears on the tiled doorstep. More recently this shop (11) is 'Finn's Hairdressers'. It opens into Drumming Well Lane. 'Finn's Hairdressers' shared a door-number, denoting that there has been a change from what was once a sole business that, along with the workspace, has been split into two! Mr White even sold pianos in his shop! For a short time in the late-1980s the shop ran as a print-sellers and picture-framers. The 'Martin Charles Bridal Gallery' opened after Martin had completed graduated from Northampton and London Universities. He spent time as a design assistant for Gianni Versace in Milan before starting his own label. His bespoke bridal shop has been running since 2011.

Number 15 is a seventeenth-century house with a carriage-way at its west-end (the entrance to Turner's Yard). It has a newer (late-nineteenth-century) shop window, a low door and eighteenth-century sash windows. The large shop windows were smaller bays in the Victorian era. The house has an old coaching entrance adjacent to it. This was useful as Mr Turner (1857-1930) ran a basket and coffin

---

[277] Oral history, Joyce Hardick.

business with his workshops in the yard. Charles John Turner was a cabinet maker who used the ground floor, when William Coles shared the building with him during the late-1930s. Thereafter, 'Hewitt and Company' ran a specialist pottery and glassware shop here, with "windows full of China and twinkling crystal vases, plates and other useful items". This building is now a private house. In 1973, number 15 belonged to the Hewitt family where they sold old maps, works of art, antiques, carpets and fine quality glassware. The Potter family lived here in the 1970s, but they kept the original shop name. Jean Atkins recalls that Kathleen Munford (a trained ballet dancer, who worked in London theatres and trained others) worked in Hewitts' (Potter's). This glassware and pottery shop was open until the 1980s. It was run by Pat Smith for a time, yet the name remained unchanged. It is now a private residence (located near the zebra-crossing to the old 'Secondary' school).

Turner's Yard lies between 15 and 17 West Street. In the pre-war years, Maurice Meadows lived at number 1 with his wife, Minnie. Number 2 was home to Mrs S.E. Perkins, Mr J.W. Davis lived at 3. Mr William Arthur Wallinger and his wife, Beatrice (née Harris) lived at number 4 (aged in their fifties at the time).

The following three West Street buildings (17, 19 and 21) were originally connected as a public house. The building dates to around 1700 and are small, listed buildings. Number 17 was the home of Mr Wilfred Oliver Christy (1901-1970) and 19 and 21 were the 'Nag's Head' inn, which the Christy family also owned and ran. This contiguous building (19 and 21) was the 'Nags Head' and half is 'Tavern House', bed and breakfast (which is believed to be part of the "Ship Inn" properties). In the 1970s 21a was 'Oundle Galleries'. Very "in vogue" with the era, 'Oundle Reproductions' opened here and sold replica furniture in the 1980s. It was managed by Grace Jones (prior to her move to be the manager of "Oundle Cobbler"). In the 1980s and 1990s, the building functioned as "KikiSams" to the right of the small corridor and "Village Carpets" (Steve Cottingham's carpet shop) had the left side of the building. Mary Prosser lived at the back. The whole shop is currently reunited as "KikiSams" toys and child-wear. To further confuse matters, 21 shares its number with number 23. 21-23 is now "R.N.V. Accountants" financial services. (23 was listed as uninhabited during 1939). There was a patch of empty land (which had once held a house that burned down) between them. It was built on in the 1970s. The new building has been made to look as if it was always there, but it is obviously newer on close inspection.

In the 1930's numbers 25 and 27 were the properties of Mr A. Steeles (who was a stationer). Number 27 was sold and developed into a newsagent, sweet and toy shop run by Mr James. It sold Matchbox toys, which were small boxes with toy cars inside. They were well made and very affordable. Children loved them. Mr Jonathan J. Ives (1909-1975) lived at number 29 during the 1930s.

Mr George Edward Barks (1908-1972) lived at number 31 during the pre-war years. In 1937 he married Mary Kirby in Peterborough. In the early 1970s it was Mr James's newsagents shop. Many Oundle teenagers were employed in their first job (on an early-morning newspaper-delivery route) from here.[278] It became Mrs Sandra Longman's dry-cleaners and is now 'Raffaele' hairdressers and 'Eastern Spices' curry and kebab takeaway.

Number 33 is 'Yorke House'. The house was built further back from the road than its neighbours. It has the remains of a preserved mediæval undercroft beneath its frontage (which is bordered by a low wall). The cellar, brick-lined and vaulted, was used for storage since mediæval times. Mrs Lucy Ethel Siddons (née Barnes), the recent widow of James Carvil Siddons, moved to live here after his death in 1937. (She died in 1957, aged 85.)

Number 35 is a privately owned building. This was 'Paul's' green-grocer's shop in the early 1970s. This small shop and the adjacent 'Age Concern' and the 'Oxfam' shops initially had connected top floors. These were often used as living quarters or for storage. In the 1930s, number 35 was vacant, but at 37 there lived a boot and shoe-maker, Mr Johnny Bull. The "Age Concern" building was formerly the Misses Margaret and Vivian Seamark's shop that sold clothing and haberdashery in the 1960s. Both of the sisters were born in Oundle in the first decade of the twentieth century. Their shop was where to go "if you needed to line your bottom drawer for your wedding".

---

[278] Sharon Jackson, Wendy Mudza and Rosemary Moynehan, to name but a few.

The Cunnington family ran a fruit and veg shop at number 39, before it sold to Fred W. Lane and they moved over the road. In the 1970s, Fred Lane's shop had unused ground at the back, but was built-up in a similar-style to those nearby. Mr Lane's shop (number 39) is now 'Age Concern'. In the 1960s and early 1970s people played music, so they needed sheet music and vinyl records. Fred sold both sheet music and also recharged the old-style batteries from the pre-war years.

Joyce Gaunt lived in East Road and recalls the 1940s and 1950s Victor Sylvester instrumental band, which produced music played at local ballroom dances. She mentioned that this had continued until the American troops came, "then it was Glenn Miller dance music and the jitterbug". 'In the mood', 'Moonlight serenade' and swing music were very popular. In the 1930s, she was frequently asked to take the family 'accumulator' from East Road to get it recharged at the Lanes' shop at 39 West Street. She said the "accumulator", a heavy box-like apparatus for storing energy (like a rechargeable battery), worked the 1930s radios and record players. Mr F.W. Lane sold wireless' (radio's), televisions and other electrical items. He was also a photographic dealer. He lived at and traded from 41a in the 1930s and 1940s. The Reverend E. Lee was resident upper-floor resident (39) in 1939.

In 1939, Mr. Charles Frederick Barwell lived at 41. He was born in 1860 and died in 1943. The large, double glass-fronted building at 41 was later "Hooton's" grocers. Old Mr Hooton was called "Mr Hooter" by the children.[279] His son, "Ted" Hooton and his wife, Doris, had an extensive family, many of whom followed the family shop-keeper tradition.   After Hooton's, number 41 became the 'International Stores'. The International Stores were run by Mr Crick. The cashier and book-keeper was Beryl Gilbert (née Shutt). Paul King's mother worked here. Then, Peter (Pete) Goodman ran it as "Goodman's" shop. He ran the garden centre portion in the back of the shop. In the 1960s Pete took on the whole shop. (Pete's daughter is recalled as being a Brownie in the 1970s. The family had a small spaniel who would go with Pete to the pub (usually the Ship). Pete was an outdoors man. He enjoyed rock climbing and owned all his own equipment. Pete took the Brownies rock climbing in Matlock, Derbyshire, in the 1970s. Always a keen

---

[279] Oral history, Ruth Keans.

gardener, he started Elton garden centre. When his mother became elderly, she left West Street and entered 'Stonglands' apartments. (Mrs Teresa Jackson had her flat after her demise.) Their shop is now the 'Oxfam' Shop.

Victoria Yard was named for the Queen and the (subsequently named) public house. It was commonly known as Jinks' Yard as this was where the Jinks family lived. The yard runs by the side of the Oxfam shop via a shared way. In Victorian times this was where the Jink's family cart could be seen parked by their house. They were carriers, but also were highly faithful, as they had a room in their West Street House for mass (from 1807-1880). John Clifton recorded in his 1782 diary, "A badger baiting this afternoon at Jinks little yard at the White Hart, and most of the sliving, jeering, looty Wallens gave their attendance. Some of them gave a penny to be let in to see it". His tone sounds (correctly) disapproving. The houses in Victoria Yard are now private, yet give access between West Street and Milton Road. It dates to the mid-1900s. During WWII this shop sold hardware and garden items. There were a "couple of steps at the back" to see the garden items and hardware was seen throughout the rest of the shop. The original shop encompassed both the current 'Oxfam' shop and adjacent 'Age Concern'. Jean Atkins remarked that the upstairs rooms, above both shops, had their own ghost (or just creaky boards!). Miss Atkins was the regional organiser for Oxfam, so knows the origins of the stores here. Jean left school at fourteen and joined the land army. She spent her life running charity foundation departments around the world (including the Girl's Friendly Society, Cheshire Homes, the Prison's service, the RNIB and other charities).

Mick Crick said, "My father, Reginald, was the manager of The International Store (a high class grocery chain) in West Street Oundle. I was a small child during the war years and, as Christmas approached, I was always very excited about the celebration. On Christmas morning mum would be busy in the kitchen preparing our feast. Just before lunch was put on the table, dad would draw the curtains and lock the doors. We had a large, square dining table and dad, my brother John, my sisters, Girlie and Janet and I would sit at the table and mum would bring in the food. We would have roast cockerel, pheasant, rabbit and pork pies, with lots of potatoes and home grown vegetables, followed by plum pudding and lashings of thick Jersey cream. Many years later, I asked my eldest sister, Girlie, why dad drew the curtains and locked the doors before the Christmas feast was put on the table. She told me that everyone was on wartime rations, but our dad was the 'Corporal Jones' of his day and did 'under the counter' deals with all the local farmers and, if Fred Bennett walked by our house and saw what was on our table, all hell would be let loose in the town!"[280]

Number 43 was formerly named "The Chestnuts", owing to the trees in the rear gardens. It is a beautiful old house with a courtyard and bay windows. In the early 1900s the building gained a new frontage after a fire. Andrew Spurrell's great-uncle, Bernard Turner, lived here. Then Captain Peter R. Thompson (MRCVS) resided here during the pre-war years of WWII.

Paine's Alms Houses are listed buildings. Paine's Cottages (east) and the Manse (west) are linked by a front-wall and an Elizabethan gateway. They were the original wings of a fifteenth-century house. (The bay-windows were added later). The houses belonged to Sir Walter Mildmay (1523-1589) of Apethorpe Hall (recently renamed as a Palace). Mildmay was Queen Elizabeth I's chancellor. His house stood in West Street (east of the current Stahl Theatre). His main Hall (that spanned the back land between the buildings) no-longer exists, but the wings on each side of the courtyard garden (behind the gateway) are parts of the original Tudor houses.

Minister, John Paine (occasionally transcribed as Payne) founded the alms houses after the death of Walter Mildmay in 1598. Paine was a Minister of the Dissenting Congregation. He lived in the Manse to the western side of the alms houses. His chapel was next to them (the Stahl). These buildings are the best-preserved courtyard and mediæval houses in the town.[281] In 1801, John Paine rebuilt parts of them to provide the residences for Protestant families (nonconformists, who did not agree with the terms and governance of the Church of England). This beautiful stone building looks as if it was a comfortable home. According to an agreement dated 21st May 1801, John Paine

---

[280] Mick Crick, personal testimony.
[281] Most of Oundle tenements from this period were cottages, farms (virgates) and burgages. They were retained by Peterborough Abbey.

conveyed the alms houses to a group of trustees. With four "tenements situated at Chapel End in Oundle upon trust to place therein poor persons or families of or attending the congregation of Protestant dissenters in Oundle".[282]

Nineteenth-century Oundle held a strong non-conformist tradition. Nearly a third of the population (who were Presbyterians, Calvinists and Congregationalists) supported a dissenting Protestant chapel. This former Congregational Church was built on the site of the "Great Meeting", which was an earlier independent place of worship. A commemoration-stone on the wall that reads "This independent church was founded 1690 and rebuilt in 1864". Most of the walls were created from the remains of other buildings. On the wall of the west wing is a marker stone that reads "D.G. 1753". In 1939, Paine's Alms Houses were still in use and housed Mrs Emma J. Batson (who passed away in 1950, aged 91) in number 1. Miss Rebecca Adams (1849-1939) and Mrs Sarah J. Hayes (1858-1945) lived at number 2. Number 3 was empty in the late-1930s, but Mrs Gertrude Limmage (1886-1966) lived at number 4. These imposing buildings are now private houses.

In October 1942, a 'new' minister, the Rev. George Castley conducted a Sunday harvest thanksgiving service at the Congregational Church. Yet the church was ill-attended, except for times of "special festivals". The old Congregational Church became the United Reform church and then the Stahl Theatre. Cannon Cartwright is held to have been the vicar. In the late 1960s and 1970s the Congregationalist minister was the Reverend Amy Howell. When she sang in the Sunday morning service her voice would wake up Jackie Kirkpatrick (who lived over the road). Jackie alleged that there were hidden tunnels beneath West Street from the Parish Church to the basements of various old buildings in West Street (including the Secondary Modern school grounds, the Ship Inn and other locations in the town). I also recall Mr Leo Dunham telling us about this while we were in school during the mid-1960s. He had said that many of them had collapsed and were not safe or navigable.

---

[282] http://www.british-history.ac.uk/vch/northants/vol3/

Until the 1970s, the Stahl Theatre remained the Congregational Chapel and was part of the original alms house complex. The building underwent restoration and alteration (including a glass lean-to extension) to provide a venue to plays and events in the late 1970s. At that time some bodies were discovered under the theatre floor, dating to when it was a Congregational Chapel. Oundle School theatre opened in 1980.

Mr Dennis T. Coleman lived at number 45 during the 1930s. Dr Ivor P. Spurrell (surgeon) and his family lived at 47, which was called the "Queen Anne House". It is a large building (by the Stahl). The front dates to 1824, but the remainder is much earlier (and is from the 1600s). It was so named, as Queen Anne is reputed to have visited her former lady-in-waiting who lived there. Andrew Spurrell grew up in the Queen Anne's house (when it was a surgery). The top floor was originally used as living quarters; the surgery and waiting-room were based on the ground floor. Andrew has fond memories of living here with his family. Nearby, at 49 are the School Music Rooms; home of Mr Arthur Stafford (who married Agnes Horn in 1913) during the 1930s.

House and shop are allied at 51 and 51a West Street. Mr S.G. Dyson's clock and watch-repair shop, was (for half a century) run by Polish émigré, Emil Skiba, who kept his father-in-law's name to continue the business and the family-run 'Green Man Antiques' (opposite at 51a).

In the early 1920s, Sydney George Dyson launched his original 'Dysons' shop here. It was initially a furniture shop, but when his son-in-law, Emil Skiba, took over the shop the business changed to being a clock and watch sales and repair shop. Emil escaped from Siberia after it was invaded by the Soviet forces in 1939. He walked 1,600 miles to freedom. He fought at the battle of Monte-Cassino (Italy) in the war. The business is directed by Sydney Dyson's granddaughter, Jo Elwood, thus this has been an ongoing, family-run clock business since 1952. The shop has pendulum clocks, balance clocks and other antique clocks for sale, with the oldest clock dating to the 1700s. Emil received an award for his Polish army service in WWII at the Polish Embassy in London in 2010 (at the same ceremony as fellow Oundle resident, Lucjan Mudza of North Street, who received a silver cross as the surviving child of a family deported to Siberia, Kazakhstan and northern Russia by the Soviet regime after September 1939).

An early 1960s treat was to "do a Harry Worth" in Skiba's window on our way home from Saturday Catechism classes or Church (usually the former as we didn't have adults watching). Harry Worth was a comedian who appeared in his own show on the BBC. He started each show with his standing in a shop window so that half of his body was hidden and the other half symmetrically reflected in the glass. Then he would lift the leg that could be seen so as to appear to float! We children regularly did this in the window of the clock shop next-door to the Church! (Harry Worth's 1960s comedy series "Here's Harry" is remembered for an opening sequence in the shop window that has since gone on to become known as "doing a Harry Worth". The series ran sixty episodes between 1960 and 1965.)[283] Also, on Saturdays we would spend our Saturday Sixpence (a small silver coin, which is about the size of a current penny) in Hindman's sweet shop over the road as a reward for "being good".

The 'Victoria' public house was formerly an Oundle parish poor-house (workhouse). As the 'Victoria Inn' it commemorated the Queen of the time (and known locally as the "Vic", it ran for over a hundred years until its closure In the 1950s). A 1724 workhouse ledger records[284] that "for the past five years Oundle was burdened with the poor and taxes". To combat this the trustees purchased a "House for the Maintenance and Employment of the Poor", who were considered to be "full of Idleness, as they were of Complaints", so seven governors (trustees) and two overseers were chosen to look after them. They also appointed a Master and Mistress to organise provisions for the house and to keep the inmates who were able, "employed to work". It went on to say that "there are now in the House, six old Men, five old Women, and nine Children; the Women and Children are employ'd in Spinning and Knitting: And the Men and Boys, who are able, are sent to Plow for the Farmers, and feed and look after their Cattle at home; the profits from their labour, which is generally about six Shillings per Week, the Master of the House accounts for once a week to the Trustees; and the Expenses of the House, which he also lays before

---

[283] BBC1 series 'Here's Harry' (1960-65), set in "Acacia Avenue", had a cast of four. It portrayed a bumbling man, irritated by bureaucracy, living with a cat, 'Tiddles' and never-seen, Aunt Amelia Prendergast, had a cast of four; 'Harry Worth' (1966-69).
[284] The National Archives and Workhouse organisation.

them, is usually about 40s. The Overseer's bill before used to rise to half a Crown in the Pound per Annum often, and seldom or never less than 2 shillings, they now come to no more than 10d. or 11d., so that, upon a fair Calculation, the Town is eased of two Thirds of their Charge, and yet I assure you the Poor are provided for in a very plentiful manner, and have everything necessary or convenient in Life." [285] Ruth Keans recalls the 1960s when the old workhouse had been reduced to a home for old men. She said that "Tom and George were dumb and suffered from dwarfism. The two men took the hand-cart down to the town each day to collect the shopping for the Master. Mr Groves was in charge then". The building served an antique shop in the 1980s and is now a private residence.

St. Wilfrid's Church (the former Zion chapel) was built in 1852. It is an unassuming, flat-fronted building that was used until the 1960s, when the Catholic congregation relocated to the Most Holy Name of Jesus Church (known as 'the Jesus Church'). The incumbent priest lives in the house on the corner of the Benefield and Stoke Doyle roads. Mr and Mrs Eaton lived in a house on South Road, over the road from the dairy, but in the 1960s Mrs Eaton was a stalwart of the Roman Catholic Church, where she taught Saturday catechism classes and Sunday-school. This ex-church building is now flats.

During the mid-1930s number 53 was the 'Victoria Inn' public house, which was the home of Frederick (Fred) Storey and his wife, Alice (née Allen), who were married in 1935. Mr William T. Taylor lived at number 55. (He died in 1949, aged 77.) Herbert M. Ely at 57 lived next-door with his new bride. Herbert married Lily Sturgess (in Thrapston) in 1935. Benjamin Thurlby was born in 1890. He lived with his wife, Florence Willis. They married in 1913. The couple lived at number 59. Ben worked as a scrap metal merchant. (Later, his thatched house was devastated by fire.) Next-door was where a tailor, Arthur Bellairs lived and worked (61) during the 1930s. He died in 1940 at the age of 58. From the early 1960s to 1965, Miriam Knight (née Woods) lived at number 63, which is at the bottom of Inkerman Yard.

---

[285] The Society for Promoting Christian Knowledge is the oldest Anglican mission organisation. It was founded in 1698.

Continuing in West Street: 63 was the home of W.C.E. Sauntson. Number 65 is Cottesmore House. Mr T.W. Curwain lived at 67 and Miss A. Caborn at 69.

House 69 was the original shop for 'Rachels' (clothing) from 1970-1984, before its later move to the town centre. At 71 lived Mr S. Bennett, who was a Justice of the Peace. Number 73 was Mrs Dugdale's house in 1938. Number 73 belonged to Mrs W.A. Lane. It was used the premises of a ladies' hairdressers' salon; specialising in permanent waving, tinting and bleaching. By the 1960s this had become Lilian's hairdressers. (Lilian had been one of the stylists working for Mrs Lane.) Mrs E.R. Smith lived at 75. Mr C.A. Pulley lived at number 77. Mr J.T. Smith lived at 79, next to 'Claridge and Company' grocers. The Misses Newborn lived at 83. At 85 was Major A.L. Butcher (who had gained a military cross). Mrs B.A. Close lived at 87. James Harrod lived at number 87 during the 1930s. He worked as a slater and roofer. Mr E. Stafford lived at 89.

Inkerman Place and Yard

Inkerman Place (sometimes referred to as Inkerman Yard) had only twenty-four residences. In 1939 number 1 was the home of James E. Haslegrave, 2 was empty, 3 was the home of Walter J. Brudenell and his family. Number 4 was empty and numbers 5 to 8 were not listed as housing. Mr William E. Smith lived at 9 (he died in 1947, aged 85). He was next-door to Alfred W. Elderkin and his family lived at number 10. (Alfred died in 1949, aged 69.) In 1940 his daughter, Queenie, married Reginald Carvell. Herbert John Swann lived with his family at number 11, with Mrs C. Wilmott next-door (at 12). Mrs M. Holmes lived at 13. Mr E. Giddings lived at 14. Mr C. Fox lived at 15. Mrs L. Cox lived at 16. Mr A. Bird was at 17 and number 18 was empty in 1938. Mr Samuel Ingham lived at 19 (who died in 1951 aged 75), next-door to Mr Walter G. Lee at 20 (who married "an Oundle lass", Nancy Sharpe, in 1930). 21 was empty in 1928, but 22 was the home of S. Stretton and family. Mr Alfred J.M. Allen lived at 23. He married Ivy Langley in 1914. They lived next to Mrs Jane E. Stretton at 24. (Jane lived until 1953 when she was aged 84).

Robert and Elizabeth Butt (who were better known as Bob and Eliza) lived in Inkerman Yard (before moving to 113 Benefield Road). They married in 1909 and had five children (four girls and a boy). The first of their children was Violet (known as 'Vi') who was born in 1912. She was followed by Beatrice (1914), Grace (1919), Eileen (1922) and Robert (1932). Bob and Eliza's second child, Beatrice, was known by her family at "Flip" (although the reason for this is not remembered.) Beatrice died at the grand old age of 103 in January 2018. She was the last of her generation of the Butt family. Bob's sister, Grace married Arthur Ball in 1939. She remained in the Oundle area when her siblings moved away. Oundle School had their own Power Station, in Blackpot Lane and Bob Butt worked there until he retired. Eliza Butt worked as an embalmer. She lived from 1889 to 1969.

The Butt family's Inkerman Place house was on the right. In the middle of the yard between the houses there was a stony area and at the end of the row there was a communal 'outhouse' toilet. All of the families from the yard shared the facilities. The census of 1881 shows that Elizabeth Saddington (1838-1915) lived at 1 Inkerman Yard. She lived with her husband, Edward Afford and their son, Walter Edward Afford. Later, the Tyers family lived at number 1. The Prior family were at number 3. At number 5 there lived a woman named May and her daughter, Joyce (in the cottage next to the Prior family). Mr and Mrs Chester lived in the yard with their daughter, Sheila. (They lived at 11 or 12 Inkerman Yard.) During WWI Frank Rollerson and his family lived at number 18. (His teenaged son, who was also named Frank, died in the war and is commemorated on the memorial). The Bennett family lived in Inkerman Yard in the late 1890s until the early 1900s, before they moved to Barnwell. Levi Rose (was born in Thurning in 1867) and Elizabeth Abbot (was born in 1863) were married in Oundle in 1888. In the 1911 census they are listed as living at number 3 Inkerman Yard. In 1891, Levi worked as an agricultural labourer and in 1901 his occupation was listed as "waggon filling", as he worked as a "Great Northern railway man". It appears that by 1911 he was working on a local farm as a general labourer again.[286] There were only four houses to the left within the yard. In three of these, the residents of the 1960s were Alan Brackley (4), the Mowbray family (6) and the Friday family

---

[286] http://www.terrys.org.uk/charts

(8). The Friday's house was on the left and backed-onto Ben Thulby's scrap yard. The Bamford family lived on the other side of the archway.

In the wartime, the "British School" was based on the main road, beside "Lilian's hairdressers", and was in an old building, behind the cottages of Inkerman Way. It took in children before the Council School. It also functioned as a wartime base of the "Oundle Maid's Club", run by Miss A.M. Wood. Miss Boult (whom, I was told "was in some way related to Sir Peter Scott")[287] ran the Oundle Brownie group in this building during the 1960s. She lived in North Street. She had a passion for training girls in how to be self-sufficient and able. This rather reflects the era she had lived though. She had the "suffragette spirit" by living through a war, when women made a leap in self-sufficiency and self-regard.

Inkerman Way meets Victoria Yard and stood at the rear of Spurlings, with its large garden and big house (now an infill housing estate). There are large, wrought-iron gates at the rear of the Stahl and Paine's Alms Houses that mark the entrance to Oundle School property. The Inkerman Way houses and bungalows are set back in a row from the road. Inkerman Way was originally lined with stone cottages that were demolished to make way for new homes that were built in 1962. The original Victorian buildings provided high-density housing for twenty-four families. These were built as a response to growth and a need for accommodation in the 1850s. The name venerates the Crimean battle of Inkerman of 1854 (which, despite being a victory led to over two-thousand British casualties).[288]

75 West Street is listed as a Grade II town house with an attractive walled garden. This was Sue Crick's 'guest house' that provided temporary accommodation. 'Ashworth House' was also a Japanese restaurant. It was recalls the family who lived here in the 1900s. Mr Leslie Ashworth, was the son of an Oundle School engineer. He was very innovative and kept up to date. He owned the first crystal-set wireless in the town. Children were taken to the Ashworth's house to hear the radio (as it was quite a novelty).

---

[287] With thanks for this information to Sheila Denley.
[288] For further reading, A.W. Kinglake, "*Invasion of the Crimea*", in 8 volumes. Pub. Blackwood, Edinburgh: 1863–1887 (1863).

'Waterland House' stands at 81 West Street.[289] After this, at the far end of the street is a large store. It functioned as a grocer's in the 1930s and traded as 'Claridges' grocers, selling beer, wine, spirits, frozen-foods and ice-creams during the 1940s-1950s, under proprietors L.A. Waters and J.A. Osborn. The 'West End Stores' convenience shop was run by Nancy 'Nan' Smith. At the time the 'Spar' (generic) items they stocked were cheaper than those sold by other shops in the vicinity. Nan's daughters, Patricia (known as 'Tishi) and Karen (who were twins) attended the local primary in the 1960s. The store continued to run as a grocery shop under various guises until the 1990s. Now, Guy Bolsover's shop sells 'fitted' kitchens.

Next was a lane next to Miss Newborn's house, before the small, West Oundle Garage and repair-store; accessed via the lane. Finally, 87 is the last house in the street. In 1938, number 87 was the home of Mr Josiah Jones Harrod. He was a slate repairer and roofer. He came to Oundle for work from his Stamford home. (Josiah lived from 1893-1970.) Number 87 is attached to a smaller building on its left. It has a lower roof-line and is the first house in Benefield Road. This is designated by a wall-sign by the Drill Hall car park.

The end of West Street and the junction of Benefield and Stoke Doyle roads is the area was formerly called Chapel (or Chappel) End. It is the site of the mediæval chapel of St. Thomas of Canterbury. Leland referred to this chapel (circa 1540) as "the church or chapel of St. Thomas now of our Lady". The site is now occupied by a Church built in 1879 by the Watts-Russell[290] family. It was designed by A.W. Blomfield in the shape of a Greek cross with a central octagonal tower. The Roman Catholic Church acquired the "Church of the Holy Name of Jesus" in 1971 on Stoke Hill (location of the gate). In 1940, a space on the inside left of the Church-gate was dug and filled with a large, round concrete platform. This plinth had a "swivel-placement spike" embedded in it that could hold a 'Tommy gun".[291]

---

[289] This is a houses with no name (or number). H. Gilbert Barnes, secretary of Oundle & District Sweet Pea and Horticultural Society, lived at Melton House, West Street, in the early 1970s. His house name is no longer apparent.
[290] Lord of the Manor of Oundle and Biggin.
[291] Oral history, Percy Arnett.

Mr Binder, then Mr J. Dixons owned the grocery shop at the apex of Binder's Row, West Street and Stoke Hill. The thatched shop caught fire and burned down in the 1960s. It is believed that a blow-torch was being used by decorators (around the wooden window frames) and had set fire to the shop. Kathleen Shiels (whose father was one of the firemen called to the site) recalls that "They were doing the roof at the time. They gave away ice-cream as there was nowhere else to put it!"[292] Binder's Row meets with West Street, but is not numbered as part of Benefield Road. Mr Ellis Owen Roberts' (1900-1976) shop was also in Binder's Row.

...oooOOOooo...

SOUTH ROAD

South Road (south side)

Beyond the East Road junction is the corner (formerly a sorting office and ARP station). The rear garden of Lime House and spinney were near to the road, behind the wall. The name it was known by was the 'Cobthorne Furlong' (from the 1800s). In the 1930s Mrs K. Richardson lived at number 1, then later, Lawrance E. Modd (*sic.*[293]; born in 1939 and lived here with his parents). Mr William Ellis Horn (born in Oundle, 1907-1972; married Janet Palmer in 1954) lived at 2 and at 2a was Mrs M.L. Straw's home, named 'Ewelme'. 3 South Road is "Chapel Hill House". This new stone house is adjoined-to a building that was formerly part of Lime House. Part of it has an inset chapel window. Number 15 is side-on to the road, followed by a row of Victorian houses in front of Bassett Place. The Hadyn Terrace houses started with number 3, but were been more recently renamed. Haydn Terrace has four Victorian houses, now numbered 23 to 29. In the 1930s Miss Elizabeth Healey lived at number 3 (who died here in 1954, aged 87) and equally long-lived neighbour, Miss Lydia E. Spencer at number 4 (who died in Oundle in 1956, aged 83). Ralph Groom lived at 5. Mr R.G. Saunders, M.A., taught at the School and resided at number 6 for the duration of his work years.

---

[292] Oral history, Kathleen Shiels.
[293] Spelt like this in the original source.

377

Bassett Place

The "Chester Cottages" were brick-built in 1885. They stand behind Haydn Terrace. There are gates to rear gardens from this lane, which on exploration (less than 100 yards) reveals a row houses. The seven houses in Bassett Place are in an L-shape behind the eastern side of South Road. Numbers 1, 2, 3 and 4 Bassett Place are two-bedroomed, stone-built, Victorian, terraced cottages with rear gardens. The latter houses (5, 6 and 7) are red brick. These were built in 1894, with a section named 'Albany Place' dating to 1904. The houses are traditional with fan-lights above the doors that open onto quarry-tiled floors. A sign on the buildings reads "Albany Place".

The land and small ford were originally owned by Mr Bassett, who acquired it in the early fifteenth-century. The ford crossed a shallow stream from the River Nene that people could cross to travel to the market. The ford was probably in use long before any West Street houses were built; when North Street and St. Osyth's Lane were the main town. The Austell Survey (1565) recorded that three young men were drowned here in 1750. The quiet lane has been further developed since 1926. Rowley Scotney lived behind Bassett Place in the Odd Fellows' House. Like the Masons, in the late eighteenth-century, the Oddfellows were illegal "friendly societies" (with no political or religious connections). Government informers were paid to infiltrate meetings at Lodges, so members used secret signs and passwords. A brick-built garage or shed is evident on the main road. It was the property of 'Tommy' Head, who used it for parking his charabancs (an early form of a bus that was used for pleasure trips). Thereafter, it belonged to Frank and Horace Dugdale and was used mainly as storage for two of his cattle-lorries. Frank Dugdale (Frank was born in 1907) wanted to obtain the land behind his barn, but it was never his. It was sold as part of the purchase of a house in Herne Road, which meets at its rear garden-gate. Hence, this land is a short-cut to the householders' garden and their Bassett Place garage.

In the late 1930s the people living in Bassett Place included Mr Eric Vessey (born in Oundle in 1904). He lived at number 1. Mr William H. Titman and his wife lived at number 2 and at 3 were Mr Charles William Stapleton (who was born in Thrapston) and his wife, Ellen (née Swann). They were married in in Oundle in 1903. (Charlie lived from 1876-

1943.) Mr Charles Bird (1872-1948) lived at number 4 and Mrs Martha Johnson at number 5 (1876-1952). Mrs M. Smith lived at number 6 and Miss Harriet Elizabeth Bolton (1869-1950) at number 7. The resident at number 8 was Arthur Riddle and at number 9 was Mr Thomas Christopher Wills.

By the 1980s, Diane Wyles and her family lived in Bassett Place. They were neighbours of Stephen J. and Sharon R. Cottingham. Sharon and Steve held a Christening 'reception' in their cosy 'first real home' (in 1980) for their first-born daughter, Darryl. A lasting memory is of Sharon's mother, Teresa Jackson playing hopscotch on the paving slabs with a group of children. They were gathered outside at the front of the building on that day and were happily engaged by Teresa while other guests had their tea inside. Aubrey 'Clanger' Clarke and his wife (known by some as 'Mrs Clanger'!) also lived in this row. Aubrey was held as a prisoner-of-war thirty miles from Nagasaki, Japan. He heard the explosion of the atom bomb. He died in 1998. He is best remembered for his bike, his mac tied together with string around the waist and his beret hat. Sheila Denley said that "it is best to describe him as looking like Michael Crawford in the 1973 BBC television comedy series, 'Some Mothers Do 'Ave 'Em'." Sheila also recalls that he had names for all of his pigs. A particular favourite pig was named "Sunflower". Sunflower was quite a character and would climb on the roof of the sty where she could be seen from the Denley house windows!

Dyson's coal merchant business ran from the old house and barn buildings at number 41 South Road. The house now has a beautiful garden and its resident, Tracey Mathieson, runs a floral business named 'Foxtail Lily'. Since 2006 it has sold wedding bouquets and flowers for special occasions from the barn shop. The next house in this road was where Roy and Dorothy Sumner ran their milk-delivery business. Sheila Denley (now Stables) shared information on Roy's milk deliveries to Wadenhoe village, which he did for over forty years (1952-1995). He would happily ride on his dray, while singing the ancient music-hall ballads that he had learnt from his dad. Roy was known for his Oundle milk supplies and deliveries during the 1960s and 1980s. He lived in (43) Bradley Cottage (built in 1812), a detached, stone family home with a supply-depot yard and garden. The business finally closed when Roy retired and his children (Richard, Mary, Rachel and Claire)[294] grew-up and moved away. They make frequent visits to the town, often to exhibit their creativity in local galleries. Richard Sumner is a talented stone-mason, who has worked to create tops of cathedrals and other buildings. His sisters, Mary and Rachel are artists in their own right, making superb silk pictures and stitched-fabric creations. The family held regular exhibitions in local galleries (at the Yarrow and Dolby galleries) besides further afield. Their home (before the numbering change was 8 South Road) was, formerly, an L-shaped cottage. It was for sale by auction in the summer of 1954 when Roy bought it.

Its sale poster reads: "With Vacant Possession - 8 South Road, Oundle, a pleasantly situated freehold cottage. Southam and Sons are favoured with instructions to Offer by Auction at the Cottage on Thursday 26th August, 1954 at 6 p.m. prompt. Subject to conditions of Sale to be then and there produced: The detached freehold cottage known as 'Bradleys Cottage' of stone and slate erection standing in its own grounds on the south side of the road, and comprising living room 13ft x 10ft with tiled hearth, kitchen with range and cupboard, 2 bedrooms. Wash house with copper and water tap. Lavatory connected with sewer. Stone, brick and tile barn with loft over. Lean to shed. Large garden with carriage entrance from street and having an area of nearly half an acre. Electricity and Town Water are installed. The property has a frontage of 78ft or thereabouts to South Road, and lends itself for reconstruction and improvement. Vacant Possession will be given on completion of purchase. Further particulars and "Order to View" may be obtained from the Auctioneers, Thrapston ('Phone 9) and Oundle ('Phone 3152) or from the Solicitors. Messrs Sherard and Coombs, New Street, Oundle ('Phone 3106)"

There are new houses and bungalows from here along this road (mostly dating to the post-war years). Some were built along this road following the playing fields, which were used by the Secondary Modern School until its closure in 1972. Many reminisce about the past games

---

[294] This very talented family were all artists and exhibited at the Dolby and Yarrow Galleries. Mary (a silk and textile artist, painting and printing, with degrees from Northampton and Surrey Schools of Art, and Bristol University) is very sadly missed. She died in 2016, aged 58.

of hockey or football on the freezing sports field. I particularly hark back to the 1960s winter-games (as it was netball for girls on the hard court that doubled as the playground in the summer), in a short hockey-skirt and matching rhubarb-maroon legs (that had previously been alabaster when wearing long socks or 'tights' and indoors), half-heartedly chasing a very hard white ball and secretly hoping it would never hit me.[295]

The terrace of houses at the south-west end of South Road were known as Cabbage Row, due to the nineteenth-century market gardens that were planted nearby. The road, which was formerly known as 'South Back Way' in the 1800s, has been steadily in-filled by new houses since WWII. The old brewery cottages run along this part of the road. David Wills lived here when he was first married. He said that the numbers for South Road started at this end of the road. Now the house numbering starts at the other end!

At the end of the road, the Anchor Brewery malting's lasted from 1854 to around 1904. The brewery was allied to the 'Anchor Inn' (Duck's Nest) in St. Osyth's Lane. The malting's have recently undergone recent renovation as modern housing, along with the warehouse (with hoists) and nearby worker's cottages.[296] A stone and brick-built brewery house and offices are on the corner of South Road and Mill Lane. Stables and other buildings stood behind the house and a pyramid-shaped, malt-kiln roof is glimpsed from the road.

Herne Road (north side)

Most of the houses built in Herne Road date to the 1960s and 1970s, although in the late 1800s and early 1900s the road had the town 'Quoits Club'. The houses nearer to South Road are older than those further along the road. There were only eight houses on this side of the road in the 1930s. Now, it has a mixture of all ages, styles and use of materials.

Ioan Thomas noted that the "great loop of the River Nene to the south of Oundle is called the Herne, which comes from the Old English word meaning corner or bend." When the paved road surface ends, a track

---

[295] Anna Fernyhough.
[296] Oral history, David Wills.

to the fields runs along Herne Road and then loops back to join the Ashton Road. This loop is known as the "Donkey Track" or the "Donkey Race Track". For many years, students from the senior schools were sent out to keep fit by running along the 'Donkeys' as part of their compulsory afternoon exercise regime. (I note here that some stopped for a crafty break or cigarette on the route, when they were not being observed by their teachers.) The A605 bypass changed this practice as it perilously runs along part of the A605. The old railway track was much safer to traverse! It is still possible to walk from Ashton Road and meet the end of the Herne, which is a circular route.

The low wall at the beginning of the road looks older than those around it. The first house (number 1) is very individual. Mr Edwin Brudenell lived here in the pre-war years. It has a newer brick-built section attached to the older stone part that has a bay window that looks south, below an apex part of the roof. It is joined to the following houses in a terrace. The numbers 3, 5 and 7 are early twentieth century brick houses, bearing the name "Hern Terrace". In the 1930s, Sergeant-Major H. Edwards lived at number 3. The Misses King lived at 5 and Albert J. Belton lived at 7. He lived here until 1941, when he died (at the age of seventy-six). Numbers 9 and 11 are similar semi-detached houses, but are set back further from the road.

In the pre-war years Miss Martha A. Browning lived at number 9. Martha died in 1944, aged 79. A widow, Mrs Fanny E. Wright lived at number 11. Her husband, Frederick, had died in 1934, when he was 63 years of age. William Ernest Dolby lived at number 13. (He was born in 1859 and he died when he was 81). Mr Cecil E.A. Fieldsend (who was born in Brigstock in 1881) lived at number 15 for many years until his death in 1956. Most of the older houses have been modernised with attic-conversions, yet keep their original bay-windows. A large, detached house at number 13 dates to slightly earlier than its neighbours, with attractive wisteria growing over its date stone. Here, a small gate leads to the rear (to Bassett Place). Yvonne Cottrell and her husband, Peter, lived in one of the newer bungalows. Yvonne worked as a volunteer at Peterborough Hospital until her sudden demise in early 2017 at the age of eighty.

New bungalows, numbers 17, 19, 21 and 23 are adjacent to the corner, where the newly constructed roads merge with Herne Road. Nearby houses are all twenty-first century constructions and designs, beginning with a road to the left, which has been named Red Kite Drive. School View and William Court are roads leading off from Red Kit Drive. They link (via a footpath) with Old School Avenue (where the Red Cap School once stood), leading to Churchill Walk, Croxton Close and Herne Lodge. Webb Close is named after Miss Webb, who ran the Red Cap School. Roads link to Ashton Road and East Road by public footpaths (but are not traversable by vehicle). Queen's Court is comprised of a range of houses dating to 2015. Number 27 Herne Road is a bungalow that is set back from the road via a drive. Number 29 is similar. The end of the old 'donkey track' lane is a no-through-road, where land was formerly quarried (near to Prince William School) so there was no issue with new building. Prior to the start of building, a Bat Report and a review of badger activity was made to check if there would be any possible incursion into habitats. The study showed that there was no threat to wildlife, so building commenced. Prince William School is the immediate neighbour, so anyone living near should be 'student friendly' during term times!

Prince William School is a secondary 'academy' school and sixth form college, located at the end of Herne Road. It opened and closed on its inaugural day as nothing had been completed, including the toilets! Today it is up and running smoothly. 'Cheremy Grange' and a private residential dwelling, Beaumont House, are to the South of the site and are directly opposite the school entrance. The School sports pitches extend to the east, until they meet the A605 road that bypasses Oundle. A footpath continues and crosses the A605 and leads to a field walk over the river to Ashton. The school was built in 1971 and was named in honour of the late Prince William of Gloucester of Barnwell Manor. The buildings at this end of the road halt above the flood plain of the River Nene.

Prince William School has grown since opening. The County Council's Cabinet granted final approvals for the change to a two-tier education system in 2014, including the implementation of the new influx of children and change in educational structure in September 2015. It opened and closed on the same day, as the toilets and other features had not been completed over the summer and the school was not habitable. It has an on-site pre-fabricated Army Cadet building that is used as a Day-Nursery.

Herne Road (south side)

In the 1930s there were only fifteen houses in the whole road. The first house on the south side is number 2, a Victorian red-brick built with attractive, oval windows either side of the main door. It is a large detached house set in its own garden. This is where the Carpenter family lived until they moved to North Street. Mr William M. Freeman lived here with his family in the pre-war years. There are detached private garages and space next to this along Herne Road. There is a modern bungalow (number 4), set at a jaunty angle to the road. Nurses Cates and Lonsdale lived here in the pre-war years. Nearby is number 6, a modern, red-brick house with apparent, new extensions. Mr H.W. Bolton lived at (6) 'Belmont' in 1939. Mr Edward W.V. Freeman lived at the 'Cottage' (former 8). Edward had married Margaret Stokes in 1929. They lived with their children, Christine and Thomas, who were born in 1932 and 1935, respectively. (8a is a bungalow that was built more recently as an infill building.)

Mrs A.E. Goosey lived at (10) 'Rockside' in a detached, two-storey, red-brick house surrounded by well-matured trees. Number 12 is a large building where Mr W. McMichael and his family lived in the 1930s. The house at 14 is a small, bungalow-style, two-storey house. Number 16 is a white, detached, two-storey, family house and this is where Mr and Mrs Harry Titman lived. Both were teachers at the local state school. Harry taught woodwork and Margaret taught mathematics and sports. Both were busy in clubs and societies and both were stalwarts of the local country dancing groups.

Numbers 18 and 20 are newer. The house at 22 is a two-storey, detached house, set well back along a drive. In the 1970s, Basil and Cynthia Kimpton (née Wild) lived here. "Mrs Kimpton" taught typing and secretarial skills to secondary school girls. She was the secretary of Oundle Women's Institute. Their house had fields beyond and between the houses.

Opposite the Prince William School at 24 Herne Road is Cheremy Grange. Mr. L. Baker lived at 'Cheremy' in the 1930s. At that time its house number was listed as 14. This red-brick, three storey building was a home for the elderly that closed in 2005, after seventeen years of service. A new law meant its manager was no longer qualified to run the residential care home without updating her qualifications in business and management (despite 37 years of nursing experience). The building now houses offices. Chestnut House, 26 Herne Road, is a new construction on land associated with Cheremy Grange. New red-brick buildings are alongside the original building, fenced separately, in the pleasantly green and tree-lined road. A white picket fence denotes the boundaries to the property. Numbers 28, 30 and 32 are large, white, detached houses within a gated area. These are in a mock-Georgian style, with porticos over the main doors. 32a Herne Road faces eastward and is an L-shaped bungalow. The farm-track leads east. From this viewpoint there are continuous fields as far as the eye can see (to the north, east and south).

Bassett Ford Road and Riverside Close

Leading down-hill from South Road, just after the Herne Road junction, is Bassett Ford Road. It is a "no-through road" and only leads to the houses and the fields. It was originally just a track leading to the kissing-gate and the fields and river walk to Barnwell Mill. Bassett Ford Road originally had only one house at its apex junction, but now there are many houses stretching the full length of the eastern side. Most of the new houses date to the 1980s (with some newer). The houses are mostly confined to the northern and eastern side of the road. The houses in Riverside Close command a lovely view over the flood-fields and river. Sheep are generally pastured in these meadows.

The road leading over the fields to the open air swimming pool and the river via the (now non-extant) Jubilee Bridges turns at the junction to Riverside Close from Bassett Ford Road. In his autobiography, 'My Oundle', Leslie Black stated that "The town bathing place was over the meadows from Basset Ford Road, near a staunch. At one time the approach to it was from Barnwell Road opposite Barnwell Mill, but a pre-Sanderson headmaster opened the Jubilee Bridges to make access easier. Before their swimming pool was built it was used by Oundle School. It had a 'pit' and shallows (except when the staunch gate was down). The Urban Council supplied a caretaker-cum-lifeguard and changing rooms." Geoff Black noted that in the late 1960s, "the local lads from Oundle and neighbouring villages, such as Barnwell, met at the Lido (the outdoor pool) and behaved as lads do, with laddish behaviour and lots of mucking about, jumping in, shouting and having fun!" My memories of this are of the 1970s, with the surface of the water being very green with scum and algae and with a very low river level.

American airmen frequented the town (and flew overhead), army trucks passed through and tanks were occasionally seen along the Glapthorn Road. (After the war had ended and before the US airmen left the area, they bought bicycles for all of the Polebrook children as a generous 'thank you and goodbye' gift.) There were spells when locals donated clothing and food parcels (that were sent out to servicemen overseas).

During the war years, Clark Gable[297] was stationed at nearby Polebrook airfield (that was built for the RAF in 1940 on Rothschild land). American troops came in and extended the runway using local concrete and a base made from gravel dug from what now form lakes in Barnwell Country Park. The USAF flew sorties from the airstrip and lived in Polebrook. In 1943, Clark Gable would visit Oundle on a borrowed motorbike and was frequently seen visiting the pubs, shops and local outdoor swimming pool. This collected gaggles of girls who wanted to "oggle a real-life Hollywood star",[298] which proved difficult for him, as he was "a friendly, but quiet man". It was said that "He didn't stand on ceremony" and "would rather not be noticed or singled-out for preferential treatment".[299] Most of the locals thought that he was easy-going. "He strolled down the street saying 'hi' to people he passed. He would sign autographs and chat, but also made a point of visiting the children in local schools. Gable also, apparently, "used rookeries in the fields for target practice". No-one mentioned if he was a 'crack-shot'! Joyce Hardick (née Gaunt) recalls that Clark Gable often drank in the 'Rose and Crown' and other local 'watering-holes'.

---

[297] William Clark Gable (1901-1960) was based at RAF Polebrook from May to November 1943 as an observer-gunner on USAF B17 Flying Fortresses.
[298] Barbara Chester and 1940s friends visited the river-pool to see Clark Gable swim.
[299] Percy Arnett, Cynthia Arnett, Joyce Hardick, *et.al.*

Other well-known visitors in the wartime inlcuded Ella Formby (who played the ukulele like her more celebrated brother, George) and Bob Hope. (Joyce has photographs of these stars.) Jackie Ganderton[300] recalls that her aunt, June Gaunt, worked in St. Osyth's Lane in the Clarke's bicycle shop.[301] When their parents ran the 'Rose and Crown' public house, Ella Formby stayed with them. She was in ENSA[302] and like her well-known brother, George, entertained the forces by playing the ukulele. Frank and Margaret Gaunt had lodgers who stayed with them. Some of the Oundle girls met and married men from the US Forces and moved to the USA. The men in the forces were always generous with items that were restricted in the war time. June loved the 'new' 1940s fashions. Joyce Hardick recalls that she has some photographs of her and her sister, June, showing the beach and after a shopping trip to London, where an American Captain bought her a fashionable Easter bonnet.

South Road (north side)

At the end of a high wall we reach the back entrance to 'Bramston' and School staff housing. Bramston Close was built on the Newman family's gardens and the field where there was once a cow-shed. Mr Newman was the Head of Bramston House in the 1970s. His family also owned the field over the road.[303] Many houses in South Road have been remodelled and renovated over time. Large gateways open to the lawns of the Oundle School-masters' houses. In the late 1930s, many of the residents lived off South Road and worked for Oundle School. At number 17 was the home of the Reverend Cecil Howard D. Cullingford, M.A. He was born in London in 1904 and married in Bristol in 1933. He lived here with his wife, Olive. Next-door Mr S. Champ lived at number 18. He was an Honorary Associate of the Royal Academy of Music. Living next-door at 19 was Mr R. Carpenter. John Alfred Tatam (1894-1977) lived at number 20, who held a Music Baccalaureate and also an Associate of the Royal Academy of Music. The staff housing compound caters for staff and their families. In more recent years those best

---

[300] Jackie married John Ganderton.
[301] See Jackie's photograph of June outside the shop where she worked.
[302] The Entertainments National Service Association, established in 1939, provided entertainment for allied armed-forces in World War II.
[303] Ibid.

remembered include Alan G. and Eleanor M. Rayden[304] and their family and the Collier family. For many years, Mr and Mrs John Eaton lived in the house named 'Mayfield', which stands just along South Road from these. The Eaton's lived in a house that led up-to and backed onto the market place shops. The Sue and Philip Norman talk about cutting through to their garden from their own backyard via a gulley. It made a handy short-cut for small children!

In South Road, Mr R. Dyson and sons, coal merchants, were at number 7. At number 8 was Mr A. Neath. Miss C. Clark lived at number 9. Cheryl Forscutt recalls that Miss Clark had a soil path. She noted that soil paths and old cobbled pathways are becoming a thing of the past. Cobble paths do remain in parts of Oundle, but usually in private gardens. Miss Clark and Mr 'Charlie' Douglas had an allotment garden along the road that they shared. Living at number 10 was George Furnell and his wife, Ellen (née Durance), who married in 1917. Mr William G. Ley lived at number 11. (He died in Oundle in 1939, aged 70.) Mr E.A.J. Richards lived in final house in the road, number 12.

Amps car-park stretches between South Road and West Street. Their wine salesroom is accessible from both roads. This was originally the garden to the pharmacy. There was a large lawn and flower garden that stretched far southward from the shop. It was sold to Michael Amps by the Hilton family. The old sheds (where stretchers and first aid equipment had been stored by Mr Whitwell)[305] became the Amps' wine store; uphill through a narrow passage to West Street, which emerges between the 'Tesco' and 'Boots' pharmacy. Their rear exits by 'Navarac' (64). The former (Co-op) Store land at the rear was used for residents since the 1980s; formerly Bancroft and Bateman's (West Street). 'Peterborough Steam Laundry' collected 'work' from homes and designated agents. Mrs Pawson of the 'Boot Stores' in West Street was a local dry-cleaning agent. Houses that are numbered 66-72 have been reconstructed and 72a, "Trewithen" is built off the road.

---

[304] Eleanor Rayden is a daughter of the late Canon C.M. Cockin of St. Peter's Church.
[305] The last St. John's Ambulance member to use it was Leslie Black. He pushed it to Glapthorn village to treat a man with a broken leg. He then pushed the patient to Oundle railway station and accompanied him to Peterborough Hospital for treatment. Wendy Bollans recalls that the brown canvas stretcher was still in the store-room behind the chemist shop in 1970!

Ship Lane gives access to the 'Ship Inn' and its rear car-park (and north to West Street on foot from this car-park entrance). The Ship driveway and car-park accesses both roads. Alongside the lane is a two-storey, detached house, which was once owned by Sergeant Wild (before he moved to live in the police-house on Mill Lane). The Bamford family also lived on the corner of Ship Lane, with their children, Heather (who married Bob Seaton) and Neil. 'Tradell' glazing suppliers ran from this building in the 1990s before they relocated to Barnwell, circa 2007.

Nearby, at 92 South Road is the Veterinary clinic and surgery. It opened in 2000 after a move from its former home at Lorne House in Jericho. Lorne house is a large, two-storey, Georgian house with gardens, whereas the new South Road veterinary clinic is a single-storey, plain and utilitarian building. The current vet's surgery was the kitchens and canteen (school hall) of the old (county-council) secondary school. Some residents have memories of people who worked there. One name in particular stands out: one of the cooks was Mrs Spriggs. Now the people we meet in the building have names like Nick Park (who is definitely not related to Wallace and Gromit!).

New houses were built on the old playground to its rear since 2015. The Auction Mews houses stand here and are accessed via a shared drive from the vet's. There are also recent houses by the old brewery in an area renamed "Brewery Court". Paul Bancroft, Chartered Accountants offices are located beside what were the electricity store-rooms. Stretched between West Street and South Road was the site of the Oundle Union Brewing Company (established in 1836 was sold to Smiths' brewery in 1853, when the brewing moved to Blackpot Lane). A building on the site recalls its final public house name. It is near to and on the land of a public house that had its front located on West Street, previously known as the 'Unicorn', the 'Mason's Arms' and the 'Old Hind' (and rebuilt and known as 'Avondale House' in the late 1800s). Houses 96-108 and the "Drying House" are new dwellings and conversions from older buildings that were associated with the brewery land. The Union Brewery Counting House and stable area is still accessible from South Road. Its former Brewing House and school, 'Townley House', is a private dental surgery. Staff have stories to tell about 'overall-wearing worker' spirits who are at times apparent time within the building.

In the nineteenth-century, the Danford family owned the land in West Street, stretching south to South Road. Danford's Close was constructed by builders in 1966 and 1967. Danford's Road leads to a pathway to Danford's Yard. Danford's was built for Oundle Urban District Council in 1963, after a demolition order on the cottages that stood in Danford's Yard.

The name 'Yard' was purposely omitted from any new housing plans: 'Yard' having 'humble' connotations. The Women's Institute hut once stood here and Miss Haynes "lived in the top house". The rear of Coles' builders' yard stretched from West Street to South Road. The original number 10 was Percy C.E. Clarke's home. He was a building contractor and specialised in general repairs. In the 1960s and 70s, Percy converted old cottages, added bathrooms and worked as a decorating contractor registered with the Federation of Master Builders.

Whitwell's Yard

The Whitwell Yard 'bespoke' apartment development is largely designed in an L-shape. The town-house names and Yard name were inspired by nearby Fotheringhay Castle and its historical inhabitants. The remains of the Castle were reputedly incorporated into the fabric and facia of the Talbot Inn by William Whitwell. The houses comprise of ancient names: Latimer House, Parr House, Devonshire House, Aragon House, Tewdr House (sic.), Griffin House, Shrewsbury House, Whitwell's Lodge and Stables.

South Bridge Close

This Close has been built since the late 1970s. It is beside the fields that were (until Tudor times) named Saint Sythe's Meadows. South Bridge Close is close to the river and the old bridge. The land in the Close (between West Street and South Road) has been developed for housing since 1970. From the turn of the last century to the 1950s this land was used by circuses and fairs that visited the town. It is to the rear of the old 'Wagon and Horses' public house. Close-by is the fifteenth-century 'Manor House', which is taller than its surrounding buildings. (Note that the Manor house has been referred to as "Wakerley manor".) It can be clearly seen over the roof-tops from South Bridge Close and Mill Road. It was originally part of a much larger

Manor and was the home of Mrs Diana Ashby (1912-1999). Nearby allotments, available to rent (by the fields opposite the road) until the 1970s, abutted with the Mill Road cottages and brewery buildings.

MILL ROAD

Mill Road (east side, travelling south)

Mill Road eighteenth-century cottages were built near to a working Oundle Water Mill. It was within a back-water at the South Bridge. Some of its stones and foundations can be seen at low water. To the east side of the road is a row of single-storey workmen's cottages. These have been much restored in the past few years. They date to the 1600s and were built one by one, so successively age. (Numbers 3 and 5 are the earliest.) Belying their age, they have dormer gables in the roof. Number 5 has a well-preserved stone window. There is clear variation in the sizes of the stonework among the large stones of number 8 and the much smaller stones of number 9. From mediæval times, the tenements were divided so that they could house as many people as possible. The terraced homes were behind "Wakerley Manor" (also called the Manor House). They faced empty land and a view down to farmland in the 1600s. The interiors were steadily improved by indoor bathrooms. The roof of the sixteenth-century 'Manor' or 'Priest's House' can be seen above Mill cottages.

In the 1930s, Mr Thomas S. Mawdesley was a solicitor who lived and worked at 16 Mill Road as it was a 'Sun Insurance' office (founded in 1710). Dealing with insurance transactions, it is listed in the Town Directory for "fire, accident, motor, marine, burglary, live-stock and plate-glass" cover. Percy Arnett recalled that "In Mill Road, the Weatherington family were in the first house. Elderly Mr Fox lived at the back in a cottage, down a passageway. Leslie Clipston also lived in one. Mr and Mrs Berry and their daughter, Jean, lived in another". Percy added, "I can't recall who was in the next one, but there was an old bloke. I did a paper round before the war and when I went to deliver it the old bloke always asked for a cup of tea with no milk or sugar. The Brindsley family were next."

The tall building glimpsed behind the row as an old, steep roof, has been known by several names: "Wakerley Manor", "the Priest's

House" and the "Priory". It a fragment of a Manor that survives from the sixteenth-century. The gable-roof is timber-framed and the plasterwork is patched and shows evidence of partitioning. The (South Road-Mill Road) Manor is accessed via a cottage passageway and is best viewed from the Jesus Church at the top of the hill or from the bridge at the bottom. Nearby, on the corner is a house that was part of the Oundle Anchor Brewery (dating between 1854 and 1904). The Georgian building is large and plain, with a brick face and stone back-walls. Just into South Road there is a brewer's warehouse with hoists and another row of workers cottages. The cottages have been renumbered and updated in recent times.[306]

Mill Road (west side, travelling south)

The police station and police house led down the west side of Mill Road, just along from the courts and registrars' office. During the 1970s, the police station had a very memorable telephone number - "Oundle 2222". The Magistrates' Court and police station buildings provided housing for the police superintendent and his assistant. The superintendent in 1930s was Mr Osborne. In the 1970s Sergeant Mike Clamping and his family lived in the police house. The house adjoined the courthouse, which dates to 1877. It is a two-storey, period stone building. For a few years the building was utilised by the Town Council (after its move from the Victoria Hall, circa 2000). Recently, the building was divided into offices with working units in the courtyard.

The 'free entry' Oundle Town Museum (established in 1981) is located in the old magistrates' court and police station (with cells) that had the Oundle Registry Office (upstairs). The museum made a move from the Drill Hall and now hosts 'rolling exhibitions' in the lower rooms and static displays in part of the upper floor. Just ask and the volunteer staff are happy to lock your children into the old cells for a short time! This 'Courthouse' building stands on the corner of "Chappel End" [sic] on Stoke Hill. It currently has a dog-grooming business in the courtyard workshop (3). The museum used the Oundle School Anglo-Saxon Hoard for its "2000 years of Oundle Town" exhibition. Until November

---

[306] Oral history, David Wills and Percy Arnett.

2017, the exhibition was based on war-time Oundle. In the early 1800s, Nathaniel Ball owned all of the the land between the Court House and the Nene.

'Apollo House' is a large, (mostly 1880s, but incorporating earlier buildings) Georgian house, where Mr and Mrs John Crawshaw and their children lived from the 1960s. Until the millennium this was the last solid house on this side of the road. Since the millennium, houses have been built from this to the river. Wildlife proliferates in the trees and banks of the river. Kingfishers and heron are occasionally spotted alongside the more common ducks, swans and hedge-sparrows. From the bridge, people enjoy the calming sights of fish swimming in the shallows below. Reflecting our past, there are sheep in the meadows and red kites in the skies.

The 'south bridge' has seven arches (five are somewhat smaller than the central two). For a short time the bridge was protected by a 'weight limit' and barriers that prevented larger vehicles from entering via this southern route while the bridge was restored to use. Its barriers (and some cars) bore the result of drivers with poor spatial awareness! Nearby Barnwell Country Park has lovely riverside and lakeside walks. It is easy to walk to from Oundle and lures families with its picnic areas and play facilities, alongside a small café, visitor's centre, bird-hides and fishing platforms. Throughout the year the park hosts free entertainment for the community, which includes a summer brass-band day (when five or six bands take turns to play through the day). The park borders the old lock and mill which are upstream, just outside the town limit. Since 2014, 'Oundle Mill' (formerly a pub, restaurant and hotel) has closed, owing to being twice flooded by high Nene water-levels.

STOKE HILL (formerly 'Chappel End')

Stoke Hill (south side)

The Anglo-Saxon Charters describe the land-boundaries that were subject to leases, diplomas, wills and writs (from around 963 A.D.) onward. They mention the mill "leet" or "leat-watercourse" dug to supply water to the watermill (or its mill pond). From around the sixth century the land from the Stoke Doyle Road to Mill Lane belonged to the mill owner. Tenements were built for workers as the town grew. By 1565, the miller lived in the tenements in Chapel End (now the Old Dairy) that stretched down the road to the mill that stood by the river.

Stoke Hill is the start of the Stoke Doyle Road. Here stood the mediæval chapel dedicated to Thomas Becket (who was the Archbishop of Canterbury from 1162 to his murder in 1170).[307] Until the Watts-Russell family built the current chapel, the "Most Holy Name of Jesus Church", the land in the centre of the roads, the old dairy and the houses west of this, plus the land to the north of 'the green' (where up to five building stood) was all owned by Mrs Sukey Tookey (who died in 1845).

The church name is shortened to "the Jesus Church", which is of Roman Catholic denomination. It is surrounded by roads. When it moved location from St. Wilfrid's in the 1960s, an old joke was that St. Peter's Church congregation finished their service half-an-hour earlier so that they could knock their rivals over when crossing the road after leaving their service!

The town's former police station and courthouse is on this corner, with front access to the road. In the 1930s it was designated as 1 Stoke Hill, with a carriage-way leading behind, via a courtyard, to a covered gateway on Mill Road. To the 1800s this was designated as the Bridewell (a sixteenth-century prison or house of reform for petty offenders). Nathaniel Ball also owned all of the land on Stoke Road that did not belong to Mrs Tookey and William Fox (who owned the farm). William owned the "Dairy Farm" on Stoke Road in the 1820s. His son, Charles Fox, inherited it from him. By the twentieth century it was owned by Albert S. Bierton and his sons.

On 7th October 1955, the 'Peterborough Advertiser' reported 'a vehicle' (most likely a tractor and trailer from the description) that was owned by farmer, Sidney Rowell, from 'the Orchard', Benefield Road, was involved in an accident. The vehicle was driven by his 20-year-old son, David, when it became detached from its tow, somewhere opposite the Jesus Church, on Stoke Hill. He badly damaged a pedal-cycle that was owned Mr J. Frederick. The outcome of the incident was

---

[307] bbc.co.uk/history/historic_figures/becket_thomas.shtml

not reported, but in all probability was resolved amicably as fault was easy to establish.

On the same side of the road (note that odds and even numbers do not swap sides on this road), at number 2 is the Old Dairy building, which belonged to the dairy farm at the bottom of the hill. Joyce and Hans Hardick lived in this house with their family, but subsequently moved to the farm at the bottom of the hill. The window that was part of the shop can be clearly seen. The window could be opened to allow children to purchase ice-creams through it.[308] Mr Sydney (known as 'Syd') Rowell was the dairy farmer (born in 1893) who lived here with his wife, Winifred, and their family. His farm was at the bottom of the hill (with his dairy at the top). His milk was delivered by a horse and 'float' cart. Householders put their jugs out on the doorstep to be filled as he did his rounds.

In 1939, Mr E.G. Johnson was the police inspector living at 1 Stoke Hill. Mr Sidney Rowell's dairy was next-door at number 2. Adjoined to the Old Dairy is are two striking, connected, Georgian-style buildings. Next door, 'New House' was converted into the girls' boarding-rooms in 1997, but was first used as for boarding in 1907. Despite its name, the original building is one of the oldest school houses in Oundle. It is believed that Oliver Cromwell lodged in 'New House' during the 1600s and the interior most likely dates to two centuries earlier. It is a many-windowed building (including two in the roof space). During the late 1800s, the house was known as 'Knaptoft House' and Thomas Wilson (a farmer) lived here. He was the Chair of the Board of Guardians. New House is now the property of Oundle School and is residential student accommodation. Abutted to this and a storey lower is a stone-built house, with new windows and doors, as the brickwork is altered around them. The main house was owned by Mr H.M. King, a master at the school, before it was purchased by the School. Part of New House (School property) was a Wesleyan meeting house and Baptist Chapel that was founded in 1800. (The nearby early-Victorian Chapel at the terminus of West Street dates to 1852.) A carriage-way leads beyond to a courtyard. The House Master in 1938 was Gerald T. Burns, who oversaw both 3 and 4, which have been consolidated as 'New

---

[308] David Wills has memories of this.

House'. Number 4 is a beautiful, Jacobean house, roughly contemporaneous with the 'White Lion', bearing a date 1648 above the upper windows.

In the 1930s, living at number 5 were Alfred and Grace Marlow. The couple were elderly. Alfred was a retired postman. The farm cottages are set back from the road along with number 5. In the 1950s they were part of Rowell's farm. Edward and Ruth Shrives lived at number 6. Ruth served at the WVS in the canteen. Edward was the farm foreman. Their daughter, Barbara, was a showroom attendant and was also a member of the St. John's Ambulance. During the war years, William C. Horsford lived at number 7 with his wife, Ada, and their daughter, Doris (who was born in 1900). He was a retired gentleman and helped as an ARP warden. At 8, Mrs Louisa Binder was a retired widow who lived with her 'companion' and help, Charlotte Barwell. Number 9 was the home of Reginald Buckland and his wife, Anne. Reginald was a stationers and printers clerk. Number 10 was the home of a widow, Mrs Sarah Binder.[309] Sarah Elizabeth Binder (née Dolby) was born in 1865 and died in 1939, aged 83. She had married her late husband, Charles Ernest Binder (1859-1932) in 1896. Charles predeceased his wife by seven years. At number 11 there was Mr Charles W. Vessey. He was born in 1899. Prior to the war, Charles was a widower, who worked as a butcher's assistant. Number 12 was the home of Mrs Fanny Stokes (wife of John Stokes), while Mr A. Andrews lived at 14.

Stoke Hill (north side)

There are two cottages at the start of Stoke Hill, by a "concealed entrance". Numbers 11, 12 and 13 are terraced, two-storey, Victorian houses. They are on the corner (near Binder's Row) at the junction of Benefield Road and Stoke Road. No longer extant on this corner was the 'Falcon' pub (that was later named the 'Rose and Crown' – and is not to be confused with the Inn of the same name in the town centre). Over two centuries ago, the 'Woolpocket' inn stood over the road from the 'Wagon and Horses' and a couple of doors down from the 'Cross Keys' (at number West Street 89). The Most Holy Name of Jesus Church

---

[309] Note that women took their husband's names, so were also listed under their husband's initials.

396

is in the middle of all of the roads. Opposite the gate stands 10 Stoke Hill, the Roman Catholic "Priests House". The "Priests House" once belonged to Dr Crow (who was captured by the Japanese). She had been a professor of the Royal College of Gynaecology in Singapore. She was taken to a prisoner of war internment after Singapore fell to the Japanese in 1942. (It was not relieved until 1945.)[310] The Governor General during the fall of Singapore was Sir Shelton Thomas. In the late-1960s, Eileen Crow (her younger sister) was the Headmaster's secretary at Oundle School. The sisters bought the parts of the house and converted them into three flats. Later, Dr Crow sold the flats to the Roman Catholic Church and the house was renamed the "Priests House". The house is a stone-built and is adjoined to a large Georgian building (9). Nearby there is a stone house, named 'Vine House', which is joined to a three-storey "cottage" (number 7).

Newer properties stand nearby, as Oundle's "new-growth" extends westward. Number 2 is a bungalow with a south-facing lawn. It dates to around the millennium. All buildings from here on are new, apart from 10, a detached (1977) house. Alma (née Black)[311] and her husband, Paul Coles, lived on Stoke Hill with their children, Nicola (a district nurse) and Simon.

Stoke Doyle Road

On the south side of the Stoke Doyle Road there is mostly farming land as far as one can see. On the north side of the road there are new houses that have been built in Warren Court in the last thirty years. In Stoke Road during the 1930s, Mr C.B. Taylor lived at the cemetery lodge. His nearest neighbour was Mr Thomas Gray at the Isolation Hospital. Mr John Horsford lived here with his family and Mr William J. Hasslegrave with his. They were both farmers at Oundle Lodge. The 'Lodge' is also where Mr George L. Gent and his sons farmed. Mr A. Brindsley lived at Wakerley Cottage and Mr T. Allen at Wakerley Lodge. In 2015, planning permission was requested for the erection of agricultural buildings for Oundle Lodge on the Stoke Doyle Road. Plans were to make a system for managing vehicle-wash water and drainage, for managing slurry and dirty water. Fields and pastures stretch

---

[310] For further reading see http://www.pows-of-japan.net/articles.htm online.
[311] Alma sadly died in late 2017 and is missed by all who knew her.

beyond here to Stoke Doyle village. Ruth Keans (née Moisey) originally came from Stoke Doyle. Percy Arnett recalls that despite living in Oundle for all his life, in 1948 he played dominoes for the Stoke Doyle team as he worked in that village. He says that he still enjoys a game of dominoes if he can get it. 'Sudborough House' is where the Victorian mortuary stood. The mortuary has been demolished. Wood Lane has just a few houses along it, but the Victorian built houses are large and have wonderful views over the town and surrounding fields.

An old, narrow bridge spans a stream of water from the Nene, over the field to the south. David Wills stated that the original road went straight (due west) and did not turn the tight corner over the low bridge. Viewed from a distance, the line can be seen where the original carriageway led. A new estate, Warren Bridge, stands on the west side of the Oundle cemetery. (Some refer to it as "the cemetery estate".) Within the burial ground stands a Victorian chapel (1850s) that stood vacant and unused for about sixty years. The chapel was utilised in 1980s for storing the Oundle Amateur Theatrical Society (OATS) costumes and props. The small, stone chapel was in need of refurbishing, as it had been many years since it was used for non-conformist and conformist burials. David mentioned that, "Methodists and Baptists were buried in the south of the cemetery, while Anglicans were buried on consecrated ground to the north." The chapel has been sold, restored and is now a private house. The cemetery-gate Lodge is also a dwelling.

Further along this road is the old, red-brick Sanatorium. It stands alongside newer buildings. Leslie Black recalled in his memoirs that the 'fever-cart' was often seen in Oundle in the early 1900s. The horse-drawn yellow-cab travelled back and forth to the Sanatorium Isolation Hospital. It carried locals with respiratory problems, diphtheria, scarlet fever and infectious diseases. They were borne by the fever-cart to prevent the sickness from spreading. Many people going to the 'San' were unable to walk to the outskirts of town unaided. After WWI, those with influenza (and other respiratory tract infections) were taken to this clinic. The epidemic of "Spanish flu" debilitated Oundle and the nearby villages. Anne Gray's grandmother was one of those died from it. This (1918) deadly influenza pandemic was carried back from France by sick troops returning from the war.[312] A children's playground rhyme from the same era that was used for skipping and hopping games goes, ""I had a little bird. Its name was Enza. I opened the window and ... In-flu-enza."

BENEFIELD ROAD

Benefield Road (northern side)

The road stretches from the Drill Hall to Biggin Grange (A427 road), between Oundle and Benefield. The first houses from the junction are classed as West Street and Binder's Row. The Benefield Road begins just prior to the Drill Hall car-park. In the 1930s, Ted and Emily Ashby lived at 7. Ted was a railway engineers' labourer. Number 9 is the Drill Hall. Drill halls first began following the formation of the Rifle Volunteer Corps in 1859. The Company of Rifle Volunteers was first established in Oundle in connection with the County Battalion in 1894. The Rifle and Pistol Clubs had their base behind the building. In the 1960s, Glynn Evans, David Barrow, Eric Cotton, Freddie Otto (who gave driving lessons), Brian Sumner, Roy Sumner (who was a miik-man), Basil Kimpton, Maurice Burrows, David Kirkpatrick (who was a hairdresser), Les Barber, Dick Able, Gordon Clark and Leslie Titman (who taught the Secondary School woodwork and technical-drawing classes) were all members of the club (to name but a few). Drill halls began to close after a reduction in Territorial Army personnel after the Second World War.

Unused, the Oundle Drill Hall has been converted to into dwellings during the twenty-first century. In the 1930s John and Eileen Adams lived here. John was a sergeant in the 5th Battalion of the Northants Regiment. By 1937, Mr S. Bond and his family lived at the Drill Hall. The Council renovated the building in 1993, adding a kitchen, hall and meeting rooms used for the community and as a base for the Youth Club. The museum was housed upstairs and the building was used as a polling station, until it was sold in 2012 and thereafter divided into eight refurbished flats. This created a reduced-size town car-park nearby.

---

[312] The 1918-19 Spanish 'flu' virus killed forty-million people and is thought to be the deadliest disease in recent history.

On the recommendation of the Housing Committee, the chairman and the surveyor were asked to inspect suitable sites on Benefield and East roads. In 1938 the Oundle Urban District Council building was constructed on the Benefield Road by Mr Charles R. Cunnington. Milton Road (with its access to Oundle Cricket Club and School Houses) leads off to the north from this junction. In 1937 the 'Ashworth Brothers' garage was located at number 1 Benefield Road. It is said to have been built on a field purchased from Dr Turner. Mr Robert Bailey Rothwell Ashworth (1894-1959)[313] lived in number 3. He was a trained engineer who ran the garage. During WWI he was an observer in the RAF. Robert married Miss Jessie Carley in Uppingham in 1924. Jessie worked as a hotel manageress. Their son, Bryan, was born in Oundle in 1929. He attended Laxton School (where he was quite unhappy). Bryan later trained and worked as a consultant neurologist in Edinburgh. As a child, Andrew Spurrell rode his pony in the field to the south of the garage. Later, Mr Francis and Mr Marshall owned, developed and manned the two garages that bore their names in the 1960s. They were located on opposite sides of the road. Townhouses have recently replaced both garages. Richard (Dick) Francis (a mechanic) bought the business on the north side (by Milton Road). Archie Marshall joined the firm when Dick had bought the field opposite and built the 'Shell' garage (now Peacock Villas). Both men were skilled motor and electrical engineers. Archie Marshall also ran a radio, cycle and television showroom at 1 West Street (now 'Beans' café). The Benefield Road garage was an Austin Rover dealership. The two men ran a 'family' business with "over forty-five years" in the trade. They took on local staff who gave "individual attention to you as a person and not so much a number!" Their advertising continued, "It costs no more, often less!" Richard Willimont conducted their after-hours sales. (He later ran the garage on Station Road.)

On the corner wall there was a lozenge-shaped sign for "St. Ann's" (without an 'e'), designating where the school stood, before it became part of the garage. The museum has the commemorative stone that reads: "St. Ann's in the Grove 1862". St. Ann's Court recalls the private infant school that stood near this land. The corner houses on the Benefield Road date to the mid-to-late-1980s. Numbers 3, 5 and 7 are

---

[313] Robert had moved to Nottingham by the end of his life.

terraced houses (by Milton Road). The first house on the corner is named "Filbert Villa" (3).[314] It is a Victorian stone house. Its bay-front extends to the roof. This house is slightly grander than its neighbours. Originally, the land had many hazel trees growing on it.[315] From the late 1800s to 1911 (when she died), Miss Louisa Smith lived in this house. She was the sister of the brewery owner, John. Harold Williams, a bank accountant, and his wife, Minnie, lived here during the 1930s. At number 5 there lived William Stretton and his wife, Dora. Adjacent to them was Mrs Annie Gann (at number 7). She was a widow in her late seventies during the pre-war years. "The Gardens", 7b, is a stone, two-storey house. It stands next to a much newer house (7a).

Toll-gates and Turn-pikes

On 28th March 1840, the 'Northampton Mercury' announced that the North Oundle and Weldon 'Turnpike Road' had opened. The Benefield Road originally started at this juncture, where the toll-gate (or toll-bar) crossed the road. In May 1852, Edward and Esther Quincey became the proud parents of Thomas Quincey. They lived in Ashton, but (according to the baptismal register for 1838-1858) Edward worked as the "toll-gate keeper" in Oundle. In 1846 Mrs Peggy Rowse (who was a toll collector) had her children baptised (possibly on the death of their father). By 1855, Augustine Roddis worked as a toll collector[316] and one year later, in 1856, William Smith was the toll-gate keeper. A year later, John Woodcock is listed as a toll collector, along with Augustine Roddis, a shoe-maker and gate-keeper. By the 1930s, people living still recalled the main toll-gates surviving on the Benefield Road and in Elmington (by the corner-turning to Cotterstock). Five tolls originally controlled the access to Oundle, its market and all of the onward routes via the town.

The Oundle tolls and market dues of 1535 were five pounds and nineteen shillings, which, when added to fines and manorial dues was a hefty sum. Four centuries later, the 1939 Directory reports that the

---

[314] A 'filbert' is a Hazelnut (hazel-tree nut or 'cobb nut'). St. Philbert (608-684 AD) saint's day is at the time nuts were harvested, roasted and stored. Hence its name.
[315] Oral history, David Wills.
[316] Oundle Baptismal Register, 1838-1858.

Barnwell Road Toll House was still standing, just beyond Mill House. It is hard to ascertain when it ceased to be used.

In the 1930s, the Benefield Road 'Toll House' (9) was the home of retired School Master, Joseph Rippener. He lived here with his wife, Lillian. It is a charming, plain, stone-built house (grade-II listed). The original part dates from the early eighteenth-century. It has many features from the period, including its original flagstone floor. The house has been extended, over the last century.

Continuing along the Benefield Road

Mr Thomas Knight and his wife, Dora, lived at number 11 during the early 1930s. In 1937, Miss Spriggs lived at 11. Throughout the 1930s and 1940s, 13 was home to P.A. Palmer and his family. Number 15 was the home of Herbert and Gladys Arnett. Five of their six children lived with them. The exception was Joyce, the eldest, "who lived with gran and grandad before emigrating to America". Kathleen, Percy and Elsie (who later married Walter Bladon),[317] Jean (now Griffin) and her younger brother, Brian lived at home. Percy said it was "amazing to think that five children were brought up in a one-up-one-down house".

"Peddler" Palmer was a friend of the Bladon children. (Peddler later worked as a local coalman.) One day, when Percy, Kay and Peddler played outside in the fields, they heard a noise. Percy recalls, "It was a baby crying. Brian had been born!"[318] Percy said that he and Edward Bird were chums and were always in trouble in school, except they were good at arithmetic and were so far ahead that they had separate lessons from the rest of the class. Percy said that his tastes changed and he "later preferred geography"! At home in the 1930s, Percy was teased by his sisters that Barbara (Chester) was his girlfriend. (In 2017, Barbara chuckled and said that this was the first she time had heard of it!) Percy tells of a time in school when he was around the age of eleven. John Cunnington (who was the same age as Percy) lost his temper and swore at Mrs Perring. They were in the primary school top class and she expected better control from him, so she caned him for his impudence.

---

[317] Walter Bladon, Elsie's husband, died in February 2017, aged 82.
[318] Percy Arnett, personal information.

'Cherry Orchard' was a small enclave of houses that stood on this site. From the 1920s to the 1950s, four cottages stood side-on to the road. They were set-back on a 'ledge' or buttress, amidst orchards full of greenery and cherry trees. Barbara Chester was born in one of the four off-road houses that were here in the 1930s. Her family moved within her first year. She said that Mr Wade, the local butcher, had bought the cottages to "knock some down and convert the rest into a big house". The converted property (17 Benefield Road) is within Cherry Orchard Yard. The combined, converted, two-storey house is a grade-II listed building. It was originally several cottages that date to the 1700s. In the middle-section of this house there is a thatched cottage. It stands hidden at the back of 'Toll House' and is one of the remaining two thatched cottages in Oundle.

Percy Arnett said that 'Cherry Orchard' originally had two houses in it, but then two more were built. He went on to say that there were three families living in it when his family lived there. The Arnett family moved to number 32 Benefield Road when Percy was eleven. The numbering in the road has changed since the 1930s. At number 13 were the Marlow family and at 15 were Percy's family. Alfred (Alf) Lagdon, an electrician, lived at numbers 17 and 19 (which had been knocked together into one dwelling). Living with Alf were John Morgan (a watch and clock maker) and Leonard Carbyle (a tailor's 'cutter').

Percy said that the children from the houses would play over the road in the meadows and in the stream at the bottom of the hill. He said that his sister, Kathleen (known as Kay) would "slide down the hill on a tin" (metal tray). Percy recalled that she had no fear and "went under the barbed-wire at the bottom and straight into the brook!" Likewise, when June and Joyce Gaunt were children they lived in the Benefield Road and spent long hours playing in the brook with buckets and spades. (See photograph.)

The three (Cherry Orchard) properties have since been demolished. In the early 1800s, a lane known as Birds' Yard was nearby. Here is a row of terraced houses. Numbers 19, 21, 23 and 25 are first row with wrought-iron railings on the frontage. The houses are all similar in style and are constructed of stone. Mr H.B. Williams lived at number 19 in 1937. Later, Alexander Meunier (an insurance agent) lived here with his wife, Freda. Mrs Edith Robinson lived at 21 in 1937. (She died in

1963, aged 90.) Thereafter, Alfred Compton lived at 21. He was a carpenter and wheelwright who lived with his wife, Eileen and their son, David. Eileen's sister (Violet) and her mother (Mary) also lived with them. Number 23 was the home of Sydney and Bertha Clark and their family. They later moved to a few doors along the road. Sydney worked as a deliver-van driver. At number 25, William Weldon lived with his wife, Daisy, and their family. William worked as a plumber and general builder.

Number 27 is listed as 'Keppel Cottage'. It was reported in the 'Northampton Mercury', 13th February 1841, for "Eligible investment to be sold by auction. The following Valuable Estates viz., Lot 1. All that newly-erected Messuage or DWELLING HOUSE, with the stable, outhouses and appurtenances, situated near the Tollbar on the Benefield Road, in Oundle aforesaid, used as a Public House known by the sign of "The Admiral Keppel" and now let to the Oundle Union Brewing Company." The land alongside the public house was also advertised and sold: "Also all that excellent GARDEN, ORCHARD and CHERRY-HOLT, adjoining the above-mentioned messuage, planted with 500 choice Fruit Trees of various descriptions, containing altogether by recent admeasurement 3A. OR. 6P more or less." In 1937, Arthur Malan lived here. Number 27 was still known as "Keppel Cottage" in the 1930s. It is a large building with two bay-windows and an arched front door. It is the last in the terraced row. Beyond it is a large hedge and private residence. The public house "The Admiral Keppel" was named after a much-admired admiral, who was court-martialled and acquitted during the American War of Independence. The Inn was renamed in his honour by devotees.[319]

The houses numbered 29, 31 and 33 no longer exist, but during the pre-war years they were still being lived in as family homes. Number 29 was the home of Charles Forster and his family. Widow, Edith Abel lived at number 31, with her son Stanley and daughter, Gertrude. John William Mason (a joiner) lived here with his wife, Lottie. Their son, John lived in number 35. Pilot Officer John Herbert Mason DFC, was born in 1921 and served with the 50th Squadron. He was killed in action in

---

[319] The Oundle Pub and Brewery Trail, Oundle Museum Trust, 1997 and 2002.

France in May 1944. He was posthumously awarded the Distinguished Flying Cross medal. Generations of the Mason family still live in Oundle.

Numbers 35 and 37 have a shared driveway, surrounded by mature gardens with trees. Number 35 is "Walnut Cottage". It was Miss Howitt's home in 1937 as her mother, Selina Howitt (née Afford) had died in 1936. Number 37 was home of Charlie Smith, who was a Private in the Regular Army 5th Northants. He married Edith Hemmant at the end of 1934. Number 39 is a very large two-storey, 'European-influence' design, house with lawns to the front. It has a short drive behind a low garden wall. It is appropriately named 'Orchard House' after the cherry trees that were here until the 1950s. In 1937, Mr E.S. Baxter lived at number 39.

Stephen Coales and his wife, Elizabeth (née Brinsley [1874-1943]) lived at number 41. There was a difference in the Coales' ages, as they married (in 1889) when she was fifteen and he was twenty-seven. Later in their lives they were both listed as 'incapacitated'. (Their house has been demolished.) A row of a stone-built terraces numbered 43, 45, 45a and 47 are built sideways-on to the north of the road. The first, 'Stoneleigh', is where Miss Amelia Patchett lived in the 1930s. At 45, there lived Percy Kirby (who was a guard in the army). He lived here with his wife, Elizabeth. In 1937, Mrs E. Mason lived next-door at number 45a. She lived here with her husband, Mr Charles W. Mason.

Charles and Ivy Evans lived at 45a before the Mason's. Charles Evans was an 'assistant-borer' and tractor driver who did 'heavy work'. Ivy lived a long and happy life. She was born in East Road in 1915. Her father was a swimming attendant at the school, but she enjoyed "bathing place" by the river. Her sisters attended the British School and Ivy, who was younger, attended the County Council School. In April 1943 she and six friends met and established the Oundle women's section of the British Legion. Mrs Donegani (from East Road) was the secretary of the group and Mrs Laxton (who lived in the Market Place) was the President. The group met at the Laxton's home (in part of their outfitter's shop). During WWII, Miss Caborn and Ivy cooked foods as an evening meal (supper) for the soldiers who were stationed in the Rectory. Throughout her life Ivy bore the Legion standard in the course of successive Remembrance Days. She worked in the Oundle school laundry.

At 47 was Mary Ann Smith (born in 1867), who lived alone. The town guide for 1937 lists Mrs J. Smith as living here. Separate from these dwellings, there is a new family house that stands on the corner of Prince William Road. On the corner is a large Yew tree. It is in what was Lottie Mason's garden. The original house was level with the new houses at the start of the road. The original buildings were up-hill, slightly to the north and cut in a stone yard.

Recent roads leading off the Benefield Road

The inspiration for Prince William Road, Wyatt Way, Whitwell Close, Mildmay Close and Clifton Drive comes from local benefactors and land-owners. There have been several new roads constructed along the Benefield Road since 1973. Their chosen names may intrigue the curious and budding historians. The 'Road', 'Way' and 'Close' designations commemorate Oundle's renowned, deceased and notable locals. Prince William Road is named for Prince William of Gloucester. He was the grandson of George V and also a cousin of Queen Elizabeth II. He grew up in Barnwell and was frequently seen when shopping in Oundle. He died in tragic circumstances when his plane crashed at the Goodyear International Air Trophy Show in 1972. His father, Prince Henry, was gravely ill at the time. Princess Alice did not wish to tell him of their son's death for fear of the consequences. She disclosed in her memoirs that he probably learnt of his son's death from reports on the television.[320]

Robert Wyatt and his wife, Joan, were the 'merchant' relatives of Sir Thomas Wyatt who lived in Oundle.[321] Together Robert and Joan co-founded the 'Guild of Our Lady of Oundle' in the late fifteenth-century. They funded the small Oundle guild school (1485-1556) with its classes held in the Parish Church. When widowed, Joan founded a chapel. Robert was buried in the chapel of St. John the Baptist (in 1494). When Joan followed him to the grave, she left money to the Gild, to her chapel (John the Baptist) and to the chapels of the Holy Trinity and St. Thomas.

---

[320] "The Memoirs of Princess Alice, Duchess of Gloucester", 1983.
[321] Leyland identifies Robert Wyatt a 'merchant'.

Robert and Joan also left money in their wills for the repairs of Ashton and Oundle bridges. Joan "endowed the fraternity with revenues for two priests" who [at the suppression of the monasteries] each had a salary.[322] A story from their family in the reigns of Richard III mentions Sir Thomas Wyatt's imprisonment in the Tower of London. The story goes that Thomas was saved from starvation by befriending a cat who brought daily sustenance for him. The story does not go into great detail as to whether the 'food' was palatable, but is presumed to be rodent kills!

A room that were "early priest's quarters" caused a stir when it was reviewed during recent restorations at St Peter's Church. The room is about four metres square with two windows and a fireplace. It is understood that this was the (fifteenth century) school-room where William Laxton was taught. It is also thought that the school room was first built as part of the alms house that was commissioned by Robert and Joan Wyatt in 1485.

Mr William Whitwell was a 'gentleman' from Oundle. He lived in the Berrystead in 1626 and provides his name for Whitwell Close. (See the Market Place pages for more detail concerning Mr Whitwell.)

Mildmay Close recollects and honours Sir Walter Mildmay of Apethorpe (1523–1589), Chancellor of the Exchequer to Queen Elizabeth I. He was involved in and controlled the execution of Mary, Queen of Scots, in nearby Fotheringhay in 1587. He visited Mary just before her final warrant was signed, prior to her end. Mildmay controlled influence as the Commissioner for Edward VI on the dissolution of the chantries and guilds. He most-likely protected the boys' School (Laxton) from closure. Among other notable deeds, Mildmay founded Emmanuel College in Cambridge. He was rewarded for his services to the monarchy with a grant of land (including Apethorpe 'Palace' or 'Hall', as it was known throughout the twentieth century).[323] A century later, King James I visited Mildmay in Apethorpe. It is reasonable to assume that when he stayed there he is also sure to have passed through Oundle. It may be that he also visited nearby

---

[322] "The Works of Henry Howard and of Sir Thomas Wyatt, the Elder", by Henry Howard, Earl of Surrey. Two edited volumes, printed by T. Bensley, London, 1816.

[323] For information on Whitwell or Mildmay, see section in this book on West Street.

Fotheringhay castle and decided to 'raze it to the ground' as it was where his mother met her grisly end.

Clifton Drive has new two-storey, detached houses. There are open fields behind them. The drive is named for eighteenth-century diarist, master carpenter and joiner, John Clifton. He lived in West Street. He also acquired and renovated a small cottage in New Street by the "Red Lion gates". (See the Oundle School photograph of this building before it was demolished to make way for the Great Hall.) It has been suggested that Clifton was the Parish Church sexton, administering in the church and Church yard, besides acting as bell-ringer and a grave-digger. His main occupation seems to have been carpentry. Clifton often employed the help of his colleagues John Gann and William Weldon, in his wood-working labours.

Benefield Road (north side continued)

The house on the corner is accessed via a five-bar gate and is of a modern construction. Numbers 49 to 61 are in a row of seven older stone-built, terraced cottages with a patch of lawn separating the houses from the public footpath and the road. They are situated on the corner of Cordwainer Gardens.

Industrious Terrace

Herbert Platt (a widowed gardener) lived at number 49. His brother and sister, Arthur and Rose Platt lived with him (and were all aged in their seventies by the time WWII began.) The people who lived at number 51 were the Clarke family. Mr Richard Clarke was a retired, Urban District Council labourer. Richard lived with his wife, Isabella, who worked as a Council office cleaner. At 53, Sydney Hillock (an engineers' labourer) who lived with his wife, Irene, and their daughter, Joyce, in a one-bedroom stone cottage. They had a large garden that was well tended. At number 55 there was Oliver Shrive (a cowman) and his wife, Annie. They lived with their daughter, Monica, who worked as a shop assistant at the newsagents.

Number 55 bears a plaque on the stone, front-wall, "C. Afford. Industrious Terrace. 1859". This would be where Cook Afford lived with his parents, George (a builder) and Elizabeth, who moved to here in 1851. It is likely that Cook's father, George, built the row of houses.

Cook (who also became a stonemason) was born around the time when they moved from the 'Wagon and Horses'. Cook married in 1882 and, by 1901, he and his family lived next to his father.[324] Mr Thomas Platt lived at 57 during the early 1930s. He was born in Oundle in 1841. Thomas died in 1937, aged 96. In 1939, Ronald and Evelyn Coales and their son (who was also named Ronald) lived here. (Ronald [senior] was a council labourer.)

Number 59 was the home of Mr Albert Platt (a council labourer and ARP decontamination man) in the 1930s. Albert was born in 1880 and lived to be seventy-seven years of age. The building he lived in was converted into the home and shoe shop of Ebenezer (Ebbie) Walton (junior). His father (also a cobbler) lived a little further down the road. The shoes Ebbie sold were housed in the hallways and rooms of number 77, as well as his family. Ebbie travelled around the town in his van, collecting shoes that needed repairing and selling footwear. His round on Saturday mornings saw him delivering shoes that were ordered the week before. He let families pay weekly and collected their payments when they could afford it. Mr Walton's workshop was out in the back garden and he grew cacti in his greenhouse. Many parents bought their shoes from him, especially those with large families.

Children played in the road where the Walton family lived. Their back gardens have been developed for housing and this area is known as Cordwainer Gardens. They were named in memory of the family. The name is still used in the names of guilds, such as the "Cordwainers' Company".[325] This road now has new, late-twentieth and early twenty-first century stone-built houses. The last house in the terraced row, before Cordwainer Gardens, has an added extension porch. In the 1960s, Janek and Sylvia Czwortek lived at number 61 with their children, Carol and Stephen. Janek (Johnny) always enjoyed meeting his friends for 'a pint' over the road in the 'Black Horse' pub. Here he would meet up with Bob Butt and Mr Pridmore. In the 1930s, Mr Oliver

---

[324] "A Collection of Oundle Families", pp. 14-23.
[325] A shoemaker made new shoes from new leather. A cobbler repaired shoes. Traditionally, a cordwainer was a skilled craftsman who used fine goatskin leather. www.cordwainers.org

Walton (a motor and agricultural engineer and repairer) lived at number 61 with his wife, Olive. Alice Edwards lived with them.[326]

To confuse readers further, Mr Ebenezer Walton, senior, was also a boot-dealer and repairer. He and his wife, Sarah, lived at number 63. They had a daughter, Gertrude, who worked as a clerk of accounts and also was an ARP warden. Their family included Rebecca, Ebenezer (junior, known as 'Ebbie', who was also a boot repairer)[327] and Susan. Ebenezer Walton (junior) grew up and had three daughters: Frances,[328] Jackie and Vivien, who attended the primary school in the early 1960s. Mr 'Ebbie' Walton was (like his father) a traditional shoe-repairer and salesman.

Many people recall with fond memories that to late-1970s, the family when they lived in the middle-terrace house, opposite the pub. People could always buy their shoes 'on tick' (credit) from him. His shoe store was inside the house, which must have been very cramped with the hallway full of "nothing but shoe boxes". Mr Walton's brother had three sons, two of whom are still in Oundle. Their names were Brian, Derek and Adrian Walton. Currently, a gate leads to 'Cordwainer Gardens'. Beforehand, this was a gap between the houses (where the Czwortek and Walton families lived). The gap led to houses known as 'the Pits'.

The Pits were a group of old cottages (roughly in the position of the Prince William estate). It is worth noting that Number 1 'the Pits', backed onto the Walton's house. In 1936, Bertie Arthur Pridmore lived at number 1 and by 1939, Arnold Upex, who worked as a carpenter (aged 19) lived here. Mrs Betsy M. Pridmore was at number 2 in 1936. Number 3, 'The Pits', was Leonard Cottingham, who was an "armourer and weapon-trainer". His wife, Mildred, Trevor (a young baby) and two other people lived here. Mr John T. Fletton, a retired groundsman and his daughter, Gertrude, lived at number 4. At number 5 was Mr Ernest W. French and his wife, Annie. Mr James R. Gilbert, a doctor's servant, lived at number 6 with his wife, Olive, and their son, Michael in the

---

[326] The 1939 pre-war register.
[327] Oral history, Susan Wyles.
[328] Frances may have been named for her paternal grandmother, Frances Walton (née Blankenship).

410

1930s. At number 7 was Ted and Emily Ashby. Ted worked on the railways as an engineers' labourer. Mr R. James Hall and Annie (his wife) lived at number 8 with their son, Percy. Ruth Smith was an evacuee, who lived with them.[329] Mr Leslie Black recalled sitting with a dying man in the Pitts when the Sanatorium was full of flu victims. On the western corner of Cordwainer Gardens (63) is a pretty, restored cottage. In 2012, there was a dispute regarding the building of three detached houses adjacent to the cottage. The residents of the time believed the intended houses would infringe on their property and create traffic problems for the road.

Numbers 63 and 65 are listed as nineteenth-century, grade-II buildings. 63 and 65 were listed as grade-II buildings. Both are two-storey stone buildings. Number 63 has three windows (one down and two upstairs). In the 1930s, Ernest S. Clark (born in 1882), a painter and decorator, lived at 65 with his wife, Florence. Richard Murphy lived in this house in the 1960s (opposite the 'Black Horse' pub).

Mrs Christiana Binder, who was the wife of Henry Binder, lived at number 67 in 1937. In the early 1930s, Mr William Machin (a physical training instructor; A.P.T.S.) and his wife, Kathleen had lived here. Others lived in the same household, but are not listed in the register. Mr and Mrs Sidney Clark lived here in the 1960s.[330] (They had previously lived at number 23.) Number 69 is an early nineteenth-century, grade-II listed building. It is a two-storey, stone house with three stone-lintel windows and an original gabled porch. Mr Henry P. Butler (a builder's merchant manager In the 1930s) and his wife, Matilda, lived here with their son, Henry Ingham Butler. Lodging with them was George W. Brewster (who worked as an assistant school master) and Florence Cordurell (who was an assistant teacher). In 1994, Dr Hadfield and his family lived here. In 2009, the resident at number 69 requested that a detached dwelling could be built on their land. Finally, seven years later the plot (behind number 69) was sold and a new large detached house (69a) was built in 2016.

---

[329] 1939 register.

[330] These are Anne Gray's paternal grandparents as her real grandmother died in the Spanish 'Flu' (influenza virus) epidemic just after WWI and Mrs Clark was her step-granny.

Number 71 is "The Old Pottery" is down a private lane. This house was once a pair of seventeenth-century stone cottages that were remodelled over thirty years ago. At number 71 during the 1930s this was the home of Albert and Nellie Brinsley. Albert was a general farm worker who grew-up in Mill Lane.[331] The following five houses were built in the late eighteenth-century (they are odd numbers, 73 to 81). They are grade-II listed, two-storey stone cottages. Number 81 is an extended semi-detached and 85 is a detached house. At 73 was Mrs Caroline Clarke. She was an elderly widow who lived alone. In the 1800s number 73 was the "Three Horseshoes" pub. Herbert Pailing and his wife, Elsie lived at number 75. (Herbert was a stationer's assistant.) In 1937, Miss Smith is listed as living with them.

Also in the 1800s, a widower named Charles Smith (who worked as a market porter) lived next-door (number 77) with his daughter, Daisy. Living with them was Mr Arthur Smith. He was a retired farmer. At 79, Miss Mary Killingsworth lived in a cottage named 'Rivendell'. Living at number 81, 'Jasmine Cottage' were George Bent (a retired night-watchman) and his wife, Mary. Albert E. Bennett lived in the semi-detached, pre-war council houses war. Albert was described as an Urban District Council "road man". He was single and lived at number 83 with his younger siblings, Ernest and Edith. Ernest was also a bachelor. He worked as an auxiliary postman. Their sister Edith (who was described as 'incapacitated') lived with them.

Prior to the onset of WWII, Robert Spriggs and his wife, Agnes, lived at number 85 with their son, James. Robert was a "road-man" for Northamptonshire County Council. James worked as a P.A. Institution (workhouse) porter. At number 87 was a widow, Daisy Rogers, with her brother, Mr G.E. (Edward) Rogers. Edward worked in the town as a butcher's assistant.

Mr Gerald E.J. Lee lived at number 89. 'Gerry' (as he was known) was born in 1917. Both of his parents shared the same surname (Lee) before they married (just prior to the First World War). Gerry was described in the 1939 register as "a travelling theatrical entertainer". He lived with his brother, Lincoln H.V. Lee, who worked as a travelling musician (born in 1915) and Marjorie ('Mona') Lee, who was a

---

[331] A Collection of Oundle families', pp. 48-51.

travelling actress. She was born in 1919. In 1942 Gerald married Miss Ellen Harvey.[332] 'Captain' Harvey (Gerald's father-in-law) annually travelled with his two daughters and their big cats (mainly lions and cheetah) on tour to the London Palladium, the Hippodrome and other renowned stage events. See section in this book for more information.

At number 91 was Gladys Rawlings. She was born in 1905 and worked as an actress, but in 1939 she was listed in the register as "an unpaid domestic". There were five lodgers also in the same house, including Mr John T. Rawlings. Next-door at 93, there lived William Pheasant, Phoebe (his wife) and their family. William (known as Bill) was a Church caretaker. Their son William (junior), was a cowman. Also in the same abode lived a general farm labourer, Ernest A. Limmage. After the war, this became the home of Angela Taney's family.

Residents in pre-war years were as follow: at number 97, was Hannah Mears. She worked as a char woman. She lived here with her daughter, Florence. She subsequently married Mr Baker. Next-door, at 99, were Charles and Caroline Coleman (both listed as 'incapacitated'), who lived with several lodgers. Henry and Beatrice Smith were two of them. Henry was a road-worker and Beatrice worked as a 'char woman' (cleaner). Another lodger was Martha Perrett. By the 1960s, Henry and Beatrice Smith, lived here by themselves. Number 95 was the home of Annie Jacob, who lived with her son, Frank Jacob.

Number 101 was the home of Thomas Clarke, his wife, Mary, and their family. He was known as a "pig man". More than likely he worked on a local farm looking after the swine. Living next door (in 103) were William Fletton (who was a council labourer), his wife, Mary and their daughter, Violet (who worked in retail sales). In 1937, George H. Durrant lived here. He was born in 1918. Next-door (in 105) Thomas Pridmore (a general labourer) and his wife, Agnes, lived with their sons, Thomas (who was born in 1926) and their younger child, Bert. During the war years they also had Peter Neal living with them. He was a ten year-old evacuee. He was only one year younger than Thomas (junior). At number 107 there was George E. Harrodyne[333] (a council labourer).

---

[332] Sharon Cottingham, personal testimony.
[333] At times written as 'Harradine', the name is from a Northants village, Harrrowden.

He lived with his wife, Beatrice, and their children, Dorothy (aged 5) and Herbert (aged 4).

A widow, Eliza Rawson (née Martin) lived at 109, with her daughters Margaret and Cynthia. They first lived in Victoria Yard before moving to Benefield Road. Eliza's daughters were: Margaret Iliffe (née Martin; mother of Daphne Elizabeth ['Betty'] Iliffe[334]), Fanny, Annie, Bertha, Hilda, and Cynthia (who married Jack Bryce and lived in Gordon Road). Margaret was born in 1893. She worked as a Ward-Maid in the P.A. institution (the workhouse, otherwise known as the 'Spike'[335]). There was also a son, Peter Martin. (Eliza may have married twice as Peter was a 'Martin'.) Also living in the household was Nelly Marshall, a sewing maid. The family moved to the end of Benefield Road in 1930. Betty's children, Di, Sue and Neil have lived in this road for much of their lives.

At 111, George Baxter was a "jobbing builder for repairs and demolition" who often worked for the council. He lived with his wife, Fanny (née Martin, who was Margaret's sister from 109, next-door) after they moved from Victoria Yard in the 1930s. Also at this address were Doreen O'Neary (born 1925; who later married into the Martin family) and Eileen, an evacuee from Middlesex.

At house number 113 there were Mr Robert Edward (Bob) Butt and his wife, Eliza (née Jacobs). Eliza usually wore a 'hessian apron' as she worked as a mortician, preparing and laying out.[336] Numbers 95 and 97 are late nineteenth-century semi-detached houses. From here on, all of the houses to number 113 are the same age and type. The only exception to this is number 115, which is a large detached house that was built in the early 2000s.

Heron's Wood Close is a separate, short, cul-de-sac road leading to the north from the Benefield Road. This Close was built in 2008. It originally was just land, a house and orchard. The wood behind the houses was

---

[334] Betty Iliffe (born 1930), wed Cyril Wyles. Di, Sue and Neil are their children.
[335] "The Spike" by George Orwell (1931) details a night in a workhouse ward, as he posed as a vagrant (a social experiment for his writing). Published by Adelphi, 1931. Republished as "Down and out in Paris and London", Penguin Books, 1933.
[336] Oral history, Di and Sue Wyles. See also section: 'War and Peace' (Arthur Ball's Memories of Robert Edward Butt).

planted in 1965, by Oundle School. Sue and Diane Wyles recall seeing the trees being planted. The Close and 'woodland' property overlooks fields. The woodland was planted in the 1960s and contain a cairn memorial for Lieutenant John Heron Rogers. John was an ex-Oundle School student (1929-1933) who was died during the war (1941).

When Percy Arnett was aged eight or nine, he went for a walk with his friend, Clifford Holmes, "over the fields and up to Biggin, but we somehow got lost and we ended up at the 'Willards' in Glapthorn Road" (now a doctor's house). He said, "We'd never been there before and had to ask directions to get home again. It was amazing that that we ever got that far!"[337]

Continuing along the Benefield Road beyond the town limits are Biggin Grange and the Grange Farm. Biggin Hall and its associated lands are just beyond the Oundle boundary sign. The land originated as a monastic farmstead, but the hall dates to the sixteenth century. The Manor at Biggin close to Benefield Castle. The castle was a thirteenth-century stone ringwork, timber fortress that replaced a fortified Norman manor house. It is thought to have been a fort that was built during the anarchy of King Stephen's reign (1138–44). In 1208 King John seized it for debts. In 1264, while Henry III was a prisoner, he issued an order to the knights living in Benefield Castle (noting that peace had been made between the king and his barons) that they were not to leave the castle or "do any ill" nearby. In 1265 the men from the castle plundered the Biggin Manor-house, crossed the river into Oundle and took a number of cattle. The Oundle men retaliated and recovered much of the herd. Shortly thereafter the castle was dismantled. By 1300 only the site remained with a moated-platform just west of the church.

Biggin Hall is the family home of the Watts-Russell family who have close historic bonds with Oundle. Jesse Watts-Russell was born in Oundle (1786-1875) and married in 1810, at the age of twenty-three. His wife, Mary, was born around 1784 in Oundle. They had one son, Jesse David Watts-Russell. He married Mary Neville Wright in 1835. Mary came from Benefield and was two years younger than Jesse. They

---

[337] Oral history, Percy Arnett.

had one daughter, Josephine Watts-Russell (later Mrs Birch). The family still reside in the Hall.[338]

Their descendant, Ivo Watts-Russell went to Oundle School, then Kettering Technical College. In the 1980s, Ivo formed the 4AD record label. Elusive though he is, his aesthetic instincts were creative. He has lived a reclusive life in Santa Fe, New Mexico in the United States of America since 1994.

Benefield Road (south side, Binders' Row to the Golf Club)

Binder's Row was a terrace of houses that caused quite a stir when they burned down in the 1960s. The row was named for the family who lived there. John Coleman Binder was born in 1863, the youngest of nine children. He grew-up and took on his father's shop in Benefield Road. He married when he was 38 and lived with his wife, Louisa Clara (née Middleton) at 8 Stoke Hill in their later years. He was 51 years old when war broke out in 1914 and kept a diary of events. He died in 1933 (aged 70) and Louisa in 1944 (aged 88). Newer houses have replaced the ancient houses that burned down in the 1960s. Benefield road, proper, started over the road from Milton Road.

Mrs Sarah J. Askham lived at number 2. She shared her house with Winifred Hiscock. At number 4 was Marcus Fox.[339] He worked as a solicitors' clerk (in 1901). By 1939 he was the clerk to the registrar of births, marriages and deaths. A builder's foreman, Mr James Morrison lived at number 6 with his wife, Jane. By the late-1030s they were aged in their sixties. The houses that followed were 'related' in more than one sense, as the Spriggs' family were all relations. In 1901 Percival "Frederick" Spriggs lived at number 8. He was "a car man" who lived with his wife, Alice, and their children, Malcolm and Carole. Later, Fred Carter lived here (by 1937). In 1901 Harriett Spriggs (a widow) lived at number 10 with her daughter, Ivy. Harriet stayed with her mother until she was joined in matrimony. Mr John T. Spriggs and his wife, Annie, lived at number 12. Percival (from number 8) was the son of John (at

---

[338] A 'grange' is defined as a country house with a farm granary barn. Medieval Latin 'granica' (villa) 'grain house or farm'.

[339] See "A Collection of Oundle Families", pp. 112-119.

12) and the grandson of Harriet and her late husband, Thomas Spriggs (at 10).

In 1936, Mrs Emma Roughton lived at 14. By 1939, William and Mildred Carter lived at this address. They lived with their one year old son, Michael. Bill worked as a master baker. Mr Frederick George Dolby ("George") was a general farm labourer. He lived at number 16 with his wife, Joyce, and their son, Peter ("James Peter") who was born in 1936.

Living at number 18 were Charles and Emily Clarke with their son, Percy. Percy was a brick layer's apprentice. At number 20 and living next to their son (Charles, at number 18) were Joseph Clarke and his wife, Mary. Joseph was a general labourer. The couple lived with their unmarried sons, Percy (a 'coal hawker') and George. At 20a were John and Olive Youngs. John worked on the maintenance staff at Oundle School. Prior to 1939, he was a 'fitting' instructor. They lived with their daughters, Elizabeth (born in 1900; married Mr Ward) and Valerie (born in 1929).

South of the Benefield Road and Milton Road junction are 'Peacock Heights' (development on the old Francis and Marshall's garage site). The garage was demolished in the early 1970s. These town-houses were built since 2000. Next-door is 20c, a new, detached house that meets garden of 22. Number 22 is the detached house where Bernard Roworth Turner lived with his wife, Maud. Dr Ivor Spurrell and his brother came to live with their 'Uncle Bernard' while recovering from illness and stayed.[340] Bernard was a renowned surgeon and medical author. He co-authored "Day books of a country practice, Oundle, Northants", by Doctors George W.B. Calcott, Edward Somerset and Bernard R. Turner (1893-1916), which is retained at the Royal College of Physicians, London. Bernard died in 1957, aged eighty-five. His large house is suitably named 'Turners'.

After 'Turners' there are Council rented allotments between the houses. In 1934, two allotment huts caught fire and Mr Coles and Bill Brinsley lost their tools and huts! Percy Arnett remembered that "there was the Carter's grocery shop at 24 Benefield Road" when he

---

[340] See Memories by Andrew Spurrell in this volume.

was a child. "It was the first building after the allotments and I remember the day they closed and sold off all the sweets cheaply". This old shop (24) is stone-built and dates to the early-nineteenth-century. It served as the business and home of Mrs E. Carter, who was a grocer in the late-1930s until it had a shop fire. Thereafter it only served as a dwelling. At 26 lived Harold Prior (a bricklayer), his wife, Edith, and their family. Next-door (28), James Dolby was a vegetable gardener. He lived with his wife, Kathleen. Miss Frances Child lived with them, until she married Mr Wilmott. Number 30 was the home of Mr John T. Bell. Slightly later, Ernest Ely and his wife, Annie lived here. Ernest was a motor-driver at the sports ground.

Living in the group of council house: (at 32) were Florence Richards (a dressmaker) and her sister, Jessie Richards (who acted as housekeeper). At number 34 were Edith and Harold Bamford and their family. Harold was a corn-dealer manager and special constable. Numbers 24 to 34 are stone-terrace houses and 32 to 38 are a group of two-storey terraced-houses. Jack Richardson lived at number 36. In the 1930s he was a local railway clerk. During the war years he was a member of the air observer corps. Jack lived with his wife, Gladys, who was in the women's voluntary service. Peter Richardson, their son (born in 1920) joined the RAF. They lived together with three other members of the family. Later, Wilfred and Barbara Welsh (née Shrive) family lived at 36 Benefield Road. They lived here with their children, Alan, Judith and David.

In 1937, Leonard Wilfred Bird lived at number 38. He was born in 1905. He lived here with his wife, Miriam (née Horn). They married in 1933. Later, William and Rose Upchurch lived here (38). William was a school caretaker. At number 40 (prior to 1936) Kenneth J. Hollowell lived here. Kenneth was born in Peterborough in 1909 and died in Northampton in 1973. Suitably, the middle of his life was spent in between those two locations: Oundle. Later, Harold (a carpenter and joiner) and Sarah Mowbray were in this house. Also living in the household was Thomas Dyson, a lodger, who prospered as a school-master. At number 42 was John Monk (who was born in Stamford in 1882). He lived here in the early 1930s. It then became the home of James and Edith Titman and their son, Leslie. James was a school porter. Leslie was a naval inspector. 'Les' later married and taught woodwork at the Secondary Modern School. Number 44 was the home of Dorothy and Cyril Elwood. Cyril was in the RAF (Volunteer Reserve). At 46, were Muriel and Richard Abel. In number 48 was Ada Beeham, who lived on her own (she was aged in her fifties in the late 1930s). At number 50 was the elderly Mrs Harriett Gregory (aged 88). Number 52 was the "Black Horse" and Mrs Elsie Clarkson was the licensee. Also living here was Kate Gallimore (who was born in 1904). 'Sunningdale' (52b) was the home of Mr Harold Wallis. (He was born in 1911 and married Eleanor Hudson in 1937.)

Numbers 40 and 42 form a 'semi-detached' building. Like the houses either side, these have a white rendering. The following similar style, two-storey buildings form a group of five dwellings. Benjamin Smith lived at 'Wyncote Cottage'. This was a separate dwelling alongside the "Black Horse" (still classed as 52). Benjamin was a joiner, who lived with his housewife wife, Gladice. Arthur Clarkson and his wife, Elsie, kept the 'Black Horse Inn' public house at number 52 in the 1960s and 1970s. In spite of its original historic grade-II listing, this building has sadly been demolished. New houses were built on the site in the early 2000s. There are six mews houses on the site that is aptly named 'Black Horse Court'. The three-storey, stone town-houses (built in 2004) have an arch to the courtyard parking within. Next-door is "Red Kite Lodge". At 52a is a white bungalow. James Cherry was a retired police sergeant, who lived in the bungalow with his wife Edith and their son, Ronald. Ronald was a carpenter and joiner. The house has newer buildings in what would have been its rear garden. 52b is a detached house that was constructed on part of the old 'Black Horse' property. Clifton Drive was built in the early 1980s. Its name celebrates the diarist John Clifton (1728-1784).[341] 52c was the home of Virginia and David Francis. David was the son of Dick, the owner of the nearby garage (see earlier in this section). Next-door is a white house, named 'Little Gables'.

During the late-1930s, Wilfred Blackwell lived with his wife, Margery and their family lived at 54. It was later the home of Mrs Bradshaw. Tom ('George') and Joan ('Ruth') Smart lived at 54. They lived with their daughter, Elizabeth, who attended the local primary school in the 1960s. Their house was purchased by Stuart Forscutt and his family in

---

[341] For more information, his diaries are in Northamptonshire Record Office.

1999. Number 54 was since merged with 56. At 56 were Ursula and Herbert Peploe (a carpenter) and their son, Bernard (who worked as a printer in the 1930s). Later, Florrie Taney lived here with her daughter, Angela (until 1982). In number 58 were William and Elizabeth Bell. William worked as the postman.[342] Subsequently, Harry and Nora Eillingsworth lived here in the 1960's, with their two sons, Arthur and Alan. Number 60 was the home of house painter, Charles Cunnington. He lived with Agnes, his wife and their children.[343] This red-brick building is part of the terraced row (54-62; four dwellings). In the 1930s Eric Garratt and his wife, Edith, lived at 62. Eric was a "brewery maltster and lorry driver". After the Garratt's moved, Christopher and Winifred Maggie Wills (née Curtis; who were married in late 1933) lived here with their family. They were stalwarts of the Church. Their son, David (now in his eighties) and his wife, Sheila (née Martin) live in the house where his father was born in early 1906. It has been extended into part of next door over the years, but is largely the same property. David is proud of his home, its history and its lovely garden. At number 64, Herbert Gee (born 1877) lived alone. He worked as the railway crossing-keeper. (Number 64 has been demolished, but gates still lead to the rear of the former houses numbered 64 and 66.) Number 66 was empty in the late-1930s. There is a coach-entrance halfway along the building. Number 68 is the last house before the new Pexley Court expansion. Percy Clarke (1878-1948) lived at number 68 with Jessie (born 1890), Hilda (1908) and Daphne M. Clarke (1930). Percy was as a plumber and decorator. There were two other people in the household whose names are not recorded. (Later, Daphne wed Mr Gordge [sic.] and Hilda married Mr Small). John and Blanche Smith lived at number 70 with their children, Una (born 1920; later Mrs Robinson) and Philip (1927). John worked as a joiner and carpenter.

Number 72 is a bungalow, opposite Pexley Court junction. Houses 86, 88 and 92 are classed as 'old-build' flats or maisonettes. From here, all of the houses are modern. Wakerley Close and the town limit beyond. The last bungalow was demolished for the new estate (Lytham Park). Joyce and John Robinson lived here. Clifton Drive, Pexley Court and Lytham Park, are on the south-side of the road.

---

[342] See "A Collection of Oundle Families", pp. 38-41.
[343] Ibid. pp. 91-94.

Pexley Court was built around 1998, using the name of a cow-pasture field between Oundle and Biggin Hall. It ran through Pexley Wood to the north and was noted in the Austell survey (1565). Wheat was grown in the field (1778) and a "highway robbery" took place in 1779.[344] The Pexley fields may also be haunted! Locals note night-time noises heard and "uniformed men". Are these soldiers Roundheads and Cavaliers (remnants from civil war of the 1600s)? Finally, the name Lytham is in error as it was meant to be "Latham" Park.[345] The road, built in 2009, honours Parson Latham, despite the spelling! All of the new roads are cul-de-sacs.

Oundle Golf Club is a member's-owned golf club founded in 1893. The course is eighteen holes and has a lounge bar purveying full meals, snacks and a range of drinks. The Club presented the NGU County Championships in 2007 and, in 2015, the first County Championships of the Northamptonshire Golf Limited; an association of male and female golf clubs from Northamptonshire.[346] Harley Way is a new area of development that leads alongside the Golf course. It is on the road leading to Lyveden Manor (a country house on a mediæval site).

Milton Road and the Old Primary School

Originally this part of the road was named North Back Way (in the 1885 survey). The houses in Milton Road were developed since the 1880s. There were two next to the Church National School and the infant school, St. Anne's in the Grove. The discrete housing area off Milton Road was built around 1995. It has approximately seven dwellings and is named St. Anne's Court after the small school that was on the corner of Benefield Road and 'Milton Lane'. (Oundle museum has the St. Anne's in the Grove marker-stone.) The houses opposite the old Primary School were built in the 1890s. In the 1900s a block of four houses were built.

By the late-1930s most of the properties in Milton Road belonged to Oundle School. Mr F.G. Stretton lived at number 1. At number 3 was 'Jim' Graham. At number 5 was Mr Samuel G. Squire, M.A. He was the

---

[344] Ioan Thomas.
[345] Information from David Wills.
[346] www.oundlegolfclub.com

master at St. Anthony House. In 1928, Samuel was married in Oundle church to Miss Rita F. LeGrand-Jacob.

Over the road (on the north side) there were further families living in school properties. Number 2 was the home of Mr John M. Siddons, who was an engineer. Oundle School master, W.G. Walker lived at number 4, with fellow teacher, William Llowarch, at number 6. (Both held Master's degrees.) The Methodist minister, Reverend J.E. Matthews lived at 8. Number 10 was the home of Mr Felix T. Allen (who died in Oundle in 1940, aged 54). In charge of Sidney and Grafton Houses were two masters, Mr Bernard Vickers Kingham (who died in 1962 aged 73) and Mr A.C. Cutliffe, respectively. At 14, Laxton and Crosby Houses were Mr I. Hepburn, M.A. and Mr W.G. Walker, M.A.[347] Mr John Miller Siddons (who was born in Oundle in 1858) lived in at number 2 for an extended period. He worked for the school as an engineer. Robin and Freda Rowe lived with their family in the end house (by the chapel grounds) in the 1960s. Their neighbours were Lucy and Cornelius (known as Neil) Moynehan and their children, Peter, Rosemary and David. Neil taught in the Blackpot Lane foundry. The School Languages Department stands at the junction.

On the south side of Milton Road, after gate from the Great Hall garden (Oundle School), are Drumming Well Lane and the former site of St. Peter's C. of E. Primary School. Its logo was the crossed keys of St. Peter. The school is heavily associated with the parish church: St. Peter's Church of England. The school dates to 1842, a time when there were three primary schools in Oundle. Known as the "National" church school it collected fees for attendance. There were separate entrances for boys and girls. In 1876 the Reverend Hopkins ran the school. After the end of the First World War, the children were given a day of 'Armistice holiday' from school to celebrate the formal declaration of peace on 24th October 1919.[348]

In 1932, John Barton retired and Mrs Mabel Perring was employed as the headmistress. She served as such for many years and was aware of her pupils welfare needs. As alluded to earlier in this book, she pre-

---

347 Directory information.
348 The peace Treaty of Versailles formally ended WWI. It was signed by Germany and the Allied Powers on 28th June 1919.

arranged for a dentist and a nurse to visit and check all of the children. The school gained a radiogram. This allowed children access broadcast news. The school was refurbished in 1937 and two years later, was inundated with over a hundred-and- forty evacuee children, who were billeted around the town. By 1942 each class suddenly held up to sixty-eight children!

Mr Venner was taken on as Head in 1950. He introduced a 'house system', with patron saints of UK as their house names. An extra classroom was built in 1956, yet the toilets remained in the playground! The school gained some land from next-door that gave pupils more playground space, until it was developed into a reception foyer and offices in the late-1960s. In 1957, Alan Denley became the Headmaster and he selected a Head girl and boy (for the first time); Gillian Fellowes and Roger Lefort. Shoe inspections began and hand-washing was a must. Alan Denley appointed his neighbour, Diana Rivett, as the school secretary. In 1964 the old raised verandah leading to the classrooms was enclosed. Like other properties in Oundle, it was no surprise when a brick-lined well (dating to the early 1800s) was suddenly discovered in the front of the school, sourced by underground aquifers. The school finally closed in 2016 (when Northamptonshire middle-schooling ceased). The Primary school moved into the Middle School property on Cotterstock Road. The school had a farewell open-day in May 2016.[349] Records and photographs were displayed for ex-pupils and townsfolk to see. It was a day to remember.

As Oundle School advanced, Headmaster Frederick William Sanderson wanted to provide housing for his growing number of staff. In late 1919 and early 1920 he bought two villas in Glapthorn Road and two houses in Milton Road. The houses were all transferred to the Grocers Company the following year, together with a workman's cottage Inkerman Yard. Sanderson also purchased 'Avondale'. Its residents (in 1920) were Mr. and Mrs. Marshall. They remained in the house after its purchase as Sanderson was content to wait until they were ready to move.

---

[349] With thanks to the Denley family and Oundle Primary School for information.

The British School on Milton Road was also acquired by Oundle School. The National Archives hold the British School records and accounts (1843-1903) to the date when it eventually closed. Sanderson's (unfulfilled) notion was to transfer the Music classes to the British School building (as it would to allow a master to live in the 'music room' house in Milton Road). In May 1920 Sanderson wanted to buy the town cricket ground. In January 1921 he purchased the 'Local Close' (now 'Home Close'). The Foundry was erected in a corner of Local Close.[350] The town Cricket Club remains on Milton Road and is on the corner, opposite to Sydney and Grafton, Laxton and Crosby School Houses, swimming pool and sports facilities.

GLAPTHORN ROAD

Glapthorn Road currently has one-hundred and fifteen residences along its length; with an average value of £491,250, compared to an average property value of £365,365 for the rest of Oundle, denoting that this is a fine road to live in. Most of the houses are large with decent gardens, making Glapthorn Road the eligible to live in and showing a certain level of prosperity.[351] Ioan Thomas holds that in 1885 there were just eight Glapthorn Road houses (from Milton Road to Cotterstock Road, by the 'George' Inn).[352] Most of these dwellings were in a cluster near to the windmill.

Glapthorn Road (east side, travelling north)

On the corner of Blackpot Lane, there is an Anderson shelter dating to the WWII. Bevil Allen recalls pre-war times in Laxton School, when he was a "day boy" who helped to dig the air-raid shelter in front of the building at the corner of Blackpot Lane and Glapthorn Road (the new construction was renamed 'Sci-Tec' in 2016). Boys dug in the "hottest of weather and the lower they dug the harder it got" (as they then had to haul the soil up to the top in a bucket). This was not the preferred shelter for boys in the Laxton, as Bramston House garden had a shelter was over the road from the Church yard and cloisters. In 1941, David M. Lawes of Laxton Grammar School spoke about finance at a talk entitled "Money Talks. Speak up Oundle". This was then designated

---

[350] F.W. Sanderson.
[351] Glapthorn Road is often documented with an 'e' at its end (before 1900).
[352] With kind permission of Ioan Thomas, collected "Oundle Street Names".

the slogan for "Oundle War Weapons Week". It came from a suggestion by Lawes, but was the winning title from a competition judged by Mrs B.R. (Emma) Turner. Andrew Spurrell has a photograph in his album of three small children in pith helmets, each carrying a banner reading "Give a Bob". This was for weapons week. Whether this made any difference to the war effort in Oundle is not known. David Wills recalls the "war weeks", when clothes and foodstuffs were collected to send to the the armed forces. The war ended when Bevil was seventeen. He heard that a group of school boys stole a bus, which they took on a round-trip to Peterborough and back. He said that there was "exuberance as the end of war was declared". Bevil also remarked that all "pubs were full of people celebrating together, no matter who they were and not caring if they knew each other or not". He went on to say that "everyone joined in together, towns-people, boys and teachers. "No-one complained or caused any trouble about who was doing what. It was like a united sigh of relief that the war had ended."

By the old dug-out shelter at the south-eastern corner of Glapthorn Road, there is a new, state of the art, science and technology building and nearby, is the Patrick Engineering Centre. They were built in 2016 on the site of the old Oundle School Foundry and Workshops. This is where boys could cast items in aluminium or brass. In the 1940s, the School blacksmith's shop was here (as the school had owned a farm and horses). The current building overlooks the Home Close, a wonderful, green field used for sports. It is full of daffodils in the spring and has a wild-flower bank by the 'run-off' water from the roof of the Sci-Tec building. The field is used by Oundle School on sporting occasions and for parking on school 'speech' and open days. It has also been used when Oundle School terms had ended (for fetes and the old town Carnivals). The pitch is an aesthetically pleasing sight with so much of Oundle being redeveloped for housing.

Nearby, the green, copper roof-tops of Sanderson and Dryden houses and can be seen from the road. Sanderson House was built in 1938 and is named after the Headmaster, Frederick W. Sanderson (who was here from 1901 to 1922). Sanderson was an educational reformer, who died in Oundle at the age of sixty-five, whilst serving as the Head of the School. Dryden is situated overlooking Home Close and the science building. It was also built in 1938 and takes its name from the local seventeenth-century poet, John Dryden (who was born in nearby Aldwincle). In the late-1930s Mr H. Cauldwell was the Housemaster at Dryden House, concurrent with William G. Walker the Sanderson Housemaster. 'The Ramblers' at 2 Glapthorn Road is a large Victorian house. During the 1930s this was the home of William Rippiner. He was a teacher and the secretary of the Oundle Friendly Society, Oddfellows branch.[353] He lived here with his wife, Annie. (Flora Howe was the Rippiner's live-in housekeeper.) Hetty Bell recalls going to his house to take the "the payment money" for their family's health subscriptions. The people of Oundle paid into "Sick and Dividing Clubs" as an insurance for illnesses. Hetty said that at the time she was not sure what the money was for, but realises now that it was payment for "hospital insurance". As Hetty had to have an operation (in Northampton) it was a very sensible expense.

Number 4 was the home of Evelyn and Robert Upcott. Robert was a modern-languages school-master, besides as a Territorial Army lieutenant at Oundle School. Number 4 is a detached house with bay windows. It is distinctively different from its neighbour. 4a and 4b are detached houses near to a public footpath to Millfields. The 'Mytton' fresh meat business is run from 4a. The family deliver to local butchers and markets.

Set along a drive, just off the Glapthorn Road is the Mackey's house. This site once held a large house, gardens, an orchard and a windmill. Oundle 'Tower Mill' was a limestone-building from the late-1600s and early 1700s. In 1800, Richard Ragsdell owned the windmill and fields off Glapthorn Road. There were a few houses scattered nearby, but not many. A little later, miller, Robert Callow and his family owned and ran the mill (circa 1830). His family also owned and worked a mill at Castor. In Oundle, the four sails that worked the mill were detached in 1908, but corn-grinding continued with the use of a "gas-engine". This was sustained until the mid-1930s (and is remembered by older residents). In the 1950s, the adjacent field was farmed by the Oundle School "Young Farmer's Club" under the auspices of William Cartwright (a language teacher).

---

[353] See section in: "A collection of Oundle Families", by Margaret Brewster.

The windmill ceased grinding before the Second World War, when parts and equipment were taken away as scrap-metal. It was then allowed to "fall into a sorry and dilapidated state". In 1955, Mr Crawley bought land from New House. For a short time, Mr and Mrs 'Crump' Crawley lived in it and ran a motorcycle repair shop. In 1964, 'Crump' had the mill demolished as his wife wanted to live in a "proper house". Once the debris was cleared away, a new bungalow was built with "nice fitted cabinets in the kitchen". Family friends helped with the task.[354] The house and land was sold to the Mackley family in 1966. Gwendoline (née Little) and Brian married in early 1957 and lived with their daughter, Nicola, who was born in 1968. The house was renovated and for many years Brian Mackley repaired cars in his small, friendly, repair garage on the land. The current buildings date to the late-1960s and early 1970s.

Living at number 6 were Marion and William Chown. William was a master-grocer and provisions merchant. The couple lived with their children, Kathleen and John. Houses 6 and 6a are south-facing. They have gardens to their frontages (the south side). A windowless (side) wall runs parallel to the road. In the 1930s, number 8[355] was the home of Sidney and Fannie Pargeter (née Richards). They married when she was just fourteen and he was thirty. (Sidney died in 1967, aged 74.) Their daughter, Dorothy, lived with them until her marriage to Jack Davey (1952). Sidney worked as a local government sanitary inspector. Their house is set in its own garden, bordering that of (6) Mill House. It was later the home of Mr Brian Mackley and their family. Brian Mackey ran his own small, private garage. In 2009, Brian extended the house. A shared-drive to the main road runs along the south face of both houses, parallel to the road. There is also a Council-maintained walk (cut-through) that leads to the newer Millfields houses.

Until this century, 8a had decorative wrought-iron peacocks, butterflies and a windmill on its gates. These were black and painted with local images (peacocks and butterflies from nearby Ashton Wold) and a windmill image from next-door. It was formerly the home of Miss Marriot, then the house belonged to Vic and Dora Thorington (from the 1960s to the millennium). On their demise the property was sold.

---

[354] Family of Sue Crick (née Crawley).
[355] This building has had a recent loft conversion.

The bungalow and gates were demolished and a large, three-storey building built in its place. The new house is made of stone. 8a is overlooked by the older house to the right (8). Old number 10 was where widower, Edward Perkins lived in the 1930s. He worked as an agricultural-implement machinery-agent. Edward lived with his daughter, Mary. She was a preparatory school music teacher. Nearby, 10 and 10a are new, as is 10c 'Burgage House'. Numbers 12 and 14 are semi-detached, pre-war, art-deco style houses. In the 1930s, at 12 'Fairholm' (now 'Bramley'), there lived Richard Yeld. He was a retired, Indian-carpet manufacturer. He served as a Major in the Indian Army Reserve and his household was quite extensive. He lived with his wife, Mrs Mary W. Yeld. Phyllis Martin (born in 1908) was their live-in housekeeper. Phyllis resided in the Yeld household with her daughters, Rosemary (born in 1935) and Ann (1938). Also living at this address, there was Stella Hayward, a children's nurse. Valentine Baldwin also lived and worked here as a domestic servant. 12a was the home of George Osborn and his wife, Dorothy. He worked as a power house engineer. At 12a during the late-1930s was Mr B.C. Smith.

Also in the pre-war years, 12b was the home of Leslie Redhead. He was a Master bread, cake-maker and confectioner. He also sold wines and spirits. Leslie ran a cake shop in West Street with his mother. (Their name still appears on the doorstep tiles of the Bridal shop.) His wife, Olive, and daughter, Marie Gillian Redhead lived above the shop. At 12c, Miss Amy Julia Pashler was a retired lady living 'by private means', who continued to reside here after her mother, Mrs T. Pashler died. A companion, Theodora Bird, lived with her. At 12d was the home of Mr George Rippiner. He was a retired school master and Headmaster. He became the Head after his brother, Joseph (who lived at number 2), retired as the Head of the Council School. His wife, Lavinia, lived with him, alongside their daughter, Dorothy. (She was also a teacher.) 12e was the home of William and Hetty Montgomery. He worked as a cricket coach with the school. At 12f, lived Esmonde and Philip G. Cotton (born in 1900). Philip worked as a boot and shoe-maker, repairer and shop-keeper in the Market Place. He was also a special constable in the Observer Corps.[356] A recently modernised bungalow

---

[356] "A collection of Oundle families", pp. 86-90.

stands at corner of New Road. (Its garden and garage access New Road.)

On the northern side of the New Road junction are 14 and 16 (late Victorian buildings). In 14, were James Champion, a bank official (in the ARP ambulance corps) and his wife, Alice (who was in the women's voluntary service). Phyllis Parkinson lived with them. The house on the corner of New Road is dated to 1865. George Manning (1885-1965) lived here. He was a plumber and member of the Gilbert and Sullivan Operatic Society. Subsequently, the Clark family lived here in the 1960s. Their daughter, Gillian, attended the local schools. She was in the PWS hockey team, tutored by Miss Chamberlain, with other girls from her year. She is a local hairdresser.

Frederick Jackson, a Master and mathematician at Oundle School, lived at number 16 with his wife, Jessie. She was a school-mistress at Laxton Grammar School teaching the 'day boys' from the town. Jessie was a member of the St. John's Ambulance Brigade. Next-door, at 18 lived Emma Chew. She lived "by private means" and died in 1946 (in her eighties). Her daughter, Crystabel Lorinne, lived with her. (Crystabel married Eric Turnill in 1952). Doris Swift and Mary Aldred also lived at this address in the 1930s. They were both teachers.

'The Wic' (number 18) is an updated Victorian creeper-clad, stone, L-shaped house. In contrast, 18a "Waimera" is a newer red-brick construction. Mr Herbert Palmer lived at number 20 during the war years. He taught Chemistry at Oundle School. He was also an Air-Raid Warden and a Northants County Constable. His wife, Emily, was also in the ARP. She worked in the Reports Centre. Also living in the house was Eva Cochrane. Eva was an elementary-school teacher.

Here I add, as a small aside, a personal anecdote from the day when I visited the Abingdon museum in Northampton with my mother and family friend, Edwina Halverson. Edwina was looking at a dummy in a display and said, "Look, it's a traffic warden". Mum (from the next room) heard and called out, "If it's war-time people on display, it's probably an ARP". Edwina, asked, "How can I tell?" Mum replied, "If he's got a whistle he's an air-raid warden and if he's got a notepad he's a traffic warden." and she was right. He had a whistle!

At 20, a three-storey, detached, Victorian building was the home of Mr H.C. Palmer, a Master at Oundle School. Numbers 22 and 24 are Victorian semi-detached "villas" named 'Florence' and 'Albert'. They were named after their neighbours (who were probably the builder and his wife): Albert and Florence Binder at 34a. 'Binder's Cottages' have coloured-brick patterns and clover-leaf shapes on their roof finials. At 22 there lived Mr Maurice Lakeman (a secondary school, mechanical engineering teacher). He was also an air-raid warden. His wife, Elizabeth was a housewife. Mr Frank Spragg lived at number 24. He was a school master and also a Captain in the Territorial Army. He was on the "general list" (as category B3, "deemed only suitable for sedentary work"), so had not been called for service in the pre-war years. His wife, Adeline, and their children lived with him. Mr Millin B. Selby lived in the detached Victorian house (26). Millin was a retired farmer who lived with his young wife, Jessie. Their lodgers were Hilda Marvell (a school teacher) and Robena Priestman (a widow).

Jocelyn Collier lived at 28 'Lambourne House' when she was in her forties. (Her late husband was Major Albert E. Collier.) Mr Horace W. Elsey lived at 'Cecil House', number 30. He was a widower in his fifties, who worked as a bank cashier. His housekeeper was Florence Taney. The house is red-brick with front and rear lawns. Kate and Archibald Chadwick lived at 32 (known in the pre-war years as 'Orchard House'). He was a school-master, aged in his fifties. At 34 in a small, red-brick bungalow, lived Harriett Rands. She was an "unpaid domestic". Harriett shared her house with Mary Curwain. 34a is a large house in its own grounds. It was formerly known as 'Coombe Brae'. Mrs Florence Binder (born in 1886) lived here. She had been married to Arthur H. Binder and for a time when they were first married, they lived with Arthur's parents (William and Mary Ann) in West Street. Before his retirement, Arthur had worked as a jeweller. He had died in 1936. Florence had retired six years earlier. During the war years, Annie Squire (born the same year as Florence) and Denis B. Squire were living with her.

Number 34 is a detached Victorian house with bricking and windows. This house has three others nearby (34a, b and c), built into spaces in the late-1900s. 36, 'Hill Crest' is a sizeable house. It was the home of William and Lucy Wood. William was a retired draper. 36b is set back from adjacent buildings and is a new mock-timbered house (built in 2003) with the name "The Sycamores". Mrs and Mr North lived at the large and impressive, 'Somerby House' (38) before the First World War. It was mentioned that number 38 had been the main house while 36 was "the house where the servants lived". In 1875 it was the final house in the road. From this house a dirt-track road led to Glapthorn.

Prior to the First World War number 38 was the home of John and Julia North. John was a retired butcher. In the same household was Doris Townsend. She worked as a 'companion and help'. She was a member of the Women's Voluntary Service. She lived with John and Julia in their large, semi-detached property (attached to and on the right of number 40). Number 40 was the home of Mrs 'Maud' Ault. She was an "unpaid domestic" housewife, born in 1878. She lived here alone after her husband, William H. Ault died (in 1932) at the age of fifty-seven. Much later, this became the home of the Watson family. They lived in number 40 from the 1960s until the early twenty-first century. This house stands on the corner of Springfield road. It was the home of John and Heather Watson. Heather was a homemaker and foster-carer. She and her somewhat recalcitrant husband raised their family of three girls, three boys and two adopted girls. The Watson children, Sue, Bridget, Alice, Robert, Charles and Patrick grew up in this house alongside Si and Lizzy (their adoptive sisters who required some help for their disabilities). She was very proud of her heritage and often talked about her own mother who had 'Romany in her blood'. Heather always raised money for charity, particularly the NAB (Northamptonshire Association for the Blind). Her adoptive daughter, Si, had lost her sight at a young age. Heather was a stalwart of the Polebrook Church, after having a disagreement with the vicar of the day at St. Peter's. He complained about the noises the young, disabled children made in church one day. She quoted, "Suffer the little children to come unto me and forbid them not: for of such is the kingdom of God" and "voted with her feet" by taking her family to Polebrook church where they were welcomed and had no such issues! Heather helped to run the Polebrook Brownie pack and was a local 'Avon' lady. She also assisted for a time at the PHAB club (a group for physically handicapped and able bodied people, which was held in Fletton House). Heather died in 2010 in Sue Ryder Care at Thorpe Hall Hospice.

To continue her memory, her grand-daughter and daughter-in-law are both named Heather.

Numbers 38 and 40 are large, Edwardian, three-storey family homes. They are semi-detached houses with encaustic patterned and quarry-tiled floors. The large garden to the rear of number 40 runs alongside Springfield Road. The zebra-crossing by the Springfield Road junction has new houses on the west side in the newly designated 'Lyvden' area. This site was developed on the old cricket fields around 2015. A name that echoes this is "Cricketers Way".

Number 42 is on the corner of Springfield Road. During the 1930s, Samuel Broadbelt lived in house 42 with his wife, Myrrah. He worked as a division road surveyor for the NCC and was a member of the Civil Defence Service De-Contamination, Rescue and Road Repair unit for the ARP. Mrs Enid Chew (née Kent) and her family (Elizabeth, Anne [now Massey], Cathryn and Kate) lived here during the years between the 1960s and 1990s. Elizabeth became a radio-therapist at Peterborough Hospital. In the 1990s, 'Value' cars were hired from here. During the 1930s Mr Ronald Kerr-Muir lived at 42a. He taught chemistry at Oundle School and was a Second Lieutenant in the Territorial Army. He lived with his wife, Margaret, who was a V.A.D. In the 1930s, their neighbours (at 44 Glapthorn Road) were Alec and Clara Wright. Alec worked as a dispenser and was in the Observer Corps. The Wright's lived with their family, Charlotte E.R. Curtis, Edith Richards and Alexander Richards. (Note that some family members were not listed in the register). Charlotte died in Peterborough in 1946, aged 84. Edith Richards (1905-1974) never married. Also living in this household in the pre-war years were Christopher and Winifred Wills. Their son, David Wills lived with his aunt (Mrs Clara Wright) while he was growing up. She ran a Christian Youth Club in her house. During the war years David would cross the road and play in the (spring) fields with his friends over the road from his aunt's house. He said that they liked to play in the derelict Victorian brick-works nearby. Although this does not sound particularly safe! David recalled that at the junction (just before the 'George' pub) there was a road block. The road had been narrowed to a vehicle's width to slow traffic entering and leaving town. It could be closed off with large (road-roller-like) concrete blocks. As a boy he would take his toy periscope to look over the barrier.

Frank Stokes was a widower who lived at 46. He worked in the accounts department as a 'collector' for the Brewery. His daughter, Monica married Mr Cheney. Frank's son, Stanley, was an inspector of machine tools in the air ministry. At number 48 were Mrs W.B. 'Mary' Binder and her son, William. He was a coach-builder, joiner and air-warden. They lived with their relative Horace Brudenell (who was a widower). Number 50 was the home of Miss Edith Rawlinson. Edith was a spinster, who was born in 1900. Henrietta Elliot (who was incapacitated) and Mrs C.N. 'Mary' Elliot lived with Edith. The job of the Elliot's was to do the 'home duties'. Mr Harry Saunders lived at number 52 during the years leading up to WWII. He married at the turn of the century and died in 1948, aged 69. His wife, Emma had predeceased him six years earlier, aged 63. Edward Johnson lived at 54 and John D. Pridmore lived at 56. John died in 1964 (aged 74). Mr Charles ('Charlie') Douglas worked as a clock-maker and watch repairer in the Market Place. Charlie lived with his wife, Mabel at their home (number 58). Next-door, number 60, was where Mary J. Salsbury (senior) lived. She 'performed household duties' as a housewife and lived 'by private means'. She lived with her daughter Hilda, who was a café and 'sweet-house' proprietor. (Mary Salsbury died in Oundle in 1967, aged 99.)

During the 1930s, Phyllis and Nicholas Dolby lived at 62. Nicholas was a registered accountant and an air-raid warden. Phyllis was a registered accountant managing clerk. Later, Reg and Dorothy Sutton lived at 62. Reg was very civic-minded. He worked as a telephone engineer, but his heart was with the people and children of Oundle. His actions and activities were motivated by (and showed concern for) the public good. A humanitarian, he was well-loved; forever doing community service, heading charities and events. Reg was Oundle's representative on Northamptonshire County Council, he pushed to establish Prince William School and was a member of Oundle and District Care Committee. Reg loved photography and the history of Oundle. His wife, Dorothy died in 2003. Reg died in 2011 after living his life for others.

During the Second World War, William and Bessie Brown lived at number 64. William was a cricket coach and store-keeper at the school. He was also a telephonist in the auxiliary fire service. Number 66 is where Emily Osborn lived with her family: Richard Osborn was a brewer's clerk and Emily took care of the household. At 68 were George and Katharine Gilbert. George worked as a "sugar-beet fieldsman" and served as an air-warden.

George and Lillian Ray lived at number 70. George was a dairy farmer. He later passed his dairy business down to his son, Desmond. A butcher's assistant, Lionel Leverton lived with them. Miss Marjorie Golds also stayed with the Ray family during the war years. Des' father, George Ray started the dairy and milk business that his son continued. George came to live almost a hundred years ago. He originally came from Broughton near Huntingdon. Des was born in 1927, just before the family moved to Cotterstock, bought a house and started their dairy farm. George rented the farm-land from Mr Assiter in North Street. By the 1960s, the Ray's milked in the region of seventy cows per day. They also kept pigs. Parents would visit with their children to look at the litters when they arrived. It was a pleasant walk from Oundle town centre to the outskirts of the town to see the pigs and cows. George died aged 63, in 1965. Des said that when Mr Assiter died, the farm was sold. Des couldn't afford to buy it and "Jim Richardson bought it". Des then continued milk sales with "bought the milk in" from Keith Wright's farm, which was near St. Ives. (His rival was milk salesman, Roy Sumner, who also 'bought-in' milk to deliver. Des said that Mr Sumner started his delivery business after the Ray family.) In the last few years of his work as a milkman, the milk he sold was purchased from the Co-op. Des closed his milk business when he was aged 66. (He is now 91.)

Des and his sister, Pamela grew up on the farm and he said that they were content that they did. Des said, "As a nipper we played at our end of the town. Some people went everywhere, but we were not allowed to. We were at 70 Glapthorn Road and Bevil Allen lived on the other side of the road, further up so we had friends nearby". Initially, Andrew Spurrell bought his old house in Glapthorn Road, before it was sold to Keith Johnson and his family. Keith was a butcher with a business in the town centre.

434

From his youth Des recalled the children tobogganing "in the fields at the back of the farm". "When we were kids we went to the Cotterstock field (by the sewage plant) to go tobogganing" as there is a good slope. It is where children today follow suit (when there is any snow). He said, "I think half the town came here to play". Des Ray and his wife, Madeline (née Rawlings and Wilber) live on the Cotterstock Road, close to where he was raised. Their daughter, Judy, lives nearby.

During the 1930s, their neighbour at 72 Glapthorn Road was a single lady who lived alone. This was Miss Fanny Sherard (who was born in 1866). At 74 there lived Stanley Jeakins. He was the manager of a local grocery and foodstuffs department. In the war years he also served as an ARP and was enrolled with the NCC constabulary. He lived here with his wife, Alexandra and their family. During the war years they shared their house with two evacuees, Margaret Gibbons and Jean Pearce. (The girls were both born in 1925 and attended the local primary school for the duration of the war.) Number 76 was not built until after the war. The houses that followed this section of the road were built as post-war semi-detached Oundle "School housing" for employees.

George and Nancy Slote and their daughters, Wendy and Margaret, lived in the school housing from 1952. George worked for Oundle School as a general maintenance man. Nancy worked at the School Tuck Shop and was also worked part-time at Gordon and Audrey Knight's grocery store in Rock Road. Number 78 was also a school house (attached to 76). Mr (Fred) and Mrs Read lived at number 78 in the 1950s. They had no children and moved to York after retiring from the School. In the pre-war years, number 84 was the home of Ephraim W. Rands and his family. Ephraim moved to Brigstock after his retirement. (He died aged 66 in 1948.) Number 86 was the home of Mr Stanley Wilson. Number 88 was the home of Mr G. Cope and 90 was the home off Mr A. Collard and his family. Number 92 is amusingly named 'Ywurry'. It was the home of C.J. White and his family. Mr R.F. Wheatley, B.Sc., taught at the School and lived at number 96. In the 1930s a single occupant, Miss Joanna Turner lived at number 98. By 1939, Mr J.R. Turner also lived at 98. It is presumed that he moved in with his daughter. Mr A.E. Lane lived at house 100.

Glapthorn Road (west side, travelling north)

Glapthorn Road meets the Blackpot Lane and Milton Road crossroads and is a continuation of New Street. On the corner is the Oundle School Adamson Centre, which re-opened in 2013 as a Modern Languages Department. The Adamson Centre, formerly the 'Sir Peter Scott'[357] building, has had its interior completely redesigned in the last few years. Named for its benefactor, former pupil David Frederic Dobell Adamson (who attended during the war years), left a bequest intended to "improve facilities for and give opportunities to students to learn to speak and communicate in foreign languages."

The Oundle School Chapel of St Anthony was consecrated in 1923 and was built as a memorial to the fallen of WWI. It contains intricate stained-glass windows that were designed by John Piper and constructed by Reyntiens in the mid-1950s. Heather Cunnington (*née* Melton) said, "My father worked in the schools grounds". She said, "I have a photograph of him clearing the snow during the winter of 1961. One of the men in the photograph was my father, Reg Melton. He was opposite St. Anthony's school house in Milton Road. He is just outside the School Chapel."[358] (See photographs.)

Nearby, the Yarrow Galley building opened in 1918 on the first Speech Day after the war ended. It was sponsored by Sir Alfred Yarrow in memory of his son, Eric, who died in 1915 at Ypres. The gallery became permanent exhibition rooms in 1970 to host exhibitions by students, local and national artists. Eric Yarrow's statue stands west of the chapel and was created by an art master.

A statue that was relocated from the front of the School Chapel to the front of the Yarrow Gallery is a striking bronze statue of a naked boy with his arm raised. It is known as "Here Am I, Send Me". The sculpture, by Kathleen Scott, was possibly modelled on her son, Peter. To compound any possible inaccuracies, when Sir Peter Scott gave a visiting-lecture at the school he stood on the stage, held up his hand and said "It Is I". Forty years ago the statue was stolen, but was quickly

---

[357] 1909-1989.
[358] Photograph by kind permission of Heather Cunnington (*née* Melton).

recovered by the police as its feet were "sticking out of the getaway-van's doors".

The first house on the road is past the Yarrow. This is 1 Glapthorn Road. In 1973 this was the home of Sergeant Barry Armitage. His constable lived at number 1a with his family in the other half of this semi-detached building. Locals always called them "the police houses" and didn't bother with numbers! Over the last twenty years these buildings ceased to be police houses, were sold and extended. Number 3, 'Abbott House', is a purpose-built retirement home. The building has replaced the old two-storey, flat-roofed building. The old building is nearer to the road, awaiting sale. The old building was 'women only' in the 1960s (as Fletton House took only men). The new building is open to a small community of men and women. There was once a house here that was the home of Mrs Edith Oldfield. She was the Secretary of the Dr Barnardo's 'Young Helper League'. A new residence has been built for the use of the Abbott House matron and her family. Lynn and Lesley Norman (non-identical twins) once lived here.

Fletton Way and the Workhouse Complex

To the rear of these houses is Fletton Field. It is quite near to the Workhouse (that was built in 1836). John Smith originally owned the Fletton land in 1899. He sold the 'Field' to the Guardians of the Poor of the Oundle Union. Community activities have taken place on this land ever since.

Slightly behind Abbot House stands the old workhouse chapel, which was built in 1896 by architect, Ninian Comper. Sharon Jackson (now Cottingham) and I[359] visited the chapel and old workhouse buildings with Reg Sutton during the early 1970s, when the building was near-derelict. We recall the old bell (that is still intact) and the huge stove that was just inside the main door (to the west). The Beatitudes (Biblical verses from St. Matthew) were escribed around the tops of the high walls of the Chapel. They read: "Blessed are the poor in spirit, for theirs is the kingdom of heaven. Blessed are they who mourn, for they shall be comforted. Blessed are the meek, for they shall inherit the earth. Blessed are they who hunger and thirst for righteousness,

---

[359] Personal memories, Anna Fernyhough and Sharon Cottingham.

for they shall be satisfied. Blessed are the merciful, for they shall obtain mercy. Blessed are the pure of heart, for they shall see God. Blessed are the peacemakers, for they shall be called children of God. Blessed are they who are persecuted for the sake of righteousness, for theirs is the kingdom of heaven."[360]

The building was carefully converted around twenty-five years ago, with new floors above ground level and was transformed into a comfortable, two-storey, private residence (renamed 'Magdalen House'). It was converted into a house in the 1980s. In the early 1990s it operated as a bed-and-breakfast. During its time as a bed and breakfast I was lucky enough to have friends staying there for a couple of nights. This gave me the opportunity to go inside. I liked the way in which the clever redesign had worked, despite the upstairs windows being at floor level. All in all, this is a successful, cosy house. Via a side-route to the workhouse from the chapel, a short path leads behind the doctor's surgery to Stronglands Court.

Accessed via Fletton Way, Mason House (commemorates Oundle Councillor, Mrs Lottie Mason) stands behind Fletton House, the 'Hub' and its car-park. In 2013, this large, red-brick building changed from being the offices and waiting-room for the Care Trust to a residential day-assessment centre (with detached rooms for the elderly). It was offered for sale as an office conversion or residential dwelling. Nearby, 'Stronglands Court' bungalows are for retired people. Although under one roof, these are warden-assisted individual apartments. These were originally built in 1983 for people with mobility issues. It was named after a furlong in Hill Field.[361] The library and doctor's surgery are conveniently next-door. Mrs Ivy Evans had lived in New Road until she became old and moved to Stronglands. Her daughter, Joyce, helped in the move. Teresa Jackson lived here until she was too unwell to care for herself, so moved to Abbott House. Around 2001, Teresa Jackson lived here. She enjoyed looking out of her window at the firemen (and passers-by) who accessed their building from here. One day she looked out of her window and called to a passing fireman, "Could you get me some bread and milk, please?" People were very willing to

---

[360] The Bible, New Testament, Sermon on the Mount (Matthew 5:3–11).
[361] From the Anglo-Saxon furlong; a "furrow long" length when ploughing.

help.[362] One day, an ice-cream van visited and Teresa went out to buy everyone in the residences an ice-cream. Stronglands thus retains a sense of independence, security and community.

The Workhouse

The workhouse had a two-storey entrance-block, flanked by lower wings. The porter's room was in the centre with the board-room. At the back were four wings that led from an octagonal hub. The "Poor Law Institution", known as the "Oundle Workhouse" dated to around 1834. It was where the current doctors' surgery building stands. The original institution was designed for the poor, old, ill (mentally and physically), the destitute (from a lack of work during times of high unemployment) or for anyone without relatives able to provide care. Unmarried, pregnant women were often rejected by their families, yet the workhouse accepted them during and after the birth. It carried with it conditions, which needed due consideration before entry. Workhouses were not prisons, but were not far from being so.[363] Inmates could request to enter, but once accepted, they lost their voting rights (until the law was repealed in 1918). Some workhouse inmates are listed in the baptismal register for Oundle (1838-1858). On 29th May 1854, a baby, Patrick Woodford, the "son of the late Thomas Woodford" (a labourer) and Hannah Woodford, was born and baptised in the Union Workhouse. The officiating Curate, J.M. Holt, performed a private baptism. The register notes that it is a "rare occurrence to note a dead husband" as "late". The baby was institutionalised from birth (a hard start to life in the town).[364] The workhouse fell into disrepair. Times and methods were fast changing. Workhouses around the country closed as they were seen to be outdated and Dickensian. Oundle workhouse was demolished in the early 1970s and the new surgery building opened in 1993.

Nearby stands part of the workhouse complex: the Library. It stands at the original drive entrance to the workhouse and was part of the original complex that was used by the Board of Governors. It was

---

[362] Rowena Brown (née Jackson), personal history.
[363] The Oundle Poor Law Union formally began in 1835, overseen by an elected Board of Guardians.
[364] Baptismal register for Oundle, 1838 -1858. NRO 249P/5.

extended in the 1960s to accommodate more books. My first visit to the library was in the early 1960s. I recall the very first book borrowed. It was a biography about the Russian ballet dancer, Anna Pavlova.[365] It had lots of interesting ballet pictures and facts that I wanted to read again and again! The library is housed in the separate lodge and board-room block that was erected slightly later than the workhouse. It stands to the left of the gated entrance. A stone gatepost survives, but is covered in creeper. An infirmary was erected to the south of the workhouse in 1900. The chapel was funded by charitable contributions and was erected in the 1890s. On its inaugural opening a collection was taken from the attending dignitaries to help to pay the outstanding building debt. The institution inmates who attended that day were each given sixpence to drop into the Chapel collection-box.

Originally, the workhouse had accommodation for one hundred and fifty inmates and in 1926 was considered to be a poor-law institution. Mr Thomas A. Pywell was the Master at the Oundle Institution (number 1). Mr H. Jones was an NCC Divisional Surveyor who lived at 1a. Fletton House was the home for destitute old gentlemen from the 1950s to the 1970s. Sharon Jackson (now Cottingham) and I conducted 'community service' here just prior to going away to university. Some of the elderly men we met in the early 1970s had been in institutions throughout their lives. One old gentleman had been born in a workhouse and grew up there. He had never known a typical 'family life' or a small house. He had performed 'workhouse tasks' and jobs as a part-time labourer throughout his life. The 'Glapthorn Road Hospital' and 'Infirmary' on this site was a 'cottage hospital' from the 1940s to the 1960s. Health-visitors monitored infants between birth and the age of five. In 1973 Miss J. Woods and Miss D.E. Barnard were just two of these.

In 2016, Fletton House accommodated the Hub cafe, the Oundle Town Council offices, the Registry Office, Oundle Community Pre-School, fitness classes and other activities (including parties) in its room-rental spaces. Annually, from the 1930s the Council schools were visited by a Nit Nurse. Children were expected to line-up quietly in single-file while the nurse checked their scalps. The Nit Nurse would sometimes visit

---

[365] Anna Fernyhough, personal history.

individual classes and children would quietly queue to have their heads checked for nits (head-lice). This was a necessary, but not pleasant experience. The nurses were under the auspices of the local doctor. (Nurse Pulley was the school visiting nurse of the 1960's.)

After the war, during the 1940s and part of the 1950s, the workhouse was renamed Glapthorn Road Hospital. In the north-wesernt corner was a casual ward. It served as overnight lodging for tramps and vagrants. Nearby was a large patch of healthy rhubarb, which supplemented the purchased food and was cooked in the workhouse kitchens. The central workhouse block was demolished. The surviving parts were adapted for local use. The public library was converted from the old Board-rooms, with their cast-iron stove and tiled floors. Fletton House was primarily a home for elderly men from the 1960s to 1970s. The able-bodied amongst them functioned as local workmen. They would be issued a packed lunch and a beer, spend the day labouring, before returning to Fletton House in the evenings. The complex had a mortuary at the rear (that was demolished),[366] but Fletton House, its chapel and library buildings remain as survivors of the old Workhouse complex.

Dr Michael Lewis opened the new Glapthorn Road surgery in 1983. Dr Oliver Stovin was a young protégé of Dr Lewis and moved to the new building with him, but retired in 2015 after twenty-six years at Oundle Surgery. During his time at the surgery he saw patient numbers grow and sundry changes to the National Health Service. The current surgery has been extended, firstly with an atrium and then with a new half, making the surgery double its original size. In the summer of 1994, there was another new innovation: Oundle gained a female doctor, Ros Wilmot. She qualified in 1975 and came to Oundle with her husband and daughters, Jane and Eleanor. At last, those females who were easily embarrassed could discuss their problems with a woman. There are far too many doctors to list here, but Dr Leiber, Dr Pearson and Dr Richardson were amongst the first doctors to work in the new building.

The Registrar of births, deaths and marriages was Mr M. Berridge. He lived in the Entrance Block, Glapthorn Road Hospital (1973). The

---

[366] Information from Jean Atkins.

superintendent registrar, Mr J. Ford, also lived here. The original Oundle Registry Office was converted into a house and, subsequently, was demolished to make way for the police station. Beyond this point is the Police Station and the Fire-station. Number 7 is divided into three flats. Once upon a time, this house was used by Community Service Volunteers employed by Fletton House in the early 1970s. They cared for and entertained the old gentlemen. (They were usually students who had just left University.) Three of these whose first names remain in my mind, were Rosy, Ray and Roy. (I am sorry that we do not recall their surnames!). They painted pictures, helped by Prince William students, along the corridors and up the stair wells to make the cavernous place seem brighter.[367]

Continuing along the Glapthorn Road

Pavilion Drive leads to the Oundle School boarding-houses for girls. Each House has a resident matron to care for students (in a pastoral and administrative way). Student rooms vary between houses, most have a mixture of dormitories and bed-sits (allocated according to seniority). Wyatt and Kirkeby Houses for girls opened in 1990. At the terminus of Pavilion Drive are sports fields and cricket grounds, which are linked by pathways to the swimming pool and Milton Road. The annual Oundle School Leavers' Ball takes place in a marquee on the Two Acre pitch (behind Fisher and Crosby Houses) and in the sixth form club. Each July, it runs from early evening to the early hours and is celebrated with a firework display that townsfolk are welcomed to attend to watch. In the 1960s, the Oundle town swimming pool members had a card that they could purchase to allow them to swim here. Fees were 6d (six old pennies) per swim. This was available in the holiday, after the School terms had ended. Mr George Slote worked for Oundle School in the 1950 and 1960s. One of his roles was as a swimming pool attendant. He was a strong swimmer and enjoyed keeping the pool well-maintained.[368] Mr John W. Hogg was the school swimming instructor. Before 1923, on the land of the current pool car-park there was the old School chapel. This is where art classes were taught. It was demolished after the Second World War, but was known (by the boys) as the 'Tin Tabernacle'. It was a green and dull-cream

---

[367] Anna Fernyhough, personal history.
[368] Margaret Brewster (née Slote), personal history.

coloured, wooden structure with a corrugated-iron roof. When it rained the boys couldn't hear what was being said by the teacher.

The old School Sanatorium on Glapthorn Road has a lovely airy balcony for recuperation, reminding us of houses from "Gone with the Wind".[369] In the late-1930s the School Sanatorium matron was Sister Leverton. The Old Sanatorium was later divided into flats. In 1973, the secretary to Oundle Young Wives Group was Mrs A. Bosworth, who lived in Gayes' Cottage by the Oundle School playing-field on Glapthorn Road. The school owned a brown horse-drawn cab that carried sick boys to the sanatorium. It was said that in the end of year 'japes' some of the school leavers took the cab and burned it on the Home Close. It is believed that Oundle School retains the skeleton of the (white) horse that pulled the school 'Sani-cab ambulance' to and from the clinic. The sanatorium building has attractive Victorian ironwork. People moved in occupational-spheres and it was reported that "Mrs Rudd, late of the Oundle School Sanatorium, has been appointed Matron of Latham's hospital. There were eight applications."[370] No longer used as a 'health centre', in the 1980s, the School sold uniforms on the upper floor of this building. A new sanatorium was built in the 1990s between the girls' houses.

Mr Thomas E. Marshall was at number 5 and, at 5a was a teacher, Mr G.S. Rees. He lived in a house named 'Grey Gable' that was located just within Pavillion Drive. The school laundry was at 7 and was run by Mr H. Parnell in pre-war years. In 1925 at the Oundle School Laundry, Irene Motson[371] wrote a fascinating account of her life. She worked as a laundress after WWI, which was a difficult vocation, yet Irene fondly recalled her "life in simpler times". Irene was sixteen when she gained her job in the school laundry. She worked from 8.30 until 5pm with breaks for lunch and refreshment. Days were tiring, but Irene enjoyed it. Each day the laundry was brought in and taken to the wash-house. It was sorted, put into large steam-machine drums, then put through rollers. Girls would 'feed' and catch the clean laundry as it came

---

[369] Styled with a colonnaded front. See the 1939 epic film, "Gone with the Wind", which depicts colonnaded houses (with roof-support columns) in Georgia, USA.
[370] *'Northampton Mercury'*, 9 January 1914.
[371] Irene Motson, unpublished document: "Memories of Oundle School Laundry", courtesy of Oundle School.

through. Long, ironing tables completed the job. Laundry was then put into large baskets, collected and returned to Houses.

Mrs Denny, Mrs Horne and Mrs Setchfield were responsible for the house-master's wife's and matron's laundry. This was the best work and prepared individually. Saturday mornings were spent scrubbing the floors and cleaning, before time was their own. Sundays meant Chapel, taking the Sunday-school with "Florrie". The lawns could be used in holidays, "as a break". At Christmas, the boys were packed and taken to the train. Then, the Great Hall had an annual dance for domestic staff. Irene was paid "two and six a week", but had her own room, "hot water on tap in the bathroom" and a "sitting room with a good fire in it". Her working life in the laundry was a happy time.

David Wills' father, Chris, was in the Royal Observer Corps and a local postman. His station was off Glapthorn Road, just "behind a couple of fields beyond the Oundle School Laundry". David visited the post with his dad and was fascinated by the 'plotting table'.

A new house designated for the Oundle School deputy-head, stands to the left of the driveway. Nearby, on the right, the School recently sold land for the construction of a housing estate. It was completed by 2017 and stands opposite Springfield Road junction. It stretches westward, almost to Biggin Grange. This landscape was the site of a mediæval deer park. It was in the vicinity of (and south-east of) Biggin Hall, in the wooded area known as 'Park Wood' and dates to the late 1100s. The land went to the Bishop of Peterborough, but was transferred to the Earl of Gloucester in 1292. Biggin Hall is the home of the Watts-Russell family. (The hall is not open to the public.)[372]

New houses were constructed opposite Springfield Road (on what was Oundle School land) in the past couple of years. These new development houses are named 'Laxton Gardens'. The nearby Rockingham Hills houses were built around 1972. The names of the new roads were derived from local links to gentry (as the land belonged to Rockingham castle estate).

The 'George' public house is at 91 Glapthorn Road. The 'George Inn' was run by Mr T. Marriott in the pre-war years, but is better

---

[372] Biggin Grange Deer Park: www.parksandgardens.org

remembered as run by proprietor, Mr L. Peacock in 1973. His son Richard, attended the Secondary Modern School and later Kettering Technical College with other local children. As teenagers Sharon (Jackson) and I remember spending time with Richard and groups of our school friends at the pub, but never drinking! The pub provided morning coffee and cooked food, which continues to this day. They also provided weekly and overnight caravan parking in the 1960s and 1970s. The rear 'George' land was reserved for more permanent caravans. Mr 'Jimmy' Lowe, a history teacher at the Oundle Secondary School lived here during the late-1960s and early 1970s. This was during the time that the Peacock family managed the pub. Since this time, the interior has been much improved and extended. Doors and walls have been opened and additional room-space added to the southern side, giving the interior a lighter aspect.

Tilley Hill Close

The Tilley Hill Close cul-de-sac was built in the 1950s by the Oundle Urban District Council. Sergeant Askew lived in the 1950s loop-road when these houses were relatively new developments. Ioan Thomas tells of a local tale tells of Captain Tilley, who lived in the stone house opposite the entrance to the Close, which is the origin of the name it bears. In 1856, there was an accident on the fringe of the town on Tilley Hill when a horse escaped and caused havoc.[373] It was suggested that Mr Tilley was a smuggler who used a tunnel from his house to the river. Others suggest that Tilley's ghost can be seen waiting on the corner by the 'George', but this may be the effect of another 'spirit'! Many of these houses were let by Oundle Council as social housing for low income earners.

In 1973, Mrs Evelyn A. Rootham (née Bunning, when she lived in North Street) was the secretary of the Oundle Women's Institute. She lived at 2 Tilley Hilll Close, in a semi-detached house (like others in the cul-de-sac). Evelyn was born in 1930. She married Gordon Marks in 1942. Subsequently, she married John Rootham in 1952. They had two daughters, Jennifer and Helen, who lived with them at this address. The rear gardens are mainly lawn with some plants and trees, but some have brick-built sheds and storage. Next-door, number 6 was the base

---

[373] Information with thanks to Ioan Thomas.

of our local ambulance service and home of Mr R. Nodwell was the ambulance man. For a time in the 1960s, Peggy Thurlby and her family lived in two of the houses on the close that had been "knocked together". She later moved to New Road. 17 Tilley Hill is Mr Marshall's well-established local construction firm. In 1973, at 26 was a constable in the Oundle Police Force.[374] This loop-road dates to the 1950s.

The Gaunt family moved from Havelock cottages to be residents at 119 Glapthorn Road. Here they lived next to Mrs Fanny Carter. Joyce recalled their neighbour, who loudly remarked that she "didn't like "posh people with televisions" and wondered if she was referring to them. Joyce said that all of the children who lived nearby played in the spinney and fields. They walked through the spinney to get into Des Ray's fields. Jackie, Joyce and Virginia (née Gaunt) said, "Everyone played there. We built dens to play in and took biscuits to eat." At other times "we played hopscotch on the paving slabs with chalk and did handstands by the wall. We were never bored." "We skipped, used hoola-hoops, played 'kiss-chasing' and were busy all of the time."

Evenings were a time for families: Joyce said, "We used toasting forks to toast bread and crumpets over the fire." Jackie joined in by telling us that "... the coal-man came to deliver coal for the fire. We put coal on the fire and chopped sticks. We would have a tin bath once a week in front of the fire. Then it was off to bed with a stone hot-water bottle and in the mornings there would be 'Jack Frost' on the windows' as there was no central heating then. We all had layers of blankets – not duvets."

Joyce's niece, Jacqueline Ganderton (née Burgess), mentioned her younger brother. She said that in the 1950s, "When Stephen was small, he crawled over to the open fire and the kettle-stand in the hearth". Jackie said that "He knocked the kettle over and had an awful scald." This was a terrible shock for the entire family. As this was before mobile-phones were developed and household telephones were very rare, "To get the doctor, we had to go to the red telephone boxes. If you were about to give birth, someone would have to rush over to the phone-box to phone the doctor. Dad biked to the phone-box to call the nurse when my brother was born." "It was the Glapthorn Road box he

---

[374] A Police Constable also lived at 13 Springfield Road (early 1970s).

went to, as the Tilley Hill Close phone-box was only put there later." She said, "Mrs Allaby looked after mothers after they had given birth". (She was the Spurrell family's nanny in the 1930s.) Mr David Allaby (an Oundle School master) taught Joyce how to play 'Lexicon'. She still enjoys playing this card-based crossword game.

After the Tilley Hill cul-de-sac, the Glapthon Road continued for only a short distance. Number 13 was the home of J.W. Mason and his neighbour at 15 was C.G. Dew (a stonemason). At 17 was Mr H Sharp. Bevil and Margaret Allen (and their family) lived at number 121a during the 1970s. The Allen's recall the land to the rear, which had cows and a brick shed. These are all long gone.

Rockingham Hills Estates leading off the Glapthorn Road

New estates have been created since the turn of the twenty-first century. Newbold Close, Walcot Close, Creed Road and Hillfield Road are new roads that were built. Hillfield's name denotes that it was one of the three 'Open Fields of Oundle' that were considered part of the Parish. These are where the town's early settlements were situated. Most of the newer road names commemorate Oundle patrons. Hillfield Road is appropriately at the top of a rise in the land.

Creed Road commemorates Jemima Creed, who ran a school in Ashton. In 1548 the cemetery and chapel of 'Ashton in Oundle' and the cemetery and chapel of Oundle (St. Thomas') were sold by the Crown to Francis Samwell. The site is said to be that of the Manor House. A new chapel and schoolhouse was built here in 1708, under the will of Jemima Creed (the daughter of John Creed of Oundle).

In late 1674 the Rectory Manor-house, land and tithes were sold by William and Bridget Page to Bernard Walcott and his wife, Elizabeth (née Page). They moved into the Rectory around five years later. An annual rent of just over thirty-two pounds was paid to the 'Crown' (James 1 and later to his son, Charles I). The Rectory on North Street was then sold to several people and shared. This meant that William Walcott could buy the rights to it (1750) and keep it clear of any rent previously paid to the Crown. Dr William Walcott died in 1806. He and his late wife, Mary Creed (related to the owners of Cobthorne), left the property to their son William, who died in 1827 (aged 74). At this point the property went to the Simcoe family who disposed of it.

As an aside, it is believed that there are tunnels beneath the Rectory that lead to a house in North Street, to the Church and beyond to buildings in West Street. I recall Leo Dunham talking about this with the class when I was in school.[375] I believe that he said he had been into some of the passages, which were unsafe and blocked off in parts. The story was somehow related to the Secondary Modern School buildings. Another subterranean passage is said to stretch from the Berrystead to the Church. I would dearly love to know the truth about these underground passages and determine their age and use.

The name 'Newbold' was created in error. It was initially proposed by Oundle Town Council that a suitably new road name was 'Newborn Close'. The name should have been a lasting memorial to Meta Olga Newborn (who was born in Oundle and lived here from 1891 to 1976). She never married and spent her life working as a well-loved teacher in the Oundle Council School, West Street, for over forty-five years. Her two sisters also taught in the school. Many students remember them with appreciation and gratitude.

Wentworth Drive was largely constructed in 1999 and 2000. Despite some opposition to building in this location, the build went ahead and historic finds verified that people resided here long before. Below ground level were archaeological remains from a Roman camp, with ditches and a walled enclosure. There was also an Anglo-Saxon cemetery dating from the early mediæval period.[376] Roman pottery and broaches were uncovered near to the new building site. Late Bronze Age pits and pottery were also found. There were indications of pottery-making techniques dating from before 650 BC. A roundhouse was found that dated to the late Iron Age. Early mediæval pottery, a bone comb and metal grave goods were also unearthed.[377]

Wentworth Drive, Sondes, Monson, Siddons, Seymour, Watson and Culme Closes are all roads that were built in the last forty years. Roads built beyond Tilley Hill Close towards Glapthorn village are all named

[375] Anna Fernyhough, personal and oral history.
[376] The Early Middle Ages (6th-10th century) followed the Roman Empire occupation.
[377] Library of Unpublished Fieldwork Reports, York: Archaeology Data Service.

for land-ownership links with families from Rockingham Castle. The castle was the home of naval commander Saunders Watson (who died in 1988) and Elizabeth Culme-Seymour. The houses in Seymour Place date to 1973.

Sondes Close was built around 1980 and relates to Oundle's connection with the Sondes' family of Rockingham. It was built in 1988 and has historical links with the Wentworth, Sondes, Monson, Culme-Seymour and Watson families of Rockingham Castle, who were the landowners. Siddons Close was built around 1992. It and Seymour Place were built on the old brickworks that were owned by George Siddons. The bricks produced here were used in the construction of the Victoria 'Town Hall' at the turn of the twentieth-century. Siddons was a coal merchant and owned an agricultural supplies business.

Cotterstock Road

The 'George' inn is at a meeting of the ways. At this juncture, the road splits. To the left is Glapthorn and Southwick and right branch to Fotheringhay and Cotterstock. Mr John Miles helped to build the current Southwick water-tower. He travelled around building water-towers and at that time stayed with the Horner family. (He met his wife-to-be, Mrs Dorothy Black, when she was working in Abbott House. They married in 1953.) The rest is history!

The nearby village of Southwick is linked with Oundle. It has a strong attachment to reformers, such as Sir Thomas Fowell Buxton (1786-1845) who worked with William Wilberforce (1759-1833) for the liberation of slaves and other social reforms. His wife, Hannah Buxton was the sister of prison reformer, Elizabeth Fry (1780-1845). Hannah Buxton was the great, great grandmother of Edith Capron (of Southwick Hall).

During the 1930s Cotterstock Road had only three houses and no house numbers. Mr Philip Gurney Coombs (1891-1972) lived at 'Pembroke House'. Mrs J.T. Robinson lived in 'Cottonwood'. (She was the widow of John T. Robinson.) Mr Henry H. Morris lived in 'Mayfield'. All houses along the Cotterstock Road were constructed since 1926, on what were pasture fields. (Some built very recently.) Until the nineteenth-century, the Stamford Road followed an old track towards

Cotterstock and Fotheringhay, then via a green lane to the west of Nassington. Solicitors, Mr Sloan and Mr Coombs, both had houses in the Cotterstock Road.

Oundle and Kings Cliffe Middle School (that is now the local primary school [since a move in 2016]) was built along the Cotterstock Road, Oundle, in 1980. There is access at the back to Glapthorn Road. Ray Close is on the site of the paddock that was owned by the Ray family. Old Mr Ray and his son, Desmond, were farmers. The family had herds of cows and delivered milk to residents of Oundle from the 1930s until the 1960s. I recall walking along to see the cows with my mother and my sister in her pushchair. We would tear up chunks of grass from outside the gate to tempt the cows over to eat from our hands. In the autumn we went picking blackberries and rose-hips from the hedgerows.

Built around 1996, number 137 is a detached brick bungalow. It has a bay wall with windows by the front door and it stands in its own garden. 139a Glapthorn Road is a large, two-storey, detached house (with the upper storey in the roof-space) that was built in 2017. This is the end of the town, but who is to say where the town boundaries will end tomorrow.

Springfield Road, Lime Avenue and Bellamy Road

Springfield Road connects to Lime Avenue, Bellamy Road, Nene View and other roads. These roads have all been developed since the 1960s. Prior to their urbanisation there were allotments and fields. These were often the sites of discarded bottles. Cheryl Forscutt recalls that children would go to the allotments and collect the 'Fanta', 'Corona' and other glass bottles that gardeners had left. They would then recycle them for a few pennies. A deposit on the bottles was a useful source of pocket-money for youngsters of the 1950s and early 1960s. Mrs Beech would give back the deposit on handed in glass bottles. Later, in the 1980s, Hugh Jones owned a small grocery shop in Bellamy Road and later in New Road. Some recall a small pond at the front of the Bellamy Road's "Springfield Stores".

The 1960's bungalows and 'family housing' were mostly built for the Council. They were constructed in an arc (to the north). Most join

450

Glapthorn Road in the north-western part of the town. The houses in the road are all of a similar style. When bought by their tenants the houses were updated (usually with parking and new front-doors) to create individuality. Springfield Road numbers 2 to 20 are in a cul-de-sac. As are houses 42 to 64. These buildings are mostly designed as upstairs and downstairs flats. They were for built for rental from the local Council. Road names often depict natural features of the land. Springfield Road was built on town allotments and fields, which ran with natural springs. Hillfield Road is demarked as it is at the top of a rise in the landscape or hill as is its link-road, Greenfields Drive. These roads were developed in after the millennium.

Lime Avenue was built on land where two lime kilns had stood. It is one of the first roads built off the Cotterstock Road. Lime kilns were used for the calcination of limestone forming quicklime. Kiln use in regional areas turned out to be unprofitable and gradually stopped between the world wars owing to the new large-scale production from factories. The fields were west of Springfield and uphill (towards Benefield and Biggin Grange). There are a mixture of council houses and privately-owned buildings in these newer Oundle roads. Number 49 Springfield Road, was once a tobacconists!

Jennie Shaw has an affection for the old town after living here for forty years. She says that she is still "a relative newcomer to Oundle"! Matthew Seward lived in Bellamy Road and his comment was that "There's not a lot of history in Bellamy Road". In fact, it was built on land that was bought from the Church and now has a mix of private and council houses. Its name commemorates a Charity established in 1658 from the will of Clement Bellamy of Yarwell. As one of Oliver Cromwell's officers, he provided scholarships in Cambridge and local apprenticeships here.[378] Houses were built from 1965 to 1970. There was a small shop near the corner in the 1970s that sold sweets and groceries, which is now a private house. Until the 1960s, the land where these current roads stand was almost totally given over to rented 'grow your own' allotments.

---

[378] Smalley Law, p. 85.

Nene Way was built as a connecting road by Lime Avenue. It dates to the same years and reflects the views that it has over the Nene valley.

NEW ROAD

New Road (south side, travelling east)

In the 1800s, New Road was nothing more than a farm track with ditch-like rain-gullies to the southern side that formed a stream.[379] Children would float sticks and boats on the water in this stream. This childhood occupation continued until the road was developed to the bottom of the hill.

In the pre-war years there were not many houses or residents in New Road. In 1938 there was Charles ('Charlie') T. Cunnington at number 1. Living at number 2 was William B. Bell and family. Number 3 had Mr Ernest Streather (who was born in 1899). Arthur E. Fancourt lived at number 4 (until his death in 1949, aged 68) and Mr Reginald Willie Cheetham lived at 5. (He was born in 1893). At number 6 was Frank William Whymant (who was born in 1901). He worked as a bootmaker. Mr George Spencer lived at number 7. At 8 was Mrs Susannah Hancock (the widow of Henry Hancock) and Mrs Lily Streather (née Williams), who was the wife of Ernest Streather at number 9. They married in 1913, but lived apart. At number 10 were Mr Harry Black and Mr Matthew George Mould. George worked as a builder. (He was born in 1891). At 11 was Mr William Johnson. Number 12 was the home of John W. Caborn. He married Mary in 1901 and died in 1943, aged 67. Mary died in 1958 (aged 85). Living at number 13 was Mr Harry Winham. By 1939, those living at 7 were Mr Geoffrey Spencer (a freelance painter and decorator) and his family. Hetty Bell clearly recalls the stream and the games children played in it. In the 1930s, she lived with her family in the "second house" from the top of the road, "next to the policeman". During the late-1980s, the Cunnington family's lived in the first house, Mr and Mrs Keith Sauntson at 3 and Mr and Mrs Lacey (parents of Janet) were at number 5.

New Road currently acts as a 'rat-run' for cars and heavy goods vehicles wanting to avoid the town centre and the weight-limited South Bridge. It acts as a route between the A605 and Corby. It has the

---

[379] Oral history, Hetty Carter (née Bell).

second-highest number of transitory vehicles in town. With narrow pavements, poor road surfacing and a children's park at the base of the hill, there is concern for its lack of traffic control. The town-centre has been 'traffic calmed' by reducing the speed limit to twenty miles-per-hour, but many other roads still suffer from the number and speeds of vehicles passing through. Often, heavy traffic moves at speeds above the limit. This is the foundation for the residents' safety concerns. (In 2012 a resident was knocked-down by a vehicle!) Large-scale building developments have exacerbated the safety issues on New Road and Glapthorn Road. Business is good, housing is booming, but the infrastructure of Oundle cannot cope. Since 2014 the situation has worsened. The local roads were only 'tarmac' covered in the late-1800s and early 1900s, before this they were made up of rough stones and silt. Perhaps the time has come to look after what we have.

Millfields is a cul-de-sac that was built is on the land of the 'Red House' and where a stone-built windmill stood. Prior to its demolition, the mill and land was sold to an airman who was there for about a year. It had ceased to work and the sails needed repairing. Mr Crawley then bought the property. The mill was subsequently demolished.

Beyond Millfields is a row of semi-detached houses with sizeable gardens. Oundle School owned the houses for their workers, but they were subsequently sold to their occupants. Stuart and Ruby Laxton lived in the first semi-detached house. Stewart Laxton's father owned a tailor's shop that was part of what is now Bramston House. His mother worked in the WVS canteen in Crown Court. Stewart (aged 16 in the war) and Ken (the older brother, born in 1927) attended Laxton School. Stewart's brother, Don married Viva Lee in 1946, Margaret (his sister) married John Hawkins in 1947, Jean married Donald Mableson in 1953 and Stewart married Ruby Stringer in 1951. Stewart remains a stalwart of the Oundle Bowls Club.

New Road has a row of semi-detached houses. They are identical (or mirror-imaged) and share side walls. These houses are followed by a short terrace of houses. On the south side of the road, the terraced houses are numbered 17, 19, 21 and 23. During the 1950s and beyone, 19 was the home of David and Shirley Weatherington. These form a block (with the 'Lantern Take-Away' at number 23). Bert and Lily Ely lived at 21 (next to Beech's corner shop). The Lantern (23) was formerly Cyril and Beryl Beech's shop. Cyril was a photographer. Their son, John, also enjoyed photography. Beryl worked in the shop. She sold a variety of household products, from tea to sweets. There was a glass display case just inside the door with Mars bars and other treats. Sharon Cottingham recalls that Beryl Beech was "a lovely lady with a slight tic". Others recalls that "She didn't like people lingering too long in the shop" or that "it was quite small inside." Beryl is most often thought of, as she "was always good to children of the 1960s who came in for sweets." The shop is now the 'Lantern'. It provides delicious Chinese and English take-away food. Lisa is very helpful and organises orders for food that can be collected when ready.

Victorian houses were built in terraces as people moved into town from the countryside. The kitchen is usually found at the back, with gardens to the front and rear. As houses were built before people owned cars, often the gardens have been altered to allow parking. Some of the semi-detached houses in New Road have done this, unfortunately the terraces are directly onto the street without front gardens, so parking is more difficult.

The (one-way) entrance to Gordon Road divides the terraces, as a second block begins on the other side. Numbers 25, 27, 29 and 31 New Road are symmetrical. For a while, Sharon (Cottingham's) aunt, Jessie Richmond (née Roughton; Dennis' elder sister) lived at number 27 with her husband, Don. There are two newer council houses on New Road at 33 and 35. (These houses are set slightly back from the others.) 'Ruff' Clark lived in 33 and Noel Marshall and his wife, Vera (née Thompson) lived next-door (in 35) with their children, Paul, Leza (later, Smith) and Carl. They had married in 1956. Noel was born Christmas Day, 1929 and died in 2014. His sister, Mary (née Marshall) Hudson was born in 1932. (She later moved to Glapthorn.) Numbers 37 and 39 are likewise, corner semi-detached houses, but they are set at an oblique angle to New Road. Ron Brackley lived at 37 prior to Mr and Mrs White. Tony and Marlene Black moved in (from 1978) when they swapped houses with the White family in Gordon Road.[380]

After Ivy Evans had lived here (in the 1940s), the Hamilton family lived in number 39, followed by Colin and Marilyn Smith. The Smith's had

---

[380] Oral history, Heather Black.

married in their teens and had three sons, Anthony, Simon and Darren. 'Ant' was born in New Road, followed by Simon (while they were living in Gordon Road in 1978.) They firstly lived in one of the newly built St. Peter's Road houses in the 1960s, then in the Gordon Road house in 1970 (for twenty-eight years) before moving back to St. Peter's Road again.

Marilyn tells of a funny story that happened while the family were living in Gordon Road in the late-1980s. One morning she "went outside to get in the washing that had been hanging outside overnight". Her sons had a tent that they had left erected in the garden. Suddenly a voice came from the tent. "Hello Mrs Smith". (She jumped!) The voice continued, "I knew that you wouldn't mind if I slept here overnight. I got locked out at home!" She said that her children had friends to stay all the time, so she didn't mind at all. Colin and Marilyn noted that when their boys were growing-up there was "not a lot of surplus cash to fill the front room". As they mainly used the sitting room and kitchen (at the back) they kept a pool table, a dart board and "a room full of boys and their friends" in the front. Marilyn said that "at least they knew where the children were and that they were warm and safe". During the coal miner's strikes in the 1970s there was no heating, but the family had a functioning fireplace that had double uses; to heat the one room and for simple cooking. Marilyn said, "The boys loved to toast crumpets and teacakes over the fire with a fork". Doing this reminded Marilyn of her own childhood and gave her children a taste of the past.

The exit from Gordon Road meets New Road. Gordon Road was once a two-way road, but is now one direction owing to constriction caused by cars that are parked in the road. On the lower side of Gordon Road, the houses, yet again, slope (looking into both roads). Number 41 New Road was the home of Mr and Mrs Evans, Jackie, Jean and Peggy (née Fox). At 43 were the Hillook family. When they moved John Leayton (Ruth and Anne's brother) lived here. There is one further semi-detached building in New Road. Number 45 was the home of Mr and Mrs Marshall. Mrs Marshall was known locally as "Granny Marshall". She sold British Legion Poppies every year to the householders in Gordon Road and New Road. Both Sharon Cottingham (née Jackson) and Cheryl Forscutt (née Miles) grew-up in Gordon Road during the

1960s and "always remember her with fondness". Number 47 is other part of the Marshall's semi-detached house. This is where "Mr Burrows, Johnny Horne and Joey" lived. They partly faced into New Road. In the past twenty years most of the Gordon Road houses were purchased from the Council. New owners have improved and renovated them. Most have large back gardens with a smaller 'parking' space or garden at the front.

After the war years the local fields housed Thurston's fair, which filled two fields with its rides and caravans. The (mill) fields lay behind the gardens at the (up-hill) northern side of Gordon Road. On the south side of Gordon Road was the recreation ground (known as the "Rec") with its big slide. Children would coat the surface in candle-wax to make the slide-down faster. There were also sit-in rocker boats and a wooden roundabout (that have been long gone from this spot).

A dyke ran between the recreation ground and the corn-fields behind Pick Arthey. Another wide dyke that was "full of water-cress and caddis flies", was in the Ray's fields. (Children would go and collect both and take them home!) "Assiter's Wood" is on the Cotterstock Road. (Mr Assiter also owned the Havelock Cottages on East Road.)

The New Road bungalows along the northern side have lovely views of the recreation ground and park. The World War Memorial Field lies at the base of the hill, near to the Malting's converted residences. The 'Recreation Ground' was designated as a Memorial Ground and is documented on this site from the early 1950s. There are free facilities for basketball, football, play areas (one enclosed for younger children), skateboard ramps and space for picnics.

From its inception, the field had play equipment (by Station Road) and a field for playing football. It once had a hard-surface tennis court in the north-western corner, but this now has a solitary netball-post. Children of the 1960s and 1970s could be heard singing "See-Saw Margery Daw" at the tops of their voices as they rocked. The annual November 5th, "Guy Fawkes night" bonfire was here in the late-1960's, after dark. Often there were two bonfires (built by the local children from surrounding roads). Cheryl Forscutt remembers that "there would be rival gangs who would destroy each other's bonfire to take the bits to build up their own". She went on to say that "Cook's field was opposite the park. It was a good site for collecting bits and pieces. The corn would have been harvested a short time before and the cut corn was good for making dens out of the bales (until they were moved). The loose straw was good as kindling for lighting bonfires fires".

Sharon Cottingham and I[381] recall fairs that visited the recreation ground (pocket park) in Oundle in the 1960s. I believe that most stalls charged a few pennies to have a go at winning something. The amusements included attempting to hook-a-duck, throw and embed a dart into a playing-card (that had been glued to an almost impenetrable wooden board), a rifle range and push a ticket from a straw with a knitting needle to win a prize. Prizes seemed reasonable for the cost. Sometimes you won and sometimes you didn't, it was all part of the fun of the fair. Slightly more infrequently, people won a big prize: a teddy or large stuffed toy, a China vase or chalk ornament. Sharon Cottingham recalls that once the chalk ornament started to degrade, break or wear away, children would use them outside on the pavements. She recalls winning a 'chalk dog' from one particular fair. When it chipped, she used it to draw with on the paving slabs outside the house. The chalk washed away at the next heavy-rain shower. (I believe that modern, plastic, fairground prizes hold much less charm.)

Small fairs visit annually. Unfortunately, in 2017 it rained very heavily in the week that the fair came, so their profits must have been poor.) During the 1960s and 1970s Oundle fairground bumper-cars summoned the locals from their houses with loud music blasting from speakers. I recall hearing the recorded sounds of Diana Ross and the Supremes' 'Baby Love' song being played over and over again. This is as a long-embedded memory. Even today, I can't hear this tune without recalling fun-fairs.

A circus visits Oundle annually, sets up a big top in the World War Memorial Field and stays for a week. Once upon a time, there would be excitement to see wild and exotic animals in cages that were brought out to perform, but current regulations have curtailed this. Now pets and people perform acrobatics. Old entertainment included clowns, acrobats, aerial and high-wire acts, trained animals (dogs and

---

[381] Anna Fernyhough, personal memories.

horses), trapeze acts, musicians, dancers, tightrope-walkers, jugglers, magicians, unicyclists and stunt artists. Pinder's Circus and the Circus Ginnett visit annually. As animals are expensive to maintain, the traditional style circus is slowly disappearing. In 2012, circus' received 'bad press' when a local circus man failed to ensure that his elephant's requirements were met. (A welfare group filmed the 'Anne' the elephant being mistreated). The outcome was that she was relocated to a Safari Park. The family still live locally, but no longer keep wild animals. They train and revere their performing horses that travel to shows all around the UK.

'Oundle Tyre and Exhaust Centre' is a small one-storey, 1950s-style garage. This garage stocks a wide variety of tyres and is known for their repairs being fair in price and fast to respond. Behind Pick Arthey garage are several Council rental garages for residents who need parking facilities. The rear of Pick Arthey enters the road by the park. The garage offices and workshops are built of stone, but the repair shed has a corrugated roof and is quite cold to work inside in the winter months. The rooms over the 'kiosk' were, at one time, rented as accommodation for staff. Over the road from the park and garage is the long, red-brick wall and windows of the Riverside Maltings. These face east onto Station Road, the Nene river and flood-fields. The Riverside Maltings were originally part of the brewery complex. The houses here were converted in the 1980s and are currently listed as 'retirement residences'. The main house was known as 'Nene Cottage' and was used by the warden of the Maltings in the 1980s.

The ladies living in the Maltings might like to know that certain youngsters knew how to climb in through a window and explore inside the red-brick buildings. They also tried to look for a well that was said to be in or near the kitchen of the house. Local children went 'scrumping' for apples in the rear orchard. The old brewery Inn (their house) and land was rented from Smith's brewery by Colonel McMichael. He sold second-hand furniture (from their Station Road house). Often the furniture was purchased from local country houses. Bridget McMichael lived here and attended Miss Webb's School. She and her friends skated on the river whenever it froze. Cheryl Forscutt noted that although the orchards had very good apples they also had resident ghosts. Near the house were planks to walk along that went out into the river from the bridge wall. The brackets for the planks are still in the stonework where long gone barges were kept tied (until the early 1970s). The barges delivered the coal that was then stored in the yard. Roads were not as developed a hundred years since, so barges were more easily used to transport items to Oundle. The 'Maltings House' garden was always immaculate, with stooping willow trees and grass lawns.

Later, Mr and Mrs Hindman (not related to the family in West Street) lived in the house with their daughter, Dawn (who married Alan Colver in the 1970s) and their son, Harry. The Hindman's also sold furniture. Cheryl tells a story of her brother, Michael, who was not easily spooked. She said that the layout of the 'maltings' is quite different now. At that time there was the house, a barn (to the left) that had once been the stables and by the river, the garden. Her brother was playing with Harry Hindman and a bunch of their friends. They were running in the gardens and in and out of the straw hayloft and lower-barn when Michael saw a group of "children dressed in Victorian clothing with white aprons sitting by the barge ties". They had completely vanished by the time the boys went out for a closer look. The Hindman's subsequently put an article into the newspapers to describe strange events they were experiencing. Cheryl said that their report may have been an early 1970s publicity-stunt article to alert people to their sales. It was also said that the last occupiers (before their conversion into domiciles) considered having the property exorcised, but did not as the "children did no harm and seemed contented and happy". The family sold and moved to Peterborough in the late-1970s, where they sold cars. One thing that Cheryl did mention is that Michael was not "easily phased", but he was bothered by the incident and didn't visit again.

New Road (north side, travelling east)

On the hill, there are four houses at the top before the Rock Road junction. The corner house faces on to Glapthorn Road, yet its garden and parking face onto New Road. The first house (number 2) was for many years the Thurlby family home. It was so for over thirty years. Mrs Margaret (Peggy) Thurlby kept a very large, tended garden to the south of and at the back of her property. There she had a greenhouse and grass lawns. After her death around the start of the twenty-first

459

century, the garden was sold and a house was built on the land. The new house is number 4 is in what was Peggy's garden. The Thurlby family was large. Mr Ronald J. Thurlby married Miss Margaret Tobin in early 1950. Between 1952 and 1964 they had eight children: Eamonn, John, Francis (known as Frank), Clare, Loretta, Vincent, Deidre and Desmond (the twins). Deirdre married Philip Norman.

By the late 1970s Mrs Thurlby was a recognized and well-known member of the Roman Catholic Church and community. She always wore a hat. By the 1970s she had gravitated from here white, fluffy "Church hat" to a green one. Peggy always went into Flower's Chemist to buy her hair dye. She used "Loving Care" black dye. One day she went into the chemist to ask if they had any. They had sold out, so recommended that she try the other chemist in town. The next time that she was seen, her fluffy, bright green hat looked new. On closer inspection, it was. It was her hair! The colour she had purchased had reacted with her hair and had turned it green. Peggy was advised to go over to the hairdressers to sort it out.[382]

Opposite Millfields (a cul-de-sac) is Rock Road. These houses were built adjacent to and west of the New Road farm house, which for many years was the home of the Clack family. (For many years Michael Clack served as a town councillor.) Originally, this old farm house was the only house amidst fields. It stands slightly back from the road with a pleasant and private rear garden. Until the 1970s, the garden and orchard was much larger. It was sold and divided into brown-site building plots for new housing. This 'garden' is now the 'Orchard Close' cul-de-sac. There are six houses on this land. Further down the hill-side (to the north side of the road) there is a new detached bungalow built on a short spur-road (2016). Number 47 New Road and its neighbours were been built since the 1960s. Number 16 has "2001" on its apex.

ROCK ROAD

Rock Road was an L-shaped extension from a short New Road. At the time, Springfield Road did not exist and was just fields and allotments. It now connects two roads: New Road and Springfield Road. The houses in Rock Road date from the 1860s. Many are classic Victorian

---

[382] Wendy Bollans, personal memories.

terraced houses. They were initially constructed by the two Rock brothers who had formed a company, bought the land and built on it. (Hence the name of the road.) Most of the properties have gardens to the rear.

The first group of houses are largely brick constructions with sash windows. Many have been replaced with the modern plastic equivalent. Number 2 was constructed around the 1870s. From the rear (east) the terraced houses appear to be very tall, which is an illusion as they are built on the hillside. The roof tops have altered little since they were built, aside from dormer windows in the attic of number 18. Some houses have the original terracotta chimney-pots on their rooftops. Four houses went up for sale by auction in October 1887. At the time of their sale, Edward Freer, Mr E. Dove, Mrs (Rebecca?) Cliffe and Mr Josiah Thorpe lived in the four houses.

The houses are distinctly Victorian inside. To keep themselves warm, the household would have a fireplace, often with a grate, in every room. Fire-surrounds were made from stone, marble or wood. The interiors of the houses have been modernised to include a bathroom and toilet. The original cooking ranges and fireplaces have been replaced to include up to date heating systems and cooking facilities. Jill Plowright said that until the 1960s all of the toilets were at the bottom of the gardens. If you spotted someone going out in the garden with their coat on, they were off to the toilet.

The road was about half the length that it is today. It began in the middle (now even numbers 12 to 26) and then was built to stretch along to the corner house (larger than others in the row) at the New Road end of the terraced houses. On the opposite side of the road, odd numbers 9 to 15 were constructed around the same time. Rock Road was built forming an L-shaped extension from the short New Road. At the time (late-1800s) Springfield Road did not exist and was mere fields and allotments. It now connects two roads: New Road and Springfield Road. The houses in Rock Road date from the 1870s. Many are classic Victorian terraced houses. They were initially constructed by the two Rock brothers who had formed a company, bought the land and built on it. (Hence the name of the road.) Most of the properties have gardens to the rear. On the north-side of the road the odd numbers 3 to 31 are similar buildings. The houses numbered 29 and 31 are newer and bear the date 1914.

This group of houses are largely constructed of pale brick with sash windows. Many of the original sash windows have been replaced with modern equivalents in recent times. Number 2 was constructed in 1870. From the rear (east) the terraced houses appear to be very tall, which is an illusion as they are built on the hillside. The roof tops have altered little since they were built, aside from dormer windows in the attic of number 18. Some houses have the original terracotta chimney-pots on their rooftops. Four houses went up for sale by auction in October 1887. At the time of their sale, Edward Freer, Mr E. Dove, Mrs (Rebecca?) Cliffe and Mr Josiah Thorpe lived in the four houses.

These houses are distinctly Victorian inside. To keep themselves warm, the household would have a fireplace, often with a grate, in every room. Fire-surrounds were made from stone, marble or wood. The interiors of the houses have been modernised to include a bathroom and toilet. The original cooking ranges and fireplaces have been replaced to include up to date heating systems and cooking facilities. Jill Plowright said that until the 1960s all of the toilets were at the bottom of the gardens. If you spotted someone going out in the garden with their coat on, they were off to the toilet.

The road was about half the length that it is today. It stretched from the first house (larger than others in the row) on the corner of New Road to the end of the terraced houses. Chris Barcock said that the householders "would all come outside their houses to line the street to watch important events happening in the road", such as local weddings, for example, when the Bamford's daughter was married. Families got to know their neighbours very well.

Rock Road (west side, travelling north)

The house on the corner is in New Road and was nicknamed the 'lighthouse'. In the pre-war years the corner house belonged to the Weston's, then later the Brampton's. Its rear gate opens onto Rock Road. The "jitty" leads around to the back gardens for the row.

Just beyond the jitty is number 1. In 1939 Mr Harold Rufus Wills (David Will's uncle) lived here in the pre-war years. He lived in the end terraced-house in the 'jitty'. (His uncle, Frank Wills and his wife, lived at number 17 during the same pre-war years.) Harold was born in 1889. He married Gertrude Toyne in 1912. Number 1 became the Skingley family home in the 1960s (their children were Diane, Philip and Suzanne [the latter married Andrew Purvis in 1975]). They were related to the James' (over the road). Number 1 originally had its front door at the front, but this was bricked-in and the side door is now used. Wilf Plowright and his family lived at number 3 during the pre-war years. Miss May Hardy lived in this house (3) during the 1960s. In the 1911 census, Henry Binder and his wife, Elizabeth Chappell, lived at number 5. (They had only been married for a year.) They lived here with Gertrude (Elizabeth's daughter with her late husband). Mr Alfred Gore was at number 5. He lived to be sixty-nine (and died in 1954). Mr Arthur E. Cunnington and his family were at number 7. Arthur lived until 1965 (when he was the 'ripe old age' of 96). Mr E. Clapcott and his family lived in number 9.

Mr William H. Hardy and his wife, Alice (née Vessey) married in 1930 and lived in the semi-detached house (number 11) thereafter. Robert Skingley and his wife, Winifred (née James), married in 1945. They completed their family with three children: Philip, Diane and Suzanne. Their children attended the local primary school throughout the 1960s. Later, the Secondary Modern School magazine announced proudly that Philip had been offered a place at York University. (In these days it was quite exceptional for children to scholastically achieve as the local schooling was not geared to academic success.) The Skingley family house at 11 Rock Road was the first semi-detached house (with bay windows). After the Skingley's moved, Mrs Molly Slater made her home at number 11. Molly worked in Hunt and Coombs solicitor's office. She was the secretary of the Oundle Gilbert and Sullivan Players. The "G and S" group was first initiated in 1958 from the remains of the Oundle Operatic Society. Their first show was 'The Pirates of Penzance' performed in 1959. By 1973 Molly was a stalwart of the Oundle and District Care Committee.

In the 1930s Mr Alfred William Taney lived at 13. Alfred and "Auntie Bessie" Taney lived at 13. Mr Taney (Angela Hudson's uncle) was a fireman. Annie and Edward ('Ted') Plowright lived at 15. They lived with Thomas Wade Stretton (who was known as 'Jack'). He was Annie's brother. Alfred attended his own house-fire as he was the Oundle Fire Chief. He was born in Oundle in 1893 and died in 1969, aged 76. (Two of his sons, Harry and Bill followed his lead and became Oundle Fire Chiefs.) Mr Thomas Wade Stretton and his family shared the accommodation at 15 in the 1930s. In the 1960s, 15 was Mrs Taylor's house. Twentieth century infill houses (15a and 15b) were built on the land adjacent to the original number 15. The land had been part of a large garden that was next to the Victorian houses. Six houses (17 to 29) are within a terraced block. Number 17 is taller and has an apex roof, creating a distinctively different look from the rest of the row. During the pre-war years, number 17 was the home of Mrs Annie Munton. Mr and Mrs Willis later lived at 17. Mr Willis was a local postman. Mrs Clarice Anderson (née Pywell) was born in 1916 and lived at number 19 Rock Road over the Second World War years. She had married Sydney Anderson in late 1937. In the coming three years she had given birth to Dorothy, Dulcie and Robert. By the 1950s she was considered to be as "an elderly lady in Rock Road". The Gaunt family lived at number 19 in 1957. After her marriage, Joyce lived with her husband, Hans in the Ashton Road farm cottage, then Stoke Hill, they then moved into the new (1960s) houses at the end of Rock Road (number 49).

Mr William J. Stretton lived at 21 with his family. Frank Woodman and his family lived at number 23. Frank died in 1939, aged 58. Next door, George H. Bridge and his family lived at 25 during in the 1940s. The Bridge's house was considerably newer than the others in the row. Later 'Bill' Pheasant lived at number 25 in the 1950s and 1960s. (Mr Pheasant was Teresa Jackson's [Gordon Road] sister's father-in-law, just to demonstrate how inter-related Oundle folk are.) Mr Pheasant was the church gardener. Number 29 was where Herbert Ernest Roughton and his wife, Jessie (née Rycroft). They married in 1914. Mr Thomas Oughton and his wife, Ethel (née White) married in 1923 and lived at number 29 with their son, Thomas and daughter, Yvonne (who lived here as a small child). Thomas died in 1945, aged forty-six. (I was informed that "Auntie Ethel" Oughton was related to the Jackson and White families of Gordon Road).[383]

---

[383] Oral history, Gerry White.

Private Reginald Barrett (who died in WWI) was the son of Edward and Hannah Barrett. Reggie grew up in Rock Road. His parents later moved to Gordon Road.[384] Mr Robert W. Taylor and his wife, Marjorie (née Cunnington) made their family home at number 31. This house was built in 1914. In the 1930s, this was the last house in the row. The newer houses are semi-detached. They stretch along the more recent part of Rock Road (from the last of the terraces to the rented bungalows at the terminus). These were all built post-1940.

At the far end of the road there was a large mound that could be climbed. It blocked the view from the road, but from the top of the mound children had access to the fields beyond. The fields belonged to local farmers, the Ray family. The council houses and flats that are now at the northern end of Rock Road (and the other infill dwellings) were not built until the late-1950s and early 1960s. Gill Giddings recalled played at the end of the road, which was known as "the green". In the 1940s and 1950s the children were safe to play in the dead-end street. Sue Crick noted that "the children held their own May Day processions for the road and all of the residents helped out and made the occasion fun. The youngsters would parade down the road with their own 'Queen of the May' and would crown her at the top of the mound at the end of the road. She had her own attendants and everyone in the road would come out to watch".[385]

The houses at the end of the road were originally Council-built around the same time as Springfield Road was developed on the fields with streams and springs. Now, in the 'newer' houses, Aldous' building contractors are at number 33. Number 35 and 37 are flats. The houses here are divided by upstairs and downstairs flats. With eighteen terraced houses to the east of the road and smaller groups of terrace to the west, this road has some semi-detached properties and bungalows at the north end. Some Council rental houses are maintained by Spire Homes. They have small front and rear gardens and have a view of the compact community-garden at the end.

---

[384] Reginald died during a Turkish counter-attack and was buried in the War Cemetery in Jerusalem, Israel.
[385] Oral history, Sue and Mick Crick.

More recently, new families have moved in to the comfortable residences in Rock Road. Samantha (Sam) and Christian Marshall came to Oundle in recent years to start their family life here. Sam said that Oundle is "home from home". It is "a place where you can feel welcomed and safe. It is one of the most beautiful places in Northamptonshire." Sophia, their (toddler) daughter has known no other home and "can grow up here and be part of Oundle's future".[386]

Rock Road (east side, travelling north)

Even-numbers 2 to 12 were constructed in 1870 as a terrace adjoining those between 14 and 30. They are pale-brick terraced houses. Numbers 14, 16, 18 and 20 are a slightly different construction and included a laundry house, wash and bath house for the row. The Rock Freehold Land Society of London[387] bought land on Glapthorn Road and New Road. By March 1884, fifty-three plots had been laid in the two roads. Twenty-four were sold to one purchaser (for £20). By 1885, there were eleven houses and by the turn of the century, twenty-four. Number 31 bears the date 1914 and was the last house in the road until the 1940s.

On the eastern side, building developers the Rock brothers lived in number 2. After living across the road on the corner (at 4 New Road) Mr Charlie and Mrs Mabel Fisher lived at 2 Rock Road in the early 1930s. (Without knowing it at the time of purchase, Mabel Fisher's great-niece and her family bought the house in 1987.) After the Fisher family, Mrs Alice Beesley (1891-1975) moved in. She married (Fred) in 1897, but by the time she lived here in the late-1930s, she was a widow. (Frederick Beesley died in 1936, aged 64.) A little later, the Bamford's lived here. Simon Upchurch and his family were in number 2 in the late 1970s. Local teachers, Teresa ('Terri') and Tim Crews married (in 1977) and lived here with their two small daughters until 1987. In 1935 Mr William Bertie Binder lived at number 4. By 1939 Mr James Richard Toon (1895-1971) lived here with his family. James married Elizabeth Sawford (in 1914). Their children James (born in 1916), Kathleen (1918) and Eileen (1921) resided her. The house was passed to the unmarried daughter, 'Kath', (a nanny, lunch-time-

---

[386] Personal interview, Samantha Marshall (30/09/2017).
[387] Predecessors of the Northern Rock Building Society.

supervisor and pre-school aid). She lived in Rock Road for her entire life.

In the late-1930s Mr Frederick B. Bennett (1898-1973) and his family lived at number 6. Mrs Ward and her family lived at 6 thereafter. Mr Cecil James Weston (who was born in 1908) lived at number 8 in the late-1930s. Mr Weston was followed by Ethel Binder, who lived here until August 1975. At this point John Eaton moved in to number 8. Later, during the 1980s Sue and Charles Young lived in this house with their two fledgling sons, Christopher and Andrew. They remarked that the fire surround in the house was constructed from a wartime parachute box from Polebrook airfield. The banister hand-rail on the staircase was made by Derek Gunn (the local undertaker in Barnwell). Just before the Second World War began Mr and Mrs Keafoot lived in number 10. Thereafter, several families who rented the property were USAF staff from the local air bases. In the 1930s Mr John G. Sabin lived at 12, then Mr and Mrs James and their son, Jarvis, lived in here in the 1960s. Mr James was the brother of Mrs Skingley (at number 11). Michael Amps lived here in the 1980s and then the Clarke family. Mr J.H. Newton and his family lived at 14 during the 1930s. At 14 (in the 1960s) were Mrs Palmer and her daughter, Joan. (She had also lived in St. Osyth's Lane.) Mr T. Cooper lived at number 16 in the 1930s. Mrs Newton and her children, Peter and Chris later lived here.

At 18 were Mr S.T. Rowell and his family. Jill Giddings lived here after this. Subsequently, in the early 1990s, 'Sam' lived at number 18 with his owners, William ('Bill') and Heather DeGaunza and their three young sons, William, Daniel and Oliver. Bill was a police constable in the local force. Sam was a black Labrador. He was generally "a good, old dog". He rarely moved very far or very fast, as he was 'getting on in age'. One day Heather decided to give the front door a fresh coat of paint. She went inside after finishing and left the door slightly ajar, so that the paint would not stick. After a while she noticed that the family dog, Sam, wasn't in his usual spot. He was missing! After searching high and low, she just could not find him. Meanwhile, PC DeGaunza was on duty and had been called out on a case. The local pet shop (in Crown Court) had reported that a dog with no collar had "let itself in and was happily munching from a barrel of pigs ears" that were displayed on the floor. The shop owners were afraid to do anything with the dog as they didn't recognise him, also he didn't seem to be with anyone. To his embarrassment, Bill arrived to find that the dog in question was his own! He said that there would be no charges (other than for the pigs' ears) and due to Sam's past-history of good behaviour, he would only be cautioned with any past offences taken into account.[388] Sam seemed to learn his lesson and didn't do this ever again. From the turn of the twenty-first century, Jonty Shingles (1957-2016) and his family lived at number 16. Jonty was a well-liked, local figure. He grew-up in North Street as the son of Mr Shingles the (1960s and 1970s) Laundimer Housemaster. Jonty was described as "a lovely man, with a larger than life personality to match". (Jonty's sister, Buffy, lived near to him in Rock Road.)

Mr J.W. Brown lived at number 20, then it was owned by a lady known as "Auntie" Mabel Brown. [389] Sue Crawley grew up in 22 Rock Road. She recalls that the local children played in nearby fields (at the north end and off the eastern side of the road). She said that they didn't stray far. After number 22, there was an archway and narrow passage that leads behind all the gardens (that is a public right-of-way along the back to New Road). The six houses used it for taking their bikes and prams to the backs of their houses. Tony Rowell (born in 1946) lived here after the Crawley's. His wife ran the wool shop (Oundle in Stitches) next to Trendall's. Sidney Rowell worked a painter at Oundle School. He and his wife, Amy, had three children: Tony, Alan and Margaret. Mr John H. Rowell (1877-1944) lived at 22. He lived all his life in Oundle.

Mrs (John) Fleckner lived at number 24 in the late 1930s. After this time, number 24 was the Richards family home. Mr Arthur Richards and his wife, Clara (née Spinks) married in 1911. They lived here with their children, Lilian, Eileen, Beatrice, Evelyn, Douglas and Edna. Mr Arthur J. Richards lived at 26, before Mr "Sammy" Black and his family moved in. At 28 were Mr J. Cook and his family. They had two children, Delaphine (who married Mr Askew and was a police-wife) and her brother. Number 28 was rented to American servicemen and their families from the nearby Molesworth and Alconbury bases in the

---

[388] This appeared in the local Anglia Television news and in the local papers, as Bill's colleagues had 'called it in'!

[389] Oral history, Sue Crick (née Crawley).

1970s. The Shiels family (Michael was a fireman) moved here into 28 North Street in 1970s. At 30 lived Mr James H. Brown (1860-1939). Later, Gordon Knight and his wife, Audrey (née Hooton), who ran a small shop that sold everything as a general store (tinned items, food stuffs, toilet roll and tea!) at 30 Rock Road. The shop was in the room at the front of their house. They lived here with their daughters, Debra and Louise. For a few years Nancy Slote worked at the Knight's shop. Gordon and Audrey "were great to work for" and made Nancy feel very welcome. Audrey had a 'naughty' sense of humour and, at a party at number 2 in the mid-1990s she turned up in a cheeky corset (she was around seventy at the time)! She was lively and was great fun.

Number 32 is part of the classic, Victorian terraced property. Mr Charles M. Tilley (the Co-op manager) and his wife, Sarah, lived at number 32 for a long time. They married in 1913. Living here in the 1960s was Miss Pearl Hopkins. She lived alone. Pearl was the Co-op milk 'girl'. One year my sister and I made a "Guy Fawkes" for bonfire night (at the local Football field). 'Guy' was life-sized and wore old clothing stuffed with newspaper. The face was painted and he had a real cigarette stuck in its mouth! When Pearl delivered the milk that November morning, she got "such a shock" when she opened the door to the passageway! She thought that she had found a collapsed man there so mum had to sit her down and give her a cup of tea to let her recover![390]

Numbers 36 and 38 were the last of the terraced houses on the south side of the road. They belonged to the Co-op. (It is believed that 32 and 34 were also.) A passage leads between the houses as a shared-access to their back gardens. In number 32 (the first house) there lived Mr H. Goldsmith. He was the local ambulance driver. (His neighbours were thrilled and remarked that "he had a 'phone"). Beryl Cox (née Hill) was born in the upstairs bedroom of 34 Rock Road in 1932. Her father was a Co-op bread delivery-man. When Beryl left school she worked at the Siddon's coal yard. Beryl married Ernie Cox in 1934. Ernie worked as a School electrician. She lived next to her parents after she married, so the related families knocked an arched-doorway through inside to join the houses. Technically, Eric lived with Beryl in the house that she was

---

[390] Wendy Bollans, personal history.

born in. Mr and Mrs John E. Hill (Beryl's parents) lived at number 36. John Hill was born in Oundle in 1906.

Beryl recalled that "you couldn't see the fields from the end of the road" when she was a child, "as there was a high hedge at the end of the road", which was just beyond her house. She went on to state that "Mr Ray owned the fields and Lorna Coombs kept her horses there. Between the house and the hedge was a strip of grass, which we called the Green". Beryl remembered that "during the war there were bins for putting waste food in". "Also, for some time there was a lion named Mushie, who was kept in his cage there. The poor old thing was so old by then he had no teeth, but he kids loved him. Mrs Irene Channing looked after him, as she lived along Rock Road." In the 1940s, the locals would all come outside their houses to 'line the street' and watch important events, such as local weddings, for example, when the Bamford's daughter was married. Families got to know their neighbours very well. Beryl told me, "From the back of my house I could see the allotments and the Station and the boats on the river. Lovely views!" She looked down the hillside and said, "I could see right up to Morborne" (which people on the eastern side of the road can still see from their bedroom windows). Beryl has a very good memory. She said, "I know the name of everyone who lived in the street in the 1930s, but of course people stayed in one place then. I hardly know anyone in the street now." This is a sad reflection of the changing society in which we all live.

Mr J. Wright lived at 38. The Coleman family lived here after him. Mr A.F. Gray was at number 40 with his family. Miss Flora Howe lived at 42. Flora never married. She lived from 1874 to 1947.

Two new houses in the road are numbers 42a and 50a. They were built in what was once the large garden of the house next-door. This was originally (in the 1940s) a green space between the terraced houses and the big detached house. On the eastern side of the road this one large house that stood apart from the row was owned by the Gallagher family. Mr Gallagher was a school master at Oundle School. He lived here with his family and husky dogs. It was the home of the Lee family before they moved to Gordon Road. Whilst living here Gerry Lee was visited by "Old Mother Riley", which was the talk of the road.[391] In the 1960s this was Barbara and Stuart Wiggins' house. All the houses on this side of the road have excellent views of the Nene valley and surrounding fields, particularly from their upper floor windows. Now Council-built semi-detached and bungalow houses lead to the end of the road.

Opposite the junction with New Road is Millfields. Millfields is a T-shaped cul-de-sac that denotes the mill and land that stood at the end of the road. Its entrance opens on to New Road. On the land between the field and its junction with New Road stood a house (Hetty Carter and others of her generation recall it clearly). The large and impressive abode was named the Red House. Hetty said that it had a 'wonderfully extensive' orchard. The windmill was a landmark until the 1950s. Many houses now stand on the site. They were built in the 1970s and 1980s. The cul-de-sac is linked with Glapthorn Road via a pedestrian cut-through.

GORDON ROAD

Gordon Road was not built as a loop-road, but a short, straight cul-de-sac. Originally, it had five terraced-houses on the right with slightly larger detached-houses on the left. It ran a short distance to the fields and allotments to the south. Most of Gordon Road was built in the 1940s as Council Housing. There were a few red-brick houses in a row, but for the most part, it was built in an arc, linking with New Road at both ends in 1950. (Houses were then built on fields that had stretched to the brewery in Blackpot Lane on the south-eastern side.) Gordon Road had fifteen terraced houses (at the north-west end) plus four terraced houses placed diagonally (on either side in New Road) that were built at the turn of the twentieth century.

Gordon Road was named in 1905 on the twentieth anniversary of General Gordon's death. The Victorian Major-General Charles George Gordon (1833-1885) had been sent (by the government and Prime Minister, Gladstone) to suppress a rebellion against the colonial powers (who had occupied their country). Gordon had died whilst

---

[391] Oral history, Jill Giddings (née Plowright). Note that Old Mother Riley was a music hall act (1934-1954). The Irish washerwoman and charlady act was played by (and was the concept of) Arthur Lucan. Later Roy Rolland's role (1954-1980s).

fighting against Mahdist warriors in Khatoum, Sudan. He had ties to Northamptonshire with friends in nearby Twywell. General Gordon became a national hero when the news of his demise reached England.

The original numbering was for just a short, Victorian terraced-row that later was part of the outer-loop. (See Map of Gordon Road showing the sets of original and new numbering.) The terraced-house numbering only went to 15. In 1939, the two blocks of terraced houses were 1 to 15 consecutively. The new and old numbering for house 1 is the same.

In the 1940s, Frank Jackson and his family moved to live in Gordon Road. He had problems with his lungs that stemmed from tuberculosis, so he worked locally for the District Council in the East Road depot. During WWII, he was seconded and sent to put telegraph-poles into the fen dykes to prevent enemy boats travelling along them and catching England unaware.[392] In the non-war years, the river was frequently used for transporting items. Some of these items, up to the end of the 1940s were Peterborough bricks from the brick company there. They transported these and other goods to Wansford, Oundle, Thrapston and Northampton.

For the 1952 Coronation celebrations, householders placed chests with fancy cups and items on the concrete lintels above their front doors.[393] Gerry White lived here with his parents in the 1960s. In the pre-war years, Gerry's grandad was Ron White. He worked as a miller at Cotterstock. His grandmother was the post mistress. His father was born in 1917. Doris Englefield was Gerry White's mum. She was in the Land Army, members of which were distributed to assist allied Polish camps and to the German P.O.W. camps. So she knew all of the local farmers and travelled around doing visits. Gerry lives in Australia, but visits Oundle on trips back.[394]

Gordon Road (old outer loop)

Harold Martin lived at number 1 Gordon Road. He was a cabinet maker and undertaker. His wife was named Hilda. They shared their house

---

[392] Oral history, Sharon Cottingham (née Jackson).
[393] Oral history, Gerry White.
[394] Ibid. 23/08/17 – visit.

with Florence Church (born in 1909) and her children. Today there is no number 2, but number 3 was number 2 before the road was extended. At number 3 (previously 2) in the 1930s, there lived Charles and Annie Carter and their family. Charles was a House porter for Oundle School. In the 1960s this house still belonged to the Carter family. (Mrs Carter was Mrs Nancy Trotman's mum.) Prior to the war years, at 5 (previously 3) lived Mrs Agnes Green and her daughter, Dorothy ('Dolly'). Agnes was a widow. Next-door at number 7 (previously 4) there were the Miss Tilley's, Minnie and Ethel. They were retired dressmakers, who were aged in their seventies in the late 1930s. Later, in the 1960s, this was the home of Mrs Ada Plowright (née Martin) who lived here alone. At 9 (the old number 5) there lived Mr John Mould. He worked as a grocer's assistant. He lived with his wife, Lydia (who was born in 1881) and their family, Edith, Muriel, Harold and Thomas E. Mould (possibly known as 'Eric'). Muriel Mould (Eric mould from 57's mum). At 11 (previously 6) was Harriett Peploe. She lived alone. Mrs Ivy Dann (née Martin) was the sister to Ada (from number 6). Ivy lived here with her family (formerly with her parents at number 1]. She returned to the place from where she had been evacuated (in the war) to live here. At this point, there is a passage between houses numbered 12 and 13 (formerly 6 and 7) that leads to the rear gardens.

Number 13 (formerly 7) was where Edward Buswell lived with his wife, Margaret Jeanette (also "Janetta Margretta"). He was a railway man, goods checker. The couple lived with their son, Albert ("Bertie"), who worked as a builder's labourer. Bertie was born in 1920. He married Sharon Cottingham's "Auntie Marjorie" (Cynthia Marjorie Jackson) in 1956. She alleged, "He had a big motor-bike". (I gather that this was not a euphemism!)

From 1939 to the 1960s, number 15 (formerly 8) was the home of Mrs Florence Baxter, who was known as "Granny Baxter" and her son, George W.L. Baxter ("Les"). Les fixed electrical items in part of their house. He kept a shed over the road "by the chickens", where he kept his repair equipment. Les unfortunately had a large goitre on his neck that created his "softly spoken" voice. When he died "there was a sale of hundreds of items, mostly clocks and watches" (as his job was fixing time-pieces). It was held in the old Scout Hut on the corner of St.

Peter's Road. Marilyn Smith and Gwen Hayward helped to organise the sale.[395] Next-door at number 17 (formerly 9) was where Herbert Hackney lived with his wife, Edith. He worked as a butcher's assistant. This was later the home of Mr and Mrs Albert ('Bert') Taney. At 19 (old 10), in 1939, lived Mrs Rebecca Balderson. She was a home nursing auxiliary and was a widow. Dorothy Edwards lived with her. At 21 (old 11, the bigger house at the end of the terraced group) was Albert Cotton, bootmaker. He lived with his wife, Emily. They were the parents of the Cotton (shoe shop) dynasty. They lived with their children, Ena and Hector and their little brother, Jack Cotton, who was born in this house in 1924. When their brother (Philip Cotton) left school at the age of fifteen, he opened the shoe shop business with his older brother, Jack. Jack was responsible for repairing the shoes brought in. When the Cotton family moved, Mrs Shuttleworth lived here. Neighbours said that she was "never seen". Teachers, Bevil and Margaret Allen lived at number 21. Their house looked out at fields in this era, before the Council houses were built.

From number 21 onward the houses are new and date to the 1940s. On the outside loop, at number 23, lived Mr Quincy, who was here In the 1960s. He taught recorder groups at the Oundle Secondary Modern School. Number 25 was where Mr Charles H. Weatherington (1881-1970) lived with his wife and their family. The family eventually grew up and moved out. Richard was always known as "Itchy" as his younger brother, Pip, couldn't pronounce his name. The nickname stuck with him. At number 27 were Mr and Mrs Compton. Miss Ward (now Saunston) lived with her family at 29 Gordon Road, until 1990. Mr John and Mrs Marion Donegani took on the house in 1963 with their four children: Michael, Douglas, Carole and Marilyn lived at number 29 (from 1949 to 1963), while Nan Donegani resided at number 30.

There is a path to the allotments. Sharon Cottingham mentioned that this is where her "Uncle Dennis (Roughton) had an allotment, along with Mr Barnes." Mr and Mrs Harry Marshall lived at number 31. Harry was a chimney-sweep and their son drove a lorry. Mr and Mrs Hitchin lived at 33. Mr and Mrs Ronald White lived at 35 with their children,

---

[395] Marilyn Smith, personal history.

Gerald (Gerry) and Shirley. Ron was a mechanic at East Road NCC Depot. Ron drove Frank Jackson to St Peter's Church with his daughter, Sharon on her wedding day, when she married Steve Cottingham. Later, number 35 was the home of Mr and Mrs Marshall and their children: 'Wibby', George, Noel and Mary. Mr Edward Thomas ('Ted') Marshall worked for Oundle School. He was born in 1896, three years after his brother Arthur ('Fred') Marshall from North Street. For a time the Marshall family lived in the Oundle School Sanatorium before moving in to Gordon Road.

The Wilcox family lived at number 37 in the 1950s and then it was the home of Mr and Mrs Trotman and their children, Jane, Robert, Stephen and Andrew. The Campbell family first lived at 39, then the Crick family were here from 1966 to 1969. The Lee family moved to 39, a slightly smaller house, when their children started to leave home. It had a deep well in the back garden. Mr and Mrs Trayford lived at number 41. Later, Janet Roberts moved in to 41 after living at number 14. Frank and Teresa Jackson lived at 43 from 1951 to 2004, with their children, Lorna, Glynis, Sharon, Rowena, Maria and Robert.

Sharon has "a picture of my cousins Margaret and Billy Pheasant that was taken in the long back garden of 43 Gordon Road. You can see that the ground is dug over, but there are no vegetables or flowers. Sometime later it was all seeded to lawn". Sharon recalls the corn-fields and allotments behind her childhood home stretched all the way to Blackpot Lane. It was an idyllic playground for growing children. After the Jackson children grew, left home, married, and had children of their own, Frank died and Teresa lived here alone for a time before moving to 'Stronglands'.

Number 45 was where John and Dorothy Miles and their children, Alma (Black),[396] Lynette (Black), Anthea (Miles), Lesley (who lived for only three days after her birth in 1956), Julie, Michael and Cheryl ('the twins') and, last but not least, Kevin resided until the 1970s.[397] Cheryl explained that her mother, Dorothy, married her first husband, Reginald Black, in the pre-war years. Reginald died in WWII when Alma was just a tiny baby. Johnnie Miles was Dorothy's second husband.

---

[396] Sadly deceased in late 2017.
[397] Family history, Cheryl Forscutt (née Miles).

Together they had a further six children. The Miles family lived at number 45 for fifty-eight years. The Palmer family moved in after this. Next-door, 47 was the home of Mr and Mrs Melton. Next-door were Mr and Mrs Peggy Pilgrim (at number 49). Mr and Mrs Harold Edwards and their children, Brian and Gordon, moved here after the Pilgrims. Mr Edwards had a box brownie camera (see Sharon Cottingham's story).

Mr and Mrs Willett lived at 51. Mr and Mrs Coles and Arthur Coles lived at 53. Then Mr and Mrs Eric Mould (Tarzan) moved here with their children, Susan, Eileen, Linda, John and Jayne. Number 55 was the home of Tom and Violet Knight and 57 was the home of Mr and Mrs Eric Mould. Eric worked at the NCC yard and was known as Tarzan. Mr and Mrs Fellowes lived at 59 and 61 was the home of Mr and Mrs Ray Sharpe and their daughter, Doreen. Their home was beside the recreation ground path. On the other side of the pathway was Mr and Mrs Jack Bryce, who lived at 63 with their son, Andrew, until his heart-rending, accidental early demise. Andrew sadly drowned while canoeing with friends on the river. Subsequently, the Underwood family lived here.

Number 65 was the home of the Goodacre family and then Mr and Mrs Brackley and their son, Roy. Mr and Mrs Midlane lived at 67 with their children, David and Pat (now Coles). David was one of the founder members of Oundle Amateur Theatrical Society (O.A.T.S.). Mr and Mrs Horner lived at number 69, before Henry and Betty Wiggins and their sons. Mr and Mrs Townsend lived at 71. 73 was the residence of Alan Cherry and his wife. Next-door William ('Bill') and Phyllis Condor (née Marshall) lived at 75. They had no children, but Lizzie Marshall of North Street was Phyllis' mother. Living at number 77 were Charles and Dorothy Hobbs (who married in 1941). Charlie was a local postman. Mr and Mrs Carroll lived next-door at number 79 with their sons, John and Cyril. Mr and Mrs Cosham lived at 81 (1950 to 1968) with their daughter Susan (now Sansby). Sue left Oundle in 1983. In the last house of the road lived Wilfred "Wilf" Ray, his wife, Clarice and their children, Michael, Terry and Corrinne. Mr and Mrs White lived here after the Ray family.

Gordon Road (old inner loop)

Number 4 (formerly 15), a semi-detached house, was the home of Rex and Gwendoline Nightingale and their family. Rex was a public assistance institution relief officer. This was later the home of Mrs Joan Fellows (1960) with her children, John and Anne. Joan was a primary school teacher. Neighbour, Mr Jesse Hill (born in 1884) lived at number 6 (formerly 14) with his wife, Annie (known as "Clara"). He was a public school hairdresser. Also living here was Doris Boursnell. Doris was an evacuee who lived with Jesse and Annie during the war years. In the 1960s this was the home of Miss Rowlett.

Number 8 (formerly 13), was the home of William Richards. He was a furniture upholsterer and an ARP voluntary ambulance-driver. He lived with his wife, Maud and their family. This was later the business and home of Stanley (Stan) and Pamela (Pam) Beesley, who ran their family, industrial and commercial photography and film-processing service here. They were hired for important events: school May Days, Christmas', speech days and weddings. Pam, also a photographer, was a Brownie Leader for many years. They lived here with their children, Chris, Sally and Richard (a talented artist and leatherworker). Richard and Chris played in a local pop band. (See photograph and following pages for further information.) The new number 10 (formerly 12) is like 8, 6 and 4, in that they are all semi-detached and stand opposite the old terraced houses. 10 was the home of George and Elizabeth Sharpe. George was a retired postman. After Mrs Sharpe had moved, Mr and Mrs Danny Jackson lived here. (The new-build properties were built after this house.)

Gordon Road (new inner loop)

Number 12 was the first of the newer houses in Gordon Road. First there were Mr and Mrs Charles ("Charlie") Foster in number 12. It was later the residence of George and Hetty Carter and their young children, Jonathan and Paul, who were here until the early 1960s. When they moved out, Mr and Mrs Lilley moved in. Mr Arthur and Mrs Phyllis (née Wallinger) Groves lived at number 14 with their children (Wendy and Neil) in the 1960s. At 16 were Mr and Mrs Dennis

Roughton. Sharon Cottingham said that "Dennis was my dad's cousin and he was always known as Uncle Dennis" (and "Aunty Eileen"). They lived here in 1971.

There was one occasion in 1971 or 1972, when (on a spontaneous whim) Sharon and I were taken to a party in Cottingham village near Corby. The party went on for longer than we had anticipated and we needed to wait until Mr Blackman (who had driven us to the party with his son and other Laxton school boys) returned to collect us. On her arrival Sharon asked to be dropped at the corner, as she didn't want to be taken all the way to the house. On the quiet walk to her home along Gordon Road she passed 'Uncle Dennis' standing by his gate. He said with a chuckle, "Do you know they've been looking for you? I'm going to stay here and listen to this. It's going to be good!" (It was! Sharon and I were on a ban from meeting after school for quite a while after that!)[398] During the 1960s, there were Mr and Mrs Cunnington at number 18. Mr and Mrs Barnes lived at 20. Number 22 was the home of Mr and Mrs Burdett, then (later) John and Mary Clark from 1947 to 1968. After the Clark's Mr Archie Marshall (who owned the garage and TV shop) moved in and lived here. Val Palmer lived here afterwards.

At 24 were Mr and Mrs Moorehead, then Mr and Mrs Peggy Thurlby. Mr Gerald and Mrs Ellen Lee (née Harvey) lived next-door at 26. As their family grew and shrank they moved houses within the road. When Gerry lived in Gordon Road, amongst his neighbours were the Beesley's. Pam and Stan's eldest son, Chris Beesley sang and played in a local rock band (or bands) and his friends. It is believed that one band name was 'Oddessy'. Gerald Lee had written many songs in his theatrical life and had a demo-record made of some of the songs. Gerry decided to write some song lyrics for Chris' band, which they performed in public, but in 1979 Gerry's work was plagiarised by the popular singer, David Essex,[399] who had made a couple of small variations and added his own name as the song-writer. The song (and the single) was "Goodbye First Love". It was also released on Essex's 'Imperial Wizard' album. Gerry immediately recognised this music as his own, and so did the Oundle band it had been given to. No acknowledgement appeared for Gerry, so he complained to the record

[398] Anna Fernyhough and Sharon Cottingham, personal history.
[399] This popular singer starred in the stage-musical "Godspell" in the 1970s.

producers. David Essex immediately withdrew the singles of the song from being sold, but could do little about the multi-tracked LP (long-playing) records. After an interesting court case, the outcome was that Gerry was repaid his royalties and the issue was smoothed-over.[400] The Lee's lived in the large, family house for many years. (Mr and Mrs Ted Hooton lived here in the mid-1950s, after some of their children had grown, married and moved away.)

At 28 were Mr and Mrs J Sanders. Their son, Tim was part of Chris Beesley's band. Next-door, at number 30, there was Mrs Belcher (then Mrs Clarke moved in after her). At 32 lived Mr and Mrs Hastings. (The Goodman's moved in to 32 afterwards.) Norman Bunning and his wife lived at 34. Norman was the son of James and Edith Bunning (nee Taney). He was born in 1943 and lived all his life in Oundle. Later residents at 34 were "Spook" Upex and his family. At 36 there were Mr and Mrs Palmer, then the Goodman's, then the Hasting's. Next-door were Mr and Mrs C. Gryst (at 38). Alf and Ida Kemp lived at 40 by the Underwood family at number 42. For many years Henry and Betty Wiggins lived at number 69. (Betty died in 2017, aged 92.) Betty and Henry had six sons: Nigel (emigrated), Ian, Graham, Stuart (who married Barbara Wright), Granville (who married his school sweetheart, Julie) and Cary. Henry worked at Laxton Junior School until his retirement. Mark Fernyhough recalls Henry being a kind man, who "rubbed our knees when we fell over and told us everything would be alright".[401]

...oooOOOooo...

---

[400] Tim Lee, personal history, interview 08/06/2017. Particular thanks for the loan of the "cuttings-diary" of Mr. Harvey (senior) by 'Ginger' Lee 08/06/2017.
[401] Mark Fernyhough, personal history.

Big Cats and Little Cats – Julian and Tim Lee

Oundle and the Butlins' Connection

The Lee family first came to Oundle in the 1900s with a travelling theatre. They liked the town and stayed. They staged "Maria Martin and the Red Barn".

The then Oundle resident, Mr Gerald (Gerry) Lee, first lived in Benefield Road (later in Gordon Road) and "helped to fund Billy Butlin's holiday business in post-war Skegness with his savings". The venture was new in holiday ideas, as prior to this holidaymakers stayed in hotels and boarding-houses. Tim Lee, said that his dad was "paid back every penny that was borrowed by the Butlin's family and he was held in high regard by the Butlin family". Billy Butlin had established and built the holiday business. Bobby Butlin continued directing the Butlins' Holiday Camps from 1968-1984 after taking over when his father (Sir Billy Butlin) retired. The scheme was quickly endorsed and enjoyed by self-catering, holidaying families of post-war England.

Around 1968, Gerry Lee worked at Fairline Boats in Oundle, where he worked alongside the manager David Wills. Gerry is best regarded for his life spent as a pantomime cat act. Once, to advertise the local production he sat on the roof of a house in Benefield Road. He spoke on "Desert Island Discs" and discussed "being on the stage" with Roy Plomley. On the recorded BBC radio programme he talked about the eight gramophone records he would take to a desert island. He discussed how his character,' Billy the cat' (a fast kitten as other actors had the slow cat routines) ran around on stage and upset the Dame in pantomimes. He said that wearing the hot costumes was problematic and custom-made costumes cost £50, which was "very dear", so he made his own with a half-mask that was more comfortable than a full mask. With tongue-in-cheek, he remarked that "The kiddies pushed me and I fell over the edge of the stalls, but I landed on a fat lady, so everything was alright."

Gerry appeared on stage as a cat in many, many pantomimes, including "Dick Whittington" and "Puss in Boots". He said that he ran and jumped, climbed and hopped. He was challenged by a "ten-foot leap" onto a window to push open the bars, then twist-leap onto a table and spin around. When the table was not set-up properly, he fell and broke his collar bone! In different pantomimes he played a range of characters: dog, monkey, bear, goose, crocodile, horse and cow. All of them had routines and dance steps. He said that playing a goose was very hard as the costume was an iron frame with straps that did not allow him to sit (or stand) properly. He was asked if he would do it again and he replied, "I only do it if I have to."

His family are proud of him and his favourite 'stage' character: Tom the kitten. Gerry raised money as a 'cat' (and in the Freemasons as a Water Rat!) by using his celebrity status for charity purposes.[402] In 1946 "youngsters were delighted by the agile cat descending from the gallery", when the pantomime cast at the Theatre Royal, Huddersfield (1943-1944), included Gerry. He was described as a children's favourite "in his persona as his cat character".[403]

An early (1938) programme for the "Would You Believe It!" show in the Empire Theatre, London, presented a line-up with publicity (and troupes) that would be frowned on today for being 'politically incorrect'. The show displayed Fredel ("Is he a Man or a Wax Dummy?"), Elroy the armless artiste, the Man with the Xylophone Skull, the Besplays with their Unbreakable Doll, Lofty and Pippi, "the famous midget from Olympia, London", the impressionist George Meaton and 'Mushie' "the forest-bred lion"(!). Mushie lived in Oundle and belonged to the Lee family.

Gerry E.J. Lee met and married Miss Ellen E.L. Harvey when they were both relatively young. In early 1942 they were 'on tour' in Halifax, North Yorkshire. Ellen came from a different branch of "showbiz family entertainment", but she and Gerry, but they made a good team. In December 1942 there was an announced that the wedding of "two artistes appearing with the Royal Allied Circus had taken place at the Register Office in Halifax". The couple were "married in the afternoon

---

[402] The Lee family have a book of information and cuttings about their father. For 1949, it says: "Something extraordinary has happened in the Grand Order of Water Rats, for a Cat has entered its portals. In this, the diamond jubilee year of the Order, Gerry Lee, the Cat, is a member of this distinguished Order of Water Rats".
[403] Gerry Lee spoke of his theatrical life and favourite music on "Desert island Discs" (on the BBC Home Service in the early 1960s. Information with thanks to Tim and 'Ginger' Lee.

and went straight to the theatre to prepare for the evening show". An announcement noted that Gerald Lee was 'the Cat' of the circus and his bride "a female lion-tamer". Ellen had tamed two cats!

Ellen was born in London. She grew up touring the world with her father. They were in America at the outbreak of war and they returned immediately to England. Ellen's father was Jack Harvey, a showman and entertainer. Jack established Ellen with her own lion, Mushie, who (when at home) usually lived in the field at the end of Benefield Road (in his own trailer).

Gerald was, by all accounts, "quite a character". In the 1960s Gerry (and whoever he chose to take with him) would take his horse and trap from his house in the Benefield Road to a "No parking sign in town where he and his friend, Billy Russell, would tether their horses". (Both men paid little or no heed to the sign!)

Mushie (the lion)

Ellen and her family toured and exhibited their lion (taking Mushie on the Oundle train) from his acquisition in early 1940, while Ellen was working in a Cheltenham munitions factory.

During his life "in entertainment", Mushie had been trained to eat steak from Ellen's face and forehead. He only did this twice nightly (or "he would have been too full to eat"). He was introduced to audiences and was presented by Jack Harvey, Ellen's father. The act starred "Mushie the Forest-Bred Lion" and consisted of Ellen Harvey dressed in full military uniform in the centre of the stage. Sometimes they would tussle and wrestle! In a 'beauty and the beast' style act, she would lie-down with Mushie, then stroke and cuddle him to represent what a "softie" he could become for her. Then (tamed) the 'beast' would eat raw meat from her chest, face and mouth. In his heyday, Mushie would lick and eat "a steak, about 3 inches by 3 inches" from Ellen's face while she reclined on the stage.

Billed at the London Palladium as the "forest bred lion" he was later described in the 'Yorkshire Post' (November 1948) as coming "from Abyssinia". It also said that he had "never performed his stage act behind bars". Ellen would "risk death" by putting her head inside his mouth. (As time went by Mushie became fairly old and toothless, so

'Miss Ellen' had to pick her moment and "wait for him to yawn before putting her head inside his gums"!) In his dotage Mushie needed cut-up and minced food for the stage show. One report stated that in the act he "couldn't chew raw meat, so it had to be chopped into tiny pieces before being placed on her ample bosom!"[404]

A cutting that the family kept in their little brown press-book is noted as from the 1946 'Eastbourne Gazette'. It stated that "Mushie is as harmless as a kitten". He would writhe on the floor with Ellen and allow his chum, a diminutive white terrier, to have "fun and games with him". Mushie's final test of self-control always came when he was expected to eat a lump of raw meat off Miss Ellen's face. "It is rather a nasty moment for the audience when Mushie's mouth opens with a roar of delight and his teeth close over the meat." Mushie was large and described as weighing four-and-a-half hundred-weight with a good appetite. In 1943 he had his own ration card that needed to be stamped for his meals of a "hundred weight of horse meat".

All usually went well in the performances, but in one performance a teenage boy was injured. A cutting in the family scrap-book from the 1944 'Manchester News' sensationalised the event with the headline: 'Boy Jumps on Lion's back'. This critique painted the generally gentle 'Mushie' in a bad light, yet hospital medics tended their patient for "non-routine injuries". John Robinson (aged fifteen) attended Manchester's 'Belle Vue' Circus with his parents on Christmas day. While they were watching "a wrestling match act between Ellen Harvey and her five-year-old lion" John left his seat and ran into the ring. To the amazement and shock of those watching, he jumped onto the lion's back. Mushie was not used to this sort of treatment. He shook John from his back and pulled him to the floor. The audience shrieked as the animal trainers ran in and dragged the big cat off the boy (and presumably the boy off the lion). Mushie released his grip and John was taken to Hospital. Mushie was checked for injuries and the act resumed with Ellen carrying-on with her performance. John was treated for a lacerated leg at the Hospital and promptly discharged. It was said that he took home "a wad of hair that he had ripped from

---

[404] Information from Markllewellin.blogspot.co.uk/2010/08/corrie-legend.htm

Mushie's back" and an autographed picture of Ellen Harvey. One wonders what the boy's parents thought he was doing!

A few years later, there was a story in the papers stating that the nineteen year old, Ellen was bitten by seven year old (male) lion, Mushie, who she had trained as a 'wrestling stage act'. The inclusion of wild animals in stage performances was somewhat acceptable at the time. Mushie did not always live alone. He had plenty of attention from Ellen and his fans. Not only was Speck frequently seen within his travelling cage, in 1946 he shared his home with Pongo, a small lion cub. It was thought that Pongo would join the act or eventually replace the fully grown lion, but Pongo was not a fast learner. As a local favourite and celebrity, Mushie had a canine friend, Speck (a terrier) who appears in photographs with the lion. Speck joined in with some of the Mushie's acts. He also appeared in advertising and articles about his friend! Tim Lee commented that Speck "may look different on some of the photographs as the family had more than one dog named Speck"!

An incident occurred during 1948 at an evening performance at the 'Palace Theatre' in Reading. It was reported that Mushie had "seemed agitated all afternoon" before the performance. The bite was sensationalised in the press who described Ellen's hand as having "his teeth sinking to her bone". Ellen completed the remainder of her act before seeking medical attention and during her second act that evening "was wrapped in bandages"! It was claimed that in the later performance Mushie was back to his "usual self" and ate raw meat from Ellen with no safety issues. A similar occurrence happened about a year later. By 1948 it was said that Mushie had bitten up to twenty-four people! Ellen always maintained that she was "none the worse" for her scratches and bites.

Ellen gained the unofficial world record as the youngest female lion tamer. Another lovely story comes from 1949 when there was a new panic in Reading, when someone reported seeing a lion. Mr Harvey was woken and taken by the police to the warehouse where Mushie was being kept. There were fears for the night watchman as he was nowhere to be seen. On getting hold of a ladder to enter the building, the stage manager arrived in his pyjamas (with a key). On entering the building the police and family found that both Mushie and the night watchman were both sound asleep.

It seems Miss Ellen and her companion were very popular attractions in the 1950s and performed at different theatres around the country! Throughout the 1950s, Gerry and Ellen's children were born and lived in Oundle. This was their home and base when not touring with their acts. Ellen and Gerry would often collect their son, Julian, from school in their horse and cart. This they kept in the field by Mushie's cage. For much of their married life the Lee family lived in Gordon Road. Ellen and Gerry Lee's children were: Peter, Wendy, Roger, Geraldine, Paul, Julian (known as Ginger), Timothy (Tim) and Simon. Simon, the youngest, was born in 1964. Of Ellen, her son Tim said that his "mum was so kind that all of our friends would turn up to play" in their house and garden. He said, "She wouldn't mind, even if she'd been working in the fields all day. She always cooked a nutritious stew or something tasty for everyone." Their Gordon road neighbour, Sharon (Jackson, now Cottingham) recalls that "Ellen was a gentle, lovely lady".

When not entertaining audiences Mushie lived in his field at the end of the Benefield Road. Ruth Lee (née Robinson) said that her parents' home was near the field where Mushie lived. Ruth recalls that she could hear Mushie roaring and "roaring at night when all was quiet". She suggested that it was quite a calming sound as if he was talking to himself.

Tim said that at times small children were allowed to ride on his back when he took a walk down the road with Ellen "to exercise and stretch his legs".

Many of Ellen and Gerry's children live with their families in Oundle. They are rightly proud of their touring heritage and have favourable memories of the family lion.[405] Gentle Mushie was frequently walked down the main road to the station or exercised along the Benefield Road. Ellen sometimes used the land behind the "Wagon and Horses" and the yard behind the station for overnight stays when leaving or returning from touring. Mushie was a town favourite, as not every town has its own lion. Children loved to watch him. Ellen was not the

---

[405] Personal and family information, with kind permission of Julian Lee and Tim Lee.

only star in the Harvey family as her sister, 'Rene' (Irene Channing) entertained as a tightrope-walker. Both sisters married and settled in Oundle. Irene's son, Michael, lives in Oundle. To honour these memories, Tim Lee and his family currently have a pet cat named "Mushie".

...oooOOOooo...

Occupation Road

Occupation Road is an off-shoot of New Road and part of St. Peter's Road. Its name relates to the 'occupiers' of land. Early maps show a footpath leading to Cotterstock. Dog walkers of today frequently use the same trail. It was a former site of the Oundle Public Swimming Pool (1960s). The land currently has the local Tennis Club, Bowling Club and Rugby Club on its length. There are also public allotments along the road with an entrance via the Bowling Club. (The bowling club was on the left-hand side of Herne Road before moving to Occupation Road.) During the mid-1960s, there was a community swimming pool on Occupation Road. The local Secondary Modern School and the Oundle Youth Club would use it for swimming lessons during the school week. At other times it was open to the public. There was a café at the entrance which provided hot drinks. Granville Wiggins recalls that they would serve hot Bovril in the little hut. Most of the "youth of the day" spent their pocket money here. Children loved swimming at the pool. Rowena Brown (née Jackson) recalls how her lips would go blue while swimming in the cold water. "Then I'd change and get warm for a short time, before changing back into my wet costume again and get back in the water again." She recalled, "I'd always finish with a bottle of Coke and a packet of Quavers". (The pool had a lifeguard on duty when it was open and this was safer than the deep river and riverside-pool.) This pool was where the tennis courts and club-house currently stand.

The Oundle Rugby Club was formed in 1976 by a group of rugby enthusiasts at the "Ship" (with a mutual desire for a local rugby club). The group began by negotiating a field to play on and by dismantling an old tea-room, before transporting and reassembling it as the first club house in Occupation Road. It has been extended over the years; the southern half (changing-rooms) is the original building. It has been observed that regular firework night bonfires were held here until

486

rubbish was fly-tipped on the land prior to events. At this point these community celebrations were moved elsewhere. The corner of the field is not cultivated as it is the boggy area from the ditch and nearby wildlife preserve, Snipe Meadow. (See below.)

St. Peter's and St. Wilfrid's Roads

The houses in St. Peter's Road were all built since the 1960s. The odd numbers from 35-67 are north facing bungalows, designed in twos. Number 67 lies behind the tennis courts, where the road narrows. The houses here are a mix of Council-rented dwellings and private residences. St. Peter's Road was named for the Parish Church and was built on land formerly held by it. This new road was constructed on fields at this north-eastern extremity of Oundle. St. Peter's Road merges with Occupation Road and New Road (by the recreation ground). Nearby St. Wilfrid's Road and Latham Road were also Council-built in the 1960s and were named to commemorate Oundle saint (Wilfrid) and local benefactor Parson Latham.

Extremity Edges, Fields and Footpaths

The railway line ran by the Riverside, where you could walk along the disused railway line to Barnwell in the late-1960s. The rail-lines crossed the river via the Black Bridges and led the trains past the football field and onward to Barnwell, Thrapston and Kettering to Northampton (see the photograph of the Black Bridge). The Black Bridge proceeded the Cheremy Bridge. The Jubilee Bridges were footbridges over the Nene in the south "Bassett" fields. The North Bridge and South Bridge carried vehicles into Oundle by road. All of the bridges into Oundle were originally mediæval and aided travel and trade with a manorial income from Oundle market and tolls. Before bridge construction, Oundle's southerly access was across the low-point of the Nene at Bas-Ford (off St. Sythe's Lane).

Built in 1565, Warren Bridge crosses the brook on the road to Stoke Doyle. The lane ran behind the stream and tenements. The Spittle-Close Hospital was at the western end of the town. This converted into the Isolation Hospital and Sanatorium during the war years. The buildings are located in Wood Lane, which has had new building after 2000. Stoke Doyle Road was mainly used by those unwell (with TB and other infectious diseases on route to the hospital), mourners and other visitors to the nearby cemetery, in addition to daily labours riding, cycling or walking to the nearby villages to the west.

Willow-tree "osiery beds" (growing the flexible wood that could be coppiced for baskets) were beside the "Riverside Inn" and river. The footpath and "the Quicks" went northward to Cotterstock along the rail line. At one point in the 1960s there was a 'blazing, line fire'. It spread and the neighbouring coal-yard caught alight. The fire brigade were called and eventually the fire was extinguished.

Snipe Meadow is wetland area, situated on the banks of the River Nene north of Oundle Wharf. It is a very important site for protecting endangered Snipe and Redshank. The meadow provides nesting sites for Snipe with minimised disturbance. Walkers enjoy the riverside setting and its wildlife. The meadow has a 'County Wildlife Site' status and has mire and marsh. There is an access point opposite the main pitch of the Rugby Club at the end of Occupation Road and St Peter's Road. Snipe Meadow has a board-walk that is suitable for wheelchair access. It runs from the pitch to the river and its footpath. The wooden walkway was repaired in late 2017. The nearby sewage works were built in 1961. They are at the end of a track leading northward to Cotterstock Road. This is a favourite dog-walking area, particularly in the summer months.

2000 and Beyond

An early English proverb of St. Marher (1225), repeated by Geoffrey Chaucer, says it all: "Time and tide wait for no man". 'For though we sleep or wake, or roam, or ride, time forever flees away; it will tarry for no person.'

Oundle market town thrives, prospers and grows. The residents of the town have a strong bond with the past and present - and are ready for the innovations of the future. Town history helps us gain an affinity and insight into our 'local' sphere through perceived past events, present concerns and challenges of our future. 'Transition Oundle' established plans to help Oundle families and businesses reduce our carbon footprint and protect our town for future generations. The project considers energy use, food, transportation, work, lifestyles and has run a lottery-funded the 'Oundle: On your bike!' project (2012-2013). They have also supported the Rock Road Community Garden project (2015-2016) along with new business start-ups during in 2016.[406]

The Oundle and District Twinning Association was formed by Christine and Barry Barcock in 1993. In 1994 the Mayors of Nauort (Germany) and Oundle signed twinning chapters. Regular visits by residents of both towns take place and friendships have already grown between the people of the twinning groups. The town of Andresy, Paris, formed an alliance with Oundle in 2001. It has also participated in mutual visits, friendship and member exchanges.

We have come full-circle within this book. From the early farmer's markets and small schools to the more established versions of the same. Local people can make a difference. Using our local resources and taking care of our inhabitants is key. This is our town and ours is the design of what is yet to come. Oundle is a safe and healthy community. We take a pride in our town. New families wish to live in our desirable location and frequently move into the local community and expanding town. There was a recent change of perception as to how local state schools function. In the past few years there were meetings between educators and town parents who were asked for their collective opinion on how local schools should proceed. (Not all parents came away from this with their concerns met.) Perhaps it is a time for local authorities to listen to what is being said and plan accordingly.

Living anywhere (not just in Oundle) poses many questions. How do we choose to live out our lives in our places of work and in our leisure times? We need to save some of our green spaces and not sell-off or over-develop what makes us Oundle. How can we learn from the past? How do we choose to live our lives? Are we happy and safe in our places of work and how do we spend our precious leisure time? Many of our older generation whom I spoke with in interviews for this book looked back with nostalgia and they looked ahead. Oundle has facilities and services to make use of. Let's use them.

---

[406] https://transitionoundle.org.uk

We should maintain and keep our green spaces. On a large scale: Is it wise to sell-off or over-develop what makes us Oundle? On a smaller scale, the green areas and fields we have around us need to be cared for by ALL of us. I recall Alan Denley (in the early 1960s) telling a hall of gaping children that if we unwrap a sweet "Don't drop the paper. Put it in your pocket and put it in the bin at home". Our town is not as badly littered as some, but if every person takes their cans, papers, dog-waste, wrappers and bottles home we can keep the town clean and healthy. We need to repeat Alan's words and make sure that our children are aware of their environment. (This really does last for life!) Individuals must decide for themselves how they want live out their lives in their work and leisure time.

In uncertain times when Oundle is faced with a potential loss of our health-care and emergency services, it is time to notice and say"This is what we want", while hoping that those in authority have the good sense to hear. We are a polite community (as a whole), gracious and willing. We must tell our stories and be proud of our past. I hope that our memories give a peek into the past that will be preserved in the present and teach us to conserve the future of Oundle.

...oooOOOooo...

THE IMPENDING FUTURE

Oundle is a fascinating town of school and people. It has relatively humble beginnings centred on the river and its location, nestled into the side of a hill. Oundle has grown and developed since its prehistoric roots and continues to grow and thrive, thanks in part to the market centre of the town.

New businesses continue to pop up and change as times determine and tastes change. A shop that sold records may have mutated and may sell foodstuffs and stores that sold groceries may now sell second hand items, but whatever changes, Oundle remains a 'heart' in the countryside; never far from a field or riverside spot.

What keeps some families here may be enough to drive others away. Families like that of Sue Stamper, Sue Saunston and the Donegani family left to work elsewhere, while others like Mick and Sue Crick moved away to retire. Many seek work in the larger towns and cities and the 'knowing everyone' (and everything about them) issue of small villages and towns is slowly fading into the past. My own children have enjoyed living elsewhere as 'no one knows anything about us here', and this is their preference. My preference is knowing my neighbours and enjoying the conviviality of stopping every five minutes while walking into the town to chat with people I know. To reiterate and paraphrase what Richard Ormston has said, "Some days you just can't walk a hundred yards down the street without talking to half of Oundle. You just can't expect to be in a hurry!"

I hope that time will not wither Oundle or transform it into a sprawling mass of 'satellite-town' housing, with buildings packed into the spaces linking us to nearby Peterborough and Corby without a patch of countryside to be seen. We are unique, individual and quite different in our ways when compared with the other towns in the vicinity. We lost a railway link, but we have thrived by remaining rural. Some of Oundle's young people find the town lacking in suitable jobs and an absence of social life or have simply moved away, as they cannot afford the cost of housing. We have a community that is in part made up of friendly newcomers, commuters and long-term residents who have their historical roots here. Families may come and go, but Oundle hangs on to the past in many ways. Our town is quaint. It bears a specific character, reassuring to its inhabitants, sublime and safe. The public school looks after many of the character houses and is an integral part of what Oundle is. The town may be limited in scope, but has much to offer. We discover ourselves if we delve a little deeper into the shops, societies, green spaces, eating places and – the very essence of the town - the people who live here. Oundle local shops and houses are beautiful buildings in an amazing setting. We own a history that we can be proud of. However, this lovely rural area is accessible to nearby urban areas, which is a very good reason for us to counter over-urbanisation. We live here because we love our town.

Do we ever consider who lived in our house before we did? Will people wonder about us and remember us when we are gone? My prime reason for gathering these memories is that in a few years' time, if not collected and shared, they will be permanently lost to history.

Oundle does not wish to rush into the future. The town and its people are happily settled in their personal and historical roots.

Author: Anna Fernyhough, Articles and Publications

"*Serfs, Slaves and Shifta: Modes of Production and Resistance in Pre-revolutionary Ethiopia*", by Timothy Derek Fernyhough. I finalised and posthumously published my late-husband, Tim's book, with publishers: Shama Books, Addis Ababa, Ethiopia (2010). ISBN: 9994400290 and 9789994400294.

In "Women, Gender History and Imperial Ethiopia", in T. Hunt and M. Lessard (editors), *Women and the Colonial Gaze* (Basingstoke: Palgrave, 2002), Chapter 15, with T.D. Fernyhough, pp. 188-201.

In W.H.C. Frend and A. Cameron, "Survey Excavation on the Long Field at Rookery Farm, Great Wilbraham," *Proceedings of the Cambridge Antiquarian Society* 81 (1992), Section on "The Bones", pp. 11-13.

With T. Riley & K. McGowan, *A Final Report on Excavations at the George Ward and Fultz Archaeological Sites in the Shelbyville Reservoir, Illinois,* (U.S. Army Corps of Engineers, St. Louis District, 1983).

"The Raspberry Mound Mortuary Site (11-Mt-5), Shelbyville Reservoir, Illinois: an analysis of skeletal material". M.A. Thesis, 1983 ©, based on original research, University of Illinois, USA.

"*The Traditional Role of Women in Imperial Ethiopia,*" Steward Journal of Anthropology, 13, 2 (1982), pp. 69-82.

In 2012 on returning from teaching in Ethiopia, I established and ran the Little Ducklings Pre-School, Barnwell, where I remain a Director.

Contributor: Margaret Brewster, Articles and Publications

"A Collection of Oundle Families", Upfront Publishing (2016), ISBN-10: 1784564281 and ISBN-13: 978-1784564285.

"Woodstone 1841-1945", Fast-Print.net/bookshop; 1st edition (2009), ISBN-10: 184426615X and ISBN-13: 978-1844266159.

Margaret runs a family history group at the Bretton Library, Peterborough.

Figure 1: Map to show Oundle to circa 1500

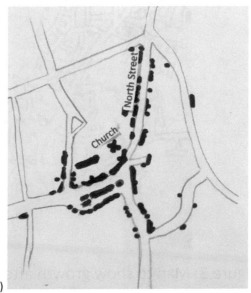

(Not to scale)

Figure 2: Map to show Oundle to c.1900

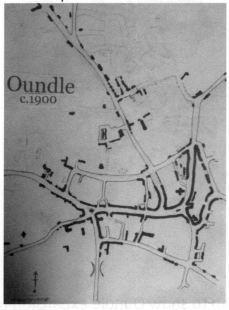

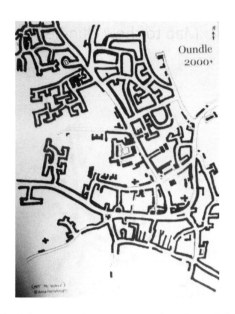

Figure 3: Map to show growth after 2000 A.D.

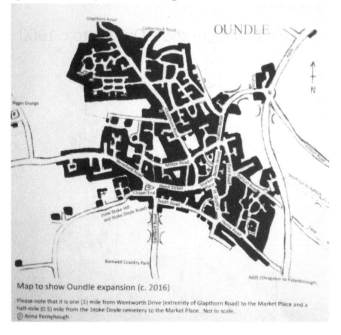

Figure 4: Map to show Oundle expansion (c. 2016)

494

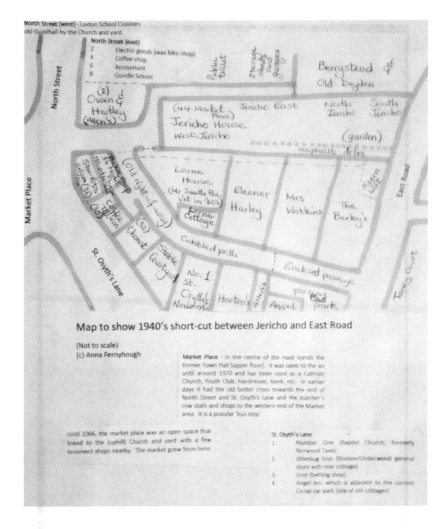

Map to show 1940's short-cut between Jericho and East Road

(Not to scale)
(c) Anna Fernyhough

Map labels:
North Street (west) - Laxton School Cloisters old Guildhall by the Church and yard.
North Street (east)
2 — Electric goods (was bike shop)
4 — Coffee shop
6 — Accountant
8 — Oundle School

North Street

(2) Owen & Hartley (Allen's)

Public toilet

Storage sheds and garages

Berrystead & Old Dryden

(44 Market Place) Jericho House
Jericho East
West Jericho
North Jericho
South Jericho
(garden)
asphalt drive

Market Place

(Old right-of-way)

Lorne House (Mr Smith the Vet in '60s)
Lorne Cottage
Eleanor Harley
Mrs Watkins
The Beebys

Fancy Court
East Road

Cobbled path

Enclosed passage

St. Osyth's Lane

Staple Courtyard
No. 1 St. Osyth's Nicholds
Hooton's
Angel
garages
Cub Park

Fancy Court

Market Place - in the centre of the road stands the former Town Hall (upper floor). It was open to the air until around 1970 and has been used as a Catholic Church, Youth Club, hairdresser, bank, etc. In earlier days it had the old butter cross towards the end of North Street and St. Osyth's Lane and the butcher's row stalls and shops to the western end of the Market area. It is a popular 'bus stop'.

Until 1066, the market place was an open space that linked to the (uphill) Church and yard with a few tenement shops nearby. The market grew from here.

St. Osyth's Lane
1 — Number One (Baptist Church, formerly Norwood Taxis)
2 — Jitterbug toys (Hooton/Underwood general store with rear cottages)
3 — Grot (betting shop)
4 — Angel Inn, which is adjacent to the current Co-op car park (site of old cottages)

Figure 5: Map to show 1940's short-cut between Jericho and East Road

495

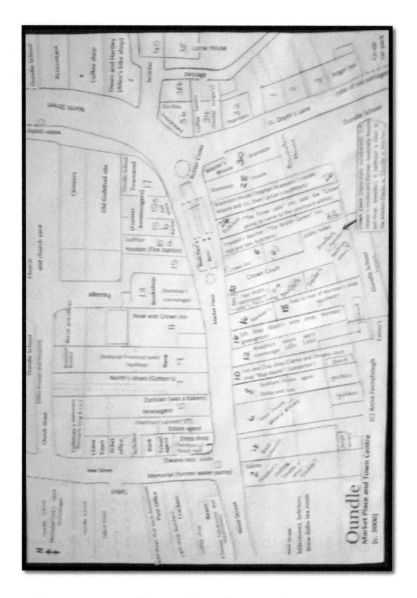

Figure 6: Oundle Market Place and Town Centre,

c. 2000

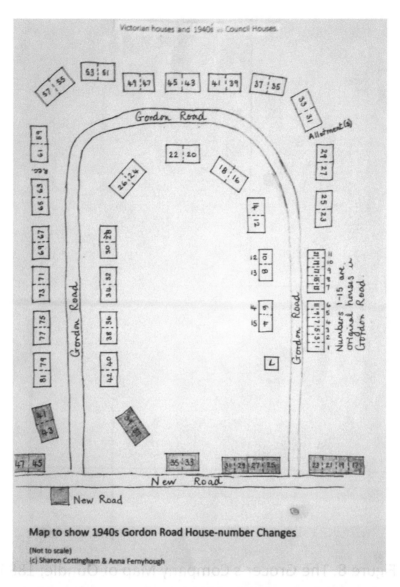

Map to show 1940s Gordon Road House-number Changes

(Not to scale)
(c) Sharon Cottingham & Anna Fernyhough

Figure 7: Map to show 1940's Gordon Road House-number Changes

Plan of Layout and Numbering of Gordon Road Houses

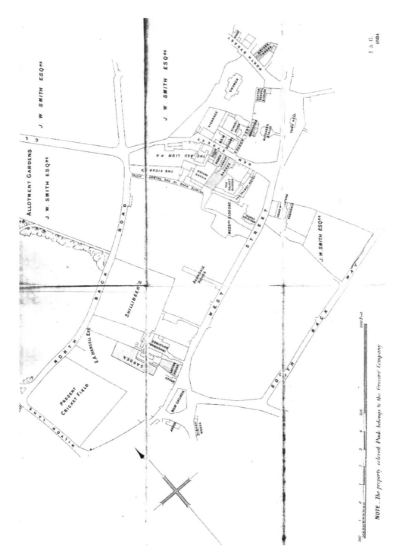

Figure 8. The Grocer's Company Map of Oundle, 1884.

(Kindly produced with the permission of the Worshipful Company of
Grocers, Oundle School.)

Figure 9. Map of Oundle, 1901.

(Kindly produced with the permission of the Worshipful Company of Grocers, Oundle School.)

APPENDICES

An 'Ephemeral' Timeline

Prehistoric - 43 A.D.	**Neolithic and Iron Age** archaeological finds and later **Bronze Age** Beaker remains (1982 on the A605 dig at the Oundle-Ashton site).[407] An Iron Age hamlet was a likely trading-hub for local farmers and crafts-people.[408]
44–410	**Roman:** Roman settlement remains have been found on the upper and lower hillsides in Oundle. Roman remains include buildings, a farmstead, amphora, pottery and graffito, a Roman cemetery and enclosures with stone buildings.[409]
410–597	**Anglo-Saxon:** Saxons (the *Undalas*) settled here (bequeathing us the name *Undala* that became Oundle). 'Undala' is thought to mean 'unsettled' (with no home-base).[410] St. Wilfrid's Church was on the site of St. Peter's Church and dates from the Saxon's to the 1700s. Oundle was an asset of Peterborough Abbey. Leofsi (son of Bixi) razed Oundle monastery and lay-waste locally. It was later repaired.[411] Archbishop Wulfstan (of York) was buried here (957).[412] Bishop (later saint) Ethelwold (Æthelwold [909–984 A.D.]) visited properties here that the Danes destroyed.

---

[407] BC is also BCE ('before Christian era'). AD is CE ('Anno Domini' or 'Christian Era').

[408] Office for National Statistics: Oundle CP: Parish headcounts, July 2015.

[409] The ARCHI database notes 846 sites near Oundle (10km). Northamptonshire Archaeological Society promotes the study of Northants archaeology and history.

[410] 'The Anglo-Saxon Chronicle: a collaborative edition', Vol.7, ed. D.N. Dumville, Simon Keynes and Simon Taylor.

[411] "A History of England: From the First Invasion by the Romans, Volumes 1-2", by John Lingard: *Hist. Elien* (Anglia Christ.), p. 122. (1819 and 1827).

[412] www.british-history.ac.uk/vch/northants/vol3/pp85-101

597-1066	**Middle Ages (Mediæval):** Oundle's patron saint, Cett(a) dates to the 7th century. The Anglo-Saxon (Secgan) manuscript says he was buried in our monastery.[413] Mediæval buildings included a market butter-cross and buildings. The Talbot (Tabret) timber-frame dates to 638 A.D. It was later rebuilt with stone (early 1600s).
1066-1154	**Norman:** Oundle is recorded in the Domesday Book as holding farming-land, a mill and thirty-six houses. Oundle is not cited as contracting the Black Death (when nearby places were affected).
1154-1485	**Plantagenet:** In 1230, Henry III visited Oundle and granted an annual (Ascension fortnight) fair.[414] In 1465 a grammar school was established, where William Laxton was educated. In 1556, he founded Laxton Grammar School with administration regulated by the 'Worshipful Board' from the Grocers' Company. The Ship Inn (a 14th-century coach-inn) was built. Most of St. Peter's church dates to the thirteenth-century. In Oundle in 1297 the Bishop of Durham's men were assaulted and goods bought at Oundle market for their bishop (Anthony Beck) were stolen.[415]

---

[413] "Cett 1". Prosopography of Anglo-Saxon England. *Morris, Carwyn Hywel.* "The Concept of Territory in the Late Anglo-Saxon and Early Medieval Cult of Saints in England" *(PDF). E-theses.bham.ac.uk. p. 5.* Also: "Cett - oi". *Oxfordindex.oup.com*

[414] www.british-history.ac.uk/vch/northants/vol3/pp85-101

[415] In 1276, Beck was the precentor of York and archdeacon of Durham.

1485–1603	**Tudor:**[416] In 1565 Oundle streets were re-named.[417] Tudor houses (intact or as single walls) are common in the town.

- Wine merchant, William Abell, born in Oundle in 1584, was the son of Thomas Abell and Suzanna Barker. From 1598 to 1602, he a London Vintners' Company apprentice. He owned the Ship tavern, off "Old Fish Street". Married with 4 children, he was 'raised to the Vintners livery' (1614) and Master in 1637.
- Oundle data was listed by John Leland (Leyland; 1503–1552).[418]

1603-1714	**Stuart (and Protectorate):** In 1611 Nicholas Latham founded North Street Jacobean alms-houses and Blue-coat School. The 'Rose & Crown Inn', 'White Lion' and 'Anchor Inn' were built (early 1600s). Paine's Alms-houses date to c. 1650. Cobthorne and its stables were built in 1656 by Cromwell's Major-General, William Boteler. Bramston and Yorke Houses date to this period.

- Peter Hausted, playwright & preacher, was born here in 1605. He died of combat wounds or plague in the siege of Banbury in our Civil War.

1714-1837	**Georgian (Hanoverian):** In 1743 Black Watch rebels were captured at Ladywood, near Oundle. They deserted in protest at being sent 'abroad' to England instead of being allowed to patrol the Scottish Highlands.[419] Berrystead House was built.

---

[416] Early Modern Britain.
[417] John Leyland, 1503-1542.
[418] en.wikipedia.org/wiki/John_Leland_(antiquary)
[419] "The Black Watch - The Mutiny". Electricscotland.com

- John Clare was born in 1793 "at Helpstone, a gloomy village in Northamptonshire" (*sic.*). He was of "waukly constitution", but his twin sister, "a fine lively, bonny wench" died shortly after their birth. He married Martha (nee Turner), known as "Patty" and had nine children (many of whom died as babies). His life was hard, yet he felt at one with the countryside. Through his life John Clare's main worry was change to the rural landscape. His poems reflect the pastoral scenery around him, yet the landscape was being transformed by enclosures between 1809 and 1817. The Enclosure Act allowed 'hemming in' small landholdings to create one large farm. Once enclosed the use of the land was limited to its owner. It ceased to be common communal land. Northamptonshire's fencers and hedge-planters left Clare devastated.
- Ebenezer Prout, musical theorist, was born in Oundle in 1835.

1837-1901

Victorian: The Market House was built after the Improvement Act (1825). Streets were "improved" by the "removal of the Butter-Cross, the Shambles, etc." and market day changed from Saturday to Thursday, a stock market added; "provision was made for lighting the town with gas or oil".[420] Workhouses were built, plus a railway station (1845) and Baptist chapel (1852).

---

[420] A new fair was started in October, the old Ascension-tide fair, Whit Monday pleasure fair and St. Valentine's fair for horses were kept but the St. Lawrence's fair was discontinued. www.british-history.ac.uk/vch/northants/vol3/pp.85-101.

1901-1910	**Edwardian**: The Victoria Hall (1902) and Great Hall (1908) were built.

- H.G. Wells (1866-1946), friend of F.W. Sanderson (see below), sent his sons to the School and wrote a tribute book 'The Story of a Great Schoolmaster' in 1924.
- Frederick William Sanderson, Head, Oundle School (1857-1922).[421]

1910-2000s	**Windsor**: Oundle survived two world wars with little harm to the fabric of the town, yet bearing the loss of life of those who fought. Extensive building development on 'brown-field sites' and fast growth at the town edges arose since the 1940s. All schools grew. Oundle School Cripps Library opened in 1988 and the Prince William School opened in 1971.

- Clough Williams-Ellis, 1883-1978, architect, educated at Oundle School (O.S.). His famous project was designing Portmeirion village and Llangoed Castle, North Wales.
- Sir Peter Scott (1909-1989) attended O.S. He studied natural sciences. His mother, Kathleen Scott, sculpted a young boy statue that stands by the Yarrow Gallery.[422]
- Gerald Touch was educated at O.S. He lived in Thrapston. He worked in intelligence and, prior to WWII, helped develop radar.
- Cecil Arthur Lewis, co-founder of the British Broadcasting Company attended O.S.[423]

---

[421] Frederick William Sanderson (1857–1922) was a favoured headmaster at Oundle School.

[422] "Here Am I, Send Me" sculpture by Kathleen Scott, FRSBS (1878–1947). From a Bible passage, "Whom shall I send?" (Isaiah 6:8). Peter's father, Robert F. Scott explored the Antarctic. In WWII Peter was awarded a DSC for bravery.

[423] Cecil Lewis (1898–1997) earned a Military Cross as a "dog-fight" pilot in WWI. He had a writing and BBC career.

- Billy Bragg (born in 1957, Stephen William Bragg) is a singer, songwriter and confident, left-wing activist lived in North Street. [424]
- Bruce Dickinson, lead-singer and musician of rock-band, Iron Maiden, attended O.S.[425]
- Christopher Alexander, architect and computer scientist, attended O.S. (1954).[426]
- Ivo Watts-Russell, founder of independent record label '4AD' (born in Oundle in 1954), lived at Biggin Hall and attended O.S.[427]
- Louise Mensch, local MP (a "Blair's Babe"), lived in Oundle until her resignation from Parliament and move to the USA (2012).
- Richard Dawkins (born in 1941) is a scientist who was educated at O.S.[428]
- Rowan Atkinson (TVs 'Mr Bean' and Black Adder's 'Baldrick') lived in nearby Apethorpe when his son attended O.S.
- Reginald Eli Sutton (1917-2011) was a senior chorister at Peterborough Cathedral. Reg loved to sing. On leaving school in 1934, he joined the engineering department of the Post Office telephone division. He volunteered to join the Royal Navy in 1942 and served on the 'HMS Rodney'. After the war he returned to the post office. Reg married Dorothy in 1940. They had two children and moved to Oundle in 1951. (Dorothy died in 2003.) For many years Reg was an Oundle District Councillor. He became a Governor at Prince William School (1971-

---

[424] Billy came (1978) to write rock music. His Oundle work includes "A New England".
[425] Paul Bruce Dickinson, musician, author & broadcaster, attended Oundle School until his expulsion (1971). Bullied, he said school was "systematic torture". He co-founded the School war-games society, cadets and live-ammunition explosions!
[426] Christopher Wolfgang Alexander is a design theorist and Berkeley professor, USA.
[427] Ivo lives in USA and currently works in art and photographical publishing.
[428] Clinton Richard Dawkins, (Oxford Professor) ethologist and evolutionary biologist.

1981), Oundle and King's Cliffe Middle, Oundle Primary and Warmington Primary Schools. Reg took life in here seriously, but had a great sense of humour. He was a founder member of the Oundle Gilbert and Sullivan Players, on the Board at Latham's and a member of the Rotary Club. Every society he joined appreciated the efforts he made on their behalf. In June 1997 he received an Order of the British Empire medal (MBE). He is sadly missed.

- George Paul Blagden (born 1989) is an actor, who attended O.S. He played Athelstan in the TV series 'Vikings' and was King Louis XIV in 'Versailles'.

(With apologies to anyone unlisted.)

APPENDIX B.

List Showing Growth of Housing and Roads Pre- and Post-1965

1.	Barnwell Road	1.	Bramston Close
2.	Bassett Ford Road	2.	Brewery Court
3.	Bassett Ford Place	3.	Bridge View
4.	Bellamy Road	4.	Clifton Drive
5.	Benefield Road	5.	Creed Road
6.	Blackpot Lane	6.	Cricketers Way
7.	Church Street	7.	Culme Close
8.	Cotterstock Road	8.	Eastwood Road
9.	Crown Court	9.	Fletton Way
10.	Danfords Close	10.	Gallery Lane
11.	Danfords	11.	Greenfields Drive
12.	Drumming well Lane	12.	Harley Way
13.	Duck Lane	13.	Herons Wood Close

14. East Road	14. Hillfield Road
15. Glapthorn Road	15. Kings Road
16. Gordon Road	16. Latham Road
17. Lime Avenue	17. Lytham Park
18. Herne Road	18. Mason Close
19. Inkerman Way	19. Mildmay Close
20. Market Place	20. Millfields
21. Mill Road	21. Monson Way
22. Milton Road	22. Nene View
23. New Road	23. Nene Way
24. New Street	24. Newbold Close
25. North Street	25. Pavilion Drive
26. Rock Road	26. Pexley Court
27. Occupation Road	27. Prince William Road
28. Cherry Orchard (Close)	28. Red Kite Drive
29. Ship Lane	29. Riverside Close
30. South Road	30. Riverside Maltings
31. Springfield Road	31. Rockingham Hills
32. St. Osyth's Lane	32. Rowell Way
33. St. Peter's Road	33. Seymour Place
34. Stoke Doyle Road	34. Siddons Close
35. Stoke Hill	35. Sondes Close
36. Tiley Hill Close	36. South Bridge Close
37. Turner's Yard	37. Spurlings
38. West Street	38. St Ann's Court
	39. St Christopher's Drive
	40. St. Wilfred's Road

The way of things to come?

Expansion in Oundle since the 1960s. The above column shows roads that were extant in 1960. Oundle has more-than doubled in size since 1965! The column to the right have been added since this date.

Note that names are NOT repeated. Names listed on the right are ALL new roads with housing.

(Also note that some newer roads have not yet been designated with names.)

41. Sutton Road
42. Taney Court
43. The Old Quarry
44. Victoria Road
45. Vine Close
46. Wakerley Close
47. Walcot Close
48. Warren Bridge
49. Watson Close
50. Webb Close
51. Wentworth Drive
52. Whitwell Close
53. Wood Lane
54. Wyatt Way

Appendix C. Gordon Road Houses - original (to 1940) and new numbering (post-1940)

1940-2017, current numbers (inner & outer hoop)	Pre-1940 numbers (outer hoop)	Notes
1	1	This has not changed.
3	2	
5	3	
7	4	
9	5	
11	6	
13	7	
15	8	
17	9	
19	10	
21	11	
10	12	Since 1940: EVEN number = inner row ODD numbers = outer row of houses.
8	13	inner hoop
6	14	inner hoop
4	15	inner hoop

Gordon Road (old numbers went to 15).

Old numbers ended at 15, as these were the original pre-1940 houses in Gordon Road.

Numbers beyond this have remained static and have not changed.

ACKNOWLEDGEMENTS AND THANKS

(Listed by first interview date)

With grateful thanks to
01/04/2017 – Margaret Brewster (*née* Slote)
08/05/2017 – Barbara Mudza (*née* Chester)
17/05/2017 – David and Sheila Wills (*née* Martin)
17/05/2017 - Sharon Cottingham (*née* Jackson)
18/05/2017 - Josephine Black (*née* Smith)
19/05/2017 – Joyce Hardick (*née* Gaunt)
19/05/2017 – Robin Moore
23/05/2017 – Abbott House residents:
Barbara Smith (*née* Gibson)
Bevil Allen and Margaret Allen (*née* Sharpe)
24/05/2017 – "Chatter-box" Coffee Tavern group:
Elsie Bladon (*née* Arnett), Barbara Mudza
(née Chester), Joyce Hardick (*née* Gaunt), Gill
Ganderton, Val Prior, Jennie Shaw and Gwen
Mackley
31/05/2017 - Ioan and Alice Thomas
31/05/2017 – Gwen Mackey (telephone conversation)
08/06/2017 – Angela Hudson (telephone interview)
08/06/2017 - Tim Lee
08/06/2017 - 'Ginger' Lee
09/06/2017 - Hetty (*née* Bell) and George Carter
09/06/2017 - Elspeth Langsdale, Oundle School Archives
12/06/2017 - John Hadman, Oundle Museum
11/07/2017 - Angela Hudson (*née* Taney)
14/07/2017 - Rob Baxter (telephone interviews)
19/07/2017 - Cheryl Forscutt (née Miles) and her family
Christopher Denley and Sheila Stables (*née* Denley)
19/07/2017 - Sue Stamper (*née* Knight)
20/07/2017 - Sue (*née* Norman) and Charles Young
28/07/2017 Linda and Terry Bamber (Oundle Scouting)
03/08/2017 - Ann Greetham (*née* Colclough)
11/08/2017 - Gerry White
11/08/2017 - Sue (*née* Crawley) and Mick Crick

23/08/2017 -	Jackie Ganderton
	Virginia Francis (*née* Gaunt)
	Bunty (*née* Hardick) and Joyce Hardick (*née* Gaunt)
02/08/2017 -	Elsie Bladon (*née* Arnett)
05/09/2017 -	Margaret Moore (*née* Plant)
	Mollie Pratt (*née* Weston; Bamford)
	Heather Cunnington (*née* Melton)
	Jean Allen (*née* Barnard)
	Susan (Susie) Moore
	Susan Stamper (*née* Knight; Afford family)
	Marilyn Smith
06/09/2017 -	Chris Beesley
07/09/2017-	Matthew G. Seward
	Jill Giddings (*née* Plowright)
	Jennifer Lane (*née* Beesley)
	Mary Moorehead (*née* Harris)
12/09/2017 -	Jean Atkins
	Wendy Bollans (*née* Mudza)
	Granville Wiggins (email communication)
	Arthur Ball
	Janet Brackley (short conversation)
	Finola Stovin
	Hanneke Soans (Oundle Town Council Office)
29/09/2017 -	Julia Langridge
30/09/2017 -	Jeremy (Jay) Thurlby
	Peter and Sheila Hooton (telephone conversation)
	Anne Cooper (*née* Leayton) and Ruth Leayton
	Pat Bird
	Samantha Marshall (*née* LaTorre)
05/10/2017 -	Bernard Kay
	Ruth Keans (telephone conversation)
04/10/2017 -	Eric Heath (with Margaret Brewster)
	Geoff and Josephine Black (*née* Smith)
07/10/2017 -	Judith Burton (*née* Welsh)
09/10/2017 -	Percy and Cynthia Arnett
11/10/2017 -	Tony and Rita Hilton
12/10/2017 -	Beryl Cox (*née* Hill)
	Joyce Marriott

	Pat and Patrick Coles
	Des Ray
13/10/2017 -	Andrew and Nita Spurrell
	Sylvia Burdett (*née* Lincoln)
24/10/2017 -	Jean Taylor (*née* Hooton)
	Janice Newall (*née* Hooton)
27/10/2017 -	Sue and Diane Wyles
	Wendy (*née* Mudza) and Michael Bollans
01/11/2017 -	Margaret Saunston (*née* Wade; Asplin)
	Esther and Anna Wild
10/11/2017 -	Marilyn (*née* Haines) and Colin Smith
	Kathleen Shiels
11/11/2017 -	Phyllis Beeby
	Stewart Laxton
16/11/2017 -	Thelma Quinn (*née* Allen)

With Thanks for Information, photographs and maps

Arthur Ball (AB)
Ann Greetham (*née* Colclough) (AG)
Ann Gray
Angela Hudson (AH)
Andrew Spurrell (AS)
Barbara Mudza (BM)
Chris Denley and family (CD)
Cheryl Forscutt (CF)
Diane and Susan Wyles (D&SW)
David Wills (DW)
Elspeth Langsdale, Oundle School Archives
Granville Wiggins (GW)
Hetty Bell (HB)
Heather Cunnington (HC)
Joyce Hardick (JH)
Kathleen Shiels (KS)
Margaret Brewster (MB)
Marilyn Smith (MS)
Oundle Museum Trust (OMT)
Oundle Town Council (OTC)
Reinette Broadhurst (RB)

Richard and Gill Ganderton (R&GG)
Sharon Cottingham (SC)
Susan Norman (SN)
Susan Young (SY)
Thelma Quinn (TQ)
Tim and Ginger Lee (T&GL)
Wendy Bollans (WB)

For assistance in facilitating this work

Margaret Brewster (support, news and archive research)
Mark Fernyhough (proof-reading services)
Kit Fernyhough (cover production and layout)
Sharon Cottingham (numerical assistance and support)
The staff at Fast-Print (publishing)
The Worshipful Company of Grocers and Oundle School
Elspeth Langsdale, Oundle School (archival information)
Oundle library, Charlotte Williams (information)
Julie, the Manager and her staff at Abbott House
Oundle Volunteer Action
Oundle Museum Trust
Oundle Historical Society
The Coffee Tavern (for withstanding meetings)
Talbot Hotel staff (withstanding meetings and interview days)
    ... also to my (ever-patient) family and friends.

For permitting the use of resources

10/05/2017 - 'Oundle's War' talk by the U3A Military History
              Group (for Oundle Museum).
21/05/2017 - Oundle Museum, Angela Hudson.
09/06/2017 - Elspeth Langsdale, Oundle School Archives.
12/06/2017 - John Hadman, Oundle Museum, theMuseum Trust.
22/07/2017 - Lesley and Steve Cheney (on behalf of their late-
              grandad, Bob Cheney, regarding Latham's and Oundle
              By-pass information).
Various dates - Margaret Brewster for house-numbering, the 1939
              Register and directory information.
08/09/2017 - Talk on Airfields around Oundle; Historical Society
              meeting.

28/10/2017 -   Robin Ackroyd (author, for spontaneous advice).

Various: to the many Oundle residents whom I may have spoken with 'in passing' and have not specified or mentioned herein.

Newspapers and maps (various editions)

British Newspaper Archive, regarding Johnston Press

Cambridge Independent Press, with thanks to Iliffe Media Limited

Northampton Mercury, with thanks to Elizabeth Bundy, Data & Copyright Executive

Oundle Chronicle, 2016 Best Newspaper Shine School Media Awards

Peterborough Citizen & Advertiser, with thanks to Johnston Press PCL

Stamford Mercury: with thanks to the Stamford Mercury Archive Trust

Ordnance Survey – various maps

Web sites

Ancestry   freepages.genealogy.rootsweb.ancestry.com

Births, Marriages & Deaths   freebmd.org.uk

British History   www.british-history.ack.uk

Elspeth Langsdale, Archivist at Oundle School

        archives@oundleschool.org.uk

        grocershall.co.uk

Ordnance Survey   ordnancesurvey.co.uk

Oundle Town Council   oundle.info/about-oundle/history

        oundle.gov.uk

        east-northamptonshire.gov.uk

Northants County Council   northamptonshire.gov.uk

Robin Moore   charitywalks.wordpress.com/cancer-charities

Rockingham Forest Trust   Heritage Resource Centre

Rugby Club   www.pitchero.com/clubs/oundlerfc

U3A   u3asites.org.uk/oundle/links

Nene Archaeology

        archaeologydataservice.ac.uk/catalogue/adsdata

Northamptonshire Record Office

N.R.O. holds records of Oundle workhouses, including Guardians' minutes (1835-1930), births register (1877-1913), deaths register (1848-1914), admissions & discharges (1836-1926), Punishment books (1870-1915) & Lunatic register (1876-1929); the Creed registers (1869-89, 1896-1914).

workhouses.org.uk/Oundle

BIBLIOGRAPHY

Alice, Princess "*The Memoirs of Princess Alice, Duchess of Gloucester*". Published by Harper Collins. Illustrated edition. ISBN: 0002166461, 1983.

Baxter, Richard "*The Certainty of the World of Spirits Fully Evinced*", published by Joseph Smith, London, 1834.

Bishop, Ian "*Oundle: a celebration in colour*", Jema Publications, Moulton, Northampton, 2001.

"*Exploring Oundle and surrounding villages: a tour of Oundle and villages within a six mile radius of the town*", ISBN 187146823x, Jema Publications, Moulton, Northampton, 1995.

Black, Leslie 'My Oundle', a booklet for Oundle Church, c. 1991.

Brewster, Margaret "*A Collection of Oundle Families*", Fast Print Publishing, Peterborough, 2016.

Britton, John "*A History of the County of Northamptonshire*", Volume 3, edited by William Page, Victoria County History, London, 1930.

Brown, M.W. '*Northamptonshire*', Cambridge County Geographies. Cambridge University Press, 1911.

Butler, Mia, & Eaton, Colin
'*Ladies of Distinction in Northamptonshire: a pot-pourri of charismatic women from all walks of life*', John Nickalls Publications, Wymondham, 2005.

Coleman, John Binder

"*Life in a Northamptonshire Market Town during the Great War, 1914-1918: the diary of John Coleman Binder, Grocer, Baker and Town Councillor in Oundle*", Oundle Museum Trust, 2013.

Downes, Michael

"*Oundle's War: Memories of a Northamptonshire Town, 1939-1945*", Nene Press, Oundle, 1995.

Gray, Douglas

"*The Oxford Book of Late Mediæval Verse and Prose*", edited by Douglas Gray, p. 573 ("Wonc n. dwelling; Wonc: dwell, be accustomed to"), Clarendon Press, Oxford, 1985.

H.M.S.O

Letters and Papers, Foreign and Domestic, Henry VIII, Volume 4, 1524-1530. Edited by J S Brewer. The Letters and Papers of Henry VIII were originally published by Her Majesty's Stationery Office, London, 1875. Free content www.british-history.ac.uk/letters-papers-hen8. (Sponsored by the Arts and Humanities Research Council.)

Hill, Peter

"*Around Oundle and Thrapston*", images of England, Tempus Publishing Limited, ISBN 075240749x, 1997.

"*A History of Hostelries in Northamptonshire*". Amberley Publishing, 2010.

Hope, Robert Charles

"The Legendary Lore of the Holy Wells of England: including rivers, lakes, fountains and springs". (R.C. Hope, 1855-1926) Published by Elliot Stock, London, 1893.

Howitt, Arthur

"Oundle Reminiscences", pamphlet, n.d.

Kenrick, M.J. *"Oundle Bypass"*, Northamptonshire Highways and Transportation division, Northamptonshire County Council, Dowsett Engineering Construction Ltd. (pamphlet), 1985.

Lowdell (Hornstein), John Gatherer
"Oundle: A record of its memories". Document held by Oundle School (c. 1895).

Maull, A, & Masters, P. *"Excavations of a Roman farmstead on land west of Glapthorn Road, Oundle, Northamptonshire,1999-2001"*.
Northamptonshire Archaeology, 2004. *Library of Unpublished Fieldwork Reports* York, Archaeology Data Service,
https://doi.org/10.5284/1002098 -
Department of Archaeology, The King's Manor, University of York, YO1 7EP.

Northamptonshire Police
"A pictorial history of 150 years of the Northamptonshire Police (1840-1990)." Booklet produced through sponsorship, Northamptonshire Police, Dickenson Colour & Commercial Printers Ltd., Kettering, 1990.

Notestein, Wallace *"A History of Witchcraft in England from 1558 to 1718"*. Awarded the 1909 A.H.A. Herbert Baxter Adams Prize for European History. Published by the American Historical Association, 1909, Washington, D.C., USA.

Oundle U.D. Council *"Oundle: Urban District Official Guide"*. Oundle Urban District Council publication, 1973.

Rowbottom, Benjamin, & Sutton, Reg. E.
"The Latham Story: an account of Latham's Charities of Barnwell and Oundle and of his Schools", a booklet, The Trustees of the Latham's Charities, (n.d.)

Rundle, Ray
"Shadows from the Past: the Oundle war memorial men 1914-1918", Inkwell Printing, Barnwell (2007). Also, *"Shadows from the Past: the Oundle war memorial men"*, Oundle Museum Trust, n.d.

Smalley Law, William
"Oundle's Story: a history of town and school." Hard Press Publishing. ISBN. 97812908314444; Re-printed from W. Clowes and Sons Ltd., London, first printed 1922.

Spellman, Judith
"Voices of the Nene Valley", Tempus Oral History Series, Tempus Publishing Ltd., Stroud, ISBN 0752424416, 2001.

Starmer, Geoffrey
"Breweries in Northamptonshire", an article in the *'Bulletin of Industrial Archaeology in CBA Group 9'* newsletter. Editor: G.H. Starmer, Northampton, 1970.

Stow, John
"A Survey of London. Reprinted From the Text of 1603", published by Clarendon, Oxford, 1908. Regards the name "Oundle (Owndale)." John Stow, 'Index of places', in *'A Survey of London. Reprinted from the text of 1603'*, ed. C.L. Kingsford (Oxford, 1908), pp.452-467. See also: British History Online www.british-history.ac.uk/no-series/survey-of-london-stow/1603/pp452-467.

Stow, John, & Howes, Edmund,

"Annales, or a general Chronicle of England". Section on "The Life and Raigne of K. William the firft", by John Stow & Edmund Howes, p. 122: "... where were wonc to dwell many lay people, which ground began to compaffe about wich a ftrong wall of ftone and gates" (sic. the long 'S' appears as 'f' in writing until circa 1800), London, 1625.

Osborne, Alice, & Parker, David

"Oundle in the Eighteenth-century: as recorded by John Clifton in his diaries", ISBN 0902544209, Spiegl & Company Press, Stamford, Lincolnshire, 1994.

Parker, David

"Oundle in the News: local newspapers as a source of historical information about Oundle", ISBN. 0902544659, Spiegl & Company Press, Stamford, Lincolnshire, 1998.

"Oundle in the News: part 2", published by Peter Spiegl and Company, Stamford, Lincolnshire. ISBN: 0902544365, 2001.

"Oundle in the News: part 3", published by Peter Spiegl Press, Stamford, Lincolnshire. ISBN: 978-0902544178, 2004.

"Oundle Wills and Headstones, 1820-1858: wills and headstones as a source of information in the study of family and local history", published by Peter Spiegl and Company, Stamford, Lincolnshire. ISBN: 0902544527, 2009.

Sawyer, P.H.

"Anglo-Saxon Charters: an annotated list and bibliography", Royal Historical Society no. 787; London, 1968.

Thomas, Ioan   *"Oundle Street Names"*, Oundle Museum Trust (pamphlet), n.d.

Wilbraham, Roger   *'An attempt at a Glossary of some Words used in Cheshire'*, by Roger Wilbraham, Esq., F.R.S. (Fellow of the Royal Society) and S.A. Communicated in a Letter to Samuel Lysons, Esq., V.P. F.S.A., 8th May 1817, pp. 13 & 41, chapter in *'Archaeologia: or miscellaneous tracts, relating to antiquity'*, published by the Society of Antiquaries of London, Volume XIX, Bayer, Staatsbibiothek. ISBN 36623534390011, London, May, 1817. The Society of Antiquaries of London, 1821.

Oundle Bibliographic Reference List for Further Reading

Baker, George   *"A History of the County of Northampton"*, edited by William Page (London, 1930). Originally published by Victoria County History, London, 1906 and 1930. *British History Online* at www.british-history.ac.uk/vch/northants/vol3/pp30-40 & ibid. pp83-95 [accessed 6 December 2017]. Note: George Baker (1781–1851) was the original author of the unfinished work, "History of Northants".

Bishop, Ian   *"Oundle: a celebration in colour"*, Jema Publications, Moulton, 2001.

"Exploring Oundle and Surrounding Villages: A tour of Oundle and villages within a six mile radius of the town". Jema Publications, ISBN-13: 978-1871468236, 1995.

Butman, D., & Lui, J.   "The Commercial Development of Oundle Market Place in the 20th Century", unpublished paper (25 pages), Oundle Upper-Sixth Form, n.d.

Cheetham, J. Keith   *"On the trail of Mary Queen of Scots"*, Luath Press Limited, Edinburgh. ISBN 01316581763, 1999.

Clark, Betty   *"A Lifetime of Memories: Oundle and Stamford"*. Published by Spiegl Press, Stamford, 1997.

Doubleday, H. Arthur, (ed.)
    "The Victoria History of the County of Northampton", edited by H. Arthur Doubleday. Published by the Advisory Council of the Victoria History, Archibald Constable and Co., Ltd., Volume 3; pp. 85-101 (1902). Reprinted for the University of London Institute of Historical Research by Dawsons of Pall Mall, ISBN 0712904492 (1970).

Eastman, Avalon   *"Oundle School Memorial Book of the First World War, 1914-1918"*. Avalon Eastman, ISBN-10: 0955293103, 2006.

East Northamptonshire Council
    "Oundle Conservation Area Character Appraisal", ENC with the Conservation Studio, 2009.

Flower, Raymond   *"Oundle and the English Public School"*. Publisher: Stacey International, 1989.

Hill, Peter   *"Around Oundle and Thrapston"*, images of England, Tempus Publishing Limited, ISBN 075240749x, 1997.

"Folklore of Northamptonshire", History Press, Stroud, ISBN 9780752435220, 2005.

Hodgekins, Terrence, *et.al.*
"Old Oundle", compiled and edited by the 'Book Committee', Rotary Club, Oundle. ISBN 0950674303. Printer: Stanley Hunt Ltd., Rushden, 1985.

Hounsome, Tony
"Lady Lilford's Triumph: A history of the ecialist Titles, Peterborough, 1992. Oundle Festival of music and drama, 1909-1992", Oundle Museum Trust, printed by Sp

Jeremiah, Josephine
"The River Nene: A Pictorial History". Published by Phillimore, Chichester, ISBN: 9781860772573, 2003.

Kinglake, A.W.
"Invasion of the Crimea", in 8 volumes. Published by Blackwood, Edinburgh, 1863–1887 (1863).

King, Alfred, and Son
"List of Old Oundelians Serving in His Majesty's Forces, January 1943". Published by Alfred King and Son (Printers), Oundle, 1943.

Knight, R.J.
"Portrait of Oundle". Published by the Oundle School Appeal Committee, Oundle, 1959.

Latham, Robert, and Matthews, William
"The Diary of Samuel Pepys", Volume II (1661), edited edition by R.C. Latham and W. Matthews. ISBN: 071351552X. Published by G. Bell and Sons Ltd., London, 1973.

Peat, C., & Newcomb, R.

"The Lincoln, Rutland, and Stamford Mercury: or, Boston, Gainsboro', Grantham, Newark, Retford, Louth, Horncastle, Grimsby, Peterboro', Oundle, Wisbech, Lynn, Spalding, Sleaford, Alford, Brigg, Baton, Hull, &c. Weekly Advertiser. Friday, April 27, 1787". ("Lincolnshire News": A Lincolnshire newspaper.) Published and printed by C. Peat and R. Newcomb, High-Street, Stamford, 1787.

Pevsner, Nikolaus

'Northamptonshire' (Buildings of England Series), Penguin, 1973 and 1999.

Jones, Owen R.

"Northamptonshire", Zincographic folding map (Black and White with division boundaries in red). Her Majesty's Stationery Office, (RE) Ordnance Survey Office, Southampton, 1885.

Lunis, Natalie

"Eerie Inns". Published by Bearport Publishing, USA. , (See article re. Talbot Hotel). ISBN: 9781627240901, 2014.

Manwaring, Kevan

"Northamptonshire Folk Tales (Folk Tales: United Kingdom", 9780752467887, History Press Ltd. (2013).

Moore, Robin

"A Walker's Diary", Published by 'A Robin Moore Production', 1995.

Moss, Julia

"Education in Oundle", Oundle Museum Trust (pamphlet), n.d.

"Religious Dissent in Oundle: from the Reformation to the Early Twentieth Century", ISBN 9780953731893, Oundle Museum Trust, 2008.

Oundle Historical Society

"*Oundle's Sporting Life: town sports' clubs – past and present*", compiled and produced by Oundle Historical Society, Occasional Paper No. 1, 1992.

Oundle Museums Trust

"*Life in a Northamptonshire Market during the Great War 1914-1918: The Diary of John Coleman Binder, Grocer, Baker and Town Councillor in Oundle*". John Coleman Binder, ISBN: 9780992723200. Published by Oundle Museum Trust, Oundle, 2013.

Oundle School

"*A-Z (Centenary) of Oundle School*". Published by Oundle School, UK, 1976.

Oundle School

"*Portrait of Oundle*", by the Oundle School Photographic Society, 1968, (1968). Author Anon. Edited and published by the Oundle School Appeal Committee, 1959.

Sawyer, P.H.

Anglo-Saxon Charters: an annotated list and bibliography, Royal Historical Society no. 787; London, 1968. Reprinted by Beekman Books; 1st Edition, 1968.

Shapiro, James

"*Oundle Exposed: Photos of life at a public school*". Published by Oundle School, Oundle, 1982.

Society for Promoting Christian Knowledge

"An ACCOUNT of several WORK-HOUSES for Employing and Maintaining the POOR; setting forth The Rules by which they are Governed, their great ufefulnefs to the publick, And in Particular to the PARISHES where they are Erected. As alfo of feveral CHARITY-SCHOOLS for Promoting Work, and Labour", Printed and sold by Joseph Downing in Bartholomew Clofe, near Weft Smithfield, MDCCXXV (Oundle section on pp. 92-93 of 112 pages), S.P.C.K., 1725.

Stock, Thomas
"Rockingham Castle" (booklet), Rockingham Publications; 1st. edition, 1984.

Taylor, J. H.
"The Geology of the Country around Kettering, Corby and Oundle: (Explanation of Sheet 171)". Published by geological survey, London, Memoirs of the Geological Survey of Great Britain, 1963.

Terrett, I.B.
'Northamptonshire'. In H.C. Darby and I.B. Terrett (eds.), The Domesday Geography of Midland England, p. 416; Cambridge, 1971.

Thomas, Alice
"Oundle in the Georgian Age", Oundle Museum Trust (pamphlet), n.d.

"Early Nineteenth-century Oundle and the Improvement Act of 1825", Oundle Museum Trust (pamphlet), n.d.

Thomas, Ioan

"Richard Creed's Journal of the Grand Tour, 1699 – 1700". (A transcription of the journal of R. Creed's tour to Rome with the Earl of Exeter.) *ISBN 0-9537318-4-7*. Oundle Museum Trust, n.d.

"Sewers and Water Supply in Nineteenth-century Oundle: Local government initiatives and central government directives". Oundle Museum Trust. ISBN 0953731863 (spiral bound), 2003.

Walker, William George

"A History of the Oundle Schools", The Grocers' Company, Hazell, Watson and Viney Limited (printing & publishing, Aylesbury, 1839 to circa 1991), 1956.

Wall, Mick

"Iron Maiden: Run to the Hills: the Official Biography" (third edition). Sanctuary Publishing. ISBN: 1860745423 (2004).

Wells, H.G.

"The Story of a Great Schoolmaster: being a plain account of the life and ideas of Sanderson of Oundle". Herbert George "H. G." Wells. Published by Chatto and Windus, ISBN 13: 9781473333574, London, 1924.

Wilson, Ronald

"Northamptonshire's Country Parks", Northamptonshire County Council Countryside Services, Northampton, ISBN 0947590137, 1993.

INDEX